# POST-KEYNESIAN GROWTH THEORY

## NEW DIRECTIONS IN POST-KEYNESIAN ECONOMICS

**Series Editors**: Louis-Philippe Rochon, *Laurentian University, Sudbury, Canada* and Sergio Rossi, *University of Fribourg, Switzerland*

Post-Keynesian economics is a school of thought inspired by the work of John Maynard Keynes, but also by Michal Kalecki, Joan Robinson, Nicholas Kaldor and other Cambridge economists, for whom money and effective demand are essential to explain economic activity. The aim of this series is to present original research work (single or co-authored volumes as well as edited books) that advances Post-Keynesian economics at both theoretical and policy-oriented levels.

Areas of research include, but are not limited to, monetary and financial economics, macro and microeconomics, international economics, development economics, economic policy, political economy, analyses of income distribution and financial crises, and the history of economic thought.

Titles in the series include:

The Financialization Response to Economic Disequilibria
European and Latin American Experiences
*Edited by Noemi Levy and Etelberto Ortiz*

Crisis and the Failure of Economic Theory
The Responsibility of Economists for the Great Recession
*Giancarlo Bertocco*

A Modern Guide to Rethinking Economics
*Edited by Louis-Philippe Rochon and Sergio Rossi*

Monetary Policy and Crude Oil
Prices, Production and Consumption
*Basil Oberholzer*

Finance, Growth and Inequality
Post-Keynesian Perspectives
*Edited by Louis-Philippe Rochon and Virginie Monvoisin*

Aggregate Demand and Employment
International Perspectives
*Edited by Brian K. MacLean, Hassan Bougrine and Louis-Philippe Rochon*

Credit, Money and Crises in Post-Keynesian Economics
*Edited by Louis-Philippe Rochon and Hassan Bougrine*

Economic Growth and Macroeconomic Stabilization Policies in Post-Keynesian Economics
*Edited by Hassan Bougrine and Louis-Philippe Rochon*

Post-Keynesian Monetary Theory
Selected Essays
*Marc Lavoie*

Capital Movements and Corporate Dominance in Latin America
Reduced Growth and Increased Instability
*Edited by Noemi Levy-Orlik, Jorge Alonso Bustamante-Torres and Louis-Philippe Rochon*

Post-Keynesian Growth Theory
Selected Essays
*Marc Lavoie*

# Post-Keynesian Growth Theory

Selected Essays

Marc Lavoie

*Professor Emeritus, University of Ottawa, Canada*
*Professor Emeritus, University of Sorbonne Paris Nord (CEPN), France*
*FFM Fellow, Institut für Makroökonomie, Düsseldorf, Germany*

NEW DIRECTIONS IN POST-KEYNESIAN ECONOMICS

Edward Elgar
PUBLISHING

Cheltenham, UK • Northampton, MA, USA

Cover image: cover photos used with permission; top left (Michał Kalecki) courtesy of Jan Toporowski, top right (Nicholas Kaldor) courtesy of Frances Stewart, bottom left (Joan Robinson) courtesy of Wikicommons and bottom right (Luigi Pasinetti) courtesy of Giovanni Pasinetti.



Published by
Edward Elgar Publishing Limited
The Lypiatts
15 Lansdown Road
Cheltenham
Glos GL50 2JA
UK

Edward Elgar Publishing, Inc.
William Pratt House
9 Dewey Court
Northampton
Massachusetts 01060
USA

A catalogue record for this book
is available from the British Library

Library of Congress Control Number: 2022931123

This book is available electronically in the **Elgar**online
Economics subject collection
http://dx.doi.org/10.4337/9781802206951

Printed on elemental chlorine free (ECF)
recycled paper containing 30% Post-Consumer Waste

ISBN 978 1 80220 694 4 (cased)
ISBN 978 1 80220 695 1 (eBook)

Printed and bound in the USA

# Contents

*Acknowledgements* vii
*Foreword* Eckhard Hein ix
*Introduction* Marc Lavoie xvii

**PART I BASIC KALECKIAN MODELS OF GROWTH AND DISTRIBUTION**

1 'The Kaleckian Model of Growth and Distribution and its Neo-Ricardian and Neo-Marxian Critiques', *Cambridge Journal of Economics*, **19** (6), December 1995, 789–818 2
2 'Traverse, Hysteresis, and Normal Rates of Capacity Utilization in Kaleckian Models of Growth and Distribution', *Review of Radical Political Economics*, **28** (4), 1996, 113–47 32
3 'Kaleckian Effective Demand and Sraffian Normal Prices: Towards a Reconciliation', *Review of Political Economy*, **15** (1), January 2003, 53–74 67
4 '*Cadrisme* within a Post-Keynesian Model of Growth and Distribution', *Review of Political Economy*, **21** (3), July 2009, 369–91 89
5 'The Origins and Evolution of the Debate on Wage-Led and Profit-Led Regimes', *European Journal of Economics and Economic Policies: Intervention*, **14** (2), 2017, 200–221 112
6 'Interest Rates in Post-Keynesian Models of Growth and Distribution', *Metroeconomica*, **46** (2), June 1995, 146–77 134
7 'The Neo-Pasinetti Theorem in Cambridge and Kaleckian Models of Growth and Distribution', *Eastern Economic Journal*, **24** (4), Fall 1998, 417–34 166
8 'Capacity Utilization, Inflation, and Monetary Policy: The Duménil and Lévy Macro Model and the New Keynesian Consensus', with P. Kriesler, *Review of Radical Political Economics*, **39** (4), Fall 2007, 586–98 184

**PART II KALECKIAN MODELS WITH AUTONOMOUS NON-CAPACITY CREATING EXPENDITURES**

9 'Convergence Towards the Normal Rate of Capacity Utilization in Neo-Kaleckian Models: The Role of Non-Capacity Creating Autonomous Expenditures', *Metroeconomica*, **67** (1), 2016, 172–201 198
10 'Long-Run Convergence in a Neo-Kaleckian Open-Economy Model with Autonomous Export Growth', with W.J. Nah, *Journal of Post Keynesian Economics*, **40** (2), 2017, 223–38 228
11 'Convergence in a Neo-Kaleckian Model with Endogenous Technical Progress and Autonomous Demand Growth', with W.J. Nah, *Review of Keynesian Economics*, **7** (3), Autumn 2019, 275–91 244

12 'The Role of Autonomous Demand Growth in a Neo-Kaleckian Conflicting-Claims Framework', with W.J. Nah, *Structural Change and Economic Dynamics*, **51**, December 2019, 427–44 261
13 'Overhead Labour Costs in a Neo-Kaleckian Growth Model with Autonomous Non-Capacity Creating Expenditures', with W.J. Nah, *Review of Political Economy*, **32** (4), 2020, 511–37 279
14 'Trend and Business Cycles with *External Markets*: Non-Capacity Generating Semi-Autonomous Expenditures and Effective Demand', with B. Fiebiger, *Metroeconomica*, **70** (2), May 2019, 247–62 306

**PART III TWO-SECTOR GROWTH MODELS**

15 'The Hicksian Traverse as a Process of Reproportioning: Some Structural Dynamics', with J. Henry, *Structural Change and Economic Dynamics*, **8** (2), June 1997, 157–75 323
16 'Pasinetti's Vertically Hyper-Integrated Sectors and Natural Prices', *Cambridge Journal of Economics*, **21** (4), July 1997, 453–67 342
17 'Traverse in a Two-Sector Kaleckian Model of Growth with Target-Return Pricing', with P. Ramírez-Gastón, *Manchester School of Economic and Social Studies*, **LXV** (2), March 1997, 145–69 357
18 'Demand-Led Growth and Long-Run Convergence in a Neo-Kaleckian Two-Sector Model', with J.H. Kim, *Korean Economic Review*, **33** (1), Summer 2017, 179–206 382

# Acknowledgements

The editors and publishers wish to thank the authors and the following publishers who have kindly given permission for the use of copyright material:

American Economic Association for article: 'Traverse in a Two-Sector Kaleckian Model of Growth with Target-Return Pricing', with P. Ramírez-Gastón, *Manchester School of Economic and Social Studies*, **LXV** (2), March 1997, 145–69.

Elsevier for articles: 'The Role of Autonomous Demand Growth in a Neo-Kaleckian Conflicting-Claims Framework', with W.J. Nah, *Structural Change and Economic Dynamics*, **51**, December 2019, 427–44; 'The Hicksian Traverse as a Process of Reproportioning: Some Structural Dynamics', with J. Henry, *Structural Change and Economic Dynamics*, **8** (2), June 1997, 157–75.

John Wiley & Sons for articles: 'Interest Rates in Post-Keynesian Models of Growth and Distribution', *Metroeconomica*, **46** (2), June 1995, 146–77; 'Convergence Towards the Normal Rate of Capacity Utilization in Neo-Kaleckian Models: The Role of Non-Capacity Creating Autonomous Expenditures', *Metroeconomica*, **67** (1), 2016, 172–201; 'Trend and Business Cycles with *External Markets*: Non-Capacity Generating Semi-Autonomous Expenditures and Effective Demand', with B. Fiebiger, *Metroeconomica*, **70** (2), May 2019, 247–62.

Korean Economic Association for article: 'Demand-Led Growth and Long-Run Convergence in a Neo-Kaleckian Two-Sector Model', with J.H. Kim, *Korean Economic Review*, **33** (1), Summer 2017, 179–206.

Oxford University Press for articles: 'The Kaleckian Model of Growth and Distribution and its Neo-Ricardian and Neo-Marxian Critiques', *Cambridge Journal of Economics*, **19** (6), December 1995, 789–818; 'Pasinetti's Vertically Hyper-Integrated Sectors and Natural Prices', *Cambridge Journal of Economics*, **21** (4), July 1997, 453–67.

Palgrave Macmillan for article: 'The Neo-Pasinetti Theorem in Cambridge and Kaleckian Models of Growth and Distribution', *Eastern Economic Journal*, **24** (4), Fall 1998, 417–34.

SAGE Publishing for articles: 'Traverse, Hysteresis, and Normal Rates of Capacity Utilization in Kaleckian Models of Growth and Distribution', *Review of Radical Political Economics*, **28** (4), 1996, 113–47; 'Capacity Utilization, Inflation, and Monetary Policy: The Duménil and Lévy Macro Model and the New Consensus', with P. Kriesler, *Review of Radical Political Economics*, **39** (4), Fall 2007, 586–98.

Taylor & Francis for articles: 'Kaleckian Effective Demand and Sraffian Normal Prices: Towards a Reconciliation', *Review of Political Economy*, **15** (1), January 2003, 53–74; '*Cadrisme* within a Post-Keynesian Model of Growth and Distribution', *Review of Political Economy*, **21** (3), July 2009, 369–91; 'Long-Run Convergence in a Neo-Kaleckian Open-Economy Model with Autonomous Export Growth', with W.J. Nah, *Journal of Post Keynesian Economics*, **40** (2), 2017, 223–38; 'Overhead Labour Costs in a Neo-Kaleckian Growth Model with Autonomous Non-Capacity Creating Expenditures', with W.J. Nah, *Review of Political Economy*, **32** (4), 2020, 511–37.

Every effort has been made to trace all the copyright holders but if any have been inadvertently overlooked the publishers will be pleased to make the necessary arrangement at the first opportunity.

# Foreword: Becoming a post-Keynesian economist with Marc Lavoie

*Eckhard Hein*

It is a great honour and pleasure to contribute this foreword to Marc Lavoie's selected essays on *Post-Keynesian Growth Theory*. I am very grateful to Louis-Phillipe Rochon for the invitation to adapt my contribution to a panel celebrating Marc's retirement from the University of Paris 13 and from running the International Master Programme 'Economic Policies in the Age of Globalisation (EPOG)' at the joint AFEP, IIPPE and AHE conference in Lille, 3–5 July 2019, for this purpose.

This contribution is a very personal review on my connections and collaborations with Marc Lavoie, which is partly chronological and partly not. I have never been formally a graduate student under the supervision of any eminent international post-Keynesian, but I moved towards post-Keynesian economics more or less on my own, studying the important works of Marx, Keynes, Kalecki, Harrod, Kaldor, Robinson, Sraffa, Steindl, and those of the then living post-Keynesians. Only at a later stage in my career, after I had obtained my German doctoral degree, I got in personal contact with the leading international post-Keynesians, whom I had studied extensively before, like Amit Bhaduri, Basil Moore, Philip Arestis, Malcolm Sawyer, Tom Palley, Amitava Dutt, Robert Blecker, Steve Fazzari, and several others. But with hindsight, it was the work of and then the personal contact with Marc Lavoie that left the largest impression on me. Therefore, I will shed some light on Marc's most important contributions to post-Keynesian economics from my very subjective perspective, and also on some of his activities on the European side of the Atlantic Ocean. What I have to present will not attempt to be comprehensive at all, and maybe it will tell more about me than about Marc – apologies for that in advance.[1]

## 1. Studying Marc Lavoie's work before meeting him (1992–2000)

In the first half of the 1990s, I did my dissertation work at the Free University of Berlin on *Money, Effective Demand and Capital Accumulation: Considerations from Marx's, Keynes's and Post-Keynesian Perspectives*. I was supervised by a Marxian economist, Klaus Peter Kisker, and the German Monetary Keynesian Hajo Riese acted as a second supervisor. Having worked through Marx and Keynes, I got somewhat lost with all those post-Keynesian contributions, the different strands, the controversies around endogenous money and exogenous interest rates, the different views on the treatment of capacity utilisation as an endogenous variable beyond the short run, etc. Then, however, I discovered Marc Lavoie's (1992) book, *Foundations of Post-Keynesian Economic Analysis*, which was an eye-opener and guide for many years. In effect, in the introduction of my dissertation, which then was published as a book in German (Hein 1997),[2] I subscribed to what Marc had called a 'post-classical' approach to economics according to four presuppositions: the epistemology follows realism instead of neoclassical instrumentalism, the ontology is classified as organicism instead of individualism, the rationality as procedural rationality instead of substantive rationality, and the focus of analysis is seen to be on production as opposed to the neoclassical focus on exchange. Built on that, I then discussed the differences and commonalities of Marx's and Keynes's contributions on money, effective demand, distribution and capital accumulation, and got into the different strands of post-Keynesian economics, with a focus on the Kaleckian tradition in particular.

Of course, in this period I studied Marc Lavoie's papers on endogenous money – and always found his arguments in favour of horizontalism most convincing, in particular those exposed in Lavoie (1996). However, what attracted me most in Marc's work were his attempts at including monetary variables, interest and credit, into Kaleckian models of distribution and growth. That is what I was struggling with in my own dissertation work. In this context, I had discovered the modern Kaleckian distribution and growth models as a bridge between Marx and Keynes, allowing one to deal with distributional conflict and the principle of effective demand in a unified framework, and with the Bhaduri/Marglin (1990) and Kurz (1990) models even allowing for different regimes, wage- or profit-led. Yet all of this was missing an explicit role for money, credit and interest. Marc's contribution to a book edited by Rühl and Mongiovi (Lavoie 1993), and in particular his paper in *Metroeconomica* (1995, Chapter 6 this volume) paved the way for my own work. On the one hand, I changed the accumulation function of Marc's models starting with the post-Kaleckian Bhaduri/Marglin investment function, and on the other hand, I introduced an interest-elastic mark-up, which gave rise to further variations and cases for the model – the usual PhD work.[3]

## 2. Meeting Marc and keeping personal contact ever since (2001– )

Since I was somewhat of a latecomer with regard to participating in international conferences, the first time I met Marc in person was at a conference at the Free University of Berlin in late March 2001, celebrating the retirement of Hajo Riese. The conference was organised by Victoria Chick who then had a visiting professorship at the Free University. At that conference, I also met some other eminent post-Keynesians for the first time; I remember, in particular, Basil Moore and a young Giuseppe Fontana. All of them were very friendly and it was a pleasure to talk to them – the international post-Keynesian community was so different from German mainstream academics with its dominant orthodox views and hierarchies.

Most importantly, I was impressed by Marc's openness and his interest in my own work and struggles. I think this was when we started to exchange e-mails and I, as the younger post-doc, started to send my ideas and paper drafts to him for comments. In these exchanges, I had to learn that Marc had worked on many areas and questions which I found interesting. Most importantly, he had already published papers on issues that I was just starting to think about. Therefore, at some point, before starting to work on an elaboration of my own models, I used to ask him first, whether he had already done what I had in mind! Sometimes he said yes, but sometimes also no – maybe there were more 'yes' than 'no'? I don't remember.

In this period, the early 2000s, Marc, among other things, was working on his book with Wynne Godley on *Monetary Economics: An Integrated Approach to Credit, Money, Income, Production and Wealth* (Godley/Lavoie 2007), which became the reference work for modern stock-flow consistent (sfc) modelling. In the same period, I was working on a book on *Money, Distribution Conflict and Capital Accumulation: Contributions to 'Monetary Analysis'* (Hein 2008), using simple small-scale analytical models, which, at least I hope, are also stock-flow consistent. But I did not apply sfc simulation models. Of course, needless to say that the Godley/Lavoie book had a much bigger impact on the post-Keynesian community than my own slim little volume.

## 3. Working with Marc I: Defending the Kaleckian model against Harrodian and Marxian critics (2008– )

Since the early 2000s Marc and I had regularly met at conferences, in Berlin, Copenhagen, Dijon, New York, etc., and we thought that we should spend some time together in order to have more time for discussions and also to try some joint work. Therefore, in May/June 2008, together with my then PhD student Till van Treeck, we visited Marc at the University of Ottawa for two weeks. During these two weeks, we worked on a joint project on instability issues in Kaleckian models, but we also spent some leisure time together. I remember the nice barbecue with Camille and Marc in their house and the billiards we played in the basement. Marc also took us to Montreal and on our way back we watched a fencing world cup tournament – it is well known that Marc had been an Olympic fencer in the 1970s/80s, and so we learnt a lot about fencing, too!

But we also did serious academic work. Marc had already dealt with the Marxian and Harrodian critique of an endogenous rate of capacity utilisation in the Kaleckian distribution and growth model beyond the short run (Lavoie 1995, Chapter 1 this volume; 1996, Chapter 2 this volume). In these papers, he showed that the supposed Harrodian instability would be contained by an endogenous adjustment of the firms' assessment of the normal rate of utilisation. I had two papers on the endogeneity of the 'stable inflation rate of employment' (SIRE) and the 'stable inflation rate of capacity utilisation' (SIRCU) (Hein 2006c, 2006d), which in the Duménil/Lévy (1999) Harrodian/Classical models were considered to determine the normal or target rate of capacity utilisation.[4] Moreover, Till van Treeck, together with Thomas Dallery, had been working on a paper based on Marc's chapter in a book edited by Mark Setterfield (Lavoie 2002), arguing that firms have multiple targets in the long run, the achievement of which may be mutually inconsistent (Dallery/van Treeck 2011). Therefore, we decided to join forces and to provide a comprehensive review and critique of the different Harrodian/Marxian models, on the one hand, and a systematic presentation of the Kaleckian responses and defenses, on the other hand. For publication, we had to split the long working paper we had produced. The first part dealing with a critique of Harrodian/Marxian models by Duménil/Lévy (1999), Shaikh (2009) and Skott (2010, 2012) was published in the *Cambridge Journal of Economics* (Hein/Lavoie/van Treeck 2011). The second part, providing a survey of Kaleckian solutions, came out in *Metroeconomica* (Hein/Lavoie/van Treeck 2012).[5]

However, Marc was not content with this state of the debate and so continued to contribute to it. In his later work, he introduced the main idea of the Sraffian super-multiplier models, the notion that growth is driven by an autonomous growth rate of non-capacity creating demand (autonomous consumption, residential investment, government expenditures or exports), into Kaleckian distribution and growth models. In Lavoie (2016, Chapter 9 this volume) and several joint papers with Won Jun Nah (Chapters 10–13 in this volume), he showed that these models allow for taming Harrodian instability under certain weak conditions, adjusting the economy to some given normal rate of utilisation in the long run. Most importantly, these models allow for preserving the Kaleckian results with respect to the paradox of saving and the paradox of cost at least for the growth path, but not for the growth rate. Such models may have good explanatory power when it comes to explaining the observed data (Chapter 14 this volume). What has been missing in these models, however, was the financing of autonomous demand growth and the related debt dynamics. I have started some work on this (Hein 2018b, Hein/Woodgate 2021), and I am grateful to Marc for his comments on some of the drafts.

## 4. Working with Marc II: The ILO project on wage-led growth (2011–2012)

I think in late 2010 Marc approached me and told me that some people at the ILO had asked him to run a project on 'wage-led growth', as an alternative to the growth regimes that had led us into the 2007–09 financial crisis and the Great Recession, the debt-led private demand boom regime and the export-led mercantilist regime. We were all very excited that a UN organisation was interested in post-Keynesian work on wage-led and profit-led growth, and Marc, together with Engelbert Stockhammer, set up a group of researchers, including Özlem Onaran with Giorgos Galanis, Servaas Storm and Ro Naastepad, Simon Sturn and Till van Treeck, and myself with Mathias Mundt, a then graduate student of mine. We produced long working papers for the ILO on the concept of wage-led growth, on the determinants of falling wage shares, on the nature of the demand regimes in OECD countries, on productivity growth issues within this concept, on the role of overall income inequality and on financialisation, the crisis and the requirements for wage-led growth. Marc, together with Engelbert, produced a very helpful and valuable piece clarifying some of the basic issues (Lavoie/Stockhammer 2013a), which I am still using for teaching purposes, and they co-edited a book on *Wage-led Growth: An Equitable Strategy for Economic Recovery* (Lavoie/Stockhammer 2013b) containing shortened versions of all our contributions. Most importantly, we presented the project at an ILO conference in Geneva in 2012 and several results of the project were then picked up by the ILO (2012) *Global Wage Report: Wages and Equitable Growth*. I think it was through this project that Marc got involved a bit more into the wage-led/profit-led demand and growth debate in post-Keynesian economics, from which he had abstained so far, and contributed some more conceptual and theoretical work (Lavoie 2017, Chapter 5 this volume).

## 5. Working with Marc III: Textbooks on *Post-Keynesian Economics* and *Distribution and Growth after Keynes* (2012–2014)

In 2012, both Marc and I started to work on some textbooks. He produced an updated and extended version of his 1992 book which then became *Post-Keynesian Economics: New Foundations* (Lavoie 2014), and I was working on a translation, update and extension of a 2004 German book on distribution and growth (Hein 2004b), which then was published as *Distribution and Growth after Keynes: A Post Keynesian Guide* (Hein 2014). In this process, we exchanged draft chapters of our books and commented extensively on each other's drafts. I must say that I benefitted a whole lot from Marc's insightful comments and suggestions. In the course of this process, we had the chance to work and discuss intensively when Marc visited Berlin for the FMM summer school 2013 (more below), coming a couple of days earlier and staying at my place. This was a very hot summer in Berlin, and I remember that we stayed in the apartment in the morning reading and discussing, but then we went out and, among other activities, had a nice and sunny boat-trip on the lakes between Berlin and Potsdam. In late 2014, we jointly presented our books at the annual FMM conference in Berlin. Guess which book has had a bigger impact on the community since then? Looking at Google Scholar quotations in late July 2021, my book has had 250 quotes, whereas Marc's has had 1102 – no surprise to me at all! Two shorter joint pieces emanated from this collaboration, too: A contribution on post-Keynesian economics to *The Elgar Companion to John Maynard Keynes*, edited by Robert Dimand and Harald Hagemann (Hein/Lavoie 2019), and a chapter on post-Keynesian theories and policies of full employment in a Swedish book, edited by Tony Johansson, on wage bargaining beyond the NAIRU (Lavoie/Hein 2015).

## 6. Working with Marc IV: FMM summer schools, *EJEEP* and EPOG (2008– )

Marc has not only produced dozens of eminent papers and several important books, he has also contributed to building and stabilising the post-Keynesian community. In 2008, Torsten Niechoj, Engelbert Stockhammer and I, with the financial and administrative support of the Hans Boeckler Foundation, started with the Berlin graduate students summer schools of the FMM, the Forum for Macroeconomics and Macroeconomic Policies (then the Research Network Macroeconomics and Macroeconomic Policies). Since 2009, these summer schools have taken place every second year – except for the Corona crisis year 2021. Marc has been a continuous lecturer at the FMM summer schools since the very beginning, usually taking over the opening lecture on 'History and method of post-Keynesian economics' or the one on 'Money, credit and central banks in post-Keynesian economics', or even both. These were also the chapters he contributed to the 'summer school book', which Engelbert and I edited, *A Modern Guide to Keynesian Macroeconomics and Economic Policies* (Hein/Stockhammer 2011). We all, and in particular the summer school students, appreciated that Marc usually stayed for the whole week at the very nice summer school location – with access to a lake – and was thus always available for discussions.

During the summer schools, Marc and I used to do some sports, usually jogging every second day before breakfast. Then, I think it was in 2015, Marc asked me whether I would like to play some tennis. I knew that he had become almost a 'semi-professional player' in order to keep up with his wife Camille, also a 'semi-professional'. I had played some tennis since I was in my early twenties, but only at a low level and I had not actively practised for a couple of years, so my expectations were not very high. To be honest, I don't remember the exact results of our matches anymore: Was it 6–0, 6–0 or did I manage at least a 6–1, 6–0? Anyway, although I had no chance whatsoever, at least I had some fun. I am not sure whether this was also true for Marc...

In 2012, Marc also joined the board of managing editors of the *European Journal of Economics and Economic Policies: Intervention (EJEEP)*, a journal which had been set up by some young German and Austrian colleagues in 2004, and which I had joined in 2008. In the course of the years, Marc's experience has helped a whole lot in improving the quality of the journal. He has organised and edited several special issues, and he has taken over responsibility for the review process of many papers. Together we have done several interviews with senior post-Keynesian colleagues, like Robert Blecker, Amitava Dutt, John McCombie and Tom Palley, and published them in the journal (Hein/Lavoie 2015, 2016, 2018, 2020). I think we both consider these interviews as an important feature of *EJEEP*, and maybe for the identity of the post-Keynesian community, too.

Finally, I have to mention the Erasmus Mundus Master Economic Policies in the Age of Globalisation (EPOG). When the main coordinator of EPOG, David Flacher, left the University of Paris 13, a senior professor was meant to take over, and it was Marc who had to take on this new role. I remember that he first bitterly complained, because running a programme was not exactly what he had come to Paris 13 for! But then he accepted 'the normative power of facts' (as the Marxians used to say) – and he helped to stabilise the programme, together with his colleagues at the University of Paris 13 and at the other universities involved, among them my Berlin School of Economics and Law.

## 7. Perspectives

I am very glad that I have had the privilege to meet Marc and to work with him a bit. I sincerely hope that this will continue for a long time to come! I am grateful for his help, support and friendship. I am sure Marc will continue to contribute to post-Keynesian economics – not only with this selection of important essays on distribution and growth. Currently he is working on another edition of his *Foundations of Post-Keynesian Economics* and I am looking forward to reading and discussing it – and to working with him in the context of *EJEEP*, FMM summer schools and beyond.

## Notes

1. For further aspects of Marc's work and life, see the interview I did with Marc for our journal, the *European Journal of Economics and Economic Policies: Intervention* (Hein 2018a).
2. Two later English papers summarised some of my findings with regard to Marx, Keynes and the post-Keynesian (Hein 2004a, 2006a), and I made another somewhat broader attempt at linking Marx and the post-Keynesians recently (Hein 2019).
3. A further elaborated and refined English version of my work was published somewhat later as Hein (2007) and companion piece using a neo-Kaleckian model setting as Hein (2006b).
4. This model had also been criticised by Lavoie/Kriesler (2007, Chapter 8 this volume).
5. If I remember correctly, we did not only work on our joint project but we also discussed our contributions to Mark Setterfield's *Handbook of Alternative Theories of Economic Growth*, to which we were invited to contribute (Hein/van Treeck 2010, Lavoie 2010).

## Bibliography

Bhaduri, A., Marglin, S. (1990), 'Unemployment and the real wage: The economic basis for contesting political ideologies', *Cambridge Journal of Economics*, **14**, 375–93.

Dallery, T., van Treeck, T. (2011), 'Conflicting claims and equilibrium adjustment processes in a stock-flow consistent macro model', *Review of Political Economy*, **23**, 189–211.

Duménil, G., Lévy, D. (1999), 'Being Keynesian in the short term and classical in the long term: The traverse to classical long-term equilibrium', *Manchester School of Economic and Social Studies*, **67**, 684–716.

Fiebiger, B., Lavoie, M. (2019), 'Trends and cycles with external markets: Non-capacity generating semi-autonomous expenditures and effective demand', *Metroeconomica*, **70** (2), 247–62.

Godley, W., Lavoie, M. (2007), *Monetary Economics. An Integrated Approach to Credit, Money, Income, Production and Wealth*, Basingstoke: Palgrave Macmillan.

Hein, E. (1997), *Geld, effektive Nachfrage und Kapitalakkumulation. Eine Betrachtung aus Marxscher, Keynesscher und post-Keynesianischer Perspektive*, Berlin: Duncker & Humblot.

Hein, E. (2004a), 'Money, credit and the interest rate in Marx's economics: On the similarities of Marx's monetary analysis to post-Keynesian economics', *International Papers in Political Economy*, **11** (2), 1–43.

Hein, E. (2004b), *Verteilung und Wachstum: Eine paradigmenorientierte Einführung unter besonderer Berücksichtigung der post-Keynesianischen Theorie*, Marburg: Metropolis.

Hein, E. (2006a), 'Money, interest and capital accumulation in Karl Marx's economics: A monetary interpretation and some similarities to post-Keynesian approaches', *European Journal of the History of Economic Thought*, **13** (1), 113–40.

Hein, E. (2006b), 'Interest, debt and capital accumulation – a Kaleckian approach', *International Review of Applied Economics*, **20**, 337–52.

Hein, E. (2006c), 'On the (in-)stability and the endogeneity of the "normal" rate of capacity utilisation in a post-Keynesian/Kaleckian "monetary" distribution and growth model', *Indian Development Review*, **4**, 129–50.

Hein, E. (2006d), 'Wage bargaining and monetary policy in a Kaleckian monetary distribution and growth model: Trying to make sense of the NAIRU', *Journal of Economics: Intervention*, **3**, 305–29.

Hein, E. (2007), 'Interest rate, debt, distribution and capital accumulation in a post-Kaleckian model', *Metroeconomica*,

**58**, 310–39.
Hein, E. (2008), *Money, Distribution Conflict and Capital Accumulation: Contributions to 'Monetary Analysis'*, Basingstoke: Palgrave Macmillan.
Hein, E. (2014), *Distribution and Growth after Keynes: A Post-Keynesian Guide*, Cheltenham, UK and Northampton, MA, USA: Edward Elgar Publishing.
Hein, E. (2018a), 'Interview with Marc Lavoie: The vigorous critique of the neo-Kaleckian or post-Kaleckian growth model is a measure of its success', *European Journal of Economics and Economic Policies: Intervention*, **15** (1), 2–11.
Hein, E. (2018b), 'Autonomous government expenditure growth, deficits, debt and distribution in a neo-Kaleckian growth model', *Journal of Post Keynesian Economics*, **41** (2), 216–38.
Hein, E. (2019), 'Karl Marx – an early post-Keynesian? A comparison of Marx's economics with the contributions by Sraffa, Keynes, Kalecki and Minsky', *European Journal of Economics and Economic Policies: Intervention*, **16** (2), 238–59.
Hein, E., Lavoie, M. (2015), 'Interview with John McCombie: I think there's absolutely no way out for them: An aggregate production function does not make any sense at all!', *European Journal of Economics and Economic Policies: Intervention*, **12** (1), 1–6.
Hein, E., Lavoie, M. (2016), 'Interview with Thomas I. Palley: We need to confront more forcefully the neoclassical position and show the absolute impossibility of the world they describe!', *European Journal of Economics and Economic Policies: Intervention*, **13** (3), 255–64.
Hein, E., Lavoie, M. (2018), 'Interview with Robert A. Blecker: People will come searching for us post-Keynesians if the political atmosphere is encouraging', *European Journal of Economics and Economic Policies: Intervention*, **15** (3), 250–58.
Hein, E., Lavoie, M. (2019), 'Post-Keynesian economics', in: H. Hagemann and R. Dimand (eds), *The Elgar Companion to John Maynard Keynes*, Cheltenham, UK and Northampton, MA, USA: Edward Elgar Publishing, pp. 540–46.
Hein, E., Lavoie, M. (2020), 'Interview with Amitava K. Dutt: I never held models as depictions of anything real; models are just to understand some mechanisms', *European Journal of Economics and Economic Policies: Intervention*, **17** (3), 278–85.
Hein, E., Lavoie, M., van Treeck, T. (2011), 'Some instability puzzles in Kaleckian models of growth and distribution: A critical survey', *Cambridge Journal of Economics*, **35**, 587–612.
Hein, E., Lavoie, M., van Treeck, T. (2012), 'Harrodian instability and the "normal rate" of capacity utilisation in Kaleckian models of distribution and growth – a survey', *Metroeconomica*, **63**, 139–69.
Hein, E., Stockhammer, E. (2011) (eds), *A Modern Guide to Keynesian Macroeconomics and Economic Policies*, Cheltenham, UK and Northampton, MA, USA: Edward Elgar Publishing.
Hein, E., van Treeck, T. (2010), '"Financialisation" in post-Keynesian models of distribution and growth – a systematic review', in M. Setterfield (ed.), *Handbook of Alternative Theories of Economic Growth*, Cheltenham, UK and Northampton, MA, USA: Edward Elgar Publishing.
Hein, E., Woodgate, R. (2021), 'Stability issues in Kaleckian models driven by autonomous demand growth – Harrodian instability and debt dynamics', *Metroeconomica*, **72** (2), 388–404.
ILO (2012), *Global Wage Report: Wages and Equitable Growth*, Geneva: ILO.
Kurz, H.D. (1990), 'Technical change, growth and distribution: A steady-state approach to "unsteady" growth', in H.D. Kurz, *Capital, Distribution and Effective Demand*, Cambridge, UK: Polity Press.
Lavoie, M. (1992), *Foundations of Post Keynesian Economic Analysis*, Cheltenham, UK and Northampton, MA, USA: Edward Elgar Publishing.
Lavoie, M. (1993), 'A post-classical view of money, interest, growth and distribution', in G. Mongiovi and C. Rühl (eds), *Macroeconomic Theory: Diversity and Convergence*, Cambridge, UK: Cambridge University Press.
Lavoie, M. (1996), 'Horizontalism, structuralism, liquidity preference and the principle of increasing risk', *Scottish Journal of Political Economy*, **43**, 275–300.
Lavoie, M. (2002), 'The Kaleckian growth model with target return pricing and conflict inflation', in M. Setterfield (ed.), *The Economics of Demand-led Growth*, Cheltenham, UK and Northampton, MA, USA: Edward Elgar Publishing.
Lavoie, M. (2010), 'Surveying long-run and short-run stability issues with the Kaleckian model of growth', in M. Setterfield (ed.), *Handbook of Alternative Theories of Economic Growth*, Cheltenham, UK and Northampton, MA, USA: Edward Elgar Publishing.
Lavoie, M. (2011a), 'History and methods of post-Keynesian economics', in E. Hein and E. Stockhammer (eds), *A Modern Guide to Keynesian Macroeconomics and Economic Policies*, Cheltenham, UK and Northampton, MA, USA: Edward Elgar Publishing.
Lavoie, M. (2011b), 'Money, credit and central banks in post-Keynesian economics', in E. Hein and E. Stockhammer (eds), *A Modern Guide to Keynesian Macroeconomics and Economic Policies*, Cheltenham, UK and Northampton, MA, USA: Edward Elgar Publishing.

Lavoie, M. (2014), *Post-Keynesian Economics: New Foundations*, Cheltenham, UK and Northampton, MA, USA: Edward Elgar Publishing.
Lavoie, M., Hein, E. (2015), 'Vägen till full sysselsättning (The road to full employment)', in: T. Johansson (ed.), *Lönebildning bortom NAIRU* (*Wage Bargaining beyond the NAIRU*), Stockholm: Landsorganisationen Sverige (LO), pp. 134–53.
Lavoie, M., Stockhammer, E. (2013a), 'Wage-led growth: Concept, theories and policies', in: M. Lavoie and E. Stockhammer (eds), *Wage-led Growth: An Equitable Strategy for Economic Recovery*, Basingstoke: Palgrave Macmillan.
Lavoie, M., Stockhammer, E. (2013b) (eds), *Wage-led Growth: An Equitable Strategy for Economic Recovery*, Basingstoke: Palgrave Macmillan.
Shaikh, A. (2009), 'Economic policy in a growth context: A classical synthesis of Keynes and Harrod', *Metroeconomica*, **60**, 455–94.
Skott, P. (2010), 'Growth, instability and cycles: Harrodian and Kaleckian models of accumulation and income distribution', in M. Setterfield (ed.), *Handbook of Alternative Theories of Economic Growth*, Cheltenham, UK and Northampton, MA, USA: Edward Elgar Publishing.
Skott, P. (2012), 'Theoretical and empirical shortcomings of the Kaleckian investment function', *Metroeconomica*, **63**, 109–38.

# Introduction to *Post-Keynesian Growth Theory*

*Marc Lavoie*

## Early thoughts

My first encounter with post-Keynesian growth theory was during the 1975–76 Honours Seminar in Modern Classics, which was a compulsory full-year undergraduate course in Economics at Carleton University, located in Ottawa, given by Thomas K. Rymes. The Seminar touched diverse fields in economics, ranging from Walrasian exchange and production theory, as well as neoclassical growth theory, and then moving on to the monetary framework with Keynes, Patinkin, Clower, Leijonhufvud and Friedman. Other professors also gave occasional lectures, for instance on the theory of the firm, the principal/agent distinction, shirking by workers and the theory of capital markets. Rymes had done his PhD at McGill University, in Montreal, which at the time and until the early 1980s was the main centre of Cambridge-style Keynesian economics, from which Canadian colleagues such as Mario Seccareccia, Louis-Philippe Rochon, Omar Hamouda, Gilles Dostaler and Morris Altman graduated at either the MA or PhD level. Rymes devoted two lectures to the Cambridge capital controversies (reswitching and capital reversals in two-sector models) and productivity accounting in December 1975. I only found out a year later, when browsing through shelves in a London bookstore, that he had written a whole book on the Cambridge controversies and its implications for productivity measurement, with a very favourable preface by none other than Joan Robinson (Rymes, 1971). He started the 1976 lectures by tackling Harrod's growth model and the neo-Keynesian or neo-Cambridgian models as they were then called. These were the models proposed in the mid-1950s and early 1960s by Joan Robinson, Nicholas Kaldor and Luigi Pasinetti.

Like many students, I suppose, I was fascinated and puzzled by Pasinetti's long-run solution to the macroeconomic determination of the profit rate, $r = g/s_c$, which only depended on the growth rate of the economy and the propensity to save of capitalists, regardless of the propensity to save of workers. So much so that when I moved to the University of Paris 1 Panthéon-Sorbonne for my graduate studies in the Fall of 1976, my first major paper was devoted to 'L'introduction de la firme et de la finance dans le modèle de croissance et répartition de Pasinetti' (The introduction of the firm and of finance in Pasinetti's model of growth and distribution), which also discussed Kaldor's neo-Pasinetti theorem. I elected to write my doctoral dissertation on a topic closer to monetary economics, however, and so my main interest became the post-Keynesian theory of endogenous money. When I got a position at the University of Ottawa (first, as a temporary position in 1979, then a tenure-track one in 1981), I opted to teach the graduate course in growth economics, and my lecture notes gave rise to my 1987 book, *Macroéconomie: Théories et controverses postkeynésiennes* (*Macroeconomics: Post-Keynesian Theories and Controversies*), which dealt with the Cambridge controversies, in particular its implications for the measurement of technical progress and the national accounting identity problem when testing neoclassical production functions, a problem that had been underlined by Anwar Shaikh and Herbert Simon.[1] The rest of the book mainly discussed newer post-Keynesian growth models and their institutional extensions, for instance the model of Adrian Wood (1975) and various versions of the neo-Pasinetti theorem.

The first chapter of the second half of the book, devoted to the post-Keynesian alternative, examined the foundations of post-Keynesian macroeconomics. The chapter dealt with the shape of cost curves, the claim that firms usually operate at a normal rate of capacity utilization which is much below full-capacity utilization, and the distinction between direct and overhead workers which had been underlined by both Tom Asimakopulos (1975), who was then a professor at McGill University, and by Donald Harris (1974), the father of US Vice-President Kamala Harris. Harris was a professor at Stanford University, who taught well-known post-Keynesians like Robert Blecker, Steve Fazzari and the late Tracy Mott.

Whereas the post-Keynesian models of the 1950s and early 1960s relied on changes in profit margins at normal capacity utilization to explain the positive relation between profit rates, profit shares and the rate of accumulation, faster growth at higher rates of utilization could explain the positive relation between profit shares and growth without changes in profit margins, thanks to the presence of overhead labour. However, just like Fernando Vianello (1985), whom I had met at the Trieste Summer School in 1984, I could not fathom how the relation between the growth rate and the profit rate could keep holding while the economy would revert back to a normal rate of utilization with a faster rate of accumulation. How the transition could actually be achieved, as I noted then, was a most interesting problem, especially in a two-sector model. That was the problem of the so-called *traverse*. Surprisingly it seems, I only became aware of the papers on the neo-Kaleckian model of growth and distribution shortly after my book came out, when I attended the 1987 Kaldor conference held jointly at the New School and at the Levy Economics Institute. Reading the papers by Robert Rowthorn (1981) and Amitava Dutt (1984), with their endogenous rate of utilization, both in the short and the long run, was a revelation.

I quickly integrated the neo-Kaleckian models in both my undergraduate course on post-Keynesian economics and in the graduate course on growth. The lectures gave rise to my 1992 book, *Foundations of Post-Keynesian Economic Analysis* (Lavoie, 1992). Usually, colleagues first publish papers in journals and later adapt them and link them to form a book. I proceeded the other way around. My interpretation of the various controversies and discussions surrounding the neo-Kaleckian model first appeared in the 1992 book (the writing of which was finished in September 1991), and it is only later that I produced and submitted articles around this topic. The only exception is a presentation that I made at a conference organized by Gary Mongiovi and Christof Rühl (at the time a student of Harald Hagemann and Heinz Kurz), at the University of Hohenheim in Stuttgart, in July 1990 (Lavoie, 1993). The conference had a remarkable format: each of us had nearly an hour to present and the question period lasted 30 minutes. Except for Malcolm Sawyer (!), all the participants were (relatively) young economists: Arie Arnon, Avi Cohen, Christian Gehrke, Chidem Kurdas, Fiona Maclachan, Juan Carlos Moreno Brid, Marco Musella, Carlo Panico, Fabio Petri, Peter Skott and Hans-Michael Trautwein. I presented what I called a post-classical model of growth, in an attempt to integrate Kaleckian, Sraffian and Eichnerian views. The rate of accumulation was a function of the rate of utilization, the profit share and the difference between the profit rate and the interest rate. The profit share itself was a positive function of the power of firms, the growth rate and the interest rate, while the saving function split corporate retained earnings from saving by households. The conditions of the effect of changes in the exogenous part of the profit share and in the interest rate were derived by using the Maple software, which seems to have impressed the participants at the time!

The above thus should help to understand how I got involved in developing models of growth and distribution, despite monetary theory and policy being my main field of research, and despite having ventured into other fields, such as sports economics (with two books and about 25 papers) and language economics (half-a-dozen papers). I am grateful to Alan Sturmer from Edward Elgar for giving me the opportunity to collect in a single volume the main papers that I have written on the topic of growth and distribution. I have tried to avoid repetitions as best as I could when making the selection. I also need to thank Louis-Philippe Rochon for having suggested this endeavour and for having collected the permissions necessary for reproduction.

**Part I: Basic Kaleckian models of growth and distribution**

The first chapter in Part I of this book, devoted to the basic Kaleckian models of growth and distribution, was published in 1995 in the *Cambridge Journal of Economics*. It is one of my five most cited articles (according to Google Scholar). It presented the critiques that Sraffian and Marxian authors were already addressing to the newly-created neo-Kaleckian model, attempting to present some justifications or counter-arguments. As Eckhard Hein recalls in his foreword, the response to these earlier critiques and to more recent ones was extended half-a-dozen years later in two joint papers, found in Hein et al. (2011, 2012).

One of those possible responses was that the normal rate of utilization could itself be influenced by the current rate of utilization – a form of hysteresis. This is the topic of Chapter 2, the 1996 *Review of Radical Political Economics* article. This proposition is highly controversial still today and it has given rise to several theoretical and empirical works. It was alluded to in the previous 1995 paper, which explains why some authors refer to it when discussing an endogenous normal rate of utilization, but the proposition and its hysteresis-based traverse is much better developed, depicted and formalized in the 1996 article. One of the intents of the article is to question Duménil and Lévy's (1995, p. 136) statement to the effect that 'while it is possible to be *Keynesian in the short term*, one is required to be *classical in the long term*'. I must say that Gérard Duménil and Dominique Lévy were very gracious since they had helped me in formalizing the details of the model that intended to disprove their claim. There is an error in the acknowledgment footnote: the paper was not first presented in March 1993 but rather in March 1995, when I was visiting Curtin University, replacing Phil O'Hara for six months. This gave us an opportunity, me and my spouse Camille, to visit her sister who was then living in Perth, and for our three children to see their three cousins within their Australian environment. At the end of the six months, however, I felt that the French of the cousins had greatly improved while the English of my kids had only made moderate progress!

Chapter 3, a paper published in the 2003 *Review of Political Economy*, was another effort, after the 1993 chapter, at integrating the Sraffian views with the Kaleckian ones, while also questioning Duménil and Lévy's statement about the need to be classical in the long run. It points to the similarities between the Sraffian normal rate of the profit and the target rate of return in pricing theories *à la* Lanzillotti (1958). This paper focuses on the role of the rate of interest in determining the target rate of return of firms, but also on the consequences of assuming that the target rate of return is being influenced by the actual rate of profit. The crux of the paper, found in its latter sections, is the integration of a conflicting-claims theory of inflation to this endogenized target rate of return. Within this framework, the actual profit rate will become equal to the target rate of return desired or assessed by firms, but at a rate of utilization that in general will be different from the normal or standard rate of capacity utilization. Thus, with the addition of conflict inflation, the rate of capacity utilization remains endogenous in the long run.

The 2009 *Review of Political Economy* paper (Chapter 4) focuses on the consequences of taking overhead labour into account. The title '*Cadrisme* within a post-Keynesian model of growth and distribution', is inspired by the use of the word 'cadrisme' by Duménil and Lévy when describing modern capitalism with its well-paid managers. The paper was published in a special issue in honour of Nicholas Kaldor, and I thought it was fitting to underline the fact that Kaldor, already in 1964, had remarked that an expansion of output would lead to a higher profit share despite holding constant the markup on direct costs, on account of overhead costs. The main purpose of the paper was to go beyond Dutt (1992) and Rowthorn (1981), who had integrated overhead labour within their model, but without taking into account the possibility that firms would raise their markups whenever overhead labour costs would be on the rise, in an attempt to pass onto consumers this cost increase. Once again, the crux of the matter is the assumption that firms follow target-return pricing and hence pursue a target rate of return; they wish to obtain a normal rate of profit when the firm is operating at the standard rate of capacity utilization. I had tackled this topic in a previously published paper (Lavoie, 1996), but with little impact, and hence I believed it was worth giving it another go in a slightly different way.

The presence and importance of overhead labour in our economies and in the empirical debate over whether countries are in a wage-led or profit-led regime is the theme of the fifth chapter of Part I, published in the 2017 *European Journal of Economics and Economic Policies: Intervention*. This is another topic of contention among heterodox economists, with most Marxian-influenced post-Keynesian authors, of a Goodwinian pedigree, usually believing or finding that economies have a profit-led demand with a profit-squeeze mechanism, while Kaleckian authors believe or find that countries are in a wage-led demand regime, or at least that domestic demand is wage led (by contrast to total demand, including net exports, which may be profit led). Besides the rate of utilization, the controversies extend to rates of accumulation, employment and productivity. The paper shows that debates over whether demand is wage led or profit led have been going on for a long time, sometimes in a confusing way, but that some earlier contributions are worth reading again. The main point of the paper is that the presence of overhead costs, ever more important today, may give the false impression under some empirical methods, that demand is profit led. This is because, as pointed out earlier, with a given markup, an increase (decrease) in economic activity will raise (lower) the profit share. A clear example of this occurred at the beginning of the Covid-19 pandemic and lockdown: as production faltered, the wage share in the USA and in Canada went up by almost ten percentage points. Goodwinians would have said that the steep rise in the wage share provoked a drastic fall in economic activity!

The next three chapters of Part I focus on the role of money and finance within growth models. The title of the 1995 *Metroeconomica* paper (Chapter 6) is explicit: 'Interest rates in post-Keynesian models of growth and distribution'. The paper sets forth a series of models where the interest rate would play a role. At the time there were relatively few contributions putting together the post-Keynesian theory of endogenous money and growth theory. As Eckhard Hein mentioned in his foreword, the various models found in the article were an inspiration for a whole series of articles of his, which were gathered in particular in his book *Money, Distribution Conflict and Capital Accumulation: Contributions to Monetary Analysis* (Hein, 2008). The paper was initially based on some of the analysis found in my 1992 book and in the Hohenheim chapter, but the Italian referees provided highly useful comments, as well as suggestions for changes and simplifications, which led to a completely revamped paper and one additional model. This was my Minsky–Steindl model, found in section 5 of the paper, which had symmetric saving and investment functions, and where the corporate debt-to-capital ratio could exhibit dynamic stability or instability. Of particular interest, in one of the configurations, dynamic instability entailed an endogenous (anti-Minskyan or Steindlian) negative relationship between the debt ratio of firms and their rate of accumulation.

I mentioned earlier that I had been mesmerized by Pasinetti's Cambridge equation, and also fascinated by Kaldor's neo-Pasinetti theorem, which came to a similar conclusion, namely that the propensity to save of households had no impact on the macroeconomic profit rate. In my 1987 French book, I had devoted a whole chapter to the neo-Pasinetti theorem and its valuation ratio (similar to Tobin's q ratio), linking it to the work of Richard Kahn, Robin Marris and Scott Moss. While the neo-Pasinetti theorem of 1966 had generated several comments in its days, it had been more or less ignored until Jorge Araujo (1995) gave it a new look. This attracted my attention and I decided to see how it could be set within a neo-Kaleckian model with an endogenous rate of utilization. This became the 1998 article published in the *Eastern Economic Journal* (Chapter 7). One of the key lessons was that an exogenous increase in the growth rate, with an endogenous rate of utilization, under weak conditions, did not lead to a decrease in the valuation ratio, in contrast to the standard interpretation of the neo-Pasinetti model assumed to be stuck at its normal level of capacity utilization, where an increase in investment and a decrease in the propensity to save of households always led to a fall in the valuation ratio. Hence, even if firms had investment functions incorporating the valuation ratio, it could still be argued that firms are free to accumulate as they please within wide limits, as Joan Robinson had earlier claimed.

One drawback of the neo-Pasinetti model is that even though the valuation ratio is supposed to be associated with an implicit interest rate (in an inverse relationship, as shown by Richard Kahn, 1972), there is no money in the model. All savings are made in the form of purchases of stock market shares, a drawback that was quickly noted by Paul Davidson (1968). The obvious amendment is thus to add money deposits to the portfolio choice of households. This I attempted to achieve in a paper that I submitted, but the referees were quick to point out that I was mishandling capital gains. As we say in French, this was *un mal pour un bien*, because I asked Wynne Godley, whom I had met a few months before, to help me with this accounting issue. It led to nearly ten years of collaboration with Wynne, first on this enhanced neo-Pasinetti model (Lavoie and Godley, 2001–02), and then on the book describing the stock-flow consistent approach (Godley and Lavoie, 2007).

The last paper of Part I (Chapter 8) was written with Peter Kriesler when he came to the University of Ottawa on a sabbatical with his family for a few months during our Summer. In fact, his visit was a very productive affair since we ended up publishing three papers together. The paper chosen here to illustrate our collaboration appeared in the 2007 *Review of Radical*

*Political Economics*. Its main purpose was to show that the Duménil and Lévy (1999) heterodox macroeconomic model ended up having the same properties as the mainstream 3-equation model that was so popular in academia at the time, and which can be found in most mainstream macro textbooks today. The 3-equation model, also called the New Consensus, as is well known through the writings of Philip Arestis (2009), has attracted the attention of several post-Keynesian economists, as found in the book edited by Giuseppe Fontana and Mark Setterfield (2009), because it relies on a central bank reaction function that determines the interest rate, being implicitly assumed that the supply of money and bank reserves are endogenous. I had myself designed a closed four-quadrant illustration of the New Consensus, and provided a post-Keynesian amendment of it, introducing path dependence and hysteresis, thus showing that inflation targeting could bring about a negative impact on the real economy both in the short run and in the long run, in contrast to the claims of the New Consensus (Lavoie, 2006). Coming back to Duménil and Lévy, Kriesler and I showed that their model behaved in a way that was analogous to the Consensus View. In addition, their model also reproduced the lessons that could be drawn from the supply-led New Endogenous Growth theory. Our approach was vindicated when I presented the paper at the University of Paris 13, with Dominique Lévy in attendance, who recognized that indeed their model seemed to be isomorphic to that of the New Consensus. Our point then, was that if anybody is on the lookout for some alternative to the Washington Consensus, it was unlikely to be found within Marxian macroeconomics.

**Part II: Kaleckian models with autonomous non-capacity creating expenditures**

One of the main criticisms addressed to the basic neo-Kaleckian model, or for that matter to the post-Kaleckian model of Bhaduri and Marglin (1990) and Kurz (1990), is that the rate of capacity utilization does not converge to its normal value in the long run. The critique is that firms will not allow their rate of utilization to forever diverge from what they consider to be the normal or optimal rate; at the very least the actual rate should cycle around the normal rate. Related to this was the critique that the neo-Kaleckian model would fall prey to Harrodian instability – Harrod's principle of dynamic instability – as firms tried to correct the situation. Another critique is that whereas the neo-Kaleckian model pretends that an increase in the wage share leads to an increase in the growth rate, most empirical studies look at the short-term effects of a change in the wage share, and hence, in the case of a wage-led economy, assess that an increase in the wage share leads to an increase in the level of economic activity; but they do not demonstrate that such an increase in the wage share leads to an increase in the growth rate of economic activity.

In 2012, Olivier Allain, who had previously written a synthesis on the neo-Kaleckian model of growth and distribution for the French public, sent me a working paper of his where he offered a response to all three of these criticisms. He combined standard Kaleckian investment and saving functions with an autonomous government expenditure growing at a constant rate, adding to these a Harrodian instability mechanism. Surprisingly, under weak conditions, this combination produced a model where the economy converges to its normal rate of capacity utilization, with the standard properties of the neo-Kaleckian model being reproduced provided they were interpreted in levels rather than in growth terms (Allain, 2015). In other words, an increase in the wage share would produce a temporary acceleration in the growth rate of economic activity, which would then come back to the exogenous growth rate set by government expenditures. The increase in the wage share would thus lead to permanent rise in the *level* of economic activity and in productive capacity. The same would happen with a decrease in the saving rate.

When I read Allain's paper I realized that there was a great degree of similarity with the so-called Sraffian supermultiplier approach which had been put forward by Franklin Serrano (1995), Graham White (1996) and Heinrich Bortis (1997), and I alerted Allain to the similarities. Their argument was that firms adjust their production capacity to secular or trend effective demand, and hence, provided there is no persistent mistake in the assessment of long-term demand expectations, there is a tendency for the economy to grow on average at the normal rate of capacity utilization. I had encountered again this argument when I participated, in May 2002, in a workshop organized by Amitava Dutt at the University of Notre Dame, when Serrano had presented a version of his model, and then again at the Sraffa conference that had been organized at the University of Roma Tre in 2010, when Óscar Dejuán (2013) had presented arguments to that effect. At the time I felt that there was no coherent dynamic mechanism that would explain how one would get from some arbitrary rate of utilization towards the normal rate of capacity utilization.[2] Serrano and Freitas (2007), in a paper published in Spanish, provided the mechanism that could bring the economy towards the normal rate of utilization. This mechanism was the combination of a non-capacity-generating autonomous consumption component, thus making the average propensity to save endogenous as argued previously by Serrano (1995), with a flexible accelerator model of induced investment, where the share of investment in output increases whenever the actual rate of utilization is higher than the normal rate. While all the ingredients were present in that paper, it did not provide a formal stability proof of the mechanism. This proof was finally delivered in the paper of Freitas and Serrano (2015), and has since given rise to an expanding empirical and theoretical literature in support of the Sraffian supermultiplier.

Allain's autonomous expenditure in his Kaleckian growth model was government expenditure, so I thought it would be interesting to follow the line pursued by Serrano and introduce instead an autonomous consumption component in the Kaleckian model, along with the Harrodian instability mechanism, as Allain had done, and see what would happen. I introduced a sketch of the model in my 2014 book (Lavoie, 2014). This gave rise to the first chapter of Part II (Chapter 9), the article on 'Convergence towards the normal rate of capacity utilization in neo-Kaleckian models', which I only submitted in January 2015 and which was published in *Metroeconomica* in 2016. This paper, along with that of Allain's (2015), has also attracted quite a bit of attention. This was not so at the beginning, however. I remember presenting the sketch of the model during the 2013 post-Keynesian summer school, organized by Eckhard Hein, Engelbert Stockhammer and the Forum for Macroeconomics and Macroeconomic Policies (FMM) in Berlin, getting the impression that the presentation had fallen on deaf ears, as it generated not even a single question. A few years later, Laura de Carvalho commented that this variant of the neo-Kaleckian model of growth and distribution was the new fashion in post-Keynesian economics, as well-known authors such as Eckhard Hein, Amitava Dutt and Tom Palley also engaged with this kind of specification![3] I also believe that this variant of the neo-Kaleckian model has helped in achieving a rapprochement between Sraffians and other post-Keynesians.

The next four chapters of Part II were all written with Won Jun Nah, now a full professor at Kyungpook National University, in Daegu, South Korea. Won Jun came as a visiting professor at the University of Ottawa for a full year in 2015, accompanied by his wife and his two daughters. Nah had published papers in Korean, based on DSGE models, but having taken a few courses in Marxian economics in his youth, he was searching for alternative approaches to economics. He had seen me make a presentation in Daegu, back in 2011, when I had been invited at the annual meeting of the Korean Association of Political Economy, and felt that he could find these alternatives by visiting the University of Ottawa where I was with my long-time colleague, Mario Seccareccia. Nah followed the course on the history of economic thought that Mario was giving. He also spent a considerable amount of time meticulously going through my 2014 book on post-Keynesian economics, finding many misprints and having long discussions about its contents, in particular about demand and growth regimes. Indeed, when back in Korea, he became involved in the income-led programme that was launched by the Korean government (Joo et al., 2020). Just before departing however, in the Fall of 2015, he jotted down the equations that would be needed to study what the neo-Kaleckian model would look like if the autonomous non-capacity-generating expenditure consisted of exports (driven by world demand) instead of consumption or government expenditures. This became the paper that we published together in the *Journal of Post Keynesian Economics* in 2017 (Chapter 10).

We then thought that the principle of autonomous non-capacity-generating expenditure combined with the Harrodian dynamic instability principle could be applied within many other contexts. By December 2016, we had submitted the paper that was eventually published in September 2019 in the *Review of Keynesian Economics* (Chapter 11), where we considered the impact of endogenous technical progress in a model with autonomous consumption growing at an exogenous rate. It took a long time for the paper to be published since it was accepted in February 2018 – a lesson for young scholars who are eager to get their works published as quickly as possible. We recovered a previous paradoxical result achieved by Cesaratto et al. (2003) in their discussion of the Sraffian supermultiplier mechanism, that is, the fact that technological change does not generate faster growth. For technical progress to have a positive impact on the growth rate of the economy, faster technical change needs to generate an increase in the growth rate of the non-capacity-creating autonomous components of effective demand. As we argued in our article, this could happen, for instance, if the accelerated pace in the introduction of novel and fashionable products induces an increase in the growth rate of autonomous consumption.

By December 2016, Won Jun had also written down the first draft of the paper that incorporated the conflicting-claims framework into the neo-Kaleckian growth model with autonomous consumption. This framework is popular among post-Keynesians to explain wage and price inflation, in particular when the real-wage target of workers is said to depend on the rate of employment. We submitted the paper in September 2017 and the article was eventually published in the 2019 December issue of *Structural Change and Economic Dynamics* (Chapter 12). Once again, there were some delays, as it took nearly a year for minor changes to get approved! An interesting feature of the article is that we provide simulations based on the theoretical model and some appropriate calibration which generates stability despite the presence of the Harrodian instability principle. The long-run version of the model also incorporates convergence towards a steady employment rate, in contrast to several neo-Kaleckian models where the issue of unemployment is not explicitly dealt with, thanks to an endogenous growth rate of the labour force.

The fourth paper that resulted from my collaboration with Won Jun Nah took into account the distinction between direct and overhead labour, just as I had previously done in two papers of Part I, but this time while considering autonomously growing consumption expenditures and with the addition of the Harrodian dynamic instability principle in the long-run version. As readers may guess by now, or as they will find out when they will read my 2017 piece in the *European Journal of Economics and Economic Policy* (Chapter 5), I thought overhead labour and target-return pricing played a crucial part in understanding fluctuations in the profit share and hence had to be studied within the context of non-capacity generating autonomous expenditures. I had suggested the idea to Won Jun in July 2017, spurred by the completion, within the EPOG programme at the University of Paris 13, of the Master thesis of a student of mine, Lílian Nogueira Rolim, who dealt with the econometric consequences of overhead labour for the assessment of wage-led demand.[4] By October we had a draft with the main equations. The paper was eventually submitted to the *Cambridge Journal of Economics*, but the editors and the referees thought the relevance to equations ratio was too low. A simplified version of the paper, where we assumed an exogenous normal rate of utilization instead of an endogenous one, thus perhaps making the paper less controversial, was eventually submitted to and published in 2020 in the *Review of Political Economy* (Chapter 13). An interesting feature of the paper is that while an increase in the relative remuneration of overhead managerial labour has no certain effect on economic activity in the short run, increased inequality in wage distribution leads to a definite fall in the average growth rate of the economy during the traverse to the new long-run equilibrium.

The last paper of Part II (Chapter 14) was written with Brett Fiebiger, an Australian who was a post-doctoral scholar at the University of Ottawa for nine months, thanks to grants from the Institute for New Economic Thinking (INET) and the Social Sciences and Humanities Research Council of Canada that my colleague Mario Seccareccia had managed to obtain in the early 2010s to study the political economy of new fiscalism. When, later, I also got a grant from INET to study central banking and its crises, we once more solicited Brett's help. I think it is fair to say that both Brett and I greatly benefitted from this interaction, as we continued our collaboration much beyond his stay in Ottawa, having published together no less than five articles. In the meantime, Brett got very much interested in the empirical issues surrounding the role of non-capacity-generating autonomous expenditures, or more precisely what he calls semi-autonomous expenditures. As said earlier, this topic attracted the attention of many well-known post-Keynesians, but it also attracted the attention of several detractors. With working papers and submissions flying back and forth, Neri Salvadori and Heinz Kurz, as the editors of *Metroeconomica*, decided to devote a special issue to the topic. The paper written with Brett Fiebiger, devoted to a mixture of theoretical and empirical approaches to the role of what we called non-capacity-generating semi-autonomous expenditures, was accepted in September 2017, but as the special issue had to await laggards, it appeared in *Metroeconomica* in May 2019. The paper can be considered to be a critique of Harrodian or Goodwinian critics (such as Peter Skott) of the neo-Kaleckian approach. The paper also underlines the importance of residential construction – hence household investment – in generating economic activity, at least in the US economy. The companion paper that we refer to as Fiebiger (in press) in the article, was finally published as Fiebiger (2018), and is certainly worth reading as it demonstrates that corporate investment follows (and does not accompany) increases in economic activity, thus also showing the relevance of the Sraffian supermultiplier and its induced investment.

**Part III: Two-sector growth models**

Besides Mario Seccareccia and I, two full professors at the University of Ottawa in the 1980s had some relationship with post-Keynesian economics. Anna Koutsoyiannis was part of the staff for a short while. She had written a terrific second-year microeconomics textbook, which contained several chapters devoted to limit-entry pricing and to what she called average pricing, as well as a critique of marginal pricing (Koutsoyiannis, 1975). Her textbook thus dealt with the ideas of authors such as Sylos-Labini, Hall and Hitch, Cyert and March, Lanzillotti, and Andrews, the latter having been her colleague at the University of Lancaster. The second professor was Jacques Henry. He had been trained as a neoclassical development economist, but he met his Damascus moment when he spent a sabbatical in the Sahel desert, realizing that their inhabitants were thoughtful and wise individuals despite following none of the development models of neoclassical economics. He then searched for alternative models, found Sraffian economics and later the rest of post-Keynesian economics, in part through discussions with Mario and I. In 1985, he wrote a working paper, called 'Traverse as a process of reproportioning', which was presented at a conference held at the University of Ottawa in 1987. The paper was intended to be part of a book devoted to traverse analysis, but for reasons that we could not elucidate, the paper was not included in the book, each of the three editors blaming the others for the refusal. Jacques Henry passed away at the age of 55 in 1989, at about the same age and same time as Alfred Eichner, both deaths being dramatic losses for post-Keynesian economics. Jacques had left his traverse paper aside, and I decided to resurrect it, as I felt that his draft was much more original than the editors of the book had thought and hence merited an effort to revise it in the hope of obtaining proper publication.

Sraffian economics, at least at the time, only dealt with stationary or steady states. It was Hicks (1965) who first attempted to analyze how an economy would transit from one equilibrium to another (with a lower or higher growth rate of the labour force) within a two-sector Sraffian model with fixed coefficients, producing a consumption good and a fixed capital good utilized in both sectors – a specification which can also be found in Robinson (1956). His traverse, and the one analyzed in the first article of Part III (Chapter 15), published in 1997 in *Structural Change and Economic Dynamics*, can be dubbed a neoclassical traverse, because it analyzes the transition under the condition that full employment of labour and full capacity utilization in both sectors are being maintained.[5] For this to happen, there has to be a reproportioning of the capital stock and of the labour force, which justifies the title of the article, 'The Hicksian traverse as a process of reproportioning'. Both Hicks and Henry argued that all the interesting action in economics occurs during the transition, during the traverse, in other words, in historical time (and not in logical time at the steady state) as Joan Robinson would put it. While others had previously shown, through stability analysis, that for the traverse to be possible, the capital-to-labour ratio in the consumption sector had to be higher than in the investment sector, the originality of our paper was to describe graphically the actual path followed by both quantities and prices, both in the stable cases and in the unstable cases. In particular, the consequences of the unsuccessful traverses were mathematically and graphically spelled out, with in one case fewer and fewer consumption goods being produced and in the other with fewer and fewer capital goods being produced. We also showed that the price traverse resulted from the quantity traverse required for reproportioning, prices changing to ensure that aggregate demand would match the quantities being supplied from one period to the next.

In some sense, the second paper of Part III (Chapter 16), titled 'Pasinetti's vertically hyper-integrated sectors and natural prices', published in a 1997 issue of the *Cambridge Journal of Economics*, also deals with transition and reproportioning of the production structure. The title is perhaps misleading as it deals with two views of vertical integration – Pasinetti's view and what I called the standard view. The paper arose from my interaction with my former undergraduate teacher, Tom Rymes (also a tennis partner), who had his own approach to vertical integration – which I called the standard view. The purpose of the paper, as in many other instances when I have written papers, was to clarify my own views on the subject and to provide a pedagogical understanding of Pasinetti's concept of hyper-vertically integrated labour coefficients.[6] I thus designed the simplest model that could handle structural change, that is, a three-sector model, with two sectors producing consumption goods and one sector producing a basic good – the machines used in all three sectors. There is thus a clear interdependence between the three sectors, which produces many problems when the two consumption sectors are not growing at the same rate. I retrieve results which are similar to those observed in the previous article, that is, growth is unsustainable when the two consumption sectors grow at exogenously-given growth rates. I compared this model with the equivalent model that arose from Pasinetti's view of vertical integration and his efforts to get around the stability problems provoked by this interdependence, by assuming that each consumption sector has access to its own industrial source of machines, as if the investment sector is composed of two firms, each feeding itself and only one consumption sector. The cost to pay to avoid the interdependence is that when computing natural prices (where the profit rate is equal to the growth rate), following Pasinetti, the same machine needs to be valued at two different prices, depending on the consumption sector that it is associated with. The only other way out is to assume within the standard view of vertical integration that there is flexibility in the utilization of the capital stock, that is, firms dispose of excess reserves of capacity with endogenous rates of capacity utilization.

And this is exactly what was assumed in the next paper, one also published in 1997, this time in the *Manchester School of Economic and Social Studies* (Chapter 17). The paper looks at what happens in the traverse in the case of a two-sector model whose structure is similar to the one used to analyze the Hicksian traverse, but without assuming full employment, assuming instead fixed prices, target-return pricing (without uniform rates of profit) and endogenous rates of utilization. In other words, the paper examines reproportioning during the traverse in a two-sector neo-Kaleckian model of growth and distribution. The article arose as a result of the preliminary work that was conducted in his major paper by an MA student at the University of Ottawa, Pablo Ramírez-Gastón. Investment in each sector is assumed to be a simple function of the rate of capacity utilization of the sector, so this is what determines the growth of the economy. In contrast to the Hicksian/Sraffian model, the successful realization of the traverse does not depend on the investment sector being less capital-intensive than the consumption sector. Also in contrast to the Hicksian/Sraffian case, in a successful traverse, the proportion of capital held in the investment sector is not necessarily positively tied to the rate of capital accumulation. The cause of this is the endogeneity of the rate of utilization, as reflected by a fundamental equality, given by $g = u_i/a_{ki}(1 + \kappa)$, where $g$ is the overall rate of capital accumulation, $u_i$ and $a_{ki}$ are the rate of utilization and the capital-to-capacity ratio of the investment sector, while $\kappa$ is the proportion of machines held in the consumption sector relative to the machines found in the investment sector. If the rate of utilization is stuck at its normal level, at constant technical coefficients, a higher growth rate must necessarily be associated with a lower kappa.

Except for Amitava Dutt (1988) and the paper described above, until very recently, virtually no one tackled the topic of the two-sector Kaleckian model of growth and distribution. Along with Fujita (2019), Nishi (2020) and Fanti and Zamparelli (2021), the last paper of Part III is one of the few articles which dared to do so. This is the paper that I wrote with Jung Hoon Kim, on the basis of a chapter of his doctoral dissertation at the University of Ottawa back in 2007 (Chapter 18). The article was published in 2017 in the *Korean Economic Review*. As in the previous paper, it relies on target-return pricing, but with an investment function that incorporates both the rate of utilization and the rate of profit, and it examines the traverse to the new long-run equilibrium position when changes are made to the propensity to save out of profits or to the target rates of return of either sector. It also examines a series of different closures, in the same spirit as Dutt's (1988) paper. One such closure is based on the assumption that the rate of accumulation in the investment sector is equal to the rate of growth of the consumption sector, modulated by the discrepancy between the profit rates of the two sectors. With such a variant, there is convergence towards a uniform rate of profit, provided the speed of adjustment of profit rate differentials is smaller than the propensity to save out of profits.

A fully-adjusted position, as Vianello (1985) called them, could be achieved if in addition it is assumed that target rates of return are raised whenever the actual profit rate exceeds the target rate of return. With this modification, the rates of utilization of both sectors converge to their normal value. The paradox of thrift still holds because a higher propensity to save leads to a lower growth rate. However, this last closure links up with the models described in Part II, because an increase in real wages will only lead to a temporary increase in the growth rate of the economy and in the rate of capacity utilization during the transition towards the new steady state. As in the models of Part II with autonomous non-capital-generating expenditures, the initial imposition of higher real wages will induce a level (instead of a growth rate) of economic activity and productive capacity which is higher than if no such change had been imposed. The overall lesson taken from this last study is that the results obtained with the help of these sophisticated two-sector models are roughly isomorphic to the results achieved with simpler one-sector models, thus justifying their use.

## Conclusion

Post-Keynesian authors have given much attention to the issues connecting growth and income distribution. Today, income distribution – income and wealth inequality – is very much a topic of interest among scholars of all horizons. Growth, by contrast, is a contested terrain, with many authors looking for ways to slow down growth, or even achieve zero growth or degrowth, instead of speeding up growth in the hope of achieving full employment, because of ecological concerns and the carbonization of the economy. Along with many post-Keynesians of my generation, I have not given much thought to the degrowth possibilities or necessities. It should be pointed out, however, that several ecological economists are now using the tools of post-Keynesian economics, Kaleckian, Sraffian or Goodwinian models and the stock-flow consistent approach, to develop alternative macroeconomic models that incorporate environmental issues without relying on standard mainstream assumptions. As our economies will transition towards a greener economy, the concept of the traverse, as described in some of the articles of Part III, will become ever relevant.[7] A number of post-Keynesians are already engaged in this search, some within the confines of agent-based modelling.

## Notes

1. I tackled again this issue in Lavoie (2008, 2018).
2. In particular, I offered an examination and critique of White's (1996) investment function and mechanism in Lavoie (1999).
3. There was a small algebraic error in the computations of the determinant and the trace of the Jacobian, which was corrected by Skott (2017).
4. A quite different version of her work was eventually published as Rolim (2019).
5. A somewhat revised version of the paper, with much cleaner figures, was published in French in Henry and Lavoie (2002).
6. I returned to this topic in Seppecher et al. (2018), in an agent-based model with three industries making consumption, intermediate and fixed capital goods, where markups were randomized, showing that the prices of the consumption good ended up being very close to Pasinetti's natural price, proportional to the unweighted sum of the direct, indirect and hyper-indirect labour coefficients.
7. To give a single example, see Nguyen-Huu and Pottier (2020) on energy transition.

## References

Allain, O. (2015), 'Tackling the instability of growth: a Kaleckian-Harrodian model with an autonomous expenditure component', *Cambridge Journal of Economics*, **39** (5), September, 1351–71.

Araujo, J.T. (1995), 'Kaldor's neo-Pasinetti theorem and the Cambridge theory of distribution', *Manchester School of Economics and Social Studies*, **63** (3), September, 311–17.

Arestis, P. (2009), 'New Consensus macroeconomics and Keynesian critique', in E. Hein, T. Niechoj and E. Stockhammer (eds), *Macroeconomic Policies on Shaky Foundations: Whither Mainstream Economics?*, Marburg: Metropolis, pp. 165–86.

Asimakopulos, A. (1975), 'A Kaleckian theory of income distribution', *Canadian Journal of Economics*, **8** (3), August, 313–33.

Bhaduri, A. and S. Marglin (1990), 'Unemployment and the real wage: The economic basis for contesting political ideologies', *Cambridge Journal of Economics*, **14** (4), December, 375–93.

Bortis, H. (1997), *Institutions, Behaviour and Economic Theory: A Contribution to Classical-Keynesian Political Economy*, Cambridge: Cambridge University Press.

Cesaratto, S., F. Serrano and A. Stirati (2003), 'Technical change, effective demand and employment', *Review of Political Economy*, **15** (1), 33–52.

Davidson, P. (1968), 'The demand and supply of securities and economic growth and its implications for the Kaldor–Pasinetti versus Samuelson–Modigliani controversy', *American Economic Review*, **58** (2), May, 252–69.

Dejuán, Ó. (2013), 'Normal paths of growth shaped by the supermultiplier', in E.S. Levrero, A. Palumbo and A. Stirati (eds), *Sraffa and the Reconstruction of Economic Theory: Volume Two: Aggregate Demand, Policy Analysis and Growth*, Basingstoke: Palgrave Macmillan, pp. 139–57.

Duménil, G. and D. Lévy (1995), 'A post-Keynesian long-term equilibrium with equalized profit rates', *Review of Radical Political Economics*, **27** (2), 135–41.

Duménil, G. and D. Lévy (1999), 'Being Keynesian in the short term and classical in the long term: The traverse to classical long-term equilibrium', *Manchester School of Economics and Social Studies*, **67** (6), December, 684–716.

Dutt, A.K. (1984), 'Stagnation, income distribution and monopoly power', *Cambridge Journal of Economics*, **8** (1), March, 25–40.

Dutt, A.K. (1988), 'Convergence and equilibrium in two sector models of growth, distribution and prices', *Journal of Economics*, **48** (2), 135–58.

Dutt, A.K. (1992), 'Stagnation, growth and unproductive activity', in J.B. Davis (ed.), *The Economic Surplus in Advanced Economics*, Aldershot, UK and Brookfield, VT, USA: Edward Elgar Publishing, pp. 91–113.

Fanti, L. and L. Zamparelli (2021), 'The paradox of thrift in a two-sector Kaleckian growth model', *Metroeconomica*, **72** (3), July, 526–38.

Fiebiger, B. (2018), 'Semi-autonomous household expenditures as the *causa causans* of postwar US business cycles: The stability and instability of Luxemburg-type external markets', *Cambridge Journal of Economics*, **42** (1), January, 155–75.

Fontana, G. and M. Setterfield (eds) (2009), *Macroeconomic Theory and Macroeconomic Pedagogy*, Basingstoke: Palgrave Macmillan.
Freitas, F. and F. Serrano (2015), 'Growth rate and level effects: The stability of the adjustment of capacity to demand and the Sraffian supermultiplier', *Review of Political Economy*, **27** (3), July, 258–81.
Fujita, S. (2019), 'Mark-up pricing, sectoral dynamics, and the traverse process in a two-sector Kaleckian economy', *Cambridge Journal of Economics*, **43** (2), March, 465–79.
Godley, W. and M. Lavoie (2007), *Monetary Economics: An Integrated Approach to Credit, Money, Income, Production and Wealth*, Basingstoke: Palgrave Macmillan.
Harris, D.J. (1974), 'The price policy of firms, the level of employment and distribution of income in the short run', *Australian Economic Papers*, **13** (22), June, 144–51.
Hein, E. (2008), *Money, Distribution Conflict and Capital Accumulation: Contributions to Monetary Analysis*, Basingstoke: Palgrave Macmillan.
Hein, E., M. Lavoie and T. Van Treeck (2011), 'Some instability puzzles in Kaleckian models of growth and distribution: A critical survey', *Cambridge Journal of Economics*, **35** (1), May, 587–612.
Hein, E., M. Lavoie and T. Van Treeck (2012), 'Harrodian instability and the normal rate of capacity utilization in Kaleckian models of distribution and growth – a survey', *Metroeconomica*, **63** (1), March, 39–69.
Henry, J. and M. Lavoie (2002), 'La traverse de Hicks dans son modèle horizontal bisectoriel: Le réaménagement de la structure productive', *L'Actualité économique*, **78** (1), March, 87–114.
Hicks, J.R. (1965), *Capital and Growth*, Oxford: Oxford University Press.
Joo, S., K. Lee, W.J. Nah, S.M. Jeon and D.H. Joe (2020), *The Income-Led Growth in Korea: Status, Prospects and Lessons for Other Countries*, Sejong: Korea Institute for International Economic Policy.
Kahn, R.F. (1972), 'Notes on the rate of interest and the growth of firms', in R.F. Kahn, *Selected Essays on Employment and Growth*, Cambridge: Cambridge University Press, pp. 208–32.
Koutsoyiannis, A. (1975), *Modern Microeconomics*, London: Macmillan.
Kurz, H.D. (1990), 'Technical change, growth and distribution: A steady state approach to unsteady growth', in H.D. Kurz, *Capital, Distribution and Effective Demand: Studies in the Classical Approach to Economic Theory*, Cambridge: Polity Press, pp. 210–39.
Lanzillotti, R.F. (1958), 'Pricing objectives in large companies', *American Economic Review*, **48** (5), December, 921–40.
Lavoie, M. (1987), *Macroéconomie: Théorie et controverses postkeynésiennes*, Paris: Dunod.
Lavoie, M. (1992), *Foundations of Post-Keynesian Economic Analysis*, Aldershot: Edward Elgar.
Lavoie, M. (1993), 'A post-classical view of money, interest, growth and distribution', in G. Mongiovi and C. Ruhl (eds), *Macroeconomic Theory: Diversity and Convergence*, Aldershot: Edward Elgar, pp. 3–21.
Lavoie, M. (1996), 'Unproductive outlays and capital accumulation with target-return pricing', *Review of Social Economy*, **54** (3), Fall, 303–21.
Lavoie, M. (1999), 'Investment functions in Sraffian and Kaleckian models', *Économie appliquée*, **52** (1), 119–25.
Lavoie, M. (2006), 'A post-Keynesian amendment to the New Consensus on monetary policy', *Metroeconomica*, **57** (2), May, 165–92.
Lavoie, M. (2008), 'Neoclassical empirical evidence on employment and production laws as artefact', *Revista Economía Informa*, **351**, March–April, 9–36.
Lavoie, M. (2014), *Post-Keynesian Economics: New Foundations*, Cheltenham, UK and Northampton, MA, USA: Edward Elgar Publishing.
Lavoie, M. (2018), 'Production functions, the Kaldor–Verdoorn law and methodology', in P. Arestis (ed.), *Alternative Approaches in Macroeconomics: Essays in Honour of John McCombie*, Basingstoke: Palgrave Macmillan, pp. 303–30.
Lavoie, M. and W. Godley (2001–02), 'Kaleckian models of growth in a coherent stock-flow monetary framework: A Kaldorian view', *Journal of Post Keynesian Economics*, **24** (2), Winter, 277–312.
Nguyen-Huu, A. and A. Pottier (2020), 'The Hicksian traverse revisited: Conditions for the energy transition', *Structural Change and Economic Dynamics*, **54**, September, 102–11.
Nishi, H. (2020), 'A two-sector Kaleckian model of growth and distribution with endogenous productivity dynamics', *Economic Modelling*, **88**, June, 223–43.
Robinson, J. (1956), *The Accumulation of Capital*, London: Macmillan.
Rolim, L.N. (2019), 'Overhead labour and feedback effects between capacity utilization and income distributions: Estimations for the USA economy', *International Review of Applied Economics*, **33** (6), 756–73.
Rowthorn, B. (1981), 'Demand, real wages and economic growth', *Thames Papers in Political Economy*, Autumn, 1–39.
Rymes, T.K. (1971), *On Concepts of Capital and Technical Change*, Cambridge: Cambridge University Press.
Seppecher, P., I. Salle and M. Lavoie (2018), 'What drives markups? Evolutionary pricing in an agent-based stock-flow consistent macroeconomic model', *Industrial and Corporate Change*, **27** (6), December, 1045–67.
Serrano, F. (1995), 'Long period effective demand and the Sraffian supermultiplier', *Contributions to Political*

*Economy*, **14**, 67–90.
Serrano, F. and F. Freitas (2007), 'El supermultiplicador sraffiano y el papel de la demanda efectiva en los modelos de crecimiento', *Circus*, **1**, October, 21–37.
Skott, P. (2017), 'Autonomous demand and the Harrodian criticism of the Kaleckian model', *Metroeconomica*, **68** (1), February, 185–93.
Vianello, F. (1985), 'The pace of accumulation', *Political Economy: Studies in the Surplus Approach*, **1** (1), 69–87.
White, G. (1996), 'Classical competition, Keynesian adjustment and composite dynamics: A critical perspective', *Économie appliquée*, **49** (4), 5–36.
Wood, A. (1975), *A Theory of Profits*, Cambridge: Cambridge University Press.

# PART I

# BASIC KALECKIAN MODELS OF GROWTH AND DISTRIBUTION

*Cambridge Journal of Economics* 1995, **19**, 789–818

# The Kaleckian model of growth and distribution and its neo-Ricardian and neo-Marxian critiques

Marc Lavoie*

This paper analyses the newer Kaleckian models of growth and distribution and the criticisms that have been addressed to them by neo-Marxian and neo-Ricardian authors. The models discussed assume overhead labour costs and target return pricing. The main issues are the form of the investment function and the notions of normal rates of profit and of normal rates of capacity utilisation. Despite the relevance of (and often the similarity between) the neo-Marxian and neo-Ricardian critiques, it is shown that the main features of the Kaleckian growth model may still be preserved.



## 1. Introduction

Post-Keynesian economics is still mostly known for the models of growth and distribution that were developed by Kaldor (1957), Robinson (1962) and Pasinetti (1962) in the late fifties and in the early sixties. For this reason, it is important to distinguish between those earlier models of growth and the newer models that have been recently proposed by post-Keynesian authors associated with the Kaleckian tradition. We shall call neo-Keynesian the older models, while we shall call Kaleckian the newer ones.

There are two major related differences between the two groups of models that one should note. First, the neo-Keynesian models, because they are still being inspired by the framework developed by Keynes, are basically set in a world of competition, whereas the post-Keynesian models of Kaleckian inspiration are part of an oligopolistic framework. The second difference between the two models is that the older neo-Keynesian model implicitly presumes that in the long period the economy runs at full capacity or that the rate of utilisation of capacity is fixed at a given normal level, whereas in the newer post-Keynesian model the rate of utilisation of capacity is endogenous and is not assumed to be equal to a normal value, even in the long period (Kurz, 1993, 1994).

Manuscript received 18 September 1992; final version received 20 September 1993.

*University of Ottawa, Canada. This paper was presented at Carleton University and at the meetings of the Eastern Economic Association in March 1992, and also at the LATAPSES research centre of the University of Nice at Sophia-Antipolis in June 1992. Besides the participants at those presentations, I would like to thank Richard Arena, Trish Cahill, Mario Seccareccia and Peter Skott for their comments at various stages of the paper. An anonymous reader of the journal also provided helpful and perceptive comments, which led to substantial revisions of the paper. This article was made possible by a grant from the Social Sciences and Humanities Research Council of Canada.

0309–166X/95/060789+30 $12.00/0 

There are important consequences to the adoption of those differing assumptions, despite the other similarities of the two models. Perhaps the most crucial one is that in the neo-Keynesian *one-sector* model there is a necessary long-period inverse relationship between the real wage rate and the rates of profit and of accumulation.[1] As Amadeo (1986B) recalls, neo-Keynesian models share this antagonistic description of accumulation with neo-Marxian models, and it is in conformity with the old classical notion that in the long period a unique and inverse relation between the real wage rate and the rate of profit must obtain. By contrast, in the Kaleckian model, there is *usually* a positive long-period relationship between the real wage rate and the rates of profit and of accumulation.[2] This implication of the Kaleckian model of growth conforms with standard post-Keynesian short-period results, where increased real wages induce higher rates of capacity utilisation.[3]

It seems that the Kaleckian model of growth and distribution was originally developed independently by Bob Rowthorn and Amitava Dutt (Amadeo, 1987, p. 75), but the main results of their model were also arrived at by Del Monte (1975) in a paper published in Italian. Several other works have been published using a very similar framework. The exact growth model to be presented here is closest to the one displayed by Rowthorn (1981).

There are four crucial aspects according to which the ensuing model may be unambiguously called a *Kaleckian* model of growth and distribution. First, there is the investment function, about which more will be said later. Second, prices relative to direct costs are influenced by a broad range of factors, often summarised under the phrase 'degree of monopoly', and are thought to be little influenced by the level of demand. Prices are of the cost-plus type, within the context of oligopolistic market structures. Third, marginal costs are assumed to be constant up to full capacity, and overhead labour costs are taken into account. Fourth, in contrast to earlier Kaldorian hypotheses, the rate of utilisation of capacity is assumed to be generally below unity, and labour is assumed not to be a constraint.[4]

The long-period results at which Kaleckians arrive, notably the positive relation between the real wage rate and the rate of accumulation, have been questioned by various neo-Ricardian and neo-Marxian authors. The aim of the present article is to present these various criticisms *within the framework of the Kaleckian model*, and to show that there are substantial similarities between the formal neo-Marxian critique and the less formal neo-Ricardian objections to the Kaleckian model. It should be pointed out that such

[1] In a two-sector model the negative relation between real wages and the rate of accumulation need occur only under the classical hypothesis of no savings out of wages (Spaventa 1970, p. 140).

[2] Again, in a one-sector model, the positive relation between real wages and accumulation need occur only under the classical hypothesis of no savings out of wages (Nichols and Norton, 1991; Lavoie, 1992, p. 345). This is an additional objection to the cooperative capitalism view implicit to the Kaleckian model (Sarkar 1993).

[3] For instance, Nell (1985, p. 176) writes: 'Is it, in fact, the case that a rise in the growth rate at full capacity can only come about through a fall in real wages? This is certainly the neo-Keynesian tradition, and it is also in the spirit of Ricardo and Marx, but is it really true? The serious question is whether this is a good way to theorise about increasing the growth rate when the economy is operating at what is regarded as the normal level of capacity utilisation, let alone during a period of stagnation'.

[4] This is an obvious Kaleckian feature, as the following quotation demonstrates: 'A considerable proportion of capital equipment lies idle in the slump. Even on average the degree of utilization throughout the business cycle will be substantially below the maximum reached during the boom. Fluctuations in the utilisation of labour parallel those in the utilisation of equipment. The reserve of capital equipment and the reserve army of the unemployed are typical features of capitalist economy at least throughout a considerable part of the cycle' (Kalecki, 1971, p. 137).

comparisons are possible because it now has been recognised by economists of various schools that excess capacity *may* play a role both in the short and in the long period. We shall see that most of the objections to the Kaleckian model can be regrouped around discussions of the investment function on the one hand, and around the meaning of normal rates of profit and normal rates of capacity utilisation on the other hand. Possible answers to the objections will also be discussed.

The paper focuses on the simple Kaleckian model, set without reference to the financial sector nor to the external sector.[1] The possibility of introducing a rate of interest distinct from the rate of profit, although work has been done to this effect, will be disregarded.[2] Problems associated with a multi-sector framework are also ignored and as a consequence neither the question of a uniform rate of profit,[3] nor the issues brought up by Steedman (1992) with respect to the validity of the mark-up approach, will be discussed directly. In particular, the capital–capacity ratio will be taken as constant, and it will be assumed that changes in real wages have no impact on the choice of technique.[4] It will be further assumed that the short-period supply of output can be immediately adjusted to demand, as is usually supposed in Keynesian models.[5] We start by presenting the essentials of the Kaleckian model of growth and distribution.

## 2. The canonical Kaleckian model

*The profits cost equation*

There are three crucial equations in the Kaleckian model. We start out with the derivation of what Rowthorn (1981, p. 8) and Steindl (1979, p. 3) call the profits function, which we shall call the profits cost equation. From national accounting, we have that the value of output is equal to the sum of the wage costs and the profits on capital:

$$pq = wL + rpK \tag{1}$$

where $p$ is the price level, $q$ is the level of real output, $w$ is the normal wage rate, $L$ is the level of labour employment, $r$ is the rate of profit, $K$ is the stock of capital in real terms. This may be rewritten as:

$$p = w(L/q) + rpK/q \tag{2}$$

In most Kaleckian models, only variable labour is taken into consideration. Here, in the Kaleckian tradition of Asimakopulos (1975) and Steindl (1979, p. 3), we follow Rowthorn (1981) and Kurz (1991) by taking into account fixed or overhead labour ($L_f$) as well as variable labour ($L_v$).[6] We then make use of the following definitions:

The amount of labour employed:

$$L = L_v + L_f \tag{3}$$

[1] See Taylor (1991) and Sarantis (1990–91).

[2] See Skott (1989), Taylor (1991), Dutt (1992) and Lavoie (1995).

[3] For discussions about gravitation and the convergence towards classical prices of production, a reader is referred to the special issue of *Political Economy* (1990). The likelihood of convergence in the specific case of multi-sector models of cost-plus prices is discussed in more detail in Boggio (1992).

[4] See Kurz (1986, 1990) for studies on the meaning of normal rates of utilisation in the context of the choice of technique. See Kurz (1991) and You (1994) for studies of technical progress.

[5] In the terms of Duménil and Lévy (1987, p. 140), the model is one of equilibrium dynamics.

[6] The importance of overhead labour for growth models has been lately underlined by Nichols and Norton (1991).

The rate of utilisation of capacity, with $q_{fc}$ full capacity output:

$$u = q/q_{fc} \tag{4}$$

The capital to capacity ratio:

$$v = K/q_{fc} \tag{5}$$

The average or marginal productivity of variable labour:

$$y_v = q/L_v \tag{6}$$

The requirements in fixed labour, assumed to depend on output capacity rather than actual output:

$$y_f = q_{fc}/L_f \tag{7}$$

The ratio of fixed labour to variable labour, the latter being defined at full capacity output, is assumed to be fixed. Calling $f$ such a ratio, it follows from its definition and from equations (6) and (7) that $f$ is equal to:

$$f = y_v/y_f \tag{8}$$

With these definitions, equation (2) can be rewritten as:

$$p = w(1 + f/u)/y_v + rpv/u \tag{9}$$

Equation (9) gives us the price of a unit of output in terms of the labour costs per unit of output and the profits per unit of output.[1] Note that the first element of the right-hand side of equation (9) is simply average cost per unit at the actual rate of utilisation of capacity. From this equation, we obtain the profits cost equation in terms of the real wage rate:

$$r = (u/v)[1 - (w/p)(1 + f/u)/y_v] \tag{10}$$

Kaleckian models are often expressed in terms of the *gross* profit margin $m$. To do so, we have to introduce a pricing equation. Post-Keynesians usually rely on some cost-plus pricing procedure. We shall consider two of these. The first one is the simple mark-up procedure on unit direct costs. Here, as we deal with a single vertically-integrated sector, all direct costs come down to labour costs, so the mark-up pricing procedure becomes:

$$p = (1 + \theta)w/y_v \tag{11}$$

The gross margin of profit $m$, or Kalecki's degree of monopoly, is a simple function of the mark-up $\theta$. It is given by:

$$m = \theta/(1 + \theta) \tag{12}$$

From the above three equations, we obtain the profits cost equation of the Kaleckian growth model:

$$r = u(m/v) - (1 - m)f/v \tag{13}$$

The rate of profit is a function of the rate of utilisation of capacity and of various parameters, including the gross profit margin.

[1] One could introduce a parameter, say $\sigma = w_p/w$, which would signal the ratio between the average salary paid to overhead labour, $w_p$, and the average wage paid to variable labour, $w$. With such an addition, there would be no change to the equations, except that the product $\sigma f$ would replace the parameter $f$ wherever it appears (cf. Nichols and Norton (1991), and Lavoie (1992, ch. 6)).

*Target return pricing*

While Kaleckians themselves seem to have favoured mark-up pricing, one is not forced to adopt this type of cost-plus pricing procedure. Indeed, it has been argued by Lee (1985) that pricing procedures are to a large extent dependent on accounting procedures, and that the latter have long been sophisticated enough to support normal cost pricing procedures, also called by some full cost pricing. Such pricing is based on unit costs, or rather standard unit costs, rather than unit direct costs only. A particular specification of normal cost pricing is target return pricing, and it seems to be prevalent today (Lanzillotti, 1958; Shipley, 1981). A well-known example of target return pricing is General Motors.

> GM begins its pricing analysis with an objective of earnings, on the average over the years, a return of approximately 15 per cent after taxes on total invested capital. Since it does not know how many autos will be sold in a forthcoming year, and hence what the average cost per unit (including prorated overhead) will be, it calculates costs on the assumption of *standard volume*—that is, operation at 80 percent of conservatively rated capacity. A *standard price* is next calculated by adding to average cost per unit at standard volume a sufficient profit margin to yield the desired 15 per cent after-tax return on capital. (Scherer, 1970, p. 174)

Some Kaleckians seem to agree to this sort of pricing procedure, without necessarily using it explicitly. For instance, Asimakopulos (1975, p. 319) argues that 'mark-ups are designed to cover, over time, both overhead costs and profits. Their values would thus be dependent on the standard rates of utilisation of productive capacity used to calculate standard costs as well as on some expected rate of return'.[1] We can find an explicit pricing formula for target return procedures that is almost as simple as the mark-up equation (11). To do so, we define the *standard* rate of utilisation of capacity, $u_s$. First note, with the help of equation (9), that unit costs at standard volume are equal to: $w(1+f/u_s)/y_v$. Target return pricing would then be such that:

$$p=(1+\theta')w(1+f/u_s)/y_v \qquad (14)$$

What then would $\theta'$ be equal to? Suppose that the replacement value of the stock of capital is $pK$, while the target rate of return, to which we shall also refer as the *standard rate of profit*, is $r_s$. Required profits for the period are then $r_s pK$. With a standard rate of utilisation of capacity of $u_s$, corresponding in the period to a level of output of $q_s$, the required profits for the period must be equal to $r_s vpq_s/u_s$. This must be equated to the total profits that are to be obtained by marking up unit costs at the standard rate of utilisation of capacity: $q_s\theta' w(1+f/u_s)/y_v$. After some manipulation, a simple pricing formula for target pricing procedures emerges:

$$p=\left(\frac{u_s+f}{u_s-r_s v}\right)\frac{w}{y_v} \qquad (15)$$

Of course, the equation makes sense only if the denominator is positive, that is, if $u_s>r_s v$. The inequality must by necessity be fulfilled since it implies that wages are positive, i.e., profit income is smaller than total income. When this target return pricing formula is combined with equation (10), the profits cost function becomes:

$$r=[(f+r_s v)u-(u_s-r_s v)f]/v(u_s+f) \qquad (16)$$

[1] Asimakopulos's model is very similar to the one presented here. It includes overhead labour costs, but is set in the short period only.

One should note that if the actual rate of utilisation of capacity $u$ turns out to be equal to the standard rate of utilisation of capacity $u_s$, the actual rate of profit $r$ is then equal to the target rate of return $r_s$ embodied in the margin of profit of the pricing procedure. This can be seen more clearly by rewriting equation (16) under the form of equation (17).

$$r=r_s\left(\frac{u+f}{u_s+f}\right)+\frac{(u-u_s)f}{v(u_s+f)} \tag{17}$$

Since equation (16) is linear in $u$, it clearly shows that the standard and the actual rate of utilisation of capacity cannot be equal unless the standard and the actual rates of profit are equal. This result will be quite useful in Section 4.

*Effective demand*

The previous equations define a rate of profit seen from the cost accounting side. Effective demand has not yet been taken into account. In the neo-Keynesian models, the rate of accumulation is taken to be exogenous, so that the Cambridge equation can be interpreted as fully representing the notion of effective demand. A crucial feature of the Kaleckian model is its investment function. The Cambridge equation must thus be reinterpreted as a savings function. With the standard assumptions, i.e., there are no savings out of wages and salaries or the Pasinetti (1962) conditions apply, the savings function in growth terms becomes:

$$g^s=rs_p \tag{18}$$

with $s_p$ the overall propensity to save out of profits.

We now come to the investment function, which, as will be seen, has been the main subject of contention. Both Rowthorn (1981) and Dutt (1984; 1990) use Kaldor's (1957) investment function expressed in growth terms:

$$g^i=\gamma+g_uu+g_rr \tag{19}$$

where $\gamma$ is some parameter, which must be positive in the models without overhead labour (Dutt, 1990, p. 25), but which can be negative in the models with overhead costs.

Note that investment decisions depend positively on both the rate of profit and the rate of utilisation. Putting together equations (18) and (19), one obtains what Rowthorn (1981, p. 12) calls the realisation curve. We shall call it the effective demand equation:

$$r=(g_uu+\gamma)/(s_p-g_r) \tag{20}$$

The steady-state solution to this Kaleckian model of growth and distribution can be obtained by combining the profits cost equation and the effective demand equation. In the case of the simple mark-up procedure, we use equations (13) and (20). A graphical solution is offered in Fig. 1. The model is stable provided:

$$s_p>g_r+g_uv/m \tag{21}$$

The model contains two crucial features. First, Keynes's paradox of thrift holds, even in the long period. A decrease of the propensity to save would shift up the effective demand curve, labelled ED in Fig. 1, and hence generate higher rates of profit, utilisation and accumulation. The paradox of thrift proves to be very resilient to critiques, although it will not be discussed any further. Second, there is the paradox of cost: any increase in costs raises the rate of profit (Rowthorn 1981, p. 18). This can be shown by taking the partial derivative of equation (13) with respect to $m$. This derivative is obviously positive.

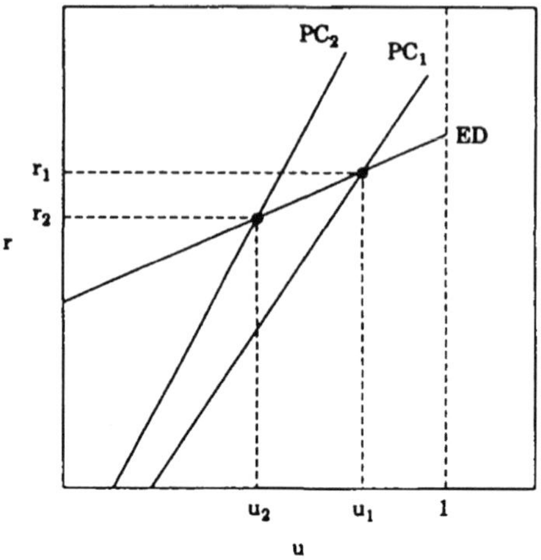


**Fig. 1.** *The paradox of costs: lower real wages induce a lower rate of profit.*

An increase in the mark-up or in the gross profit margin $m$ thus entails an upward shift of the profits cost curve, labelled PC in Fig. 1. A lower real wage rate is thus associated with a lower rate of utilisation, a lower rate of profit, and hence a lower rate of accumulation.[1]

Since these positive relations go against the classical beliefs that accumulation requires sacrifices and that labour and capital interests are necessarily dissonant, it will surprise no one that some neo-Ricardian and neo-Marxian authors have questioned those implications of the Kaleckian model, on various grounds.[2]

## 3. The critique of the Kaleckian investment function

*On the similarity between the neo-Ricardian and the neo-Marxian critiques*

Besides the rejection of mark-up prices as relevant long period prices, the main neo-Ricardian response to the positive relation between real wages and profit rates has been the denial of the relevance of a rate of utilisation that would be different from its standard rate. The neo-Ricardians call this standard rate the normal rate of capacity utilisation. Two approaches have been taken. One is to deny that the rate of utilisation in the long period may be any different from its normal rate. We shall deal with this position later. The second approach is to deny that the current rate of utilisation has any impact on investment decisions.[3] This is the position that we now tackle.

[1] From his Kaleckian model of accumulation, Del Monte (1975, p. 243) concludes: 'Our model confirms what is usually observed in the real world, that is, an increase in the degree of monopoly diminishes the rate of utilisation of plants and the rate of growth. When firms decide to reduce the real wages of workers, the result is not an increase in the rate of profit, but rather a decrease in the rate of profit, because the higher degree of monopoly has led to fall in the rate of utilisation of capacity' [my translation].

[2] Ironically, but rightly so, Kurz (1993, p. 78) attributes to the neo-Keynesians the belief that 'the distributive conflict holds full sway over the long period', adding that such a position cannot be accepted.

[3] Some neo-Ricardians have adopted the first position, only to later switch to the other. Vianello (1989, p. 188) writes that 'it was only after reading Dr Ciccone's article that I realised that I had no need to bring in the tendency of productive capacity to adjust when arguing away the alleged influence of current on expected capacity'.

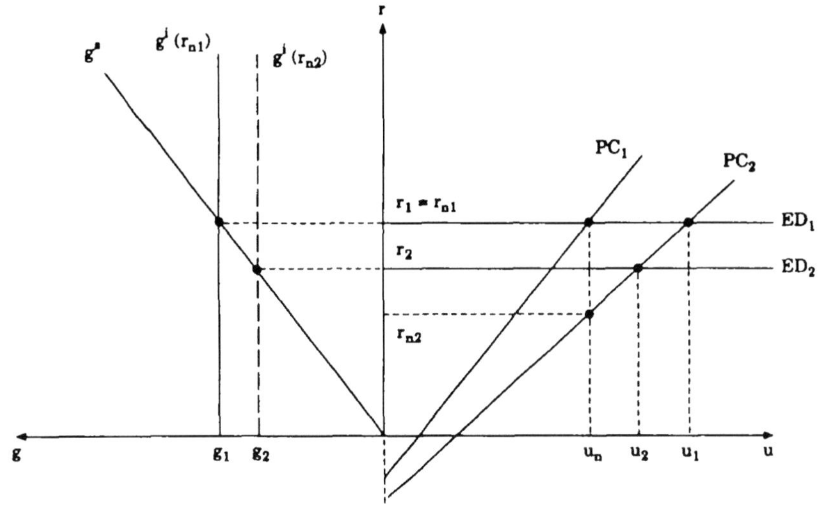


**Fig. 2.** *The classical view: a lower normal rate of profit induces lower accumulation.*

While some neo-Ricardians recognise that the rate of utilisation in the long period may be different from its normal rate, they dispute that current profitability could have any influence on expected profitability. This objection is related to the investment function. The view of both Ciccone (1986, p. 26) and Vianello (1989), and also of Garegnani (1992, p. 56) and Kurz (1992, p. 22), is that new investment depends on expected profitability, computed at normal prices based on the normal rate of utilisation of capacity. This means that the investment function depends on the (expected) normal rate of profit rather than on the actual rate of profit. The justification for this is that entrepreneurs cannot make future plans under the assumption that capacity will be perpetually over-utilised. Plans must be made according to profitability at normal use of capacity. The rate of profit that represents 'the guiding light for investment and pricing decisions, cannot possibly be either an abnormally high or an abnormally low one' (Vianello, 1985, p. 84). Assuming as an extreme case that the actual rate of utilisation has no impact on the investment function, the neo-Ricardian investment function could be written as follows, with $r_n$ denoting the (expected) normal rate of profit:

$$g^i = \gamma + g_r r_n \tag{22}$$

Vianello's (1989) main argument is that Kaleckian authors fail to understand that expected profitability is hindered by a rise of real wages, even if actual profitability stays constant in the short and medium run. This fall in the expected normal rate of profit eventually leads to a fall in investment activity, and hence to a fall in the actual rate of profit, thus justifying to some extent the pessimistic expectations. This reasoning is illustrated in Fig. 2. Suppose we start from a fluke situation in which the savings and the investment functions, $g^s$ and $g^i(r_{n1})$, are such that the rate of utilisation and the actual rate of profit happen to be at their normal rates, $u_n$ and $r_{n1}$. The initial profits cost curve is given by $PC_1$ and the effective demand curve must be $ED_1$. Now let us assume an increase in the real wage, with no change in the technical coefficients. This implies a downshift of the profits cost curve to $PC_2$. In the short period, with no change in the rate of accumulation, and hence no change in the actual rate of profit, the actual rate of utilisation of capacity rises to $u_1$. It is this rise in the rate of utilisation that allows actual profitability to stay constant, despite the rise in wage costs.

According to Vianello, however, this situation will not last. Entrepreneurs will revise their view of the normal profit rate, taking into account the new real wage rate. The new normal profit rate $r_{n2}$ is given by the intersection of the new profits cost curve $PC_2$ and the normal rate of utilisation $u_n$. The desired rate of accumulation—given by equation (22)—falls to $g^i(r_{n2})$, thus inducing a downshift of the effective demand curve to $ED_2$. At the end of the process, the normal and the actual rates of utilisation will usually diverge, as will the actual and normal rates of profit. The new actual rate of profit, that is $r_2$, is below the initial rate of profit $r_{n1}$, despite real wages having increased and despite the rate of capacity utilisation being endogenous. Although the rate of utilisation does not necessarily equal the normal rate of utilisation nor unity, the negative relation between the real wage rate and the rate of profit is recovered, as the neo-Ricardians would have it. Similarly, the long-period negative relation between the real wage rate and the rate of accumulation is restored.[1]

One need not, however, make the extreme assumption that the actual rate of utilisation of capacity has no induced effect on the investment function. One may presume that firms take normal profitability into account while still responding to the actual rate of capacity utilisation.[2] Noting that normal profitability is related to the normal rate of capacity utilisation in accordance with equation (13), that is, the profits cost equation, the 'neo-Ricardian' investment function of equation (22) would then become:

$$g^i = \gamma + g_u u + g_r r_n \tag{23}$$

This is precisely what Bhaduri and Marglin (1990) offer as an investment function. They contend, as do Kurz (1991) and other neo-Marxians such as Epstein (1994), that the investment function, if linear, should be of the following form:

$$g^i = \gamma + g_u u + g_m m \tag{24}$$

Here, as before, $m$ represents the gross margin of profit, derived from the mark-up on variable costs, and $g_m$ represents the sensitivity of investment to changes in the margin of profit. Bhaduri and Marglin seem to argue that investment activity depends on a single variable, the actual rate of profit. That rate can, however, be decomposed into the rate of utilisation of capacity and the *net* share of profits $\pi$ in national income, that is:

$$r = \pi u / v \tag{25}$$

[1] I believe Fig. 2 is a correct graphical representation of Ciccone's and Garegnani's literary models. Once the new normal profit rate has been inserted within the new investment function, the relation between the $ED_2$ and $PC_2$ curves could be such that the actual (average) profit rate $r_2$ is smaller or larger than (or even equal to) the normal profit rate $r_{n2}$. According to Ciccone, while prices gravitate around their normal values, the actual rates of capacity utilisation need not. Here I understand Ciccone (1986, 1987) and Garegnani (1992) as saying that while prices and investment decisions incorporate the normal profit rate $r_{n2}$, the actual rate of utilisation $u_2$ may on average be greater or smaller than $u_n$.

[2] For instance, Garegnani (1992, p. 62) writes that 'the normal rate of profits will be that on which [the entrepreneurs] will base their decision to invest—a rate which, as we saw, will need bear no close relation to a ratio between aggregate actual net profits and aggregate existing capital'. But he also recognises that 'a high past level of utilization of the plant might well result in a higher amount of investment, and a larger new plant . . .' (1992, p. 56).

In the special case where there is no overhead labour, the net share of profits $\pi$ and the gross margin of profit $m$ are identical. Strictly speaking, when there are overhead costs, an investment function based on the definition of the actual rate of profit should depend on the net share of profits $\pi$ rather than the gross margin of profit $m$. We shall return to this distinction, which is only relevant, at least in one-sector models, in the case incorporating overhead costs.

Broadly speaking then, the argument of Bhaduri and Marglin is based on equation (25). They say that an increase in the actual rate of profit may be due either to a rise in the actual rate of capacity utilisation or to a rise in the margin of profit. When investing, firms would separate the effects on profits due to effective demand from those which follow from the firm's ability to cut its costs relative to prices. Bhaduri and Marglin (1990, p. 391) demonstrate that the canonical Kaleckian investment function, equation (19), when compared to equation (24), imposes restrictions on the relative response of investment to the two constituents of the profit rate. In their own equation, the rate of utilisation plays no role in addition to that played as part of the actual rate of profit.

While the arguments advanced by neo-Marxians and neo-Ricardians may appear different, they are in the end identical. This can most easily be seen by getting rid of overhead costs in the profits cost equation (13), and finding the normal rate of profit corresponding to a normal use of capacity: One gets:

$$r_n = mu_n/v \tag{26}$$

As long as normal capacity utilisation $u_n$ and the capital to capacity ratio $v$ are constants, any change in the gross margin of profit $m$ implies a change in the normal rate of profit $r_n$. Clearly, then, the investment function proposed by Marglin and Bhaduri as a replacement for the Kaleckian investment function is a variant of Vianello's case against the use of current profitability as an argument of the investment function. Bhaduri and Marglin (1990, p. 388), as well as Vianello (1989, p. 183), argue that Kaleckians have omitted the depressing cost effects of higher wages on economic activity. Equation (26) makes clear that the proponents of equation (24) suppose that, if the rate of profit is to be taken into consideration in addition to the rate of capacity utilisation, it should be calculated at the normal rate of utilisation. Those who are saying that the margin of profit $m$, rather than the actual rate of profit $r$, should enter the investment function in addition to the rate of utilisation of capacity are making an argument which is no different from the assertion that the normal rate of profit $r_n$, rather than the actual one, should be included in the investment function in addition to the rate of utilisation of capacity. The neo-Ricardian and the neo-Marxian objections to the Kaleckian investment function are thus in the end identical.

*Kaleckian responses to the critiques*

That the Kaleckian investment function implies unwarranted restrictions seems to be a fairly valid point, which cannot be disputed on logical grounds. Indeed, this point may even be attributed to the Kaleckians themselves, since it is Steindl who argued that one needs to distinguish 'between those shifts to or from profits which are due to effective demand, and those which result from changed price-cost relations independent of demand' (1979, p. 3).[1] The use of equation (24) combined to the rest of the Kaleckian model allows Bhaduri and Marglin (1990), as well as others such as Kurz (1991) and

[1] Steindl made the same point earlier: 'The net profit margin can, in fact, change for two quite different reasons: either because of a change in utilisation of capacity, with an otherwise unchanged structure of costs and prices; or the net profit margin can change at a *given level of utilisation of capacity*' (1952, p. 46).

Taylor (1991, ch. 3), to demonstrate that several regimes are possible, and that there may or may not be a positive relationship between the real wage rate and the rate of accumulation. It must be noted, however, that Bhaduri and Marglin (1990, p. 385) do not put much weight on this investment function to justify the possibility of a profit squeeze regime. They consider their results more compelling when associated with an open economy. The income elasticity of imports could eventually lead to a deterioration of the trade balance, annihilating the expansionary effects of higher real wages (cf. Blecker, 1989). Staying within the confines of a closed economy, however, several reasons can be advanced in favour of the Kaleckian investment function over the Marxian/neo-Ricardian investment formulation.

One may hesitate to incorporate the margin of profit (or the normal rate of profit) as one of the determinants of the investment function in a macroeconomic model for at least five different reasons. Most of these reasons have to do with factors entrepreneurs face when operating in an economy set in actual time. First, it is not clear that an increase in the margin of profit that corporations try to impose at the normal degree of capacity utilisation necessarily implies better profitability. This follows an argument put forward by some neo-Ricardians. According to Pivetti (1988, p. 282), 'the interest rate determines the markup of prices over nominal wages'. An increase in the margin of profit may thus be the result of an increase in the perceived permanent rate of interest.[1] This does not necessarily entail good news for the entrepreneurs in contrast to the rentiers. Second, as has been argued by Dutt (1990, p. 223), firms may be looking at the overall economy, rather than at their own situation, to judge the expected profitability of their investment plans. If this is so, firms would not be able to assess the current normal rate of profit as the neo-Ricardians explicitly argue. The available information would only allow entrepreneurs to estimate the actual rate of profit. As a consequence, the rate of profit rather than the margin of profit or the normal rate of profit again would have to be the variable entering the investment function. Third, the choice of the proper variable in the investment function may depend on the time horizon involved. If the lifetime of the investment project is shorter than the number of years expected to be needed for the actual rate of utilisation to come back to its normal rate, it would be more reasonable for firms to base their decisions on actual rates rather than normal rates. This last argument, and the one to follow, would probably convince economists concerned with sequences of short runs, such as the Kaleckians, whereas they would have less impact on those economists more preoccupied with the atemporal long-period analysis, such as the neo-Ricardians.[2]

A fourth reason, based on the dynamics of effective demand in actual time, could also be offered in favour of the Kaleckian investment function. Going back to the example given in Fig. 2, it can be shown that in the transition period during which the rate of capacity utilisation increases from $u_n$ to $u_p$, the growth rate of sales is higher than that prevailing in the initial steady-state. We know from equations (1) and (5) that $q/K=u/v$, and hence in growth terms that:

$$\hat{q}=g+\hat{u}-\hat{v} \tag{27}$$

[1] The margin of profit would then be written as:

$$m=m_e+m_i i$$

where $m_i$ is a positive parameter and $i$ is the nominal or real rate of interest. See Dutt (1992B) and Lavoie (1992, ch. 6).

[2] See, among others, Halevi and Kriesler (1991). For a distinction between long-period positions as a notional state and long run as a duration of time, see Caravalho (1992, p. 19–25).

Even though the rates of profit and of accumulation are assumed constant from one steady-state to another, an increase in real wages will induce both a higher rate of capacity utilisation and a transitional increase in the growth rate of sales ($\hat{q}$). The result is intuitive: the rate of utilisation rises because sales are rising faster than the installation of new capacity. This should have a positive impact on the expectations and animal spirits of entrepreneurs in a world of uncertainty, independently of its impact on the rate of profit, and regardless of the fall in the gross margin of profit or in the rate of normal profit.

The final and crucial justification of the standard Kaleckian investment function, however, is the finance frontier (Agliardi, 1988, p. 284). Unless investment expenditures are entirely financed by retained earnings, firms can only invest as long as they can convince banks that they are worthy borrowers. Retained earnings are thus an important element of the investment function, *independently of any effect that a high rate of capacity utilisation may have on the desire to invest.* The normal rate of profit, or the margin of profit, may be a good indicator of profitability of investment to be expected for the future; but the realised rate of profit is also a good indicator of the borrowing possibilities of firms.[1]

The independent influence of the rate of utilisation over investment has been verified empirically by many authors, notably by Fazzari and Mott (1986–87): in a time-series study, they show that the sales and retained earnings of firms each have a positive impact on investment expenditures, while their flow of interest payments has a negative influence on investment. Similarly, Chamberlain and Gordon (1989) show that capacity utilisation and profitability net of interest payments are significant determinants of investment. Those findings are entirely compatible with the investment function proposed by Kaleckians in general and Steindl in particular. They highlight the importance of the rate of utilisation, independently of its effect on the realised rate of profit.

*Profit shares with overhead labour*

A major reason for which the investment function and the results of the standard Kaleckian model have been questioned is that some authors do not believe that the canonical Kaleckian model and its main stagnationist view correspond to the stylised facts of the last two decades. In the Kaleckian models without overhead costs, a rise in real wages is necessarily associated with a rise in the share of wages and with a rise in the rate of accumulation. Neo-Marxian authors, however, note that in the recent past rising wage shares have been associated with lower rates of accumulation.[2] A sample of this view is presented below:

> Recent trends in income distribution and economic growth in the OECD countries seem, at least at first sight, to cast doubt upon the stagnationist view. A number of studies have found that wage shares rose and profit shares fell in the United States and other western countries sometime after the mid-to-late 1960s. This distributional shift roughly coincides with the period of 'stagflation', or slower growth, accompanied by inflationary pressures. (Blecker, 1989, p. 395)

[1] This factor was underlined not only by Kalecki (1971, p. 111) but also by Robinson (1962, p. 86). In addition, the importance of realised profits, in contrast to normal profits, on the availability of finance for firms desiring to invest has been recognised more recently by neo-Ricardian authors: see Garegnani (1992, p. 62) and Roncaglia (1990, p. 110).

[2] See also Auerbach and Skott (1988) and Sarkar (1993). It must be said in defence of Blecker that Nell makes a very similar argument to support the Kaleckian model. Nell argues that the neo-Keynesian and Marxian inverse relation between real wages and growth cannot be valid, because since the 1940s 'the share of wages and the rate of growth *both* increased' (1985, p. 176).

It must now be noted that the model that has been developed above is impervious to that critique. There is no inconsistency between low shares of profit and low growth rates or low rates of utilisation in a Kaleckian model incorporating overhead costs, as we now show. Recall the definition of the rate of profit given by equation (25). The share of profits (net of fixed wage costs) is thus $\pi = rv/u$. Using this algebraic definition of the share of profits, we can substitute into it the effective demand function and the profits cost function, given by equations (20) and (13), to obtain the profit share as seen from the demand and supply sides respectively.

$$\pi^d = [vg_u + v\gamma/u]/(s_p - g_r) \tag{28}$$

$$\pi^s = m - (1 - m)f/u \tag{29}$$

It can be seen immediately that a rise in the degree of monopoly $m$ leads to a shift of the $\pi^s$ curve only, the shift being an upward one. As to the impact on the equilibrium share of profits, two cases arise depending on the sign taken by $\gamma$ (Rowthorn, 1981, p. 21). When this parameter is positive, the $\pi^d$ curve is downward sloping, as illustrated in Fig. 3(a). A fall in real wages, that is an increase in the degree of monopoly, leads to an increase in the share of net profits from $\pi_1{}^*$ to $\pi_2{}^*$. Under these conditions, it would thus appear that the movements of the share of profits are countercyclical. The share of profits increases when the rate of utilisation, the rate of profit and the rate of accumulation all decrease as a result of the lower real wages. A specific instance of this case is the Dutt/Amadeo model without overhead costs, in which the $\gamma$ term cannot be negative, and where the $\pi^s$ curve is horizontal.

In the Kaleckian model with overhead costs, however, the $\gamma$ term can be negative. Such a situation occurs if positive profits are required for firms to invest. The $\pi^d$ curve is then positive, as is shown in Fig. 3(b).[1] As in the previous case, an increase in the gross margin of profit $m$ shifts up the $\pi^s$ curve. This time, however, the share of profits falls from $\pi_1{}^*$ to $\pi_2{}^*$. The movements of the share of profits are thus procyclical. The share of profits decreases, as does the rate of capacity utilisation, despite the increase in the gross margin of profit. In this case, which is just as likely as the other, the share of profits and the rate of accumulation increase together, just as they did in the earlier post-Keynesian models of Robinson and Kaldor. Readers may also verify for themselves, in both parts of Fig. 3, that a variation in the demand parameters that induces an upward shift of the $\pi^d$ curve results into an increase of both the rate of utilisation and the share of profits. This implies that for a given margin of profit the rate of accumulation and the share of profits increase together.

The stylised facts that have been observed in OECD countries are thus consistent with the stagnationist model: high mark-ups and low real wages may induce both slow growth and low net profit shares. High mark-ups are not synonymous with high profit shares in Kaleckian models with overhead costs. As Weisskopf (1979, p. 354) warns: 'Because of the overhead labour phenomenon, a rise in the share of total wages (hourly wages plus salaries), and hence a decline in the share of profits may result from a decline in the rate

[1] Note that the $\pi^d$ curve necessarily has a smaller slope than the $\pi^s$ curve. This requirement arises out of the necessity for the steady-state rate of capacity utilisation to be positive and because of the stability condition. Heuristically, it also can be seen that the $\pi^d$ curve cannot cut the $\pi^s$ curve from below, by noting that an increase of the mark-up would lead to an increase in the rate of utilisation, an impossible result within the strict Kaleckian model presented here.

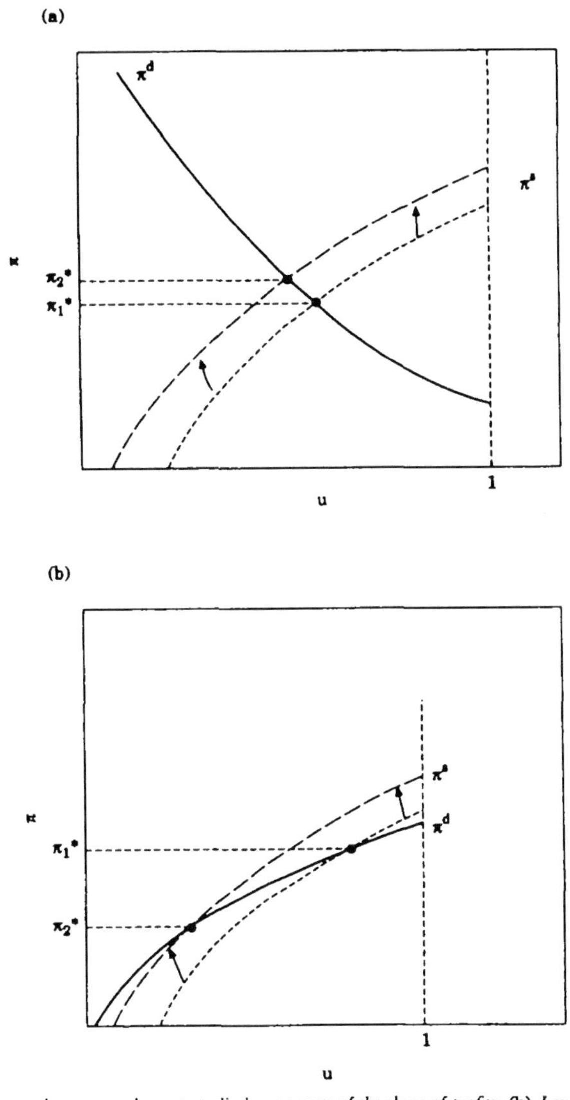


**Fig. 3.** (a) *Lower real wages, and countercyclical movements of the share of profits;* (b) *Lower real wages, and procyclical movements of the share of profits.*

of capacity utilisation as well as a rise in the strength of labour'. The analysis of Fig. 3(b) also shows that one need not go beyond the confines of a one-sector model to prove that a higher real wage rate may be associated with a lower wage share, as Steedman (1992, p. 148) cautions us, provided the effects of effective demand and variable rates of capacity utilisation are taken into account.

## 4. Implications of various definitions of the normal rate of capacity utilisation on the Kaleckian investment function

In previous discussion it was assumed that the actual rate of capacity utilisation can be different from the normal rate of utilisation in the long period. There are, however, several authors who believe that such a characterisation lacks consistency, or who contend that such a steady-state contains the seeds of its own destruction. We shall discuss in turn the implications of such criticisms for the investment function and the pricing equation. All the objections centre around the definition and meaning of a normal or standard rate of capacity utilisation.

In the course of the discussion, the concept of a *fully adjusted position* will be considered. Such a position will be defined as a situation which results from an adjustment process that occurs across long-period positions. The object of the adjustment process is to provide a convergence between the normal targets of the firm and their realised values. While the term 'fully adjusted position' is borrowed from Vianello (1985), it will be shown, in contrast to Vianello's use of the term, that even in fully adjusted positions the rate of capacity utilisation may still be considered endogenous.

Most of the discussion in Sections 3 and 4 will focus on whether the possible adjustment processes are stable or not. It should be pointed out that all conclusions are only valid for the linear model presented here; they would have to be reconsidered in a non-linear system where, for instance, there may be limit cycles such that instability would abound near the centre of gravitation of the long-period equilibrium, but where the stability would prevail away from this centre of gravitation.[1]

*The normal rate of utilisation as cost minimisation*

It has been argued by Kurz (1986) that the normal rate of utilisation of capacity could not be something defined by conventions. 'The normal rates of utilisation of the various items of plant and equipment are conceived to be in compliance with the principle of cost minimisation' (Kurz, 1986, p. 43). The normal rate of capacity utilisation is defined in this view according to the optimal choice of technique. This, however, cannot be considered a valid objection to the approach taken here. As Caserta (1990) points out, excess capacity has three dimensions. Utilisation can be increased by a more speedy operation of a plant, by longer or more numerous shifts of operation, or by putting to work machines that were previously idle. Only this last sort of excess capacity should be taken into consideration in models of the Kaleckian type (Caserta 1990, p. 151).[2] Cost minimisation deals with the other two meanings of excess capacity.

One can thus assume that each plant or segment of plant is being operated at its most efficient rate, in compliance with the proper principles of cost minimisation. The full capacity of a firm is then the sum of all of its capacities so defined (Eichner 1976, p. 62). When the rate of utilisation of capacity is below unity, some of the segments or some of the plants are not being utilised at all. It does not mean that plants are being run inefficiently with inappropriate shifts. As Dutt (1990, p. 230) points out, while firms may control the pace at which each plant is being used, they have no control over the overall degree of capacity utilisation at the macroeconomic level. Cost minimisation and excess capacities are not incompatible: cost minimisation deals solely with the pace at which a

[1] See, for instance, Skott (1989) and Dutt (1992A).

[2] Many economists object to this third notion of excess capacity, and hence to Kaleckian models in general, by arguing that firms use fluctuations in inventories to adapt to the fluctuations in demand (cf. Kurz, 1986, p. 53).

plant normally should be operated. This is generally unrelated to demand factors that set the actual rate of capacity utilisation and to the strategic and conventional considerations that determine the normal rate of capacity utilisation.

*The normal rate of utilisation as a target*

The rate of utilisation being clearly defined over the set of all plants, rather than at the level of the plant segment, we may now deal with the main objection to the Kaleckian long-period approach. This objection to the long-period inequality between the actual rate of capacity utilisation and the normal one is based on the presumption that the normal rate is a target of the firms. This is a criticism of Kaleckian models that can be found in Auerbach and Skott (1988) and in Committeri (1986; 1987). In their view, the normal rate of capacity is an optimal rate of utilisation that firms try to achieve, at least over the long run. Therefore, entrepreneurs would not be content unless the targeted rate of capacity utilisation is realised: 'It is inconceivable that utilization rates should remain significantly below the desired level for any prolonged period' (Auerbach and Skott, 1988, p. 53). The only possible steady state is one in which the actual rate of utilisation is equal to its normal or targeted level. This leads to the belief that the only consistent steady-state analysis is one where those two rates are equal, i.e., what Vianello and others consider to be 'fully adjusted positions'.

This is an embarrassing objection to the Kaleckians.[1] If the actual rate of capacity must eventually be equal to a *given* normal rate, then the rate of utilisation is not an endogenous variable in the long period any more. The objection is particularly valid since Kaleckians have sometimes referred to the normal rate as the 'planned' degree of utilisation of capacity (Steindl, 1952, p. 129; Amadeo, 1986B, p. 83), thus reinforcing the belief that the normal rate of capacity utilisation is a target of firms, which must be fulfilled in the long period. The complications arising from such an interpretation can be clearly spelled out by using an investment function suggested by Steindl (1952, p. 128) and reintroduced by Amadeo (1986A, 1986B). This investment function is based on the distinction between undesired and desired excess capacity, or between the actual rate and the normal rate of capacity utilisation, respectively denoted by $u$ and $u_n$.

$$g^i = \gamma + g_u(u - u_n) \tag{30}$$

The investment function is illustrated in Fig. 4, where the actual rate of accumulation is to be found at the intersection of the $g^i$ and the $g^s$ curves.[2] If the actual rate of utilisation turned out to be equal to the normal or desired one, the actual rate of growth would be equal to $\gamma$. As Committeri (1986, p. 173) and Caserta (1990, p. 152) point out, if firms are content with the degree of capacity utilisation that is being achieved and do not desire to have it changed, one concludes that the rate of accumulation desired by firms should be equal to the expected growth rate of sales. It is clear from equation (30) that the exogenous parameter $\gamma$ then represents this expected growth rate of sales. If, as is shown on the graph, it is assumed that the actual rate of capacity utilisation $u_1$ is smaller than the planned rate $u_n$, the actual rate of growth $g_1$ must be smaller than the expected growth rate of sales $\gamma_1$. Committeri argues that this cannot be a consistent solution: in a proper steady-state model, expectations of sales growth and of spare capacity should be realised.

[1] Halevi and Kriesler (1991) and Sawyer (1994) also come to grip with that objection.

[2] Note that the $g^s$ curve is identical to the profits cost function, equation (13), except for a multiplicative constant arising from the savings function, equation (18), such that: $g^s = s_p[u(m/v) - (1 - m)f/v]$.

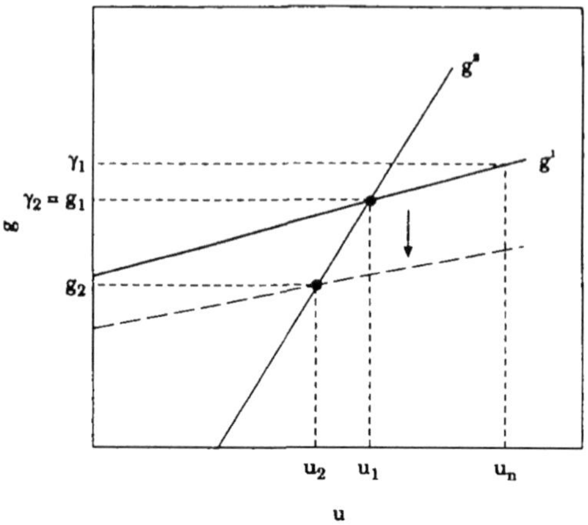


**Fig. 4.** *Firms revise the expected rate of sales growth, at a constant standard rate of capacity utilization: instability.*

At this stage, four possibilities arise: firms take into account this divergence between actual and expected rates of growth of sales in their investment function; firms revise their expectations of sales growth; firms revise their targeted normal rate of capacity utilisation; firms revise both their expectations of sales growth and their normal rate of utilisation. All four possibilities will be dealt with.

*Taking the expected growth rate of sales into account*

Suppose first that firms incorporate the discrepancy between sales expectations and realisation within the investment function. Investment function (30) would now be:

$$g^i = \gamma + \alpha(g - \gamma) + g_u(u - u_n) \qquad (31)$$

Capital accumulation would accelerate whenever the actual growth rate of sales exceeds their expected growth rate $\gamma$. Such a function is proposed by Eichner (1976, p. 197), to take into account the fact that the actual growth rate may diverge from the *secular* growth rate, and hence says Eichner, from the *expected* growth rate. Such a function, however, adds little to the existing model. There still will be steady-state positions where expectations and targets are not being realised. This can be seen by solving equation (31) and verifying that it contains all the features of equation (30):

$$g^i = \gamma + g_u(u - u_n)/(1 - \alpha) \qquad (32)$$

The second possibility is the one underlined by Committeri and Kurz. Firms could react to their unrealised sales expectations by modifying their expectations of sales growth. The $\gamma$ coefficient would then vary according to the realised values of the rate of growth. If firms react in an adaptive manner, the expected growth rate of sales at each period would then be:

$$\gamma_t = (1 - \varphi)\gamma_{t-1} + \varphi g_{t-1} \qquad 0 < \varphi < 1 \qquad (33)$$

In the case depicted in Fig. 4, the $\gamma$ coefficient would go down to $\gamma_2$. This implies that the investment curve $g^i$ should shift down, the actual rate of growth should drop to $g_2$, and the actual and normal rates of utilisation of capacity should diverge even further. The

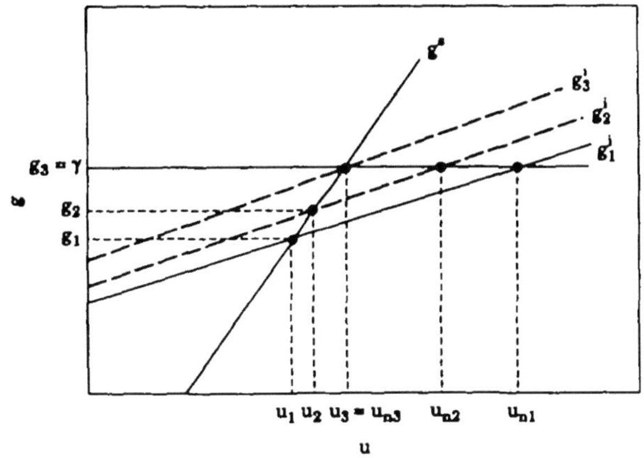

Fig. 5. *Firms revise the standard rate of capacity utilization, at a constant expected rate of sales growth: stability.*

conclusion of this exercise, *if the normal rate of utilisation of capacity is considered to be a target and if firms respond to their unrealised sales expectations*, is that the model is unstable (Committeri 1986, p. 175). As Kurz (1994, p. 415) points out, this is reminiscent of Harrod's instability principle. There is no fully adjusted position besides full capacity utilisation, or else it must be *assumed* that the rate of utilisation in the long-period position is always equal to its normal level.

*Revising the normal rate of capacity utilisation*

The third possibility that arises from considering the normal rate of capacity utilisation as a target rate is the following: one would expect the target to change according to historical variations in the actual rate. The normal rate of utilisation $u_n$ ceases to be an exogenous variable that contributes to determine the actual utilisation and accumulation rates. This was recognised early on by Amadeo (1986A, p. 155) and Ciccone (1986, p. 35). Of course it may be said that if the normal rate of utilisation tends towards the actual rate of utilisation, the steady-state rate of utilisation is still endogenous, although in the fully adjusted position the normal and the actual rates are necessarily equal.

In this third case, it will be supposed that the expected rate of growth of sales $\gamma$ is an expectation based on unchanging secular trends—a somewhat unKaleckian assumption.[1] Investment equation (30) thus depends on the perceived secular growth rate of sales, i.e., it does not depend on the actual growth rate: $\gamma$ is a given, in contrast to what has just been assumed in the Harrodian instability case. Let us also suppose that the normal rate of capacity utilisation responds to the actual rate of capacity utilisation in the following manner:

$$u_{n(t)} = (1 - \tau)u_{n(t-1)} + \tau u_{(t-1)} \qquad 0<\tau<1 \tag{34}$$

The fully adjusted impact of the above two assumptions can be observed in Fig. 5. Let us start, as in Fig. 4, from a situation where the initial rate of growth $g_1$ is below $\gamma$, and hence where the rate of capacity utilisation $u_1$ is below the normal rate $u_{n1}$. This will

[1] It should be pointed out that a similar assumption is required for the stability of multi-sector growth models that study the possibility of classical gravitation: investment depends on a given steady-state rate of growth $\gamma$, which is supposedly known (Caminati, 1990, p. 24).

induce a fall in the normal rate of capacity utilisation, along the lines of equation (34), say to $u_{n2}$. This fall in the normal rate of capacity utilisation will in turn induce an upward shift of the investment function $g^i$. The new actual rate of capacity utilisation $u_2$ will now be higher than the previous actual rate $u_1$, and it will be closer to the normal rate of capacity utilisation, while the new rate of accumulation $g_2$ will also be higher. This process will continue until the actual and the normal rates of capacity utilisation, $u_3$ and $u_{n3}$, converge with each other, at which point the rate of growth of the economy will be exactly equal to $\gamma$. In such a model, there is thus a convergence towards the expected secular growth rate of sales: as Committeri (1986, p. 174) would have it, producers 'would be content with what they are doing'. This would also be reflected in the long-period equality between the actual and the normal rates of utilisation. Despite this equality, however, the rate of utilisation is still endogenous.

The value of the fully adjusted rate of capacity utilisation depends on the expected secular rate of growth $\gamma$ and on the parameters defining the $g^s$ curve, in particular the margin of profit and the propensity to save. While the rate of utilisation is endogenous, many of the properties of the canonical Kaleckian model do not hold any more. There is still a positive relationship between the animal spirits of the entrepreneurs (the $\gamma$ parameter) and the rates of accumulation, profit and utilisation. However, the paradox of cost and the paradox of thrift only hold in a degenerate version. An increase in real wages has no impact on the fully-adjusted rate of accumulation and its rate of profit, although it will induce a higher rate of capacity utilisation; similarly, a decrease in the propensity to save has no impact on the rate of accumulation, although it will induce higher rates of profit and of utilisation. The rate of accumulation in the fully adjusted position is not endogenous any more. The model thus contains a mix of Kaleckian and neo-Ricardian features.

*A possibility devoid of definite solutions*

One need not assume, however, that the expected rate of growth is given to safeguard the Kaleckian model. Both the expected growth rate of sales $\gamma$ and the normal rate of utilisation $u_n$ may react to discrepancies with their realised values, in accordance with equations (33) and (34). This is the fourth possibility: it would deprive the model of definite solutions, since there would be no point of anchor for the model, but all the usual Kaleckian results could be restored. Whether stability or instability prevails in such a model would depend on the relative speed with which $\gamma$ and $u_n$ would react. Since the adaptive behaviour of the normal rate of utilisation provided stability (the third case), whereas the adaptive behaviour of the expected growth rate brought instability (the second case), intuition tells us that a necessary condition for the stability of this fourth case is that $\tau$ be larger than $\varphi$.

Let us illustrate this fourth case with the help of Fig. 6. Let us assume that initially, through luck or the adjustment mechanism to be described, the economy is in a steady-state where the actual rate of accumulation of the economy is equal to the expected growth rate of sales $\gamma_1$, and where the actual rate of utilisation is equal to its normal rate $u_{n1}$. This is given by the intersection of the curves denoted by $g^i_1$ and $g^s_1$. Suppose there is now an increase in real wages, or a fall in the propensity to save. This implies that the savings curve shifts to the right, from $g^s_1$ to $g^s_2$. The new steady-state rate of accumulation and rate of capacity utilisation will now be higher, at $g_2$ and $u_2$. Because these rates are not equal to their target values, such a situation cannot last. The adjustment mechanisms described by equations (33) and (34) will now come into play.

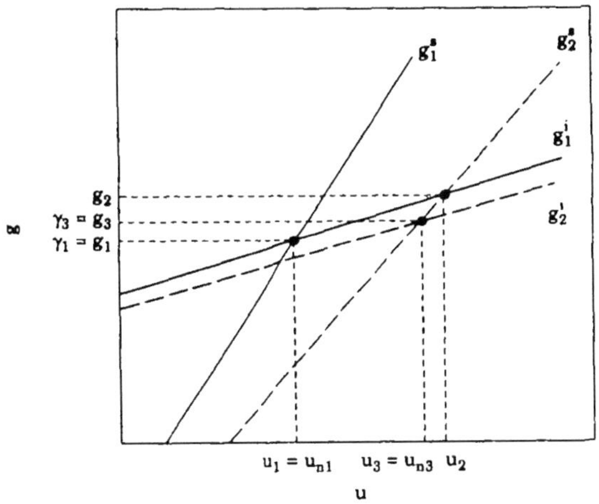


**Fig. 6.** *Firms revise both the standard rate of capacity utilization and the expected rate of sales growth.*

Both the expected growth rate $\gamma$ and the normal rate of utilisation $u_n$ will rise, and consequently shift the investment function.

The crucial question is whether the $g^i$ curve will shift up or down. This depends, as can be seen from equation (30), on whether the change in desired accumulation induced by the increase in the normal rate of utilisation, $-g_u du_n$, will surpass the change in desired accumulation induced by the increase in the expected growth rate of sales, $+d\gamma$. If the expected growth rate of sales is the more sensitive to actual values, the $g^i$ curve will shift up and instability will sway the model. If the normal rate of capacity utilisation is the more sensitive, the $g^i$ curve will shift down to $g^i_2$, as illustrated in Fig. 6, and stability will prevail.[1] This adjustment mechanism will continue until finally the normal and the actual rates of utilisation are equated at $u_{n3}$, at which point sales growth expectations and the rate of accumulation will also be equated $\gamma_3$. The fully adjusted position will lie somewhere on the $g^i_2$ curve, between $g_1$ and $g_2$. The revised model is thus deprived of a definite solution; rather there exists a set of possible solutions.

The fourth possibility in its stable incarnation thus offers some middle ground between Kaleckians and their critics. On the one hand, the actual rate of capacity utilisation is necessarily equal to its normal value in the fully adjusted position, as many critics would have it. The normal rate of utilisation is, however, itself endogenous across long-period positions. All the standard Kaleckian results follow from this endogeneity of the actual and normal rates of utilisation. In particular, as shown on Fig. 6, the paradoxes of cost and of thrift both hold. Starting from a fully adjusted position, an increase in the real wage rate, or a decrease in the propensity to save, induces higher rates of profit and of accumulation in the new fully adjusted position. While fully adjusted positions are associated with normal values of the rate of capacity utilisation, this does not imply that the wage–profit curve is given for different fully adjusted positions, even though techniques are given.

[1] More exactly the stability of the adjustment process requires $\tau(\gamma u/s_p + A) > \varphi(\gamma/g_u + A)$, where $A = (1 - m)f - mu_n$. This implies, given stability condition (21), that $\tau > \varphi$ is an insufficient condition.

Following a suggestion by Dutt, Amadeo properly described the proposed adjustment mechanism, but without a graphical illustration.

> Indeed, one may argue that if the equilibrium degree is systematically different from the planned degree of utilization, entrepreneurs will eventually revise their plans, thus altering the planned degree. If, for instance, the equilibrium degree of utilization is smaller than the planned degree ($u^* < u_n$), it is possible that the entrepreneurs will reduce $u_n$. The reduction of the planned degree would shift the investment function in such a way that the new equilibrium degree will be greater than the initial one. If entrepreneurs keep revising their plans, eventually both degrees of utilization will coincide. Even if this is the case, however, the objective of this model is to show that the equilibrium degree of utilization—be it equal to or different from the planned degree—is endogenously determined. (Amadeo, 1986A, p. 155)

To preserve the *endogenous* determination of the rate of utilisation within fully adjusted positions, one must thus argue that the adjustment of the normal rate of capacity utilisation occurs faster than any possible adjustment of the expected growth rate of sales. This is actually the position taken by those neo-Ricardian who favour an endogenous rate of utilisation in the long period. For instance, while Ciccone believes that 'the effectively experienced utilization of capacity influences the utilization considered normal only very slowly' (1986, p. 36), he points out that in his analysis the rate of accumulation is an 'independent given' (1987, p. 109). Similarly, when discussing Ciccone's model, Committeri (1986, p. 179) speaks of 'a secular path of accumulation' that would be little affected by fluctuations in demand.

## 5. The convergence towards normal rates of profit and of utilisation and the pricing equation

### *The normal rate of utilisation and target return pricing*

Up to now the analysis has emphasised the shape of the investment function. It was, however, mentioned in Section 1 that the target rate of return and the standard degree of capacity utilisation have an impact on pricing, and hence on the profits cost function. Let us assume in the following that the normal rate of profit about which the neo-Ricardians are talking is no different from the target rate of return or the standard rate of profit used in target return pricing, and that the normal rate of capacity utilisation is the same concept as the standard rate of capacity utilisation.[1] This will allow us to formalise some neo-Ricardian objections to the Kaleckian model of growth and distribution, focusing this time on the pricing decision and on the normal rate of profit. Let us start with a long quote by one of these neo-Ricardian critics:

> The possibility of capacity utilization being different from its planned degree in the long run would have an important implication for theories of distribution and accumulation . . . The *realized* rate of profit emerging from the interplay between distribution and effective demand may not be inversely related to the real wage, even in situations that the authors seem not to think limited to the short period; another way to say this is that the . . . normal rate of profit $r_n$ (i.e. the rate of profit technically obtainable at the normal utilization degree with [the real wage rate] taken at its current level) may diverge from its realized rate, even for long periods of time. Now, we do not wish to quarrel with this reasonable proposition: the *observed* rate of profit is very unlikely to coincide with $r_n$, even in terms of averages covering long periods of time, although we might suspect that after all, there must exist *some* connection between the two rates. The model, however, contains no element

[1] As noted by Reynolds (1987, p. 179), 'the target rate of return can possibly be thought as corresponding to the long-run rate of profit, as in Sraffa's model'.

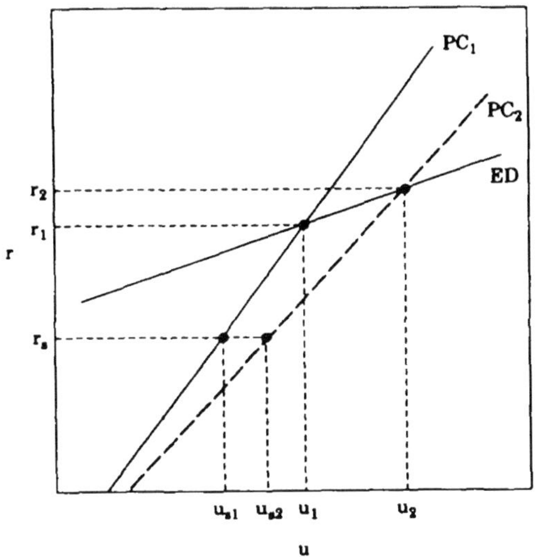


**Fig. 7.** *Firms revise the standard rate of capacity utilization in the pricing formula: instability.*

for the exploration of this connection, as it implies a persistent and systematic divergence between [the actual and the normal degree of capacity utilization]. (Committeri 1986, pp. 170–171)

Committeri's critique of the Kaleckian growth model is the macroeconomic version of the objection addressed towards multi-sector pricing models based on a vector of exogenous target rates of return (Boggio 1992, p. 284). How are those rates supposed to be determined? Should not a complete long-period theory include an explanation of how they are formed or modified? We first deal with the standard rate of capacity utilisation and then with the target rate of return.

Let us go back to equation (16), which represents the profits cost function set in the context of target return pricing procedures. Let us how deal with a change in the standard rate of capacity utilisation which figures in the pricing formula. An increase of this standard rate is equivalent to a reduction of the margin of profit, and its implies an increase in the real wage rate. It follows that an increase of the standard rate of utilisation of capacity must be associated with a downward shift of the profits cost curve. This is illustrated in Fig. 7. The initial profits cost curve is $PC_1$, to which corresponds a standard rate of utilisation of capacity $u_{s1}$ and a target rate of return $r_s$. The effective demand curve being assumed given, that is the investment function is of the usual Kaleckian type (equation 19), the actual utilisation and profit rates in the initial situation are $u_1$ and $r_1$ respectively. In the situation drawn, the actual rate of utilisation exceeds its standard level, and hence so does the actual rate of profit. Let us suppose that firms react to this discrepancy by changing the standard rate of utilisation contained in the target return pricing formula, according to the formula given by equation (34), $u_s$ here playing the role of $u_n$. What is to be shown is that tampering with the standard rate of utilisation of capacity in the pricing equation will resurrect Harrod's instability problem.

Suppose that as a result of the high actual rate of utilisation, the new standard rate of capacity utilisation incorporated in the pricing formula is raised from $u_{s1}$ to $u_{s2}$. Let us further assume that the standard rate of profit is left unchanged. It can be seen in Fig. 7 that the new actual rate of utilisation $u_2$ will be even larger than in the previous period, while the discrepancy between the actual rate of profit and its standard rate has grown even larger, to $r_2 - r_s$. Letting the standard rate of utilisation of capacity respond to the fluctuations in its current rate thus exacerbates the overuse or the lack of use of capacity. Of course, there is an upward limit to this phenomenon: the rate of utilisation can be no higher than unity; but no such limit exists on the downward side. We are back to the conclusions drawn by Committeri in the unstable case of the investment function; the model is unstable, or the degree of capacity utilisation must be assumed to be equal to unity or to its normal rate.

One is tempted to conclude that the standard rate of utilisation of capacity is a purely conventional parameter, because it cannot be otherwise for structural macroeconomic reasons. If price makers were to revise their view of the standard rate of capacity utilisation according to the values taken by the actual rate, the economy would be highly unstable. Indeed it is well known that firms that employ target return pricing hardly ever change the standard rate of utilisation that is present in cost-plus pricing procedures. For instance, until the events of the last decade, the standard rate of utilisation of capacity incorporated in the pricing formula used by GM underestimated the rate of utilisation that was actually realised in most years by the company. As a consequence, 'the realized return on invested capital has averaged well over the 15 per cent target rate' (Scherer, 1970, pp. 174–175).

*The normal rate of profit and target return pricing*

Let us now deal with changes in the target rate of return, i.e., the standard rate of profit $r_s$. It is clear from equation (15) that an increase in the standard rate of profit leads to a rise in the profit margin $m$. It is equally clear from equation (16) that the profits cost curve shifts up when the standard rate of profit $r_s$ is increased in the target return pricing formula. It is at this juncture, it seems, that the arguments in favour of the inverse relationship between real wages and accumulation are the strongest. If firms respond to the overutilisation or to the underutilisation of capacity in the manner described by orthodox theory, that is by lowering prices in the latter case and by raising them in the former, the possible range of the actual rate of utilisation in the long period should be smaller than if the gross margin of profit is truly exogenous.[1] If firms diminish the target rate of return whenever the actual rate of profit exceeds the standard rate, the possible range of the actual rate of capacity utilisation would be diminished to the point of uniqueness: in the fully adjusted position, the actual rate of capacity utilisation could only be equal to its standard rate. Let us then suppose that firms react to a discrepancy between the actual and the standard rate of profit, and set the target rate of return in the following manner:

$$r_{s(t)} = (1 - \mu) r_{s(t-1)} + \mu r_{(t-1)} \qquad 0 < \mu < 1 \tag{35}$$

Combining equations (35) and (15), we see that whenever the rate of profit exceeds the target rate of return, firms react by increasing the target rate of return and the margin of profit. What happens is illustrated in Fig. 8. The effective demand curve and the

[1] Similarly, Sawyer (1994, p. 220) and Garegnani (1992, p. 70) argue that the propensity to save $s_p$ is not a constant: with high rates of accumulation firms tend to retain a higher proportion of their earnings. This compensates for the favourable impact of the rate of accumulation on the actual profit rate, and as a result the fluctuations of the actual profit rate around the normal rate would be dampened.

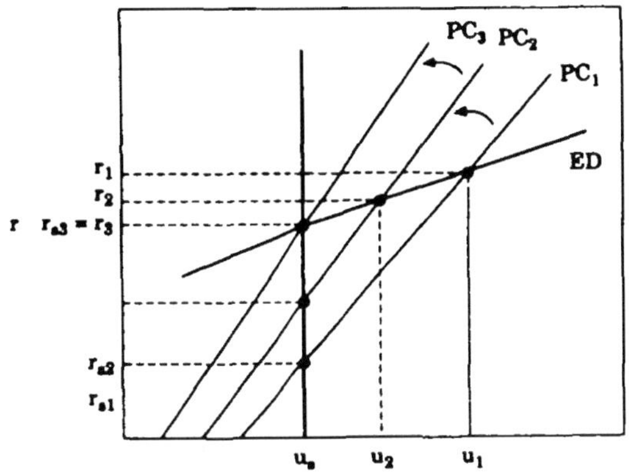


**Fig. 8.** *Firms revise the target rate of return in the pricing formula: stability.*

standard rate of utilisation of capacity are assumed to be given. Let us start from a situation where the profits cost curve is $PC_1$, corresponding to a low target rate of return $r_{s1}$. Under this situation, both the actual rate of profit and the actual rate of utilisation are high, at $r_1$ and $u_1$. This situation will not last as firms revise the target rate of return, moving it up from $r_{s1}$ to $r_{s2}$. The profits cost curve shifts to $PC_2$, yielding a rate of profit that is still higher than the standard rate, but where the difference between the two is now smaller than initially. This process will go on until the target rate of return is set at a level of $r_{s3}$, at which point the actual rate of profit will be equal to it, while the rate of utilisation will be equal to its standard rate $u_s$. Note that changes in the target rate of return induced by the actual levels of the rate of profit tend to stabilise the model. An increase in the target rate of return, caused by an excess of the actual rate of profit over the standard rate, pulls down both the actual rate of profit and the actual rate of utilisation.

The rate of utilisation can only be an endogenous variable in the long period if the adjustment of the target rate of return to the actual conditions is sluggish, and preferably non-existent. This is all too evident in pricing equation (17), where it is obvious that the standard and actual rates of utilisation are equal if the standard and actual rates of profit are equated. If there exists a process insuring this latter equality, the actual rate of utilisation in the fully adjusted position becomes a predetermined variable, equal to the given conventional standard rate. The various cost and reaction parameters being given, the standard rate of utilisation of capacity thus determines the rate of profit that is consistent with it, through the effective demand function. This determines then the real wage rate and the rate of growth. The neo-Ricardian causal nexus presented in Section 2 and in Fig. 2 has been brought back. Furthermore, the inverse relationship between the rate of growth and the real wage rate that characterised earlier neo-Keynesian models is recovered. Because the rate of utilisation is given, an increase in the exogenous determinants of the growth rate—the expected secular growth rate that Eichner talks about—induces an increase in the rate of profit and a fall in the real wage. This is represented in Fig. 9 by an initial upward shift of the effective demand curve, from $ED_1$ to $ED_2$, due to an increase in the $\gamma$ parameter. This is followed by an induced upward shift of the profits cost curve, from $PC_1$ to $PC_2$, corresponding to a hike

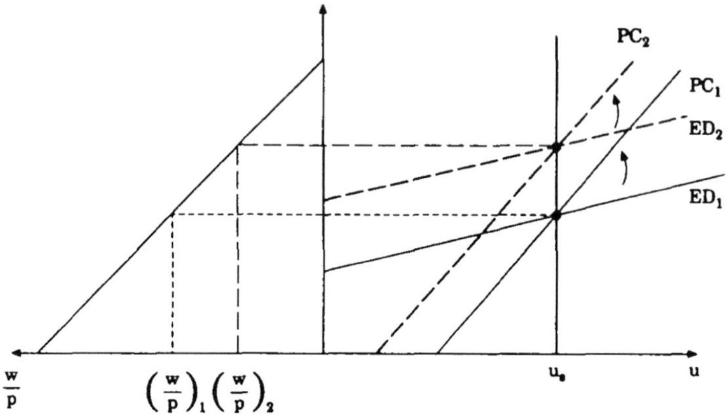


**Fig. 9.** *The Eichner–Wood–Cambridge variant of the classical case.*

in the margin of profit. At the end of the process, the rate of growth and the rate of profit have risen, but the real wage rate has fallen, as they would have in the neo-Keynesian model.

Thus, as Marglin (1984, p. 125) correctly points out when discussing the neo-Keynesian model, 'the key assumption is that the rate of capacity utilisation varies on the path between steady-growth configurations, but not across steady-growth states'. In the present terminology, the rate of capacity utilisation varies between long-period positions, but not across *fully adjusted* positions.

It should be noted that the results arrived at with the help of equation (35) are very similar to the story provided by Eichner (1976, 1987) and other post-Keynesians who have emphasised the financial needs of investment growth and their effect on the profit margin of corporations.[1] In those models, a faster pace of investment induces firms to increase their margin of profit in search of additional internal funds to finance this investment. In the Eichnerian model, as in the earlier neo-Keynesian models of Kaldor and Robinson, increased investment is associated with higher prices relative to wage unit costs. Effective demand and growth rates have an impact on margins of profit. For those authors, while in the short period the actual and the standard rates of capacity utilisation may diverge, it is not so in the long period. The reason for this is that they *assume* that the standard rate of profit will be adjusted to the actual trend of the growth rate, and hence to the actual rate of profit, as in Fig. 9. This leads Wood (1975, p. 129), for instance, to say that his model is a 'long run model of the determination of the share of profits at normal full capacity use'. The requirement of a normal rate of capacity utilisation implies, however, that faster accumulation is inexorably linked to lower real wages and disposable income (Eichner 1976, pp. 278–279). By contrast, in the Kaleckian model, an increase in the exogenous determinants of the growth rate is conducive to faster accumulation without real wages changing, while higher real wages are conducive to faster accumulation. The relation between real wages and the accumulation rate is thus reversed in the Eichnerian model when compared to that of the

[1] We may include the models proposed by Wood (1975) and Harcourt and Kenyon (1976) among the Eichnerian models. See Nell (1992, ch. 17) for a detailed critique of each of these Eichnerian models.

Kaleckian model (Agliardi, 1988). The opposition is striking, since the Eichnerians and the Kaleckians equally rely on firms setting prices within an oligopolistic industrial structure.

The above analysis thus shows that to insist on realised targets gives full justification to the position taken by many neo-Ricardian authors. If an adjustment mechanism equates the actual rate of profit and the target rate of return, normal prices eventually prevail, and the long-period inverse relation between the real wage rate and the rate of accumulation must also prevail.[1] This inverse relation is upheld despite the presence of all the standard Kaleckian features.

It could be possible to argue, however, along the lines presented when discussing Fig. 6, that both the standard rate of utilisation and the standard rate of profit of the target pricing formula could respond to actual values. One would again obtain a model without definite solutions, but where, in the stable case, higher real wages in fully adjusted positions could be associated with higher rates of accumulation and higher rates of profit, despite the actual rates of profit and of capacity utilisation being equal to their standard values.

Another avenue, which would add a Kaleckian formalisation of inflation and real wage determination to the present model, could also have been pursued to retain all the radical results of the Kaleckian model. It has been shown by Lavoie (1992, pp. 417–421) that the addition of a conflicting-claims theory of inflation drives a wedge between the target rate of return *assessed by firms* ($r_s^*$) and the target rate of return *actually incorporated into prices* ($r_s$). Within such a model, the adjustment mechanism described by equation (35) equates the actual rate of profit with the target rate of return assessed by firms ($r=r_s^*$), but not with the target rate of return incorporated into prices ($r \neq r_s$). It follows, in contrast to the belief of many neo-Ricardians (Ciccone, 1987, p. 110), that even in fully adjusted long-period positions, actual prices are not equal to normal prices, i.e., those prices that would bring into equality the target rate of return incorporated into prices and the actual rate of profit if the economy were operating at normal capacity.[2] As a consequence, the rate of capacity utilisation is still free to vary from its standard or normal rate. The key characteristics of the Kaleckian model, that is, the endogeneity of the rate of utilisation of capacity, in the short period, in the long period and in fully adjusted positions, is preserved within a model with definite solutions.

## 6. Conclusion

The main features of the Kaleckian model of growth and distribution have been shown to be based on its pricing equation, its investment function and the endogeneity of the rate of capacity utilisation. In particular, the model has been extended to a pricing procedure based on target return pricing. It has been demonstrated that the neo-Marxian critique of the investment function is very similar to the neo-Ricardian objections to the same investment function. Various arguments have been advanced to justify the particular investment function put forth by Kaleckians, despite the logic of the criticisms.

[1] Normal prices prevail in this simple one-sector world. Boggio (1986) has shown that in multi-sector models of target return pricing, cost-plus prices with an arbitrary vector of target rates of return also converge towards normal prices with a uniform rate of profit, when the target rates of return slowly respond to demand conditions Such a model, however, contains none of the so-called Keynesian features present in our Kaleckian model.

[2] Note that Boggio (1992, p. 287) comes to a similar conclusion within the context of a multi-sector model: with inconsistent claims between workers and firms, the vector of actual profit rates is not equated to the vector of target rates of return in the long period.

It has also been shown that the Kaleckian model, when overhead labour costs are included, is impervious to the criticism that it does not fit the recent stylised facts.

The notions of normal (or standard) rate of capacity utilisation and of normal (or standard) rate of profit have also been extensively discussed, since the inequality between those two rates and the long-period solutions of Kaleckian models has come under heavy criticism, mainly from neo-Ricardian authors but also from other non-orthodox economists. The main issue is whether the normal rate of utilisation or the normal rate of profit must be seen as target variables that firms endeavour to realise. In the case of the investment function, it has been shown that the normal rate of capacity utilisation can be slowly revised according to its own actual rate without the model losing all of its Kaleckian characteristics. This requires, however, that the expected growth rate of sales, imbedded in some Kaleckian investment functions, remain given or adjust even more slowly than the normal rate of utilisation to actual conditions. In the latter case, although the actual rate of capacity utilisation ends up equating the normal rate of utilisation, the positive relation between the real wage rate and the rate of accumulation is sustained in fully adjusted positions. Such a surprising result is due to the fact that both the actual and the normal rates of utilisation are endogenous across fully adjusted positions, so that the wage–profit frontier at the normal rate of utilisation is not fixed any more. The drawback of this formalisation, however, is that the model is left with a set of solutions, rather than a definite one. Furthermore, if the expectations of sales growth are quickly modified in reaction to the actual rates of growth, the model becomes unstable.

Looking now at the pricing part of the model, it was shown that the normal rate of utilisation cannot respond to the actual rate of utilisation, otherwise the model once more becomes unstable. On the other hand, the normal rate of profit may respond to the actual rates of profit without disturbing the stability of the model. As some critics have already noted, however, such an adjustment mechanism makes exogenous the rate of capacity utilisation, and consequently it destroys the Kaleckian positive relation between the real wage rate and the rate of accumulation. Such a model behaves more like the neo-Keynesian model of Robinson and Kaldor, showing features akin to Eichnerian growth models. The positive relation between real wages and accumulation is, however, recovered when one adds to the model a conflicting-claims theory of inflation and real wage determination.

In view of the analysis pursued in this paper, and in view of the results obtained with regard to the convergence of full cost prices towards production prices, we may now assert that pure production prices must be seen as the notional version of the more realist cost-plus prices. One would agree with Boggio (1990, p. 57) that 'the most promising way forward, in terms both of realism and of definiteness of results, is to develop the full-cost models'.

### Bibliography

Agliardi, E. 1988. Microeconomic foundations of macroeconomics in the post-Keynesian approach, *Metroeconomica*, vol. 39, no. 3, 275–297

Amadeo, E. J. 1986A. The role of capacity utilization in long-period analysis, *Political Economy*, vol. 2, no. 2, 147–185

Amadeo, E. J. 1986B. Notes on capacity utilization, distribution and accumulation, *Contributions to Political Economy*, vol. 5, 83–94

Amadeo, E. J. 1987. Expectations in a steady-state model of capacity utilization, *Political Economy*, vol. 3, no. 1, 75–89

Asimakopulos, A. 1975. A Kaleckian theory of income distribution, *Canadian Journal of Economics*, vol. 8, no. 3, 313–333

Auerbach, P. and Skott, P. 1988. Concentration, competition and distribution, *International Review of Applied Economics*, vol. 2, no. 1, 42–61

Bhaduri, A. and Marglin, S. 1990. Unemployment and the real wage: the economic basis for contesting political ideologies, *Cambridge Journal of Economics*, vol. 14, no. 4, 375–393

Blecker, R. A. 1989. International competition, income distribution and economic growth, *Cambridge Journal of Economics*, vol. 13, no. 3, 395–412

Boggio, L. 1986. Stability of production prices in a model of general interdependence, in Semmler, W. (ed.), *Competition, Instability, and Nonlinear Cycles*, Berlin, Springer-Verlag

Boggio, L. 1990. The dynamic stability of production prices: a synthetic discussion of models and results, *Political Economy*, vol. 6, no. 1–2, 47–58

Boggio, L. 1992. Production prices and dynamic stability: results and open questions, *Manchester School of Economic and Social Studies*, vol. 60, no. 3, 264–294

Caminati, M. 1990. Gravitation: an introduction, *Political Economy*, vol. 6, no. 1–2, 11–44

Caserta, M. 1990. The steady-state model of capital utilisation: a comment, *Studi Economici*, vol. 41, 139–153

Chamberlain, T. W. and Gordon, M. J. 1989. Liquidity, profitability, and long-run survival: theory and evidence on business investment, *Journal of Post Keynesian Economics*, vol. 11, no. 4, 589–610

Ciccone, R. 1986. Accumulation and capacity utilization: some critical considerations on Joan Robinson's theory of distribution, *Political Economy*, vol. 2, no. 1, 17–36

Ciccone, R. 1987. Accumulation, capacity utilization and distribution: a reply, *Political Economy*, vol 3, no. 1, 97–111

Committeri, M. 1986. Some comments on recent contributions on capital accumulation, income distribution and capacity utilization, *Political Economy*, vol. 2, no. 2, 161–186

Committeri, M. 1987. Capacity utilization, distribution and accumulation: a rejoinder to Amadeo, *Political Economy*, vol. 3, no. 1, 91–95

Del Monte, A. 1975. Grado di monopolio e sviluppo economico, *Rivista Internazionale di Scienze Sociali*, vol. 83, no. 3, 231–263

Duménil, G. and Lévy, D. 1987. The dynamics of competition: a restoration of the classical analysis, *Cambridge Journal of Economics*, vol. 11, no. 2, 133–164

Dutt, A. K. 1984. Stagnation, income distribution and monopoly power, *Cambridge Journal of Economics*, vol. 8, no. 1, 25–40

Dutt, A. K. 1990. *Growth, Distribution and Uneven Development*, Cambridge, Cambridge University Press

Dutt, A. K. 1992A. Conflict inflation, distribution, cyclical accumulation and crises, *European Journal of Political Economy*, vol. 8, 579–598

Dutt, A. 1992B. Rentiers in Post Keynesian Models, in Arestis, P. and Chick, V. (eds), *Recent Developments in Post-Keynesian Economics*, Aldershot, Edward Elgar

Eichner, A. S. 1976. *The Megacorp and Oligopoly: Micro Foundations of Macro Dynamics*, Cambridge, Cambridge University Press

Eichner, A. S. 1987. *The Macrodynamics of Advanced Market Economies*, Armonk, M. E. Sharpe

Epstein, G. 1994. A political economy model of comparative central banking, in Dymski, G. and Pollin, R. (eds), *New Perspectives in Monetary Macroeconomics*, Ann Arbor, University of Michigan Press

Fazzari, S. M. and Mott, T. L. 1986–87. The investment theories of Kalecki and Keynes: An empirical study of firm data, 1970–1982, *Journal of Post Keynesian Economics*, vol. 9, no. 2, 171–187

Garegnani, P. 1992. Some notes for an analysis of accumulation, in Halevi, J., Laibman, D. and Nell, E. (eds), *Beyond the Steady State: A Revival of Growth Theory*, London, Macmillan

Halevi, J. and Kriesler, P. 1991. Kalecki, classical economics and the surplus approach, *Review of Political Economy*, vol. 3, no. 1, 79–92

Harcourt, G. C. and Kenyon, P. 1976. Pricing and the investment decision, *Kyklos*, vol. 29, no. 3, 449–477

Kaldor, N. 1957. A model of economic growth, *Economic Journal*, vol. 67, 591–624

Kalecki, M. 1971. *Selected Essays in the Dynamics of the Capitalist Economy*, Cambridge, Cambridge University Press
Kurz, H. D. 1986. Normal positions and capital utilization, *Political Economy*, vol. 2, no. 1, 37–54
Kurz, H. D. 1990. Effective demand, employment and capital utilisation in the short run, *Cambridge Journal of Economics*, vol. 14, 205–217
Kurz, H. D. 1991. Technical change, growth and distribution: a steady state approach to unsteady growth on Kaldorian lines, in Nell, E. J. and Semmler, W. (eds), *Nicholas Kaldor and Mainstream Economics*, London, Macmillan
Kurz, H. D. 1993. Accumulation et demande effective: quelques notes, *Cahiers d'économie politique*, vol. 22, 59–82
Kurz, H. D. 1994. Growth and distribution, *Review of Political Economy*, vol. 6, no. 4, 393–421
Lavoie, M. 1992. *Foundations of Post-Keynesian Economic Analysis*, Aldershot, Edward Elgar
Lavoie, M. 1995. Interest rates in post-Keynesian models of growth and distribution, *Metroeconomica*, vol. 46, no. 2, 146–177
Lanzillotti, R. F. 1958. Pricing objectives in large companies, *American Economic Review*, vol. 48, no. 5, 921–940
Lee, F. S. 1985. Full cost prices, classical price theory, and long period method analysis: a critical evaluation, *Metroeconomica*, vol. 37, no. 2, 199–219
Marglin, S. A. 1984. Growth distribution, and inflation: a centennial synthesis, *Cambridge Journal of Economics*, vol. 8, no. 2, 115–144
Nell, E. 1985. Jean Baptiste Marglin: a comment on 'Growth, distribution and inflation', *Cambridge Journal of Economics*, vol. 9, no. 2, 173–178
Nell, E. J. 1992. *Transformational Growth and Effective Demand: Economics after the Capital Critique*, London, Macmillan
Nichols, L. M. and Norton, B. 1991. Overhead workers and political economy growth models, *Review of Radical Political Economy*, vol. 23, no. 1–2, 47–54
Pasinetti, L. L. 1962. Rate of profit and income distribution in relation to the rate of economic growth, *Review of Economic Studies*, vol. 29, no. 4, 267–279
Pivetti, M. 1988. On the monetary explanation of distribution: a rejoinder to Nell and Wray, *Political Economy*, vol. 4, no. 2, 275–283
Reynolds, P. J. 1987. *A Synthesis of Kaleckian and Post Keynesian Economics*, Brighton, Wheatsheaf
Robinson, J. 1962. *Essays in the Theory of Economic Growth*, London, Macmillan
Roncaglia, A. 1990. Is the notion of long-period positions compatible with the classical political economy, *Political Economy*, vol. 6, no. 1–2, 103–111
Rowthorn, B. 1981. Demand, real wages and economic growth, *Thames Papers in Political Economy*, Autumn, 1–39. Reprinted in *Studi Economici*, vol. 18, 1982, (3–54), and also in M. C. Sawyer (ed.), *Post-Keynesian Economics*, Aldershot, Edward Elgar
Sarantis, N. 1990–91. Distribution and terms of trade dynamics, inflation, and growth, *Journal of Post Keynesian Economics*, vol. 13, no. 2, 175–198
Sarkar, P. 1993. Distribution and growth: a critical note on 'stagnationism', *Review of Radical Political Economy*, vol. 25, no. 1, March, 62–70
Sawyer, M. 1994. Prices, capacity utilisation and employment in the post-Keynesian traditions, in Dutt, A. K. (ed.), *New Directions in Analytical Political Economy*, Aldershot, Edward Elgar
Scherer, F. M. 1970. *Industrial Market Structure and Economic Performance*, Chicago, Rand McNally
Shipley, D. D. 1981. Pricing objectives in British manufacturing industry, *Journal of Industrial Economics*, vol. 29, no. 4, 429–443
Skott, P. 1989. *Conflict and Effective Demand in Economic Growth*, Cambridge, Cambridge University Press
Spaventa, L. 1970. Rate of profit, rate of growth, and capital intensity in a simple production model, *Oxford Economic Papers*, vol. 22, no. 2, 129–147
Steedman, I. 1992. Questions for Kaleckians, *Review of Political Economy*, vol. 4, no. 2, 125–151
Steindl, J. 1952. *Maturity and Stagnation in American Capitalism*, Oxford, Basil Blackwell
Steindl, J. 1979. Stagnation theory and stagnation policy, *Cambridge Journal of Economics*, vol. 3, no. 1, 1–14
Taylor, L. 1991. *Income Distribution Inflation, and Growth: Lectures on Structuralist Macroeconomic Theory*, Cambridge MA, MIT Press
Vianello, F. 1985. The pace of accumulation, *Political Economy*, vol. 1, no. 1, 69–87

Vianello, F. 1989. Effective demand and the rate of profit: some thoughts on Marx, Kalecki and Sraffa, in Sebastiani, M. (ed.), *Kalecki's Relevance Today*, New York, St. Martin's Press
Weisskopf, T. E. 1979. Marxian crisis theory and the rate of profit in the postwar US economy, *Cambridge Journal of Economics*, vol. 3, no. 4, 341–379
Wood, A. 1975. *A Theory of Profits*, Cambridge, Cambridge University Press
You, J. 1994. Macroeconomic structure, endogenous technical change and growth, *Cambridge Journal of Economics*, vol. 18, no. 2, 213–233

[2]

Review of Radical Political Economics Vol. 28(4)113–147(1996)

# TRAVERSE, HYSTERESIS, AND NORMAL RATES OF CAPACITY UTILIZATION IN KALECKIAN MODELS OF GROWTH AND DISTRIBUTION

*Marc Lavoie*

ABSTRACT: The paper deals with the main objection addressed against the Kaleckian model of growth and distribution, i.e., the endogenous rate of utilization need not be equal to its normal rate in the long run. Various mechanisms are introduced to bring the Kaleckian model to a fully adjusted position, where the realized and normal rates of capacity utilization are equated. When hysteresis effects are considered, Kaleckian results may be sustained even in fully adjusted long-run positions.

## INTRODUCTION

The aim of the present article is to deal with the main objection addressed against the standard Kaleckian model of

Department of Economics, University of Ottawa, Ottawa, Ont. Canada K1N 6N5; email: mlavoie@ uottawa.ca.
This paper follows numerous written and verbal discussions I had with Mark Setterfield from Trinity College (Connecticut). An earlier version of the paper was first presented at Curtin University in March 1993, then at Murdoch University and Newcastle University, and also at an URPE session of the ASSA's in San Francisco. The paper was written while I was a Visiting Professor at Curtin University, in Perth, Western Australia, and it benefitted from comments by Heinz Kurz, Bill Mitchell, Barkley Rosser, Julio Silva, Mark Setterfield, Peter Skott, and Graham White. The minutious comments of the referees—Gary Mongiovi, Gil Skillman, Gérard Duménil, and Dominique Lévy—were very helpful. Special thanks go to Duménil and Lévy who helped me to formalize the consequences of the models. The usual disclaimers apply nonetheless.


Published by Blackwell Publishers, 238 Main St., Cambridge, MA 02142, USA, and 108 Cowley Rd., Oxford, OX4 1JF, UK.

growth and distribution.[1] As it is usually depicted, the rate of utilization in Kaleckian models is endogenous both in the short run and in the long run, and so need not be equal to its normal rate. In the long run, say the critics of the Kaleckian model, the actual rate of capacity utilization should be equal to its *normal* or *standard* rate. Such a long-run situation constitutes a *normal equilibrium* or a *fully adjusted position*.

The debate about whether or not the realized rate of utilization converges toward or gravitates around its normal value is of great importance for heterodox economists. If the realized and the normal rates tend to equate, it may well be that the Keynesian results obtained in the short run would be overturned in the long run, thus yielding classical (or neoclassical) results. The dispute between Kaleckians and classical Marxists, if these reversals were indeed to occur in models where the constraints set by the normal rate of utilization are properly taken into account, would thus be very similar to the controversies between Keynesians and monetarists that marred the early neoclassical synthesis. As is well-known, the monetarist point of view—that Keynesian effects in the short run are necessarily overturned in the long run—prevailed until the new Keynesians put hysteresis effects to the forefront. Here, within the framework of Kaleckian models, it will also be shown that the consideration of hysteresis effects—seen mainly from the demand side—modifies the terms and the results of the debate.[2]

The structure of the paper is the following. In the first section, we recall the positions held by various non-orthodox authors and schools of thought on the paradox of thrift and the paradox of costs. In the second and third sections, the main components and features of the simplest Kaleckian model of growth and distribution are presented, including the two paradoxes just mentioned. The fourth section explains how the Kaleckian and the classical positions can be reconciled, through a reversal of the short-run Keynesian\Kaleckian effects, leading to standard classical results in the long run,

---

[1] Such a model can be found in Dutt (1990) in particular. The discussion is limited to one-sector models. About the additional issues linked to a two-sector Kaleckian model, see Ciccone (1991), Glick and Campbell (1995), Park (1995), Dutt (1995A, 1995B), and Lavoie (1996) among others.

[2] The association of hysteresis effects and endogenous normal rates of capacity utilization has some empirical counterpart. For instance, in their empirical study of Australian wage inflation, Watts and Mitchell (1990) reject the hypothesis of *a natural* rate of capacity utilization and endorse the presence of hysteretic effects on both the steady-state rate of unemployment and the normal rate of capacity utilization.

with the realization of the normal rate of capacity utilization. In the following sections, the *normal* rate of capacity utilization becomes an endogenous variable. In the fifth section, hysteresis effects are introduced via the pricing function only. The paradox of thrift is shown to extend to long-period normal equilibria, whereas the paradox of costs may or may not. In the sixth section, the normal rate of utilization of capacity is endogenous both in the pricing function and in the investment function. When fully adjusted positions are compared, the propensity to save has no impact on the rate of accumulation, whereas the paradox of costs again may or may not hold. In the seventh section, hysteresis effects are introduced through the investment function only. Both the paradox of thrift and the paradox of costs are impervious to the imposition of normal equilibria. A Keynesian (or Kaleckian or post-Keynesian) stance may thus be justified, despite granting relevance to an analysis based on fully adjusted positions.

## PARADOXES AMONG NON-ORTHODOX SCHOOLS OF THOUGHT

Whereas neoclassical economists seem to have some common ground over which they can debate the worthiness and the adequacy of their models or of their theories, such a common approach did not seem to characterize the various non-orthodox schools of thought until recently. Over the last few years, however, there have been several attempts to organize discussions around a common framework, either in the discussion of prices of production or for strictly macroeconomic questions. With respect to the latter, the Kaleckian model of growth and distribution seems to have generated a great number of contributions from authors of all persuasions, be they post-Keynesians, neo-Marxists, or Sraffians. In that sense, the Kaleckian model is a good candidate for a potential post-classical synthesis, i.e., a synthesis of the views that could arise from post-Keynesians and Kaleckians on the one hand, and Marxists and Sraffians on the other.[3]

This does not mean, of course, that there are not any subjects of contention between the various participants to the post-classical synthesis. This is particularly clear when one

3 The expression "post-classical" was first used by Henry (1993) in 1982. The expression has been endorsed, with the same meaning, by various authors: Eichner (1986), Hagemann (1992), Lavoie (1992), Duménil and Lévy (1993).

looks at table 1, where the various opinions regarding the possibility of the paradoxes of thrift and of costs are examined within a framework where dynamic productivity effects are excluded by assumption.

Table 1
Long Run Relationships

<table>
<tr><th></th><th>Classicals<br>Classical Marxists<br>Robinson's inflation barrier</th><th>Cambridgians<br>Robinson, Kaldor<br>Eichner, Wood</th><th>Kaleckians<br>Modern Sraffians<br>Keynesian Marxists</th></tr>
<tr><td rowspan="2">A higher rate of accumulation is associated with</td><td colspan="2">Lower real wages</td><td>Higher real wages or constant real wages</td></tr>
<tr><td>A higher propensity to save</td><td colspan="2">A lower propensity to save</td></tr>
</table>

As can be seen, the whole spectrum is in fact covered by the various non-orthodox authors. Post-Keynesians of the Cambridge (UK) variety (sometimes called neo-Keynesians) and classical authors alike believed that higher real wages are necessarily associated with lower rates of accumulation. The cause of this agreement is that both sets of authors, even more modern ones such as Eichner (1987) and Wood (1975), consider long-run equilibria to mean situations where the realized and the normal rate of capacity utilization are equated. Cambridgians however believed in Keynes's paradox of thrift, i.e., lower propensities to save are associated with higher rates of accumulation. Robinson held an intermediate position, since she acknowledged that under certain conditions—those of the inflation barrier—a higher propensity to save might allow a higher rate of accumulation (Robinson 1956, 48). The belief that higher rates of savings lead to faster accumulation is also upheld by classical Marxists (Marglin 1984).

At the other end of the table one can find Kaleckian and Sraffian authors, who endorse the paradox of thrift and who do not believe that higher accumulation rates must be associated with lower real wages, even in the long run. Recent writings by Sraffians show that many of them, just as Kaleckians, believe that in the long run the realized and the normal rates of capacity utilization need not be equated to each other.[4] From there follows their rejection of the necessary inverse relationship between the accumulation rate and the real wage rate.

The alliance between the followers of Kalecki and those of Sraffa is ironic considering that towards the end of her life Joan Robinson appeared to be quite critical of Sraffa's followers, whereas she was quite enthusiastic about Kalecki's writings. What is even more ironic is that Robinson, in her two major books (1956, 1962), took the Cambridgian stance which is quite opposite to the one defended by modern-day Kaleckians. As was pointed out by Marglin (1984: 125), Robinson assumed that the rate of capacity utilization could change during the transition between two long-run equilibria, but she assumed away these output changes when comparing long-run growth rates.

We now present the Kaleckian model in its most simple form, showing how the endogeneity of the realized rate of utilization generates the paradoxes of cost and of thrift. We shall define as the classical camp those who object to these paradoxes on the grounds that realized rates of capacity utilization eventually must be back to their normal levels in the long run.

## MAIN COMPONENTS OF THE KALECKIAN MODEL

The macroeconomic Kaleckian model of growth and distribution is built on three equations: an investment function and a savings function, which basically determine effective demand and profit rates from the demand side, and a cost function, which explains the profit rate from the supply side.

The investment function is the most contentious of all these functions, as one could guess. All Kaleckian models assume that the rate of accumulation desired by firms depends on the rate of profit or on the rate of capacity utilization, or on some combination of these two rates. In the simplest formulations, the investment function depends on the current

---

4 See for instance Ciccone (1986), Garegnani (1992), Kurz (1994), Roncaglia (1995), and Park (1995). For Kurz (1994, 410), "the economy is subject to the principle of effective demand at any moment of time and thus also in the long run," and later he adds: "It cannot be expected that, in an economy subject to the principle of effective demand, productive capacity will, on average, be utilized at the desired level." No one will be surprised to see that Nell (1985), who has always been at the juncture between Kaleckians and Sraffians, also takes this position in his critique of Marglin (1984).

rate of capacity utilization $u$, and on some exogenous parameter $\gamma$, which may represent entrepreneurial animal spirits, financial constraints, or the expected secular rate of accumulation.[5] The rate of accumulation set by entrepreneurs is thus $g^i$:

$$g^i = \gamma + g_u u \tag{1}$$

where $g_u$ is a parameter expressing the sensitivity of the rate of accumulation to a change in the rate of utilization. All parameters, here and later on, are assumed to take a positive value.

In a slightly more refined version, the desired rate of accumulation depends on the *difference* between the realized and the *normal* rate of capacity utilization $u_n$:

$$g^i = \gamma + g_u(u - u_n) \tag{2}$$

Another simple investment function is one where investment only depends on profitability. Such an investment function has certainly been popular, and it can be found in particular in Robinson (1962). This function decomposes the Kaleckian model into a recursive variant where effective demand determines the rate of capacity utilization without the latter having feedback effects. An instance of such a function is given by equation (3), where $g_r$ is the sensitivity of the rate of accumulation to a change in the profit rate $r$.

$$g^i = \gamma + g_r r \tag{3}$$

Other investment functions, which give rise to a greater variety of cases, assume that the investment function depends on the rate of utilization and the *normal* rate of profit $r_n$, i.e., the rate of profit which entrepreneurs expect to realize on their new investment if future realized rates of capacity utilization turn out to be equal to their normal value.

$$g^i = \gamma + g_u u + g_r r_n \tag{4}$$

In this paper, we shall consider only investment functions

---

5 Trigg (1994) has recently argued that this Kaleckian investment function has nothing to do with Kalecki's own depiction of investment behavior. Be that as it may, we shall still speak of Kaleckian models, keeping in mind that they may have more to do with Steindl (1952) than with Kalecki.

(1) and (2), leaving aside equations (3) and (4).

The savings function $g^s$ is the least contentious of all three functions of the Kaleckian model. In the Kaleckian model, as in other similar non-orthodox models, the classical savings function, because of its convenience, seems to be the usual savings function. Savings out of wages are assumed to be zero, while the propensity to save out of profits is $s_p$ In accumulation terms, this is the well-known Cambridge equation:

$$g^s = s_p r \tag{5}$$

More complex formulations can be thought of, some going beyond the classical function, some elaborating on the components of profits, taking into account for instance the fact that firms have their own retained earnings while households may hold either shares or fixed-interest assets (Dutt 1992; Lavoie 1995B). We shall stick however to the simple and useful classical savings function.

Finally there is the profit-cost function, i.e., the determinants of the rate of profit seen from the cost side. The simplest of these profit-cost functions is one assuming the constancy of the various parameters as the rate of capacity utilization changes. Calling $m$ the share of profits in national income and $v$ the capital/output ratio at full capacity, we have:[6]

$$r = um / v \tag{6}$$

It is quite obvious that the $m$ parameter could be either a positive function of the rate of capacity utilization, when there is overhead labor for instance, or could be a negative function of capacity utilization, if there are decreasing returns or if workers manage to extract higher real wages from firms when their rates of utilization get higher. But again, to deal with the most basic aspects of the model, the $m$ parameter will be assumed to be a constant. This means that we shall omit overhead labor and capital depreciation allowances, and assume constant returns to scale.[7] As a result the share of profits in national income depends in a straightforward manner on the markup over wage costs used for pricing

---

6 With $K$ the stock of capital, $Y$ the level of output, $C$ capacity output, and $P$ the level of profits, we have by definition: $r \equiv (P / K) \equiv (P / Y)(Y / C)(C / K)$.

7 Models with overhead labor costs and capital depreciation can be found in Rowthorn (1981) and Lavoie (1992, 1995A).

purposes. A higher markup, i.e., a higher profit margin, implies a higher $m$ and a lower real wage rate at given labor productivity.

The reader may note that there is a straightforward relationship between the normal rate of profit $r_n$ and the profit share $m$. If the markup is set so as to achieve a normal rate of profit (or a target rate of return) when firms are producing at normal capacity utilization, then the markup must be such that:

$$m = r_n v / u_n \tag{7}$$

At this point the reader may wonder what the definition of a *normal* rate of capacity utilization is. It should be pointed out that the interpretation of the normal rate is not a microeconomic one, but rather a mesoeconomic and macroeconomic one.[8] It is assumed that each segment of a plant is operated at its optimal level, as defined by the engineers, under the standard requirements of cost minimization. Companies have several plants, but expect that in normal conditions some of the segments will not be running. One may then wonder why firms would continue to upkeep such plants. The reasons have to do with the presence of uncertainty, as was pointed out by Steindl (1952: 2). Firms hold on to excess capacities to face an uncertain future, just as agents hold on to cash balances for liquidity purposes. These reserves of capacity allow firms to respond quickly to changes in demand and in its structure, and in addition they are a deterrent to entry by new firms.[9] The normal rate of capacity utilization is thus a convention, defined by the above considerations and by historical experience with regards to the rates of capacity that can be expected to be realized on average, as a consequence of macroeconomic conditions.[10]

---

[8] For a discussion of the various meanings of a *normal* rate of capacity utilization, see Kurz (1994: 417) and Lavoie (1995A: 803). See also Larson (1991).

[9] For a more extensive discussion, see Lavoie (1992: 124-6).

[10] If past experience is not part of the conventions that help to determine the normal rate of utilization, e.g., $u_n$ is fixed by the variance of $u$ but not by its own past values, as some suggest, then $u_n$ would be akin to an exogenous variable and there would be no room for the mechanisms contemplated in sections 5 to 7. See Lavoie (1992: 330-1).

## MAIN FEATURES OF THE KALECKIAN MODEL

We may now present the main results of the canonical Kaleckian model, as represented by equations (2), (5), and (6). Because of the chosen investment function, the model may be set in the $(u, g)$ space. Combining equations (5) and (6), the savings function may now be rewritten as:

$$g^s = (s_p m / v)u = \alpha u \tag{8}$$

where $\alpha$ is equal to the term between brackets.

The model is now reduced to the investment function given by equation (2) and the savings function given by equation (8). Setting $g^i = g^s$, as illustrated on figure 1, we get the steady-state rate of capacity utilization:

$$u^* = \frac{\gamma - g_u u_n}{\alpha - g_u} \tag{9}$$

Figure 1

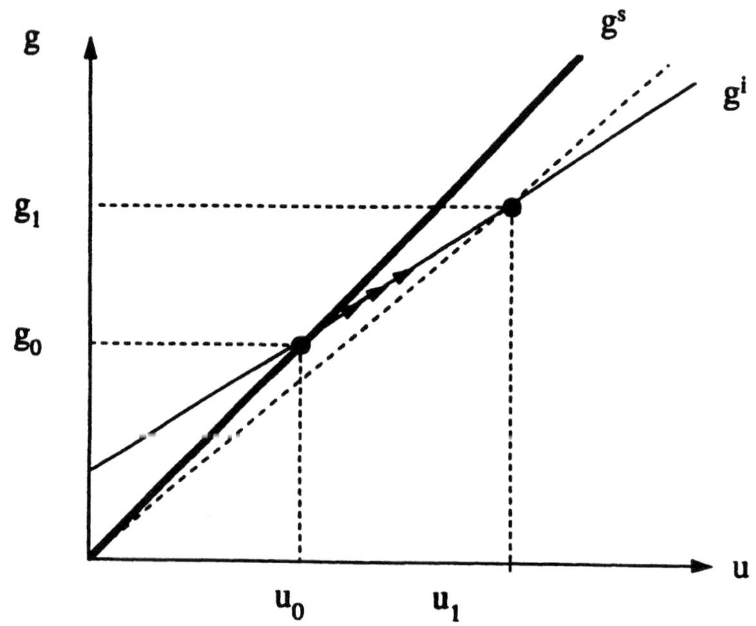


and the steady-state rate of accumulation:

$$g^* = \frac{\alpha(\gamma - g_u u_n}{\alpha - g_u} \qquad (10)$$

where the denominator, $\alpha - g_u$, must be positive to fulfil the standard short-run stability condition and where $\gamma > g_u u_n$ is required to get a positive rate of utilization.

It should be noted that although entrepreneurs have been made to respond to any divergence between the realized and the normal rates of capacity utilization (in equation (2), the long-run rate of utilization $u^*$ will not equal its normal rate $u_n$, except by fluke. The macroeconomic consequences of individual microeconomic behavior, as expressed by the investment equation (2), are not those that were intended by each entrepreneur.

Both the paradoxes of thrift and of costs can be illustrated in figure 1. Because of the requirements of short-run stability, the slope of the savings curve is assumed to be steeper than that of the investment curve. Start out from the rate of accumulation $g_0$ and $u_0$, where the investment and savings curves intersect. Suppose there is a decrease in either the propensity to save $s_p$ or the profit margin (the profit share $m$ drops). This implies a decrease in the $\alpha$ parameter of equation (8), and the savings curve must rotate downwards. The new rates of growth and of capacity utilization are now $g_1$ and $u_1$. Hence a lower rate of savings leads to faster accumulation—the paradox of thrift—while a higher real wage leads to faster accumulation and higher realized profit rates—the paradox of costs as Rowthorn (1981: 19) was first to call it.[11] During the transition, the rate of growth of sales exceeds that of capacity accumulation, while the rate of capacity utilization increases, until it reaches $u_1$. The positive effects on effective demand that are induced by higher propensities to consume and higher real wages are extended to the Kaleckian long run, i.e., when the rate of growth of sales and the rate of accumulation are equated.

Of course, there are more complicated models that can give rise to multiple constellations. For instance, if one adopts the investment formulation given by equation (4), the paradox of costs will arise for some values of the parameters, while it will not arise for other values. This investment equation is essentially the one adopted in growth models by Bhaduri and Marglin (1990), Kurz (1990), and Taylor (1991). Another way to remain agnostic as to the impact of real wages on growth rates

11 This can be checked from equation (10), where $dg^* / d\alpha < 0$.

is to assume equation (3). Because the model becomes decomposable, changes in real wages have an impact on rates of utilization, but none on rates of accumulation. To assume a non-constant and non-linear profit margin variable—as do various Marxist authors (You (1994) for instance)—will also lead to multiple sorts of relations. However, in all these models, as in the standard Kaleckian model, the long-run rate of capacity utilization is not constrained to be equal to its normal rate. Whatever their intrinsic merits and their ability to reproduce results which are acceptable to both Kaleckians and Marxists, depending on parametric values, they do not respond to the fundamental critique made against Kaleckian models in general.

What the critics of the Kaleckian model argue is that this model cannot be complete unless some mechanism drives the model to a long-run solution where the realized rates of profit and of capacity utilization are equated to the normal rates of profit and of capacity utilization (Committeri 1986; Auerbach and Skott 1988; Skott 1989: 55; Duménil and Lévy 1995; Park 1995).[12] As mentioned in the introduction, we call this particular long-run solution the *fully adjusted position*, as suggested by Vianello (1985). The constraint of the fully adjusted solution in non-orthodox models is somewhat similar to the constraint of the Friedmanian natural rate of unemployment or that of the Wicksellian natural rate of interest in neoclassical models. With respect to the fully adjusted position, the case is made that a normal rate of utilization, or a normal rate of profit, cannot forever be considered normal unless it is realized in the long run. Models of growth and distribution can thus only be consistent if there exists some mechanism leading the model to a fully adjusted position (or if the model gravitates, as in limit-cycles, around the fully adjusted position, as in Skott (1989)).

The intent of the following sections is thus to present and to develop mechanisms that will tow the standard Kaleckian model towards a fully adjusted position, i.e., toward a long-run equilibrium where the realized and the normal rates of capacity utilization are equated, along with the realized and normal rates of profit.[13] What we are interested in is the

---

[12] This was also Keynes's opinion when, as the editor of the *Economic Journal*, he objected to one of Kalecki's papers where Kalecki assumed that the rate of capacity utilization could be different from its normal value even in the long run: "For I am still innocent enough to be bewildered by the idea that the assumption of all firms always working below capacity is consistent with a long-run problem" (Keynes 1983: 830-1).

[13] Dutt (1990: 59; 1995A: 150) himself has offered a quick-fix solution: because of uncertainty, there is no unique normal rate

*traverse* towards the fully adjusted position, i.e., we want to know if there exists a passage from one such equilibrium toward another (Hicks 1965: 184). We shall examine whether or not the paradoxes of thrift and of cost survive the transition toward these fully adjusted positions. In other words, taking for granted that fully adjusted positions are the standards through which long-run models should be evaluated, we want to make sure, as Joan Robinson would put it, that these positions can be reached in *historical* time.

## KEYNESIAN IN THE SHORT RUN, CLASSICAL IN THE LONG RUN

Starting out from a Kaleckian model with Keynesian features, Duménil and Lévy (1994, 1995) have recently proposed a traverse toward a fully adjusted position. Their results are entirely compatible with the classical Marxist tradition. They contend that while one can be Keynesian (or Kaleckian) in the short run, or even in the long run as Kaleckians define it, one must reject the paradoxes of thrift and of cost when fully adjusted positions are compared. One should endorse classical beliefs when dealing with properly defined long-run positions.[14] The arguments brought forward by Duménil and Lévy are very similar to those advanced by Robinson (1956) when presenting the case of the so-called inflation barrier, the case which brings her most clearly into the classical camp. For Robinson, as for Duménil and Lévy, price inflation induces the monetary authorities to intervene in such a way that firms become financially constrained.[15] These constraints diminish the animal spirits of the firms or they directly inhibit firms from investing.

To demonstrate that one can be Kaleckian in the short run or in the Kaleckian long run but must be classical when

---

of capacity utilization; entrepreneurs will not bother changing their behavior as long as the realized rate of capacity utilization is within an acceptable range.

14 "More generally, basic Keynesian assumptions make sense only in the short term. In our opinion, the synthesis between the two trains of thought must combine the Keynesian perspective in the short term, and the classical perspective in the long term" (Duménil and Lévy 1995: 139). On this issue, their viewpoint is symmetric that of the new Keynesians of the first kind, as Greenwald and Stiglitz (1993) call them. The position of these new Keynesians is that demand-led Keynesian equilibria make sense in the short run, but not in the long run.

15 See Lavoie (1990) for a graphical illustration of Robinson's inflation barrier.

dealing with fully adjusted positions, Duménil and Lévy basically start out from the standard Kaleckian model already presented in the previous sections.[16] To this they add various behavioral equations, linked in particular to the rate of inflation $\pi$. Their model, with $\beta$ and $\in$ as reaction parameters, is as follows:

$$\pi = \beta(u - u_n) \tag{11}$$

$$\dot{\gamma} = - \in \pi \tag{12}$$

Equation (11) follows directly from Duménil and Lévy's (1995) equation (4). It simply says that the rate of price inflation $\pi$ increases with the discrepancy between the actual and the normal rate of capacity utilization. It is not quite clear why this should be so, at least from a post-Keynesian perspective, but the above is compatible with the old Phillips curve.[17] Equation (12) gives us the time derivative of $\gamma$, the parameter in investment function (2), which must now be interpreted as a proxy for the ability of firms to borrow. Equation (12) follows from the various arguments put forth by Duménil and Lévy (1994). It implies that as long as the rate of inflation is not brought down to zero, monetary authorities will continue to impose financial constraints which will increasingly dampen the animal spirits of the entrepreneurs or thwart their borrowing capabilities. It could easily be argued that this is compatible with Kalecki's (1971: ch. 12) view of the political business cycle.

Duménil and Lévy's addition to the Kaleckian model is that the $\gamma$ parameter is now an endogenous variable, the value of which changes unless the rate of inflation is brought down to zero. But $\pi = 0$ when $u = u_n$, and hence the final equilibrium of the model corresponds to what we have called the fully adjusted position. Duménil and Lévy's model thus provides a traverse from the Kaleckian long-run position to a classical fully adjusted position. It provides, as was pointed out in section 1, the mechanism that was lacking in

---

[16]In particular, they assume, as we did in sections 2 and 3, that real wages are constant (Duménil and Lévy 1994: 6).

[17] For those who doubt that a lower than normal rate of capacity utilization would lead to deflation, as implied by equation (11), the model could be rewritten with some structurally given inflation rate $\pi_0$ as:

$$\pi = \beta(u - u_n) + \pi_0 \tag{11'}$$

$$\gamma = - \in (\pi - \pi_0) \tag{12'}$$

Robinson's (1956) analysis of output and growth.

The path of the above traverse is better seen with the help of figure 2. Let us suppose that the economy is initially at its normal rate, $u_n$, with a rate of growth of $g_0$. Let us assume, as in figure 1, a decrease in either the propensity to save or the profit margin, leading to a downward rotation of the savings curve. As before, the rates of growth and of capacity utilization rise, to $g_1$ and $u_1$. These positive effects on effective demand will not last, however. Slowly, the effects of restrictive monetary policies will take their toll, and the investment curve will gradually shift down, until the realized and the normal rates of capacity utilization are equated at $u_n$. At the end of this process, the rate of accumulation will have fallen to $g_2$, below $g_0$.

Figure 2

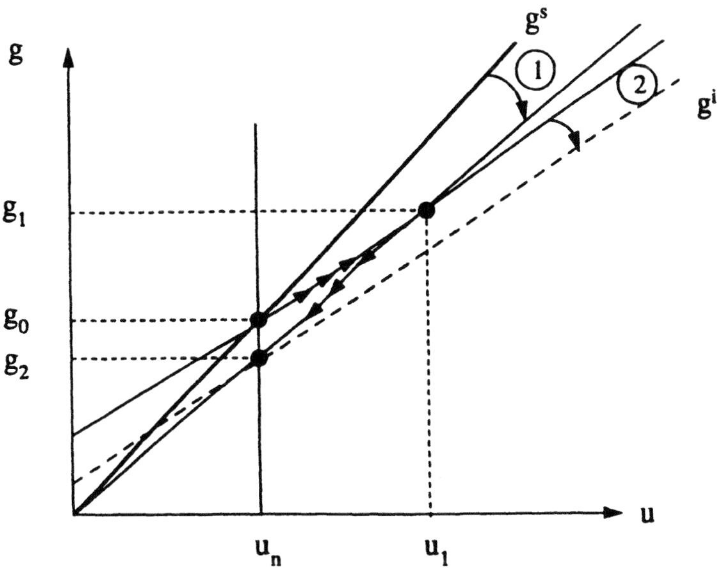


In fully adjusted positions, lower rates of saving, and higher real wages thus induce lower rates of accumulation—a result congenial to the classical (as well as the neoclassical) view. When fully adjusted positions are taken into account, Keynesian demand effects are wiped out; supply effects take over. Duménil and Lévy (1994, 1995) thus conclude that the post-classical synthesis is not illusory. Their solution to what initially appeared to be an inescapable dilemma is to forsake the paradoxes of thrift and of costs in the long run, by constructing a convincing traverse from the Kaleckian long-run position to a fully adjusted position with all the classical characteristics. In the classical perspective, a variant of the Cambridge equation determines the rate of accumulation across fully adjusted positions:

$$g^{**} = s_p r_n \tag{13}$$

Sustainable higher rates of accumulation occur either because the propensity to save $s_p$ is now higher or because the normal rate of profit $r_n$ has risen, following a fall in real wages. Here, obviously, there are no hysteresis effects, as the fully adjusted long run values of the variables $g$, $u$, and $r$ are respectively given by equation (13) and the exogenous parameters $u_n$ and $r_n$

## HYSTERESIS THROUGH THE PRICE FUNCTION

The traverse from any position to a fully adjusted position proposed by Duménil and Lévy is not however the only possible one to such fully adjusted positions. If the realized profit rates and utilization rates are not equal to the normal profit rate and utilization rate, then it seems that entrepreneurs could adapt to the actual situation by modifying the normal profit rate and the normal rate of capacity utilization.[18] Now, as can be seen from equations (7) and (2), this could occur either in the profit-cost function or in the investment function. Let us first deal with the former, while the latter case will be discussed in the next two sections. We thus consider a model consisting of equations (1), (5), (6), and (7). The parameter $m$ is now set according to the values taken by $r_n$ and $u_n$.

Let us assume that entrepreneurs have an adaptative behavior, setting the normal rates of profit and of capacity utilization according to past conventions and recent experience, as posited by Robinson (1956).[19] The normal rate

[18] Slow changes in $u_n$ induced by past values of $u$ have been suggested by Amadeo (1986: 155) and Ciccone (1986: 36).

[19] "Where fluctuations in output are expected and regarded as normal, the subjective-normal price may be calculated upon the basis of an average or standard rate of output, rather than capacity.... Profits may exceed of fall short of the level on the basis of which the subjective-normal prices were conceived. Then

of profit $r_n$ and the normal rate of utilization $u_n$ in the pricing equation may thus *slowly* vary through time according to the following differential equations:[20]

$$r_n = \varphi(r^* - r_n) \tag{14}$$

$$u_n = \sigma(u^* - u_n) \tag{15}$$

The normal rate of capacity utilization is thus slowly increased when the actual rate exceeds the normal rate. Let us see this more formally. Recall that the investment equation now being used is equation (1), $g^i = \gamma + g_u u$, so that the adjustment process plays its role only on prices, not on investment. The equilibrium value of $u$, the equivalent of equation (9), is now given by:

$$u^* = \frac{\gamma}{\alpha - g_u} = \frac{\gamma}{(s_p r_n / u_n) - g_u} \tag{16}$$

Note that, as in the case of equation (9), the denominator of equation (16) needs to be positive for short-run stability to occur. This implies that the following condition must be fulfilled:

$$\frac{s_p r_n}{g_u u_n} > 1 \tag{17}$$

Condition (17) means that the slope of the savings function $(s_p r_n / u_n)$ is larger than the slope of the investment function $(g_u)$. One can then derive from equation (16):

$$u^* - u_n = \frac{\gamma - s_p r_n + g_u u_n}{(s_p r_n / u_n) - g_u} \tag{18}$$

Similarly, from (7) and (16), one obtains:

$$r^* - r_n = (r_n / u_n)(u^* - u_n) \tag{19}$$

---

experience gradually modifies the views of entrepreneurs about what level of profit is obtainable, or what the average utilisation of plant is likely to be over its lifetime, and so reacts upon subjective-normal prices for the future" (Robinson 1956: 186, 190).

20 These two equations can be found in Lavoie (1996).

Obviously, the fully adjusted position is such that $u^* - u_n$, as this will also lead to $r^* = r_n$. From the numerator of equation (18), we see that this requires:

$$u_n^{**} = \frac{s_p r_n - \gamma}{g_u} \tag{20}$$

where $r_n$ however is itself endogenous! The lack of a definite fully adjusted solution can be remedied by putting together equations (14), (15), (18), and (19), which can be rewritten as:

$$\frac{\dot{r}_n}{\dot{u}_n} = \frac{\varphi(r^* - r_n)}{\sigma(u^* - u_n)} = \frac{\varphi r_n}{\sigma u_n} \tag{21}$$

This can be put in terms of logarithmic derivatives:

$$\frac{dr_n}{r_n} = (\varphi / \sigma)\frac{du_n}{u_n}$$

Taking the integral, and then the exponential, we can find the explicit solution to our problem:

$$r_n = Cu_n^{\varphi/\sigma} \tag{22}$$

where $C$ is a function of the initial values of the variables. Substituting equation (22) into (20), one obtains the fully adjusted solution $u_n^{**}$, which cannot be determined explicitly here:

$$g_u u_n^{**} = s_p C(u_n^{**})^{\varphi/\sigma} - \gamma$$

Let us now examine the conditions required for dynamic stability. First substitute the value of $r_n$ as given in equation (22) into equation (18). From equation (15) and the following definition:

$$\hat{u}_n = \dot{u}_n / u_n$$

we obtain the rate of change $\hat{u}_n$:

$$\hat{u}_n = \sigma \frac{\gamma - s_p C u_n^{\varphi/\sigma} + g_u u_n}{s_p C u_n^{\varphi/\sigma} - g_u u_n} \tag{23}$$

Taking the derivative of equation (23), we have:

$$\frac{d\hat{u}_n}{du_n} = \frac{\sigma\gamma[g_u - (\varphi/\sigma)s_p C(u_n)^{\frac{\varphi-\sigma}{\sigma}}]}{D^2}$$

where $D$ is the denominator of equation (23). Having started out with a two-variable differential equation system, it has been brought back to a one-variable system. For dynamic stability to prevail, we thus need the above derivative to be negative. This implies:

$$Cu_n^{\frac{\varphi-\sigma}{\sigma}} > \frac{g_u \sigma}{s_p \varphi}$$

The term on the left-hand side is $r_n / u_n$. Dynamic stability thus requires:

$$\frac{\sigma}{\varphi} < \frac{s_p r_n}{g_u u_n} \tag{24}$$

Two cases may be considered. In the first case, when $\varphi > \sigma$, dynamic stability necessarily occurs. Having assumed short-run stability, the fulfilment of equation (17) guarantees the fulfilment of equation (24), i.e., the left-hand side of equation (24) is then smaller than one, while the right-hand side is necessarily larger than one. In the second case, with $\varphi < \sigma$, dynamic stability may still occur if equation (24) is fulfilled.[21] This implies that the ratio of the reaction parameters $\sigma / \varphi$ be smaller than the ratio of the slopes of the savings and investment functions (which is more likely to occur when the slope of the savings function is steep while that of the investment function is flat). Otherwise, the model is dynamically unstable.

It can easily be shown that the first case of dynamic stability is associated with an increase in the profit margin when realized rates of capacity utilization exceed their normal rates. From equation (7) we derive:

$$\hat{m} = \hat{r}_n - \hat{u}_n - \hat{v}$$

where the hats denote rates of growth. From the above

[21] We then have: $1 < \sigma / \varphi < (s_p r_n / g_u u_n)$.

equation and equation (21), assuming no change in the $\upsilon$ parameter, we have:

$$\hat{m} = (\varphi / \sigma - 1)\hat{u}_n$$

This shows that in the first dynamically stable case, where $\varphi > \sigma$, profit margins increase when realized rates of capacity utilization exceed their normal rates. Where $\varphi < \sigma$, profit margins would decrease, and this could lead to a stable equilibrium or to an unstable situation.

The above can be illustrated with the help of figures 3 and 4. Let us first illustrate the first case of dynamic stability, with figure 3. Suppose as before that the economy starts out from a fully adjusted position given by $(u_{n0}, g_0)$. Let us assume, again as before, a decrease in the propensity to save $s_p$. This will initially induce a downward rotation of the savings function, to $g_1{}^s$, with the new long-run solutions being $(u_1, g_1)$. The discrepancy between the realized and the normal rates will induce a slow reaction as described by equations (14) and (15). Here, because of the assumptions made on the reaction parameters, the profit margin $m$ rises. The savings function rotates back upwards, until $g_2{}^s$, at which point the decreasing realized rate of utilization $u_2$ will equate the increasing normal rate of utilization $u_{n2}$. The rate of accumulation at this new fully adjusted position is now $g_2$, which is still higher than the rate of growth $g_0$ of the original fully adjusted position. In contrast to the model depicted in the previous section, the paradox of thrift is preserved when fully adjusted positions are compared. The paradox of costs, however, does not hold: the higher rate of accumulation here is linked to higher profit margins and hence lower real wages. In equation (7), we have $\gamma r_{n2} / u_{n2} > r_{no} / u_{n0}$. A similar exercise could be performed by increasing the exogenous parameter $\gamma$ of investment function (1).

On the other hand, in the second case of dynamic stability, the paradox of costs holds even in fully adjusted positions. This case is illustrated with the help of figure 4. As before, we assume a drop in the propensity to save. The higher than normal actual rate of utilization will induce changes in the normal profit rate and in the normal rate of capacity utilization. Because $\varphi < \sigma$, the profit margin decreases and real wages increase. However, assuming that equation (24) is fulfilled, this will not lead to an unstable situation where the rate of growth would take off, and a new fully adjusted position will be reached at $u_2 = u_{n2}$, with $g_2 > g_0$ and $r_{n2} / u_{n2} < r_{n0} / u_{n0}$ A fully adjusted higher rate of capital accumulation is associated with higher real wages. The paradox of costs may thus arise across fully adjusted positions.[22]

Figure 3

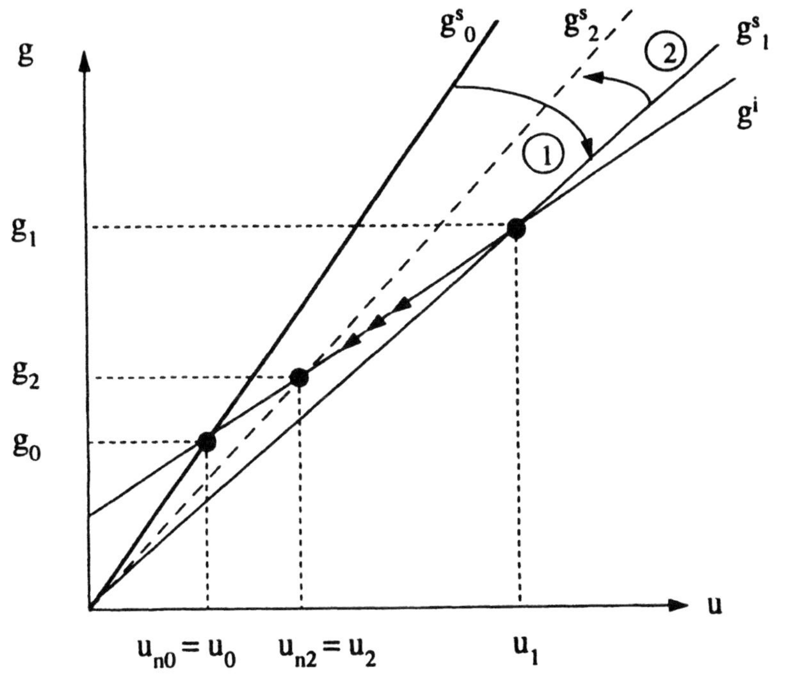


An interesting feature of the present traverse is that the model yields a continuum of possible fully adjusted equilibria. In figure 3 for instance, given the initial fully adjusted position at $u_{n0}$, and given the temporary long-run solution given by $u_1$, the new fully adjusted position can be anywhere on the investment curve between $u_{n0}$ and $u_1$. The new fully adjusted position depends *on the adjustment process during the transition*. Of course, if we know the exact form of the differential equations (14) and (15), we can find out exactly what the new fully adjusted position ($u_{n2}$, $g_2$) will be. This new fully adjusted position depends however on the previous

22 In the unstable case, there would be a series of higher real wages accompanied by higher rates of accumulation.

Figure 4

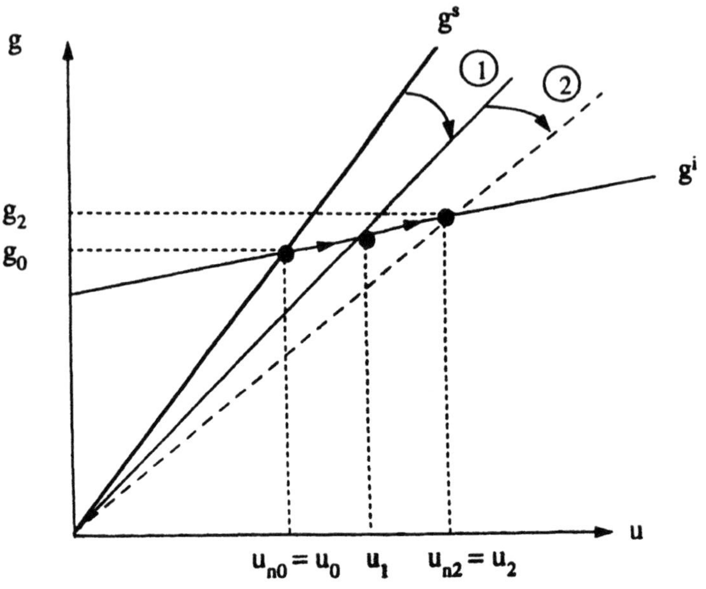


fully adjusted position, i.e., it depends on $u_{n0}$, which is itself an endogenous variable. The exact fully adjusted equilibrium thus depends on the values taken by the reaction parameters—$\varphi$ and $\sigma$—and the initial values of the variables, as is clear from equation (22). We here have a case of *deep endogeneity*, as Setterfield (1993) calls it. With deep endogeneity as modelled above, hysteresis is the general case rather than the exception, even in linear models as in the present Kaleckian model. The fully adjusted position here depends on the previous path of the economy. We thus have an instance of hysteresis, which might be defined as models where "the long run or final value of a variable depends on the value of the variable in the past, by virtue of the influence of this past value on the current alleged exogenous variables" (Setterfield 1995: 14).[23]

---

23 One may wonder whether the model is reversible. Reversibility is defined as an economy which, confronted with a shock, say an increase in animal spirits as measured by $\gamma$, comes back to its initial fully adjusted position if the shock is deleted, here if the animal spirits revert to their initial level (Setterfield 1995: 5). The answer to this question is yes, but only as long as the reaction parameters of the entrepreneurs do not change through time, as can be ascertained by the fully adjusted solution given by equation (21)

## HYSTERESIS THROUGH A COMBINATION OF THE PRICE FUNCTION AND THE INVESTMENT FUNCTION

Let us now consider precisely the model that was initially presented. As in the previous section, the pricing function depends on the normal rate of profit and the normal rate of capacity utilization, $r_n$ and $u_n$. We now assume, in addition, that entrepreneurs take the normal rate of capacity utilization in consideration when they make their investment decisions. The model thus consists of equations (5), (6), and (7), as before, whereas equation (1) is replaced by investment equation (2), where $g^i = \gamma + g_u(u - u_n)$.

The Kaleckian long-run solutions for the rate of utilization and the rate of accumulation are now given by equations (9) and (10). Let us assume as before that entrepreneurs slowly react to the divergence between the actual and the normal rates according to equations (14) and (15). Following the same procedures as in the previous section, the divergence between the actual and the normal rates of profit is given by equation (19), while the divergence between the actual and the normal rate of capacity utilization is given by:

$$u^* - u_n = \frac{\gamma - s_p r_n}{(s_p r_n / u_n) - g_u} \tag{25}$$

From the numerator of the above equation, it can be seen that a fully adjusted position will be reached when $u^* = u_n$, i.e., when:

---

for instance. In this sense the recent path of the economy has no impact on the outcome. However, if we were to write equation (15) under the following form:

$$u_{n(t)} = (1 - \sigma_{(t)})u_{n(t-1)} + \sigma_{(t)}u_{(t-1)}$$

with $0 < \sigma_{(t)} < 1$ and $\sigma_{(t)} \neq \sigma_{(t-1)}$ then path-dependence would be complete. There would be no reversibility, since the value of σ, in the solution given by equation (21), would be different before and after the shock. There is no reason to expect $\sigma_{(t)} = \sigma_{(t-1)}$. This equality is just a convenient one. In general the model is thus *irreversible*.

$$r_n^{**} = \gamma / s_p \tag{26}$$

There is thus a unique solution for the fully adjusted rate of profit. What about the fully adjusted rate of capacity utilization? Equation (22), which was obtained in the previous section, is still valid:

$$r_n = Cu_n^{\varphi/\sigma} \tag{22}$$

Combining equations (22) and (26), we obtain an explicit fully adjusted solution for the rate of utilization:

$$u_n^{**} = (\gamma / s_p C)^{\sigma/\varphi} \tag{27}$$

We find again a continuum of fully adjusted solutions for the rate of capacity utilization, which depends again on the initial values of the variables and on the reaction parameters of the entrepreneurs, i.e., on the behavior of the entrepreneurs during the traverse. In addition, along Keynesian lines, both the fully adjusted rate of utilization and rate of profit depend positively on animal spirits and negatively on the propensity to save.

A peculiar feature of the present model, when compared to the previous one, is that dynamic stability always occurs, given short-run stability, regardless of the values taken by the reaction parameters $\varphi$ and $\sigma$. In this sense, dynamic stability is not conditional. This can be seen by taking equations (15), (22), and (25), from which we obtain:

$$\hat{u}_n = \frac{\dot{u}_n}{u_n} = \sigma \frac{\gamma - s_p C(u_n)^{\varphi/\sigma}}{s_p C(u_n)^{\varphi/\sigma} - g_u u_n}$$

The derivative of the above expression yields:

$$\frac{d\hat{u}_n}{du_n} = \frac{-\gamma(s_p r_n / u_n - g_u)}{D^2} < 0$$

This derivative is always negative, since the term in brackets is necessarily positive when short-run stability prevails, as shown in equation (17). Therefore dynamic stability always prevails, provided short-run stability is assumed.

While we know that dynamic stability is not conditional on the values of $\varphi$ and $\sigma$, what about the paradox of costs and the paradox of thrift? Let us first consider the paradox of thrift. Note that since the fully adjusted solution is defined by $u^* = u_n$, it follows, given the form of the investment function—equation (2)—that the fully adjusted rate of accumulation is necessarily $g^{**} = \gamma$. Therefore, a drop in the propensity to save would only momentarily hike up the rate of accumulation. In the fully adjusted long run, the rate of accumulation would have to come back down to its (secular) level, $\gamma$. What we have in this case is a degenerate Kaleckian outcome (Lavoie 1995A: 807). There is no paradox of thrift, but on the other hand there are no negative long-run consequences to a decrease in the propensity to save. Indeed, profit rates and utilization rates in the new fully adjusted position are now higher than what they were in the old fully adjusted position.

This is illustrated with the help of figures 5 and 6. In both figures, a decrease in the propensity to save drives up the rate of accumulation from $\gamma$ to $g_1$, while the rate of capacity utilization moves up from $u_{n0}$ to $u_1$. The induced changes in $u_n$ and $r_n$ shift both the investment and the savings functions. In figure 5, where profit margins rise and real wages drop, the new fully adjusted rate of capacity utilization is given by $u_{n2}$; in figure 6, where profit margins drop and real wages rise, the new fully adjusted rate of capacity utilization is given by $u_{n3}$. Of course, the fully adjusted rate of capital accumulation remains at $\gamma$.

Figure 5

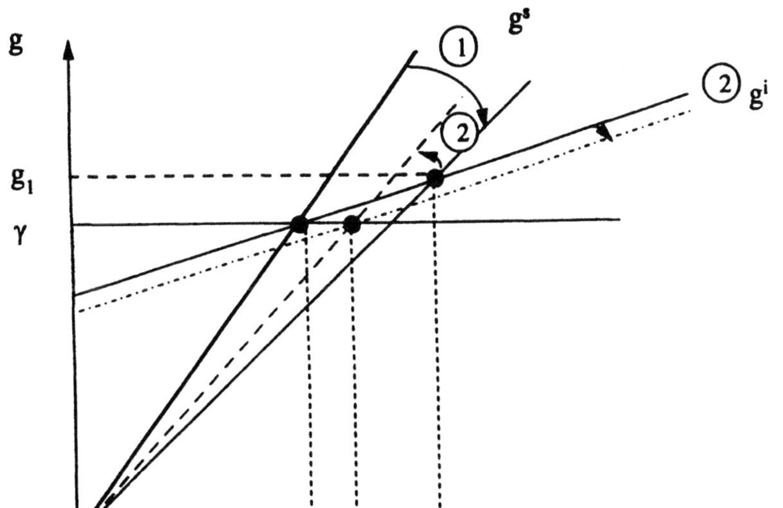

Figure 6

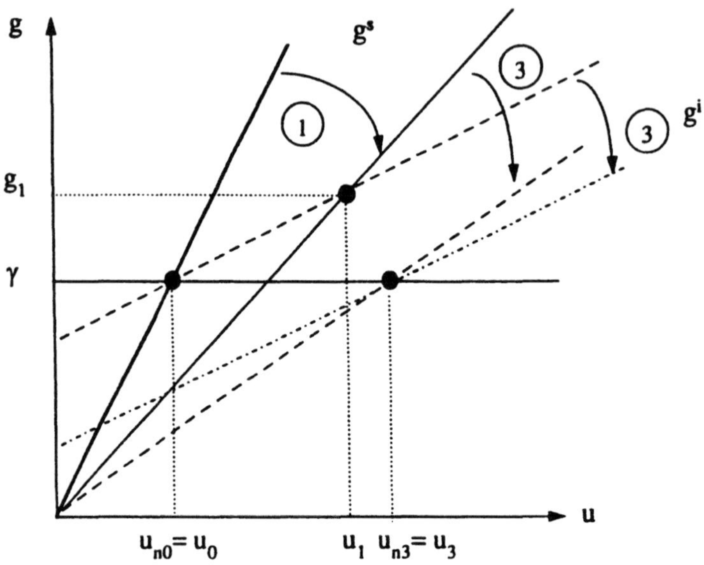


One may wonder whether real wages should be expected to fall or to rise when actual rates of capacity utilization exceed their normal levels. In the neoclassical framework or in the old Cambridgian growth models *à la* Robinson and Kaldor, real wages would fall, i.e., profit margins would rise. Demand forces in the goods market would push up prices, or seen from another angle, real wages fall with growth and increased employment, in line with the neoclassical marginal physical product of labor. On the other hand, it is not clear that such a mechanism is realistic in capitalist economies. While firms may wish to increase their profit margins when the economy benefits from over-normal rates of capacity utilization, they may well be prevented from doing so by their requirements on the labor market. Because the bargaining position of workers is much improved when the economy is running at over-normal rates of capacity utilization, it may be that while firms are targeting higher values for their normal rates of profit and of capacity utilization, realized profit margins are now lower and real wages higher. This is the neo-Marxian notion of the profit squeeze, but the mechanism is also put forth by Kalecki (1971: ch. 14) and Dutt (1995A: 149).

There is some irony here. Without this neo-Marxian short-run positive relationship between rates of capacity utilization and real wages, the Kaleckian paradox of costs does not occur, as shown at $u_{n2}$ in figure 3. On the other hand, with the neo-Marxian profit squeeze mechanism, the Kaleckian paradox of costs is maintained, as shown at $u_{n2}$ in figure 4. The same occurs with the model of the present section: a fully adjusted higher rate of accumulation, say $\gamma_2$, is associated with a lower profit margin and a higher real wage, as long as the neo-Marxian profit-squeeze mechanism works out, as it would in figure 6.

## HYSTERESIS THROUGH THE INVESTMENT FUNCTION ONLY

As was pointed out above, firms may have little control over margins of profit if these are the result of conflicting claims between firms and workers, where workers have some power to modify real wages.[24] In that case, one could argue that the evolution of what is considered to be the normal rates is of little relevance to pricing. Rather, one could argue that firms link normal rates of utilization of capacity only to the tools over which they have absolute control, i.e., their investment decisions.

Let us also consider again the endogeneity of the $\gamma$ variable that is to be found in investment function (2), as was done in section 4. The present model thus consists solely of equations (2) and (8), as it did in the simple Kaleckian model of section 3. As in the previous section, if we impose the equality between the realized and normal rates of capacity utilization, $u^* = u_n$, the rate of accumulation is necessarily equal to the exogenous parameter of the investment function, $g^{**} = \gamma$ in fully adjusted positions. This implies that the investment function given by equation (2) can be interpreted in the following way. $\gamma$ represents the expected secular rate of sales growth. To keep up with sales growth, firms must invest in new capacity at the rate $\gamma$. If the current rate of capacity utilization exceeds the normal rate, firms need to speed up the rate of accumulation to match the secular rate of sales growth while simultaneously

24 The conflict with workers will drive a wedge between the normal rate of profit targeted by entrepreneurs and the normal rate of profit actually incorporated into prices. While the normal rate of profit targeted by entrepreneurs and the realized rate of profit may become equal in the long run, these two rates will not in general be equal to the actual rate of return embodied in prices. Thus even in long-run positions, normal prices (the Sraffian or classical ones) will not necessarily arise. See Lavoie (1992: 417-21).

recovering their target rate of capacity utilization.

The above interpretation can be illustrated with the help of the following example. Suppose as always that we start off from a fully adjusted position, given by $(u_{n0}, g_0)$ in figure 7 below. Because $u_0 = u_{n0}$, we know that $g_0 = \gamma_0$. Assume a decrease in either savings rates or profit margins. The new long-run rate of utilization will be $u_1$, while the steady-state rate of growth is now $g_1$. The rate of capacity utilization is permanently higher than its normal rate, while the long-run rate of sales growth is now higher than the expected secular growth rate of sales. If the expectations and the behaviour of entrepreneurs are influenced by current values, the normal rate of capacity utilization should rise along the lines given by equation (15), while the expected secular rate of sales growth should similarly rise. We thus have two differential equations, describing the evolution of the two slowly moving variables, $u_n$ and $\gamma$:[25]

$$\dot{u}_n = \sigma(u^* - u_n) \tag{15}$$

$$\dot{\gamma} = \psi(g^* - \gamma) \tag{28}$$

As in section 3, the long-run values of $u^*$ and $g^*$ are given by equations (9) and (10). Combining these two equations to equations (15) and (28), we obtain equations (29) and (30):

$$\dot{u}_n = \sigma \frac{\gamma - \alpha u_n}{\alpha - g_u} \tag{29}$$

25 There is a hint of this interpretation in Lavoie (1992: 330), and the model as such can be found in Lavoie (1995A: 807-9). Skott (1989: 54) also deals with an endogenous normal rate of capacity utilization, but his depends on an entry-deterrent strategy only. When the actual rate of utilization exceeds the normal rate, the latter *decreases*, in contrast to what is assumed here. Dutt (1996) also supposes that normal rates of utilization are set to deter entry, but he assumes that incumbent firms *reduce* normal rates of capacity utilization when they expect a higher rate of entry than at present, i.e., as long as the expected secular growth rate of sales exceeds the current rate of accumulation. By assuming that:

$$\dot{u}_n = -\sigma(\gamma - g)$$

one would arrive at results qualitatively similar to those reached here.

$$\dot{\gamma} = \psi \frac{g_u(\gamma - \alpha u_n)}{\alpha - g_u} \tag{30}$$

The ratio of these two equations is:

$$\frac{\dot{\gamma}}{\dot{u}_n} = \frac{\psi g_u}{\sigma}$$

which can also be rewritten as:

$$d\gamma = \frac{\psi g_u}{\sigma} du_n$$

Taking the integral of this expression, we get the solution:

$$\gamma = (\psi g_u / \sigma)u_n + C \tag{31}$$

Substituting this value of γ into equation (29), the differential equation becomes:

$$\dot{u}_n = \frac{\sigma}{\alpha - g_u}[(\psi g_u / \sigma)u_n + C - \alpha u_n] \tag{32}$$

Dynamic stability requires that the derivative of equation (32) with respect to $u_n$ be negative. This derivative is:

$$\frac{d\dot{u}_n}{du_n} = \frac{\sigma}{\alpha - g_u}[(\psi g_u / \sigma) - \alpha]$$

Assuming short-run stability, i.e., assuming $\alpha > g_u$, the derivative is negative and there is dynamic stability whenever the term between square brackets is negative, i.e., whenever $\alpha > (\psi / \sigma)g_u$.[26] Since we have assumed short-run stability, a sufficient condition for dynamic stability is thus $\sigma > \psi$. It is sufficient for the speed of adjustment of the normal rate of capacity utilization to be larger than the speed of adjustment of the expected secular growth.

We may now discuss the fully adjusted solutions, $u_n^{**}$ and $g^{**}$. The fully adjusted rate of capacity utilization is such that $u^* = u_n$, which means that equation (32) is equal to zero. This implies:

26 Under Dutt's (1996) formalization, the dynamic stability condition becomes $\alpha > \psi / \sigma$.

$$u_n^{**} = \frac{C\sigma}{\alpha\sigma - \psi g_u} \tag{33}$$

Given the dynamic stability condition, we see that $C$ must be positive for $u_n^{**}$ to be positive. Equation (33) shows that with dynamic stability, an increase in the propensity to save or in the profit margin—both changes leading to a decrease in $\alpha$—induces an increase in the fully adjusted rate of capacity utilization.

What about the expected rate of sales growth and the fully adjusted rate of accumulation? Making use of equation (8), $g = \alpha u$, and equation (33), we have:

$$\gamma^{**} = \frac{C\sigma\alpha}{\alpha\sigma - \psi g_u} \tag{34}$$

Taking the derivative of this equation with respect to $\alpha$ we find:

$$\frac{d\gamma^{**}}{d\alpha} = \frac{-C\sigma\psi g_u}{(\alpha\sigma - \psi g_u)^2} < 0 \tag{35}$$

We thus have again a model of hysteresis, where the fully adjusted long run solutions depend on the past values of the variables and on the reaction parameters of entrepreneurs during the traverse to the fully adjusted position.[27] Furthermore, in the present case, both the paradox of thrift and the paradox of costs are carried over from the Kaleckian long run to the classical fully adjusted positions, as can be seen from equations (33) and (35). This model of hysteresis, due to deep endogeneity arising from equations (15) and (28), is a case of demand-led hysteresis. It is not the supply-side behavior of households which causes demand effects to have an impact on normal rates, as it would in most neoclassical models. Rather it is the demand-side investment behavior of entrepreneurs which causes path dependence.

The dynamically stable case of this model of hysteresis is

---

[27] There will be irreversibility if the reaction parameters change through time, as one would expect they would. For instance, we could have:

$$\gamma_{(t)} = (1 - \psi_{(t)})\gamma_{(t-1)} + \psi_{(t)} g_{(t-1)}$$

with $0 < \psi_{(t)} < 1$ and $\psi_{(t)} \neq \psi_{(t-1)}$.

illustrated in figure 7. Recall that the rate of utilization and the rate of accumulation had initially increased to $u_1$ and $g_1$, following a reduction in the propensity to save or in the profit margin. Because of the dynamic stability condition, the investment function now shifts down, forcing expected growth rate of sales to converge to the higher realized rate of accumulation, while the realized and the normal rates of capacity utilization converge toward each other. This will occur at the new fully adjusted position $(u_{n2}, g_2)$, where $u_2 = u_{n2} > u_{n0}$ and $g_2 = \gamma_2 > g_0$. With this behaviour on the part of the entrepreneurs, the paradoxes of thrift and costs are equally valid in the long run and in fully adjusted long-run positions. A Keynesian or Kaleckian economist need not become classical when the full consistency of the fully adjusted positions is taken into account.

Figure 7

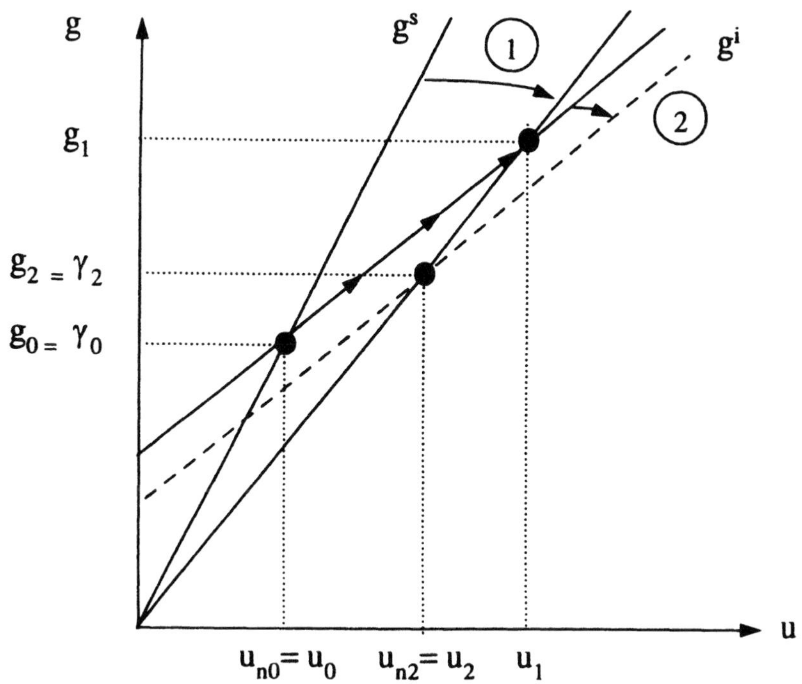

## CONCLUSION

The Kaleckian model of growth and distribution is a flexible pedagogical tool, which can be used to develop a post-classical alternative to neoclassical macroeconomic theory. The main drawback of the Kaleckian model, as seen by its critics, is that the model did not take into account the constraint of normal equilibrium. In a normal equilibrium, one where tranquillity is preserved, the realized rate of capacity utilization should equal or gravitate around its normal or targeted value. This equality defines what we have called fully adjusted positions. Critics of Kaleckian models thus question the validity of Kaleckian results, mainly the extension to the long run of the paradoxes of thrift and of costs. For these critics, fully adjusted positions are not determined by demand-side factors, but rather by supply-side considerations, namely the desire to save and normal rates of profit. Kaleckians, as a response, have questioned the usefulness of supply-side determined normal equilibria, arguing that these fully adjusted positions lack significance unless "some coherent dynamic adjustment process is specified which can describe the traverse from one equilibrium position to another, without the traverse itself influencing the final equilibrium position, that is, without the equilibrium being path determined" (Halevi and Kriesler 1991: 86).

Whereas such a traverse was lacking in previous accounts of normal equilibria, we have shown that classical authors have put forth a model which explains the transition from a position incorporating all the Keynesian/Kaleckian features to a fully adjusted position incorporating all the classical features. The dynamic adjustment process proposed by Duménil and Lévy eschews the objections raised by Halevi and Kriesler. It yields a unique fully adjusted position, which is not influenced by demand forces. Their normal equilibrium, linked to the normal rate of capacity utilization, thus in some sense plays a role similar to that of the natural rate of unemployment in neoclassical economics.

The adjustment process proposed by Duménil and Lévy is not however the only possible one. Just as hysteresis effects have put in jeopardy the concept of the unique natural rate of unemployment in neoclassical economics, hysteresis effects take away the relevance of comparative analysis based on classical equilibria with a single normal rate of capacity utilization. Simple and plausible adjustment mechanisms may give way to fully adjusted positions which preserve the Keynesian paradox of thrift or the Kaleckian paradox of costs. These fully adjusted positions, which fulfil the consistency requirement that realized and normal rates of capacity utilization be equated, can be shown to depend on the path taken during the traverse, i.e., on the adjustment process during the transition. A critical feature of these new fully adjusted positions is that their normal rate of capacity utilization is itself an endogenous variable.

A Kaleckian or Keynesian stance thus remains justified even if one considers that long period analysis with fully adjusted positions constitutes the ultimate ground to support economic policies. Kaleckians or post-Keynesians need not deny the fruitfulness of long-period analysis to retain the relevance of their models. While fully adjusted positions with classical features may arise out of Keynesian short-run equilibria, traverses towards fully adjusted positions that retain some or all Kaleckian and Keynesian features are also quite possible. Duménil and Lévy (1995: 136) claim that "while it is possible to be *Keynesian in the short term*, one is required to be *classical in the long term*." In contrast, the present study shows that this claim is unwarranted when hysteresis effects are taken into account. It is perfectly legitimate to remain Keynesian in the short run, in the Kaleckian long run, and across fully adjusted positions.

## REFERENCES

Amadeo, Edward J. 1986. The Role of Capacity Utilization in Long-Period Analysis. *Political Economy* 2(2): 147–185.

Auerbach, Paul and Peter Skott. 1988. Concentration, Competition and Distribution. *International Review of Applied Economics* 2(1): 42–61.

Bhaduri, Amit and Stephen Marglin. 1990. Unemployment and the Real Wage: The Economic Basis for Contesting Political Ideologies. *Cambridge Journal of Economics* 14(4): 375–393.

Ciccone, Roberto. 1986. Accumulation and Capacity Utilization: Some Critical Considerations on Joan Robinson's Theory of Distribution. *Political Economy* 2(1): 17–36.

__________. 1991. Book review of Amitava Krishna Dutt, "Growth, Distribution and Uneven Development." *Contributions to Political Economy* 10: 94–102.

Committeri, Marco. 1986. Some Comments on Recent Contributions on Capital Accumulation, Income Distribution and Capacity Utilization. *Political Economy* 2(2): 161–186.

Duménil, Gérard and Dominique Lévy. 1993. Book review of Christian Bidard, "Prix, production et rareté." *Journal of Economics - Zeitschrift für Nationalökonomie* 53(3): 309–313.

_________. 1994. Being Keynesian in the Short Term and Classical in the Long Term: The Traverse to Classical Long-Term Equilibrium. CEPREMAP, Preliminary draft, April.

_________. 1995. A Post-Keynesian Long-Term Equilibrium with Equalized Profit Rates? *Review of Radical Political Economics* 27(2): 135–141.

Dutt, Amitava K. 1990. *Growth, Distribution and Uneven Development.* Cambridge: Cambridge University Press.

_________. 1992. Rentiers in Post Keynesian Models. In *Recent Developments in Post-Keynesian Economics.* Philip Arestis and Victoria Chick (eds.). Aldershot: Edward Elgar: 95–122.

_________. 1995A. Monopoly Power and Uniform Rates of Profit: A Reply to Glick-Campbell and Duménil-Lévy. *Review of Political Economy* 27(2): 142–153.

_________. 1995B. Profit Rate Equalization in the Kalecki-Steindl Model and the "Over-Determination" Problem. Working paper, University of Notre Dame, October 1995.

_________. 1996. Equilibrium, Path Dependence and Hysteresis in Post-Keynesian Models. Paper prepared for a volume of essays in honor of Geoffrey Harcourt, edited by Philip Arestis and Malcolm Sawyer.

Eichner, Alfred S. 1986. *Toward a New Economics.* London: Macmillan.

_________. 1987. *The Macrodynamics of Advanced Market Economies.* Armonk: M.E. Sharpe.

Garegnani, Pierangelo. 1992. Some Notes for an Analysis of Accumulation. In *Beyond the Steady State: A Revival of Growth Theory.* Joseph Halevi, David Laibman, and Edward Nell (eds). London: Macmillan: 47–71.

Glick, Mark and Donald A. Campbell. 1995. Classical Competition and the Compatibility of Market Power and Uniform Rates of Profit. *Review of Radical Political Economics* 27(2): 124–135.

Greenwald, Ben and Joseph Stiglitz. 1993. New and Old Keynesians. *Journal of Economic Perspectives* 7(1): 23–44.

Hagemann, Harold. 1992. Traverse Analysis in a Post-Classical Model. In *Beyond the Steady State: A Revival of Growth Theory.* Joseph Halevi, David Laibman, and Edward Nell (eds). London: Macmillan: 235–263.

Halevi, Joseph and Peter Kriesler. 1991. Kalecki, Classical Economics and the Surplus Approach. *Review of Political Economy* 3(1): 79–92.

Henry, Jacques. 1993. Post-Keynesian Methods and the Post-Classical Approach. *International Papers in Political Economy* 1(2): 1–26.

Hicks, John. 1965. *Capital and Growth.* Oxford: Oxford University Press.

Kalecki, Michal. 1971. *Selected Essays on the Dynamics of the Capitalist Economy*. Cambridge: Cambridge University Press.

Keynes, John M. 1983. *Articles and Correspondence: Investment and Editorial. Collected Writings*. Don Moggridge (ed.). Vol. 12. London: Macmillan.

Kurz, Heinz D. 1990. Technical Change, Growth and Distribution: A Steady State Approach to Unsteady Growth. In *Capital, Distribution and Effective Demand: Studies in the Classical Approach to Economic Theory*. Cambridge: Polity Press.

__________. 1994. Growth and Distribution. *Review of Political Economy* 6(4): 393–420.

Larson, Bruce. 1991. A Dilemma in the Theory of Short-Run Production and Cost. *Southern Economic Journal* 58(2): 465–474.

Lavoie, Marc. 1990. Thriftiness, Growth and the Post-Keynesian Tradition. *Économies et Sociétés* 23(7): 123–134.

__________. *Foundations of Post-Keynesian Economic Analysis*. Aldershot: Edward Elgar.

__________. 1995A. The Kaleckian Model of Growth and Distribution and its Neo-Ricardian and Neo-Marxian Critiques. *Cambridge Journal of Economics* 19(6): 789–818.

__________. 1995B. Interest Rates in Post-Keynesian Models of Growth and Distribution, *Metroeconomica* 46(2): 146–177.

__________. 1996. La traverse kaleckienne dans un modèle d'accumulation à deux secteurs avec coût complet: à la recherche d'une synthèse post-classique. *Cahiers d'économie politique* 26: 127–164.

Marglin, Stephen A. 1984. Growth, Distribution and Inflation: A Centennial Synthesis. *Cambridge Journal of Economics* 8(2): 115–144.

Nell, Edward J. 1985. Jean Baptiste Marglin: A Comment on "Growth, Distribution and Inflation." *Cambridge Journal of Economics* 9(2): 173–178.

Park, Man-Seop 1995. A Note on the "Kalecki-Steindl" Steady-State Approach to Growth and Income Distribution. *Manchester School of Economic and Social Studies* 63(3): 297–310.

Robinson, Joan. 1956. *The Accumulation of Capital*. London: Macmillan.

__________. 1962. *Essays in the Theory of Economic Growth*. London: Macmillan.

Roncaglia, Alessandro. 1995. On the Compatibility Between Keynes's and Sraffa's Viewpoints on Output Levels. In *Income and Employment in Theory and in Practice: Essays in Memory of Athanasios Asimakopulos*. Geoffrey C.

Harcourt, Alessandro Roncaglia, and Robin Rowley (eds). London: Macmillan: 111–125.

Rowthorn, Bob. 1981. Demand, Real Wages and Economic Growth. *Thames Papers in Political Economy* 18: 3–54.

Setterfield, Mark. 1993. Towards a Long-Run Theory of Effective Demand: Modelling Macroeconomic Systems with Hysteresis. *Journal of Post Keynesian Economics* 15(3): 347–364.

__________. 1995. Historical Time and Economic Theory. *Review of Political Economy* 7(1): 1–27.

Skott, Peter. 1989. *Conflict and Effective Demand in Economic Growth.* Cambridge: Cambridge University Press.

Steindl, Joseph. 1952. *Maturity and Stagnation in American Capitalism.* Oxford: Blackwell.

Taylor, Lance. 1991. *Income Distribution, Inflation and Growth: Lectures in Structuralist Macroeconomic Theory.* Cambridge, Mass.: MIT Press.

Trigg, Andrew B. 1994. On the Relationship between Kalecki and the Kaleckians. *Journal of Post Keynesian Economics* 17(1): 91–108.

Vianello, Ferdinando. 1985. The Pace of Accumulation. *Political Economy* 1(1): 69–87.

Watts, Martin J. and William F. Mitchell. 1990. Australian Wage Inflation: Real Wage Resistance, Hysteresis and Incomes Policy: 1968(3)–1988(3). *Manchester School of Economic and Social Studies* 58(2): 142–164.

Wood, Adrian. 1975. *A Theory of Profits.* Cambridge: Cambridge University Press.

You, Jong-Il. 1994. Macroeconomic Structure, Endogenous Technical Change and Growth. *Cambridge Journal of Economics* 18(2): 217–233.

*Review of Political Economy, Volume 15, Number 1, 2003*

# *Kaleckian Effective Demand and Sraffian Normal Prices: towards a reconciliation*

MARC LAVOIE

*Department of Economics, University of Ottawa, Ottawa, Ontario, Canada K1N 5N6*

*Sraffians and Kaleckians alike reject the belief that higher rates of accumulation need be associated with lower real wage rates or higher propensities to save. The rejection of this proposition is mainly based on the endogeneity of the rate of capacity utilization, both in the short and the long run. This endogeneity often relies on a discrepancy between the realized and the normal rates of profit, or between the realized and the target rate of capacity utilization, a discrepancy which some authors believe is unwarranted in long run analysis. Various models that eliminate this divergence are outlined. In all these models, the normal rate of profit itself is taken as an endogenous variable. In the first two models, the normal rate of profit depends either on the realized profit rate or the rate of interest. Supply-led results may then reappear in long run analysis. In the last model, one introduces the possibility of a divergence between the rate of return as assessed and targeted by firms, and the rate of return that is actually incorporated into prices. This divergence arises because of the bargaining power of workers and their real wage resistance. Under these conditions, the demand-led results of the Kaleckian tradition are recovered in a model with definite solutions.*

## 1. Introduction

The Sraffian and post-Keynesian traditions are often associated with each other. There are historical reasons for this association, since these traditions both originated at the University of Cambridge. While all agreed that full employment, if left to market forces could only occur occasionally, substantial theoretical disputes arose between the two schools, in particular on the relevance and relative importance of long period analysis compared with short-period investigation. Despite these disputes, however, a large range of agreement has remained, in particular about a most crucial issue, the causal role played by effective demand in the theory of accumulation. The causality involved can most simply seen by making use of the well-known Cambridge equation, $r = g/s_p$. The *classical* interpretation of this equation in a world divided into two social

This paper was presented at the Eastern Economic Association, in Boston, in 1999. I wish to thank Davide Gualerzi, Gary Mongiovi, Mark Setterfield and the referees of the journal for their comments.
E-mail: mlavoie@uottawa.ca

ISSN 0953-8259 print/ISSN 1465-3982 online/03/010053-22 
DOI: 10.1080/0953825022000033125

classes, one of which (the working class) does not save, is that the rate of accumulation $g$ is an endogenous variable, which is higher when either the normal rate of profit $r$ or the propensity $s_p$ to save out of profits (earned by capitalists) is higher. This classical interpretation is consistent with the views recently developed by *neoclassical* authors within the framework of the so-called *new growth theory*. The crucial distinctive feature of these models, in contrast to the previous neoclassical Solow model, is that the steady-state rate of accumulation $g$ is an endogenous variable. Essentially, this steady-state rate of accumulation is determined by the rate of return on capital and the propensity to save. These two variables are exogenous, determined respectively in the production sphere (by technology alone) and by the preferences of consumers. Since many of these new growth models assume that all factors of production are capital, physical capital or human capital, all incomes appear as returns on capital, and hence with a single propensity to save out of income, we are back to the Cambridge equation. We are also back to the classical interpretation of this equation, since a higher propensity to save and a higher rate of profit generate a higher rate of accumulation.

The classical and the new neoclassical analyses of growth thus have much in common (Kurz, 1997). From the point of view of effective demand, these analyses are supply-led in the sense that higher savings generate higher growth rates. This must be contrasted to the post-Keynesian view of accumulation, which has been developed in Cambridge in the 1950s, according to which higher propensities to save generate lower rates of accumulation. In these models, developed in particular by Joan Robinson, the Cambridge equation is only one half of the story. It must be combined with an investment function, where accumulation depends on the expected rate of profit and various other factors, such as the optimism of entrepreneurs or the availability of credit. The introduction of this investment function has a substantial impact on the interpretation of the Cambridge equation. In the post-Keynesian model of Joan Robinson, both the rate of accumulation and the realized rate of profit become endogenous, and it is no longer possible to assert that a higher propensity to save is conducive to a higher rate of accumulation. In fact, quite the contrary occurs: a higher propensity to save generates a lower rate of accumulation. This was the dynamic equivalent of Keynes's paradox of thrift, whereby a higher propensity to save generates a lower income level in a static framework, and it generalized the role of effective demand to growth economics and the long run. To this generalization, both the Sraffians and the post-Keynesians adhered.

Despite this agreement on the role played by effective demand, the interpretation of the Cambridge equation generated a controversy between Sraffians and post-Keynesians. The latter came to interpret the rate of profit determined by the Cambridge equation as the normal rate of profit, consistent with the normal utilization of capacity. Thus, in the old Cambridge model of growth, a higher rate of accumulation came to be associated with a higher normal rate of profit, and hence, disregarding changes in saving rates or technical progress, with higher profit margins and lower real wages. This did not fit well with the Sraffian view, according to which the normal rate of profit is determined by the power struggle over real wages or by interest rates set by the central bank. Initially, most Sraffians, along with many Marxists and Cambridge authors, such as Joan Robinson, associated the long period with *fully adjusted positions* only, i.e. positions that correspond to the normal use of capacity or normal output, with a uniform rate of profit (Vianello, 1985). Most Sraffians now have explicitly abandoned at least part of this claim. The present Sraffian view is that, even in the long period, the realized utilization rate will generally be different from its normal level. The rate of capacity utilization is thus flexible, in the short run as well as in the long run, and this flexibility allows savings to adjust to a higher rate of investment, as the post-Keynesians would have it, but without profit margins having to rise or real wages to fall. This rejection of a necessary link between higher growth rates and higher profit margins, as can be found in Garegnani (1992), constitutes the main Sraffian critique of the old Cambridge model of growth, which until recently constituted the dominant post-Keynesian view of output and distribution.

It should be noted that the very same critique against the old Cambridge model of growth had been addressed by Davidson (1972, pp. 123–127) in his overview of post-Keynesian economics. Davidson noted some inconsistency among Cambridge authors: on one hand, they underlined the importance of effective demand and quantity adjustments, but on the other hand their growth models relied on the flexibility of the price mechanism. Both Kaldor (1964, pp. xvi–xvii) and Robinson (1969, pp. 261–262), however, had themselves recognized the deficiencies of their models in that regard, noting that actual profit rates could be modified through changes in the rate of utilization, without modifying profit margins. As argued by Kurz (1994), the endogenous view of the actual degree of utilization is also fully compatible with the growth models constructed by post-Keynesians in the Kaleckian tradition (Rowthorn, 1981; Amadeo, 1986; Dutt, 1990; Lavoie, 1995), and it extends Keynesian income effects beyond the short-run, where they had been contained until then. Thus, Sraffians agree that there is no reason for the actual rate of capacity utilization to equal its normal rate.[1]

Notwithstanding these large segments of agreement among post-Keynesians and Sraffians, there remain two sources of contention. First, several authors, be they Sraffians or Marxists, have claimed that long-run models where the rate of utilization is not equal to its normal value, lack logical consistency. For these authors, only fully adjusted positions are logically consistent in a long-run analysis, i.e. only equilibria where the realized and the normal rates of profit are equal, and where the realized and the normal rates of capacity utilization equal each other. Only these equilibria are *final*, because otherwise there would exist economic forces that would change the long-run equilibrium. One response to this critique has been to redefine the long run, as do Chick & Caserta (1996), calling medium-run models, or provisional equilibria, those models that achieve an equilibrium rate of growth without the actual and the normal

[1] A similar convergence of views can be observed in the case of some Marxists. For instance, as late as the early 1980s, Marglin (1984) was still assuming a fixed rate of capacity utilization in long-run analysis, while the degree of utilization becomes an endogenous variable in Bhaduri & Marglin (1990).

utilization rates being equal. The other response has been to study the mechanisms that could lead these two rates to become equal, and to analyse the consequences of these mechanisms on the theory of effective demand. But even if this problem is set aside, a second source of contention arises. According to most Kaleckians, there is no reason to expect actual prices to equal normal prices, i.e. those prices computed with normal rates of profit on the basis of normal rates of capacity utilization. For Sraffians, on the contrary, such normal prices must prevail in the long period. As Ciccone (1986, p. 24) puts it, 'the tendency towards long-period prices does not in fact seem to require the simultaneous gravitation of the effective utilization of capacity around its normal level—i.e. the level of utilization implicit in those prices'. For these Sraffians, the tendency towards normal prices does not entail a tendency for actual rates of capacity utilization to equal normal rates of capacity utilization. Another way to put it is to say that the convergence towards normal prices occurs much faster than the convergence towards normal rates of capacity utilization. My intent in the following sections is to study these two sources of contention.

The paper proceeds as follows. In the next section we present the essentials of a Kaleckian model of growth with target return pricing. In the third and fourth sections, two different adjustment mechanisms are proposed to bring the economy back to a fully adjusted position. In the fifth section we introduce a conflict-based theory of inflation. In the sixth section, it is shown that an adjustment process that takes into account the bargaining power of workers does not bring back the economy to a fully adjusted position, i.e. despite target rates of return and realized rates of return being equated, actual rates of capacity utilization do not converge towards normal rates. The last model will thus yield some ground to all views: actual prices in the long-run equilibrium are not normal prices, and actual utilization rates are not normal rates, but because the realized rates of return turn out to be equal to the target rate of return, dynamic forces are such that this equilibrium is a terminal point.

## 2. The Basic Model

### 2.1. The Profits Cost Equation

There are two crucial equations in the Kaleckian model of growth and distribution: one identifies the rate of profit from the supply side, the other from the demand side. We start out with the derivation of what Rowthorn (1981, p. 8) and Steindl (1979, p. 3) call the profits function, which we shall call the profits cost equation. From national accounting, we have that the value of net aggregate output is equal to the sum of the wage costs and the profits on capital:

$$pq = wL + rpK$$

where $p$ is the price level, $q$ is the level of real output, $w$ is the nominal wage rate, $L$ is the level of labour employment, $r$ is the rate of profit, $K$ is the stock of capital in real terms. Thus,

$$p = w(L/q) + rpK/q \qquad (1)$$

We then make the following three definitions:

$$l = L/q$$
$$u = q/q_{fc}$$
$$v = K/q_{fc}$$

The first equation shows labour per unit of output, assuming away, as is often done, overhead labour. The second equation defines the rate of utilization of capacity, with $q_{fc}$ denoting full capacity output. The third equation defines the capital-to-capacity ratio, which is assumed to depend on technology. With these definitions, equation (1) can be rewritten as:

$$p = wl + rpv/u \tag{2}$$

Equation (2) gives us the price of a unit of output in terms of the labour costs per unit of output and the profits per unit of output. From this equation, we obtain the rate of profit in terms of the real wage rate:

$$r = (u/v)[1 - (w/p)l] \tag{3}$$

The *realized* rate of profit here thus depends on the exogenous real wage rate and the degree of capacity utilization. At this stage, we have to introduce a pricing equation. Kaleckians themselves seem to have favoured mark-up pricing of the type:

$$p = (1 + \theta)wl$$

One is not forced to adopt this type of cost-plus pricing procedure. Indeed, it has been argued by Lee (1994) that pricing procedures are, to a large extent, dependent on accounting procedures, and that the latter have long been sophisticated enough to support normal cost pricing procedures, sometimes called full-cost pricing. Such pricing is based on unit costs, or more specifically standard unit costs, rather than unit direct costs only. A particular specification of normal cost pricing is target return pricing, and this seems to have been prevalent for some time, both among large and smaller firms (Lanzillotti 1958; Shipley 1981). There are obvious tight links between Sraffian versions of normal prices and the administered cost-plus prices, to be found in many empirical studies and which are endorsed by most Kaleckians. This is most obvious in Lanzillotti's version of normal cost pricing, which is based on target-return pricing. Prices are set according to the normal unit costs of the price leaders, assessed at some *standard* volume of production, on the basis of a *target rate of return*. There is no presumption that this target rate of return will be the realized rate of profit: the former will be achieved only if actual sales are equivalent to the standard volume of output. Some Sraffians give a similar interpretation of prices of production: they may be defined on the basis of a stable system of profit rate differentials; they are based neither on the best available nor the average technique, but rather on the dominant technique—that of the price leaders; they are based on the normal degree of utilization of the existing productive capacity rather than on actual output levels (Roncaglia 1990).

We can find an explicit pricing formula for target return procedures that is almost as simple as the mark-up equation. What then would the mark-up proxy $\theta$ be equal to? Suppose that the replacement value of the stock of capital is $pK$, while the target rate of return, which we might want to call the *normal* or the *standard* rate of profit, is $r_s$. Required profits for the period are then $r_s pK$. With a normal (or standard) rate of capacity utilization of $u_s$, corresponding in the period to a level of output of $q_s$, the required profits for the period must be equal to $r_s vpq_s/u_s$. This must be equated to the total profits that are to be obtained by marking up unit costs at the standard rate of utilization of capacity: $\theta wl$. After some manipulation, a simple pricing formula for target pricing procedures can be found:[2]

$$p = (u_s/(u_s - r_s v))wl$$

Of course, the equation makes sense only if the denominator is positive, that is if: $u_s > r_s v$. The inequality must, by necessity, be fulfilled since it implies that wages are positive, i.e. profit income is smaller than total income. When this target return pricing formula is combined with Equation (3), we obtain the rate of profit seen from the cost side, i.e. the profits cost function:

$$r^{PC} = r_s(u/u_s) \tag{5}$$

One should note that if the actual rate of capacity utilization $u$ turns out to be equal to the standard rate of utilization of capacity $u_s$, the actual rate of profit $r$ is then equal to the target rate of return $r_s$ embodied in the margin of profit of the pricing procedure. Since Equation (5) is linear in $u$, it clearly shows that the standard and the actual rates of profit cannot be equal unless the standard and the actual rates of capacity utilization are equal. This result will be useful when the target rate of return is endogenized later on.

## 2.2. The Effective Demand Side

The previous equations define a rate of profit seen from the cost accounting side. The rate of profit that will be realized depends on the actual rate of capacity utilization. Effective demand, which has not yet been taken into account, will help determine the rate of capacity utilization. In the simplest neo-Keynesian models, as in the presentation of Ciccone (1986), the rate of accumulation is taken to be exogenous. The impact of effective demand in the Cambridge equation is felt on the realized rate of profit, which is the endogenous variable. A crucial feature of the Kaleckian model is its investment function. The Cambridge equation must thus be reinterpreted as a savings function. With the standard assumptions, i.e. there are no savings out of wages, the savings function in growth terms becomes:

$$g^s = rs_p$$

with $s_p$ the overall propensity to save out of profits.

We now come to the investment function, which has been the main subject

[2] A similar but more complicated formula could be derived in a two-sector case, as is done in Lavoie & Ramirez-Gaston (1997).

of contention. Let us use a version of it that has often been used by Kaleckian authors. The rate of accumulation set by firms depends on the rate of capacity utilization and on the realized rate of profit:

$$g^i = \gamma + \gamma_u u + \gamma_r r$$

where $\gamma$ is some parameter that must be positive in models without overhead labour (Dutt 1990, p. 25), while $\gamma_u$ and $\gamma_r$ are positive reaction parameters.

Putting together the above two equations, one obtains what Rowthorn (1981, p. 12) calls the realization curve. To avoid confusion, and to emphasize the role of effective demand, we shall call it the effective demand equation:

$$r^{ED} = (\gamma_u u + \gamma)/(s_p - \gamma_r r) \qquad (6)$$

The steady-state solution to this Kaleckian model of growth and distribution can be obtained by combining the profits cost equation (5) and the effective demand equation (6). Doing so yields:

$$u^* = \gamma u_s/[r_s(s_p - \gamma_r) - \gamma_u u_s]$$
$$r^* = \gamma r_s/[r_s(s_p - \gamma_r) - \gamma_u u_s] \qquad (7)$$

These solutions are positive and the model is stable provided:

$$s_p > \gamma_r + \gamma_u u_s/r_s$$

## 3. A Fully-adjusted Position with an Endogenous Normal Rate of Profit

As is well known, the basic Kaleckian growth model contains two features. First, Keynes's paradox of thrift holds, even in the long run (an increase in the propensity to save decreases $u^*$ and $r^*$, and hence the rate of accumulation). Secondly, there is the paradox of cost: any increase in costs raises the realized rate of profit (Rowthorn, 1981, p. 18). A higher target rate of return in the pricing formula, i.e. a lower real wage rate, is associated with a lower rate of utilization, a lower realized rate of profit, and hence a lower rate of accumulation. While Sraffian authors do not endorse the sort of investment function that gives rise to the paradox of costs, they nonetheless agree that the paradox of costs may occur under some circumstances.[3]

Another problem arises however, which is the main subject of the present paper, that of the discrepancy between the target rate of return and the realized rate of profit. While there is no objection to these two rates being different in the short run, several authors believe that a discrepancy between the two rates contradicts the notion of a long-run equilibrium—a final equilibrium where there should exist no inducement to modify the values taken by the main variables. Sraffian authors such as Vianello (1985), Committeri (1986) or Park (1997a), and Marxist authors such as Duménil & Lévy (1994) or Auerbach & Skott

[3] Sraffian (and Marxist) authors, as is explicit in Kurz (1991, 1994), generally endorse an investment function of the type: $g^i = \gamma + \gamma_u u + \gamma_r r_s$. The paradox of costs will only arise under some parameter constellations.

(1988), insist that, in the long run, targets should be achieved. The steady-state solutions of the Kaleckian growth model, as in Equation (7), may thus be taken to be a provisional equilibrium. How then could we arrive at the final equilibrium? And would this final equilibrium be a fully adjusted position?

A possible mechanism to arrive at a final long run position would have the normal rate of profit (or more precisely here, the target rate of return) itself being influenced by the actual rate of profit. Whenever the rate of profit exceeds the target rate of return, firms react by (slowly) increasing the target rate of return and the margin of profit. A straightforward representation of this intuition yields the following time derivative:

$$\dot{r}_s = \phi\,(r^* - r_2) \tag{8}$$

Will the operation of Equation (8) ensure convergence between the actual rate of profit and the target rate of return? When the actual rate of profit is higher than the target rate of return, the latter is set at a higher value. The profit margin is thus increased. The higher profit margin (the lower real wage) slows down effective demand, thus reducing the rate of utilization and the realized rate of profit, despite the higher target rate of return. This process will continue until the target rate of return is such that it generates an actual rate of profit, which is equal to the target. More formally, this can be seen by taking the derivative of the equilibrium rate of profit, given by equation (7), with respect to the target rate of return:

$$\mathrm{d}r^*/\mathrm{d}r_s - \gamma\gamma_u u_s/D^2 < 0$$

where $D$ is the denominator of Equation (7).

This process, however, will also bring together the realized rate of capacity utilization and the standard rate of utilization. The actual rate of utilization in the fully adjusted position thus becomes a predetermined variable, equal to the given conventional standard rate $u_s$. As a result, the paradox of costs disappears. An increase in the rate of growth is associated with a decrease in the real wage rate (and an increase in the standard rate of return).

On the other hand, the paradox of thrift is sustained even in this fully adjusted position. An increase in the propensity to save has a negative impact, from one fully adjusted position to the next, on the rate of accumulation. This can be seen by putting together Equations (5) and (6), which define the profits cost function and the effective demand function. In the fully adjusted position, the realized rate of capacity utilization is always equal to its standard level, so that $u^{**} = u_s$. When solving for the very long run, when all adjustments corresponding to Equation (8) have been exhausted, it is the target rate of return $r_s$ that becomes the endogenous variable. Solving for this variable, and making use of the Cambridge equation, we obtain:[4]

$$r_{s**} = (\gamma_u u_s + \gamma)/(s_p - \gamma_r)$$
$$g^{**} = (\gamma_u u_s + \gamma)/[1 - (\gamma_r/s_p)]$$

[4] It should be noted however that, with a simplified investment function of the sort $g^i = \gamma + \gamma_u u$, changes in the propensity to save would have no impact on the fully-adjusted rate of accumulation.

An increase in the propensity to save $s_p$ yields a fully adjusted position with a lower rate of accumulation. The paradox of thrift thus appears to be quite resilient. Indeed, the results that are achieved with the addition of the adjustment process described by Equation (8) are akin to those that were defended by post-Keynesians such as Joan Robinson with the help of the old Cambridge model (Lavoie 1992, p. 357). If an adjustment mechanism equates the actual rate of profit and the target rate of return, normal prices eventually prevail, and despite the presence of short-period Kaleckian features, the economy is ultimately back to a fully adjusted position, at normal rates of capacity utilization. Now, this was precisely the basis of the old Cambridge growth model, where the paradox of thrift also held up. This was also the basis of the modern oligopolistic version of the old Cambridge model, as can be found in the Eichner-Wood model, and as it has been recently proposed again by Nell (1996, p. 396). Finally, it can be said that the present adjustment mechanism also solves a problem that was mentioned by some Sraffians: if Sraffa's pricing equations are implicitly based on fully adjusted positions, how can these positions ever be reached? The mechanism of Equation (8), with the rest of the Kaleckian model, provides the route towards fully adjusted positions that Vianello (1985) and Committeri (1986) were looking for, at least within a one-sector model.

## 4. An Alternative Process towards Fully Adjusted Positions

Duménil & Lévy (1999) have recently suggested alternative means to achieve a fully adjusted position: they suppose that demand inflation is generated as long as realized rates of capacity utilization exceed the standard rate, and hence that, in an attempt to fight off inflation, monetary authorities raise real interest rates as long as this divergence persists. This can be formalized as:

$$\mathrm{d}i/\mathrm{d}t = \zeta\,(u^* - u_s)$$

where $i$ is the real interest rate, and $\zeta$ is a positive reaction parameter.

Assuming an investment function, the arguments of which are the rate of utilization and the realized rate of profit, net of the real interest cost:

$$g^i = \gamma + \gamma_u u + \gamma_r(r - i)$$

it follows that the economy will always be brought back to a position with a constant real interest rate, where the actual rate of capacity utilization is equal to its standard rate (the adjustment will proceed as long as $u^{\square}\ \square u_s$).

For instance, if effective demand and pricing conditions, given by $ED_1$ and $PC_1$, are such that the actual rate of utilization $u_1$ exceeds the standard rate $u_s$, as is the case in Fig. 1, the behaviour of the monetary authorities will drive down the effective demand curve to $ED_0$, where the actual and the standard rates of capacity utilization are equated, that is until the actual rate of profit is brought back to the target rate of return $r_{s1}^{**}$.

Within the framework presented by Duménil & Lévy, real interest rates do behave in line with the loanable funds theory across fully adjusted positions.

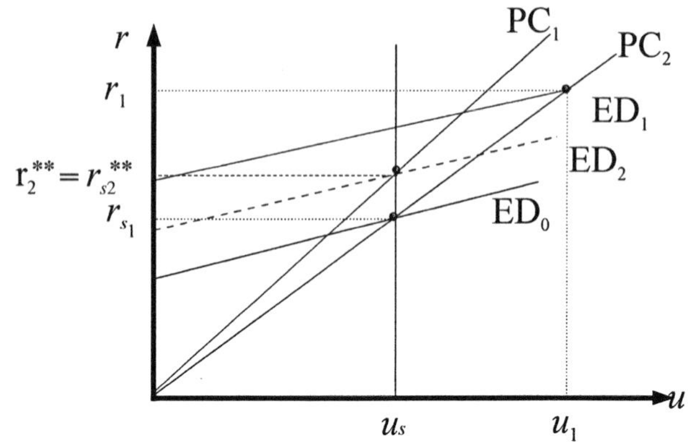


**Fig. 1.**

Evaluated at the fully adjusted position (where $u^* = u_s$), the savings and the investment functions are:

$$g^s = r_s s_p$$
$$g^i = \gamma + \gamma_u u_s + \gamma_r (r_s - i)$$

By equating the above two equations ($g^i = g^s$), we can derive the value of the fully adjusted real rate of interest:

$$i^{**} = [\gamma + \gamma_u u_s - (s_p - \gamma_r) r_s]/\gamma_r$$

It is then obvious that a higher propensity to save, or a higher normal profit rate, is associated with a lower real rate of interest when fully adjusted positions are reached. The Duménil & Lévy model generates truly classical supply-led features across long-run positions. Higher savings rates allow for faster growth and lower real rates of interest when long run equilibria are taken into account. Within such a framework, both the paradox of costs and the paradox of thrift disappear. Although the economy behaves along Keynesian or Kaleckian lines in the short period, i.e. although the model is demand-led in the short-run, the long-run behaviour of the model is consistent with the classical model of accumulation. A low propensity to save is eventually conducive to a low rate of accumulation, and low rates of accumulation are associated with low normal rates of profit and high real wages. This has led Duménil & Lévy (1995, pp. 136–137) to argue that 'while it is possible to be Keynesian in the short term, one is required to be classical in the long term'.

Could the paradox of thrift be salvaged by adding to the above equations an additional relation linking the target rate of return to the rate of interest? Following a remark made by Sraffa, it has been suggested by a number of Sraffians that the normal rate of profit is mainly determined by the rate of interest set by the monetary authorities (Panico, 1985; Pivetti, 1985; Vianello, 1985, p. 84). In particular, Pivetti (1991, p. 122) has explicitly linked full-cost pricing and target-return pricing to the trend level of the rate of interest. For Pivetti, the costing margins that firms consider normal or appropriate are calculated to yield a fair rate of return on investment. This fair rate of return—the target rate of return or the normal rate of profit—itself depends on the rate of interest that can be obtained on riskless placements. In its simplest form, as suggested by Pivetti (1985, p. 87), we have:

$$r_s = i + r_{npe}$$

where $r_{npe}$ is the net profit rate of entrepreneurs, or the profit rate of entrepreneurs net of interest (opportunity) costs, which is here assumed to be given.

This net profit rate of entrepreneurs is not the net rate of return that entrepreneurs actually manage to get; rather, $r_{npe}$ is the net rate of return that entrepreneurs add to the interest opportunity cost when setting gross costing margins and prices. The *realized* net profit rate of entrepreneurs, just like the realized profit rate, depends on the realized rate of capacity utilization. Of course, more sophisticated relations between the target rate of return and the lasting rate of interest could be put forward, relations that would not necessarily keep the net profit of entrepreneurs at a constant level, but for our purposes the simple relation as presented above will suffice.[5]

Putting together this Sraffian relation and the Duménil & Lévy mechanism where any increase in effective demand would still bring back the economy to a fully adjusted position, a lower rate of savings, comparing fully adjusted positions, would now entail a higher realized rate of profit and a higher target rate of return. This result is illustrated in Fig. 1. Assume we start out from a fully adjusted position, given by the intersection of the $ED_0$ and $PC_1$ curves, at the standard rate of utilization $u_s$ and the normal rate of profit $r_{s1}{}^{**}$. A lower propensity to save or higher animal spirits would initially push the effective demand curve from $ED_0$ to $ED_1$. The new realized rate of utilization $u_1$ would induce the monetary authorities to increase real rates of interest. These higher interest rates would lead entrepreneurs to augment target rates of return, thus inducing a rotation to the left of the profits cost curve from $PC_1$ to $PC_2$. This, combined with the negative effects of higher interest rates on investment and effective demand, as revealed by the drop in the effective demand curve from $ED_1$ to $ED_2$, would finally bring the economy to a new, fully adjusted, position, at the standard degree of utilization $u_s$, where the realized rate of profit and the target rate of return would equal $r_{s2}{}^{**}$.

The target rate of return, in the long run, has again become an endogenous variable, while the long-run realized rate of capacity utilization must be equal to its standard value ($u^{**} = u_s{}^{**}$). Mathematically, the fully-adjusted target rate of return, seen from the demand and the supply side respectively, must be such that:

$$r_s;^{**} = (\gamma + \gamma_u u_s - \gamma_r i^{**})/(s_p - \gamma_r)$$

$$r_s^{**} = i^{**} + r_{npe}$$

[5] This is the main critique addressed against Pivetti's framework (see Mongiovi, 1996, among others). There is also a very interesting critique by Serrano (1993), about how one can define a real rate of interest–as opposed to a nominal rate of interest–independently of changes in relative prices. Finally, there is the critique of Nell (1999) who argues that there cannot be such a thing as a normal rate of interest.

where $i^{**}$ is the endogenous fully adjusted real rate of interest. Solving for the fully adjusted rate of interest and for the fully adjusted rate of accumulation, we get:

$$i^{**} = [\gamma + \gamma_u u_s - (s_p - \gamma_r) r_{npe}]/s_p$$
$$g^{**} = \gamma + \gamma_u u_s + \gamma_r r_{npe}$$

The fully adjusted rate of accumulation depends ultimately on the optimism of entrepreneurs (as reflected in the various $\gamma$ parameters) and on the value taken by the net profit of entrepreneurs, as assessed by the entrepreneurs. The paradox of thrift is not recovered, even with this Sraffian version of the Duménil & Lévy mechanism. A decrease in the propensity to save leads to a temporary increase in the rate of utilization and the rate of accumulation. These higher rates however generate an increase in the real rate of interest set by the central bank. Interest rates (and target rates of return) continue to rise until the actual rate of utilization is brought back to its normal value, at which point the actual rate of profit is also equal to its normal value. This implies that the difference between the new fully adjusted profit rate $r_{s2}^{**}$ and the old fully adjusted profit rate $r_{s1}^{**}$ is exactly equal to the difference between the new and the old fully adjusted real rates of interest. Thus, when comparing fully adjusted positions, once all adjustments have been completed, it must be concluded from the above solutions that a decrease in the propensity to save does not lead to any change in the rate of accumulation.

On the other hand, an increase in the animal spirits of entrepreneurs (a rise in the parameter $\gamma$) will generate an increase in the fully adjusted rate of capital accumulation. This, however, will be accompanied by an increase in the fully adjusted real rate of interest and in the fully adjusted rates of profit—the realized rate of profit and the target rate of return being equated. In this case, there is some reconciliation between the Sraffian approach and the views that have been expressed by some post-Keynesians (Nell, 1988; Wray, 1991). For the latter, in the long run, higher rates of accumulation must induce higher realized rates of profit and hence higher interest rates and higher normal rates of profit. For the former, higher rates of interest cause higher normal rates of profit. The two views appear to be vindicated here: a higher propensity to accumulate $\gamma$ generates faster accumulation, higher real rates of interest, higher normal profit rates, and higher realized profit rates.

Are there other means to recover the paradox of thrift and the paradox of costs? It would be possible to argue that the standard rate of utilization also responds to actual values (Lavoie, 1996; Dutt, 1997; Park, 1997b). This line of research, which generates a multiplicity of solutions, many of which retain their Kaleckian properties, will not be pursued here. We shall instead track a new avenue, based on the addition of a conflict-based model of inflation. This will allow us, within a fully determined model, to retain the flexibility of the rate of capacity utilization and the positive relation between the real wage rate and the rate of accumulation (in some cases), while assuming the equality between the realized and the normal rates of profit.

## 5. A Model of Conflict Inflation

We now present a model of inflation that does not rely on excess demand. The model is based on the inconsistent income claims of firms and workers, that is, based on what has been called *real wage resistance* by some and an *aspiration gap* by others. In standard terminology, the focus of the analysis is on the wage–price spiral. As a first approximation, wage–wage inflation and other income conflicts will be omitted, as will be feedback effects from the real economy.[6] This will allow us to understand the essentials of the model of conflict inflation and to integrate it to target return pricing.

The model may be called Kaleckian because it has some affinity with Kalecki's last article, entitled 'Class struggle and distribution of national income' (Kalecki, 1971, ch. 14). Whereas before, Kalecki took the degree of monopoly to be an exogenous variable, he argues in this article that trade unions have the power to achieve reductions in the mark-up, by demanding and achieving large increases in money wage rates. This view has been summarized by Rowthorn (1977, p. 179) in the following: 'The working class can shift distribution in its favour by fighting more vigorously for higher wages, although the cost of such militancy is a faster rate of inflation, as capitalists try, with only partial success, to protect themselves by raising prices'. This reflects the notion that social forces, such as the bargaining position of workers, help to determine income distribution.

Several post-Keynesian, neo-Marxian, and even mainstream authors have constructed models of conflict inflation, as first presented by Rowthorn (1977). In all these models, the rate of inflation is a function of the degree of inconsistency between the mark-up that firms wish to target and the real wage rate that the leading key labour bargaining units consider to be fair. As is clear from the mark-up pricing equation, $p = (1 + \theta)wl$, a target set in terms of real wages can always be made equivalent to a target set in terms of a mark-up. With target return pricing procedures, this target corresponds precisely to a target rate of return. Provided there is no change in productivity, it is thus indifferent to assume that both firms and workers set real wage targets, or that they both set mark-up targets. Here we shall set the equations in terms of the target rate of return.

The basic model of conflict inflation is based on two equations (see for example Dutt, 1990, p. 83). It is assumed first that the rate of growth of money wages that labour unions manage to negotiate is a function of the discrepancy between their real wage target and the actual real wage rate. In terms of target rates of return, this means that the target real wage rate of workers is equivalent to a target rate of return $r_{sw}$. It is the discrepancy between a high actual target rate of return and a low desired target rate of return, seen from the workers' point of view, that drives up wage demands. It is also assumed that the rate of

[6] One could introduce a feedback relationship between the rate of growth of the economy and the claims of workers or those of the firms, with little modification to the results to be shown (Lavoie 1992, ch. 7). One could also introduce a relationship between the claims of workers and the rate of unemployment, a sort of Phillips curve, in which case the model would become much more complex (see Skott, 1989, and Dutt, 1994). Also, see Cassetti (2002)

growth of money wages depends on the expected rate of price inflation $\hat{p}^e$. In its simplest form, the above two ideas can be expressed as:

$$\hat{w} = \Omega_1 (r_s - r_{sw}) + \Omega_2 \hat{p}^e$$

Similarly, it may be assumed that firms increase prices when the actual mark-up is below the mark-up that they would ideally desire to set, and that the larger the differential between those two mark-ups the higher the rate of price inflation. This may be formalized in terms of target rates of return, which for the firm we may denote as $r_{sf}$. The target rate of return, as *assessed* by firms may be different from the actual target rate of return *incorporated* into prices. When firms aim at higher mark-ups, given the actual mark-up, they would speed up the rate of price inflation, being constrained however by their bargaining power on both the labour and the product markets. Assuming that firms may have to list prices before wage increases have been settled and taking into account expected wage inflation, we have:

$$\hat{p} = \Psi_1 (r_{sf} - r_s) + \Psi_2 \hat{w}^e$$

We are now able to give an explanation of why the target rate of return may fully adjust to the actual rate of profit, without the rate of utilization of capacity becoming exogenous. To do this, it has to be recognized that firms are not in a position to set the exact mark-up of their choice. One must thus distinguish between two sorts of gross costing margins: the actual costing margin, which arises from the bargaining process; and the desired costing margin, which corresponds to the target rate of return and the standard rate of capacity utilization that firms would like to incorporate into their pricing strategy. In terms of wage rates, one would have to distinguish between two wage rates: the actual real wage rate arising from bargaining; and the real wage rate targeted by firms, corresponding to the standard rate of profit $r_{sf}$ *assessed* by firms.

We may consider that there is a steady-state in a model without technical progress when the actual real wage rate is a constant; that is, when the actual and the expected rates of wage inflation are equal to the actual and expected rates of price inflation (again, technical progress is omitted for simplification). In such an equilibrium, that is with $\hat{w}$ and $\hat{p}$ equal to each other, the profit margin is a constant, and equating the two equations describing wage and price inflation, we get:

$$\hat{p} = \frac{\Omega_1 (r_s - r_{sw})}{1 - \Omega_2} = \frac{\Psi_1 (r_{sf} - r_s)}{1 - \Psi_2}$$

By solving the above equation for the target rate of return actually incorporated into prices, namely $r_s$, the distinction between the above concept and the target rate of return $r_{sf}$ assessed by firms should become clearer. There is a simple relation between the two concepts: the actual target rate of return $r_s$ is a weighted average of both the target rate of return assessed by firms and the target rate of return assessed by workers, where the sum of the weights ($\Omega$ and $\Psi$) is equal to one, and such that:

$$r_s = \Psi r_{sf} + \Omega r_{sw} \tag{9}$$

where:

$$\Omega = \frac{\Omega_1 (1 - \Psi_2)}{\Omega_1 (1 - \Psi_2) + \Psi_1 (1 - \Omega_2)}$$

$$\Psi = \frac{\Psi_1 (1 - \Omega_2)}{\Omega_1 (1 - \Psi_2) + \Psi_1 (1 - \Omega_2)}$$

This new model is exactly like the model first presented in Section 2, where no complications related to inflation had been introduced. In Equations (4) and (5), we may now introduce the value of the actual target rate of return as given by the weighted average of Equation (9). Combining Equations (7) and (9), one obtains:

$$r^* = \frac{\gamma\,(\Psi r_{sf} + \Omega r_{sw})}{(s_p - \gamma_r)\,(\Psi r_{sf} + \Omega r_{sw}) - \gamma_u\, u_s} \tag{10}$$

An increase in the target rate of return as assessed by firms, $r_{sf}$, will lead to an increase in the target rate of return incorporated into prices, $r_s$, and hence, as shown in Section 3, to a fall in the realized rate of profit $r^*$, i.e.

$$\mathrm{d}r^*/\mathrm{d}r_{sf} < 0 \tag{11}$$

## 6. Conflict Inflation with an Endogenous Target Rate of Return

Let us now endogenize the target rate of return as assessed by firms. This means that higher realized rates of profit will modify what the firms consider to be the normal rate of profit. Let us assume, then, that firms slowly adjust their assessed target rate of return ($r_{sf}$) according to the actual rate of profit ($r$), in symmetry to Equation (8) above. More precisely, as suggested in Lavoie (1992, p. 418), Equation (8) must now be written as:

$$\dot{r}_{sf} = \phi\,(r^* - r_{sf}) \tag{12}$$

In Section 3, it was argued that a long-run equilibrium is reached when the target rate of return $r_s$ is the same in two successive periods, that is when the target rate of return and the actual rate of profit are equal, as driven by the process of Equation (8). Here, in a world where trade unions have some bargaining power, the process of adjustment involves, instead, the target rate of return $r_{sf}$ assessed by firms, and Equation (12). In general, the process described by Equation (12) will thus come to an end without the fully adjusted rate of return being actually incorporated in prices. This means that the rate of capacity utilization emerging from the adjustment process is not necessarily the standard rate of utilization, and that, as a consequence, the rate of capacity utilization is endogenous despite the existence of this adjustment process. The long-run equilibrium is not, in general, a fully adjusted position.

The final equilibrium of such an economy with evolving bargaining power will thus require the additional equation, $r^* = r_{sf}$. Unfortunately, adding this condition in Equations (7) and (10) yields a quadratic equation. It is thus easier to assess the adjustment process from a graphical point of view. We can first

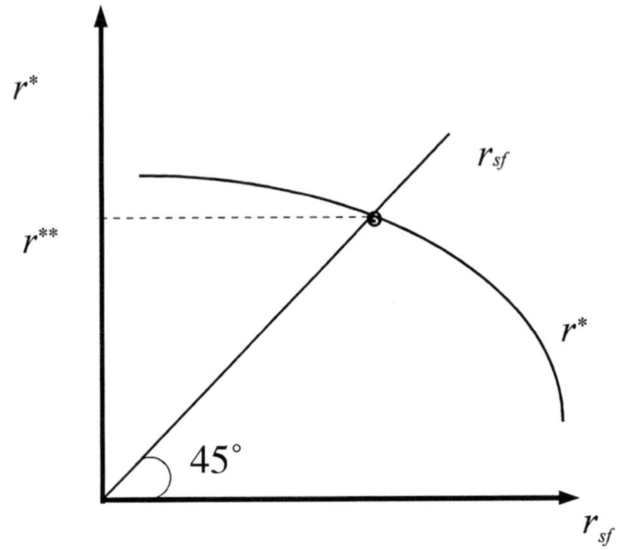


**Fig. 2.**

look at this adjustment process by considering the rate of profit only. This is done in Fig. 2. The $r^*$ curve represents the negative link between the target rate of return assessed by firms, $r_{sf}$ and the actual rate of profit that arises from effective demand considerations. For instance, when the actual rate of profit is above the target rate of return as assessed by firms, firms react by raising what they perceive to be the normal target rate of return. This, as shown by Equation (11), leads to a decrease of the realized rate of profit. There is thus a convergence process between the two rates, achieved at $r^*$. This is the long-run rate of profit.[7]

The adjustment process is more completely represented in Fig. 3. Let us start from a situation in which the real wage rates desired by firms and by workers coincide, as shown on the left-hand side of the graph, where the $\hat{w}$ and $\hat{p}$ curves intersect on the vertical axis (so that $\hat{p} = 0$). This implies that the target rate of return initially assessed by firms, called $r_{sf1}$, and the target rate of return embodied in the pricing formula, called $r_{s1}$, are equal. We have the triple equality: $r_{sw} = r_{sf1} = r_{s1}$. We can draw the profits cost curve corresponding to this situation, which is shown on the right-hand side of the graph as PC($r_{s1}$). We can suppose that the initial conditions, from the effective demand point of view, were such that the target rate of return incorporated into prices was being realized at the standard rate of capacity utilization $u_s$, i.e. $r_{s1} = r_1^{**}$ (as shown by the curve $ED_1$). Suppose now that there is a sudden increase in demand, as shown by the shift of the ED curve from $ED_1$ to $ED_2$. Under the new demand

[7] As can be seen, given the necessary negative relationship between the target rate of return and the actual rate of profit, there can only be one economically relevant long-run equilibrium; the other solution would yield a negative rate of profit.

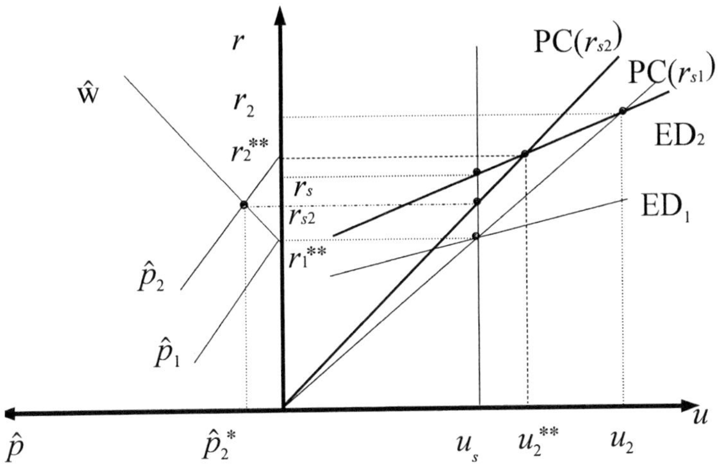


**Fig. 3.**

conditions, the actual rate of capacity utilization is $u_2$, and the actual rate of profit is $r_2$. The actual rate of profit $r_2$ is thus much higher than the target rate of return $r_{sf1} = r_1^{**}$. As a result, firms will slowly revise upwards their assessed target rate of return $r_{sf}$, along the lines of Equation (12), as is illustrated in Fig. 2.

Three phenomena will now arise. First, as firms revise their estimate of what the target rate of return is, a discrepancy arises between the real wage rate targeted by firms and the real wage rate targeted by workers. This will induce wage and price inflation, along the lines of our conflictual inflation model, while the actual real wage rate becomes different from the real wage targeted by firms. Secondly, a similar wedge arises between the target rate of return assessed by firms and the target rate of return incorporated into prices. Thirdly, as real wages diminish, the actual rate of profit falls. There is thus a convergence between the realized rate of profit, which falls, and the target rate of return assessed by firms, which rises.

The end result of this convergence process is shown in Fig. 3. Firms are assessing a target rate of return of $r_{sf2}$. Because of the bargaining power of labour, inflation occurs at a rate of $\hat{p}_2$.[8] The new profits cost curve PC($r_{s2}$) is such that the actual rate of profit, $r_2^{**}$, and the target rate of return assessed by firms, $r_{sf2}$, are equated. The adjustment process of the target rate of return has led to a new rate of capacity utilization $u_2^{**}$, which is different from the standard rate of utilization, $u_s$. The rate of capacity utilization in the long-run position is thus still endogenous, despite the presence of an adjustment mechanism.

The introduction of real wage resistance by workers thus yields a model where the equilibrium rate of capacity utilization is still endogenous, not being

[8] This rate of inflation is a steady state rate of inflation, and not just a transitory phenomenon.

forced back to its standard level of utilization, despite the adoption of a mechanism that brings together the target rate of return and the actual rate of profit. The key characteristic of the Kaleckian model, that is the endogeneity of the rate of capacity utilization, even in the long run, is thus preserved within a model with definite solutions. On the other hand, a key assertion among some Sraffians—that the rate of capacity utilization is endogenous in the long run, even when entrepreneurs equate the standard rate of return with the realized rate of profit—is also vindicated. Here, the realized rate of profit is equalized to the target rate of return assessed by entrepreneurs, although this assessed normal rate of profit is not exactly incorporated into prices, because of real wage resistance.

It should be noted, however, that the pure Sraffian or classical position is not vindicated in the present model.[9] Demand conditions being given in the long period, say by the curve $ED_2$, some authors would maintain that normal prices should be set according to the target rate of return noted $r_s$ in Fig. 3, and that prices on this basis will be the centre of gravitation of market prices. In our model, assuming that firms initially did set prices on the basis of a target rate of return of $r_{s1}$, a target rate of return of $r_s$ will eventually be assessed by firms. This target rate of return, however, is not a centre of gravitation. The target rate of return assessed by firms will continue to rise until it equates the actual rate of profit, that is until $r_{sf2} = r_2^{**}$. At that point, the target rate of return incorporated into prices, $r_{s2}$, will be lower than the target rate of return $r_s$ that would correspond to the Sraffian normal prices.

One last issue must be dealt with. It has been argued in the introduction that most Kaleckians and Sraffians agree on the fact that lower real wages need not be associated with higher rates of accumulation in the long run, even without technical change. From the analysis portrayed in Fig. 3, it is clear that the higher fully adjusted rate of accumulation, induced by higher animal spirits or a lower propensity to save, has led to an increase in the profit margin and hence to a fall in the real wage rate. Thus, while the paradox of thrift has been recovered once again, one may therefore wonder whether the attempt to safeguard some features of the Kaleckian or Sraffian analysis has not led to the destruction of other key features. This is not the case however. Even with adjustment mechanisms of the type entertained in Equation (12), a rise in the rate of accumulation may be accompanied by increases in the real wage rate.

Such a case is illustrated in Fig. 4. Suppose again that we start from a fully adjusted position, where conditions are such that the actual rate of capacity utilization is equal to the standard rate of utilization and where the targets of workers and those of firms coincide. The rates of profit are then $r_1^{**} = r_{s1} = r_{sf1} = r_{sw1}$. The economy is at the intersection of the ED and $PC(r_{s1})$ curves, while on the left-hand side of the graph, the $\hat{w}_1$ and $\hat{p}_1$ curves intersect on the vertical axis. Now consider the case where workers are more militant and request a higher real wage rate, equivalent to a lower target rate of return, say $r_{sw2}$. For didactic purposes, suppose they initially manage to impose real wages

[9] Note that Boggio (1992, p. 287) comes to a similar conclusion within the context of a multi-sector model: with inconsistent claims between workers and firms, the vector of actual profit rates is not equated to the vector of target rates of return in the long run.

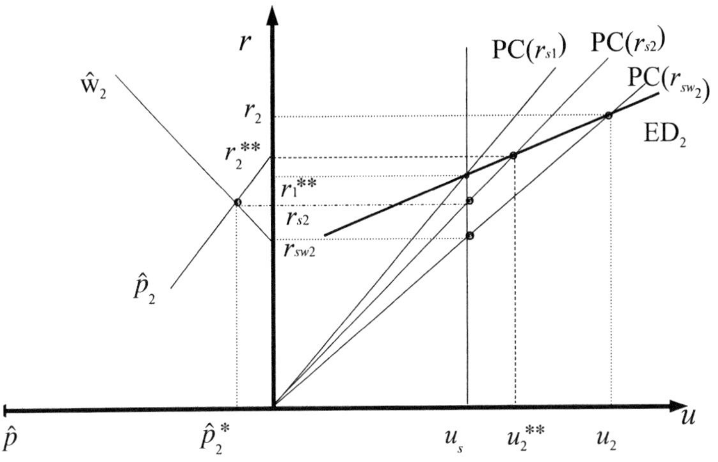


**Fig. 4.**

equivalent to this target rate of return $r_{sw2}$. This leads to a downswing rotation of the profits cost curve, from PC($r_{s1}$) to PC($r_{sw2}$). The higher real wages will induce a higher rate of capacity utilization ($u_2$), a higher rate of accumulation and higher realized rates of profit ($r_2$). This is the usual Kaleckian result. In the long run, however, the high realized rate of profit will induce entrepreneurs to increase what they consider to be the assessed target rate of return. In Fig. 4, this will be represented by an upward rotation of the PC curve, from PC($r_{sw2}$) to PC($r_{s2}$), until, finally, the falling realized rate of profit equates the increasing assessed target rate of return, such that in the end $r_{sf2} = r_2^*$. At that point, the new long-run rate of return incorporated into prices will be given by $r_{s2}$, with $r_{s2} < r_{s1}$. The new $\hat{w}_2$ and $\hat{p}_2$ curves cut each other at that $r_{s2}$ rate of profit. The new long-run rate of utilization $u_2^{**}$ is necessarily on the given ED curve, between the initial rate $u_s$ and the provisional rate $u_2$. Thus, comparing long-run positions, where the assessed target rates of return and the realized rate of profit are equated, it follows that, in this case, a higher rate of capital accumulation is associated with a lower incorporated target rate of return, and hence with a higher real wage.[10] The Sraffian and the Kaleckian key belief, that higher rates of accumulation need not be associated with lower real wages, is thus confirmed, even across long-run positions.

## 7. Conclusions

In contrast to what was initially assumed both by Marxists and by neo-Keynesians à la Joan Robinson and Nicholas Kaldor, Sraffians and Kaleckians alike contend that higher rates of accumulation need not be associ-

[10] We would still get this result if we had started from a situation where the steady state rate of inflation was greater than zero.

ated with lower real wages, even without technical progress. Such a result was linked to the endogeneity of the rate of capacity utilization. This belief, however valid within the short-run context, has been questioned on the basis that it relies on discrepancies between standard and realized rates of capacity utilization or between normal and realized rates of profit, discrepancies that are judged to be unwarranted in long run analysis. Other solutions have been offered in the past to avoid this logical problem, such as the distinction between normal and average values (Park, 1997a, 1997b), as well as the possibility of endogenous normal rates of capacity utilization (Lavoie, 1996).

Two other solutions were first considered here. The first solution, where the normal profit rate is endogenous, responding to the values taken by the realized profit rate, has transformed the Kaleckian model into the old Cambridge growth model à la Joan Robinson. When the adjustment process has been completed, the long run equilibria are fully adjusted positions, running at their normal rates of capacity utilization, where higher rates of accumulation require lower real wages and higher normal profit rates. Still, these fully-adjusted positions exhibit some demand-led features, namely the paradox of thrift. The second solution is that offered by Duménil & Lévy (199). They assume that higher than normal utilization rates are conducive to price inflation, and that central banks respond to this inflation by pushing up real rates of interest. Investment and effective demand are eventually slowed, and this slowdown continues until rates of capacity utilization are brought back to their normal value. Duménil & Lévy thus manage to transform a short-run Kaleckian growth model, with demand-led features, into a long-run supply-led classical model of accumulation, where faster growth at fully adjusted positions requires higher savings rates and higher normal profit rates. The addition of the Sraffian hypothesis that normal rates of profit are largely determined by the real rate of interest set by the central bank only partially helps to recover some demand-led features.

The solution considered here in greatest detail is also based on the endogeneity of the value taken by the normal rate of profit. However, in addition, we considered the possibility of a divergence between the rates of return assessed and targeted by firms on the one hand, and the rate of return that is actually incorporated into prices on the other hand. This divergence arises because of the bargaining power of workers and their real wage resistance. There is convergence, however, between the realized rate of profit and the rate of profit targeted by firms. Under these conditions, the demand-led characteristics of the Kaleckian model are sustained, even in long-run equilibria. Such long-run equilibria are not fully adjusted positions where the equilibrium rate of capacity utilization would equal its normal value. The utilization rate remains an endogenous variable, even in long run equilibrium. The paradox of thrift remains valid in all cases, and the paradox of costs is retained in some cases, i.e. higher rates of accumulation need not be associated with lower real wages, even across long-run positions.

## References

Amadeo, E. J. (1986) The role of capacity utilization in long-period analysis, *Political Economy*, 2 (2), pp. 147–185.

Auerbach, P. & Skott, P. (1988) Concentration, competition and distribution, *International Review of Applied Economics*, 2(1), pp. 42–61.

Bhaduri, A. & Marglin, S. (1990) Unemployment and the real wage: the economic basis for contesting political ideologies, *Cambridge Journal of Economics*, 14(4), pp. 375–393.

Boggio, L. (1992) Production prices and dynamic stability: results and open questions, *Manchester School of Economic and Social Studies*, 60(3), pp. 264–294.

Cassetti, M. (2002) Conflict, inflation, distribution and terms of trade in the Kaleckian model, in M. Setenfield (Ed.), *The Economics of Demand-led growth* (Cheltenham, Edward Elgar), pp. 189–211.

Chick, V. and Caserta, M. (1996) Provisional equilibrium and macroeconomic theory, in P. Arestis, G. Palma & M. Sawyer (Eds), *Markets, Unemployment and Economic Policy: essays in honour of Geoff Harcourt, volume two* (London, Routledge), pp. 223–237.

Ciccone, R. (1986) Accumulation and capacity utilization: some critical considerations on Joan Robinson's theory of distribution, *Political Economy*, 2 (1), pp. 17–36.

Committeri, M. (1986) Some comments on recent contributions on capital accumulation, income distribution and capacity utilization, *Political Economy*, 2(2), pp. 161–186.

Davidson, P. (1972) *Money and the Real World* (London: Macmillan).

Duménil, G. and Lévy D. (1995) A post-Keynesian long-term equilibrium with equalized profit rates? A rejoinder to Amitava Dutt's synthesis, *Review of Radical Political Economics*, 27(2), pp. 135–141.

Duménil, G. & Lévy D. (1999) Being Keynesian in the short term and classical in the long term: the traverse to classical long term equilibrium, *Manchester School of Economics and Social Studies*, 67 (6), pp. 684–716.

Dutt, A. K. (1990) *Growth, Distribution and Uneven Development* (Cambridge, Cambridge University Press).

Dutt, A. K. (1994) On the long run stability of capitalist economies: implications of a model of growth and distribution, in: A. K. Dutt (Ed.), *New Directions in Analytical Political Economy* (Aldershot, Edward Elgar), pp. 93–119.

Dutt, A. K. (1997) Equilibrium, path dependence and hysteresis in post-Keynesian models, in P. Arestis, G. Palma and M. Sawyer (Eds), *Markets, Unemployment and Economic Policy: essays in honour of Geoff Harcourt, volume two* (London, Routledge), pp. 238–253.

Garegnani, P. (1992) Some notes for an analysis of accumulation, in: J. Halevi, D. Laibman & E. Nell (Eds), *Beyond the Steady State: a revival of growth theory* (London, Macmillan), pp. 47–71.

Kaldor, N. (1964) *Essays on Economic Policy I* (London, Duckworth).

Kalecki, M. (1971) *Selected Essays in the Dynamics of the Capitalist Economy* (Cambridge, Cambridge University Press).

Kurz, H. D. (1991) Technical change, growth and distribution: a steady state approach to unsteady growth on Kaldorian lines, in: E. J. Nell & W. Semmler (Eds) *Nicholas Kaldor and Mainstream Economics* (London, Macmillan), pp. 421–448.

Kurz, H. D. (1994) Growth and distribution, *Review of Political Economy*, 6(4), pp. 393–420.

Kurz, H. D. (1997) What could the New Growth theory teach Smith and Ricardo? *Economic Issues*, 2(2), pp. 1–20.

Lavoie, M. (1992) *Foundations of Post-Keynesian Economic Analysis* (Aldershot, Edward Elgar).

Lavoie, M. (1995) The Kaleckian model of growth and distribution and its neo-Ricardian and neo-Marxian critiques, *Cambridge Journal of Economics*, 19(6), pp. 789–818.

Lavoie, M. (1996) Traverse, hysteresis and normal rates of capacity utilization in Kaleckian models of growth and distribution, *Review of Radical Political Economics*, 28(4), pp. 113–147.

Lavoie, M. & Ramirez-Gaston, P. (1997) Traverse in a two-sector Kaleckian model of growth with target-return pricing, *Manchester School of Economic and Social Studies*, 65(2), pp. 45–69.

Lanzillotti, R. F. (1958) Pricing objectives in large companies, *American Economic Review*, 48(5), pp. 921–940.

Lee, F. S. (1994) From post-Keynesian to historical price theory, part 1: facts, theory and empirically grounded pricing model, *Review of Political Economy*, 6(3), pp. 303–336.

Marglin, S. A. (1984) Growth, distribution, and inflation: a centennial synthesis, *Cambridge Journal of Economics*, 8(2), pp. 115–144.

Mongiovi, G. (1996) Some critical observations on post-Keynesian macroeconomics, in: S. Pressman (Ed.), *Interactions in Political Economy: Malvern after ten years* (London: Routledge), pp. 110–119.

Nell, E. J. (1988) Does the rate of interest determine the rate of profit, *Political Economy*, 4(2), pp. 263–267.

Nell, E. J. (1996) Transformational growth and the long period method, *Review of Political Economy*, 8(4), pp. 379–401.

Nell, E. J. (1999) Wicksell after Sraffa: capital arbitrage and normal rates of growth, interest and profits, in: G. Mongiovi and F. Petri (Eds) *Value, Distribution and Capital: essays in honour of Pierangelo Garegnani* (London: Routledge), pp. 266–293.

Panico, C. (1985) Market forces and the relation between the rates of interest and profits, *Contributions to Political Economy*, 4, pp. 37–60.

Park, M. S. (1997a) Normal values and average values, *Metroeconomica*, 48 (2), pp. 188–199.

Park, M. S. (1997b) Accumulation, capacity utilisation and distribution, *Contributions to Political Economy*, 16, pp. 87–101.

Pivetti, M. (1985) On the monetary explanation of distribution, *Political Economy*, 1(2), pp. 73–103.

Pivetti, M. (1991) *An Essay on Money and Distribution* (London, Macmillan).

Robinson, J. (1969) A further note, *Review of Economic Studies*, 36(2), pp. 260–262.

Roncaglia, A. (1990) Is the notion of long-period positions compatible with the classical political economy, *Political Economy*, 6(1–2), pp. 103–111.

Rowthorn, R. E. (1977) Conflict, inflation and money, *Cambridge Journal of Economics*, 1 (3), pp. 215–239.

Rowthorn, B. (1981) Demand, real wages and economic growth, *Thames Papers in Political Economy*, Autumn, 1–39. Reprinted in *Studi Economici*, (18), 1982, pp. 3–54, and also in M. C. Sawyer (Ed.) *Post-Keynesian Economics* (Aldershot, Edward Elgar).

Serrano, F. (1993) Book review of Massimo Pivetti, an essay on money and distribution, *Contributions to Political Economy*, 12, 117–124.

Shipley, D. D. (1981) Pricing objectives in British manufacturing industry, *Journal of Industrial Economics*, 29(4), June, pp. 429–443.

Skott, P. (1989) *Conflict and Effective Demand in Economic Growth* (Cambridge, Cambridge University Press).

Steindl, J. (1979) Stagnation theory and stagnation policy, *Cambridge Journal of Economics*, 3(1), March, pp. 1–14.

Vianello, F. (1985) The pace of accumulation, *Political Economy: Studies in the Surplus Approach*, 1(1), pp. 69–87.

Wray, R. L. (1991) Boulding's balloons: a contribution to monetary theory, *Journal of Economic Issues*, 25(1), pp. 1–20.

*Review of Political Economy,*
*Volume 21, Number 3, 369–391, July 2009*

Routledge
Taylor & Francis Group

# Cadrisme *within a Post-Keynesian Model of Growth and Distribution*

MARC LAVOIE

*Department of Economics, University of Ottawa, Canada*

ABSTRACT *The 1990s, especially in the United States, witnessed an unprecedented change in income distribution, with a large redistribution towards rentiers on the one hand, and towards the upper ranks of the managerial bureaucracy on the other hand, as became ever more obvious after the financial scandals affecting large corporations such as Enron and Worldcom. This has also been accompanied by large capital gains that benefited top-file managers as well as shareholders. Ordinary employees and workers, as a counterpart, have seen their real purchasing power stagnate. Despite all this, and in contrast to the predictions of the canonical Kaleckian growth model, many countries achieved respectable growth rates of capital and output. The purpose of the present paper is to explain this paradox and to provide a consistent post-Keynesian model of growth that would model the main features identified above, making a distinction between managerial labour, basically overhead labour, and workers, essentially direct labour – a distinction that was recommended, but never implemented by Kaldor. The model is based on target-return pricing procedures. We then study the implications of* cadrisme, *a managerial-friendly regime based on large pay packages for the managerial class.*

## Introduction

In the introduction to his *Essays on Economic Policy I*, commenting on his earlier growth and inflation models, Kaldor (1964, p. xvi) wrote that:

> The one important aspect in which I would now amend the exposition of the theory ... relates to the assumption of constant (short-period) prime costs. I did not realise then that this assumption – which makes a constant 'markup' equivalent to a constant *share* of profit in income – was not just a simplification, but was definitely misleading. In industry, short period labour costs per unit of output are not constant, but falling (mainly on account of the influence of 'overhead labour'); as a result of this, changes in the ratio of investment to output can elicit corresponding changes in the *share* of profit (and hence in the savings ratio) even if the 'mark up' is constant.

*Correspondence Address*: Marc Lavoie, Department of Economics, University of Ottawa, Canada. Email: marc.lavoie@uottawa.ca

ISSN 0953-8259 print/ISSN 1465-3982 online/09/030369–23 © 2009 Taylor & Francis
DOI: 10.1080/09538250903073396

Despite suggesting such an amendment, Kaldor never actually implemented it in his own previous models of growth. Instead, he went on, building new and different growth theories. Yet, other post-Keynesian authors, Harris (1974) and Asimakopulos (1975), eventually introduced the distinction between direct labour and overhead labour in their short-period macroeconomic models, thus showing that the principle of effective demand could deal simultaneously with the determination of output and that of income distribution.

The distinction between direct labour and overhead labour is all the more relevant given the recent evolution of macroeconomic income distribution. The 1990s, especially in the United States, witnessed an unprecedented change in income distribution, with a large redistribution towards wealth owners (rentiers) on the one hand (Epstein & Jayadev, 2005, p. 65), and towards the upper ranks of the managerial bureaucracy on the other hand (Petit, 2006, p. 47), as became ever more obvious after the financial scandals affecting large corporations such as Enron and Worldcom. This has also been accompanied by large capital gains that benefited top-file managers as well as shareholders up until 2001. This managerial-friendly regime based on large pay packages for upper-level managers and the overall managerial class has been called *cadrisme* by Duménil & Lévy (2004, ch. 7).[1] Ordinary employees and workers, as a counterpart, have seen their real purchasing power stagnate. Indeed, according to Mohun (2006, p. 360), between 1979 and 2000, the share of production or direct labour in the United States income has gone down 7 percentage points while that of supervisory or overhead labour has gone up by 10 percentage points during the same time period. Despite all this, many countries achieved high profit rates and respectable growth rates of capital and output – a rather paradoxical fact seen from a canonical Cambridge Keynesian point of view.

The purpose of the present paper is to explain this paradox and to provide a consistent model of growth that could explicitly take into account at least most of the features identified above. The model will focus on the distinction between: upper and middle management, or white-collar or supervisory labour, on the one hand; and workers, or blue-collar or non-supervisory labour, on the other hand, being understood that most blue-collar workers today are to be found in the service industries. The model to be built relies on a staff/worker distinction proposed by Rowthorn (1981) in his remarkable rendition of a modernized post-Keynesian growth model, which came to be known as the *Kaleckian* growth model. This distinction was also put forward in the papers of Nichols &

[1]For instance, the average remuneration of CEOs in the USA, as a ratio of average workers' wages has increased from 96 in 1990 to 458 in 2000 (Petit, 2006, p. 51), a period that most observers associate with the demise of managerial capitalism. One would presume that other upper and middle rank managers also benefited from this bonanza. Saez & Veall (2005) show that the top 5% income earners in Canada have dramatically increased their share of income, in particular those of the top percentile, as in the USA. This has been mainly accomplished through increases in salary income. The top 5%-income earners now get nearly 30% of all income, whereas their share remained at or below 25% from 1945 to 1995.

Norton (1991), Dutt (1992) and Lavoie (1992, 1995, 1996, 1996–97). All these authors assume that managerial staff must be understood as essentially overhead labour, the amount of which is proportional to full-capacity output, while non-supervisory workers are variable or direct labour, the amount of which is proportional to actual output.

The present paper is also a response to the claim, recently made by Tom Palley (2005), that class conflict in its traditional Marxist sense is absent from Cambridge theories of growth and income distribution. Palley's own response was to present a Kaleckian growth model, where income is split between capital and labour income, with the latter being split again between salaries being paid to the managerial classes and wages being paid to workers. As for capital income, part of it is retained by firms, while the rest is distributed to households, according to capital ownership. While we pick up the social classes identified by Palley (2005), the model that we suggest here is distinct from his because we assume, as suggested by Kaldor (1964), that the proportions of wages paid to workers and managers, rather than being exogenous variables, are responsive to the actual rate of capacity utilization, thus implying that average labour productivity and the profit share change with the level of capacity utilization.

A further feature of the model presented here is that it is designed to remedy a drawback of the approach followed by Rowthorn (1981) and many after him. Most post-Keynesian authors assume that an increase in the cost of staff labour will have no impact whatsoever on the markup or on prices. This is because prices are assumed to depend only on unit direct costs, that is on the costs encountered on workers only – variable labour. Under the conditions of monopoly capitalism, i.e., in the real world of megacorps surrounded by smaller firms, it is most likely that managerial staff costs could be shifted on to the consumer, and hence induce higher prices, at given nominal wage rates for variable labour, even though there are still excess reserves of capacity. To take this likely possibility into consideration, the markup, instead of being given exogenously or determined by the pressures of demand, will depend on target-return pricing. Thus, in contrast to what can be found in most Kaleckian models, where prices are fixed through a simple markup on direct costs, we shall assume, rather, that prices are fixed through a target-return pricing procedure, which takes into account direct as well as indirect costs, such as those incurred for managerial and supervisory staff, as in Lavoie (1992, pp. 350–352; 1996).

We shall discover that additional managerial costs may lead to slower accumulation, even when managers do not save, if the economy is running beyond its standard rate of capacity utilization. This will be contrasted with the results achieved by Dutt (1992) and Rowthorn (1981). Some additional remarks with regards to profit shares and the saving propensities of managers will then be made in the last sections of the paper.

## The Profits Cost Equation

The standard Kaleckian model of growth and distribution with excess capacity can be brought down to two equations describing the rate of profit, from the supply side and from the demand side (Rowthorn, 1981; Dutt, 1990). We start out with the derivation of the profits function seen from the cost side (the profits cost equation PC). From national accounting, we know that the value of output is equal to the sum of the wage costs and the profits on capital:

$$pq = w^*L + rpK$$

where $p$ is the price level, $q$ is the level of real output, $w^*$ is the average nominal wage rate, $L$ is the level of labour employment, $r$ is the rate of profit, $K$ is the stock of capital in real terms. This may be rewritten as:

$$p = w^*(L/q) + rpK/q \tag{1}$$

We now consider two sorts of labour: on one hand upper- and middle-class managerial labour, and on the other hand the rank-and-file workers, who may include lower-rank managers. Broadly speaking, we shall associate upper-level management with overhead or fixed labour ($L_f$), while rank-and-file workers are direct or variable labour ($L_v$). We then make use of the following definitions:

$$L = L_v + L_f$$

$$L_v = q/y_v \tag{2}$$

$$L_f = q_{fc}/y_f \tag{3}$$

$$w_v = w$$

$$w_f = \sigma w_v,\ \sigma > 1 \tag{4}$$

$$w^* = (w_v L_v + w_f L_f)/L$$

Equation (2) assumes that there are constant returns, i.e., productivity per variable worker, $y_v$, is constant up to full-capacity output ($q_{fc}$). This implies that variable and marginal costs are constant. The amount of unproductive labour is assumed to depend on full capacity output, as in equation (3). The nominal wage rates of variable and fixed workers are $w_v$ and $w_f$, and it is assumed that the latter are $\sigma$ times the level of the former, as shown in equation (4). This $\sigma$ ratio will be the focus of our analysis, since we mainly wish to study what could have been the impact of a shift in favour of managerial average remuneration relative to that of ordinary labour.[2]

To define the profits cost curve, we need in addition the following two variables: the rate of utilization of capacity $u$, with $q_{fc}$ full capacity output:

$$u = q/q_{fc}$$

[2]See the appendix for an alternative specification.

and the capital to capacity ratio $v$, assumed to be given by the existing technology:

$$v = K/q_{fc}$$

Let us call $f$ the ratio of fixed labour to variable labour, the latter being defined at full capacity output. It follows from its definition and from equations (2) and (3) that $f$ is equal to:

$$f = y_v/y_f$$

With these definitions, equation (1) can be rewritten as:

$$p = w(1 + f\sigma/u)/y_v + rpv/u \tag{5}$$

Equation (5) gives us the price of a unit of output in terms of the labour costs per unit of output and the profits per unit of output. Note that the first element of the right-hand side of equation (5) is simply average cost per unit at the actual rate of utilization of capacity. From this equation, we obtain the profits cost equation, in terms of the real wage rate $w/p$:

$$r^{PC} = (u/v)[1 - (w/p)(1 + f\sigma/u)/y_v] \tag{6}$$

It remains to decide upon the determinants of the real wage, or more precisely of real efficiency wages, $(w/p)/y_v$. In Kaleckian models, the level of the real wage, for a given productivity level, depends on the value of the costing margin. We thus need a pricing equation. Prices in Kaleckian models are usually based on a simple markup over unit direct costs. Here, as we deal with a single vertically-integrated sector, all direct costs come down to variable labour costs, so the markup pricing procedure becomes:

$$p = (1 + \theta)w/y_v \tag{7}$$

### *Target Return Pricing*

The point now at issue is the determinant of the markup $\theta$. Herein lies the originality of the model. Whereas many Kaleckians and post-Keynesian authors assume that the costing margin is applied to unit direct costs, studies have shown that most firms nowadays fix prices on the basis of total unit costs, i.e., full cost pricing. More precisely, prices are based on standard unit costs, i.e., normal-cost pricing (Lee, 1994). A particular specification of such normal-cost pricing is target-return pricing, and it seems to be prevalent today, in particular among large firms (Lanzillotti, 1958; Shipley, 1981; Lee, 1994).

A crucial element of target-return pricing is the value taken by the target rate of return $r_s$. With the new corporate governance that was fashionable over the last two decades, firms were being asked by their financial sponsors to achieve a minimum rate of return on equity, the ROE standard, conventionally (or mystically) set at 15% (Plihon, 2002). In the current model, to keep things simple, the financial side is being kept aside. Still, we may presume that if firms desire to achieve a given rate of return on equity, they would have to consistently achieve a given rate of profit. This required rate of profit, or normal profit, is the target rate of return $r_s$.[3]

We can find an explicit pricing formula for target-return procedures that is almost as simple as the markup on direct costs, given by equation (7).[4] To do so, we define the standard rate of utilization of capacity, $u_s$. First note, with the help of equation (5), that unit costs at standard volume are equal to: $w(1 + f\sigma/u_s)/y_v$. Target-return pricing would then be such that:

$$p = (1 + \Theta)w(1 + f\sigma/u_s)/y_v \tag{8}$$

What then would the markup on total unit costs, $\Theta$, be equal to? Suppose that the replacement value of the stock of capital is $pK$, while the target rate of return is $r_s$. Required profits for the period are then $r_s pK$. With a standard rate of utilization of capacity of $u_s$, corresponding in the period to a level of output of $q_s$, the required profits for the period must be equal to $r_s vpq_s/u_s$. This must be equated to the total profits that are to be obtained by marking up unit costs at the standard rate of utilization of capacity: $q_s\Theta w(1+f\sigma/u_s)/y_v$. After some manipulation, a simple pricing formula for target pricing procedures emerges:[5]

$$p = \left(\frac{u_s + f\sigma}{u_s - r_s v}\right)\frac{w}{y_v} \tag{9}$$

In terms of the simple markup pricing procedure, this implies that $1+\theta$ in equation (7) is equal to the term in parentheses in equation (9). Therefore, the

[3] In Kaleckian models, markups are usually assumed to depend on various historical factors, such as industry concentration ratios or the bargaining power of labour unions. For instance, Dutt (1990, p. 83) assumes that labour unions have a target real wage, while firms have a target markup, and hence, in line with equation (7), a target real wage. The actual real wage will be some weighted average of these two targets. Similarly, we can assume here that labour unions target a certain real wage, which corresponds to a standard rate of return, while firms aim at a standard rate of return, say $r_s^*$, whereas the actual target rate of return incorporated into prices, $r_s$, in general will be in-between these two rates (Lavoie, 1992, pp. 418–419; 2003). See also Cassetti (2003).

[4] See Lavoie (1992, pp. 256–258). In addition, such an approach to pricing would appear to bring consistency within a multi-sector framework, without adopting long-period Sraffian pricing. See Lavoie and Ramírez-Gastón (1997).

[5] By equating the two expressions representing required total profits, one obtains:

$$p = \Theta(w/y_v)(u_s + f\sigma)/r_s v$$

Then equating this new value of $p$ with the one given by equation (8), we have:

$$\Theta = r_s v/(u_s - r_s v)$$

Plugging back the required value of $\Theta$ into equation (8), one obtains equation (9). Of course, this equation makes sense only if the denominator is positive, i.e., if: $u_s > r_s v$. The inequality must by necessity be fulfilled since it implies that wages are positive, i.e., profit income is smaller than total income.

markup $\theta$ over unit direct costs is equal to:

$$\theta = (r_s v + f\sigma)/(u_s - r_s v) \tag{10}$$

The share of gross profits, that is, profits plus overhead costs, is equal to:

$$m = \theta/(1+\theta) = (r_s v + f\sigma)/(u_s + f\sigma) \tag{11}$$

while, naturally, the share of wages, the labour income going to workers, i.e., direct or blue-collar workers, is equal to:

$$1 - m = \omega = (u_s - r_s v)/(u_s + f\sigma) \tag{12}$$

We shall say more later about the share of net profits, which we shall call $\pi$, and the labour share of managers, which by residual, is necessarily equal to $m-\pi$. In the meantime, inspection of equation (12) reveals that, obviously, an increase in the $f\sigma$ term will reduce the share of income $\omega$ going to workers, while it will increase its complement, the gross profits share $m$.

Pricing equation (9) can be reinterpreted in terms of real wages. Given the technical coefficients (such as $y_v$, $f$ and $v$) and the rate of utilization used to compute standard costs, real wages are determined by the target rate of return $r_s$ actually incorporated in the pricing formula:

$$\frac{w}{p} = \frac{(u_s - r_s v)y_v}{(u_s + f\sigma)} \tag{13}$$

The profits cost equation, as appeared in equation (6), was a function of the then indeterminate real wage. The value of the real wage is now given by the elements of the target-return pricing formula. By combining equations (6) and (13), and after some manipulations, one obtains an explicit profits cost equation, equation (14), which turns out to be, as one would expect, a positive linear function of the actual rate of capacity utilization: the higher the actual rate of utilization the higher the realized rate of profit.

$$r^{PC} = \frac{(f\sigma + r_s v)u - (u_s - r_s v)f\sigma}{v(u_s + f\sigma)} \tag{14}$$

In terms of the gross costing margin $m$ this profits cost equation would be simplified to:

$$r^{PC} = [mu - (1-m)f\sigma]/v \tag{15}$$

The formula given by equation (9) clearly shows how additional costs associated with overhead labour will be passed on to consumers, in the form of higher prices. It does not matter whether managerial and supervisory staff are now paid higher wages relative to variable labour (a higher $\sigma$ ratio), or whether more managerial staff have been hired relative to the number of blue-collar workers (a higher $f$ ratio). The result is the same: markups will be raised, and hence prices will increase, *ceteris paribus*, and both the real wages of workers (equation (13)) and the share of income going to (direct labour, blue-collar) workers (equation (12)) will decrease. In a world dominated by megacorps that endorse pricing procedures based on target-return pricing, higher managerial staff costs are necessarily associated with higher prices, as well as higher gross costing margins at standard capacity utilization, unless firms simultaneously decide to reduce their target rates of return.

It remains to see whether this shift in costs towards consumers has any impact on effective demand.

## Effective Demand without Target Return Pricing

The previous equations define a rate of profit seen from the cost accounting side. We now have to tackle the issue of profit realization, i.e., the question of effective demand. The canonical post-Keynesian model has the following saving and investment functions in growth terms:

$$g^s = s_p r \tag{16}$$

with $s_p$ the overall propensity to save out of profits.

With this saving function we assume that there is no saving out of wages. In other words, neither the managers nor the workers save on their labour income. It is also assumed that either profit recipients save on their capital income, or that profit recipients save nothing out of their capital incomes, and that all saving is done by corporations, through their retained earnings. While this may look like an excessively simplified assumption, it is not too far from reality since, in countries such as the United States and Canada, saving rates on flow income by households have fallen to nearly zero in recent years.

The investment function is assumed to be the canonical Kaleckian investment function, given by:

$$g^i = \gamma + g_u u + g_r r \tag{17}$$

where $\gamma$ is some constant, which could be indifferently positive or negative, reflecting the strength of animal spirits, while $g_u$ and $g_r$ are reaction parameters to changes in the current rate of utilization and the current rate of profit.[6]

[6]More will be said later about the well-known Bhaduri & Marglin (1990) investment function. In the meantime, note that in a model without overhead costs or without capital depreciation, the constant parameter $\gamma$ would need to be positive, because the saving function would arise from the origin, forcing the investment function to have a positive intercept with the vertical axis, for otherwise, as we shall see in the next footnote, there would be no economically-meaning solution, since the slope of the investment function needs to be smaller than that of the saving function. But here, with overhead costs, the constant $\gamma$ can be negative, as will be emphasized later.

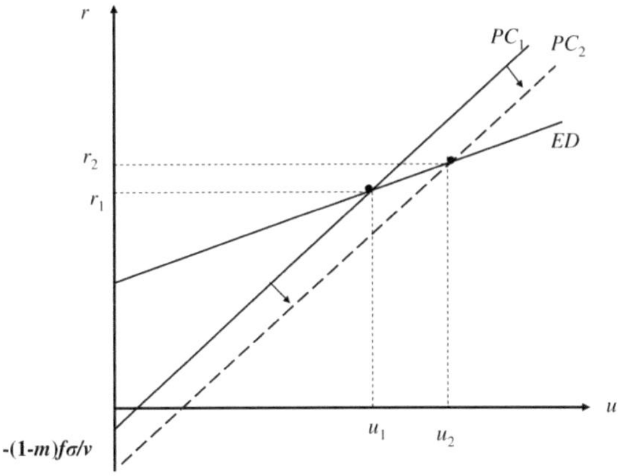


**Figure 1.** Macroeconomic impact of an increase in managerial costs, without target return pricing.

Putting together the above two equations, one obtains what Rowthorn (1981, p. 12) calls the realization curve. We shall call it the effective demand function (ED):

$$r^{ED} = \frac{(g_u u + \gamma)}{(s_p - g_r)} \tag{18}$$

The long-run solution to this Kaleckian model of growth and distribution can be obtained by combining the profits cost equation (noted PC) and the effective demand function (noted ED), both of which are upward-sloping.[7]

We first deal with the case studied by Dutt (1992). This case is defined by the combination of equation (18), which deals with effective demand, and equation (15), which represents the profits cost curve when the simple Kaleckian markup procedure is assumed to be followed by firms, that is when firms do not take into account overhead unit costs when setting prices. The graphical solution of this first case is shown in Figure 1. The graph illustrates what happens with the Dutt model when there is an increase in overhead managerial costs, that is when either the $f$ or the $\sigma$ ratio is raised. The *PC* curve shifts down, from $PC_1$ to $PC_2$, the two curves being parallel to each other. The overall impact of an increase in overhead managerial costs, without target return pricing, is quite obvious: there is an increase in both the equilibrium rate of capacity utilization and the rate of profit, and as a consequence the rate of accumulation also increases (Rowthorn, 1981, p. 18; Dutt, 1992, p. 105; Lavoie, 1992, p. 315). The paradox of costs is fully at work here: higher costs lead to higher profit rates.

[7]The model is stable if the slope of the saving function is steeper than that of the investment function, which implies that the profits cost curve is steeper than that of the effective demand curve, i.e., provided: $s_p > g_r + g_u v/m$. This, or similar conditions, will be assumed throughout.

## Effective Demand with Target Return Pricing

Dutt (1992), Nichols & Norton (1991) and Lavoie (1992, pp. 344–347) all show that this paradoxical behaviour could disappear if there is some saving out of labour income. Indeed, it is well-known since Amadeo (1986, p. 94) that the paradox of costs does not hold all the time if there are savings out of wages or salaries. But this is not what we wish to tackle immediately. Another issue, as had been pointed out by Burkett (1994, p. 119), in a comment on Dutt (1992), is 'whether firms are able to pass on unproductive outlays as higher prices'; that is, whether firms are able to pass onto consumers additional managerial costs. If this is so, as would be the case with target return pricing, the higher prices 'could limit the positive impact of such expenses on effective demand in the economy as a whole'. Higher managerial costs could thus be associated with lower realized profit rates and rates of accumulation. The paradox of costs, as applied to managerial costs, would vanish, even without savings out of labour income. This is what we now explore.

Let us instead analyze what happens when firms follow target-return pricing procedures.

The question at stake is whether an increase in $f$ or in $\sigma$, i.e., in the relative importance of managerial labour or in its relative remuneration, still leads to an increase in effective demand, and hence to an increase in the rate of capacity utilization, the rate of profit and the rate of capital accumulation. To find out, we must take the derivative of the profits cost function with respect to $\sigma$ (or indifferently with respect to $f$, since the two parameters play a symmetric role). Making use of equation (14), we find:

$$dr^{PC}/d\sigma = f(u_s - r_s v)(u - u_s)/v(u_s + f\sigma)^2 > 0 \text{ if } u > u_s \qquad (19)$$

The partial derivative is positive whenever the actual rate of capacity utilization is above the standard rate.[8] Equation (19) shows that when there is an increase in overhead costs in a model in which firms practice target-return pricing, the profits cost curve spins counter-clockwise around the fixed point determined by the target rate of return and the standard rate of capacity utilization. This is shown in Figure 2, where two graphical solutions are offered: one where the economy stands beneath the average standard rate of capacity utilization (point $A$, given by the intersection of $PC_1$ and $ED_A$), and the other where the economy operates beyond the average standard rate of capacity utilization (point $B$, given by $PC_1$ and $ED_B$).

To the initial unit overhead cost corresponds the $PC_1$ curve, while the higher unit overhead cost corresponds to the $PC_2$ curve. The impact of the rise in overhead costs on the rates of profit and of capacity utilization depends on the actual rate of capacity utilization compared with the standard one. The former depends on the position of the effective demand curve, $ED_A$ or $ED_B$.

[8] Recall that $(u_s - r_s v)$ is necessarily positive.

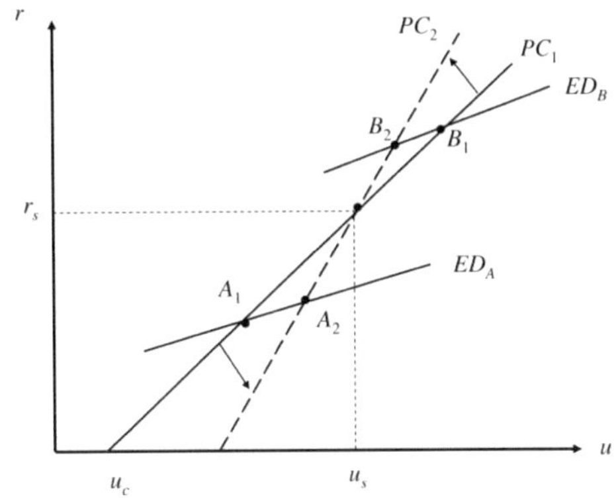


**Figure 2.** Macroeconomic impact of an increase in managerial costs, with target return pricing.

One may be puzzled as to why higher unit overhead costs would have a positive effect on the cost-side profitability of firms when the actual rate of capacity utilization exceeds its standard rate, whereas it would have a negative effect on cost-side profitability when the actual rate of capacity utilization is below the standard rate. The cause of this is that overhead labour costs are spread out over different levels of output. Following an increase in managerial labour costs, prices are raised just enough to maintain the customary rate of return when the firm is operating at the standard rate of utilization of capacity. When the firm is operating beyond the standard rate of utilization, the hike in prices more than compensates for the increase in unit costs. Reciprocally, when the firm is operating below the standard rate of utilization, the hike in prices does not fully compensate for the increase in unit costs.

This can be seen in Figure 3, where the cost curves of the representative Kaleckian firm, as they emerge from equation (5), have been drawn with direct labour costs shown as constant per unit of output, while total unit costs incorporating the fixed managerial overhead labour costs are represented by a rectangular hyperbola. The increase in the overhead labour costs is shown here by the upward shift of the unit cost curve. At the standard rate of capacity utilization $u_s$, the vertical distance between unit costs and the price level remains the same, before and after the change, indicating that the rate of profit on capital remains at $r_s$.[9] By contrast, at $u_B > u_s$, this vertical distance increases, showing that profitability is now higher than when overhead labour costs were lower. At $u_A < u_s$, the vertical distance diminishes, indicating that profitability is dropping at that rate

[9]If we leave partial equilibrium analysis, things are a bit more complicated since all prices, including those of investment goods, would need to rise, as can be seen from equation (5), which implies that price increases would need to take into account the higher value of replacement capital. This however does not change anything in the logic of the above argument.

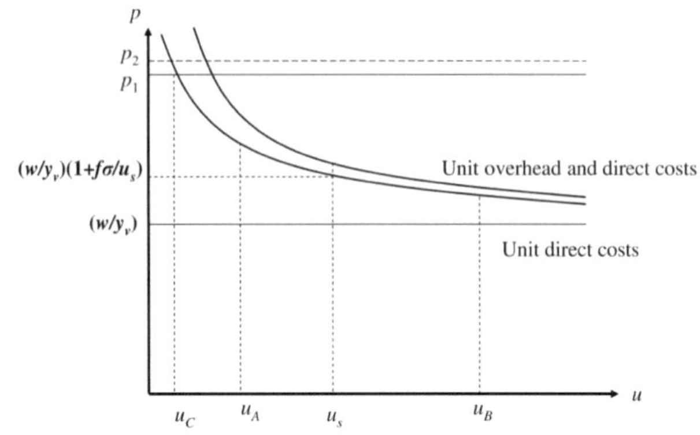


**Figure 3.** Microeconomic impact of an increase in managerial costs, with target return pricing.

of utilization.[10] An extreme instance of this case is given at rate $u_C$, where profitability becomes negative.

Having cleared up the implications of higher managerial overhead labour costs for the profits cost function, we may now study their implications for the long-run solution of the model. Let us return to Figure 2. When the economy is stagnating, i.e., when the actual rate of capacity utilization is below its standard level and when the actual rate of profit is below its normal level (as at point *A*), an increase in managerial labour costs will have positive effects on the economy. The positive effects of additional purchasing power being granted by the firms to their high and medium rank managers will overtake the negative effects induced by the rise in prices and the fall in real purchasing power of direct labour. The rate of capacity utilization, the rate of profit and hence the rate of capital accumulation will all rise as a result. The mechanism at stake here, as in Cambridge models of growth à la Kaldor and Robinson, is the principle of effective demand. At the rate of utilization $u_A$, the potential rate of profit is now lower than what it was before additional managerial labour costs were introduced. The potentially lower share of profit thus generates some excess demand at that rate of utilization, because the propensity to save out of wages is greater than that of out of profits, which drives up the actual rate of capacity utilization.

On the other hand, when the economy is in a boom, i.e., when firms are operating beyond their standard levels of capacity utilization (as at point *B*), the potential share of profit is hiked up, and hence at a given rate of capacity utilization there is an excess supply of output. As additional managerial costs are passed on to consumers, the real purchasing power of (direct) workers diminishes and drives down effective demand, along with rates of capacity utilization, profit rates and accumulation rates. Thus, even if saving from overhead workers is

[10]This effect is clearly illustrated at $u_C$. At that rate of utilization, the firm was initially making profits. The increase in overhead labour costs would push up unit costs to the new (higher) price level, and hence profits and profitability would drop to zero.

entirely assumed away, there are strong Keynesian reasons to be opposed to any increase in relative managerial or sales staff expenses. These reasons are, however, less relevant when the economy is stagnating, at low rates of capacity utilization and low rates of growth.

If higher rates of accumulation are the target of an economy, firms should increase the relative weight of their managerial expenses (as defined by $f$ and $\sigma$) when the economy is stagnating, not when it is booming. An educated guess would lead us to believe that firms tend to do the converse, expanding the relative importance of managerial staff and their remuneration when times are good, and cutting heavily (again in relative terms) into unproductive staff when times are bad. If such a behaviour is indeed that of firms, then the cyclical fluctuations in the relative importance of managerial outlays tend to dampen effective demand under all circumstances, be they those of a stagnating or a booming economy.

## The Evolution of the Net Profit Share with Target Return Pricing

We can further examine the consequences of target return pricing when managerial costs are pushed upwards. Let us study the impact of higher managerial costs on income distribution, more precisely the evolution of the net profit share.[11] Once again we can study what would happen by starting off from the profits cost curve and the effective demand curve, expressed as a profit rate. We know, from accounting identities, that the rate of profit can be expressed as $r = \pi u/v$, where $v$ is the capital to full capacity ratio, $u$ is the rate of capacity utilization and $\pi$ is the net profit share.

By taking equations (14) and (18), and multiplying them by $v/u$, we thus obtain the net profit shares, $\pi^s$ and $\pi^d$, seen from the supply and the demand sides. We have:

$$\pi^s = \frac{(f\sigma + r_s v)}{(u_s + f\sigma)} - \frac{(u_s - r_s v)f\sigma}{(u_s + f\sigma)u} \tag{20}$$

$$\pi^d = \frac{v g_u}{(s_p - g_r)} + \frac{\gamma v}{(s_p - g_r)u} \tag{21}$$

Obviously, once again because the expression $(u_s - r_s v)$ must be positive for the model to make economic sense, there is a positive relationship between $\pi^s$ and the rate of capacity utilization $u$. Thus, the profit share seen from the supply side $\pi^s$ is upward sloping in the $(u, \pi)$ plane, as shown in Figures 4 and 5.

Things are not so clear in the case of the profit share seen from the demand side $\pi^d$. The constant parameter $\gamma$ of the investment function can be indifferently positive or negative. When the $\gamma$ parameter is positive, there is a negative relationship between the profit share seen from the demand side $\pi^d$ and the rate of capacity utilization, as shown in Figure 4. By contrast, when the $\gamma$ parameter is negative,

[11]Within the context of a short-run model, see Lavoie (1998) for a simplified analysis of the profit share under different hypotheses (with or without overhead costs, with a Kaleckian or Marxist closure, etc).

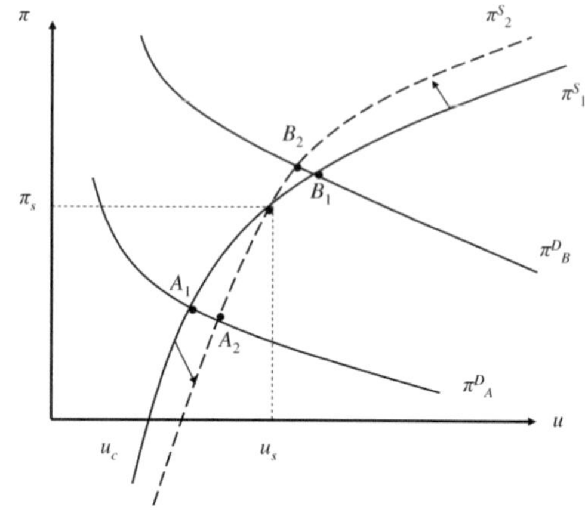


**Figure 4.** Impact of an increase in managerial costs on the net profit share, with target return pricing, when the investment constant is positive.

there exists a positive relationship between these two variables, as shown in Figure 5 (see Rowthorn, 1981, p. 21; Lavoie, 1992, pp. 341–343).

Let us again focus on what happens when there is an increase in managerial costs, more precisely in the relative remuneration $\sigma$ of the managerial staff. The derivative with respect to $\sigma$ of the profit share seen from the supply side is:

$$d\pi^s/d\sigma = f(u_s - r_s v)(u - u_s)/u(u_s + f\sigma)^2 > 0 \text{ if } u > u_s$$

Thus once more the sign of the derivative depends on whether the actual rate of utilization is below or above the standard rate of capacity utilization. As before,

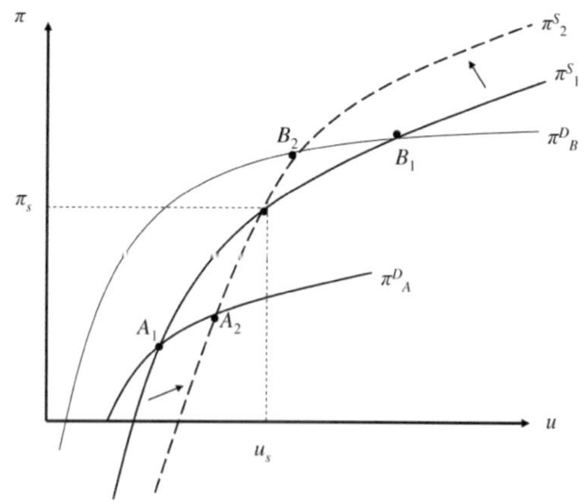


**Figure 5.** Impact of an increase in managerial costs on the net profit share, with target return pricing, when the investment constant is negative.

the profit share seen from the supply side spins counter-clockwise around the fixed point determined by the standard rate of capacity utilization and the net standard profit share $(r_s v/u_s)$. Following an increase in managerial costs, the net profit share, for a given rate of capacity utilization, increases when the rate of capacity utilization is above the standard rate of capacity utilization; and it decreases when the rate of capacity utilization is below the standard rate.

Naturally, since the above derivative is equal to zero when $u = u_s$, the net profit share remains unchanged when managerial costs are increased when the economy is operating at the standard degree of capacity utilization $u_s$. This is not surprising since we know, from the accounting identity $r = \pi u/v$, that when $u = u_s$ the net profit share $\pi$ equals $r_s v/u_s$, which is a constant.

But to find out what will actually occur to the net profit share in general, we need to consider both curves. In Figure 4, when effective demand is strong, and the rate of utilization is above its standard value, the increase in managerial costs leads to an increase in the net profit share; but when effective demand is weak, and the rate of capacity utilization is below its standard rate, the increase in managerial costs leads to a decrease in the net profit share.

Yet, the case described by Figure 5 is also possible. With a negative $\gamma$ constant, when the rate of utilization is above its standard value, the increase in managerial costs leads to a decrease in the net profit share; and when the rate of capacity utilization is below its standard rate, the increase in managerial costs leads to an increase in the net profit share.

The lesson to be drawn from all this is that the net profit share can go in any direction. By contrast, as already pointed out earlier, an increase in managerial costs necessarily leads to a reduction in the income share of workers and to an increase in the gross profit share, as shown in Table 1. It can also be shown that it leads to an increase in the labour share of the managerial staff in all circumstances, since this share is given by $m-\pi$, and since its derivative with respect to $\sigma$ is always positive, being equal to $f(u_s - r_s v)u_s/(u_s + f\sigma)u > 0$.

In addition, the net profit share is a poor indicator of the potential profitability of firms. Take the case of an increase in the target rate of return $r_s$. From examination of equations (14) and (20) it is quite obvious that:

$$\mathrm{d}r^{PC}/\mathrm{d}r_s > 0$$

$$\mathrm{d}\pi^s/\mathrm{d}r_s > 0$$

**Table 1.** Effect on the various income shares of an increase in managerial costs

| Income share | Conditions | | Effect of higher managerial costs |
|---|---|---|---|
| Workers share $\omega = 1-m$ | $\forall\, u$ | | − |
| Share of managerial salaries $m-\pi$ | $\forall\, u$ | | + |
| Gross profits share $m$ | $\forall\, u$ | | + |
| Net profits share $\pi$ | $u > u_s$ | $\gamma > 0$ | + |
| | | $\gamma < 0$ | − |
| | $u < u_s$ | $\gamma > 0$ | − |
| | | $\gamma < 0$ | + |

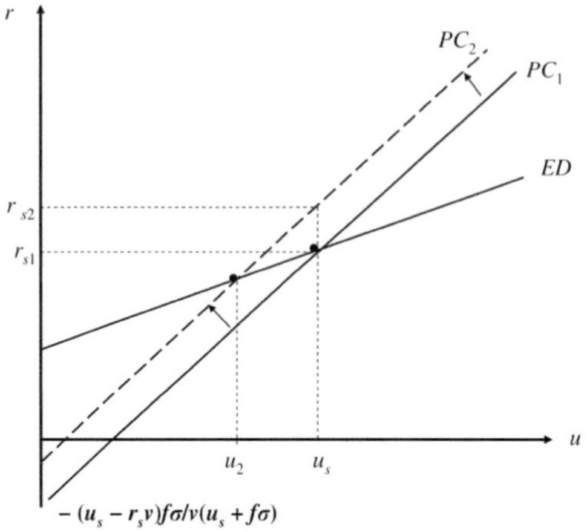


**Figure 6.** Impact of an increase in the target rate of return on the actual profit rate.

In Figure 6, it is shown that the increase in the target rate of return implemented through the pricing procedures would lead to an increase in the realized rate of profit *if* the actual rate of capacity utilization could remain at its assumed starting value $u_S$. But it won't. As a consequence of the reduction in real wages, and hence in consumption, the actual rate of capacity utilization is reduced, and eventually so is the actual profit rate. By contrast, the net profit share can either increase or decrease when firms manage to implement a higher target rate of return into their prices. In Figure 7, the higher target rate of return induces lower rates of utilization but higher net profit shares. However, in Figure 8, an increase in the target rate of return leads to a decrease in the actual net profit share.

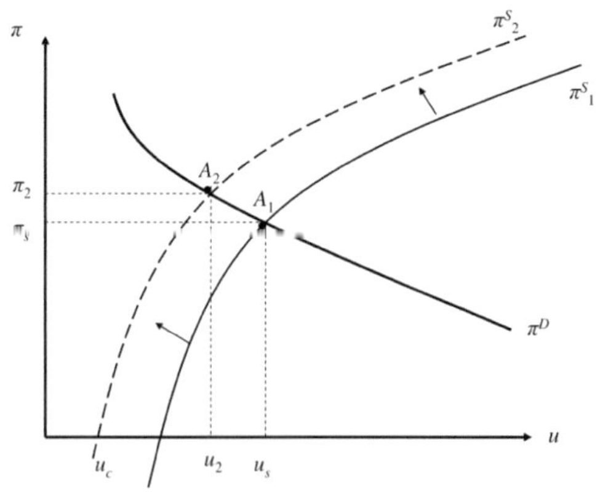


**Figure 7.** Impact of an increase in the target rate of return on the net profit share, when the investment constant is positive.

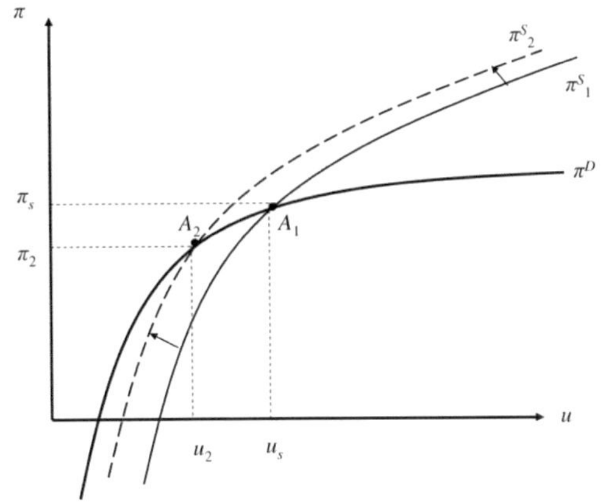


**Figure 8.** Impact of an increase in the target rate of return on the net profit share, when the investment constant is negative.

This demonstrates that the net profit share is not a reliable indicator of potential profitability when there are managerial costs, and hence there is no compelling reason to incorporate the profit share in an investment equation, as Bhaduri & Marglin (1990) do. Rather, if one is keen to eliminate the actual profit rate because it doubles up with the effect of the rate of utilization, it is the target rate of return, or the normal rate of profit, as suggested by Kurz (1991) and Lavoie (1992, pp. 332–340), that could be included into investment functions.

## Saving on Overhead Salaries

To close this paper, one may wonder whether the introduction of saving on salaries and wages can change the results obtained so far. We can proceed in a way that is nearly similar to that suggested by Nichols and Norton (1991) and Lavoie (1992, p. 344), assuming that (only) managerial (overhead) labour save out of their salaries. We can go slightly further by taking explicitly into consideration the propensity of firms to retain earnings. After some manipulation, the aggregate saving function can be rewritten as:

$$g^s = s_c r + s_{fr}(1 - s_c)r + \frac{s_{fw}\sigma f(u_s - r_s v)}{(u_s + f\sigma)v}(1 - s_{cg})r_{cg} \tag{22}$$

where $s_c$ is the corporate retention ratio while the propensity to save of managers (*fixed* labour) out of their *wage* and rentier income is respectively $s_{fw}$ and $s_{fr}$.[12]

[12]Making use of equation (3) and the definition of *f*, savings on managerial salaries are thus:

$$S_{fw} = s_{fw}\sigma w L_f = s_{fw}\sigma w q_{fc} f / y_v$$

Savings on overhead salaries as a percentage of the value of capital are thus:

We may also wish to consider that managers make capital gains on their holdings of shares, in which case we may consider in addition the propensity to save out of capital gains, $s_{cg}$, and the capital gain ratio, $r_{cg}$, which is the ratio of capital gains per unit of capital. The first term of the saving function represents the retained earnings of corporations; the second term represents managerial saving out of capital income, while the third term represents managerial saving out of salary income. As to the fourth term, it represents consumption out of capital gains, which must be subtracted from saving out of flow income.

As a result, a new effective demand relation can be derived, linking the previous investment function with this new saving function incorporating saving by managers. We now have:

$$r^{ED} = \frac{g_u u + \gamma + (1 - s_{cg})r_{cg}}{s_c + s_{fr}(1 - s_c) - g_r} - \frac{s_{fw}\sigma f(u_s - r_s v)}{[s_c + s_{fr}(1 - s_c) - g_r](u_s + f\sigma)v} \tag{23}$$

Obviously, things get much more complicated than with the earlier saving function. Basically, when saving out of salaries are assumed away ($s_{fw} = 0$), things remain as they were despite the introduction of consumption out of capital gains and saving out of rentier income. Only the first term of equation (22) remains, and hence the effective demand function behaves exactly as it did in the previous sections. In particular, it is quite obvious that the potential negative impact of additional managerial costs can be countered by a decrease in the retention ratio $s_c$ of corporations, as has been observed since the 1990s (Crotty, 2005, pp. 96–99). As shown in Figure 9, a reduction in $s_c$, or in the overall propensity to save out of profits $s_p$, will rotate up the effective demand function and lead to higher rates of capacity utilization and higher profit rates.[13] This will occur even if firms decide to restrain capital accumulation (a reduction in the $\gamma$ parameter). In fact, as we can see from equation (22), any reduction in the constant of the investment function can also be countered by either an increase in the capital gains ratio or the propensity to consume capital gains. Thus, as pointed out by Cordonnier (2006) in his enlightening contribution, the Kaleckian model can very easily explain the stylized facts of the more recent regime of capital accumulation, where corporations manage to achieve high profit rates despite slow capital accumulation and higher income shares being allocated to upper and middle rank managerial positions.

Let us now move on to the case where managers do save out of their salary income ($s_{fw}>0$). Let us first consider the case where outlays on managerial costs are increased. Whereas before this had no impact on the effective demand curve, the curve will now shift down, as a result of the increase in saving out of overhead salaries, as an examination of equation (22) quickly reveals. Indeed, taking the

---

$$S_{fw}/pK = s_{fw}\sigma w q_{fc} f/y_v pK = (s_{fw}\sigma f/v y_v)(w/p)$$

and one only needs to substitute $w/p$ by its value in equation (13) to obtain the third term in the saving function.

[13]Figure 9 illustrates the case where the sum of the constants in the $r^{ED}$ equation are negative.

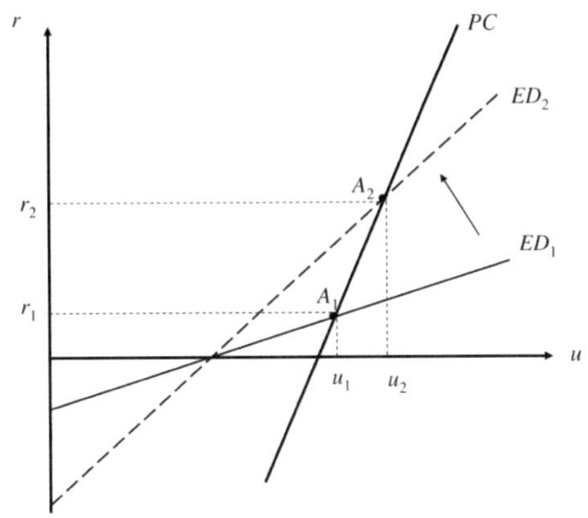


**Figure 9.** The impact of a reduction in the retention ratio of corporations on the profit rate and the rate of capacity utilization.

derivative of equation (22), we find it is always negative:[14]

$$\frac{dr^{ED}}{d\sigma} = \frac{u_s s_{fw} f(u_s - r_s v)}{v[s_c + s_{fr}(1 - s_c) - g_r](u_s + f\sigma)^2} < 0 \qquad (24)$$

The results are illustrated in Figure 10. When the rate of utilization is above its standard rate, as in situation *B*, the negative effects of an increase in managerial costs (through the rotation of the profits cost curve from $PC_1$ to $PC_2$) are reinforced by the presence of saving out of overhead salary income (which shifts down the effective demand curve from $ED_{B1}$ to $ED_{B2}$). In situation A, where the rate of utilization is below the standard rate, the favourable effects of an increase in managerial costs may be cancelled, or even overwhelmed, by the negative effects on effective demand induced by savings out of overhead salary income (the downward shift of the effective demand curve from $ED_{A1}$ to $ED_{A2}$). By making a comparison in the values taken by equations (19) and (23), at a given level of capacity utilization, it is possible to assess the conditions that are required for an increase in managerial costs still to induce an increase in the rate of utilization when it is smaller than the standard rate. The condition is given by:

$$s_{fw} < \{s_c + s_{fr}(1 - s_c) - g_r\}(u_s - u)/u_s = \alpha \qquad (25)$$

The propensity to save on managerial labour income has to be sufficiently small compared with the relative distance of the rate of utilization from its standard rate. In addition, the more stable the model, the more likely this condition is to be fulfilled.

The various possibilities are summarized in Table 2.

[14]Both $(u_s - r_s v)$ and $\{s_c + s_{fr}(1 - s_c) - g_r\}$ are positive. See footnotes 8 and 9.

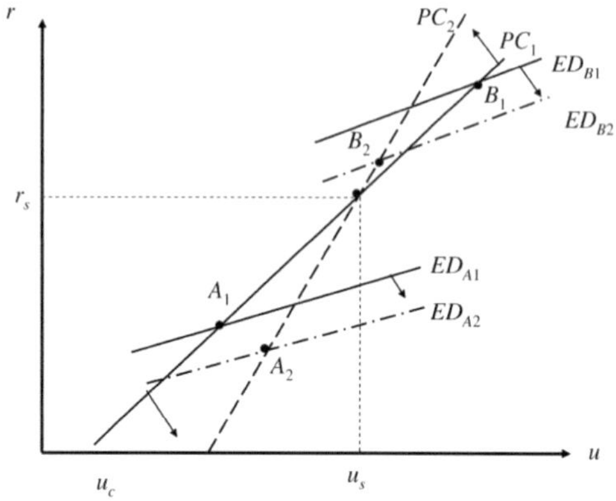


**Figure 10.** The impact of an increase in managerial costs, with target return pricing and a positive propensity to save out of managerial salaries.

**Table 2.** Impact of an increase in managerial costs on the rate of capacity utilization*

| Pricing procedure | Saving function | Conditions | | Impact of higher managerial costs |
|---|---|---|---|---|
| Markup pricing | with only saving out of profit | $\forall\, u$ | | + |
| | also with saving out of managerial salaries | $s_{fw} < s_c + s_{fr}\,(1-s_c)-g_r$ | | + |
| | | $s_{fw} > s_c + s_{fr}\,(1-s_c)-g_r$ | | – |
| Target return pricing | with only saving out of profit | $u > u_s$ | | – |
| | | $u < u_s$ | | + |
| | also with saving out of managerial salaries | $u > u_s$ | | – |
| | | $u < u_s$ | $s_{fw} < \alpha$ | + |
| | | | $s_{fw} > \alpha$ | – |

Note: $\alpha = \{s_c + s_{fr}\,(1-s_c)-g_r\}(u_s-u)/u_s$

* Conditions for a positive effect on the rate of accumulation are more stringent than those indicated for a positive effect on the rate of capacity utilization when there is saving out of managerial salaries, since we know, as revealed by Figures 9 and 10, that an increase in managerial costs will necessarily induce a reduction in the profit rate when the parameters are such that the rate of utilization is unaffected.

## Conclusion

It was argued by Nichols & Norton (1991, p. 53) that 'stagnationist models can be easily generalized to include a third class of overhead workers, a class important in modern capitalism'. This is what we have done in this paper, taking up the challenge offered by both Kaldor (1964) and Palley (2005), in the hope of showing that, as Nichols & Norton (1991, p. 53) further claim, 'a stagnationist model so generalized is capable of yielding a broader range of capitalist dynamics than the traditional stagnationist framework allowed'.

The most significant result achieved with our growth model with overhead labour is that increases in managerial costs may have either positive or negative effects on rates of capacity utilization, profit rates, growth rates and net profit shares, even when there is no saving out of wages and salaries. Furthermore, increases in target rates of return lead to reductions in the actual profit rates with the canonical Kaleckian investment function, and once again profit shares may go one way or another despite this. Thus, in contrast to what seems to be an implicit assumption of a large number of empirical studies, the evolution of wage shares or profit shares is unlikely to be an appropriate indicator of the bargaining power of labour or of capitalists, unless one succeeds in taking adequate care of cyclical effects.

## Acknowledgments

This paper was presented at the conference *Post-Keynesian Economics, Income Distribution and Distributive Justice*, the Second Bi-Annual Canada/US Eastern Border Post-Keynesian workshop, at the University of Vermont, Burlington, September 23, 2006. It was also presented to the students of the Berlin Post-Keynesian Summer School in July 2008. The paper arose as a result of my stay at the University of Lille, in June 2006, following very enlightening discussions there with Laurent Cordonnier and Franck Van de Velde.

## References

Amadeo, E.J. (1986) Notes on capacity utilisation, distribution and accumulation, *Contributions to Political Economy*, 5, pp. 83–94.

Asimakopulos, A. (1975) A Kaleckian theory of income distribution, *Canadian Journal of Economics*, 8(3), pp. 313–333.

Bhaduri, A. & Marglin, S. (1990) Unemployment and the real wage: the economic basis for contesting political ideologies, *Cambridge Journal of Economics*, 14(4), pp. 375–393.

Burkett, P. (1994) Book review of *The Economic Surplus in Advanced Economics*, edited by John, B. Davis, *Review of Social Economics*, 52(2), pp. 114–124.

Cassetti, M. (2003) Bargaining power, effective demand and technical progress: a Kaleckian model of growth, *Cambridge Journal of Economics*, 27(3), pp. 449–464.

Cordonnier, L. (2006) Le profit sans l'accumulation: la recette du capitalisme gouverné par la finance, *Innovations, Cahiers d'économie de l'innovation*, 23(1), pp. 51–72.

Crotty, J. (2005) The neoliberal paradox: the impact of destructive product market competition and modern financial markets on nonfinancial corporation performance in the liberal era, in: G.A. Epstein (Ed.) *Financialization and the World Economy* (Cheltenham: Edward Elgar).

Duménil, G. & Lévy, D. (2004) *Économie marxiste du capitalisme* (Paris: La Découverte).

Dutt, A.K. (1990) *Growth, Distribution and Uneven Development* (Cambridge: Cambridge University Press).

Dutt, A.K. (1992) Stagnation, growth and unproductive activity, in: J.B. Davis (Ed.) *The Economic Surplus in Advanced Economics* (Aldershot: Edward Elgar).

Epstein, G.A. & Jayadev, A. (2005) The rise of rentier incomes in OECD countries: financialization, central bank policy and labor solidarity, in: G.A. Epstein (Ed.) *Financialization and the World Economy* (Cheltenham: Edward Elgar).

Harris, D.J. (1974) The price policy of firms, the level of employment and distribution of income in the short run, *Australian Economic Papers*, 13 (June), pp. 144–151.
Kaldor, N. (1964) *Essays on Economic Policy I* (London: Duckworth).
Kurz, H.D. (1991) Technical change, growth and distribution: a steady state approach to unsteady growth on Kaldorian lines, in: E.J. Nell & W. Semmler (Eds) *Nicholas Kaldor and Mainstream Economics* (London: Macmillan).
Lanzillotti, R.F. (1958) Pricing objectives in large companies, *American Economic Review*, 48(5), pp. 921–940.
Lavoie, M. (1992) *Foundations of Post-Keynesian Economic Analysis* (Aldershot: Edward Elgar).
Lavoie, M. (1995) The Kaleckian model of growth and distribution and its neo-Ricardian and neo-Marxian critiques, *Cambridge Journal of Economics*, 19(6), December, pp. 789–818.
Lavoie, M. (1996) Unproductive outlays and capital accumulation with target-return pricing, *Review of Social Economy*, 54(3), pp. 303–321.
Lavoie, M. (1996–97) Real wages, employment structure and the aggregate demand curve in a Kaleckian short-run model, *Journal of Post Keynesian Economics*, 19(2), pp. 275–288.
Lavoie, M. (1998) Simple comparative statics of class conflict in Kaleckian and Marxist short-run models, *Review of Radical Political Economics*, 30(3), pp. 101–113.
Lavoie, M. (2003) Kaleckian effective demand and Sraffian normal prices: towards a reconciliation, *Review of Political Economy*, 15(1), pp. 53–74.
Lavoie, M. & Ramírez-Gastón, P. (1997) Traverse in a two-sector Kaleckian model of growth with target return pricing, *Manchester School of Economic and Social Studies*, 55(1), pp. 145–169.
Lee, F. (1994) From Post-Keynesian to historical price theory, part I, facts, theory and empirically grounded pricing model, *Review of Political Economy*, 6(3), pp. 303–336.
Mohun, S. (2006) Distributive shares in the US economy, 1964–2000, *Cambridge Journal of Economics*, 30(3), pp. 347–370.
Nichols, L.M. & Norton, N. (1991) Overhead workers and political economy macro models, *Review of Radical Political Economy*, 23(1–2), pp. 47–54.
Palley, T. (2005) Class conflict and the Cambridge theory of distribution, in: B. Gibson (Ed.) *Joan Robinson's Economics: A Centennial Celebration* (Cheltenham: Edward Elgar).
Petit, P. (2006) From one managerial capitalism . . . to another, in: B. Laperche, J.K. Galbraith & D. Uzunidis (Eds) *Innovation, Evolution and Economic Change: New Ideas in the Tradition of Galbraith*, pp. 38–52 (Cheltenham: Edward Elgar).
Plihon, D. (2002) *Rentabilité et risque dans le nouveau régime de croissance* (Paris: La Documentation Française).
Rowthorn, B. (1981) Demand, real wages and economic growth, *Thames Papers in Political Economy*, Autumn, pp. 1–39.
Saez, E. & Veall, M.R. (2005) The evolution of high incomes in Northern America: lessons from the Canadian experience, *American Economic Review*, 95(3), pp. 831–849.
Shipley, D.D. (1981) Pricing objectives in British manufacturing industry, *Journal of Industrial Economics*, 29(4), pp. 429–443.

## Appendix: An Alternative Specification of the Wage Differential

It is understood that the model is only one among several possible formalisations. For instance, in this model, the real wage of managers was a given multiple $\sigma$ of the real wage of workers. As a consequence, an increase in the target rate of return of corporations would have led to an increase in the markup and hence to a reduction in the real wage of both the workers and the managerial staff. In a *cadrisme* regime of accumulation, where finance and managers join forces to appropriate potential income shares, it might be more relevant to assume instead that the real wage of managers is a given. With this alternative closure, the wage multiple $\sigma$ becomes an endogenous variable, which depends on the target rate of return set by managers and on the real salaries which they assign to themselves through control of the corporate board of directors. This alternative closure however does not generate dynamics that are any different from those shown in the main model. This can be seen by deriving the profits cost function. Rewriting equation (5) as an explicit function of the nominal wage rate paid to managers ($w_f$), we get:

$$p = w/y_v + fw_f/uy_v + rpv/u \tag{5A}$$

We now assume that managers are paid a given real wage, $\omega_f = w_f/p$, which in fact is determined as a function of variable labour productivity, so that $\Omega_f = \omega_f/y_v$. Substituting $w_f$ by its value, $p\omega_f$, and solving for $p$, we obtain:

$$p = (w_v/y_v)\{uy_v/(uy_v - f\omega_f - rvy_v)\}$$

Assuming target return pricing, the above equation implies a modified version of equation (9)

$$p = \left(\frac{u_s r_s v - f\Omega_f}{u_s}\right)\frac{w}{y_v} \tag{9A}$$

from which we can extract the endogenized real wage of blue-collar workers:

$$\frac{w_v}{p} = \frac{(u_s - r_s v - f\Omega_f)y_v}{u_s} \tag{13A}$$

Combining equations (5A) and (13A), we find the profits cost curve

$$r^{PC} = \frac{(r_s v + f\Omega_f)u}{vu_s} - \frac{f\Omega_f}{v} \tag{14A}$$

We can see immediately that:

$$dr^{PC}/d\Omega_f = f(u - u_s)/vu_s > 0 \quad \text{if } u > u_s \tag{19A}$$

so that once again the sign of the derivative depends on whether the economy is operating above or below the standard rate of capacity utilization. This implies that Figures 2–5 still illustrate correctly what happens when managerial costs, i.e., the real wage of managers, is raised. The dynamics are not modified by this alternative mechanism of wage determination.

[5]

European Journal of Economics and Economic Policies: Intervention, Vol. 14 No. 2, 2017, pp. 200–221

# The origins and evolution of the debate on wage-led and profit-led regimes*

Marc Lavoie
Centre d'Économie de Paris Nord, University of Paris 13, University of Sorbonne Paris Cité, France and University of Ottawa, Canada

*While Kaleckian authors tend to find that economies are in a wage-led demand regime, Goodwinian authors tend to find that economies are in a profit-led demand regime. This paper avoids econometric technicalities and provides instead a historical perspective, going back to the empirical study of Boddy and Crotty and that of Weisskopf, as well as to the debates that arose in the 1980s between but also within the two main strands of heterodox macroeconomics: the Marxians and the post-Keynesians. This hopefully will help to shed some light on the more recent controversy over the existence of profit-led or wage-led demand regimes. A noteworthy feature of the paper is the emphasis on the existence of overhead labour costs and hence the distinction between managers and ordinary workers. These are likely to bias empirical measurements of demand regimes towards the profit-led regime at high-frequency data; they may also give rise to paradoxical results; and they justify the claim that an increase in the wage share of ordinary workers is likely to have a positive effect on aggregate demand even if economies are profit-led.*

**Keywords:** *overhead labour costs, wage-led regimes, profit squeeze, neo-Kaleckian models, growth and distribution*

**JEL codes:** *B5, E12*

> *'Many economists agree that Keynesian effects are important in the short run, but question whether Keynesian analysis can safely be used to guide long run economic policy toward economic growth. These debates should presumably be settled by looking at the empirical evidence as to how strong the tendencies moving capitalist economies toward full capacity utilization actually are. But econometric techniques for answering this question are themselves in dispute, and macroeconomic evidence is limited, so the policy dilemma remains unsolved.'*
>
> D.K. Foley and T. Michl (1999: 194)

## 1 INTRODUCTION

I have been asked to address the evolution of the debate on wage-led and profit-led regimes in recent decades. Ever since its conception, the FMM conference and its network have been preoccupied with matters of income distribution. It is, however, a difficult task

* Many thanks to Brett Fiebiger, Robert Guttman and Engelbert Stockhammer for providing comments on the initial version of this paper which was written for the 20th FMM conference in Berlin. The paper was subsequently presented at the post-Keynesian seminar of the CLERSÉ at Lille 1 University, at the 2017 annual conference of the French Association for Political Economy (AFEP) in Rennes, and at the 2nd Łaski Lecture organized by the Vienna Institute for International Economic Studies (wiiw) and the Chamber of Labour in Vienna. This research benefited from a previous grant on growth and inequality provided by the Institute for New Economic Thinking (INET).


Journal compilation © 2017 Edward Elgar Publishing Ltd
The Lypiatts, 15 Lansdown Road, Cheltenham, Glos GL50 2JA, UK

to address the question put to me, first, because of the sheer amount of literature devoted to the topic, but also because others have done so in the recent past.[1] Engelbert Stockhammer and Özlem Onaran (2013) have presented a survey of the main empirical results regarding demand regimes in developed and less developed countries. Eckhard Hein (2017) has devoted quite a bit of space to this topic in his review for the 2016 FMM conference of the main developments of post-Keynesian economics over the last 20 years. Peter Skott (2017: 356) has recently questioned the validity of the much-quoted econometric results obtained by Onaran and Galanis (2012), linking them to 'wishful thinking', and he has made a series of arguments to the effect that whether output growth was wage-led or profit-led was unhelpful, which, if right, would render my paper useless or obsolete. Stockhammer (2017), in a paper that was presented here at the FMM 2015 conference, has given a detailed critique of what he has called the neo-Goodwinian empirical tests of demand regimes, explaining why they often lead to the conclusion that these demand regimes are profit-led. Also in a paper that was presented at an FMM conference, but this time in 2014, Robert Blecker (2016) has delivered a detailed survey of many of the theoretical issues surrounding the notion of wage-led and profit-led demand regimes. In addition, he has provided an extensive assessment of the various econometric methods and specifications that have been used to assess whether countries are in a wage-led or in a profit-led demand regime – something that I would be incapable of doing. One puzzle that Blecker tries to solve is why, for a given country, mainly the USA, different econometric studies yield contradicting results on this issue. One wonders whether the statement by Foley and Michl quoted above is just as valid in 2016 as it was in 1999 when empirical work on wage-led and profit-led regimes was at its beginnings.[2]

In a nutshell, what Blecker argues is that studies that show that aggregate demand in the US is profit-led are most likely looking at the very short-run cyclical behaviour of the economy, while studies that show that it is wage-led take a somewhat longer view of the matter. As Blecker (2016: 386) concludes, 'the positive effects of a higher profit share on investment and net exports are likely to be felt mainly in the short run, while the negative effects on consumption are likely to be felt more strongly in the longer term', and hence, 'it is entirely possible that, in a typical business cycle, profits drive investment both up in the recovery and down in the recession, but a sustained profit share of income will not lead to higher investment or growth in the longer term' (ibid.: 387).

Now, as I have noted elsewhere (Lavoie 2014: 423–424), up until recently at least, there has been a kind of division of labour between Marxians and post-Keynesians, where Marxians focus more on cyclical behaviour while post-Keynesians tend to examine long-run growth – perhaps a remnant of Joan Robinson's growth regimes. This was pointed out also by Goldstein and Hillard (2009: 6), who made the case that there has been a split between growth theorists and crisis theorists, and that this division between business cycles and balanced growth has 'tended to run along Marxian and post-Keynesian lines'. Indeed, it could be argued that those post-Keynesians who pay attention to short-term cyclical behaviour or who pay homage to Goodwin cycles (the neo-Goodwinians as

1. Mark Setterfield (2016) notes that the *Review of Keynesian Economics* intends to devote no fewer than *four* special issues on the wage- versus profit-led growth debate initiated by the Bhaduri/Marglin (1990) article.
2. Thus while post-Keynesian Kaleckians are convinced that domestic demand regimes are wage-led, in an email (dated 17 September 2016) sent to a large group of economists, Lance Taylor writes that 'the profit-led/profit-squeeze story seems pretty well established by now', adding that 'single equation estimates of wages vs output make no sense. They are under-identified and are capturing the robust response of distribution to demand rather than the reverse'.

Stockhammer calls them) usually carry a strong Marxian background or show eclecticism that includes Marxian theory.[3] Thus, given this, and given the time-dimension findings of Blecker (2016), nobody will be surprised to discover that, roughly speaking, the authors who have provided theoretical or empirical support for a profit-led regime have some Marxian sympathies while those who have provided theoretical or empirical support for wage-led regimes have been more closely associated with a Keynesian pedigree.

To some extent, this opposition between the heterodox views based on a more Marxian slant and those based on more Keynesian–Kaleckian–Kaldorian lines will be the *fil conducteur* of my inquiry. To avoid repeating what has been done by previous authors, and because of my own impairments in econometrics, I will not survey the empirical literature on profit-led and wage-led regimes. Instead, I will provide a historical perspective to the issue, going back to the debates that arose in the 1980s between the two main strands of heterodox macroeconomics. This hopefully will help to shed some light on the more recent controversy over the existence of profit-led or wage-led demand regimes. Another particular twist of my presentation will be the emphasis that I will put on the presence of overhead labour and its impact on what can be said about wage-led and profit-led demand regimes.

## 2 IN THE BEGINNING WERE BODDY AND CROTTY

Before going back in time, it should be emphasized that the distinction between a wage-led regime and a profit-led regime may apply to at least three different categories. Most of the recent empirical action has been around demand regimes, that is whether an increase in the wage share has led to an increase in the rate of capacity utilization or in the growth rate of the economy. There is also the issue of whether an increase in the wage share or in real wages might lead to an increase or a decrease in productivity or the growth rate of productivity, in which case we might speak of a wage-led or profit-led productivity regime. And finally – and this was at one stage the main concern – one may wonder whether an increase or a decrease in the wage share or in the growth rate of real wages may lead to an increase or a decrease in employment or in the growth rate of employment, in which case we may speak of a wage-led or profit-led employment regime. In addition, there is also the issue of whether an increase in the rate of utilization or in the rate of employment will itself lead to a change in the wage share – this is what mainstream authors have called the wage curve. As recalled by Stockhammer (2017), post-Keynesian authors from the neo-Kaleckian strand have only paid a limited amount of attention to this feedback relation, because they have been concerned instead with additional determinants of aggregate demand, while those that he calls neo-Goodwinians – the Marxians or the post-Keynesians that have closer ties with the Marxian approach – have taken this feedback relation explicitly into consideration and have called it the distributive curve.[4]

This being said, how far back in time should we go? This is an arbitrary decision, as discussions about whether slowdowns in economic activity or secular stagnation must be attributed to overly high or overly low wage shares have been entertained for a long time, going back to Marx himself and authors such as Sweezy or Steindl. The modern origins of the wage-led/profit-led controversies can be found in the literature of the 1980s. The founding paper providing empirical support for profit-led employment or demand regimes would be the Boddy

3. Some neo-Goodwinian and Marxian authors (Peter Skott and Anwar Shaikh) also like to refer to themselves as Harrodians.
4. However, as pointed out and shown by Hein (2017), this does not mean that Kaleckians have not thought about the feedbacks of demand and growth on income distribution.

and Crotty (1975) study. Boddy and Crotty argued that the cycle ought not be broken into simply two parts – the slump and the expansion – but that instead it should be split into three parts, by distinguishing between the first part of the expansion, until its mid-point, and the latter part of the expansion, when the output peak is reached. Boddy and Crotty (1975: 5) contend that the 'labor share typically *rises* in the latter half of an expansion. The profit squeeze discussed by Marx does occur'. They find that 'the decline in gross share occurs well prior to the end of the expansion. The profits squeeze remains, even when profits are measured inclusive of taxes and interest payments'. With regard to the first part of the expansion, they note a decline in the wage share, as 'unit labor costs decline relative to output prices' (ibid.: 7). They attribute these changes to the evolution of the unemployment rate (the reserve army), as labour militancy (quit rates, strikes, work effort) are being reduced by high and rising unemployment rates.

Thomas Weisskopf (1979), in a highly interesting and carefully crafted paper, picked up Boddy and Crotty's idea of splitting the business cycles into three parts: the early expansion, from the trough in the level of the real output to the peak in the profit rate; the late expansion from that point until the peak in the level of real output; with the third sub-period corresponding to the recession. Recalling that the profit rate $r = umv$, where $u$ is the rate of capacity utilization, $m$ the share of profits and $v$ the capacity-to-capital ratio, Weisskopf (1979: 352) looked at the uncorrected profit shares (we shall see later what the corrected measure was). He also found that the profit share was falling in the recession, rising in the early expansion, while it was falling again in the latter part of the expansion, thus once more providing support for the profit-squeeze view, or what he called the rising strength of labour view. The trend decline in the profit rate over several cycles could also be attributed to a trend fall in the profit share.

These results, and those of Boddy and Crotty, were at the heart of what has been called the SSA school – the social structure of accumulation school – which had several similarities to the French Regulation school, both schools of thought being concerned with the large changes that had occurred with the collapsing productivity growth and the rising inflation that could be attributed to the oil shocks and conflicts over income determination. The similarities can be exemplified by the several collaborative works of members of each school, Samuel Bowles on the one hand and Robert Boyer on the other. SSA school members, in particular Bowles, David Gordon and Thomas Weisskopf, wrote a series of papers and a book where they argued that the American economy, in contrast to what had happened in the Great Depression, was suffering from a supply-side crisis, that is, a profit-squeeze crisis brought about by an overly long economic expansion, with high-employment conditions, which had overly strengthened the power of the labour force and lowered the cost of job loss to workers, giving rise to an increase in the share of wages.[5] The fall in the share and the rate of profits, according to the SSA school, had thus brought about a fall in the rate of investment and hence a secular slowdown in economic activity. As a consequence, in their view, while a redistribution of income towards labour during the Great Depression could stimulate demand and end the crisis, no such solution was possible in the early 1980s.[6] For Weisskopf et al. (1985: 261),

5. 'The full-employment profit squeeze ... has been analyzed in great detail by Rafford Boddy and James Crotty (in a cyclical context), by Andrew Glyn and Bob Sutcliffe (in a secular context), and it plays an important role in our individual and joint work as well' (Weisskopf et al. 1985: 275).
6. This is reminiscent of what one hears today from mainstream authors: before the Great Recession that started in 2008, expansionary fiscal policy and a reduction in inequality were useless; following the advent of the Great Recession and the zero lower bound on interest rates, these policies become useful.

> no such happy coincidence of short-term material interests and longer-term radical objectives is associated with the type of supply-side crisis which results when the capitalist class is too weak. The most obvious exit from the crisis is that pointed to by the right: strengthen the capitalist class, restore profits and rekindle the capitalist accumulation process.

A similar conclusion was reached by Stephen Marglin in his famous *Cambridge Journal of Economics* article. Marglin (1984a: 142) claimed the following:

> A Left program, I would suggest, must respect the logic of the economic situation. Productivity does place limits on wages, and not just physical limits. As long as profitability remains the mainspring of investment, there are economic limits that constrain the wage share. Under capitalism, profits are indeed the geese that lay the golden eggs… . A Left program must therefore accept limitations on real wages.

Presumably Marglin, at least in those years, believed that the neo-Marxian model was the appropriate one to understand capitalism, because in his book he wrote that 'the neo-Keynesian analysis leads to policies designed to stimulate investment demand or to reduce capitalists' propensity to save; the neo-Marxian model leads … to policies that will stimulate saving, or to policies that will reduce the subsistence wage' (Marglin 1984b: 101).[7] Skott (2017: 357) wonders whether left-wing economists would 'advocate an increase in inequality if it could be established that a rise in inequality tends to raise the rate of economic growth'. Well, the answer to his question has been found in the text just above. Perhaps he would not, but other progressive economists in the past have advocated real-wage restrictions on that basis.

## 3 AND THEN CAME LANCE TAYLOR

Lance Taylor (2004: 305) has more recently issued the same warning: 'wage increases as advocated by people on the Left cannot restore aggregate demand if it is in fact profit-led'. Indeed, Taylor may be somewhat over-enthusiastic about the empirical evidence providing support for the profit-led view of demand regimes when he writes that, 'as argued by Bowles and Boyer (1995) and substantiated for the United States in Chapter 9, demand in modern industrial economies appears to be profit-led' (Taylor 2004: 243). But this is not really what Bowles and Boyer (1995) arrive at; indeed they conclude that the US economy is in a wage-led demand regime, as are two of the other four countries that they examine. Epstein and Gintis (1995: 7), in their presentation of the Bowles and Boyer chapter, are more uncertain as they write that the authors have found 'mixed evidence for the stagnationist or wage-led model as the basis for a progressive strategy for restoring economic growth … . Wage increases do not *by themselves* constitute a viable strategy for supporting increases in employment. However … higher wages do increase productivity'. Thus demand and productivity would be wage-led, while employment would be profit-led.[8]

There is a strong link between the views expressed by Taylor and those that can be attributed to the SSA school. As argued above, members of the SSA school were arguing that an expansion would eventually lead to a profit squeeze – this is the so-called distributive curve emphasized by Taylor and his followers, where higher rates of utilization or

7. Using the previous notations, the neo-Marxian model as described by Marglin (1984b) can be summarized by the Cambridge equation, where the growth rate $g = s_p r = s_p umv$, with $s_p$ the propensity to save out of profits. Thus, for a given rate of utilization, a higher growth rate is associated with a higher saving rate and a higher profit share $m$.
8. More on this apparent contradiction is to follow in the section preceding the conclusion.

higher rates of employment generate higher real wages and a higher wage share. In addition, by endorsing what they called a supply-side explanation of the secular crisis attributed to the US and European economies after 1973, SSA school members were essentially arguing that the demand regime was profit-led. This is the position that Taylor endorses in his 2004 book. Observing business cycles, and being inspired by Goodwin cycles, he argues that, when looking at the wage share and the rate of utilization, the US economy shows 'negatively inclined counterclockwise spirals' (Taylor 2004: 287), and hence clockwise spirals when looking at profit shares and utilization rates. This in his view (ibid.: 291) is explained by the fact that effective demand is profit-led (there is a negative impact of the wage share on the rate of utilization), while the distributive curve is positive (higher rates of utilization lead to higher wage shares, signalling a profit squeeze). The empirical work supporting this assessment would be presented in more detail in the oft-quoted paper by Barbosa-Filho and Taylor (2006), which was subsequently subjected to the critique of Stockhammer and Stehrer (2011). A new version of this empirical analysis has been pursued by Kiefer and Rada (2015), concluding to the existence of a profit-led demand regime and a profit-squeeze distributive curve for their whole panel of 13 countries. As noted dismally by Fiebiger (2017: 19),

> a pro-cyclical profit share is commonly interpreted as providing evidence of a 'profit-led' demand regime and that, in turn, as supporting the Marxian conclusion that higher output growth requires abstinence by workers (via lower real wages). The flipside to the 'profit squeeze' theory is that a 'wage squeeze' is good for growth.

The links between the Taylor view and those of Boddy and Crotty and the SSA school are explicitly recognized by Taylor when he acknowledges that his distributive curve is what Blanchflower and Oswald call the wage curve, 'while for the Kaleckian radicals Boddy and Crotty (1975) its slope encapsulates a "cyclical profit squeeze". This usage carries over into the applied "social structure of accumulation" macro models of Bowles, Gordon and Weisskopf (1990) and Gordon (1995)' (Taylor 2004: 236). Indeed, very early on, Taylor (1983: 33) had incorporated the cyclical and profit-squeeze findings of what he then called the 'Radical economists'. He has a table with the three phases of the cycle: in the early upswing, the profit rate, profit share and rate of utilization are rising; near the peak the rate of utilization is stable, but the profit rate and the profit shares fall; in the downswing, all three variables fall.

A close link can certainly also be entertained between these earlier works and the arguments being put forward by Peter Skott in a series of papers. Skott also relies on the observed clockwise loops between the employment rate and the profit share and between the utilization rate and the profit share (Skott/Zipperer 2011) to argue in favour of his Goodwinian–Harrodian view of the economy (which he would like everyone to adopt) and to reject anything related to a Kaleckian view. A further point made by Skott (2017) in a number of places is that the rate of utilization and the rate of employment do not move together (they have their own clockwise loop), and hence that it is erroneous to omit the labour market, as do most post-Keynesian or Kaleckian growth models. Indeed, this is a point made by Bowles and Boyer (1995: 214) some time ago: 'Output and employment need not move in the same direction when productivity varies with employment'.

A possible difference between the Marxian and post-Keynesian traditions, as pointed out by Bowles and Boyer (1995: 187), is that the Keynesian tradition tends to focus on product markets whereas the Marxian tradition focuses on class conflict and the labour market. As mentioned earlier, there was some collaboration between the SSA school and the French Regulation school. Bowles and Boyer (1988: 395) present a formalization of the profit-squeeze mechanism, as changes in wage rates can give rise to what they term 'a wage-led or profit-led employment regime, respectively'. The saving and investment equations are determined by the share of profits, which itself is governed by labour effort, which in turn depends inversely on the level of employment.[9] Thus, what happens is that there is a high level of employment profit squeeze. They combine the effect of the profit share on aggregate demand with the effect of employment on the profit share (the employment version of Taylor's distributive curve) to find out whether employment is wage-led or profit-led.

The model is given more structure in Bowles and Boyer (1990), but with a given level of investment. Thanks to their effort function – an important feature of the SSA school which emphasizes the need for labour disciplining to avoid shirking – they can show that 'high employment levels necessarily preclude a wage-led employment regime… . Thus the increase in the level of employment will itself undermine a wage-led employment regime' (ibid.: 204). They conclude that: 'One important result is that taking account of labour-intensity effects yields classical results – lower wages going along with higher levels of economic activity – even under extreme Keynesian assumptions concerning savings, investment, exports, and the effects of government borrowing' (ibid.: 210). Thus within their model, even if investment and exports are assumed to be given and hence autonomous with regards to changes in unit costs, increases in real wages, which initially lead to an increase in aggregate demand, will eventually lead to a fall in output as it will induce a fall in profitability: at some point profits will be negative or will be below some acceptable target level, and hence will require a reduction in employment.

By arguing that labour productivity drops as employment goes up, what Bowles and Boyer have done is to reintroduce something that acts like the neoclassical decreasing returns. Their visual depiction of the aggregate demand relationship between real wages and employment (Bowles/Boyer 1990: 204), which has a bell shape, is identical to the graph that would depict the effective labour demand curve in a Keynesian model with decreasing returns (Schefold 1983; Lavoie 2014: 283).

## 4 SSA RECANTATION TOWARDS A KALECKIAN–KEYNESIAN VIEW

Presenting the views on profit-led versus wage-led demand regimes as a battle of wits between Marxians and post-Keynesians would however be a misrepresentation. First, it is an obvious point that the first creator of the neo-Kaleckian model of growth and distribution was Bob Rowthorn (1981) – a heterodox economist with more Marxian than Keynesian longings. Second, it must be pointed out that a number of Marxians have not bought into the profit-squeeze story or have contested that the demand regimes are profit-led. The debates between Howard Sherman and Jonathan Goldstein on the validity of the profit-squeeze mechanism are well-known among Marxians, with Sherman taking the view that components of aggregate demand other than corporate investment were responsible for the fall in the profit rate before the end of the upswing. Furthermore, just before his death, Al Szymanski (1984) was criticizing the supply-side interpretation of the crisis that had been put forward by members of the SSA school. In other words,

9. There is thus some similarity with the mechanism described by Skott (1989), according to whom high rates of employment will discourage entrepreneurs from producing further, as formalized through his output expansion function, or when Skott's (2010) investment function is said to be a negative function of the employment rate.

there has always been a number of Marxians with Keynesian tendencies who had trouble with the standard story of the SSA school.

Furthermore, Taylor himself seems to have been of two minds on the issue of demand regimes. In Taylor (1991: 72), he says that 'the stylized facts suggest that developing economies adjust to changes in the real wage in wage-led fashion when the level of output is free to vary'. This comes from his 18 country studies for the World Institute for Development Economic Research (WIDER). However, he continues by saying that 'production is frequently subject to upper bounds in the developing world. The most common are lack of capacity, a shortage of foreign exchange, and weather and the seasonal cycle which determine supplies of food and export crops' (ibid.: 73). He concludes on this by describing a non-linear aggregate demand curve in utilization and real wage space: the economy would be demand wage-led at low real wages (wage share) and demand profit-led at high real wages. An identical non-linear relationship is also introduced in the employment and real wage space by post-Keynesian Tom Palley (2011: 226): the economy would be employment wage-led at low real wages and employment profit-led at high real wages.[10]

There was also a partial turnabout of the members of the SSA school. This partial recantation can be summarized as follows: economies are generally subjected to trade-offs, and hence profit-led; but restrictive macroeconomic policies designed to redistribute income towards the upper class and the corporate sector have created such an amount of slack in the late 1970s and early 1980s that a wage growth and wage equalization strategy will benefit both the workers and the capitalists. Most intriguing was the article that Bowles et al. (1984) wrote for the magazine *In These Times*, which appeared later as a working paper. After having told us in other articles that the crisis was a supply-led one, in other words a crisis of capital shortage, created by a profit squeeze due to excessive real wages relative to productivity which had led to a downturn in investment, these three authors turn around and argue that the 'analysis of the wastefulness of the U.S. economy leads us to suggest that a left economic program be based on the macro-economic principle of wage-led productivity growth' (ibid.: 2).

Bowles et al. (ibid.: 4) note that the reigning conventional wisdom, even among the left political spectrum is the 'trickle-down distributive strategy for economic recovery', which 'sacrifices wages and living standards to boost profits and investment', so that 'raising business profitability is the way to stimulate investment and growth, and that to do this workers will have to accept a period of austerity'. This description of conventional wisdom sounds very much like Radical or SSA assessments of the time, as also endorsed by Marglin (1984a) and Taylor (2004). But Bowles et al. (1984: 6) now argue instead that 'there is a workable progressive alternative to trickle-down economics'. They further point out that 'its crucial analytical proposition is that the economies of most of the advanced capitalist nations today are slack economies, not zero-sum economies' (ibid.: 5).

They contend that the US economy is in a regime of wage-led productivity growth for the standard reasons invoked by Marx, Webb and Akerlof, that is, 'high wages contribute to productivity because they constitute an important source of motivation' and because they force 'employers to modernize or go out of business' (ibid.: 8). They add a third reason, one based on the positive effects of higher wages on aggregate demand and on the

10. In a way, this also resembles the statements made by several mainstream authors when dealing with practical issues. They recognize that higher wages or a higher minimum wage may have a favourable impact on the economy under certain conditions (when real wages are low, and hence the economy is in a wage-led regime), but they always end up claiming that the current conditions are not right, as real wages are already too high (they are so high that the economy is in the profit-led regime).

Kaldor–Verdoorn effects that they had contested in another article (Weisskopf et al. 1985: 285), arguing now that 'rising wages lead to rising consumer demand and hence to rising aggregate demand for goods and services. In the present context of inadequate final demand, this would increase productive efficiency directly and increase the rate of capital formation, thus contributing to productivity growth in the future' (Bowles et al. 1984: 9). This sounds no different from the arguments being brought forward by post-Keynesian authors today to support wage-led growth policies, with their positive effects both on aggregate demand and labour productivity. Present-day supporters of such wage-led growth strategies often face the objection that raising real wages more than productivity would lead to a fall in the profit share and in the expected or normal profit rate. But Bowles et al. (ibid.: 9) have an answer to this:

> One might nonetheless object that rising wages might not have these desirable effects if wage increases lowered the expected rate of profit on new investments and thereby reduced the incentive for business to invest. But the level of capacity utilization could be expected to improve both current and expected profit rates through the positive effect of the growth of consumer demand on capacity utilization.

It is hard to see how the strategy proposed by Bowles et al. (ibid.: 12) in this particular working paper 'differs fundamentally from that of most Keynesians', in contrast to what they claim. It is true that there are some remnants of a 'loanable funds' analysis which is antithetical to the post-Keynesian endogenous credit-money view when Bowles et al. (ibid.: 10) write that

> one might finally object that a high-wage strategy would reduce savings and hence discourage investment because of higher borrowing costs. This objection builds on the observation that workers tend to consume more and save less of their (wage) income. This argument is perfectly correct, as far as it goes; it has a long and respected history in both the Keynesian and neo-Marxian literature.

But besides this, and the statement that 'in the longer run, under conditions of full capacity utilization, continued upward pressure on wages might well provoke a decline in investment or even an investment strike by capitalists' (ibid.: 9), the similarities with the arguments brought forward by current Kaleckian advocates of a wage-led growth strategy are striking.[11]

## 5 BHADURI AND MARGLIN TO THE RESCUE

These similarities can be made more evident by comparing Bowles et al.'s (1984) arguments with the response of Edward Nell (1985) to the claims made by Marglin in his *Cambridge Journal of Economics* article, notably the claim that progressive economists must accept that real wages must be restrained. Nell started by arguing that in a mass production economy, spare capacity is the rule rather than the exception:

> Effective demand is not a matter of short-run vagaries; it is a matter of investment, i.e., of capital accumulation. The growth of capacity must keep in step with the growth of demand. This is the essence of the multiplier-accelerator process, more generally expressed as the capital stock

11. Just to bring some more confusion onto the stand of Radical or SSA authors on the issue of a wage-led growth strategy, I should add that during the Union for Radical Political Economics summer conference that I attended in Cape Cod in 1986, Weisskopf objected explicitly and vehemently to a recovery policy that would be based on higher wages.

> adjustment principle … . By contrast, the *fundamental* proposition of the Keynesian tradition is that neither in the short run nor in the long run is there any reason to suppose that this balance will be achieved at full capacity by the unregulated market, except by accident, or as a temporary phase in a cyclical movement. (Nell 1985: 175)

Nell then reiterates the argument that higher real wages are likely to generate an increase in consumer demand, and hence an induced increase in investment, as investment depends essentially on the rise in sales. Nell also picks up the Marx–Webb argument that higher real wages are likely to lead to rising labour productivity. All in all, Nell accuses Marglin and Marxian economists of providing support for conventional wisdom by assuming scarce resources when large portions of both capital and labour are idle.

> When output is determined by effective demand, investment governs current profitability, not the other way around … . First, modern economies have clearly not been operating at anything like full capacity during the past decade and a half. Raising wages would increase demand in consumer good markets. But, secondly, it would also increase the pressures on backward firms to modernise or go out of business … . In short, under suitable conditions raising wages may stimulate growth … . Marglin's framework, since it assumes Say's Law, cannot deal with these questions, and is forced to accept the position that austerity policies are nothing but simple 'economic logic', which any rational agent must accept. Conservatives could ask for no better defence. (Ibid.: 178)

Nell's arguments were formalized in the other critique of Marglin's paper, the one published by Amitava Dutt (1987), but of course they could already have been found in the neo-Kaleckian models of Rowthorn (1981) and Dutt (1984). These were models of growth where full capacity utilization was not assumed and hence where rates of capacity utilization were endogenous. Their investment functions, dependent on the profit rate and the rate of utilization, were such that growth was necessarily wage-led, a necessity that disappeared once international trade was taken into account, as shown later by Blecker (1989). It seems that these wage-led models as well as Nell's sarcastic critique of Marglin – the paper carried the name Jean-Baptiste Marglin in its title – hit a chord. By October 1987, when a large conference in the honour of Nicholas Kaldor was held at the New School in New York City and at the Levy Economics Institute, no fewer than four papers were presented with some link to the question being addressed by Nell. Skott presented his Goodwinian–Harrodian model that would be at the core of his book (1989) and which explained the business cycle as resulting from Harrodian instability and from the claim that the rate of capital accumulation is a non-linear negative function of the rate of employment. Boyer and Petit (1991) presented a growth model where they combined a demand regime and a productivity regime, which would become the prototype for the work later carried on by Servaas Storm and Ro Naastepad (2012). Heinz Kurz (1990) presented a fancy model, with three-dimensional diagrams and endogenous productivity, where investment was a function of the rate of utilization and a negative function of the real wage. Hence Kurz's model could generate either a wage-led or a profit-led demand regime, with the various combinations regarding the impact on the rate of utilization and the growth rate.

But although Kurz's paper arrived at similar results, the paper that turned out to generate the most attention, despite its rather messy presentation at the conference, was the one by Bhaduri and Marglin (1990), a version of which was published in the *Cambridge Journal of Economics*. The authors argued that the profit rate could be decomposed into a rate of utilization and a profit share, and hence that the investment function ought to depend on these two components. As I have contended on a number of occasions (Lavoie 1992), it is best to understand the profit share as being a proxy for the normal profit rate or expected profitability, for otherwise, as pointed out by two Kaleckians, Mott and Slattery (1994: 72), 'it is not clear to us why the level of the profit share, or height of the mark-up, should influence investment by itself'.[12]

In any case, the investment function proposed by Bhaduri and Marglin became highly popular among econometricians, so much that their model got called the *post-Kaleckian* model to distinguish it from the previous formalization (Hein 2014; Lavoie 2014). Besides the benefit of dealing with measurable variables (the profit share, rather than the profit rate), a big advantage of this model, as was the case with the Kurz model, is that

> particular *models* such as that of 'cooperative capitalism' enunciated by the left Keynesian social democrats, the Marxian model of 'profit squeeze' or even the conservative model relying on 'supply-side' stimulus through high profitability and a low real wage rate, fit into the more general Keynesian theoretical scheme. They become particular *variants* of the theoretical framework presented here. (Bhaduri/Marglin 1990: 388)

Thus the post-Kaleckian Marglin and Bhaduri model allowed for a (partial) reunification of the Marxian and post-Keynesian strands of heterodox macroeconomics under a single umbrella, and the rest is history.

## 6 OVERHEAD LABOUR COSTS DO MATTER

In a workshop organized by the Post-Keynesian Economics Study Group (PKSG) in the UK, Simon Mohun was asked in November 2011 to provide an assessment of the chapters found in the book on post-Keynesian economics edited by Hein and Stockhammer (2011). Mohun listed what he considered to be ten missing elements. One of them was the distinction between overhead or indirect labour and direct labour. This corresponds in the US to the distinction between supervisory workers and non-supervisory workers, the former group being identified as managers, or in French as *cadres*. It is my opinion that the omission of overhead labour has detrimental consequences on our understanding of what happens during the business cycle. It has contributed to the belief, among a number of Marxian-inspired authors, that an increase in the profit share has positive effects on aggregate demand.

Overhead labour costs were included in the neo-Kaleckian growth model of Rowthorn (1981), and could be found in some of the later versions (Kurz 1990; Nichols/Norton 1991; Lavoie 1992; 1995; 2009; Dutt 2012; Nikiforos 2015). The absence of 'permanent administrative staff' was noted by Bhaduri and Marglin (1990: 377), but despite this the large majority of the neo- or post-Kaleckian models assumed away overhead labour. As a consequence, and probably also for lack of adequate data, empirical studies devoted to the

12. Mott and Slattery (1994) also objected that Bhaduri and Marglin's investment function should depend on actual profits and not on some hypothetical measure of profits. A similar argument was made by Kazimierz Łaski, as pointed out in his obituary by Martin Riese (2016). Łaski, who had been a long-time collaborator of Kalecki and a frequent co-author of Bhaduri, always strongly objected to the concept of a profit-led economy. Łaski argued that one had to take into account Kalecki's distinction between the investment decision and the investment execution, which occurred with a time lag. As a result, lowering wages first induces a fall in consumption sales, before any change in investment expenditures can occur. The actual rate of profit thus remains unaffected while the rate of utilization falls. As a consequence, said Łaski (2004), a lower wage share would not induce firms to invest more; rather, it would induce them to reduce investment. Łaski held on to this position until the very end of his career (Łaski/Walther 2015: 140–141).

demand regimes also omitted the possibility of overhead labour. Strangely, overhead labour was very seriously taken into account in the earlier studies on the characteristics of business cycles.

Weisskopf (1979: 354, emphasis in original) mentions that 'certain types of labour – e.g. administrative, supervisory and maintenance employees – may be characterised as "overhead labour" in the sense that they must be employed in proportion to the *capacity* of an enterprise', which is exactly how Rowthorn (1981) formalized the introduction of overhead labour in his neo-Kaleckian model. As a consequence, a rise in the profit share may just as well occur as a result of an increase in the rate of utilization as it could have as a result of a drop in the strength or bargaining power of labour. Weisskopf thus proceeded to compute a 'true' wage share, corrected for this effect due to overhead labour. Once the correction is made, it appears that changes in the profit rate during the first phase of the upswing and the downswing are nearly entirely due to changes in the rate of capacity utilization. Only in the second phase of the upswing do we see changes in the (falling) profit share playing any important role in the determination of the profit rate. Table 1 shows the evolution of the various components of the profit rate, as estimated by Weisskopf (1979), uncorrected and corrected for the impact of overhead labour. Incidentally, looking at these numbers, it is hard to understand how, as assumed by Goodwinian–Marxian authors, a recovery spontaneously led by corporate investment could occur when profit rates are at their lowest. We shall later argue that external drivers are needed for the recovery.

Howard Sherman (1979) immediately interpreted Weisskopf's findings as a dismissal of the Boddy and Crotty thesis. In their book, Sherman and Evans (1984: 277) attach great importance to the role played by overhead labour costs in explaining the evolution of the profit share through the business cycle, as they claim that 'the rapid rise of output demanded and capacity utilization produce an enormous rise in productivity, mainly because of a declining ratio of overhead labor to output'. The importance of overhead labour is reiterated when they summarize their views:

> In most of expansion, the wage share declines mostly because productivity rises, which is mainly due to falling overhead labor proportionate to all labour. While productivity is rising, real wages do not rise as fast in early expansion mainly because of the institutional fact that capitalists automatically own the increased product while workers must struggle for a share of that increase through the bargaining process and other means of industrial strife. Near the cycle peak of expansion, the wage share rises a little because productivity is flat or falling while real wages continue to rise; bargaining power is high because of a high level of employment. In most of contraction, the wage share rises because of falling productivity, owing mainly to a rising percentage of overhead

*Table 1 Average annual rates of growth of the three components of the profit rate through the three phases of the business cycle, unadjusted and corrected for overhead labour costs*

| | Early expansion | | Late expansion | | Recession | |
|---|---|---|---|---|---|---|
| | U | C | U | C | U | C |
| Profit rate | +26.8 | | −10.1 | | −25.3 | |
| Profit share | +17.0 | +3.4 | −8.8 | −9.7 | −15.6 | +4.7 |
| Utilization rate | +10.8 | +27.4 | +0.5 | +1.4 | −11.9 | −32.1 |
| Capacity/capital | −1.1 | −1.1 | −1.8 | −1.8 | +2.1 | +2.1 |

*Note:* C = corrected for overhead labour costs; U = unadjusted.
*Source:* Weisskopf (1979: tables 4 and 7).

> labor to all labor. Finally, at the end of the contraction, the wage share begins to fall again because of the weakness of labor owing to high unemployment. (Sherman/Evans 1984: 200)[13]

Thus, as argued by Weisskopf and also by Sherman and Evans, in an economy with overhead labour, all else being equal, that is, with no change whatsoever in the mark-up over unit direct labour costs, an increase in the rate of utilization leads to an increase in the share of profits. Thus, unless the measures of the profit share are corrected for this effect, statistical enquiries will be biased towards finding that aggregate demand is profit-led.

But there are further problems to consider when overhead costs are explicitly introduced into a neo-Kaleckian model with the standard assumptions, such as a propensity to save out of wages equal to zero. It turns out that the profit share is a poor indicator of the potential profitability of firms. With prices determined by a target-return formula, an increase in the target rate of return might lead to an increase in the profit share, as one would expect; but for some parameter configurations, once all aggregate demand effects have been taken into consideration, a higher target rate of return might induce lower profit shares. Thus the profit share as measured by the national accountants can either increase or decrease when firms manage to implement higher costing margins or higher target rates of return into their prices, and hence reduce real wages (Lavoie 1995; 2009). What this means is that, with given labour productivity, a decrease in the real wage may actually lead to an increase in the wage share once all the effects on aggregate demand have been taken into account. As Rowthorn (1981: 21) puts it, 'this all goes to show how misleading it can be to argue in terms of the profit share, rather than the rate of profit, when the economy is operating below full capacity'. Thus one can only agree with Nichols and Norton (1991: 53) who claimed that with the consideration of a third class, that is, overhead labour, 'a stagnationist model so generalized is capable of yielding a broader range of capitalist dynamics than the traditional stagnationist framework allowed'.

This demonstrates that the net profit share is not a reliable indicator of potential profitability when there are managerial costs, and to incorporate the profit share in an investment equation, as Bhaduri and Marglin (1990) do, appears to be a second-best solution. Thus, in contrast to what seems to be the implicit assumption of a large number of empirical studies, the evolution of wage shares or profit shares, that is the slope of the aggregate demand relation between the wage share and the rate of utilization is not necessarily an appropriate indicator of the bargaining power of labour or of capitalists, unless one succeeds in taking adequate care of cyclical effects by incorporating the evolution of overhead labour costs. As Nikiforos and Foley (2012: 219–220, emphasis in original) say in a similar context:

> We have to move one step further from the characterization of an economy as wage-led if the slope of the demand curve is positive and profit-led if it is negative. We provide an alternative definition; *an economy is profit-led when a distributive or technological change against the wage share leads to a higher equilibrium level of capacity utilization.*

Unfortunately, this is more easily said than done, as it seems that only the USA has adequate data on the labour share of supervisory workers, most likely a good enough proxy for overhead labour (Mohun 2006). The explosion in the availability of data about rich households may however help compensate for this problem.

13. Retrospectively, I note that my graphical description of the evolution of the profit share and its causes through the business cycle corresponds fairly well to that of Sherman and Evans (Lavoie 2014: 426–427).

## 7 THE SHARE OF EARNED INCOME VERSUS THE SHARE OF WORKER WAGES

There is a second issue related to the fact that the pay of highly ranked managers is included within the wage share. As has been shown by Piketty (2014) and others, these managers have succeeded in increasing their share of labour income. Mohun (2014) has also shown that the wage share going to supervisory workers has dramatically increased over time in the US. Because their propensity to save is likely to be much higher than that of non-supervisory workers whose pay can be dozens of times smaller, this change in the share of labour income collected by highly paid managers is not innocuous and may once more bias the measure of the demand regime towards the appearance of a profit-led regime. This has been underlined in particular in a number of papers by Tom Palley. The argument is the following. It may be that the share of wages has gone up, but if the split between managers or overhead labour has been modified in favour of the managers, the consequences for aggregate consumption and aggregate demand are likely to be negative. Thus, while empirical studies would assess that the demand regime seems to be profit-led, this would occur because mistakenly a third class – the managers (or overhead labour) – has not been taken into consideration. Till van Treeck (2015: 162), for this reason, has also expressed his distrust at the standard empirical method to assess demand regimes on the basis of functional income.

In the neo-Kaleckian model with target-return pricing evoked earlier, things get really messy when one tries to assess the impact of an increase in the pay check taken by managers (an increase in overhead labour costs) on the rate of utilization, the rate of profit or the share of profit, even while still assuming that ordinary workers save nothing. First, the impact, once all aggregate demand effects are brought in, depends on whether the economy is operating below or beyond the standard rate of capacity utilization (Lavoie 2014: 420–421). The only sure thing is that an increase in the remuneration of overhead labour cost will induce a rise in the share of income obtained by overhead labour while it will lead to a fall in the share of income held by ordinary workers. Anything goes for the share of profits: it may rise or fall as a result of the increase in managers' pay. Empirical studies may show that a decrease in the profit share has been accompanied by a decrease in the rate of utilization, thus leading one to conclude that the demand regime is profit-led, whereas the share of income going to direct labour will have fallen.

In previous works and in a recent IMK working paper, Palley (2017) argues that a modified version of Pasinetti's model should be put forward: one ought to consider manager–capitalists, who receive salaries and hence a share of earned income and a share of profits, mainly based on their share of financial capital; and then there are the ordinary workers, who receive wages and hence a share of earned income, but who also receive a share of profits, based on their past savings. What will happen to utilization rates, profit rates and growth rates when a change occurs that will actually depend on the values taken by these various shares, the shares of profits and earned income, and the parameters of the investment and those of the various saving functions? It follows that the growth and inequality relationship depends, among other things, on what one can consider to be the deep parameters of income distribution noted above. Palley (2017) further warns that in a country where the share of earned income going to the salaries of managers has been rising, while the shares of profits and hence those of wages going to workers have been shrinking, the standard econometric assessment of the demand regime may conclude that the economy is profit-led. Thus, as in the case of overhead labour discussed above, it would be best to distinguish between the income of managers and that of ordinary workers so as to assess appropriately the demand regime. Palley (2017) also points out that, as long as the propensity to consume of ordinary workers is higher than that of managers, an increase in the share of wages going to workers will always lead to an improvement of economic activity, regardless of whether the economy as assessed in the standard way appears to be wage-led or profit-led. Thus, this should be where efforts at changing the primary and secondary income distributions should be directed to, an advice which is given empirical credence by Carvalho and Rezai (2016) and Stockhammer and Wildauer (2016).

## 8 TAKING A WIDER ANGLE

Notwithstanding the above complications, there is a growing recognition that assessing whether there are profit-led or wage-led demand regimes needs to take account of many other factors that affect aggregate demand, such as government expenditures, residential investment and the financialization process, as can be measured by the relative size of the financial sector, the importance of debt ratios and the evolution of various financial variables.

As recalled by Hein (2017), a large number of recent post-Keynesian and Institutionalist publications have pointed to the importance of conspicuous consumption and consumption emulation, as well as consumer debt. Kapeller and Schütz (2015) argue that, when these effects are taken into account, an increase in the profit share at the expense of ordinary workers that leaves the managerial class unaffected may induce the former to ask and obtain additional sources of funds by borrowing from banks in an effort to keep up with the consumption and housing expenditures of the managerial class. Thus, at least for a time, an increase in the profit share may be associated with an increase in economic activity, providing the illusion that the economy is profit-led whereas in fact it was debt-led or consumption-led.

A similar point has recently been made forcefully in the context of business cycles by Stockhammer and Michell (2017). They argue that they can generate clockwise loops between utilization rates and profit shares, despite assuming away any feedback effect of the wage and profit shares on demand, or even by incorporating a wage-led demand regime. They do so by assuming a profit-squeeze mechanism (that is, there exists a distributive curve where higher rates of utilization generate higher real wages) and by introducing a Goodwin-like predator–prey mechanism based on Minsky's financial fragility hypothesis whereby the rate of change of fragility increases with higher output and where the change in output gets slowed down by financial fragility.[14] Thus clockwise loops in the utilization rate and profit share plane do not necessarily involve a profit-led demand regime.

Brett Fiebiger (2017) has presented another explanation of the clockwise loops involving the profit share that are neither associated with Minsky cycles nor with the standard Marxian interpretation. This explanation can be associated with the so-called Sraffian supermultiplier story (Freitas/Serrano 2015) and the revised neo-Kaleckian model with autonomous expenditures (Lavoie 2016). Fiebiger argues that the evolution of what he calls the semi-autonomous household expenditures, meaning here residential investment and consumption expenditures financed by credit, have always been a key mover of (US) economic growth, not just before the Great Recession. He shows that there also exist systematic clockwise cycles between the corporate profit share and the output shares of household fixed investment and semi-autonomous expenditures with respect to the rate of employment and the rate of utilization, whereas the profit share does not closely follow

14. Ironically, their Minsky cycle is inspired by the work of Skott (1994), whose critiques of the Kaleckian view are inspired by the Goodwinian interpretation of these clockwise loops.

the output share of corporate fixed investment, especially around troughs. Indeed, he shows that while the growth rates of corporate fixed investment are strongly correlated with past GDP and corporate profits, the growth rates of economic activity and corporate profits are themselves most strongly correlated with contemporaneous household fixed investment expenditures and household semi-autonomous expenditures.

Thus, according to Fiebiger, it is the fluctuations in the fixed investment of households and their debt-financed consumption that drive most of the business cycle, with the cyclical evolution of the profit share being essentially explained by the existence of overhead labour costs. As to the investment of the corporate sector it is essentially reacting to the evolution of its sales. Fiebiger's assessment is roughly consistent with the econometric results of Stockhammer and Wildauer (2016) according to whom OECD countries are in a weak wage-led demand regime, with changes in aggregate demand being mostly driven by the evolution of household debt and property prices. It is also consistent with Barbosa-Filho et al.'s (2008: 630) remark to the effect that the US economy demand regime is 'household net borrowing led'. This was also the claim of Leamer (2007) when he titled his paper 'housing is the business cycle' and when he affirmed in his conclusion that 'it's a consumer cycle, not a business cycle' (ibid.: 51).

## 9 PRODUCTIVITY EFFECTS ALSO COMPLICATE MATTERS

Virtually everything so far has been about demand regimes. Hardly anything has been said about productivity regimes or the highly interesting works that combine the productivity regimes with the demand regimes. Taking into account the effects of higher real wages or higher wage shares will force us to take a broader look at the issue of demand or employment regimes. As was mentioned in an earlier section, Marxian authors from the SSA school did at some point advocate a wage-led productivity growth strategy, while the study of the combined productivity and demand regimes were a feature of the French Regulation school, as exemplified by the 1987 Kaldor conference paper of Boyer and Petit (1991). Noteworthy in this regard is the paper by Hein and Tarassow (2010), but I will focus on the formalization of Storm and Naastepad (2013).

Informal arguments – the same as those offered by Bowles et al. (1984), as outlined earlier – as well as empirical estimates lead us to assert that there is a positive direct effect of faster real wage growth (noted $w$ in Figure 1) on labour productivity growth (noted $p$): the Marx–Webb effect. But there is also an indirect effect, arising from the Kaldor–Verdoorn law, according to which faster output growth (noted $x$) generates faster productivity growth. Thus while in a wage-led demand regime these two effects reinforce each other, so that the productivity regime is necessarily wage-led, the two effects will go in opposite directions in the case of the profit-led demand regime, meaning that in this case the productivity regime could be either wage-led or profit-led. In addition, one would also need to assess the feedback effects of the change in productivity growth on the wage share, which would drop if the productivity change is positive. All these effects are represented in Figure 1.[15] To read the figure, one starts with the growth rate of real wages.

The bottom of the figure illustrates a problem of wage-led growth that has been underlined by Storm and Naastepad (2013; 2017). While the demand regime may be clearly wage-led, once the Marx–Webb and Kaldor–Verdoorn effects are taken into account, it is far from clear that the employment regime will turn out to be wage-led as well, since there is no guarantee that the increase in the growth rate of aggregate demand will surpass

15. Which I wish I had included in my 2014 book!

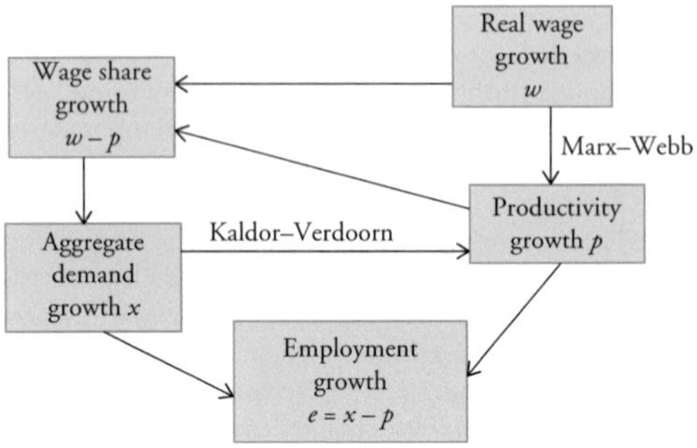


*Figure 1 Combined demand and productivity effects of an increase in the growth rate of real wages*

that of the growth rate of labour productivity (with the growth rate of employment, noted $e$, being equal by definition to $x - p$). Indeed, Storm and Naastepad argue on the basis of their theoretical model that with standard empirical estimates of the various effects, it is likely that a wage-led demand regime will correspond to a profit-led employment regime. This conclusion is less likely to occur if one modifies their theoretical model by adding, for instance, a feedback effect of the rate of productivity growth on the rate of accumulation, as Kalecki had suggested. Still, all this reminds us of the previous warning of Bowles and Boyer to the effect that output and employment growth may not move together once the productivity effects of faster output growth are taken into account: 'If productivity growth is strongly wage-led, it is unlikely that employment will be wage-led (Bowles/Boyer 1995: 145).

The obvious answer to this conundrum is that a wage-led growth strategy must also incorporate expansionary monetary and fiscal policies. This is the solution offered by Storm and Naastepad (2013; 2017) and it must be noted that, in their recent papers, advocates of a wage-led growth strategy have underlined the need for a wage-led recovery to be accompanied by expansionary fiscal policies (Onaran 2016). This is also in line with the position that was promoted by Palley (2011) when discussing a possible wage-led recovery program: besides reforming the labour market so as to give more bargaining power to ordinary workers and less to top managers and executives, there also has to be a fiscal stimulus program.

## 10 CONCLUSION

Ever since the empirical study by Bowles and Boyer (1995), a lot of effort has been devoted to finding whether economies are wage-led or profit-led. Although researchers agree that productivity regimes are wage-led, there still is no consensus among the heterodox community regarding whether economies are in a wage-led or profit-led demand regime, meaning here either the rate of utilization or the rate of growth of output. What I have contended in this paper is that, broadly speaking, while all heterodox authors involved in these debates have some ties with Kalecki and/or Kaldor, heterodox authors closer to the post-Keynesian tradition have tended to find and to argue that aggregate demand is wage-led, at least when domestic demand is considered in contrast to total aggregate demand inclusive of net exports, whereas heterodox authors who have more Marxian longings tend to find and to argue that aggregate demand is profit-led. I have shown however that this correspondence is far from being perfect, and that some authors have tended to oscillate in a very puzzling way in advocating or disparaging a wage-led growth strategy.

I have also maintained that this split goes back to the mid 1970s, with the study of Boddy and Crotty (1975) that claimed that the initial segment of the expansion in a business cycle was accompanied by a rising profit share, whereas the second segment of this expansion involved a falling profit share. This gave rise to the belief that aggregate demand was profit-led and that expansion was being halted by a profit squeeze. This finding was reinforced by the detailed study of Weisskopf (1979), who used the same three-period split, arriving at the same results with regard to the evolution of the profit share. This led members of the SSA school and followers of Lance Taylor, as can be verified from their writings, to believe that some sort of Goodwinian business cycle, based on profit-led demand and a profit-squeeze distributive curve, could explain the short-period cyclical evolution of the American economy. It has also led various authors with a Marxian background to find explanations as to why high real wages or high employment rates would eventually lead to an endogenous turnaround in economic activity.

All of this was coherent with the long-run version of the Marxian model, where higher saving rates and higher profit shares allow for faster accumulation, as was presented by Marglin (1984a). His article, however, induced responses by post-Keynesians, who objected that a medium-run analysis did not need to be associated with full-capacity utilization, and that higher real wages would speed up accumulation, as had been shown in the previous papers of Rowthorn (1981) and Dutt (1984). One can thus understand the Bhaduri and Marglin (1990) model as the Kaleckian–Marxian response to these Kaleckian–Keynesian growth models and objections, endeavouring to counteract that even with endogenous rates of utilization and Keynesian output determination, higher profit shares could induce faster growth. As we now know, the investment function of their paper, which included the profit share rather than the profit rate, facilitated empirical analysis and gave rise to the observed boom in econometric studies devoted to the determination of demand regimes.

Still, other students of business cycles, some with a Marxian background like Howard Sherman, have emphasized that the apparent positive relationship between profit shares and economic activity in the first part of the upswing and in the downswing could be almost entirely attributed to the existence of overhead labour costs – a claim that was confirmed with the help of corrected measures of wage shares by Weisskopf (1979) himself. While the rise of the labour share in the latter part of the upswing was not denied, the slowdown in economic activity before the peak was instead attributed to external factors, such as restrictive monetary or fiscal policies. More recently, it has been argued by Fiebiger (2017) that these external factors can be mostly associated with the behaviour of household residential investment and with household consumption out of credit – what he calls semi-autonomous expenditures – and hence that the slowdown in corporate investment is the result of stagnating or falling sales rather than the consequence of a fall in the profit share (or a rise in the employment rate). It would perhaps be best to say that economies are led in cyclical terms by the net financial borrowing of households. It is these effects and the presence of overhead costs that would explain the (weak) profit-led demand regimes obtained by Barbosa-Filho and Taylor (2006) and Kiefer and Rada (2015) on the basis of quarterly data and short-term dynamics.[16]

16. Kiefer and Rada (2015: 1346) appear to be somewhat mystified by the apparent long-run positive relationship between the wage share and capacity utilization. Their explanation is that in their (successful) efforts to reduce the wage share, governments have pursued austerity policies that have shifted down aggregate demand and reduced the average rate of utilization.

The presence of overhead labour, associated with supervisory workers, managers and executives poses a problem for the empirical exercises that are being pursued to identify demand regimes. In my view, and in that of Palley (2017), they are likely to bias the results towards profit-led demand regimes. Still, for those who have some confidence in the results achieved by researchers using single-equation techniques, there seems to be some consensus that domestic demand is wage-led in all countries that have been examined, while overall demand (including net exports) is wage-led in a large number of countries (Hartwig 2014; Onaran/Galanis 2014; Onaran/Obst 2016; Stockhammer/Wildauer 2016). Since productivity is also wage-led, even if some countries turn out to have their overall demand profit-led, it follows that a cooperation on a wage-led strategy that would be advocated by large international organizations like the OECD, UNCTAD, the IMF, the ILO or the G20 could turn out to be highly successful in raising economic activity and productivity, if that is the objective.[17] However, as shown by Storm and Naastepad (2013), the fact that demand regimes are wage-led does not necessarily imply that employment regimes are also wage-led. Expansionary fiscal policies are likely to be needed, something towards which the IMF seems more inclined now, or reductions in the length of the working week may be required.

In conclusion, it should be pointed out, as noted by Palley (2017), that demand regimes are not set in stone: they can be endogenized by some economic policies. For instance, a more progressive tax system or lower taxes on wage income relative to unearned income, by modifying the distribution of disposable income between classes and individuals with different propensities to consume, will transform an economic system towards a more wage-led demand regime.

## REFERENCES


Barbosa-Filho, N., Taylor, L. (2006): Distributive and demand cycles in the US economy: a structuralist Goodwin model, in: *Metroeconomica*, 57(3), 389–411.

Barbosa-Filho, N., Rada, C., Taylor, L., Zamparelli, L. (2008): Cycles and trends in US net borrowing flows, in: *Journal of Post Keynesian Economics*, 30(4), 623–647.

Bhaduri, A., Marglin, S. (1990): Unemployment and the real wage: the economic basis for contesting political ideologies, in: *Cambridge Journal of Economics*, 14(4), 375–393.

Blecker, R.A. (1989): International competition, income distribution and economic growth, in: *Cambridge Journal of Economics*, 13(3), 395–412.

Blecker, R.A. (2016): Wage-led versus profit-led demand regimes: the long and the short of it, in: *Review of Keynesian Economics*, 4(4), 373–390.

Boddy, R., Crotty, J. (1975): Class conflict and macro policy: the political business cycle, in: *Review of Radical and Political Economics*, 7(1), 1–19.

Bowles, S., Boyer, R. (1988): Labor discipline and aggregate demand: a macroeconomic model, in: *American Economic Review*, 78(2), 395–400.

Bowles, S., Boyer, R. (1990): A wage-led employment regime: income distribution, labour discipline, and aggregate demand in welfare capitalism, in: Marglin, S.A., Schor, J.B. (eds), *The Golden Age of Capitalism: Reinterpreting the Postwar Experience*, Oxford: Clarendon Press, 187–217.

Bowles, S., Boyer, R. (1995): Wages, aggregate demand, and employment in an open economy: an empirical investigation, in: Epstein, G., Gintis, H. (eds), *Macroeconomic Policy After the Conservative Era*, Cambridge, UK: Cambridge University Press, 143–171.

Bowles, S., Gordon, D.M., Weisskopf, T.E. (1984): A progressive alternative to economic and social renewal, Working paper for Policy Alternatives, no 2, Canadian Centre for Policy Alternatives.


17. The objective may change in the future, due to ecological and global warming issues.

Bowles, S., Gordon, D.M., Weisskopf, T.E. (1990): *After the Wasteland*, Armonk, NY: M.E. Sharpe.

Boyer, R., Petit, P. (1991): Kaldor's growth theories: past, present and prospects for the future, in: Nell, E.J., Semmler, W. (eds), *Nicholas Kaldor and Mainstream Economics: Confrontation or Convergence?*, London: Macmillan, 485–517.

Carvalho, L., Rezai, A. (2016): Personal income inequality and aggregate demand, in: *Cambridge Journal of Economics*, 40(2), 491–505.

Dutt, A.K. (1984): Stagnation, income distribution and monopoly power, in: *Cambridge Journal of Economics*, 8(1), 25–40.

Dutt, A.K. (1987): Alternative closures again: a comment on growth, distribution and inflation, in: *Cambridge Journal of Economics*, 11(1), 75–82.

Dutt, A.K. (2012): Growth, distribution and crises, in: Herr, H., Niechoj, T., Thomasberger, C., Truger, A., van Treeck, T. (eds), *From Crisis to Growth? The Challenge of Debt and Imbalances*, Marburg: Metropolis, 33–59.

Epstein, G., Gintis, H. (1995): Macroeconomic policies for sustainable growth, in: Epstein, G., Gintis, H. (eds), *Macroeconomic Policy After the Conservative Era*, Cambridge, UK: Cambridge University Press, 3–17.

Fiebiger, B. (2017): Semi-autonomous household expenditures as the *causa causans* of post-war U.S. business cycles: the stability and instability of Luxemburg-type external markets, in: *Cambridge Journal of Economics*, Advanced access, doi: 10.1093/cje/bex019.

Foley, D.K., Michl, T. (1999): *Growth and Distribution*, Cambridge, MA: Harvard University Press.

Freitas, F., Serrano, F. (2015): Growth rate and level effects: the stability of the adjustment of capacity to demand and the Sraffian supermultiplier, in: *Review of Political Economy*, 27(3), 258–281.

Goldstein, J.P., Hillard, M.G. (2009): Introduction: a second-generation synthesis of heterodox macroeconomic principles, in: Goldstein, J.P., Hillard, M.G. (eds), *Heterodox Macroeconomics: Keynes, Marx and Globalization*, London: Routledge, 3–23.

Gordon, D.M. (1995): Growth, distribution, and the rules of the game: social structuralist macro foundations for a democratic economic policy, in: Epstein, G., Gintis, H. (eds), *Macroeconomic Policy After the Conservative Era*, Cambridge, UK: Cambridge University Press, 335–384.

Hartwig, J. (2014): Testing the Bhaduri–Marglin model with OECD panel data, in: *International Review of Applied Economics*, 28(4), 419–435.

Hein, E. (2014): *Distribution and Growth After Keynes: A Post-Keynesian Guide*, Cheltenham, UK and Northampton, MA: Edward Elgar.

Hein, E. (2017): Post-Keynesian macroeconomics since the mid 1990s: main developments, in: *European Journal of Economics and Economic Policies: Intervention*, 14(2), 131–172.

Hein, E., Stockhammer, E. (eds) (2011): *A Modern Guide to Keynesian Macroeconomics and Economic Policies*, Cheltenham, UK and Northampton, MA: Edward Elgar.

Hein, E., Tarassow, A. (2010): Distribution, aggregate demand and productivity growth: theory and empirical results for six OECD countries based on a post-Kaleckian model, in: *Cambridge Journal of Economics*, 34(4), 727–754.

Kapeller, J., Schütz, B. (2015): Conspicuous consumption, inequality and debt: the nature of consumption-driven profit-led regimes, in: *Metroeconomica*, 66(1), 51–70.

Kiefer, D., Rada, C. (2015): Profit maximising goes global: the race to the bottom, in: *Cambridge Journal of Economics*, 39(5), 1333–1350.

Kurz, H.D. (1990): Technical change, growth and distribution: a steady state approach to unsteady growth, in: Kurz, H.D., *Capital, Distribution and Effective Demand: Studies in the Classical Approach to Economic Theory*, Cambridge, UK: Polity Press, 210–239.

Łaski, K. (2004): Macroeconomics versus 'common sense', Vienna Institute for International Economic Studies, wiiw working paper #33.

Łaski, K., Walter, H. (2015): Kalecki's profit equation after 80 years, in: Toporowski, J., Mamica, L. (eds), *Michal Kalecki in the 21st Century*, Basingstoke, UK: Palgrave Macmillan, 131–156.

Lavoie, M. (1992): *Foundations of Post-Keynesian Economic Analysis*, Aldershot, UK and Brookfield, VT: Edward Elgar.

Lavoie, M. (1995): The Kaleckian model of growth and distribution and its neo-Ricardian and neo-Marxian critiques, in: *Cambridge Journal of Economics*, 19(6), 789–818.

Lavoie, M. (2009): Cadrisme within a Kaleckian model of growth and distribution, in: *Review of Political Economy*, 21(3), 371–393.
Lavoie, M. (2014): *Post-Keynesian Economics: New Foundations*, Cheltenham, UK and Northampton, MA: Edward Elgar.
Lavoie, M. (2016): Convergence towards the normal rate of capacity utilization in neo-Kaleckian models: the role of non-capacity creating autonomous expenditures, in: *Metroeconomica*, 67(1), 172–201.
Leamer, E.E. (2007): Housing *is* the business cycle, NBER working paper, URL: http://www.nber.org/papers/w13428.
Marglin, S.A. (1984a): Growth, distribution and inflation: a centennial synthesis, in: *Cambridge Journal of Economics*, 8(2), 115–144.
Marglin, S.A. (1984b): *Growth, Distribution and Prices*, Cambridge, MA: Harvard University Press.
Mohun, S. (2006): Distributive shares in the US economy, 1964–2000, in: *Cambridge Journal of Economics*, 30(3), 347–370.
Mohun, S. (2014): Unproductive labor in the U.S. economy: 1964–2010, in: *Review of Radical Political Economics*, 46(3), 355–379.
Mott, T., Slattery, E. (1994): The influence of changes in income distribution on aggregate demand in a Kaleckian model: stagnation vs exhilaration reconsidered, in: Davidson, P., Kregel, J.A. (eds), *Employment, Growth and Finance*, Cheltenham, UK and Northampton, MA: Edward Elgar, 69–82.
Nell, E.J. (1985): Jean Baptiste Marglin: a comment on growth, distribution and inflation, in: *Cambridge Journal of Economics*, 9(2), 173–178.
Nichols, L.M., Norton, N. (1991): Overhead workers and political economy macro models, in: *Review of Radical Political Economy*, 23(1–2), 47–54.
Nikiforos, M. (2015): Uncertainty and contradiction: an essay on the business cycle, in: *Review of Radical Political Economics*, doi: 10.1177/0486613415621748.
Nikiforos, M., Foley, D.K. (2012): Distribution and capacity utilization: conceptual issues and empirical evidence, in: *Metroeconomica*, 63(1), 200–229.
Onaran, Ö. (2016): Wage- versus profit-led growth in the context of globalization and public spending: the political aspects of wage-led growth, in: *Review of Keynesian Economics*, 4(4), 458–474.
Onaran, Ö., Galanis, G. (2012): Is aggregate demand wage-led or profit-led? National and global effects, Working paper no 40, Conditions of Work and Employment Series, International Labour Office.
Onaran, Ö., Galanis, G. (2014): Income distribution and growth: a global model, in: *Environment and Planning A*, 46(10), 2489–2513.
Onaran, Ö., Obst, T. (2016): Wage-led growth in EU15 member states: the effects of income distribution on growth, employment, trade balance and inflation, in: *Cambridge Journal of Economics*, doi: 10.1093/cje/bew009.
Palley, T.I. (2011): The economics of wage-led recovery: analysis and recommendations, in: *International Journal of Labour Research*, 3(2), 219–244.
Palley, T.I. (2017): Wage- vs profit-led growth: the role of the distribution of wages in determining regime character, in: *Cambridge Journal of Economics*, 41(1), 49–61.
Piketty, T. (2014): *Capital in the Twenty-First Century*, Cambridge, MA: Harvard University Press.
Riese, M. (2016): Obituary: Kaziemierz Laski (1921–2015), in: *European Journal of Economics and Economic Policies: Intervention*, 13(3), 265–274.
Rowthorn, B. (1981): Demand, real wages and economic growth, in: *Thames Papers in Political Economy*, Autumn, 1–39.
Schefold, B. (1983): Kahn on Malinvaud, in: Eatwell, J., Milgate, M. (eds), *Keynes's Economics and the Theory of Value and Distribution*, Oxford: Oxford University Press, 229–246.
Setterfield, M. (2016): Wage- versus profit-led growth after 25 years: an introduction, in: *Review of Keynesian Economics*, 4(4), 367–372.
Sherman, J.J. (1979): A Marxist theory of the business cycle, in: *Review of Radical Political Economics*, 11(1), 1–23.
Sherman, H.J., Evans, G.R. (1984): *Macroeconomics: Keynesian, Monetarist and Marxist Views*, New York: Harper & Row.

Skott, P. (1989): *Conflict and Effective Demand in Economic Growth*, Cambridge, UK: Cambridge University Press.

Skott, P. (1994): On the modeling of systemic financial fragility, in: Dutt, A.K. (ed.), *New Directions in Analytical Political Economy*, Aldershot, UK and Brookfield, VT: Edward Elgar, 49–76.

Skott, P. (2010): Growth, instability and cycles, in: Setterfield, M. (ed.), *Handbook of Alternative Theories of Economic Growth*, Cheltenham, UK and Northampton, MA: Edward Elgar, 108–131.

Skott, P. (2017): Weaknesses of 'wage-led growth', in: *Review of Keynesian Economics*, 5(3), 336–359.

Skott, P., Zipperer, B. (2011): Cyclical patterns of employment, utilization, and profitability, in: *Journal of Post Keynesian Economics*, 34(1), 25–57.

Stockhammer, E. (2017): Wage-led versus profit-led demand: what have we learned? A Kaleckian–Minskyan view, in: *Review of Keynesian Economics*, 5(1), 25–42.

Stockhammer, E., Michell, J. (2017): Pseudo-Goodwin cycles in a Minsky model, in: *Cambridge Journal of Economics*, 41(1), 105–125.

Stockhammer, E., Onaran, Ö. (2013): Wage-led growth: theory, evidence, policy, in: *Review of Keynesian Economics*, 1(1), 61–78.

Stockhammer, E., Stehrer, R. (2011): Goodwin or Kalecki in demand? Functional income distribution and aggregate demand in the short run, in: *Review of Radical Political Economics*, 43(4), 506–522.

Stockhammer, E., Wildauer, R. (2016): Debt-driven growth? Wealth, distribution and demand in OECD countries, in: *Cambridge Journal of Economics*, 40(6), 1609–1634.

Storm, S., Naastepad, C.W.M. (2012): *Macroeconomics Beyond the NAIRU*, Cambridge, MA: Harvard University Press.

Storm, S., Naastepad, C.W.M. (2013): Wage-led or profit-led supply: wages, productivity and investment, in: Lavoie, M., Stockhammer, E. (eds), *Wage-led Growth: An Equitable Strategy for Economic Recovery*, Basingstoke, UK: Palgrave Macmillan, 100–124.

Storm, S., Naastepad, C.W.M. (2017): Bhaduri–Marglin meets Kaldor–Marx: wages, productivity and investment, in: *Review of Keynesian Economics*, 5(1), 4–24.

Szymanski, A. (1984): Productivity growth and capitalist stagnation, in: *Science & Society*, 48(3), 295–322.

Taylor, L. (1983): *Structuralist Macroeconomics: Applicable Models for the Third World*, New York: Basic Books.

Taylor, L. (1991): *Income Distribution, Inflation and Growth: Lectures on Structuralist Macroeconomic Theory*, Cambridge, MA: MIT Press.

Taylor L. (2004): *Reconstructing Macroeconomics: Structuralist Proposals and Critiques of the Mainstream*, Cambridge, MA: Harvard University Press.

Van Treeck, T. (2015): Inequality, the crisis, and stagnation, in: *European Journal of Economics and Economic Policies: Intervention*, 12(2), 158–169.

Weisskopf, T.E. (1979): Marxian crisis theory and the rate of profit in the postwar U.S. economy, in: *Cambridge Journal of Economics*, 3(4), 341–378.

Weisskopf, T.E., Bowles, S., Gordon, D.M. (1985): Two views of capitalist stagnation: underconsumption and challenges to capitalist control, in: *Science & Society*, 49(3), 259–286.

[6]

*Metroeconomica* 46:2 (1995) pp. 146–177

# INTEREST RATES IN POST-KEYNESIAN MODELS OF GROWTH AND DISTRIBUTION

Marc Lavoie*
University of Ottawa

(October 1992: revised August 1993)

ABSTRACT

The goal of this article is to make a heuristic and comparative presentation of how the major post-Keynesian models of growth and distribution integrate money, more specifically interest rates, into their framework. Five variants will be considered, all constructed on the basis of the newer Kaleckian model. It will be shown that increases in real interest rates may have surprising effects on effective demand. It will also be shown that accumulation rates and leverage ratios need not move together. The latter finding reinforces a major hypothesis of the analysis, that is, real interest rates are an exogenous distributive variable.

## 1. INTRODUCTION

One of the surprising aspects of the evolution of Cambridge theory is that, starting from Keynes's *General Theory* which described a monetary production economy, the Cambridge post-Keynesians have failed to incorporate money into their models of growth and distribution. Indeed, this was Davidson's (1972) main critique of these models and as Kregel has pointed out, 'money plays no more than a perfunctory role in the

* This research was made possible by grants from the Social Sciences and Humanities Research Council of Canada and from the School of Graduate Studies and Research of the University of Ottawa. A preliminary version of the paper was presented at the University of Nice, at the Social Sciences University of Grenoble and at York University in Toronto. I would like to thank the participants at all three seminars as well as my colleague Mario Seccareccia for their helpful comments. The present paper is a total rewrite from a previous version that was submitted to the journal. While thankful mentions to referees are sometimes of a diplomatic nature, in the present case they are a clear understatement. In fact, co-authorship could be granted to one of the referees, who provided extensive algebraic and graphical comments which led to the present version. Of course all errors that could remain are mine.

Cambridge theories of growth, capital and distribution' (1985, p. 133).[1] Until very recently, similar criticisms could be addressed to the newer Kaleckian models of growth and distribution, which add an endogenous rate of capacity utilization to an essentially Cambridge structure. This situation has changed, however, in part as a result of the arguments put forth by some neo-Ricardian authors with regards to the influence of the rate of interest on the normal rate of profit.

The present attempt to integrate money and finance into models of growth and distribution is based on one crucial assumption: the rate of interest is considered to be an exogenous variable, under the control of the central bank, while money and credit are considered to be endogenous variables, responding to the demand for them. These are assumptions often made by post-Keynesian authors of all persuasions,[2] although some specialists would not put things so crudely, arguing for instance that portfolio preferences may have feedback effects on interest rates, while firms are often credit-constrained.[3] Only the latter restriction will be taken into account, in the last part of the paper. From now on, it will be assumed that the value of the interest rate is a conventional phenomenon. Those who prefer to cling to a theory of liquidity preference may relate any change in real interest rates to a permanent and exogenous change in the liquidity preference of economic agents. It may be simpler to assume that the *real* rate of interest is under the control of the monetary authorities, or to argue, as Ciccone (1990, p. 455) does, that what the monetary authorities 'are assumed to control *through* the nominal interest rate, is precisely the real rate of interest'.[4] To a different real rate of interest will thus correspond a different monetary regime.[5]

To be valid in the long run as well as in the short run, such assumptions must be based on a non-orthodox monetary approach,

---

1 An interesting historical account of the tensions between the monetary production economy views of Davidson and the growth and distribution views of Robinson is given in Turner (1989, ch. 15).

2 See, among many others, Kaldor (1982), Pivetti (1985; 1991), Moore (1988), Panico (1988), Lavoie (1992, ch. 4) and Le Bourva (1992).

3 See Wray (1990) for instance.

4 This sort of assumption is acceptable even within the standard Wicksellian view, at least in the short run. According to this view, if the central bank follows an easy money policy, trying to keep monetary rates of interest below the Wicksellian natural rate, inflation may set in, thus reducing further real rates of interest. If the central bank tries to keep monetary interest rates higher than the natural rate, deflation will occur, thus increasing further real rates of interest. Central banks are thus always in a position to pursue a policy of low or high real interest rates.

5 An assumption made by others, Skott (1989, p. 57) for instance.

where the rate of interest is not tightly linked to the productivity of capital, in contrast to what neoclassical economists believe, and where the determination of the rate of interest is mainly a matter of monetary and income distribution policy (Rogers 1989). It will also be assumed that the pace of accumulation has no feedback effect on the real rate of interest. This is in accordance with Robinson's main view of the role of money in growth models, since she argues that 'the banks allow their total lending (and therefore the supply of money) to increase gradually, at a constant rate of interest, as total wealth increases' (1962, p. 43). If those assumptions appear excessive to the reader, he may suppose instead that inflation has for all times been eradicated.[6]

The purpose of this article is to make a heuristic and comparative presentation of how the major post-Keynesian models of growth and distribution integrate money, more specifically interest rates, into their framework. Five models will be considered along the lines described in the above paragraph. For the purpose of comparing the various approaches, the newer Kaleckian model has been chosen as the basis of comparison, although some important features of that model will be omitted. Besides the Kaleckian model, the Eichnerian or Cambridge model, the neo-Ricardian model, a post-classical model, and a Minsky–Steindl model will be presented. While the names put forth could be questioned on various grounds, it will be argued that they are adequate for the heuristic objectives being pursued. We start with a simple Kaleckian model.

## 2. THE KALECKIAN MODEL

As said in the introduction, the basis of comparison is a simplified Kaleckian model. The simplifications arise mainly to make the comparisons of the impact of changes in interest rates in the various models clearer. First, it will be assumed that there is no overhead labour.[7] This will make the net and the gross profit margins identical. Secondly, the direct influence of the rate of capacity utilization on the decisions to accumulate will be ignored in the investment function. This has the

[6] Economists often believe that higher accumulation rates induce higher inflationary pressures. However, within Kaleckian models, higher rates of growth may induce lower inflationary pressures. See Dutt (1990, p. 85).

[7] See Rowthorn (1981), Kurz (1990a) and Lavoie (1992) for models where such a feature is present.

heuristic advantage of yielding a system of equations of the decomposable type. It will also eliminate the controversial stagnationist feature of the Kaleckian model, that is the necessary positive relation between the real wage rate and the realized rates of profit and of accumulation.[8] With the following investment function, no relation whatsoever will emerge between the real wage rate and the realized rate of profit:

$$g^i = \gamma + g_r(r^e - i) \tag{1}$$

where $\gamma$ is a parameter reflecting the expected trend of future sales growth; $r^e$ is the expected rate of profit; $i$ is the permanent real rate of interest; and $g_r$ is a parameter reflecting the sensitivity of the latter two variables over the desired rate of accumulation.[9] Equation (1) is in fact the standard Cambridge investment function, as seen by Robinson (1962) for instance, with two exceptions. First, the function given here is linear, instead of having the banana shape that gave rise to two possible equilibria. Secondly, the function explicitly introduces the rate of interest, whereas Robinson (1962, p. 43) assumed that a rise in the interest rate would be implicitly reflected in a lower expected rate of profit.

The savings function, for the time being, will be the usual Cambridge equation, with no savings out of wages. It will be assumed that the distribution of profits between interest income and non-interest income makes no difference for the propensity to save out of profits, $s_p$. At a later stage, a more appropriate savings function will be considered.

$$g^s = s_p r \tag{2}$$

Combining equations (1) and (2), and letting the expected and the realized rates of profit equate, we get the well known effective demand constraint.

$$r = \frac{\gamma - g_r i}{s_p - g_r} \tag{3}$$

The graphical derivation of the effective demand constraint is to be

---

[8] See Dutt (1984) for the presence of such a stagnationist behaviour. See Kurz (1990a) as well as Bhaduri and Marglin (1990) for a modified investment function that may provide a negative relation between real wage rates and rates of profit and of accumulation within an otherwise similar Kaleckian model.

[9] Eichner (1987, p. 434) includes this very equation in his discussion of the Kaleckian investment function.

found at the top of Figure 1. The model is stable provided investment is less responsive than savings to changes in the profit rate, that is, provided that the slope of the $g^i$ function is less than that of the $g^s$ function. This requires that $g_r < s_p$, and hence a positive solution requires a positive $\gamma$.

A distinguishing feature of the Kaleckian model, compared to the old Cambridge model, is that the rate of capacity utilization is endogenous instead of being a given, fixed by conventions or technological considerations. By definition, the rate of profit can be rewritten as:

$$r = \Pi/K = (\Pi/Y)(Y/C)(C/K) = mu(1/v) \tag{4}$$

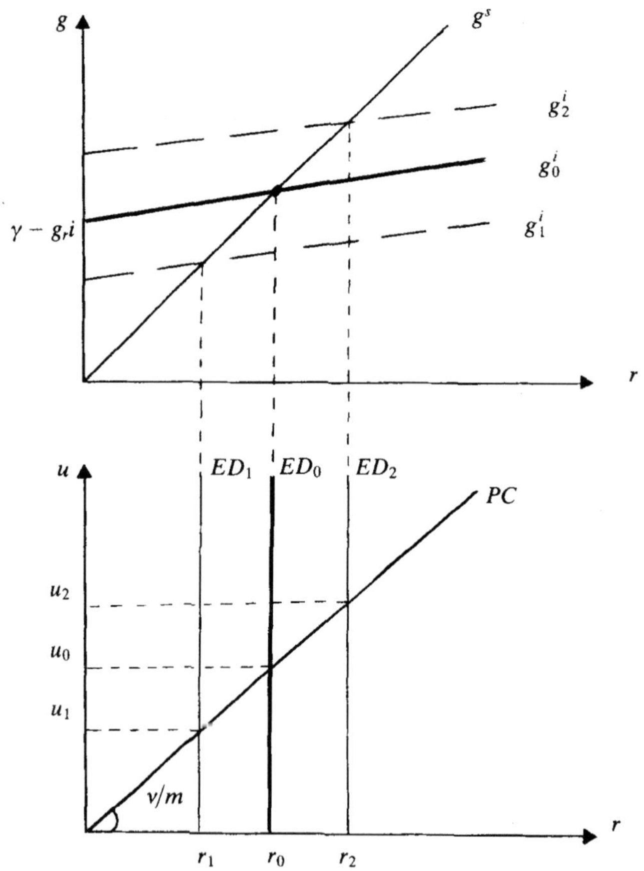


*Figure 1*

where $\Pi$ is (real) profits, $K$ is the stock of capital, $Y$ is output, $C$ is capacity output, while $m$ is the share of profits, $u$ is the rate of capacity utilization and $v$ is the capital/capacity ratio, with the latter assumed to be given. Equation (4) can be rewritten as:

$$u = (v/m)r. \qquad (5)$$

We shall call equation (5) the profits cost curve, since it determines the rate of profit, but seen this time from the cost side. However, for a rate of profit given by the effective demand constraint of equation (3), noted *ED* at the bottom of Figure 1, we see that the rate of capacity utilization $u$ depends on the margin of profit $m$, that is on the markup over variable costs set by the firms. This can be seen by looking at the standard Kaleckian pricing equation:

$$p = (1 + \theta)w/y \qquad (6)$$

where $p$ is the price level, $\theta$ the markup, $w$ the nominal wage rate and $y$ average labour productivity, and by taking note that the markup $\theta$ and the margin of profit are related to one another by the following equation:

$$m = \theta/(1 + \theta). \qquad (7)$$

In this simpler formulation, an increase in the real wage rate, that is a fall in the profit margin $m$, does not lead to an increase in the rate of accumulation but it does lead to an increase in the rate of capacity utilization. A graphical representation of the profits cost curve, noted *PC* and the slope of which is $v/m$, can be found in the bottom part of Figure 1.

We may now examine in Figure 1 the impact of a change in monetary policy reflected by an increase in the real rate of interest. As a result of this increase, the investment function will shift downwards, from $g_0^i$ to $g_1^i$, leading to a fall in the realized rate of profit and to a shift of the effective demand constraint, and hence to a fall in the rate of capacity utilization, from $u_0$ to $u_1$. In the Kaleckian model, there is no relationship between the real rate of interest and the marginal or the normal rate of profit. Symmetrical effects can be observed when the growth prospects symbolised by $\gamma$ are improved. In that case, the investment function shifts upwards, from $g_0^i$ to $g_2^i$, leading to an increase in the rate of accumulation, the rate of profit and finally the rate of capacity utilization. What has been assumed to remain constant in both cases is the profit margin, so that $m = \bar{m}$.

## 3. THE CAMBRIDGE OR EICHNERIAN MODEL

At this stage, it might be interesting to compare the results achieved in the new Kaleckian model with those that could be achieved in the old Cambridge model. A characteristic feature of the Cambridge model, at least the one put forth by Robinson (1956; 1962), is that in the long run the rate of utilization of capacity must be equal to its normal value. This feature can also be found in many macroeconomic models based on the oligopolistic behaviour of firms in a growing environment. In those models, the markup is a function of the growth rate of the firm. A particularly vivid graphical expression of this type of hypothesis can be found in the work of Shapiro (1981, p. 89). This can be expressed algebraically in the following equation:[10]

$$m = m_0 + m_g g \qquad (8)$$

Looking at things from a macroeconomic point of view, the higher the desired rate of accumulation, the higher the required profit share $m$ and hence the lower the real wage rate. This is a key result of the old Cambridge model which has generated a substantial amount of criticism from several authors associated with the Sraffian tradition (Vianello 1985; Ciccone 1986; Kurz 1990b; Garegnani 1992). It is clear that many of the recent post-Keynesian models attempting to give an explanation of the value of the markup based on the size of planned investment generate results which are no different from those of the old Cambridge models. This is particularly the case of the models developed by Eichner (1976) and Wood (1975). As it has recently been noticed by Agliardi (1988), the causality and the mechanisms underlying the Eichnerian models often run in the opposite direction to those of Kaleckian models. This is due to the additional embedded assumption according to which the economy is necessarily operating at its normal rate of capacity utilization in the long run (Wood 1975, p. 129). It follows that the rate of capacity utilization is no longer an endogenous variable in that type of model, a situation which is similar to that which could be found in

[10] A macroeconomic model incorporating this equation is presented in Lavoie (1993).

the Cambridge models. But whereas the latter models relied on competition to achieve such a situation, in the oligopolistic Eichnerian model the investment behaviour of firms or of government are assumed to be such that eventually the realized rate of capacity utilization equals the given normal rate, $u = \bar{u}_n$.

The impact of increases in the secular rate of growth of sales, given by $\gamma$, or in the rate of interest, given by $i$, is illustrated in Figure 2. The two models, the Kaleckian and the Cambridge, give identical results with respect to effective demand: the top parts of Figures 1 and 2 are identical. In both models, an increase in the inducement to invest leads

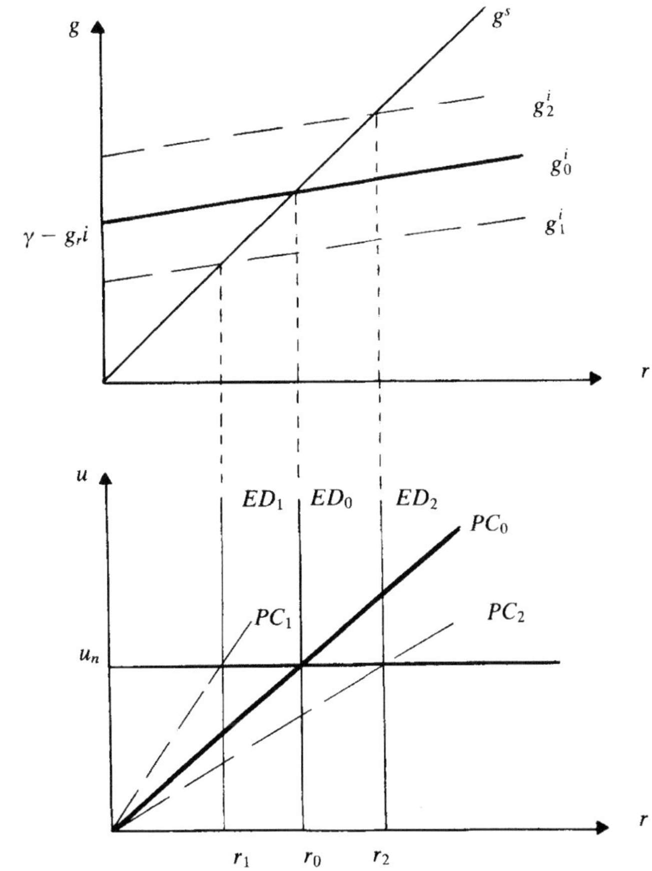


*Figure 2*

to higher rates of profit and of accumulation. In the Eichnerian and Cambridge models however, the rate of utilization is fixed at $u_n$, and hence considering equation (5), the burden of the adjustment falls entirely on the margin of profit $m$, which must increase. This is represented by a downward displacement of the $PC$ curve, from $PC_0$ to $PC_2$. We thus find again the familiar Cambridge inverse relationship between the accumulation rate and the real wage rate that some neo-Ricardians have recently questioned. Putting together equations (2) and (5), and assuming that the long run rate of capacity utilization is equal to its normal level, we get the following Eichnerian relation:

$$m = (vs_p/u_n)g \tag{9}$$

which is an extreme specification of equation (8).

As far as the rate of interest is concerned, a fall in it would generate a slowdown in the rate of accumulation in the economy. This would induce a fall in the markup and in the margin of profit, as shown by the rotation of the $PC$ curve, from $PC_0$ to $PC_1$. As in the previous case, since the rate of utilization is deemed to be equal to its normal value in the long run, a change in the parameter of the Cambridge or Eichnerian model requires an adjustment which falls entirely on the profit margin. This is fully compatible with Eichner's belief that the rate of interest has no *direct* impact on the margin of profit which is required to fulfil the financial obligations of the firm (Eichner 1987, p. 481–2). In his view, the markup and the standard rate of profit are entirely determined by the secular rate of growth of the corporation (1987, p. 355). It is only through this indirect route, according to Eichner, that the real rate of interest will have an impact on the markup. If the investment equation given by equation (1) is valid, then a higher real interest rate will be associated with a lower realized rate of profit and a lower rate of accumulation, and hence with a lower normal rate of profit. Under the conditions set by the Eichnerian model, one would thus expect a negative relationship between the real interest rate and the normal rate of profit, to be achieved however indirectly through the effective demand constraint.

## 4. THE NEO-RICARDIAN MODEL

Exactly the reverse occurs in the neo-Ricardian model. The key characteristic feature of this model is that a *direct* positive relationship between the real rate of interest and the normal rate of profit is deemed to exist. Such a relationship was initially based on Sraffa's famous sentence according to which the rate of profit is 'susceptible of being determined from outside the system of production, in particular by the level of the money rates of interest' (1960 § 44). That such a view can be called neo-Ricardian is attested by the great number of Sraffian authors who have argued in favour of it or who have endorsed it (Sylos Labini 1971, p. 270; Garegnani 1979, p. 81; Panico 1985, 1988; Vianello 1985, p. 84; Pivetti 1985, 1991; Roncaglia 1988; Schefold 1989, p. 325).

The elaboration of Sraffa's aside has however generated a great number of responses from irritated post-Keynesians (Pasinetti 1988; Nell 1988; Wray 1988). To some, it is an 'inexplicable suggestion' (Bhaduri and Robinson 1980, p. 103), which is 'excessively fanciful' (Robinson 1979, p. 180). Even some neo-Ricardians have objected to this Sraffian relationship (Schefold 1993).

As many proponents of Sraffa's aside have mentioned, several famous post-Keynesian authors, at one time or another, have however supported the possibility of a direct positive link between interest rates and profit margins.[11] The clearest exponent of Sraffa's aside is however its most ardent opponent, Joan Robinson herself. Reading the following quote of hers is like reading a summary of the neo-Ricardian point of view on this issue:

> The distribution of income between labour and capital depends . . . on the rate of profit, that is, the rate of interest *plus* the rate of net profit. If the rate of interest were (and always had been) lower or the entrepreneurs were habituated to a lower rate of net profit, the share of labour and the level of real wages would be so much the higher. (Robinson 1952, p. 96).

Compare the above with the following explanation provided by the main exponent of the neo-Ricardian view presented here:

> In the explanation of distribution . . . the normal rate of profit in each particular production sphere will be arrived at by adding up two autono-

[11] Here is a list of such supporting quotes: 'Many companies base their calculations on some "normal" rate of return . . . though the entrepreneur's normal standard is likely in course of time to be revised to match an apparently lasting change in market rates' (Sayers 1951, pp. 7–8). 'Firms often have some standard rate of profit, which includes interest, that they add to the input costs' (Harrod 1973, p. 44). 'Sustained low interest will presumably in the long run reduce the normal rate of profit' (Harrod 1973, p. 111). 'Interest costs are passed on in higher prices in much the same way as wage costs' (Kaldor 1982, p. 63).

> mous components: the long-term rate of interest ($i$) . . . plus the normal profit of enterprise ($npe$) . . .. Provided that $npe$ is a sufficiently stable magnitude, and one which is independent of $i$ and of lasting changes of $i$ . . . lasting changes in the rate of interest will cause corresponding changes in profit rates, and inverse changes in the real wage. (Pivetti 1985, pp. 86–7).

Sraffa's aside may thus be formalized by the following equation:

$$r_n = i + npe \tag{10}$$

where $i$ and $npe$ are defined as in Pivetti's statement, and where $r_n$ is the normal rate of profit, not the actual one.

It is important to stress this distinction, because some of the opposition to Sraffa's aside may be based on a confusion between the normal and the realized rates of profit. Neo-Ricardians are not arguing that higher rates of interest necessarily induce higher realized rates of profit; what they are arguing is that higher interest rates are inducing higher normal rates of profit, that is higher markups. Provided the realized rate of capacity utilization is not always equal to its normal value, a higher normal rate of profit may accompany a lower realized rate of profit. As Pivetti (1988, p. 281) points out: 'The analysis concerns the explanation of the *normal* rate of profit, in the meaning that this term has always had in economic theory, and never refers to the actual rate of profit and actual profits which are of course acted upon by demand'. In our notations, the impact of the rate of interest is on the rate of profit defined by the profits cost curve at normal capacity: a rise in the permanent rate of interest leads to a rotation upwards of the profits cost curve.[12]

This can be more clearly seen by linking equation (10) to the cost-plus pricing model. As Pivetti (1991, ch. 11) points out, Sraffa's aside may be related to theories of full cost pricing, or more specifically, to modern theories of target-return pricing. In target return pricing procedures, the margin of profit is set at a level that will provide a normal rate of profit when firms are producing at the normal (or standard) level of capacity utilization. In our much simplified Kaleckian model, this implies, from

[12] For those who are uneasy about linking Sraffa's aside to growth analysis, the following quote may bring some comfort: 'If the causal connection between the rate of interest and the rate of profit is to have any meaning at all, it must hold true in a growing as well as in a stationary economy' (Vianello 1990, p. 109).

equation (5), that:

$$r_n = mu_n/v. \tag{11}$$

By combining equations (10) and (11), it can be seen that the margin of profit $m$ is a positive function of the real rate of interest, and it can be written in the following linear form:

$$m = m_o + m_i i \tag{12}$$

where:

$$m_0 = (npe)v/u_n \tag{13}$$

$$m_i = v/u_n. \tag{14}$$

Equation (12) is thus a reduced form of the neo-Ricardian view of the determination of the normal rate of profit, as described notably by Pivetti. It can be found in a few independently written works (Dutt 1992, p. 105; Lavoie 1992, p. 362). Now, one may wonder whether $i$ is the nominal rate or the real rate of interest. Pivetti himself pays little attention to the issue, until he finally recognizes that the rate of profit should 'move in sympathy with the real rate of interest, rather than with the nominal one—the former constituting the actual price for the use of capital in production, or its opportunity cost' (1985, p. 100). Further reflection should make clear that $i$ must be the real rate. It can be noted that the real wage rate, given by equations (6) and (7), is $w/p = y(1 - m)$. Through the profit/wage frontier, this real wage must be inversely related to the real normal profit rate, and not to the nominal rate of profit. One would therefore expect the margin of profit $m$, which determines the real normal profit rate, to depend upon the real rate of interest rather than the nominal rate.[13]

This issue being settled, equation (12) allows us to use the previous graphical apparatus to analyze the impact of an increase in the real rate of interest in an economy depicted by the neo-Ricardian model. As can be seen in Figure 3, the top part of the graph is again left unchanged compared with the previous Kaleckian and Cambridge model. The main

[13] Ciccone (1990) also clearly indicates that the real rate of interest is the relevant one. Dutt (1992) supposes that $i$ is the nominal rather than the real interest rate. The conditions under which he examines the behaviour of his model, however, are such that any increase in the nominal rate of interest is accompanied by a rise in the real rate.

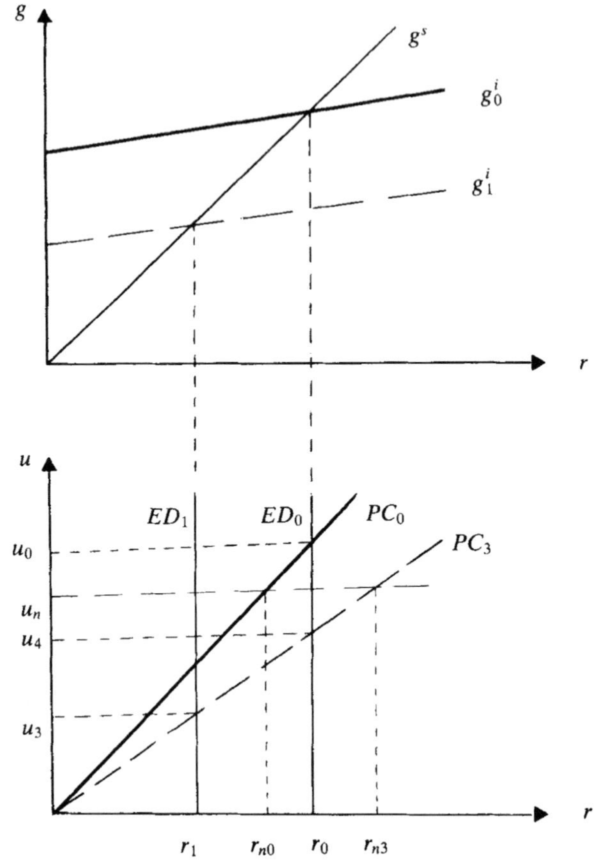


*Figure 3*

change occurs at the bottom of Figure 3, where the rise in interest rates brings on a downward rotation of the *PC* curve, from $PC_0$ to $PC_3$, as a result of the induced increase in the margin of profit. While the realized rate of profit and the rate of accumulation fall no more than they do in the Kaleckian model, the realized rate of capacity utilization falls further, from $u_0$ to $u_3$, because of the induced fall in the real wage rate. This is a consequence of the fact that the margin of profit has been raised to adjust the normal rate of profit to the new real interest rate, the normal rate of profit rising from $r_{n0}$ to $r_{n3}$.

It should be noted that the qualitative results of the analysis would not be different even if it were assumed that investment is not a function of the realized rate of profit, but instead is a function of the normal profit rate, or more precisely, a function of the normal profit of enterprise. Indeed, in trying to refute the validity of the Kaleckian model, some neo-Ricardians have argued just that (Pivetti 1985, p. 97; Ciccone 1986; Petri 1993). In our model, this would imply that the $g^i$ function at the top of Figure 3 would be a horizontal line, which would depend neither on the realized rate of profit nor on the real interest rate. The investment function, given by equation (1), would now become:

$$g^i = \gamma + g_r(r_n - i) = \gamma + g_r(npe). \tag{15}$$

If desired accumulation were given by equation (15), a lower rate of interest would induce no change in the rate of accumulation, and the realized rate of profit would remain at $r_0$. Still, the profits cost curve at the bottom of Figure 3 would shift, and the new rate of utilization would have to fall to $u_4$. Now this result contradicts some of the assertions made elsewhere by some of the same neo-Ricardian authors. Pivetti (1985, p. 99) has claimed that the direction of influence of changes in interest rates over aggregate demand cannot be predicted a priori. The main reason for this is that changes in interest rates modify the distribution of income. We must now investigate how, within our simple Kaleckian and neo-Ricardian framework, changes in interest rates could generate uncertain results. To do so, we shall construct a *post-classical* model, that is a model that entertains features of both the Kaleckian and the neo-Ricardian traditions.

## 5. THE POST-CLASSICAL MODEL

In this section, I wish to demonstrate graphically that increases in real interest rates may indeed lead to increases in aggregate demand, and hence in rates of profit, of accumulation and of capacity utilization. The demonstration relies on a modified savings function, that takes into account the distinction between retained profits and interest payments.

This new savings function is based on the dichotomy highlighted by Robinson when she claimed that 'the most important distinction between types of income is that between firms and households' (1962, p. 38). As is well known, this distinction was put to task by Kaldor (1966) in his famous neo-Pasinetti theorem, but as Davidson (1972) pointed out, the model takes no account of interest payments, the assumption being that all wealth is held in the form of shares. Here we shall devise the contrary assumption, by supposing that all wealth is held as banking deposits. Alternatively, it could be assumed that the rate of dividend payments is made in accordance with the rate of interest paid to those agents holding banking deposits or bonds. Under these simplifying assumptions, the income distributed to households as property income does not depend on whether financial capital is held through bonds or shares. This assumption will be relaxed in the next section.

Let us continue to assume the classical case of no savings out of wages. Let us suppose however that households save out of property income, that is the dividends and interest payments which they receive. Let us call $s_h$ this propensity to save out of property income by households. Their savings per unit of capital are then $s_h i$. The savings of the firms are their retained earnings. The new savings function is thus made up of two components: one related to corporate retained earnings and the other to household savings out of their share of profit.[14]

$$g^s = (r - i) + s_h i = r - (1 - s_h)i. \qquad (16)$$

This new savings function is different from the standard Cambridge relation in two ways. It incorporates the distributional impact of interest payments in its simplest form, and it distinguishes between firms and households. With respect to the former characteristic, it must be said that while several authors have incorporated the rate of interest in the investment function, it has generally been omitted from the savings function.[15] It can be seen from equation (16) that the rate of growth of savings is reduced whenever the interest rate is higher. Higher interest rates redistribute profit income from firms to households, whose propensity to save is lower than that of firms.[16] Higher interest rates thus

[14] Capital gains are omitted from the model, but including them would not alter the substance of the results obtained. This is shown by Skott (1989, p. 57) in a model which introduces banking deposits with exogenous rates of interest alongside Kaldor's securities market with its endogenous valuation ratio. Money and interest rates thus do have a role to play in a theory of growth and distribution, even when an adjusting mechanism based on an endogenous valuation ratio is at work, as is the case in the models proposed by Kaldor (1966) and Skott.

[15] Recent instances can be found in the papers of Jarsulic (1990) and Gallegati and Gardini (1991), which deal nonetheless with the importance of financial obligations for investment behaviour.

[16] Higher interest rates also redistribute income away from workers, but because the model has a decomposable form, the lower real wage has no impact on the rate of accumulation.

induce more consumption spending, not less as the neoclassical authors would say on the basis of a model of the individual agent. Taking into account income classes and the distinction between households and firms leads to radically different conclusions. Note that the positive relationship between interest rates and consumption had already been recorded by Joan Robinson.

> A permanent fall in the level of interest rates relatively to the rate of profit has reduced the rentiers' share in profits (assuming that dividends have not been raised correspondingly), and this is likely to have a more important effect in reducing the proportion of consumption to profits than any effect there may be of lower interest in increasing the ratio of consumption to rentier income (Robinson 1956, p. 253).

One may wonder why the usual Cambridge savings function, $g = s_p r$, or some variation of it, has not been kept. The reason is that $s_p$ cannot be considered an exogenous parameter any more, since its major component, the retention ratio, is now endogenous. The retention ratio is dependent on the interest rate, a factor which is not under the control of the firm. It would thus be a mistake to assume that the retention ratio is constant, unless one only dealt with states that did not differ in their monetary policy, or unless the retention ratio only applied to profits net of interest payments, as will be seen in the next section.

Let us now put together the investment and the savings function, given by equations (1) and (16), to obtain the effective demand constraint:

$$r = \frac{\gamma}{(1 - g_r)} + \frac{i(1 - g_r - s_h)}{(1 - g_r)}. \tag{17}$$

The continuous lines of Figure 4 provide an illustration of this effective demand constraint, initially set at point $A$. As before, the model is stable provided investment is less responsive than savings to changes in the rate of profit. Here, this requires $g_r < 1$. A positive solution occurs only if $(1 - s_h) > g_r - \gamma/i$, where $\gamma$ need not be positive.

Let us see what happens to the realized rate of profit when there is an increase in the real interest rate. Taking the derivative of equation (17), one gets:

$$\frac{\mathrm{d}r}{\mathrm{d}i} = \frac{1 - g_r - s_h}{1 - g_r} < 1. \tag{18}$$

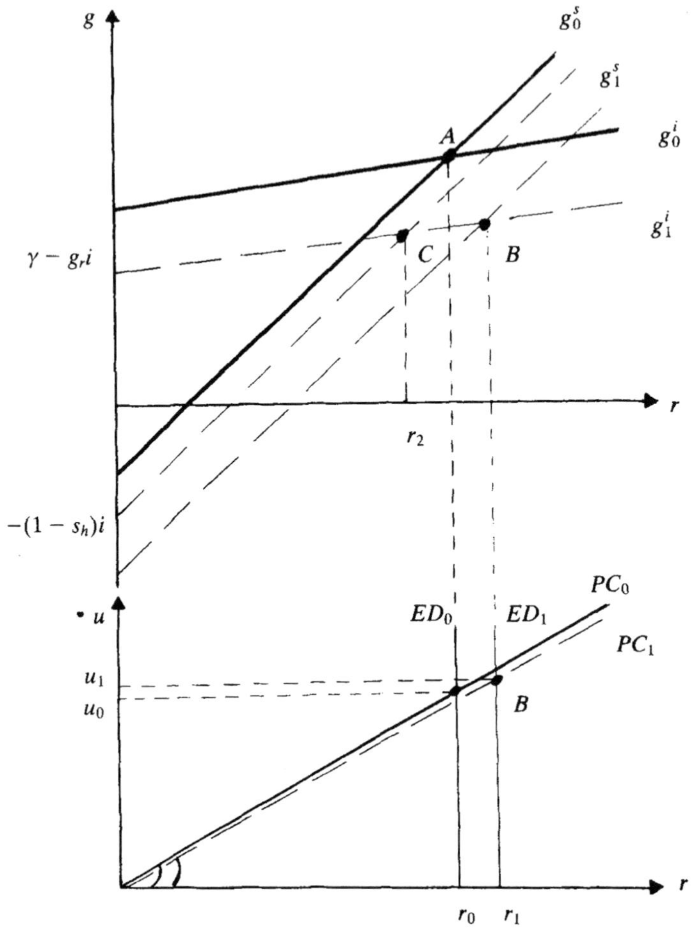


*Figure 4*

It is clear that the derivative may be positive, provided $(1 - s_h) > g_r$, that is provided households consume a large fraction of their property income compared to the unfavourable effects that high interest rates have on investment behaviour. This is the $B$ case illustrated in Figure 4, with the effective demand constraint shifting to the right, from $ED_0$ to $ED_1$. When households consume a small fraction of their property income, an increase in interest rates will lead to a fall in the realized rate of profit. This is illustrated by case $C$ in Figure 4. Thus, as is concluded by Dutt (1992, p. 119) in a similar but more complex model, the impact of higher interest rates is more likely to be negative if the holders of bonds and securities are rich people with low propensities to consume.

Similar results are obtained with regards to the impact of changes in interest rates on the rate of capacity utilization. Using equations (5), (12) and (17), and solving for $u$, one gets:

$$u = \frac{[\gamma + i(1 - g_r - s_h)]v}{(1 - g_r)(m_0 + m_i i)}. \tag{19}$$

Taking the derivative of $u$ with respect to $i$, one finds that it is positive provided the following condition holds:

$$(1 - s_h) > g_r + (m_i/m_0)\gamma. \tag{20}$$

Again, an increase in the real rate of interest may lead to an increase in the rate of capacity utilization if the propensity to consume out of property income is sufficiently large. Point $B$ at the bottom of Figure 4 illustrates such a case.

The crucial question, however, is whether there could be a positive relationship between the real rate of interest and the rate of accumulation. In the present simplified model, such a relationship could not exist. This is obvious from the derivative obtained in equation (18): the increase in the realized rate of profit $r$ is always smaller than the exogenous increase in the rate of interest $i$. This implies that the realized rate of profit, net of interest payments, is always smaller when the interest rate increases. Going back to the investment function given by equation (1), it follows that the resulting rate of accumulation must decrease when real interest rates rise. It would thus appear that the contention of some neo-Ricardians, regarding the uncertain effects of changes in the interest rate on the rate of investment, is not verified.

To come to such a conclusion would however be a mistake. It has been shown in models similar to the post-classical one presented here, but with the addition of the current rate of capacity utilization in the investment function, that a rise in the interest rate could lead to an increase in the rate of accumulation (Dutt 1992; Lavoie 1992, ch. 6). Even without taking into account the rate of capacity utilization, such a situation may occur in a modified version of the basic Kaleckian model presented here. We now turn our attention to this final post-Keynesian model.

## 6. THE MINSKY–STEINDL MODEL

### 1. Building blocks of the model

As was pointed out in the introduction, the Cambridge models of growth and distribution drew criticisms from some post-Keynesian authors because these models left out any explicit analysis of the monetary and financial aspects. Recently, there have been many attempts to build models of growth or of business cycles that incorporate financial variables, the inspiration of which has been Kalecki's (1937) principle of increasing risk and the work of Minsky (1975).[17] The goal of the last model to be presented here is to take into account financial variables, more precisely interest payments and the debt ratio, both in the investment and in the savings functions. In this sense the model will contain Minskian features.

The model may however also be associated with the name of Steindl. While Steindl's work has been given credit in the course of the Kaleckian revival, his contribution to the destabilising role that financial variables can play in a capitalist economy has been somewhat played down. Steindl (1952, pp. 113–121) provides a very perceptive analysis of the macroeconomic paradoxes, similar to the Keynesian thrift paradox, that may arise when firms or their bankers attempt to reduce debt ratios. This paradox occurs when firms decide to reduce their rate of investment whenever they find their debt ratios to be too high. Steindl's analysis is particularly interesting because he considers the effects of debt ratios on both the savings and the investment functions. It thus seems appropriate to call a Kaleckian model incorporating these effects by the name of Minsky–Steindl.

With concern focused on financial variables, from now on no attention will be paid to the rate of capacity utilization or to the profits cost curve. The model will thus basically consist of the effective demand constraint. The crucial financial variable is the debt ratio, which will be called $l$ for *leverage* ratio. The leverage ratio is here defined as the amount of loans $L$ contracted by the firms over the replacement value of capital:

$$l = L/pK. \tag{21}$$

[17] There are many such models, of which only a few are mentioned here: Jarsulic (1990), Gallegati and Gardini (1991), Franke and Semmler (1991), Moon (1991), Skott (1992). In addition, there are many recent models in the New Keynesian tradition.

While $l$ may be considered to be given in the short run, $l$ will be changing over time, unless a steady state is reached. The evolution of this variable will be considered later. For the moment let us deal with the savings function, which will turn out to be a more accurate variant of the savings function introduced in the post-classical model—equation (16). Since firms have borrowed an amount $L$ from households, either indirectly in the form of banking loans or directly in the form of bonds, they must pay out an amount of $iL$. The profits net of this amount may now be either distributed to households in the form of dividends or be saved by firms as retained earnings. Let us call $s_f$ the retention rate out of profits net of interest payments, $s_s$ the propensity to save of households holding shares, and $s_b$ the propensity to save of households holding bonds or bank deposits.[18] The savings function is now the sum of three components: the savings of the firms, the savings of shareholders and the savings of bond holders:

$$g^s = (r - il)s_f + (r - il)(1 - s_f)s_s + s_b il. \tag{22}$$

Rearranging, we get:

$$g^s = [s_f + (1 - s_f)s_s]r + \{s_b - [s_f + (1 - s_f)s_s]\}il. \tag{23}$$

The reduced form of the savings function is thus:[19]

$$g^s = s_r r - s_l(il) \tag{24}$$

with:

$$s_r = s_f + (1 - s_f)s_s > 0 \tag{24a}$$

and:

$$s_l = [s_f + (1 - s_f)s_s] - s_b >< 0. \tag{24b}$$

The most remarkable aspect of equation (24) is that $s_l$ may be positive or negative. An increased relative weight of interest payments may or may not lead to more savings. The cause of this uncertain effect, if we may go back to Robinson's quoted assertion to the contrary, is that the

18 As before, capital gains are omitted, or it is assumed that they are entirely saved.

19 This reduced form can be found in Taylor (1991, p. 130). Similar savings functions may be found in Moon (1991, p. 156) and Dutt (1992, p. 102).

rise in the interest rate leads to a decline in the dividend rate, the retention rate being assumed to be constant. Higher interest rates increase aggregate consumer spending if, as pointed out by Robinson, 'dividends are not [lowered] correspondingly'. This shows the crucial importance of institutional arrangements for the modelling of effective demand.

Let us now deal with the investment behaviour of firms. The following investment function will be assumed, which shows some symmetry with the savings function:[20]

$$g^i = \gamma + g_r r - g_l(il). \tag{25}$$

It could be argued that investment should only be responsive to profits net of interest payments, that is to the difference $r - il$. However, since firms have some liberty in fixing their retention ratio, it will be maintained that firms would not react with equal intensity to a fall in net profits arising from a fall in the realized rate of profit as from a rise in interest payments. As a consequence two parameters, $g_r$ and $g_l$, are being used. It could however also be argued that firms would not react with equal intensity to a rise in interest payments that would arise from an increase in the rate of interest as from an increase in the leverage ratio. We shall fall back on the elegance of symmetry with the savings function to justify the proposed specification, and on the following justification.

If tranquillity is defined as the ratio of realized profits to normal profits, that is $r/r_n$, whereas financial fragility is defined as the ratio of interest payments to normal profits, that is $il/r_n$, then the specification of equation (25) appears to be a reasonable one. Within a Minskian framework, one would expect investment to be a positive function of tranquillity and a negative function of financial fragility.[21] The Minsky part of the investment function would thus be justified. With respect to the Steindl part, it must be pointed out that Steindl (1952, p. 129) himself wrote down an investment equation with the rate of profit, the leverage ratio and the rate of utilization as separate arguments of the function. The real rate of interest was not included in his function, but it must be recalled that in the fifties there were only small variations in the

[20] A similar investment function, with an additional term to take capacity utilization into account, is proposed by Jarsulic (1990, p. 93).

[21] Skott (1992) argues that in general desired accumulation will be *higher* the *higher* the degree of financial fragility as defined above. I do not find his arguments convincing, precisely because they ignore the paradoxes underlined by Steindl.

interest rate. As a consequence, changes in the burden of debt could almost entirely be attributed to changes in the leverage ratio, rather than to changes in the real interest rate. Over the last dozen years, changes in interest rates have been such that they cannot be ignored any more.

With the leverage ratio $l$ being a constant in the short run, we may combine the new savings function—equation (24)—and the new investment function—equation (25)—to obtain the profit rate and the accumulation rate pertaining to the short run. One obtains:

$$r = \frac{\gamma + (s_l - g_l)il}{(s_r - g_r)} \tag{26}$$

$$g = \frac{s_r\gamma + (s_l g_r - g_l s_r)il}{(s_r - g_r)}. \tag{27}$$

Short-run stability prevails provided the savings function responds less than the investment function to changes in the profit rate. This requires that:

$$s_r > g_r. \tag{28}$$

## 2. *Results of the model*

Taking the derivatives of equations (26) and (27) with respect to $i$, one finds that the impact of an increase in the real rate of interest on the rate of accumulation is indeed uncertain, as some neo-Ricardians assert. There could be a positive relationship between the real rate of interest and the rate of accumulation, at least in the short run, as shown in Table 1. We shall call this case the *puzzling* case.

Going beyond the short run, however, the value of the leverage ratio will be changing, and this will have repercussions on the other variables

*Table 1: Uncertain effect of an increase in the real rate of interest on the realized rate of profit and the rate of accumulation in the short run*

| | $s_l < g_l$ | $g_l < s_l < g_l(s_r/g_r)$ | $s_l > g_l(s_r/g_r)$ |
|---|---|---|---|
| $dr/di$ | – | + | + |
| $dg/di$ | – | – | + |

of the model. The dynamics of the leverage ratio can be expressed by taking the logarithmic derivative of equation (21). Assuming away inflation (the markup may change, but not the price level), and using the sign ^ to denote the rate of change of a variable, we have:

$$\hat{l} = \hat{L} - \hat{K} = \hat{L} - g. \tag{29}$$

With the assumptions that have been made, the new loans contracted by firms correspond to the savings of the bond holders. In growth terms, we have:

$$\hat{L} = s_b i. \tag{30}$$

We are now in a position to find the leverage ratio that could occur in the long run. Setting $\hat{l} = 0$ in equation (29), and making use of equations (27) and (30), we get the long run value of the leverage ratio, which must be, by definition, between 0 and 1:

$$l^* = \frac{s_b i(s_r - g_r) - s_r \gamma}{(s_l g_r - s_r g_l) i}. \tag{31}$$

Taking the derivatives of the above equations leads to Table 2, which will allow us to construct the various possible cases occurring in the long run.

Table 2 shows that the main features of the model depend on a single condition, the relative sensitivity of the savings coefficients compared to the relative sensitivity of the corresponding investment coefficients. In particular, part C of Table 2 tells us under which condition the long run leverage ratio $l^*$, computed in equation (31), is a stable equilibrium. For long run stability to occur, the derivative $\mathrm{d}\hat{l}/\mathrm{d}l$ must be negative, that is

*Table 2: Puzzling behaviour and long run stability*

| | | $s_l/s_r - g_l/g_r$ | |
|---|---|---|---|
| | | + | − |
| A: (27) | $\mathrm{d}g/\mathrm{d}i,\ l = \bar{l}$ | + | − |
| B: (27) | $\mathrm{d}g/\mathrm{d}l,\ i = \bar{i}$ | + | − |
| C: (27, 29, 30) | $\mathrm{d}\hat{l}/\mathrm{d}l,\ i = \bar{i}$ | − | + |
| D: (31) | $\mathrm{d}l^*/\mathrm{d}i$ | + | − |

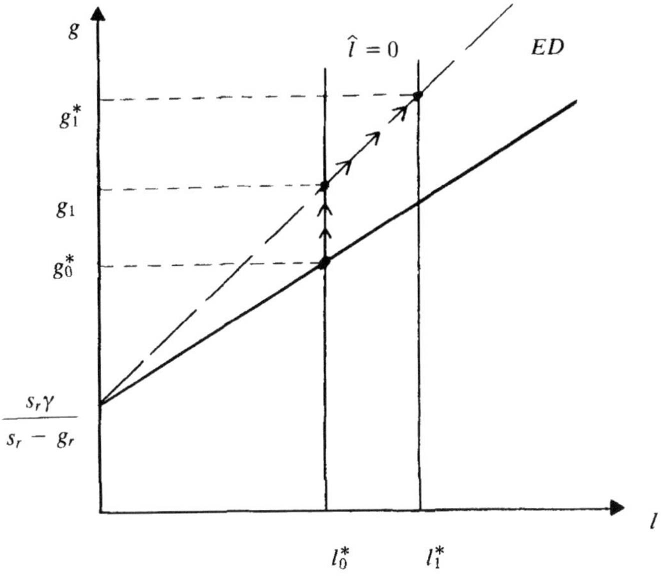


*Figure 5*

$s_l/s_r$ must be larger than $g_l/g_r$.[22] This implies in fact that both the denominator and the numerator of $l^*$ are positive. It requires that bond holders have a relatively low propensity to save, which one would expect when bond holders are poorer people, and that firms (or their bankers) show little sensitivity to changes in leverage ratios or in the weight of interest payments. This stable case is illustrated in Figure 5.

The graph illustrates what happens when the real interest rate is increased permanently. The effective demand curve *ED* rotates upwards (part A of Table 2), while the long run leverage ratio increases, from $l_0^*$ to $l_1^*$ (part D of Table 2). The long run stable case thus corresponds to what was called the *puzzling* case when discussing the short run possibilities of Table 1. An increase in the real rate of interest generates an immediate increase in effective demand and hence in the rate of accumulation, from $g_0^*$ to $g_1$. The higher interest rate induces a gradual increase in the leverage ratio of firms, accompanied by a higher rate of accumulation (part B of Table 2), until the new long run equilibrium

[22] Note that it is sufficient for $s_l$ to be negative for the long run equilibrium to be unstable. Dutt (1992, p. 104) gets a similar condition. In his model, $g_l = 0$, and hence the condition for stability becomes $s_l/s_r > 0$. His long run equilibrium is unstable whenever $s_l < 0$.

leverage ratio is reached (the stability requirement given by part C of Table 2). Therefore, while higher real interest rates lead to higher leverage ratios, a result one would expect, they also lead to higher rates of accumulation, a result that is rather unexpected. Stability in the long run sense must therefore be associated with puzzling effective demand results.[23]

Let us now consider the unstable case, that is the case where economic forces are such that the economy diverges from the long run equilibrium leverage value. This occurs when $s_l/s_r$ is smaller than $g_l/g_r$, that is when wealthy bond holders have a relatively high propensity to save while firms are rather sensitive to the evolution of their leverage ratio. Under those conditions, unless the historically given leverage ratio corresponds exactly to the equilibrium ratio, the leverage ratio will tend towards zero or towards unity. This implies that the share of capital held by bond holders tends either towards zero or towards unity. An unstable case is represented in Figure 6. The relationship between the rate of accumulation and the leverage ratio is then negative (part B of Table 2). Let us start from a situation where the leverage ratio happens to be at its equilibrium value given by $l_0^*$. The rate of accumulation will then be $g_0^*$. Let us now assume an increase in the real rate of interest. The new equilibrium leverage ratio will shift to the left, to $l_1^*$ (part D of Table 2), while the effective demand curve *ED* will rotate downwards (part A of Table 2). The increased rate of interest will induce a fall in the rate of accumulation, from $g_0^*$ to $g_1$. The higher interest rate induces a gradual increase in the actual leverage ratio, away from its equilibrium value. This will be accompanied by a decrease in the rate of accumulation. If nothing else changes, the decrease in the rate of accumulation will continue until the leverage ratio reaches unity, that is until the rate of accumulation equates $g_1^*$.[24]

Although the long run solution is unstable, the model features characteristics that one has been trained to expect. Excessively high real

---

[23] Higher rates of accumulation are also generally associated with higher rates of capacity utilization. From equations (5), (12) and (26), we know that:

$$u = \frac{[\gamma + (s_l - g_l)il]v}{(m_0 + m_i i)(s_r - g_r)}$$

so that, for a given interest rate $i$, $du/dl > 0$ whenever $s_l > g_l$. The latter condition necessarily occurs in the *puzzling* case, because of the requirements of short run stability given by condition (28).

[24] In this case, recalling the previous footnote, a fall in the rate of accumulation, the rate of interest being given, need not be associated with a fall in the rate of utilization, since the condition $s_l > g_l$ need not hold.

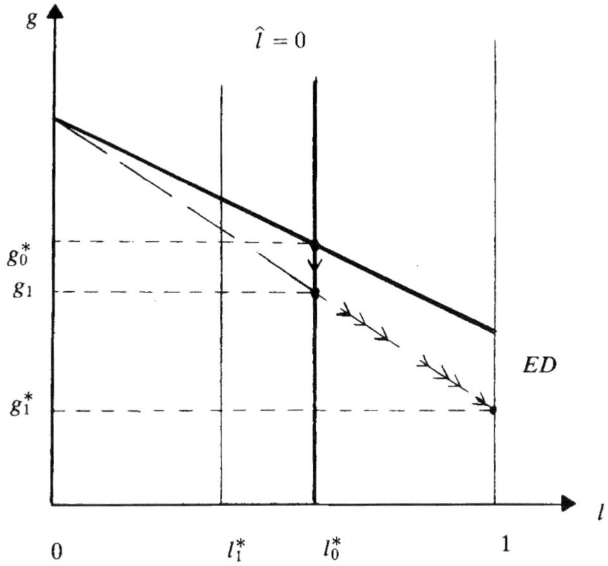


*Figure 6*

rates of interest have unfavourable consequences on the actual leverage ratio, effective demand and the rate of accumulation. Indeed, this is precisely the situation that many economies seem to be facing in the eighties and in the nineties. The ever-increasing leverage ratios, despite constant real rates of interest, are inducing entrepreneurs to cut the amount of funds they wish to borrow, in order to reestablish more conservative gearing and borrowing ratios. This is done by restraining investment expenditures. Such a behaviour is however unsuccessful. As can be seen in Figure 6, leverage ratios continue to rise although accumulation is being slowed down and interest rates stay constant.

This is a situation that was explored and described in great detail by Steindl (1952, ch. 9). It illustrates another fallacy of composition: although entrepreneurs and their bankers may wish to reduce leverage ratios in a recession, the macroeconomics may be such that this reduction need not occur. In the stable case of Figure 5, higher leverage ratios accompany higher rates of accumulation. This could be attributed to the fact that in a boom the acceptable leverage ratio usually rises, a fact emphasized by Minsky (1975, ch. 5–6) within the framework of his financial fragility hypothesis. But, as is also occasionally recognized by Minsky himself, 'the improvement of realized profits partially frustrates the planned debt-financing of investments of firms' (1975, p. 114). The targets set by individual firms may systematically be missed for macro-economic reasons. This sort of paradoxical situation would seem to occur in the case described by Figure 6 and it was clearly the subject of Steindl's attention as the following quote demonstrates.

> The entrepreneurs, even apart from their desire to reduce the initial gearing ratio, will soon be inclined to check this relative growth of their indebtedness, and their only possible reaction against it will be to reduce investment. This however will not put matters right .... Internal accumulation is reduced proportionately more than outside saving, so that the gearing ratio increases. Further reduction of investment will fall more heavily on internal accumulation than on outside savings, so that the gearing ratio will continue to increase, in spite of entrepreneurs' endeavours to reduce it by reduction of investment. Real accumulation, internal accumulation, and the profit rate will thus continue to fall and the gearing ratio will continue to rise. The outstanding feature of this *disequilibrium* is that the gearing ratio *in fact* established is continuously out of harmony with the ratio entrepreneurs *wish* to establish: this indeed is the reason for the continuing disequilibrium. There is a growing relative indebtedness against the wish of entrepreneurs, one might say an 'enforced indebtedness'. (Steindl 1952, pp. 114, 118–9).

An interesting feature of the model is that, depending on the leverage ratio actually inherited from the historical past, a drastic change in interest rates may lead to two different scenarios in the unstable case. This is illustrated in Figure 7. Suppose the initial interest rate and other parameters are such that the economy has been drifting away from the equilibrium leverage ratio given by $l_0^*$. Suppose now that the monetary authorities attempt to remedy this depressing state of affairs by reducing the real rate of interest, thus changing the equilibrium leverage ratio to its new value $l_1^*$. In the *A* scenario of Figure 7, this reduction will be insufficient because the actual leverage ratio is already too high. The rate of accumulation will increase momentarily to a higher rate, from which it will continually decrease while the leverage ratio continues to rise. By contrast, in the *B* scenario, with a lower historically given leverage ratio, the same reduction in the real rate of interest will induce a continuous rise in the rate of accumulation, while the leverage ratio will fall.

It should be noted that the B scenario gives credence to the belief that there are no inexorable forces that propel up real interest rates whenever accumulation is speeded up (Lavoie 1992, pp. 197–203). This

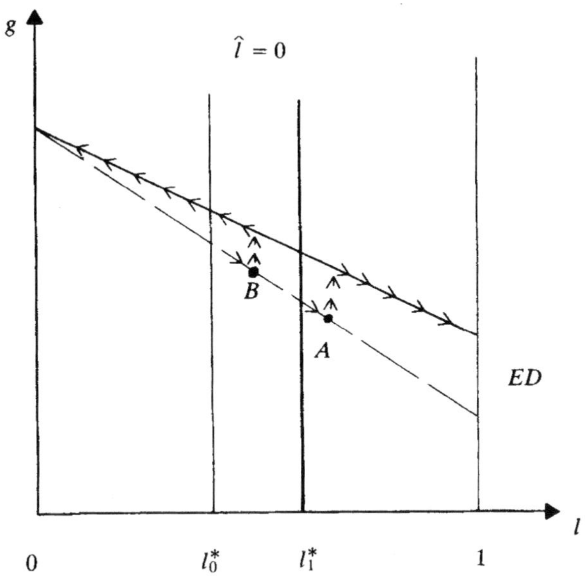


*Figure 7*

belief is based on two important features of a monetary production economy: the causality running from investment to savings, and the concept of money endogeneity. Those, among post-Keynesians, who recognize the validity of these two features while rejecting the theoretical independence of interest rates from accumulation rates, usually associate higher leverage ratios to higher accumulation rates (Wray 1990, pp. 134–8).[25] The *B* scenario of Figure 7 clearly shows that rising accumulation rates need not be associated with rising leverage ratios. As a consequence, one of the main reasons for associating rising accumulation rates with rising interest rates disappears. There are no natural forces which inescapably push up real interest rates. If real interest rates do rise, it is because the central bank has decided to modify the monetary regime.

## CONCLUSION

Five different post-Keynesian models of growth and distribution have been compared with regards to their behaviour following an increase in

[25] This relationship is often linked with Kalecki's principle of increasing risk.

the real rate of interest set by the monetary authorities. In the simple Kaleckian model, such an increase in interest rates only leads to a slowdown of accumulation. In the Cambridge and Eichnerian model, higher interest rates induce a *lower* normal profit rate, a lower realized profit rate and a lower accumulation rate. In the neo-Ricardian model, higher interest rates bring about a *higher* normal profit rate. A variant of this neo-Ricardian model, called the post-classical model, showed that increased interest rates could induce either higher or lower realized profit rates and rates of capacity utilization. Finally, it was also shown within the context of the so-called Minsky–Steindl model that higher real interest rates could lead to either higher or lower rates of accumulation. Endogenous credit-money and exogenous real interest rates can thus surely be introduced to good effect within post-Keynesian models of growth and distribution.

The Minsky–Steindl model, based on quite reasonable assumptions, showed further that long run stability is necessarily associated with the puzzling positive relationship between real interest rates and accumulation rates. The more standard negative relationship between real interest rates and accumulation rates is necessarily associated with long run instability: the economy is moving away from its equilibrium leverage ratio. If the described Minsky–Steindl model has any link with reality, and if the unstable case is the more likely, then it would appear that capitalist economies are continually in a slow traverse, with leverage ratios and accumulation rates exhibiting a negative relationship. This implies in particular that when individual entrepreneurs restrain their investment expenditures, as a consequence of high leverage ratios or in an effort to reduce their debt and borrowing ratios, they are generally unsuccessful as a group. This is the paradox emphasized by Steindl (1952): the macroeconomics is such that the efforts to reduce the leverage ratio lead to higher values of this ratio.

Another example of the paradoxical behaviour of the economy at the macro level has thus been uncovered, similar to Keynes's paradox of thrift and to Rowthorn's (1981, p. 18) paradox of costs. That such paradoxical results can be achieved within simple and heuristic models of the economy demonstrates their importance.

## REFERENCES

Agliardi E. (1988): Microeconomic foundations of macroeconomics in the post-Keynesian approach, *Metroeconomica*, 39(3), October, pp. 275–297.

Bhaduri A., and Marglin S. (1990): Unemployment and the real wage: the economic basis for contesting political ideologies, *Cambridge Journal of Economics*, 14(4), December, pp. 375–393.

Bhaduri A., and Robinson J. (1980): Accumulation and exploitation: an analysis in the tradition of Marx, Sraffa and Kalecki, *Cambridge Journal of Economics*, 4(2), June, pp. 103–115.

Ciccone R. (1986): Accumulation and capacity utilization: some critical considerations on Joan Robinson's theory of distribution, *Political Economy*, 2(1), pp. 17–36.

Ciccone R. (1990): Comment on Pivetti, in Bharadwaj, K., and Schefold, B., (eds), *Essays on Piero Sraffa: Critical Perspectives on the Revival of Political Economy*, Unwin Hyman, London.

Davidson P. (1972): *Money and the Real World*, Macmillan, London.

Dutt A. K. (1984): Stagnation, income distribution and monopoly power, *Cambridge Journal of Economics*, 8(1), March, pp. 25–40.

Dutt A. K. (1990): *Growth, Distribution and Uneven Development*, Cambridge University Press, Cambridge.

Dutt A. K. (1992): Rentiers in post-Keynesian models, in Arestis, P., and Chick, V. (eds.): *Recent Developments in Post-Keynesian Economics*, Edward Elgar, Aldershot.

Eichner A. S. (1976): *The Megacorp and Oligopoly: Micro Foundations of Macro Dynamics*, Cambridge University Press, Cambridge.

Eichner A. S. (1987): *The Macrodynamics of Advanced Market Economies*, M. E. Sharpe, Armonk.

Franke R., and Semmler W. (1991): A dynamical macroeconomic growth model with external financing of firms: a numerical stability analysis, in Nell, E. J., and Semmler, W., (eds.), *Nicholas Kaldor and Mainstream Economics: Confrontation or Convergence?*, Macmillan, London.

Gallegati M., and Gardini L. (1991): A nonlinear model of the business cycle with money and finance, *Metroeconomica*, 42(1), pp. 1–32.

Garegnani P. (1979): Notes on consumption, investment and effective demand: II, *Cambridge Journal of Economics*, 3(1), March, pp. 63–82.

Garegnani P. (1992): Some notes for an analysis of accumulation, in Halevi, J., Laibman, D., and Nell, E. J., (eds), *Beyond the Steady State: A Revival of Growth Theory*, Macmillan, London.

Harrod R. F. (1973): *Economic Dynamics*, Macmillan, London.

Jarsulic M. (1990):, Debt and macro stability, *Eastern Economic Journal*, 15(3), July–September, pp. 91–100.

Kaldor N. (1966): Marginal productivity and the macro-economic theories of distribution, *Review of Economic Studies*, 33, October, pp. 309–319.

Kaldor N. (1982): *The Scourge of Monetarism*, Oxford University Press, Oxford.

Kalecki M. (1937): The principle of increasing risk, *Economica*, 4(76), November, pp. 441–447.

Kregel J. A. (1985): Hamlet without the prince: Cambridge macroeconomics without money, *American Economic Review*, 75(2), May, pp. 133–139.

Kurz H. D. (1990a): Technical change, growth and distribution: a steady state approach to unsteady growth, in *Capital, Distribution and Effective Demand: Studies in the Classical Approach to Economic Theory*, Polity Press, Cambridge.

Kurz H. (1990b): Accumulation, distribution and the 'Keynesian' hypothesis, in Bharadwaj, K., and Schefold, B., (eds), *Essays on Piero Sraffa: Critical Perspectives on the Revival of Political Economy*, Unwin Hyman, London.

Lavoie M. (1992): *Foundations of Post-Keynesian Economic Analysis*, Edward Elgar, Aldershot.

Lavoie M. (1993): A Post-Classical View of Money, Interest, Growth and Distribution, in Mongiovi, G., and Rühl, C. (eds.): *Macroeconomic Theory: Diversity and Convergence*, Edward Elgar, Aldershot.

Le Bourva J. (1992): Money creation and credit multipliers, *Review of Political Economy*, 4(4), pp. 447–466.

Minsky H. P. (1975): *John Maynard Keynes*, Columbia University Press, New York.

Moon W. S. (1991): Taux d'accumulation et taux d'endettement dans le modèle d'accumulation post-Keynésien, *Économies et Sociétés*, 25(3), pp. 155–168.

Moore B. J. (1988): *Horizontalists and Verticalists: The Macroeconomics of Credit Money*, Cambridge University Press, Cambridge.

Nell E. J. (1988): Does the rate of interest determine the rate of profit?, *Political Economy*, 4(2), pp. 263–267.

Panico C. (1985): Market forces and the relation between the rates of interest and profits, *Contributions to Political Economy*, 4, pp. 37–60.

Panico C. (1988): *Interest and Profit in the Theories of Value and Distribution*, Macmillan, London.

Pasinetti L. L. (1988): Sraffa on income distribution, *Cambridge Journal of Economics*, 12(1), March, pp. 135–138.

Petri F. (1993): Critical notes on Kalecki's theory of investment, in Mongiovi, G., and Rühl, C., (eds.), *Macroeconomic Theory: Diversity and Convergence*, Edward Elgar, Aldershot.

Pivetti M. (1985): On the monetary explanation of distribution, *Political Economy*, 1(2), pp. 73–103.

Pivetti M. (1988): On the monetary explanation of distribution: a rejoinder to Nell and Wray, *Political Economy*, 4(2), pp. 275–283.

Pivetti M. (1991): *An Essay on Money and Distribution*, Macmillan, London.

Robinson J. (1952): *The Rate of Interest and Other Essays*, Macmillan, London.

Robinson J. (1956): *The Accumulation of Capital*, Macmillan, London.

Robinson J. (1962): *Essays in the Theory of Economic Growth*, Macmillan, London.

Robinson J. (1979): Garegnani on effective demand, *Cambridge Journal of Economics*, 3(1), March, pp. 179–180.

Rogers C. (1989): *Money, Interest and Capital: A Study in the Foundations of Monetary Theory*, Macmillan, London.

Roncaglia A. (1988): The neo-Ricardian approach and the distribution of income, in Asimakopulos, A., (ed.), *Theories of Income Distribution*, Kluwer, Boston.

Rowthorn B. (1981): Demand, real wages and economic growth, *Thames Papers in Political Economy*, Autumn, pp. 1–39. Reprinted in *Studi Economici*, (18), 1982, pp. 3–54, and also in Sawyer, M. C., (ed.), *Post-Keynesian Economics*, Edward Elgar, Aldershot (1989).

Sayers R. S. (1951): The rate of interest, in Wilson, T., and Andrews, P. W. S., (eds): *Oxford Studies in the Price Mechanism*, Clarendon Press, Oxford.

Schefold B. (1989): Distribution, prices and competition, in *Mr Sraffa on Joint Production and Other Essays*, Unwin Hyman, London.

Schefold B. (1993): Recension of Massimo Pivetti's An Essay on Money and Distribution, *Zeitschrift für die gesamte Staatswissenschaft*, (forthcoming).

Shapiro N. (1981): Pricing and the growth of the firm, *Journal of Post Keynesian Economics*, 4(1), Fall, pp. 85–100.

Skott P. (1989): *Conflict and Effective Demand in Economic Growth*, Cambridge University Press, Cambridge.

Skott P. (1992): On the modelling of systemic financial fragility, Working paper, University of Massachusetts at Amherst.

Sraffa P. (1960): *Production of Commodities by Means of Commodities: Prelude to a Critique of Economic Theory*, Cambridge University Press, Cambridge.

Steindl J. (1952): *Maturity and Stagnation in American Capitalism*, Basil Blackwell, Oxford; New Monthly Press, New York (1976).

Sylos Labini P. (1971): La théorie des prix en régime d'oligopole et la théorie du développement, *Revue d'économie politique*, 81(2), March–April, pp. 244–272.

Taylor L. (1991): *Income Distribution, Inflation, and Growth*, MIT Press, Cambridge (Mass.).
Turner M. (1989): *Joan Robinson and the Americans*, M. E. Sharpe, Armonk.
Vianello F. (1985): The pace of accumulation, *Political Economy*, 1(1), pp. 69–87.
Vianello F. (1990): Comment on Hicks, in Bharadwaj, K., and Schefold, B., (eds), *Essays on Piero Sraffa: Critical Perspectives on the Revival of Political Economy*, Unwin Hyman, London.
Wood A. (1975): *A Theory of Profits*, Cambridge University Press, Cambridge.
Wray L. R. (1988): The monetary explanation of distribution: a critique of Pivetti, *Political Economy*, 4(2), pp. 269–273.
Wray L. R. (1990): *Money and Credit in Capitalist Economies: The Endogenous Money Approach*, Edward Elgar, Aldershot.

Department of Economics
University of Ottawa
550 Cumberland St.
Ottawa (Ont.)
Canada K1N 6N5

[7]

# THE NEO-PASINETTI THEOREM IN CAMBRIDGE AND KALECKIAN MODELS OF GROWTH AND DISTRIBUTION

**Marc Lavoie**
*University of Ottawa*

The neoclassical theory of distribution is usually associated with diminishing marginal physical products, technical substitution, competition, and optimizing, where factor prices are determined by their relative scarcities. In Solow's neoclassical growth model, the long-run equilibrium growth rate is exogenous, set by the rate of growth of the labor force (and the exogenous rate of technical progress). The rate of profit is then endogenous, determined by this rate of growth, technology, and the rate of saving of the economy. In the so-called *new* neoclassical growth models, these relationships are reversed. When these models are reduced to their bare essentials, the steady-state rate of profit is the exogenous variable, while the rate of growth becomes an endogenous variable, entirely determined by the product of the profit rate and the given savings rate [Kurz, 1997].

In contrast to the above neoclassical view of growth and distribution, the so-called Cambridge school of thought emerged in the mid-1950s, with an emphasis on constant or increasing returns to scale, fixed technical coefficients, imperfect competition, behavioristic "rules of thumb", and a macroeconomic theory of income distribution [Hacche, 1979, 182]. In the Cambridge models of growth and distribution, the rate of profit is a macroeconomic variable, thus eschewing the drawbacks of assuming, as did the earlier neoclassical models of growth, that the rate of profit depends on the scarcity of capital relative to labor — a hypothesis that was shown to be based on dubious grounds during the capital controversies of the 1960s.[1] The other crucial feature of Cambridge models is the presence of an independent investment function, which insures that growth rates are endogenous variables. By contrast, neoclassical growth models generally assume that investment is driven by savings, even when steady-state growth rates are endogenous, while the old neoclassical models of the Solow type assumed more specifically that *full-employment* savings were the driving force.

In the models first proposed by Joan Robinson and Nicholas Kaldor, when savings out of wages are assumed away, the rate of profit of an economy only depends on its rate of accumulation and the propensity to save out of profits, to the exclusion of any other variable. Pasinetti [1962] generalized this result by noting that workers could earn both wages and profits, thus distinguishing between workers on the one hand and capitalists on the other, the latter earning only profits. Various neoclassical authors, such as Meade and Hahn [1965] and Samuelson and Modigliani [1966], objected to what became known as Pasinetti's paradox, that the long-run rate of profit of an economy depends only on its rate of economic growth and the propensity to save

*Eastern Economic Journal,* Vol. 24, No. 4, Fall 1998

of the capitalist class, to the exclusion of any other variable, including technological coefficients and worker's propensity to save. Neoclassical authors countered Pasinetti's paradox by showing that Pasinetti's result was just one of two possible regimes. They derived a second long-run equilibrium, where the propensity to save of the working class compared to that of the capitalist class would be such that the latter class would eventually disappear. With this anti-Pasinetti regime, as it was called by Kaldor, a way seemed open for reinstating marginal productivity analysis based on the flexibility of technical coefficients.

In response to the arguments by Samuelson and Modigliani [1966], Kaldor produced a model which he called a neo-Pasinetti theorem. The model had four connected purposes. First Kaldor wanted to produce a model, similar in spirit to that of Pasinetti, which would achieve similar results without requiring assumptions valid only in the long run. Secondly, Kaldor wanted to build a model for which no dual regime could be offered as a counterpoint. Thirdly, Kaldor's neo-Pasinetti theorem was meant as an attack on those neoclassical models where "savings governs investment." Finally, and perhaps most important, Kaldor [1978, xv] wanted "to clarify the reasons why the savings propensity out of profits must be considerably greater than the savings propensity out of wages and salaries, or of household incomes in general".

Whereas Kaldor's [1966] article is generally regarded as a neat reply to the empirical arguments supporting the likelihood of the anti-Pasinetti regime in long-run models of balanced growth, few authors have attempted to incorporate the results of the neo-Pasinetti theorem within a post-Keynesian framework.[2] Post-Keynesians have been of two minds when evaluating the importance of Kaldor's neo-Pasinetti theorem. On the one hand, it is regarded as a clear demonstration of a fundamental post-Keynesian thesis, (i.e., post-Keynesian models "are designed to project into the long period the central thesis of the *General Theory*, that firms are free, within wide limits, to accumulate as they please, and that the rate of saving of the economy as a whole accommodates itself to the rate of investment that they decree" [Robinson, 1962, 82-3]).[3] On the other hand, Kaldor's neo-Pasinetti theorem is also seen as a compromising concession to the neoclassical camp, because it incorporates an adjusting mechanism between savings and investment — the valuation ratio — which appears to be similar to the neoclassical interest rate mechanism.[4] In fact, for all practical purposes, Kaldor's *valuation ratio* is no different from Tobin's better-known *q-ratio*, which appears in many neoclassical models.[5]

This may explain why, with a few exceptions, the neo-Pasinetti theorem has been relegated to obscurity. The aim of the present paper is to offer a remedy for this lacuna, by providing a heuristic representation of the neo-Pasinetti model within the new framework developed by Kaleckians over the last fifteen years. Thus, in contrast to previous variants of the neo-Pasinetti theorem, we shall extend the model to situations where *both* the rate of accumulation and the rate of capacity utilization are *endogenous* variables. By doing so, we shall incorporate what is considered by many to be the main feature of Keynesian models in contrast to neoclassical models: the presence of an explicit and independent investment function. Furthermore, as will be shown, the incorporation of an endogenous rate of capacity utilization within the neo-Pasinetti model allows the model to retain its Keynesian results, even when investment is sensitive to the values taken by the valuation ratio. This is in sharp contrast to what occurred in previous models where the rate of capacity utilization was assumed to be constant.

The outline of the paper is the following. First, we shall recall the algebra and the graphics of the neo-Pasinetti theorem, with its two main variables, the rate of profit and the valuation ratio, when the rate of growth and the rate of capacity utilization are assumed to be exogenous. We then distinguish two different routes by which the rate of profit may adjust to its equilibrium value: through profit margins, as in the standard Cambridge models *à la* Kaldor and Robinson, and through rates of capacity utilization, as in the new Kaleckian models of growth and distribution. Just as in the new neoclassical growth models, we endogenize the rate of accumulation. We verify whether such a neo-Pasinetti model retains the properties of Kaleckian models of growth, while assuming away any feedback of the valuation ratio on the desired rate of growth. In the final section, we shall look more closely at the determinants of the valuation ratio when rates of capacity utilization are endogenous, and we shall consider in turn the impact of the valuation ratio as a determinant of investment decisions.

## THE STANDARD VIEW OF THE NEO-PASINETTI THEOREM

Although Kaldor's neo-Pasinetti theorem has generated contributions from just over a dozen authors, Araujo [1995] has recently reinterpreted it graphically.[6] While we follow Araujo in his graphics, we shall suppose that households have a single propensity to save on all income, as briefly assumed by Kaldor [1966, 318, fn. 1]. In doing so, we follow Robinson when she says that the "most important distinction between types of income is that between firms and households" [1962, 38]. In a sense, the assumption is more faithful to Kaldor since this distinction was at the core of his belief that the propensity to save out of profits is higher than the propensity to save out of wages, an assumption which drives the mechanics of most post-Keynesian models.[7] With the neo-Pasinetti theorem, Kaldor's intent is to free the determination of the profit rate from its classical dependency on a class of capitalists with a high savings propensity. By doing so, Kaldor provides additional institutional reality, introducing corporations, with leverage and retention ratios, as institutions with a role going beyond the preferences of their shareowners.[8]

The innovation in Kaldor's model is the explicit introduction of capital gains. These gains arise from the retained earnings accumulated by firms. The precise value of these capital gains depends on the valuation ratio. The valuation ratio is defined as the ratio between the financial value and the replacement value of capital. Kaldor's valuation ratio is indeed akin to Tobin's $q$-ratio, which is sometimes defined as the ratio between the market value of equity and the value of the stock of capital at replacement cost [Brainard and Tobin, 1968]. The higher the spread between the financial value of a unit of capital and the replacement cost of such a unit, the greater the capital gain per additional unit of investment. When dealing with the savings of households, one must account for the dissavings out of capital gains. In growth terms, equilibrium in the product market requires the following equality between investment and overall savings:

$$g = g^s = s_h[(u/k - r) + (1 - s_f)r)] - (1 - s_h)(v - x)g + s_f r. \tag{1}$$

The term associated with square brackets represents the savings out of wage income and out of distributed dividends; the next term stands for the dissavings out of capital gains, while the last term represents the retained earnings of the firm.[9] The notations are the following: $g$ is the rate of growth of the economy; $s_h$ the propensity to save of households; $k$ the capital to capacity ratio; $r$ the rate of profit; $v$ the valuation ratio; $s_f$ the retention ratio of firms; $x$ the proportion of investment which is financed by the issue of shares, or the external finance ratio. The latter two parameters are assumed to be given. The only innovation here is the introduction of $u$, the rate of capacity utilization, which is usually assumed constant and equal to unity.[10] In the present section we also assume that the rate of capacity utilization is a constant, but we make it an endogenous variable in the following sections.

Similarly, we may derive an equation expressing equilibrium in the financial market: the flow of supply of shares must equate the demand for shares, i.e., the supply arising from the issue of new shares by firms plus the sales of shares by households who desire to realise capital gains must equate the demand arising from the current savings of households out of ordinary income (wages and dividends). The supply flow is on the left-hand side of equation (2), while the demand flow is on the right-hand side:

$$xg + (1 - s_h)(v - x)g = s_h[(u/k - r) + (1 - s_f)r)]. \tag{2}$$

As Araujo [1995] notes, since the first condition describes the equilibrium in the product market, it is akin to an IS curve. We shall call it an ED curve, since it represents the locus of profit rates and valuation ratios for which the effective demand conditions are fulfilled. The second condition, which describes the equilibrium in the financial market, is akin to an LM curve. As a consequence we shall call it an FM curve. Equations (1) and (2) can be rewritten respectively as:

$$r = \{g[1 + (1 - s_h)(v - x)] - s_h u/k\}/[s_f(1 - s_h)], \tag{3}$$

$$r = \{-g[(1 - s_h)v + xs_h)] + s_h u/k\}/(s_h s_f). \tag{4}$$

With the rate of profit $r$ expressed as a function of the valuation ratio, the ED curve has a positive slope. In the product market, a higher profit rate, associated with higher savings, must be compensated by a higher valuation ratio, associated with larger dissavings out of capital gains. On the other hand the FM curve has a negative slope.[11] An increase in the rate of profit diminishes the share of output left to households: hence it diminishes the demand for equities. This must be compensated by a decrease in the supply of equities, a decrease that will need to be accommodated by a fall in the value of the shares sold by existing shareowners, and hence by a fall in the valuation ratio. The rate of profit plays the role of the output level in Hicksian IS/LM models, whereas the valuation ratio, as already said, plays the inverse of the role of the interest rate in such models, which is why the slopes of the ED and FM curves here are inverted compared to the standard Hicksian IS and LM curves.

The equilibrium values of the rate of profit and of the valuation ratio are given by:[12]

(5) $$r^* = g(1 - x)/s_f.$$

(6) $$v^* = s_h(u/gk - 1)/(1 - s_h).$$

While the product market is assumed to clear through variations in the rate of profit and the stock market is assumed to clear through variations in the valuation ratio, we have a two-equation system with two variables, the variations of which affect both markets as Rimmer [1993, 55] and Araujo [1995] have pointed out. What is remarkable about the neo-Pasinetti theorem is that once these two adjusting mechanisms are taken for granted, the rate of profit and the rate of growth are linked through a relationship — given by equation (5) — which is independent of the propensity to save of households. This yields the main feature of Pasinetti's model — savings of workers have no impact on the rate of profit.[13] In that context, until we examine more closely the possible determinants of the rate of accumulation, it would seem indeed that firms are free to accumulate at the rate that they wish, provided the rate of profit (and the valuation ratio) can adjust. If this is the case, "demand will be brought in line with capacity, no matter what the rate of growth of capacity", and hence "the growth rate becomes indeterminate" [Wood, 1975, 118].

In light of this indeterminacy, several commentators on Kaldor's neo-Pasinetti model have interpreted the rate of accumulation to be the natural rate of growth, i.e., the full employment rate of growth [Davidson, 1968, 259; 1972, 300; Harcourt, 1972, 220]. This need not be the case, however, as Léonard [1980, 135] and Lavoie [1987, 189] have pointed out, and as Kaldor himself acknowledged.[14] More specifically, we may introduce an independent investment function which will help determine the actual rate of growth set by the entrepreneurs.

But before we do so, let us examine what happens in the neo-Pasinetti model as firms set a higher rate of accumulation. Let us assume, as is usually done in the interpretation of the neo-Pasinetti theorem, that the rate of utilization $u$ is a constant. First, taking the derivatives of equations (3) and (4) with respect to $g$, we see that the ED curve would shift upwards while the FM curve would shift downwards. This implies, as can be seen immediately from the right-hand side of Figure 1, that the valuation ratio $v$ must necessarily be lower with a higher rate of accumulation. This is confirmed by taking the derivative of equation (6) with respect to $g$ ($dv^*/dg < 0$). Now what about the impact on the rate of profit? Once all the proper adjustments are made, the impact is necessarily positive, as can be verified by taking the derivative of equation (5) ($dr^*/dg = (1 - x)/s_f > 0$). This can also be seen on the left-hand side of Figure 1, reading along the NP curve, which represents the key feature of the neo-Pasinetti model, and which shows how accumulation is financed, in accordance with equation (5).

While it is easily understood that, when accumulation is accelerated, an excess supply of shares in the financial markets will reduce the price of shares and hence the valuation ratio, what is the mechanism that drives up the rate of profit along the NP curve? This is the topic of the next section.

**FIGURE 1**

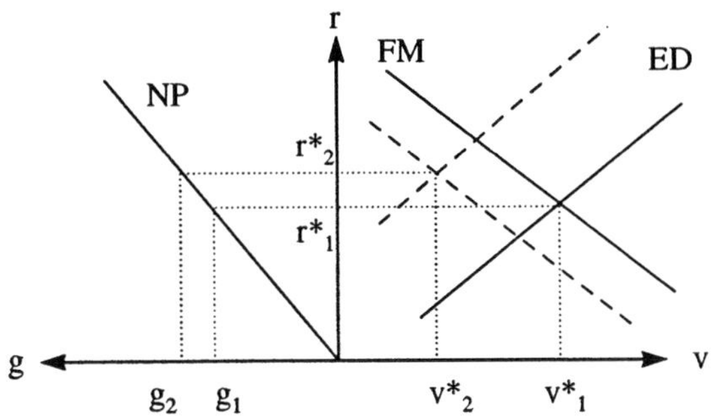


## ADJUSTMENT MECHANISMS IN THE CAMBRIDGE AND KALECKIAN FRAMEWORKS

Two adjustment mechanisms may help explain rising profit rates when accumulation is accelerated. According to the first mechanism — the Cambridge case, based either on a competitive model with full capacity utilization, or on the maintenance of normal rates of capacity utilization within an oligopolistic framework — prices and profit margins will rise when aggregate demand speeds up. This mechanism has been explored by almost all authors dealing with the neo-Pasinetti model. It is associated with the other well-known growth models of Kaldor and Robinson, but also with the more modern ones, set explicitly within an oligopolistic framework, where mark-ups set by price leaders are proportional to growth trends, just as they would be in models of growth based on assumptions of pure competition.[15]

A second possible mechanism is based on the endogeneity of the rate of capacity utilization which has been endorsed by both Kaleckians and Sraffians.[16] According to this second mechanism — the Kaleckian case, based on an oligopolistic environment with excess capacity, subjected to labor market pressures — profit margins need not be modified when growth rates rise. But the higher rates of capacity utilization will nevertheless allow for higher profit rates. We shall consider each of these mechanisms in turn.

As was pointed out in the previous section, the rate of accumulation is assumed to be given in the neo-Pasinetti model. Let us maintain this assumption for now, and consider how the rate of profit would adjust to the new rate of accumulation of the economy. First, consider the following identity, remembering that the profit rate is the ratio of profits to the value of capital:

$$r = P/K = (P/Y)(Y/C)(C/K),$$

where $P$ stands for profits, while $Y$ and $C$ are respectively output and full-capacity output. The rate of profit can thus be broken down into three components:

$$r = mu/k, \tag{7}$$

where $m$ is the share of profits in national income, while $u$ and $k$ are defined as before as the rate of capacity utilization and the capital to full-capacity output ratio.

We call this relationship the profits-cost function since profits are seen from the supply-side angle. In the simplified version of the Kaleckian model which we consider here, where overhead costs arising from labor or capital use are assumed away, the share of profits $m$ is identical to the profit margin set by firms through their pricing procedure.[17] For instance, within a simple mark-up procedure, the mark-up rate would be $\theta$, where $\theta$ is such that prices are defined as $p = (1 + \theta)\text{UVC}$, where UVC are the unit variable costs. In such a case, the share of profit, or the profit margin, is $m = \theta/(1 + \theta)$.

Let us first consider the Cambridge case, where the rate of utilization is assumed to be constant at its normal level, called $u_n$, while profit margins are flexible.[18] The profit margin must vary in line with the required rate of profit, as given by its solution found in equation (5). Making use of equation (7), we see that the profit margin must become equal to:

$$m^* = gk(1 - x)/s_f u_n. \tag{8}$$

Any increase in the rate of accumulation will thus require a higher rate of profit, and this higher rate of profit will be accommodated by an increase in the profit margin (i.e., a fall in real wages).[19] On the other hand, as is illustrated in the middle of Figure 2, a higher rate of accumulation and a higher rate of profit will be accommodated by a rise in profit margins, and a downwards shift of the profits cost function, shown here by the PC curves, while the rate of utilization remains at its normal value $u_n$. This is the mechanism sometimes contemplated by early Cambridge authors: "But let us suppose that competition ... is sufficiently keen to keep prices at the level at which normal capacity output can be sold" [Robinson 1962, 46].[20] The other mechanism, also contemplated by Robinson and Kaldor, but mainly made explicit by their followers, is that oligopolistic firms set profit margins to provide the retained earnings required to finance the secular rate of accumulation. What we have is a "long run model of determination of the share of profits at normal full capacity use" [Wood, 1975, 129].

We need not suppose however that the rate of capacity utilization is always at its normal level or equal to unity. Kaleckian authors have recently underlined the flexibility of the rate of capacity utilization, even in the long run, arguing either that no mechanism could automatically bring back the rate of utilization to its normal level, or that if such a mechanism did exist, one had to take into account the fact that the normal rate of utilization could itself become an endogenous variable.[21] As an alternative closure to the neo-Pasinetti theorem, one may consider the profit margin $m$ to be a given, while the rate of utilization is flexible and accommodates any change in de-

**FIGURE 2**

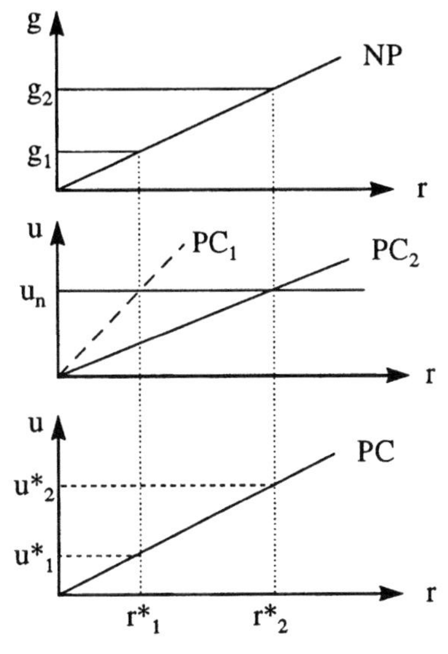


mand.[22] This corresponds to what one could expect in an oligopolistic economy with reserves of capacity. Under these conditions, the rate of utilization would vary in line with the required rate of profit. Taking again into account equations (5) and (7), the rate of utilization needs to be:

$$u^* = gk(1 - x)/s_f m. \tag{9}$$

This case is illustrated on the bottom part of Figure 2. An increase in the rate of accumulation and hence the rise in the required rate of profit are accommodated by an increase in the rate of utilization, at given profit margins (a fixed PC curve). The neo-Pasinetti theorem is perfectly compatible with rigid prices and profit margins. Here the valuation ratio and the rate of capacity utilization are the ultimate variables accommodating changes in the values of the parameters.

## AN ENDOGENOUS RATE OF ACCUMULATION

Let us now relax the hypothesis of an exogenously given rate of accumulation and take into account an explicit investment function. This will remove the indeterminacy of the growth rate. In the standard Cambridge investment function, higher expected profits are assumed to induce entrepreneurs to enter into more investment projects. For a given stock of capital, this implies that the rate of accumulation ($g^i = I/K$) decided by entrepreneurs depends on the expected rate of profit, and hence, in long-run equilibrium, on the realized rate of profit ($r = P/K$). In linear form, we have:

$$g^i = \gamma + g_r r$$

where $\gamma$ and $g_r$ are parameters that represent the animal spirits of the entrepreneurs and those of bankers who grant credit allowing firms to go ahead with their investment plans.

The advantage of such a formulation is that it provides us with a recursive model, where the rate of accumulation is fully independent of profit margins [Lavoie 1992, 302]. The drawback is that, for the rest of the model, it is as if the rate of growth $g$ were still a given variable. The results obtained with such an equation would not be any different from the ones presented in the previous section. The steady-state rate of growth would be determined in the upper graph of Figure 2, at the point where the NP curve intersects with the investment function given above.

Let us then consider an equation where investment is a function of the rate of utilization instead of the rate of profit, as many Kaleckians would have it when assuming that the rate of capacity utilization is an endogenous variable even in the long run. The logic of the argument is the following: the larger the current rate of capacity utilization, the higher the probability that some firms would hit full-capacity output as a result of the fluctuations of demand, and hence be unable to respond fully to demand and retain their share of the market. High rates of capacity utilization would thus induce more firms to enter into new investment projects, and hence, for a historically given level of capacity, induce a higher rate of capital accumulation. The investment equation in growth terms now is:

(10) $$g^i = \gamma + g_u u$$

where $\gamma$ and $g_u$ are again parameters that represent animal spirits in the economy.

If equation (10) is the investment function, what then is the equivalent of the savings function? The savings function is given by equation (5), the function showing how accumulation is financed. The profit rate, however, must be given in terms of the rate of capacity utilization, which is done by making use of equation (7), the profits-cost function. These two equations yield the $g^s$ curve of Figure 3 and the following savings equation:

(11) $$g^s = s_f m u/k(1 - x).$$

Putting together the investment and the savings function — equations (10) and (11) — yields the steady-state rate of accumulation:

(12) $$g^* = (\gamma s_f)/[s_f - (k/m)(1 - x)g_u].$$

As is usual with models of this type, equilibria are stable if the slope of the investment function is smaller than that of the savings function. This implies that the denominator of equation (12) is positive ($s_f$ must be sufficiently large), and hence that the constant term $\gamma$ must be positive for $g^*$ to have a positive solution, as is obvious from the inspection of Figure 3.

**FIGURE 3**

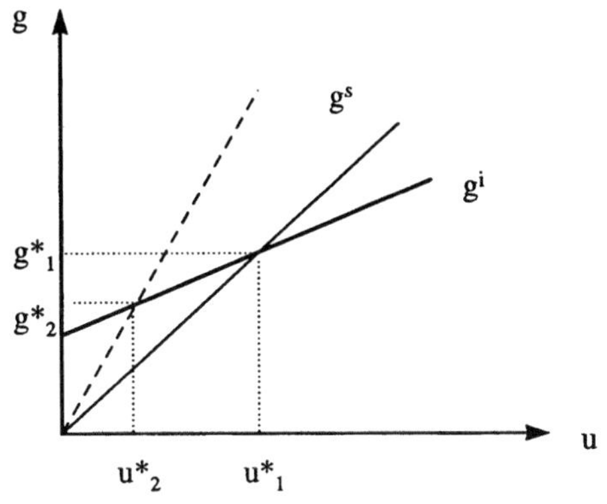


Since an increase in the retention ratio $s_f$ or in the external finance ratio $x$ will rotate the savings curve $g^s$ towards the left, such changes in parameters will lead to a fall in the steady-state rate of accumulation. Both of these changes lead to a fall in effective demand. In addition the rate of accumulation $g^*$ depends negatively on the profit margin $m$. An increase in the profit margin would again rotate the $g^s$ curve to the left, thus inducing lower rates of utilization and of accumulation, as shown in Figure 3. As a result, the rate of profit is lowered. Standard Kaleckian results (the paradox of costs: higher real wage costs lead to higher realized profit rates) are thus vitiated within the framework of the neo-Pasinetti theorem.[23] Note again that in the neo-Pasinetti model, changes in the propensity to save of households ($s_h$) have no impact whatsoever on the equilibrium rate of accumulation, as long as investment does not depend on the valuation ratio.

## VALUATION RATIOS AND GROWTH RATES

This leads us to an issue that has been emphasized by previous students of the neo-Pasinetti theorem, but which had been left aside to clear up the discussion. The issue is whether firms are truly free to accumulate as they wish, whatever the savings rate of households. Two observations have been made in the past: first, recall as we saw above by looking at equation (6), that a higher rate of accumulation, *ceteris paribus*, is associated with a lower valuation ratio; second, it can easily be shown, again by inspection of equation (6), that an increase in the propensity to save of households $s_h$ is associated with a higher valuation ratio.[24] The decisions by the managers of firms to step up growth, when the savings decisions of households remain unchanged, may thus lead to lower valuation ratios and hence lower share prices.

The first question to tackle is whether or not valuation ratios will have any impact on the investment behavior of firms. Three positions may be taken. The first is to deny that valuation ratios (and hence implicit rates of return on shares) have any impact on the real investment decisions of firms. This would particularly be the case of managerial firms living in a world of fundamental uncertainty, where neither corporate managers nor shareholders have sufficient information and knowledge to influence the behavior of each other [Moss, 1976; Crotty, 1990]. That the valuation ratio is irrelevant to the investment decisions of entrepreneurs is also the opinion of New Keynesian authors. They argue that firms hardly ever sell shares to raise capital funds and hence that the price of shares is of no significance when compared to sales expectations [Greenwald and Stiglitz, 1987, 130]. This is also Kaldor's own position on the matter:[25]

> The stock exchange value of a company can fall to say one half of the value of the assets employed in the business. But this does not change the decision as to whether it is worthwhile to undertake some investment or not; the implicit rate of return would only become relevant to the firm's decisions if the normal method of financing investment were to be the issue of ordinary shares for cash — which in fact plays a very small role. Most of the finance comes from ploughed back profits, in which case the expected internal rate of return is relevant and not the implicit rate of return.

The second position is to argue, as in the first position, that real investment does not depend on the values taken by the valuation ratio, but only under the proviso that the latter exceeds unity ($v > 1$). Otherwise, the rate of accumulation would fall to zero. This is a position taken by several authors [Moss, 1978, 317; Lavoie 1987, 176; Abraham-Frois, 1991, 198]. They argue that when the valuation ratio falls below unity, plants can be purchased through financial markets at a fraction of production cost. As Keynes put it, "there is no sense in building up a new enterprise at a cost greater than that at which a similar enterprise can be purchased" [1936, 151]. In the neo-Pasinetti model with a fixed rate of capacity utilization, as can be derived from equation (6), the rate of accumulation has clear limits. A higher than unity valuation ratio requires the fulfilment of the following inequality:

$$s_h u_n > gk.$$

Finally, there is a third position: that the rate of accumulation will be continuously affected by the valuation ratio, as it would be in Tobin's $q$-theory of investment [Brainard and Tobin, 1968]. Rimmer [1993, 112] explicitly and Moore [1973; 1975] implicitly state this position.[26] While the first position was implicitly taken in the previous section, we now explore this third position.

Suppose that firms behave partly in a Kaleckian manner, and partly in a Tobinian manner; i.e., they speed up accumulation when the rate of capacity utilization is below its normal level, but they also speed up accumulation when the valuation ratio is above unity (i.e., when the internal rate of profit on capital is higher than the implicit rate of return on shares). The investment function would then be:

(13) $$g^i = \gamma + g_u u + g_v v,$$

or more precisely, it could be rewritten as:

(14) $$g^i = \gamma + g_u(u - u_n) + g_v(v - 1).$$

Whether one adopts the second or the third position, the implication is the same: firms are not quite free to accumulate as they please. If the valuation ratio must be above unity or some other value, it could happen that the efforts of firms to speed up accumulation would be hampered and even counter-productive, unless households are persuaded to save at a higher rate.[27] If the investment function must include the valuation ratio, then the neo-Pasinetti model loses part of its recursivity.

Let us check, however, whether an increase in the rate of accumulation still leads to a fall in the valuation ratio *when the rate of capacity utilization is free to vary*. We shall find that output growth and the valuation ratio are usually *positively* related, in contrast to what occurs in the standard formalization of Kaldor's neo-Pasinetti model. In this standard interpretation, it is assumed that the rate of utilization of capacity is a given, equal either to unity or to its normal level. The variable $u$ which appears in equation (6) is thus a constant, and the negative impact of a higher rate of accumulation on the valuation ratio is thus certain, as we saw above. The contribution of the newer Kaleckian models is that these models, in contrast to the Cambridge models, old or new, do not assume that the rate of utilization is a given, even in the long run. The consequence is that, as the rate of accumulation increases, the rate of capacity utilization increases as well, as can be read from equation (9), thus providing a compensating positive effect on the valuation ratio, as can be seen from equation (6).

Let us then reconsider the equilibrium value of the valuation ratio, as given by equation (6), taking into account the flexibility of rates of capacity utilization by making use of equation (12). This valuation ratio is now given by:

(15) $$v^* = [(s_h)/(1 - s_h)][(1 - x)/ms_f - 1].$$

A higher than unity valuation ratio would thus require the following condition:

(16) $$s_h(1 - x) > ms_f.$$

The above two equations clearly show that any increase in the rate of accumulation induced by a change in one of the parameters of the investment function will have no impact whatsoever on the valuation ratio. On the other hand, an increase in the household propensity to save induces an increase in the valuation ratio, as was the case when rates of utilization were constant. It also turns out that higher external finance ratios, retention ratios, and profit margins all lead to lower valuation ratios. These results and those pertaining to the effects of these parameters on the endogenous rate of accumulation, when that rate is assumed to be impervious to changes in the valuation ratio, are presented in the table below. A higher rate of accumulation induced by a lower profit margin $m$ — as would occur in the Kaleckian model and its solution given by equation (12) — would lead to a higher valuation ratio. Similarly, a fall in the retention ratio $s_f$ or in the external finance ratio $x$, while inducing an increase in the rate of accumulation, would lead to a higher valuation ratio.[28] Finally, an increase in the household propensity to save, $s_h$, would have no direct impact on the rate of accumulation but would push up the valuation ratio.

**Impact of changes in various parameters on the equilibrium values of the valuation ratio and the rate of accumulation, as given by equations (15) and (12)**

| | $s_h$ | $s_f$ | $x$ | $m$ | $\gamma$ | $g_u$ |
|---|---|---|---|---|---|---|
| $v^*$ (15) | + | – | – | – | 0 | 0 |
| $g^*$ (12) | 0 | – | – | – | + | + |

The consequences of the above for a model in which the investment function would incorporate the valuation ratio, as in equations (13) and (14), are now obvious. Such an investment function would not alter the fundamental result of the neo-Pasinetti theorem, (i.e., it would have no impact on the claim that firms are free to accumulate as they please). Higher rates of accumulation resulting from higher animal spirits have no impact on valuation ratios, while the effect of lower retention ratios and lower profit margins on rates of accumulation and valuation ratios would be self-reinforcing: both would be increasing. The Keynesian causal mechanism — investment causes savings — and the Kaleckian paradox of costs are thus retained, even in a model where firms have a Tobinian behavior. However, an increase in the propensity to save of households would induce higher rates of accumulation, because of its positive effect on the valuation ratio. This is where introducing the valuation ratio in the investment function, as in equations (13) and (14), yields counter-intuitive results from a post-Keynesian perspective.[29]

## CONCLUSION

Kaldor's neo-Pasinetti theorem can easily be integrated into Cambridge and Kaleckian frameworks. The adjustment of household savings to the investment decisions of corporations, based on their desired rate of accumulation, is done through the valuation ratio and the profit rate, as in the original neo-Pasinetti theorem. Whereas in the Cambridge model the profit rate had to adjust through changes in profit margins, in the Kaleckian variant the profit rate adjusts through changes in the rate of capacity utilization. The validity of the neo-Pasinetti theorem thus clearly extends to under-employment situations with excess reserves of capacity; it is not limited to full-employment or full-capacity economies.

An interesting feature of this modernized version of the neo-Pasinetti theorem, in contrast to its full-capacity version, is that higher rates of accumulation need not be associated with lower valuation ratios. Indeed, in many instances a higher rate of accumulation will induce a higher valuation ratio, because higher rates of growth will generally be associated with higher rates of capacity utilization, which have a highly favourable effect on valuation ratios. The belief, expressed by Joan Robinson, that firms are free to accumulate as they please within wide limits, is thus confirmed, even in an economy where the managers of firms take into account the implicit view of financial markets. This is an important result, because it has often been argued in the past that the Keynesian aspects of the neo-Pasinetti theorem do not hold when entrepreneurs incorporate the level of the valuation ratio in their investment decisions. The domain of validity for such an objection is narrower than previously thought.

It should be noted however that no attempt has been made to take into account the main critique that has been addressed against Kaldor's neo-Pasinetti model. As was pointed out by Davidson [1968; 1972], Kaldor assumes that shares are the only available asset: households must purchase shares with their entire savings, and hence they never try to acquire money balances. An alternative position is to suppose that "when banks provide deposits to satisfy the liquidity preference of rentiers, they hold shares of firms" [Robinson, 1971, 117]. A more adequate model would have to assume that firms issue shares and take on bank loans at a fixed interest rate, while households make a portfolio choice between bank deposits (or bonds) and shares. Such a generalized neo-Pasinetti model, dealing both with stocks and flows, has been proposed by Skott [1981; 1988], showing essentially that some of Kaldor's conclusions hold even in this more realistic case.[30]

## APPENDIX

This appendix is devoted to the more general case with overhead costs. It turns out that some of the conclusions reached with the more simple case without overhead costs must be questioned. Let us first reassess the profits cost function. In the more general case with overhead costs, we may still interpret $m$ as the margin of profit over direct costs, but the profits cost relationship now becomes more complex and can be written as:

$$r = [mu - (1 - m)f - \delta k]/k \tag{7'}$$

where $f$ is the ratio of fixed to variable labor at full capacity utilization, and where $\delta$ is the rate of depreciation of capital [Rowthorn, 1981; Lavoie, 1992].[31]

Let us now consider what happens when this more complex profits cost function is used to compute the equilibrium value of the valuation ratio, i.e., when we combine the Kaleckian investment function (10) to the NP curve given by equation (5). From equation (6), we obtain:

$$v^* = \{(s_h)/[s_f k(1 - s_h)]\}\{\gamma(1 - x)k + s_f[(1 - m)f + \delta k]\}/\{m\gamma + g_u[(1 - m)f + \delta k]\} - (s_h)/(1 - s_h). \tag{15'}$$

Taking the partial derivatives of the equation above, it can be shown that, as before, a lower retention ratio, a lower external finance ratio, and a lower profit margin will induce a higher valuation ratio (and a higher rate of accumulation). In addition, a higher rate of depreciation $\delta$ and a higher ratio of fixed labor $f$ will also induce both a higher valuation ratio and a higher rate of accumulation. For these variables, the introduction of the Tobinian $q$-theory investment equation makes no difference: the effects induced by the valuation ratio are self-reinforcing. On the other hand, in contrast to the simple case without overhead costs, an increase in the parameters representing the animal spirits of the entrepreneurs, $\gamma$ and $g_u$, will induce a fall in the valuation ratio. If there are sufficiently strong feedback effects (a high $g_u$), an increase in the animal spirits of entrepreneurs may thus lead to some paradoxical results.

## NOTES

This paper was presented at the inaugural conference of the Ph.D. program of the University of Brasilia, on April 2-4 1997. The conference was organized by Joanilio Rodolpho Teixeira on the theme "Money, growth, distribution and structural change". I wish to thank the participants at the confererence, as well as Mario Seccareccia, Steve Pressman and the anonymous referees of the journal for their useful comments. The usual disclaimers apply.

1. An account of these debates can be found in Harcourt [1972]. Articles are still being published about the Pasinetti and the anti-Pasinetti regimes: see for instance Samuelson [1991] and Baranzini [1991].
2. According to Thirlwall [1987, 169], Kaldor's neo-Pasinetti theorem "was left unchallenged" by the Cambridge, Massachusetts school. In a letter to Kaldor, Samuelson and Modigliani promised that they would respond to his model, but they never did.
3. This is clearly the interpretation of Robinson [1971, 117-25] in her discussion of investment financing and of Kaldor's neo-Pasinetti model. Shapiro [1977] argues that the revolutionary character of post-Keynesian models is that investment is independent of the intertemporal consumption decisions of households.
4. See Davidson [1968, 259; 1972, 300]. A higher valuation ratio is associated with a lower rate of return on shares — a lower rate of interest. This can be shown with the help of Richard Kahn's formula, established in 1964 but published only in Kahn [1972, 214], where the valuation ratio is given by $v = (r - g)/(i - g)$, where $g$, $r$ and $i$ are respectively the rate of growth, the rate of profit and the rate of return on shares. In a letter to me, dated 9th November 1983, Kaldor says that "in fact I did not realise that the valuation ratio indicates an implicit rate of return on shares."
5. The $q$-ratio usually comes down to be equal to $q = y_k/i$, where $y_k$ is the marginal productivity of capital and $i$ is the rate of return on equity [Rogers, 1989, 121]. Since the rate of profit ($r$) and the marginal productivity of capital are presumed to be equated in neoclassical theory, omitting the rate of growth of capital ($g$), the above relationship is similar to that established by Kahn, as shown in the previous footnote.
6. These authors are: Pettenati [1967], Davidson [1968, 1972], Robinson [1971], Marris [1972], Moore [1973; 1975], Moss [1976; 1978], Léonard [1980], Odagiri [1981], Skott [1981; 1988; 1989a; 1989b], Lavoie [1987; 1990], Rimmer [1989; 1993], Abraham-Frois [1989; 1991], Araujo [1995], Panico [1997].
7. The cause of this inequality is pointed out in his very first Cambridgian model of growth and distribution: "This may be assumed independently of any skewness in distribution of property, simply as a consequence of the fact that the bulk of profits accrues in the form of company profits and a high proportion of companies' marginal profits is put to reserve" [1956, 95]. Kaldor reasserted this ten years later: "I have always regarded the high savings propensity out of profits as something which attaches to the nature of business income, and not to the wealth (or other peculiarities) of the individuals who own property" [1966, 310].
8. Kaldor's views on savings propensities are given empirical substance in Marglin [1984, 409-411].
9. Savings in growth terms are given by $S/K$, where $K$ is the replacement value of capital. $u/k$ represents output per unit of capital and $r$ is profit per unit of capital; therefore $(u/k - r)$ represents wages per unit of capital. Also $(1 - s_f)r$ are distributed dividends per unit of capital while $s_f r$ are the non-distributed dividends per unit of capital, i.e., the retained earnings of the firms. In a steady-state, an investment to the amount of $I = gK$ induces an increase in the value of all shares equal to $vI$. If however $xI$ shares are being sold in the period, the capital gain *per share* is only $(v - x)I = (v - x)gK$. The capital gain per share per unit of capital is thus $(v - x)g$. A proportion $(1 - s_h)$ of this capital gain is assumed to be realized for consumption purposes, i.e., for dissaving.

10. The only exception is Skott [1988; 1989a, 71]. In other models, the capital/output ratio $k/u$ is assumed to be constant. In neoclassical models, firms are usually assumed to be atomistic price takers and hence firms are assumed to produce at full capacity ($u = 1$), since their owners believe they can sell any amount at the going price [Dutt, 1990a, 16]. In Kaldorian models of the late fifties and early sixties, Kaldor assumed or tried to demonstrate that the only relevant equilibrium for the representative firm was one of full employment and full capacity utilization. Most of those who developed the neo-Pasinetti theorem thus kept these convenient assumptions [Skott, 1989b, 77-93].
11. Thus in the simple case where the propensity to save is the same whatever the source of income, the signs of the slopes of the two curves are the same as those arising from the case where savings out of dividends are excluded, which is the case considered by Araujo [1995] and by Kaldor [1966] in his main text. Thus the stability proof supplied by Araujo applies here as well.
12. The numerator of $v^*$, and hence $v^*$ itself, is always positive, since $u > gk$ implies that total output exceeds output from the investment industry — a condition that would necessarily have to be realized.
13. In a neo-Pasinetti model akin to that of Moss [1978], with two classes of households, workers and capitalists, where the latter have a single propensity to save, Odagiri [1981, 104] demonstrates another variant of the neo-Pasinetti theorem: $i$, the *rate of return on stock market shares* only depends on the rate of accumulation and the propensity to save of the capitalists: $i = g/s_c$. This result is obtained with the help of Kahn's relation, as defined in footnote 4.
14. "It is not *necessary* to assume full employment in order that the 'Keynesian' mechanism of adjusting the saving ratio to the investment coefficient should operate" [Kaldor 1964, xvii]. In a letter to me, dated 30th October 1982, Kaldor says that "in retrospect I much regret that I used the full employment assumption which was the cause of great confusion."
15. The more modern Cambridgian models can be found in Eichner [1973], Wood [1975], and Harcourt and Kenyon [1976].
16. See Dutt [1990a] and Lavoie [1992] for the former, and Kurz [1994] for the latter.
17. The more general case with overhead labor costs is treated in the appendix.
18. Those who wonder why firms would want to keep capacity utilization at its normal rate can assume instead that utilization is at its full capacity level, meaning then that $u = 1$.
19. Wood [1975, 109] arrives precisely at this equation, but with the assumption that $u_n = 1$.
20. Davidson caught this assumption early on: "In Joan Robinson's model... it is assumed that competition brings down market prices (and profit margins) *at the normal or standard volume of output*" [1972, 125].
21. For various formalizations of the latter case, see Lavoie [1996].
22. Changes in output levels are also identified by Davidson [1972, 308] as a possible adjustment mechanism within the framework of Kaldor's model.
23. This effect can be linked to a similar result, achieved by Dutt [1990b] in a two-class model *à la* Pasinetti, to which savings by firms has been added. The paradox of costs is also sustained when rates of capacity utilization are flexible. Naturally, a drop in the animal spirits, given by $\gamma$ or $g_u$, would also lead to a fall in the rates of accumulation and of capacity utilization, except that the $g^i$ curve would shift down instead.
24. See the discussions around these two partial derivatives in Moore [1973; 1975], Lavoie [1990], Abraham-Frois [1991].
25. This is his position as expressed in a letter to me, dated 9th November 1983.
26. Delli Gatti, Gallegati and Gardini [1990, 107] provide a mix of the second and third positions, which they call the Keynes-Davidson-Minsky theory of investment determination, by assuming that the rate of accumulation is continuously affected by the valuation ratio as long as it exceeds unity, at which point a discontinuity arises with accumulation dropping to zero.
27. According to Moore such an argument "leads back to the neoclassical conclusions of the control of the rate of accumulation by saver preferences, albeit through a quite different mechanism. A reward to property must be paid ... to induce wealth owners to hold voluntarily, and not to spend on current consumption, the wealth accumulation that results from business investment" [1973, 543].
28. Note that the retention ratio $s_f$ did not have an impact on the valuation ratio when the rate of accumulation $g$ was seen as an exogenous variable (such a result requires however that households have a single propensity to save on all sources of income, as shown by Abraham-Frois [1991, 194]). When the realized rate of accumulation depends on one of the investment functions — equations (7) or (14) — this independence vanishes.

29. As argued by both Skott [1989a, 124] and Lavoie [1990, 130], this may be Asimakopulos's best defence when he made the statement — surprising from a post-Keynesian perspective — to the effect that "the independence of investment ... from saving is not as robust as Keynes stated. The investment market *can* become 'congested through shortage of saving', even in a closed economy" [Asimakopulos 1983, 230].
30. Another related critique is that the valuation ratio may often be determined by speculative forces rather than by non-speculative ones, as is implicit in Kaldor's neo-Pasinetti theorem. This is an objection which can be found in Davidson [1968, 258; 1972, 336] and Wood [1975, 118]. Finally, linked to this, it has been argued that capital gains might not induce consumption expenditures, in contrast to Kaldor's required mechanism which has been likened to a variant of the real balance effect [Davidson, 1972, 313; Mott, 1985-86, 227].

## REFERENCES


**Abraham-Frois, G.** Krach boursier, crise financière et crise économique. *Économies et Sociétés*, March 1989, 129-42.

__________. Corporate Behavior, Valuation Ratio and Macroeconomic Analysis, in *Nicholas Kaldor and Mainstream Economics: Confrontation or Convergence?*, edited by E.J. Nell and W. Semmler. London: Macmillan, 1991, 190-204.

**Araujo, J.T.** Kaldor's Neo-Pasinetti Theorem and the Cambridge Theory of Distribution. *Manchester School of Social and Economic Studies*, September 1995, 311-17.

**Asimakopulos, A.** Kalecki and Keynes on Finance, Investment and Saving. *Cambridge Journal of Economics*, September-December 1983, 221-33.

**Baranzini, M.** The Pasinetti and Anti-Pasinetti Theorems: A Reply to K. Miyazaki and P.A. Samuelson. *Oxford Economic Papers*, April 1991, 195-98.

**Brainard, W.C. and Tobin, J.** Pitfalls in Financial Model Building. *American Economic Review*, May 1968, 99-122.

**Crotty, J.R.** Owner-Manager Conflict and Financial Theories of Investment Instability: A Critical Assessment of Keynes, Tobin, and Minsky. *Journal of Post Keynesian Economics*, Summer 1990, 519-42.

**Davidson, P.** The Demand and Supply of Securities and Economic Growth and its Implications for the Kaldor-Pasinetti versus Samuelson-Modigliani Controversy. *American Economic Review*, May 1968, 252-69.

__________. *Money and the Real World*. London: Macmillan, 1972.

**Delli Gatti, D., Gallegati, M. and Gardini, L.** Real Accumulation and Financial Instability: A Model of Profit Flows, Debt Commitments and Capital Asset Prices. *Studi Economici*, 1990 (2), 101-26.

**Dutt, A.K.** *Growth, Distribution, and Uneven Development*. Cambridge: Cambridge University Press, 1990a.

__________. Growth, Distribution and Capital Ownership: Kalecki and Pasinetti Revisited, in *Economic Theory and Policy*, edited by B. Datta, S. Gangopadhyay, D. Mookherjee and D. Roy. Bombay: Macmillan, 1990b, 130-45.

**Eichner, A.S.** A Theory of the Determination of the Mark-Up Under Oligopoly. *Economic Journal*, December 1973, 1184-1200.

**Greenwald, B. and Stiglitz, J.E.** Keynesian, New Keynesian and New Classical Economics. *Oxford Economic Papers*, 1987, 119-32.

**Hacche, G.** *The Theory of Economic Growth*. London: Macmillan, 1979.

**Harcourt, G.C.** *Some Cambridge Controversies in the Theory of Capital*. Cambridge: Cambridge University Press, 1972.

**Harcourt, G.C. and Kenyon, P.** Pricing and the Investment Decision, *Kyklos*, 1976, no. 3, 449-77.

**Kahn, R.** Notes on the Rate of Interest and the Growth of Firms, in *Selected Essays on Unemployment and Growth*. Cambridge: Cambridge University Press, 1972, 208-232.

**Kaldor, N.** Alternative Theories of Distribution. *Review of Economic Studies*, March 1956, 83-100.

__________. *Essays on Economic Policy*, Volume 1. London: Duckworth, 1964.

__________. Marginal Productivity and the Macro-Economic Theories of Growth and Distribution. *Review of Economic Studies*, October 1966, 309-319.

__________. *Further Essays on Economic Theory*. London: Duckworth, 1978.

**Keynes, J.M.** *The General Theory of Employment, Interest and Money*. London: Macmillan, 1936.

**Kurz, H.** Growth and Distribution. *Review of Political Economy*, October 1994, 393-420.
___________. What Could the 'New' Growth Theory Teach Smith or Ricardo? *Economic Issues*, September 1997, 1-20.
**Lavoie, M.** *Macroéconomie: Théorie et controverses post-keynésiennes*. Paris: Dunod, 1987.
___________. Thriftiness, Growth and the Post-Keynesian Tradition. *Économies et Sociétés*, June 1990, 123-34.
___________. *Foundations of Post-Keynesian Economic Analysis*. Aldershot: Edward Elgar, 1992.
___________. Traverse, Hysteresis, and Normal Rates of Capacity Utilization in Kaleckian Models of Growth and Distribution, *Review of Radical Political Economics*, December 1996, 113-47.
**Léonard, J.** *La répartition macroéconomique des revenus: l'enjeu des thèses de Cambridge*. Paris: Économica, 1980.
**Marglin, S.A.** *Growth, Distribution and Prices*. Cambridge (MA): Harvard University Press, 1984.
**Marris, R.** Why Economics Needs a Theory of the Firm. *Economic Journal*, March 1972, 321-52.
**Meade, J.H. and Hahn, F.** The Rate of Profit in a Growing Economy. *Economic Journal*, 1965, 445-48.
**Moore, B.J.** Some Macroeconomic Consequences of Corporate Equity. *Canadian Journal of Economics*, November 1973, 529-44.
___________. Equities, Capital Gains, and the Role of Finance in Accumulation. *American Economic Review*, December 1975, 872-86.
**Moss, S.J.** The Firm, Finance and Equilibrium in Economic Theory, in *Essays in Economic Analysis*, edited by M.J. Artis and A.R. Nobay. Cambridge: Cambridge University Press, 1976, 261-76.
___________. The Post-Keynesian Theory of Income Distribution in the Corporate Economy. *Australian Economic Papers*, December 1978, 303-322.
**Mott, T.** Towards a Post Keynesian Formulation of Liquidity Preference. *Journal of Post Keynesian Economics*, Winter 1985-86, 222-32.
**Odagiri, H.** *The Theory of Growth in a Corporate Economy*. Cambridge: Cambridge University Press, 1981.
**Panico, C.** Government Deficits in Post-Keynesian Theories of Growth and Distribution. *Contributions to Political Economy*, 1997, 61-84.
**Pasinetti L.L.** Rate of Profit and Income Distribution in Relation to the Rate of Economic Growth. *Review of Economic Studies*, October 1962, 267-79.
**Pettenati, P.** Pasinetti's Theorem in a Modern Institutional Framework, in *Post-Keynesian Theory of Growth and Distribution*, edited by C. Panico and N. Salvadori. Aldershot: Edward Elgar, 1993, 229-237. First published in Italian in *Studi Economici*, 1967.
**Rimmer, R.J.** Boulding's Theory of Distribution in a Neo-Pasinetti Framework. *Cambridge Journal of Economics*, September 1989, 453-458.
___________. *Income Distribution in a Corporate Economy*. Aldershot: Edward Elgar, 1993.
**Robinson, J.** *Essays in the Theory of Economic Growth*. London: Macmillan, 1962.
___________. *The Economics of Imperfect Competition*. London: Macmillan, 1969, 2nd edition.
___________. *Economic Heresies: Some Old-Fashioned Questions in Economic Theory*. London: Macmillan, 1971.
**Rogers, C.** *Money, Interest and Capital: A Study in the Foundations of Monetary Theory*. Cambridge: Cambridge University Press, 1989.
**Rowthorn, R.E.** Demand, Real Wages and Economic Growth. *Thames Papers in Political Economy*, Autumn 1981, 1-39.
**Samuelson, P.A.** Extirpating Error Contamination Concerning the Post-Keynesian Anti-Pasinetti Equilibrium, *Oxford Economic Papers*, April 1991, 177-86.
**Samuelson, P.A. and Modigliani, F.** The Pasinetti Paradox in Neoclassical and More General Models. *Review of Economic Studies*, October 1966, 269-301.
**Shapiro, N.** The Revolutionary Character of Post-Keynesian Economics. *Journal of Economic Issues*, September 1977, 541-60.
**Skott, P.** On the Kaldorian Saving Function. *Kyklos*, 1981 (4), 563-81.
___________. Finance, Saving and Accumulation. *Cambridge Journal of Economics*, September 1988, 339-54.
___________. *Conflict and Effective Demand in Economic Growth*. Cambridge: Cambridge University Press, 1989a.
___________. *Kaldor's Growth and Distribution Theory*. Frankfurt am Main: Peter Lang, 1989b.
**Thirwall, A.P.** *Nicholas Kaldor*. Washington Square: New York University Press, 1987.
**Wood, A.** *A Theory of Profits*. Cambridge: Cambridge University Press, 1975.

[8]

rrpe

# Capacity Utilization, Inflation, and Monetary Policy: The Duménil and Lévy Macro Model and the New Keynesian Consensus

MARC LAVOIE
*Department of Economics, University of Ottawa, Canada; e-mail: marc.lavoie@uottawa.ca*
PETER KRIESLER
*University of New South Wales; e-mail: p.kriesler@unsw.edu.au*

Received June 10, 2005; accepted April 7, 2006

**Abstract**

The article considers the adjustment toward long-run equilibrium within the Duménil and Lévy macro model, with modifications. Findings show that long-run convergence to fully adjusted positions with normal utilization is not achieved when a more realistic reaction function is proposed. Classical equilibrium occurs when a vertical Phillips curve is substituted, but the model is isomorphic to the "new consensus" model and to features of "new" endogenous growth theory.

***JEL classification:*** *E12, E40, E52, E58*

***Keywords:*** *monetary policy; central bank; inflation; capacity utilization; new Keynesian; Marxism*

In an extremely interesting article, Duménil and Lévy (1999) explore the adjustment mechanism of an economy toward a long-run equilibrium with capacity utilization at normal levels: a *fully adjusted position* as the Sraffians would call it, or a *classical long-term equilibrium* as Duménil and Lévy have it. This article clarifies a statement that they had made earlier, when they claimed that "while it is possible to be Keynesian in the short term, one is required to be classical in the long term" (Duménil and Lévy 1995: 136–37), a statement that would certainly be endorsed by some Marxist authors today, for instance Shaikh (2003, 2005). Short-run equilibrium within Duménil and Lévy's model is of the

*Authors' note:* We wish to thank Geoff Harcourt, Dominique Lévy, Malcolm Sawyer, Mario Seccareccia, and Mark Setterfield for their helpful comments at various stages of the article. This article was presented at the annual conference of the Eastern Economic Association in New York in March 2005 and at a seminar organized by Professor Jacques Mazier at the University of Paris Nord 13, in May 2005. We are also thankful to the three referees of the journal—Christophre Georges, Jon Goldstein, and Gary Mongiovi—who provided insightful comments.

*Review of Radical Political Economics*, Volume 39, No. 4, Fall 2007, 586-598
DOI: 10.1177/0486613407306824

Keynes/Kalecki type, with variability in levels of capacity utilization. One distinctive feature of their model is that it is not the forces of competition that push the economy to a fully adjusted position, but rather aspects of the macro economy coupled with the behavior of the central bank. In many ways, their analysis of the adjustment process is similar to the analysis of the so-called "new consensus" among neoclassical economists (or "new neoclassical synthesis"), which has been defined by a number of "new" Keynesian economists (such as Taylor 1999; Romer 2000; Walsh 2002; Woodford 2002), where the return to potential output is achieved through the necessary intervention of the monetary authorities.[1] This article seeks to look at Duménil and Lévy's underlying framework, comparing it with the new consensus framework, to identify their most essential similarities.

## 1. The Duménil and Lévy Model

The important aspect of the model for our purpose is their specification of the traverse which moves the economy from the Keynesian short run to the classical long-run equilibrium, defined as a position where "capacity utilization rates are 'normal'" (Duménil and Lévy 1999: 685).[2]

The short-run model takes prices as given, and allows capacity utilization to vary. In long-run equilibrium, prices are equal to prices of production with uniform rates of profit, and capacity is equal to normal or target rates.

The underlying mechanism driving their traverse is the reaction function of the central bank in the face of inflation. In Duménil and Lévy (1999) the instrument of monetary policy is the central bank's control over the money supply. However, in section 2.4.3 of their 1999 article, they make it clear that the analysis of money supply as the appropriate policy instrument is merely a simplification, and that the rate of interest can be readily substituted within their model. Indeed they do this in section 4.4 of their earlier, more extended, draft versions of the published 1999 article (Duménil and Lévy 1994, 1997). This is the course we follow, to more clearly contrast the model with that of the new consensus, where it is assumed, as in post-Keynesian models, that monetary control is essentially exercised through discretionary modifications of the interest rate by the monetary authorities. In Duménil and Lévy, monetary policy is adjusted as a result of any actual inflation rate. This, as we shall see, will assure stability of the general price level while "this stability of the

1. In the new consensus model, as pointed out by Setterfield (2004: 39), since money supply targeting is eliminated, there is no Pigou effect anymore, and hence flexible prices cannot be relied on to return to full-capacity output (or to the natural rate of unemployment). Indeed, in a survey of members of the American Economic Association, Fuller and Geide-Stevenson (2003) found that 35 percent of the economists disagreed with the statement that a self-correcting mechanism exists that brings output back toward potential output. Those that disagree probably either believe that the *discretionary* actions of the central bank provide this mechanism or think that output does not usually return to potential output.

2. The issue of whether such a long-run equilibrium corresponds to full employment or to a constant level of unemployment will not be addressed here, since it was not discussed in the Duménil and Lévy model and since it is not addressed usually by Kaleckian models. For proposals about how long-run equilibria with demand-led growth rates could equate supply-determined growth rates (the "natural" rate of growth), see Stockhammer (2004) and Dutt (2006). Presumably, like many post-Keynesians, Duménil and Lévy assume that the "natural" growth rate adjusts to the realized trend rate, through changes in immigration, labor participation, and rates of technical progress.

general level of prices ensures gravitation of the general level of activity around a normal level" (Duménil and Lévy 1999: 697).

The reaction function of the central bank is assumed to be:

$$\Delta r = \beta_1 \pi \quad (1)$$

where $\pi$ is the inflation rate and $r$ is the rate of interest. All $\beta$s are and will be positive parameters.

In both the 1994 and 1997 versions, Duménil and Lévy note that they "will not discuss here whether $r$ should be the nominal or the real rate of interest." In view of current discussions over monetary policy, it seems best to suppose that the real rate of interest is pushed up by the monetary authorities whenever price inflation exceeds some target level, so that it is best to interpret $r$ as a real rate, with $\beta_1$ a positive parameter.

As in most macroeconomic models, Duménil and Lévy—equation (16) in both the 1994 and 1997 versions—assume that investment, or more precisely the growth rate of capital, is inversely responsive to changes in the rate of interest:

$$g^i = g_0 - \beta_2 r + \beta_3 u \quad (2)$$

where $g^i$ is the growth rate of capital (the rate of accumulation); $g_0$ represents the autonomous components of growth; $u$ is the rate of capacity utilization; and $r$ is the real rate of interest (as long as $g$ is interpreted as the real rate of accumulation).

Equation (2) is analogous to an IS curve, with an inverse relation between the rate of interest and the level of economic activity $u$, since the equilibrium level of the rate of capacity utilization itself depends positively on the autonomous component of growth and negatively on the rate of interest. The equilibrium rate of capacity utilization can be obtained by confronting the above investment function in equation (2), with the standard classical saving function, which can be written as:

$$g^s = s_c R \quad (3)$$

where $s_c$ is the propensity to save out of profits and $R$ is the profit rate on capital.

As is well known, the profit rate can be decomposed into three components: $m$, the share of profits (which is a proxy for the strength of the corporate class, through the value taken by the markup over wage unit costs); $u$, the rate of capacity utilization; and $v$, the capital to capacity ratio, which is assumed to be given by technology. As a result, the saving equation can also be rewritten as:

$$g^s = s_c mu/v \quad (4)$$

This of course implies that the normal rate of profit is $R_n = mu_n/v$, where $m$ is the assumed exogenous variable that is sorted out by class conflict. The short-run equilibrium rate of capacity utilization, equating equations (2) and (4), is then given by:

$$u = (g_0 - \beta_2 r)/( s_c m/v - \beta_3) \quad (5)$$

or more simply as:

$$u = u_0 - \beta_4 r \tag{6}$$

where $u_0 = g_0/(s_c m/v - \beta_3)$ and $\beta_4 = \beta_2/(s_c m/v - \beta_3)$.

So, whenever there is inflation ($\pi > 0$) in the Duménil and Lévy model, real interest rates rise, and hence, as a consequence, rates of capacity utilization fall. This feedback mechanism will eventually lead to reductions in inflation rates, because Duménil and Lévy (1999) assume that the inflation rate is a linear function of the discrepancy between the actual rate of capacity utilization, as computed in equation (4), and some normal level of capacity utilization.[3] They have:

$$\pi = \beta_5(u - u_n) \tag{7}$$

where $u$ is still the realized level of capacity utilization and $u_n$ is the optimal level of capacity utilization targeted by enterprises (the normal rate).

Equation (7) represents a standard old-fashioned Phillips curve (it is *not* a vertical Phillips curve), where there is a straight linear trade-off between the inflation rate and the level of economic activity, without any possibility of shift in the relationship as there are no constant terms. In addition, the equation implies that inflation is nil only when the realized rate of capacity utilization is equal to the normal rate of capacity utilization. The model thus operates in some kind of competitive world, where prices are highly flexible and where they increase whenever demand exceeds normal capacity, while they decrease whenever demand falls below normal capacity. This equation, along with equation (1), implies that the rate of interest

> . . . is constant in a classical long-term equilibrium, since the capacity utilization rate is normal [$u = u_n$] and there is no inflation [$\pi = 0$]. . . . The coincidence between the absence of inflation and the prevalence of a normal capacity utilization rate is related to the behavior of enterprises. Because enterprises consider the utilization of productive capacity in the setting of their prices, price stability is associated with a normal capacity utilization rate. . . . Within our analysis, prices are a function of disequilibria between supply and demand. (Duménil and Lévy 1999: 698–99)

What happens is that the addition of the central bank reaction function and the inflation mechanism, equations (1) and (7), transforms an otherwise Kaleckian–Keynesian investment function, equation (2), into a classical (Marxist–Sraffian) investment function, where "a deviation of the capacity utilization rate from its normal value would lead to a variation of investment, instead of a constant investment" (Duménil and Lévy 1999: 692).[4]

3. This follows from their equation (1) (689) and their definition of inflation (706).

4. Because we are in a growth model, Duménil and Lévy mean that the rate of accumulation must change. Mathematically, taking the differential of equation (2), and adding equations (1) and (7), one gets:

$$dg^i = -\beta_2\beta_1\beta_5(u - u_n) + \beta_3 du$$

so that the rate of capital accumulation tends to decrease as long as the actual rate of capacity utilization is larger than its normal rate.

Although monetary variables play a role in the determination of the level of economic activity in the short run, according to Duménil and Lévy they have no real effects in the long run. The basic role of monetary variables is to push the economy to its fully adjusted long-run equilibrium, though they play no role in the determination of that equilibrium. In other words, we have the long-run neutrality of money:

> Long-term equilibrium can be defined independently of money, but monetary mechanisms are responsible for the convergence of short-term equilibria to long-term equilibrium: they are crucial *vis-à-vis* the stability in dimension of long-term equilibrium. (Duménil and Lévy 1999: 710)

The Duménil and Lévy traverse analysis represents an interesting mixture of heterodox and neoclassical theory. As we will see in the next section, the set of equations (1), (6), and (7) is very much reminiscent of the new consensus model. So is their conclusion that the system will tend to a long-run equilibrium with normal capacity (the equivalent to the NAIRU assumption), with monetary variables having no impact on real variables in the long run.

Another important element of the Duménil and Lévy analysis is their long-run neutrality of money. They argue that while the monetary system plays a role in pushing the economy to its long-run equilibrium, it does not influence that equilibrium in any way.[5] This has important implications for their underlying story. It is the assumed separation between the forces determining equilibrium and the stability factors pushing the economy to that equilibrium that bring forth their conclusion.

## 2. A Modified Keynesian Duménil and Lévy Model

However, their conclusion needs to be modified if we allow, in the Duménil and Lévy model, the inflation rate target of the central bank to differ from zero, in particular, as is usually the case, to be greater than zero. In this case, the long-run equilibrium will change depending on the inflation target, and therefore on the central bank's setting of interest rates, so that monetary policy will indirectly influence the long-run equilibrium. This restores the argument of most heterodox economists that monetary policy and the monetary system matter even in the long run. In this case the long-run equilibrium position cannot be derived independently of the adjustment path of the economy.

As we will see, the key point of departure with the new consensus model is the replacement of the latter's vertical long-run Phillips curve with a more Keynesian Phillips curve, which does allow for long-run trade-offs between inflation and the level of economic activity. Price stability, in the Duménil and Lévy model, is restored because of the reaction function of the central bank. However, Duménil and Lévy's reaction function makes central banks much more rigorous in their anti-inflationary policy than most other commentators would have them. Despite the fact that there is some argument as to the appropriate inflation target (Solow and Taylor 1999), most economists (neoclassical and

5. A similar critique of Duménil and Lévy's approach was provided by Deprez and Dalendina (1994: 72).

others) accept that central banks may target a nonzero inflation rate, while Duménil and Lévy impose a target rate of inflation exactly equal to zero.[6] In fact, if a target rate of inflation greater than zero were allowed, then the long-run equilibrium of the economy would be at a level of capacity greater than the normal rate.[7] This follows in a straightforward manner from equation (7), where $\pi > 0 \Rightarrow u > u_n$.[8]

The heterodox nature of the Duménil and Lévy model, provided some more realistic features are added to it, can be readily seen if we modify equations (1) and (7) by introducing an inflationary target $\pi^T$ greater than zero in equation (1), writing now:

$$\Delta r = \beta_1 (\pi - \pi^T) \qquad (8)$$

and by introducing into equation (7) an element of cost inflation $\pi_c$,[9] based on some institutional or structural features, now rewritten as:

$$\pi = \beta_5(u - u_n) + \pi_c \qquad (9)$$

In long-run equilibrium, $\Delta r = 0$ and $\pi = \pi^T$. Substituting the value of $\pi$ taken from equation (9), we obtain the long-run value of the actual rate of capacity utilization:

$$u^* - u_n = (\pi^T - \pi_c)/ \beta_5 \qquad (10)$$

It then becomes obvious that, all else equal, a higher target rate of inflation will be associated with a higher long-run rate of capacity utilization and a higher rate of growth. And indeed, equation (10) is essentially the result obtained by Setterfield (2004), in a model he calls the post-Keynesian alternative to the new consensus.[10] It is equally clear that a classical long-run equilibrium, with normal rates of capacity utilization, will be achieved only in the special case where $\pi^T = \pi_c$, that is when the target rate of inflation set by the central bank will turn out to be equal to cost inflation. In general, this will not necessarily be the case, even if one ventures to suppose that cost inflation ought to be determined in the long run by inflation expectations, which themselves should be anchored by the target inflation rate set by the central bank.

In other words, the reason that the Duménil and Lévy model tends to a specifically classical long-term equilibrium is not the underlying nature of the model or the adjustment process. Rather this specific result is achieved as a consequence of the choice of a very peculiar inflation target ($\pi^T = 0$), tied to a very peculiar inflation process ($\pi_c = 0$). This is indeed recognized by Duménil and Lévy (1999: 712) themselves when they say:

6. Indeed such a zero-inflation target is tied by Woodford (2002: 38) to Knut Wicksell's proposed rule for setting interest rates.

7. And hence the realized profit rate $R$ would end up being different from the normal profit rate $R_n$ in the long-run equilibrium.

8. Interestingly, long-run capacity utilization lower than normal levels is only possible if central banks target deflation. When viewed in this light, the model lacks realism.

9. As was already suggested in Lavoie (1996: 125) when discussing Duménil and Lévy (1994). This could correspond to the so-called conflicting-claims inflation theory emphasized by a large number of heterodox authors.

10. The alternative being made up, broadly speaking, of equations (6), (8), and (9).

"Economic policies may direct the system toward targets other than the stability of the general price level. . . . It would be easy to show in the model that, if such targets are defined, long-term equilibrium will be shifted to another position deviating from the normal utilization of capacity." In fact, this is true if either condition is modified, as per equations (8) or (9). In addition, these modifications mean that monetary policy will not be neutral in the long run. The traverse to the classical long-run equilibrium, based on the foundations of a non-vertical long-run Phillips curve, looks very fragile indeed.

## 3. A Modified New Consensus Duménil and Lévy Model

If Duménil and Lévy do want to recover their long-run classical equilibrium in all cases, then they need to adopt the vertical long-run Phillips curve first proposed by Milton Friedman. This is precisely what new consensus authors have done, believing that

> There is substantial evidence demonstrating that there is no long-run trade-off between the level of inflation and the level of unused resources in the economy—whether measured by the unemployment rate, the capacity utilization rate, or the deviation of real GDP from potential GDP. (Taylor 1999: 29–30)

In the short run, the inflation rate falls when unemployment is above NAIRU, and increases when unemployment is below it. This is now most often expressed in terms of output gaps: the spread between actual output and potential output. Any deviation of capacity, real GDP, or unemployment from their normal levels leads to *changes* in the inflation rate. If capacity utilization is kept above its normal level, this will quickly lead to accelerating inflation. Expressed in terms of capacity utilization, the supply constraint of new consensus models—the vertical Phillips curve—is given by equation (11):

$$\Delta\pi = \beta_6 (u - u_n) \quad (11)$$

Like Friedman (and Duménil and Lévy), defenders of the new consensus view believe that monetary policy can have real effects in the short run as summarized in a conventional IS schedule, so that equation (6) applies as well to the new consensus model, provided we ignore the additional terms that are included in the more sophisticated versions of the equation (which incorporate expected terms and autonomous shocks, as in Woodford 2002):

$$u = u_0 - \beta_4 r \quad (6)$$

Both Friedman and the new Keynesian authors strongly argue that this indicates the need for monetary policy rules. The only difference is that, while for Friedman the rule sets optimal money supply growth, for new consensus authors "the interest rate rather than the money supply is the key instrument that should be adjusted" (Taylor 1999: 47). The proposed rule would have the central bank responding to both price and aggregate demand shocks (or expected shocks). So, interest rates should be changed if inflation deviates from its target or if real GDP deviates from potential GDP. There are many variants of these rules, the best known being the so-called Taylor rule, which in terms of rates of utilization, is presented as:

$$i = \pi^T + \beta_7 (\pi - \pi^T) + \beta_8 (u - u_n) + r_n \tag{12}$$

where $i$ is now a nominal interest rate while $r_n$ "is the implicit real interest rate in the central bank's reaction function" (Taylor 1999: 50) or, in Wicksellian terms, the central bank estimate of the "natural" (real) rate of interest.

Another possible rule is to express the central bank reaction function in difference terms. Generalizing Duménil and Lévy's equation (8), the typical new consensus central bank reaction function can be written in the way suggested by Setterfield (2004, 2005), as a difference equation where the real interest rate set by the central bank reacts to both the "inflation gap" and the "output gap":

$$\Delta r = \beta_7 (\pi - \pi^T) + \beta_8 (u - u_n) \tag{13}$$

Setterfield (2005) shows that a model made up of equations (6), (11), and (13) is always stable and converges to a normal rate of capacity utilization at the target inflation rate.[11] However, the second term of the central bank reaction function, given by $\beta_8 (u - u_n)$, plays a crucial role in stability analysis. Without it, the economy would run into a limit cycle, circling the target inflation rate without ever achieving it. What happens is that the second term of equation (13) provides derivative control, a well-known stabilizing feature.[12] Substituting $(u - u_n)$ by its value in equation (11), we obtain the following reaction function:

$$\Delta r = \beta_7 (\pi - \pi^T) + (\beta_8 / \beta_6)(\Delta\pi) \tag{14}$$

With equation (14), we see that equation (13) implies that the central bank reacts to the level of, and the change in, the inflation rate. In other words, for a given current inflation rate, the central bank would impose a more punitive increase in real interest rates when inflation is quickly rising.

For Duménil and Lévy to be able to recover their conclusion that economists ought to be Keynesian in the short run but classical in the long run, they need to adopt the three new consensus equations: equations (6) (which they already have), (11), and (13). With these, monetary policy forces will always be such that there is a long-run tendency toward normal rates of capacity utilization, and hence toward fully adjusted positions (the classical long-run position), a result that is achieved in addition at the target rate of inflation set by the central bank.

11. Amusingly, before the new consensus became fashionable, Humphrey (1990) provided a similar demonstration when describing what he considered to be Wicksell's contribution.

12. The two-equation differential system becomes:

$$\begin{bmatrix} \Delta r \\ \Delta\pi \end{bmatrix} = \begin{bmatrix} -\beta_8\beta_4 & \beta_7 \\ -\beta_6\beta_4 & 0 \end{bmatrix} \begin{bmatrix} r \\ \pi \end{bmatrix}$$

where the trace is $-\beta_8\beta_4 < 0$ while the determinant of the Jacobian is $+\beta_7\beta_6\beta_4 > 0$, so that the model always converges; otherwise, without derivative control, the trace would be zero.

## 4. The Similarities with the New Endogenous Growth Models

The resemblances between Duménil and Lévy's results and the new consensus on monetary theory are reinforced when the new consensus model is reinterpreted in terms of the so-called new endogenous growth model. In the latter, in contrast with the traditional neoclassical Solow growth model, the natural rate of growth is endogenous and achieves higher levels when the economy propensity to save is higher. For instance, in Rebelo (1991), the endogenous growth rate in steady state equals $g^* = sR$, where $s$ is the exogenous average propensity to save while $R$ is the technologically given profit rate on capital (tangible and human).

In Duménil and Lévy (1999: 705), the endogenous growth rate in fully adjusted positions, achieved when $u = u_n$, is given by: [13]

$$g^* = s_c R_n = s_c m u_n / v \tag{13}$$

As in new endogenous growth models, a lower propensity to save $s_c$ eventually reduces growth rates, and so do higher real wages (or lower normal profit rates $R_n$), since they reduce the overall proportion of income that can be saved.

> In a short-term equilibrium, a lower saving rate of capitalists has the same effect as a larger real wage, that is, results in larger capacity utilization rates in the two industries and a larger growth rate; whereas in a long-term equilibrium the profit rate is not affected and a lower saving rate diminishes the growth rate. (Duménil and Lévy 1999: 705)

The interesting feature of the Duménil and Lévy model is that their model, in contrast with the new endogenous canonical growth model (see Dutt 2003), takes the effects of effective demand and class conflict into consideration, as would Keynesian or Kaleckian growth models. However, the inclusion of the specific features of their inflation equation and central bank reaction function produces a traverse toward a long-run classical model, with all the conclusions generally agreed on by neoclassical authors. For instance, lower propensities to save will eventually generate inflation through standard Keynesian demand-led effects, and hence through the reaction function of the central bank; it will induce the central bank to set higher real interest rates and slower rates of accumulation (as in new endogenous growth models). We thus have a situation where a lower propensity to save leads to higher real interest rates, as in the loanable funds story, and to slower rates of accumulation, as in new endogenous growth models.

The value taken by the real interest rate in the fully adjusted position can be obtained by substituting $u$ for its long-run value $u_n$ in equation (3). We get.

$$u_n = (g_0 - \beta_2 r)/(s_c m/v - \beta_3) \tag{14}$$

13. This is a standard result among authors of the Marxist tradition, as can be deduced from Marglin (1984: 136) or Shaikh (2005), and as pointed out long ago by Nell (1985). On this, see Lavoie, Rodríguez, and Seccareccia (2004).

from which we derive the fully adjusted value of the real rate of interest, or what Wicksellians would call the natural rate of interest:

$$r_n = (g_0 + \beta_3 u_n - s_c m u_n / v) / \beta_2 \tag{15}$$

It is then obvious that a lower propensity to save $s_c$ (or a smaller share of profits $m$) is associated with a higher natural rate of interest: the real rate that will be achieved in the long run, once the fully adjusted position has been reached.

In addition, higher real wages (when assuming no technical progress) may generate favorable short-run effective demand effects, but in the long run these higher real wages will bring about a slowdown in accumulation and higher unemployment rates. So once again the iron law of supply-side accumulation takes over in the long run, as it would in the Rebelo new endogenous growth model.

## 5. Conclusion

If we compare the new consensus model with that of Duménil and Lévy, the similarities are obvious. Both have the same specification of the IS curve, and identical central bank reaction functions (save for a target inflation rate of zero). The difference between them hinges mainly on the specification of the Phillips curve. If a more general specification is included in the Duménil and Lévy (1999) model, then their conclusion that there is a tendency toward fully adjusted positions with normal rates of capacity utilization cannot be sustained, and long-run classical features cannot be sustained. If we add the standard vertical Phillips curve to the Duménil and Lévy model, which allows Duménil and Lévy to get in a more general way the results that they are actually looking for, then we get a perfect new Keynesian model, which combines the lessons of both the new consensus on monetary policy and those of new endogenous growth theory.

We are well aware that the microeconomics of Duménil and Lévy, as can be found in detail in Duménil and Lévy (1993), are quite distinct from neoclassical analysis and are quite appealing, but it remains rather surprising to discover that their macroeconomics appear to be so isomorphic to the most popular models of the new neoclassical synthesis. We have taken the Duménil and Lévy (1999) model as an exemplar, but as pointed out in the introduction, other authors within the Marxist tradition also believe that the classical long-run equilibrium does constrain possible macroeconomic dynamics. The fact that Duménil and Lévy's model arrives at conclusions that so clearly resemble those of the new neoclassical synthesis does not mean that the former is wrong. But this clearly establishes that if we are on the lookout for alternative macroeconomic policies (an alternative to received wisdom, as embedded for instance in the Washington consensus or in the right-wing slogan TINA—"There Is No Alternative"), their justification might well have to be found elsewhere than in classical or Marxist macroeconomic theory.

By contrast, several post-Keynesian authors deny the validity of the lessons drawn either from the new consensus or from new endogenous growth theory, and thus offer some scope for an alternative, where expansionary monetary and fiscal policies, as well as a more powerful labor movement, can have beneficial long-run effects. This can be achieved in various ways: by letting the natural rate of growth, more specifically the rate of technical progress, become endogenous, as in Dutt (2005), Lavoie (2004), and also as suggested by Shaikh (2003: 140); by letting the normal rate of utilization itself become endogenous, as in Dutt (1997) and Lavoie (1996); or by rejecting the vertical long-run Phillips curve, adopting instead a horizontal Phillips curve, or rather a Phillips curve with a horizontal segment, as suggested by Tobin (1995); McDonald (1995); Hein (2002); Freedman, Harcourt, and Kriesler (2004); Palacio-Vera (2005); Fontana and Palacio-Vera (2007); and Kriesler and Lavoie (2007).

About the latter suggestion, it is rather ironic to note that whereas the vertical long-run Phillips curve is ever more entrenched in mainstream textbooks, an ever-growing number of empirical studies run against this consensual view, starting with the work of Eisner (1996), according to whom the Phillips curve in the United States was flat for low-range and middle-range rates of unemployment. Economists working at various federal reserve banks have concluded, independently, that the Phillips curve is nonlinear, with three segments, the middle-range segment of the Phillips curve, corresponding to mid-range growth rates or mid-range unemployment rates, being flat (Filardo 1998; Barnes and Olivei 2003; see also Flaschel, Kauermann, and Semmler 2005). These latter results are consistent with the idea of a *range of equilibrium rates of unemployment,* that is, a region of intermediate rates of unemployment where inflation tends to stay constant. This, added to the hysteresis literature and the idea that the NAIRU or the natural rate of unemployment is attracted toward the actual level of unemployment, as determined by aggregate demand—a conclusion also supported by a meta-analysis of empirical work (Stanley 2004)—yields much room for demand management policies.[14] Thus, we are rather optimistic about the possibility of improving the economy through proper macroeconomic policies, and we tend to take for our own the following proposition that was advanced by Wynne Godley (1983: 170) more than twenty years ago:

> Indeed *if* it is true that there is a unique NAIRU, that really is the end of discussion of macroeconomic policy. At present I happen *not* to believe it and there is no evidence of it. And I am prepared to express the value judgment that moderately higher inflation rates are an acceptable price to pay for lower unemployment. *But I do not accept that it is a foregone conclusion that inflation will be higher if unemployment is lower.*

## References

Barnes, M. L., and G. P. Olivei. 2003. Inside and outside bounds: Estimates of the Phillips curve. *New England Economic Review:* 3–18.

Deprez, J., and P. D. Dalendina. 1994. The monetary determinants of (in)stability: Some contrasts of Duménil/Lévy and the Post-Keynesians. *Review of Radical Political Economics* 26 (3): 66–75.

Duménil G., and D. Lévy. 1993. *The economics of the profit rate.* Aldershot, UK: Edward Elgar.

———. 1994. Being Keynesian in the short term and classical in the long term: The traverse to classical long-term equilibrium. Preliminary draft, CEPREMAP, April.

14. Indeed Fuller and Geide-Stevenson (2003) found that 32 percent of the economists surveyed disagreed with the statement that "there is a natural rate of unemployment to which the economy tends in the long run."

———. 1995. A post-Keynesian long-term equilibrium with equalized profit rates? A rejoinder to Amitava Dutt's synthesis. *Review of Radical Political Economics* 27 (2): 135–41.

———. 1997. Being Keynesian in the short term and classical in the long term: The traverse to classical long-term equilibrium. CEPREMAP, working paper 9702.

———. 1999. Being Keynesian in the short term and classical in the long term: The traverse to classical long-term equilibrium. *The Manchester School* 67 (6): 684–716.

Dutt, A. K. 1997. Equilibrium, path dependence and hysteresis in post-Keynesian models. In *Markets, unemployment and economic policy: Essays in honour of Geoff Harcour,* vol. 2, ed. P. Arestis, G. Palma, and M. Sawyer, 238–53. London: Routledge.

———. 2003. New growth theory, effective demand, and post-Keynesian dynamics. In *Old and new growth theories: An assessment,* ed. N. Salvadori, 67–100. Cheltenham, UK: Edward Elgar.

———. 2006. Aggregate demand, aggregate supply and economic growth. *International Journal of Applied Economics,* 20 (3) (July): 319–36.

Eisner R. 1996. The retreat from full employment. In *Employment, economic growth and the tyranny of the market: Essays in honour of Paul Davidson,* vol. 2, ed. P. Arestis, 106–130. Cheltenham, UK: Edward Elgar.

Filardo, A. J. 1998. New evidence on the output cost of fighting inflation. *Federal Reserve Bank of Kansas City Quarterly Review* 83 (3): 33–61.

Flaschel, P., G. Kauermann, and W. Semmler. 2005. Testing wage and price Phillips curves for the United States. Working paper, Comparative Empirical Macroeconomics (CEM), New School University.

Fontana, G. and A. Palacio-Vera. 2007. Are long-run price stability and short-run output stabilization all that monetary policy can aim for? *Metronomica*, 58 (2) (May): 269–98.

Freedman, C., G. C. Harcourt, and P. Kriesler. 2004. Has the long-run Phillips curve turned horizontal? In *Growth, distribution and effective demand: Alternatives to economic orthodoxy,* ed. G. Argyrous, M. Forstater, and G. Mongiovi, 144–62. Armonk, NY: M.E. Sharpe.

Fuller, D., and D. Geide-Stevenson. 2003. Consensus among economists: Revisited. *Journal of Economic Education* 34 (4): 369–87.

Godley, W. 1983. Keynes and the management of real national income and expenditure. In *Keynes and the modern world,* ed. D. Worswick and J. Trevithick, 135–77. Cambridge: Cambridge University Press.

Hein, E. 2002. Monetary policy and wage bargaining in the EMU: Restrictive ECB policies, high unemployment, nominal wage restraint and inflation above the target. *Banca del Lavoro Quarterly Review* 222: 299–337.

Humphrey, T. M. 1990. Fisherian and Wicksellian price-stabilization models in the history of economic thought. *Federal Reserve Bank of Richmond Economic Review* 76 (3): 3–12.

Kriesler, P., and M. Lavoie. 2007. The new consensus on monetary policy and its post-Keynesian critique. *Review of Political Economy* 19 (3) (July): 387–404.

Lavoie M. 1996. Traverse, hysteresis and normal rates of capacity utilization in Kaleckian models of growth and distribution. *Review of Radical Political Economics* 28 (4) (December): 113–147.

———. 2004. The new consensus on monetary policy seen from a post-Keynesian perspective. In *Central banking in the modern world: Alternative perspectives,* ed. M. Lavoie and M. Seccareccia, 15–34. Cheltenham, UK: Edward Elgar.

Lavoie, M., G. Rodríguez, and M. Seccareccia. 2004. Similitudes and discrepancies in post-Keynesian and Marxist theories of investment: A theoretical and empirical investigation. *International Review of Applied Economics* 18 (2): 127–50.

Marglin, S. A. 1984. Growth, distribution and inflation: A centennial synthesis. *Cambridge Journal of Economics* 8: 115–144.

McDonald, L. M. 1995. Models of the range of equilibria. In *The natural rate of unemployment: Reflections on 25 years of the hypothesis,* ed. R. Cross, 101–52. Cambridge: Cambridge University Press.

Nell, E. 1985. Jean Baptiste Marglin: A comment on "growth, distribution and inflation." *Cambridge Journal of Economics* 9 (2): 173–178.

Palacio-Vera, A. 2005. The "modern" view of macroeconomics: Some critical reflections. *Cambridge Journal of Economics* 29 (5): 747–67.

Rebelo, S. 1991. Long-run policy analysis and long-run growth. *Journal of Political Economy* 99: 500–21.

Romer, D. 2000. Keynesian macroeconomics without the LM curve. *Journal of Economic Perspectives* 14 (2): 149–69.

Setterfield, M. 2004. Central banking, stability and macroeconomic outcomes: A comparison of new consensus and post-Keynesian monetary macroeconomics. In *Central banking in the modern world: Alternative perspectives*, ed. M. Lavoie and M. Seccareccia, 35–56. Cheltenham, UK: Edward Elgar.

———. 2005. Central bank behavior and the stability of macroeconomic equilibrium: A critical examination of the new consensus. In *The new monetary policy: Implications and relevance*, ed. P. Arestis, M. Baddeley, and J. S. L. McCombie, 23–47. Cheltenham, UK: Edward Elgar.

Shaikh, A. 2003. Labor market dynamics within rival macroeconomic frameworks. In *Growth, distribution and effective demand: Alternatives to economic orthodoxy*, ed. G. Argyrous, M. Forstater, and G. Mongiovi, 127–43. Armonk, NY: M. E. Sharpe.

———. 2005. Economic policy in a growth context: A synthesis of Keynes and Harrod, version 3. Working paper, Department of Economics, New School University, New York.

Stanley, T. D. 2004. Does unemployment hysteresis falsify the natural rate hypothesis? A meta-regession analysis. *Journal of Economic Surveys* 18 (4): 589–612.

Stockhammer, E. 2004. Is there an equilibrium rate of unemployment in the long run? *Review of Political Economy* 16 (1): 59–78.

Solow, R. M., and J. B. Taylor, eds. 1999. *Inflation, unemployment, and monetary policy.* Cambridge, MA: MIT Press.

Taylor, J. B. 1999. Monetary policy guidelines for employment and inflation stability. In *Inflation, unemployment, and monetary policy*, ed. R. M. Solow and J. B. Taylor, 29–54. Cambridge, MA: MIT Press.

Tobin, J. 1995. The natural rate as new classical macroeconomics. In *The natural rate of unemployment: Reflections on 25 years of the hypothesis*, ed. R. Cross, 32–42. Cambridge: Cambridge University Press.

Walsh, C. E. 2002. Teaching inflation targeting: An analysis for intermediate macro. *Journal of Economic Education* 33 (4): 333–46.

Woodford, M. 2002. *Interest and prices: Foundations of a theory of monetary policy.* Princeton, NJ, and Oxford: Princeton University Press.

*Marc Lavoie is professor in the Department of Economics at the University of Ottawa, where he has been teaching since 1979. He has recently published* Introduction to Post-Keynesian Economics *(Macmillan/Palgrave, 2006) and is coauthor with Wynne Godley of* Monetary Economics: An Integrated Approach to Credit, Money, Income, Production and Wealth *(Macmillan/Palgrave, 2007).*

*Peter Kriesler has taught at the University of New South Wales since 1988. He organizes the Annual Australian Society of Heterodox Economists Conference, which is now in its sixth year. He has written on the Australian, Asian, and European economies as well as on Marxian and Kaleckian economics, and issues related to path determinacy.*

# PART II

# KALECKIAN MODELS WITH AUTONOMOUS NON-CAPACITY CREATING EXPENDITURES

# [9]

*Metroeconomica* 67:1 (2016) 172–201
doi: 10.1111/meca.12109

# CONVERGENCE TOWARDS THE NORMAL RATE OF CAPACITY UTILIZATION IN NEO-KALECKIAN MODELS: THE ROLE OF NON-CAPACITY CREATING AUTONOMOUS EXPENDITURES

Marc Lavoie*
University of Ottawa

(January 2015; revised October 2015)

## ABSTRACT

Neo-Kaleckian models of growth and distribution have been highly popular among heterodox economists. Two drawbacks of these models have, however, been underlined in the literature: first, the models do not usually converge to their normal rate of capacity utilization; second, the models do not include the Harrodian principle of dynamic instability. Some Sraffian economists have long been arguing that the presence of non-capacity creating autonomous expenditures provides a mechanism that brings back the model to normal rates of capacity utilization, while safeguarding the main Keynesian message and without going back to classical conclusions. The present article provides a very simple proof of this, showing within a neo-Kaleckian model that the Harrodian principle of dynamic instability gets tamed by the presence of autonomous consumer expenditures.

## 1. INTRODUCTION

This article presents a two-step modification of the neo-Kaleckian model. In its simpler version, an autonomous component of consumption by capitalists is added to the canonical investment function of the Kaleckian model, with this autonomous component being assumed to grow at an

* This article has been presented at the Keynesian Summer School in Berlin in July 2013, at the IMK Berlin conference in October 2013, at an INET-sponsored workshop at the Fields Institute in Toronto in November 2013, and at a seminar at the Federal University of Rio de Janeiro in December 2014. I wish to thank the participants to these events, and in particular Olivier Allain, Sergio Cesaratto, Fabio Freitas, Antonio Carlos Macedo e Silva, Won Jun Nah, Franklin Serrano and Peter Skott for their remarks. I also thank the two referees of the journal for their very substantive comments.

exogenously given rate. In this first version, the actual rate of capacity utilization is not generally equal to its normal or desired value, unless the rate of growth of autonomous capitalist consumption happens to be equal to the constant term in the investment function. In the second and more complex version, there is a Harrodian investment variable that adjusts in the long run to the discrepancy between expected growth in sales and the actual growth of capacity. The long-run equilibrium growth rate in the model is still determined by the exogenously given rate of growth of autonomous capitalist consumption, but it turns out that that under fairly weak conditions the actual rate of capacity utilization will converge towards the normal or desired rate of capacity utilization.

The model is related to a number of theoretical debates in the literature on neo-Kaleckian growth and distribution models and to empirical issues concerning the determinants of growth. Four main points are made in the article. First, it follows Franklin Serrano's (1995a, 1995b) analysis of the so-called Sraffian supermultiplier, thus called because the trend rate of output and productive capacity is determined by exogenous elements, through a multiplier effect that incorporate the accelerator effect due to induced investment. This is done by introducing a new adjustment variable (apart from the usual variables—distribution and capacity utilization) which brings saving and investment into equality. This new adjustment variable is the average propensity to save of capitalists, through the introduction of a non-proportional saving function with a constant term that in the long run grows at an exogenously given rate.

Second, the article attempts to respond to criticisms of basic neo-Kaleckian models because they (allegedly implausibly) do not produce a long-run equilibrium in which actual and normal rates of capacity utilization are equal and because they assume away Harrodian instability. It does so by producing a model that builds in Harrodian instability and ensures (conditionally) that in long-run equilibrium actual and normal capacity utilization are equalized. In so doing, the article is related to Olivier Allain's (2015) recent contribution in two ways. In his neo-Kaleckian model Allain, like Serrano, introduces a non-capacity creating expenditure that grows at a constant rate, in his case, government expenditure. And as we do here, he considers the destabilizing effects of a Harrodian investment function on his modified version of the neo-Kaleckian model, also getting conditional convergence of the actual rate of capacity utilization towards its normal value. One purpose of the present article is to provide a simpler proof of this result.

Third, the model produced implies wage-led growth, not in the sense of raising the long-run equilibrium growth rate of the economy when the wage share rises (and the profit share falls), since the rate of growth of the economy in the medium or long run is determined by the exogenous growth rate of the autonomous part of capitalist consumption, but in the sense of raising the average rate of growth during the *traverse* after the wage share increases—something that many have argued to be a suitable way of examining growth effects, that is, focusing on averages rather than steady-state values. Finally, some empirical justification is provided for the model in terms of discussions of the exogeneity of consumption growth and recent discussions of consumer debt, which provide some autonomy of consumption from income.

The outline of the article roughly follows what has been argued above. In the next section, the autonomous component of consumption by capitalists is added to the standard neo-Kaleckian model of growth and distribution, and the implications of this addition are examined. In the third section, a Harrodian accumulation behaviour is superposed to the previous model, and the conditions under which this more complex model does converge to a stable solution with a normal rate of capacity utilization are examined. We shall see that the required conditions are fairly simple. In the fourth section, there is a discussion about how the present models are related to previous contributions that have been made in the same spirit, namely those of Allain and the recent extensions of Serrano's supermultiplier model made by Fabio Freitas and Franklin Serrano (2013, 2015) and Serrano and Freitas (2015), who also demonstrate a conditional convergence towards a normal rate of utilization. The fifth section presents some empirical evidence and arguments providing support to the theoretical model. The last section concludes.

## 2. THE SIMPLE VARIANT OF THE NEO-KALECKIAN MODEL

### 2.1 *A frequent objection to neo-Kaleckian growth models*

A key feature of the neo-Kaleckian model is that the rate of capacity utilization is endogenous. In the canonical model, or even in the post-Kaleckian model *à la* Bhaduri and Marglin (1990), there is, thus, nothing that will bring back the actual rate of capacity utilization towards its normal value. A number of heterodox economists have expressed their annoyance at this feature of the standard neo-Kaleckian model. This criticism was made early on by Marco Committeri (1986), and it has been repeated more recently, for instance by Skott (2012), Duménil and Lévy (2014) and Cesaratto (2015). In the view of all these authors, a long-run equilibrium requires that the actual rate of utilization gravitates around the normal rate or converges towards it. They argue, as does Skott (1989, p. 70), that 'steady growth … is inconceivable unless the rate of capital utilisation is at the desired level'. Students of system dynamics would argue that a model without such a convergence towards the normal rate of capacity utilization would be exhibiting a missing feedback mechanism.

Several answers have been provided in response to this conundrum (Hein *et al.*, 2012; Lavoie, 2014, pp. 387–410). One broad group of answer has been to deny the relevance of this critique, for instance by arguing that neo-Kaleckian authors never had a long-run steady state in mind, thinking rather in terms of a medium-run analysis, as does Hein (2014) explicitly for instance, where the economy is exposed to all kinds of shocks and where all possible adjustments are never completed (Chick and Caserta, 1997). In other words, there is 'no such thing as a long-run equilibrium in which all relevant adjustments have been completed' (Dutt, 2011, p. 380), so that only the average of short-run positions should be of concern. As Dutt (1997, p. 450) also points out, 'long-run equilibria in these models are theoretical constructs which depict a state which is maintained *if all parameters and functions of the model are taken as given*'. But in reality they are not given. A related group of answer has been that most of the early neo-Kaleckian models, such as those of Rowthorn (1981), Taylor (1983) and Dutt (1984) did not even refer to a normal rate of utilization, presumably on the ground that although firms may have some desired rate of capacity utilization, they may be content with the actual rate as long as this rate remains within a fairly large band around the normal rate. A third answer has been that the normal rate of utilization may itself be endogenous and possibly attracted by the actual rate of capacity utilization—a form of hysteresis.[1] Finally, a fourth answer has been that many of the mechanisms pertaining to drive the actual rate of capacity utilization towards its normal value have not been entirely convincing, or that small amendments to these mechanisms have resulted in the failure to achieve convergence to normal capacity utilization, as in Dutt (2011) for instance.

Still, given all that has been said in the above paragraph, the present article starts by granting that there exists a normal or desired rate of capacity utilization, one that is exogenous, and it undertakes to find a plausible set

[1] A similar instance is provided by Skott (2005) when he argues that wage norms held by workers may be influenced by the real wages that have actually been achieved in the labour market.

of mechanisms that can lead to convergence towards this normal rate while at the same time verifying whether some of the insights of the neo-Kaleckian model, like wage-led growth or the paradoxes of costs and of thrift, can be kept. The mechanism that we propose to investigate is the one put forward by Franklin Serrano (1995a, 1995b) under the name of the Sraffian supermultiplier. His intent is to show that Keynesian results will still hold despite the actual rate of capacity utilization being brought back to its normal level in the long run. We will examine whether this can be corroborated within the confines of a modified neo-Kaleckian model.

### 2.2 *The short-run model with the Serrano proposal*

As is well-known, the canonical neo-Kaleckian model of growth and distribution is made up of three equations: an investment equation, a saving equation and an equation defining income distribution. With respect to the last equation, we shall simply assume that income distribution does not change and is proxied by the share of profit, $\pi$. We start by using the simplest investment equation that will allow us to take into account the normal rate of capacity utilization, as first proposed by Edward Amadeo (1986). This is equation (1) below, which makes an explicit reference to a normal rate of utilization or to a 'planned' degree of utilization of capacity as Joseph Steindl (1952, p. 129) calls it. This normal rate is below unity, for instance it could be at 80 per cent. This investment function $g^i$, which is the rate of accumulation of capital $K$, is based on the distinction between undesired and desired excess capacity, or between the actual rate and the normal rate of capacity utilization, respectively, denoted by $u = Y/Y_{fc}$ and $u_n$, where $Y$ and $Y_{fc}$ are output and full-capacity output:

$$g^i = I/K = \gamma + \gamma_u(u - u_n) \qquad (1)$$

It is obvious from the above equation that if the actual rate of utilization turned out to be equal to the normal or desired rate, the actual rate of growth would be equal to $\gamma$. As Committeri (1986, p. 173) and Caserta (1990, p. 152) point out, if firms are content about the degree of capacity utilization that is being achieved and do not desire to have it changed, one concludes that the rate of accumulation desired by firms should be equal to the expected growth rate of sales, or perhaps more appropriately, equal to some secular growth rate of sales. It is clear from equation (1) that the exogenous parameter $\gamma$ then represents this expected or trend growth rate of sales.[2] If it is assumed that the actual rate of capacity utilization $u$ is larger than the planned rate $u_n$, the actual rate of growth $g$ must be larger than the expected growth rate of sales $\gamma$.

We now come to the saving equation. The crucial point made by Serrano (1995b) is that the *average* propensity to save will move endogenously when there are autonomous consumption expenditures, even if both the *marginal* propensity to save and the profit share are constant. This will be the case both in the short run, when autonomous consumption is a given, and in the medium run when growth occurs, with autonomous consumption growing at some given rate, different from the rate of accumulation. The simplest way to put this is to write the saving equation $g^s$:

$$g^s = S/K = (s_p \pi u/v) - z \tag{2}$$

with $z = Z/K$, where $Z$ are the autonomous consumption expenditures of the capitalists, and hence where $z$ is the ratio of autonomous expenditures to the capital stock. As usual, $s_p$ is the (marginal) propensity to save out of profits, $\pi$ is the profit share and $v$ is the capital to output-capacity ratio, which will be assumed constant throughout. As is often assumed in this literature, there is no saving out of wages.

The main point that Serrano wishes to make is that saving (or the saving share of GDP) can adjust to investment (or the investment share of GDP) even when assuming that the marginal propensity to save, income distribution and the rate of utilization are all constant. The argument is, thus, that the 'Keynesian Hypothesis' is more general than previously thought, since it does not need to rely on an endogenous rate of utilization in the long run, in contrast to the neo-Kaleckian approach, or on an endogenous profit share, as in the earlier Kaldor-Robinson growth models. What happens is that even if $s_p$ and $\pi$, as well as $u$ are constant, the average propensity to save will be endogenous as long as $z$ is itself endogenous. This average propensity to save out of national income $Y$ can be derived from equation (2) and is equal to:

$$S/Y = s_p \pi - zv/u \tag{2'}$$

[2] Equation (1) is obviously a highly stylized representation of investment decisions. It ignores other key determinants of investment such as technological change, the profit rate or the profit share, credit or monetary conditions, the leverage ratio of firms, radical uncertainty and so on. Indeed Amadeo (1986) initially associated the constant $\gamma$ with animal spirits, and hence we could possibly link the parameter $\gamma$ to all the factors just mentioned.

Putting together equations (1) and (2) and solving for $u$, nothing special happens and all the standard neo-Kaleckian results, such as the paradoxes of thrift and of costs, still hold. An increase in the propensity to save $s_p$ or in the profit share $\pi$ leads to a fall in the rate of utilization $u$. This is obvious from looking at the short-run solution for the rate of utilization, when the ratio $z$ has not had time to change:

$$u^* = \frac{(\gamma - \gamma_u u_n + z)v}{s_p \pi - v\gamma_u} \tag{3}$$

As is usual in the neo-Kaleckian model, we assume Keynesian stability, that is, we assume that saving reacts more than investment to a change in capacity utilization, that is, $s_p\pi/v > \gamma_{u,}$ and hence we assume that the denominator of equation (3) is positive.

*2.3 The medium run with the Serrano proposal*

Let us now consider a longer run. The key idea here is that autonomous consumption expenditures grow at a certain rate $g_z$, which we assume to be given by outside circumstances. As Serrano (1995a, p. 84), puts it, it is usually assumed that autonomous components of aggregate demand grow in line with the capital stock, but 'it seems that it is rather the size of the economy itself that depends partially on the magnitude (and rates of growth) of these autonomous components of final demand'.

But assuming that $Z$ grows at the constant rate $g_z$ means that the ratio $z = Z/K$ must be changing through time, through the following law of motion that defines the growth rate of $z$:

$$\hat{z} = \frac{\dot{z}}{z} = \hat{Z} - \hat{K} = \bar{g}_z - g = (\bar{g}_z - \gamma) - \gamma_u(u^* - u_n) \tag{4}$$

The last equality is derived from the investment equation, $g^i = \gamma + \gamma_u(u - u_n)$. The bar over $g_z$ is there to recall that the growth rate of autonomous expenditures is an unexplained constant. What we wish to know is whether the behaviour of $z$ is dynamically stable or not, that is, whether it will converge to a stable value. This will happen if $d\hat{z}/dz$ is smaller than zero. Making use of equation (3), we can compute what the term $(u^* - u_n)$ is equal to:

$$u^* - u_n = \frac{(\gamma + z)v - s_p \pi u_n}{s_p \pi - v\gamma_u} \tag{5}$$

Combining equations (4) and (5) we get:

$$\hat{z} = (\bar{g}_z - \gamma) - \gamma_u \left[\frac{(\gamma + z)v - s_p \pi u_n}{s_p \pi - v\gamma_u}\right] \tag{6}$$

And, thus, taking the derivative of $\hat{z}$ with respect to itself, we find that:

$$\frac{d\hat{z}}{dz} = \frac{-\gamma_u v}{s_p \pi - v\gamma_u} < 0 \tag{7}$$

The derivative is always negative, as long as the denominator is positive, that is, as long as there is short-run Keynesian stability. This means that $z$ will converge to an equilibrium value $z^{**}$, at which value the growth rates of capital and aggregate demand will be the same as the given growth rate of autonomous consumption expenditures. This also means that the medium-run solutions that one could find, by assuming that at some point the growth rate of capital equates the growth rate of autonomous consumption, will indeed be realized if given enough time. The model is dynamically stable.

What is the intuitive understanding of the stability condition? A rise in $z$ increases aggregate consumption and therefore the rate of capacity utilization (as can be seen from equation (3)). This brings about an increase in the rate of capital accumulation through the investment equation (1). Since the growth rate of autonomous consumption is fixed, the growth rate of the ratio $z$ of autonomous consumption to capital falls.

In this medium run, $g^{**} = \bar{g}_z$, and hence making use first of the investment equation, and then of the saving equation, we can derive the two medium-run equilibria:

$$u^{**} = u_n + \frac{\bar{g}_z - \gamma}{\gamma_u} \tag{8}$$

$$z^{**} = \frac{s_p \pi u^{**}}{v} - \bar{g}_z \tag{9}$$

Obviously, if $s_p$ or $\pi$ are larger, $z^{**}$ (the medium-run size of autonomous consumption relative to capital) will be larger, but these two parameters have no effect on $u^{**}$; and if $\bar{g}_z$ is larger, $u^{**}$ will be larger. Thus, for given parameter values, $\bar{g}_z$ cannot be too large, otherwise the rate of capacity utilization would need to exceed unity, meaning that if one believes that this condition is binding, then one needs $\bar{g}_z \leq \gamma + \gamma_u(1 - u_n)$.

Furthermore, what is the effect of $\bar{g}_z$ on $z^{**}$? To find out, one has to combine equations (8) and (9), so as to obtain:

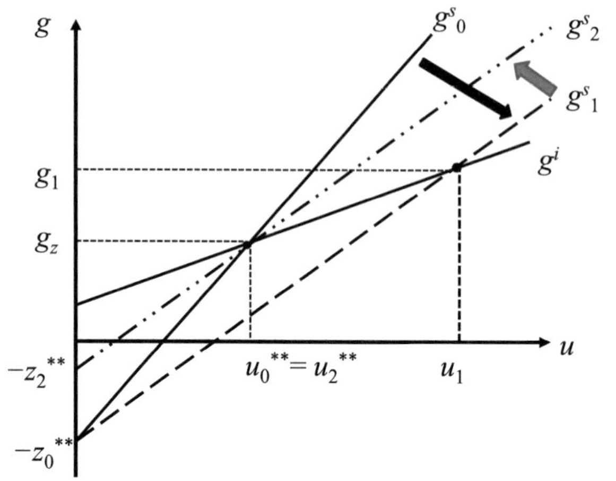


*Figure 1. The impact of a decrease in the profit share or in the marginal propensity to save out of profits with the Serrano adjustment mechanism.*

$$z^{**} = \frac{s_p\pi(\gamma_u u_n - \gamma) + (s_p\pi - v\gamma_u)\bar{g}_z}{v\gamma_u} \qquad (9')$$

Taking the derivative of equation (9′) with respect to $\bar{g}_z$ we get:

$$\frac{dz^{**}}{d\bar{g}_z} = \frac{s_p\pi - \gamma_u v}{v\gamma_u} \qquad (9'')$$

The derivative is positive provided $s_p\pi > v\gamma_u$, that is, provided there is short-run Keynesian stability, which was already assumed. Thus, as long as there is Keynesian stability, an increase in the growth rate of autonomous consumption expenditure will lead to an increase in the medium-run ratio $z^{**}$ of autonomous consumption expenditure to capital.

## 2.4 *A graphical interpretation of the Serrano mechanism*

The Serrano adjustment mechanism can be illustrated with the help of figure 1. Let us assume that the economy starts from a steady state where the rate of accumulation is exactly equal to the growth rate of autonomous consumption expenditures, with a rate of utilization of $u_0^{**}$. Let us now suppose that there is a decrease in the marginal propensity to save out of profits or in the share of profits. This will be associated with a rotation of the saving curve, from $g_0^s$ to $g_1^s$,

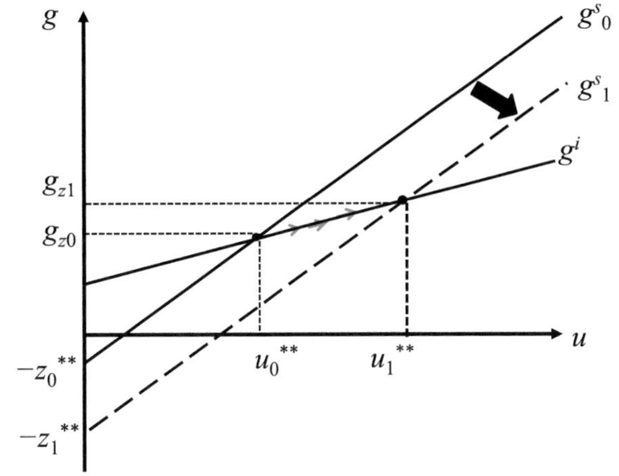


*Figure 2. The impact of an increase in the growth rate of autonomous consumption expenditures in a neo-Kaleckian model.*

as shown with the help of the black arrow, since the slope of the curve will now be smaller. In the short run, as in all Kaleckian models, this will generate an increase in the growth rate of capital and in the rate of utilization, which move to $g_1$ and $u_1$ in the short run. But the new equilibrium is only a temporary one, as the new discrepancy between $g_1$ and $g_z$ will generate a reduction in $z$ through equation (4). The saving curve will, thus, gradually shift up through time, as shown in figure 1 with the help of the grey arrow, until the saving curve reaches $g_2^s$, at which point the rate of accumulation equates the given growth rate of autonomous consumption. As to the rate of utilization, it will be back to its initial equilibrium position, such that $u_2^{**} = u_0^{**}$. The change in income distribution or in the marginal propensity to save has had no impact on the equilibrium rate of utilization. However, the *average* rate of utilization and the *average* rate of growth achieved during this whole episode are higher, the economy having been run between $u_0^{**}$ and $u_1$ and $g_z$ and $g_1$, respectively, during the whole transition. As a consequence, *at any point of time during the traverse*, the level of output and of capacity will be higher than if there had been no increase in real wages or no decrease in the marginal propensity to save.

Figure 2 illustrates what happens when there is an increase in the growth rate of autonomous consumption expenditures. As is clear from equation (4), this will generate an increase in the value of $z$, the ratio of autonomous consumption expenditures to capital. This increase will keep on going until the increase in the short-run equilibrium value of $u^*$ is sufficiently high to compensate the effect of the higher autonomous growth rate $g_z$, at which point the traverse will end. As is clear from figure 2, a higher growth rate of autonomous consumption expenditure will generate a larger value of $z^{**}$ (as seen with the help of equation (9″) and a higher value of capacity utilization $u^{**}$ (see equation (8)). Thus, the model is clearly Keynesian. Faster autonomous growth generates rates of capital accumulation and rates of capacity utilization that become progressively larger, until finally the stock of capital grows at as high a rate as that of autonomous consumption expenditures, at which point the rate of utilization takes a steady value.

### 2.5 *Discussion of the Serrano mechanism*

At this stage, five remarks can be made. First, the mechanism designed by Serrano on its own does not achieve a normal rate of capacity utilization, since $u^{**} \neq u_n$.[3] For $u^{**} = u_n$ to be achieved, the $\gamma$ parameter in the investment equation would need to equal $g_z$. In other words, entrepreneurs would need to assess the trend growth rate of sales as being equal to the growth rate of autonomous consumption expenditures. This was recognized by supporters of the supermutiplier, who used to refer to perfect foresight or to correct forward-looking expectations, without providing any further mechanisms or explanations.

Second, almost by definition, with this mechanism, we can have neither a wage-led nor a profit-led regime, as they are defined in the literature related to the post-Kaleckian growth model, since the growth rates of capital and of output eventually adjust to the given growth rate of autonomous consumption expenditures, and also because the long-run value of the rate of utilization $u^{**}$ depends neither on the profit share nor on the marginal propensity to save out of profits. As long as there is no change to any of the four parameters in equation (8), any change in the profit share or in the marginal propensity to save will have no effect on the medium-run value of the rate of utilization.[4] Thus, looking at the rate of capacity utilization

[3] A similar result is obtained by Freitas and Serrano (2013) and Serrano and Freitas (2015) when the accelerator in their model is not flexible and, thus, does not react to the discrepancy between the realized and the normal rate of utilization.

[4] Pariboni (2015) shows that if the standard neo-Kaleckian investment equation, given by equation (1), is replaced by the investment equation proposed by Bhaduri and Marglin (1990) in what is now often referred to as the post-Kaleckian model, where investment depends on the rate of utilization and the profit share, the medium-run equilibrium $u^{**}$ equivalent to equation (8) will be a negative function of the profit share, thus, showing that even the post-Kaleckian model is subjected to wage-led forces when autonomous consumption expenditures are taken into account.

achieved in the new steady states, we could say that the paradoxes of thrift and of costs no longer exist.

This leads, however, to a third remark. While the paradox of thrift and of costs are gone in the medium-run version of this model (looking at steady-state growth rates), reducing the profit share or reducing the marginal propensity to save out of profits will have a positive effect on the *levels* of capital, capacity and output.[5] This is a point that Sergio Cesaratto (2015) has emphasized recently, and it is precisely the point made originally by Serrano:

> That lower marginal propensity to save will increase the level of induced consumption and aggregate demand, and, consequently, also the long-period level of productive capacity. However, this will be a once-and-for-all effect. Once capacity has adjusted to the new (higher) level of effective demand implied by the higher (super) multiplier, the economy will settle back to steady growth at the unchanged rate given by the growth of autonomous expenditures. Therefore, on the demand side, a decrease in the marginal propensity to save brought about by the rise of the real wage will have a positive long-period level effect (on capacity output), but will have no effect on the sustainable secular rate of growth of capacity.
>
> Serrano, 1995b, p. 138.

A fourth remark is now in order. By a strange turn of events, whereas Sraffians are usually accused by other post-Keynesians of focusing on fully adjusted positions (with normal prices and normal rates of capacity utilization, as defined by Vianello (1985)), several Sraffian authors have criticized Kaleckians for focusing unduly on steady states, arguing that steady-state analysis ought to be jettisoned (Trezzini, 2011b, p. 143). In the example provided above by Serrano and in our little model, while the rate of capacity utilization would be the same at the beginning and at the end of the process, it will be higher during the transition process. Thus, on *average*, the rate of utilization and the growth rate of the economy are higher than at the starting and terminal points of the traverse. Thus, what these Sraffians are telling us is that more attention should be paid to the average values achieved during the *traverse* than to the terminal points. This is a

[5] Allain (2015, p. 1362) provides a graphical illustration of this feature, with a figure showing the evolution of the log of GDP through time, showing that an increase in the profit share in a model with autonomous government expenditure will lead to a temporary slowdown of GDP growth, which will eventually recover its initial value. GDP levels, however, will be forever lower than they would have been if there had been no change in the profit share.

recommendation with which all post-Keynesians could certainly agree (see for instance Jacques Henry, 1987), and it is one which is made quite explicitly by Man-Seop Park (1995, p. 307), who argued that the moving averages of key variables are quite distinct from their potential steady-state values, a point which was perhaps not fully appreciated when it was made.

As a fifth remark, we may say that, as a follow-up to a positive shock on aggregate demand, a *transient* higher rate of utilization, rather than a *permanent* higher rate of utilization, seems to provide a better fit to the existing data on rates of utilization. It has been argued by a number of authors that despite large short-run fluctuations of the rate of capacity utilization, the long-run variations are relatively limited, with a tendency to return towards its mean, which the critics of the neo-Kaleckian growth model interpret as being the normal rate of capacity utilization (Skott, 2012; Dejuán, 2013; Duménil and Lévy, 2014). Thus, the neo-Kaleckian model modified by the addition of autonomous consumption expenditures allows the model to be reconciled with this apparent empirical behaviour of the rate of capacity utilization.

## 3. THE COMPLEX VARIANT OF THE NEO-KALECKIAN MODEL, WITH A HARRODIAN MECHANISM

So far, we have shown that Serrano's autonomous consumption expenditure growing at a constant rate provides a mechanism that achieves convergence to a constant rate of capacity utilization, but that rate is generally *not* the normal rate of utilization, which justifies our use of a medium-run equilibrium in contrast to a long-run one. As pointe out in the previous section, the critics of neo-Kaleckian models complain that these models incorporate no mechanism driving the economy towards the *normal* rate of capacity utilization. Thus, we need to consider an additional mechanism to achieve the normal rate of utilization that Serrano and the critics are longing for. Allain (2015) has proposed the addition of such a mechanism—a Harrodian one. Thus, it will turn out that combining a Harrodian investment equation with Serrano's autonomous consumption expenditure will provide a response to those who believe that there are Harrodian instability mechanisms at work in capitalist economies as well as those who argue that the economy should gravitate around or converge towards a normal rate of capacity utilization.

For simplification purposes, we propose a slightly modified version of the standard Harrodian equation. Here, we assume that it is the *rate of change*, rather than the change, in the $\gamma$ parameter of the investment function which responds to discrepancies between observed growth rates and expected trends. Thus, the $\gamma$ parameter reacts to a discrepancy between the actual rate of accumulation $g^*$ and the expected secular growth rate of sales $\gamma$, as was suggested in Lavoie (1996, p. 139) and then by Allain (2015):

$$\hat{\gamma}=\mu(g^*-\gamma),\ \mu>0 \tag{10}$$

Taking into account the investment function given by equation (1), equation (10) can be rewritten as a function of the rate of utilization, thus, getting another standard version of the Harrodian mechanism:

$$\hat{\gamma}=\mu\gamma_u(u^*-u_n),\ \mu>0 \tag{11}$$

Making use of equation (5) once again, the Harrodian equation becomes:

$$\hat{\gamma}=\mu\gamma_u\left(\frac{(\gamma+z)v-s_p\pi u_n}{s_p\pi-v\gamma_u}\right) \tag{12}$$

We thus have a new system of simultaneous dynamic equations, given by equations (6) and (12). To find how the system behaves, we need to consider the following $2\times 2$ Jacobian matrix, called $J$:

$$J=\begin{pmatrix} \dfrac{\mu\gamma_u v}{s_p\pi-v\gamma_u} & \dfrac{\mu\gamma_u v}{s_p\pi-v\gamma_u} \\ -\left(1+\dfrac{v\gamma_u}{s_p\pi-v\gamma_u}\right) & \dfrac{-\gamma_u v}{s_p\pi-v\gamma_u} \end{pmatrix} \tag{13}$$

For the system characterized by the Jacobian (13) to exhibit stability and to converge to an equilibrium, given by the doublet $\bar{g}_z$ and $u_n$, the determinant needs to be positive and the trace needs to be negative. To find how the system described by (13) behaves, we need to look at the determinant of the $2\times 2$ Jacobian matrix, and at its trace. For the system to exhibit stability and to converge to an equilibrium given by the doublet $g_z$ and $u_n$, the determinant needs to be positive and the trace needs to be negative. We get:

$$\text{Det}\,J=\frac{\mu\gamma_u v}{s_p\pi-v\gamma_u}$$

$$\text{Tr}\,J=-\frac{\gamma_u(1-\mu)v}{s_p\pi-v\gamma_u}$$

The determinant is positive whenever the Keynesian stability condition is fulfilled. Given this short-run stability condition, the trace is negative if

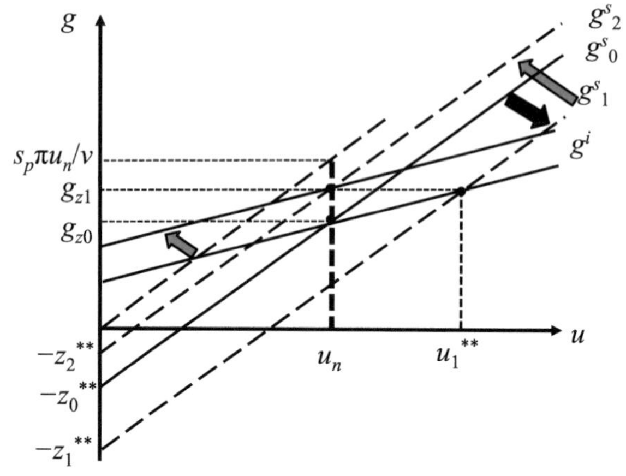


*Figure 3. The impact of an increase in the growth rate of autonomous consumption expenditures in a neo-Kaleckian model with the addition of a Harrodian mechanism.*

$\mu < 1$. Thus, the system is dynamically stable when there is short-run Keynesian stability as long as the effect of Harrodian instability is not overly strong.[6] If this is so, depending on the values taken by the parameters, this system may come back straight to its fully adjusted position, where $u^{**} = u_n$ and where $g^{**} = \gamma^{**} = \bar{g}_z$, or it may whirl cyclically towards it.

### 3.1 *A first graphical illustration*

Figure 3 illustrates what goes on when, once more, we examine the case of an increase in the growth rate of autonomous consumption expenditures, from $g_{z0}$ to $g_{z1}$. We suppose that the economy starts from a fully adjusted position at $u_n$, with the saving curve being given by $g_0^s$ and the ratio of autonomous expenditure to the capital stock being set at $z_0^{**}$. Assuming here that the Harrodian mechanism is a process that takes time to get going, the economy first moves towards the rate of utilization $u_1{}^{**}$, with

[6] While the condition $\mu < 1$ may look fairly innocuous, Olivier Allain has pointed out to me that equation (10) on its own severely restrains the strength of the Harrodian mechanism. For instance, with $\mu = 1$, and with the expected growth rate of sales $\gamma$ at 3 per cent and the actual growth rate $g^*$ at 4 per cent, the new expected growth rate of sales would only move up to 3.03 per cent. The condition $\mu < 1$, thus, implies a fairly slow convergence to the normal rate of utilization.

the share of autonomous consumption expenditures rising towards $z_1$** as indicated by the black arrow, just as it did in figure 2, but here without actually getting there. This is because the Harrodian mechanism eventually kicks in, generating an increase in the expected secular growth rate of sales $\gamma$, so that the investment function $g^i$ commences to shift upwards. As it does, driving up further the rate of capacity of utilization in the process, the growth rate of capital eventually exceeds the growth rate of autonomous expenditures. This will put the Serrano mechanism in reverse gear, with the share of autonomous consumption expenditures relative to the stock of capital now declining, as shown by the slim grey arrows. Provided its strength is not excessive, the Harrodian mechanism eventually brings back the economy towards the normal rate of capacity utilization $u_n$, with the share of autonomous expenditures eventually declining all the way to $z_2$**. This corresponds to the value given by equation (9) with $u^{**} = u_n$ and to the value given by equation ((9)') when $\bar{g}_z = \gamma$. Meanwhile, the increase in the rate of capital accumulation will be restrained by the Serrano mechanism, as it will be driven back towards the new rate of growth of the autonomous consumption expenditures, so that $g^{**} = g_{z1}$.

Figure 3 helps to understand the existence of a maximum value for the autonomous growth rate $\bar{g}_z$, for if the restriction given by inequality (14) were not to be respected, the new fully adjusted position could never be achieved, as this would require a negative amount of autonomous consumption expenditure.

$$\bar{g}_z < s_p \pi u_n / v \tag{14}$$

### 3.2 *A phase diagram analysis*

We may also examine the system of simultaneous dynamic equations with the help of a phase diagram in the $z$ and $\gamma$ space. First, from equation (12), we derive the first demarcation line where $\hat{\gamma}=0$. This will occur when:

$$\gamma = -z + \frac{s_p \pi u_n}{v} \tag{15}$$

And from equation (6) we derive the second demarcation line where $\hat{z}=0$. This will occur when:

$$\gamma = -\frac{\gamma_u v}{s_p \pi} z + \frac{\bar{g}_z (s_p \pi - v\gamma_u) + s_p \pi \gamma_u u_n}{s_p \pi} \tag{16}$$

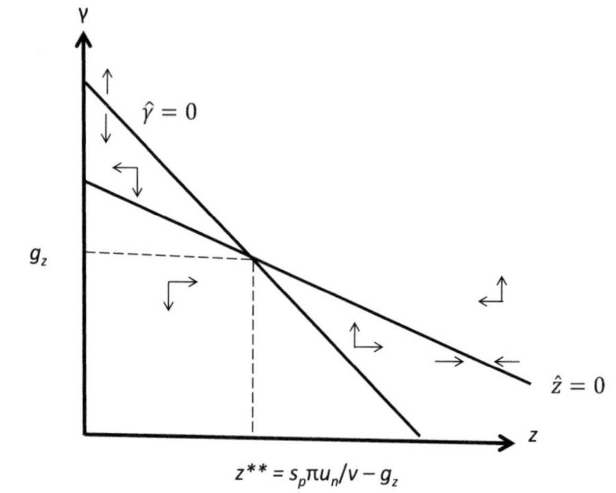


*Figure 4. The two demarcation lines tied to the share of autonomous consumption expenditures and the expected secular growth rate of sales.*

or

$$\gamma = -\frac{\gamma_u v}{s_p \pi} z + \bar{g}_z \left[1 - \left(v\gamma_u / s_p \pi\right)\right] + \gamma_u u_n \tag{16'}$$

The slope of the $\hat{\gamma}=0$ demarcation line is, thus, $-1$. As to the slope of the $\hat{z}=0$ demarcation line, we know that it is flatter than the first one, because the absolute value of the slope is smaller than 1, as long as we keep assuming the Keynesian short-run stability condition ($s_p\pi > v\gamma_u$). It can be shown that the intercept of the $\hat{z}=0$ demarcation line with the vertical axis is smaller than that of the $\hat{\gamma}=0$ demarcation line, as it should be for the two demarcation lines to cross each other, provided the condition $\bar{g}_z < s_p\pi u_n/v$ holds, as already pointed out with equation (14). The phase diagram with its streamlines is shown in figure 4. The long-run equilibrium is found at the intersection of the two demarcation lines, where $\gamma^{**} = \bar{g}_z$ and where $z^{**} = s_p\pi u_n/v - \bar{g}_z$. The dynamics of $\gamma$ are destabilizing around the stationary locus while those of $z$ are stabilizing. The cycles will be making the economy go to the long run equilibrium if the vertical dis-equilibrating movements due to changes in $\gamma$ are damper than the horizontal equilibrating movements due to changes in the autonomous consumption expenditure to capital stock ratio $z$.

Next, we examine what happens if there is an increase in the growth rate of the autonomous consumption expenditures. This is done with the help

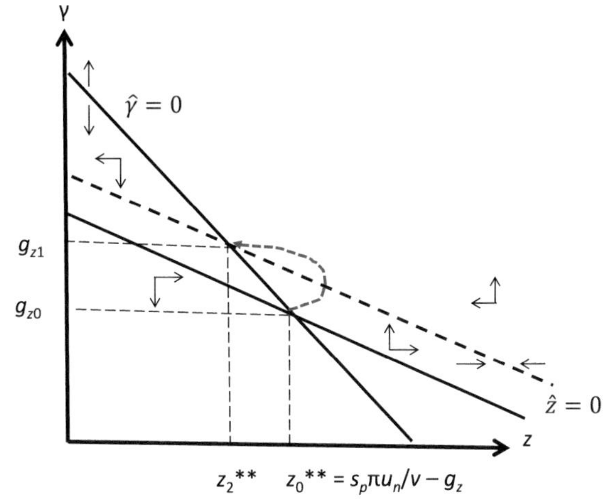


*Figure 5. Phase diagram with an increase in the growth rate of autonomous consumption expenditures.*

of figure 5. Figure 5 is the phase diagram equivalent of figure 3.The two continuous demarcation lines represent the starting position, assumed to be a long-run equilibrium with $z_0^{**}$ and where $\gamma^{**} = \bar{g}_{z0}$ and $u^{**} = u_n$. As can be verified from equations (15) and (16), the increase in $\bar{g}_z$ has no effect on the $\hat{\gamma}=0$ demarcation line, but it leads to an upward parallel shift in the $\hat{z}=0$ demarcation line, which is now given by the dotted demarcation line. The case illustrated here is one where the new long-run equilibrium is quickly achieved. As in figure 3, the faster growth rate of autonomous consumption expenditure initially leads to a higher $z$ ratio, but the increase in the rate of utilization due to the increase in autonomous expenditures, as well as the increase in the $\gamma$ parameter due to the Harrodian mechanism induce an even faster growth rate of capacity, which in the following stage causes a reduction in the autonomous consumption expenditure to capital stock ratio $z$, thus, eventually bringing back the rate of utilization towards its normal level, and, thus, achieving a new long-run equilibrium with $z_2^{**}$ and where income, capital and capacity all grow at the new growth rate $\bar{g}_{z1}$. Thus, despite the return towards the normal degree of capacity utilization, the model generates a Keynesian result.

But what happens if there is a decrease in the marginal propensity to save out of profits, given by $s_p$, or if there is a decrease in the profit share? In the simple modification of the Kaleckian model that only incorporated the Serrano mechanism, as illustrated by figure 1, the answer was fairly straightforward: since the rate of capacity utilization and the rate of accumulation were higher during the whole traverse than they would have been without the change, we could safely conclude that the paradox of thrift and the paradox of costs still held, provided they were interpreted in terms of level effects, or as average growth rates over the duration of the traverse. But what can be said once the Harrodian mechanism is added to the model?

Figure 6 provides a phase diagram of what can happen with a decrease in the profit share or in the marginal propensity to save out of profits, assuming as before dynamic stability. Both demarcation lines shift down, as shown by the new dotted demarcation lines. Because there is no change in the rate of growth of autonomous expenditures, the new long-run equilibrium value of $\gamma$ is no different from what it was originally, as is shown in figure 6. With cycles around the long-run equilibrium, there will also be phases when the economy will have lower rates of capacity utilization and growth than the long-run equilibrium values. The claim that the average growth rate over the duration of the traverse is higher with an increase in the wage share or a fall in the marginal propensity to save is, thus, not as obvious as it was when only the Serrano mechanism played a role.

Still, we can say the following. First, the fall in the profit share or in the marginal propensity to save right away will increase the rate of capacity utilization and the rate of accumulation, which will also induce an increase in the $\gamma$ parameter. This gives a clear upward bias to the growth rate. Second, as long as symmetric adjustments are assumed above and below the demarcation lines (that is, the value of $\mu$ is assumed constant), the upward movements will dominate the downward movements. These two points together insure that the reduction in the profit share or in the marginal propensity to save will generate an average growth rate that will be higher over the duration of the traverse than its starting value, despite the actual rate of capacity utilization being brought back to its normal level. Naturally, if there are asymmetrical adjustments, with slumps being stronger and deeper than expansion, this result may not hold.

## 4. DISCUSSION OF SOME OF THE RELATED LITERATURE

As pointed out earlier, the work of Serrano (1995a, 1995b), with the introduction of his autonomous consumption expenditures, is at the core of the present article. The model proposed here is, however, closest to the model and the mechanisms found in the article of Olivier Allain (2015), which was first presented at a conference in 2012. Indeed, Allain's model was the inspiration for this article. The present model and Allain's model both start with a neo-

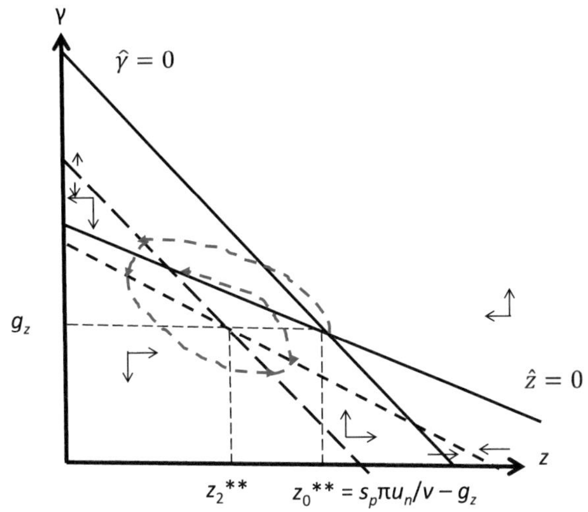


*Figure 6. Phase diagram with a decrease in the profit share or in the marginal propensity to save out of profits.*

Kaleckian framework, with an identical investment equation and a (nearly) identical Harrodian mechanism. The key difference is that Allain assumes that government expenditure grows at a constant rate and, thus, plays the role of the autonomous non-capacity creating expenditure, with the ratio of government expenditure to capital playing the role of the stabilizing factor—the $z$ variable in the present model. To avoid discussing the expansionary effects of a budget deficit and the dynamics related to debt, Allain (2015) assumes that the tax rate on income is endogenous and set to keep the budget in balance. The average propensity to save, thus, becomes a function of the tax rate and hence a function of the relative size of the autonomous government expenditure. Allain's model arrives at essentially the same results regarding growth and level effects of a change in the autonomous growth rate or of a change in the propensity to save and the profit share. Allain finds a conditional convergence towards a long-run equilibrium with a normal rate of capacity utilization. His dynamic stability condition is very similar to the one found here. Using our notation, his condition for the equilibrium to be locally stable is such that $\mu < s_p\pi u_n/v - g_z$.[7]

[7] Allain's Harrodian equation is $\dot{\gamma}=\mu\gamma_u(u^*-u_n)$. Compare with equation (11). As pointed out by one of the referees, if I had made use of Allain's Harrodian equation, based on the *change* in the $\gamma$ parameter, I would have found exactly the same condition to achieve local dynamic stability.

What about Serrano's own argument, that of the so-called Sraffian supermultiplier? There are two Sraffian positions on this issue. There are those Sraffians who have supported the analysis of the supermultiplier with its normal rate of capacity utilization, such as Heinrich Bortis (1997), Sergio Cesaratto (2015) and Oscar Dejuán (2005, 2013); and there are those like Man-Seop Park (2000), Attilio Trezzini (1995, 1998) and Palumbo and Trezzini (2003), as well as Nelson Barbosa-Filho (2000) and Moudud (2010, pp. 71–2), who have questioned the stability of the mechanism being contemplated implicitly by Serrano or who complain that he is just assuming the existence of an equilibrium at normal capacity utilization.

Indeed, Serrano (1995a, 1995b) did not present a stability analysis. This explains why his argument based on the growth rate of non-capacity creating autonomous expenditures and the endogenous average saving rate has not been more generally endorsed by other post-Keynesians or utilized in their own models. This is because, as recalled by Joseph Halevi and Peter Kriesler (1991, p. 86), to entertain the study of fully adjusted positions, one must be able to provide a 'coherent adjustment process'. Serrano could only argue at the time that as long as demand expectations by entrepreneurs are not systematically biased, the average rate of capacity utilization will tend towards the normal rate of utilization and hence that the economy will tend towards a fully adjusted position.[8]

By contrast Serrano's critics, listed above, argued that if the economy starts from a fully adjusted position, it is unlikely to remain there; and when the economy gets away from a fully adjusted position, it is unlikely to come back to it; in other words, the equilibrium at the normal rate of capacity utilization is not stable. Here we will not discuss these objections much longer as they are being scrutinized and dismissed as a misunderstanding of Serrano's initial argument by Freitas and Serrano (2013, 2015) and Serrano and Freitas (2015). For instance, Palumbo and Trezzini (2003, p. 116) would seem to agree with Freitas and Serrano when they write that 'utilization must necessarily be different from normal *on average*' and when they add that 'coincidence of demand (output) and capacity cannot be assumed either as a continuous condition … or as an average condition'. This is exactly what has been shown in the present model: the actual rate of utilization is not continually at the normal rate of utilization, nor is it there on average; it only tends conditionally towards the normal rate. And this is also what happens in the stability analysis provided by Freitas and Serrano (2013, 2015) and Serrano and Freitas (2015).

[8] The same can be said about Bortis (1997).

These two authors assume that investment $I$ is a fraction of income, so that $I = hY$ where $h$ is the accelerator, but where $h$ also happens to be the share of investment in GDP, $I/Y$. Dividing by $K$, we can rewrite this as $I/K = g^i = (I/Y)(Y/K)(Y/Y_{fc}) = (h/v)u$. In our notations, $h/v = \gamma_u$. They then assume a Harrodian adjustment mechanism similar to the one given here by equation (10), such that $\hat{h} = \mu(u - u_n)$, implying that investment takes an ever larger share of GDP as long as the actual rate of capacity utilization surpasses its normal level, thus, adopting a flexible accelerator.[9] As is the case with the neo-Kaleckian model, the rate of utilization is determined by the equality between investment and saving, but with the marginal propensity to save out of profits being assumed to equal unity while workers save nothing.

With consumption by capitalists being autonomous and growing at the rate $\bar{g}_z$, Freitas and Serrano obtain a system of two first-order non-linear differential equations, with $\dot{u}$ and $\dot{h}$ being the dependent variables. As is the case here, for Serrano's mechanism to work out, the growth rate of autonomous expenditures cannot be too large, for otherwise the share of autonomous consumption expenditures would need to be negative. Freitas and Serrano, thus, require a restriction similar to that of equation (14). As is also the case in the present model, the determinant of the Jacobian of Freitas and Serrano's (2013) dynamic system is always positive and the trace is likely to be negative if the effect of Harrodian instability is not overly strong. Freitas and Serrano (2013, p. 21) show that in their model the trace is negative and hence the dynamic stability condition is fulfilled (given the restrictive condition noted above) if the *marginal propensity to spend* remains below one during the whole adjustment process. This implies that, as a proportion of output, induced consumption out of wages plus the induced investment expenditures, including those generated by the Harrodian mechanism, must be smaller than unity. Thus, although their analysis proceeds differently, there are close similarities between the requirements for the existence and stability of the solutions of Freitas and Serrano's model and the present neo-Kaleckian model. The implications of their model with regards to the favorable level effects of a decrease in the marginal propensity to save or in the profit share are identical to those presented here.

[9] It may be worth noting that Shaikh (1991), in a paper that intended to show that Harrodian instability could be tamed, provides a convergence equation where the flexible accelerator $h$ behaves exactly as assumed by Freitas and Serrano, while the role of the exogenous growth component is taken by investment in materials needed for the growth in future production (the warranted rate). Shaikh's proof certainly mesmerized most readers at the time.

## 5. SOME JUSTIFICATION FOR ADDING NON-CAPACITY CREATING AUTONOMOUS EXPENDITURES

In this section, I wish to offer some miscellaneous justifications for the introduction of non-capacity creating autonomous expenditures in a Kaleckian model. While Keynes though that investment was the exogenous driver of the economy, presumably because he thought that it was the most unstable macroeconomic variable, there is substantial evidence that investment may best be considered as an induced variable, as argued by Serrano (1995b). For instance, Christian Schoder (2014) has recently shown that production capacities adjust endogenously to changes in current output, whereas the reverse causality does not seem to occur. In addition, there is empirical evidence that some components of aggregate demand, beyond government expenditure or exports, can be considered as more autonomous than corporate investment, although, naturally, in the long run, one could argue that there is no truly exogenous variable.

A nice piece of evidence has recently been provided by Yi Wen (2007), on the basis of Granger-causality tests and more sophisticated econometrics. Looking more specifically at *business* investment, he finds that 'Postwar U.S. aggregate data exhibit a "causal" chain among consumption, output, and investment. That "causality" runs in only one direction: from consumption growth to output growth and from output growth to capital formation' (Wen, 2007, p. 199). Thus, consumption seems to Granger-cause business investment. This poses a challenge to both standard Keynesian/Kaleckian theory and New Classical theory, since the former usually takes business investment as the causal or exogenous element of its models while real-business cycle theories assume that changes in output growth are triggered by technological shocks. Wen (2007, p. 204) claims that this inversed causality is puzzling to economists but not to people immersed in business: 'According to a businessman's intuition, production would not rise until consumption demand rises; and investment would not rise until profit rises along with the rise in production'. Nor would this empirical result of reversed causality be surprising to Sraffians in the Serrano camp.

Wen's econometric results get substantial confirmation by the recent study of Brett Fiebiger (2014), who looks at the patterns that can be observed in U.S. postwar business cycles since 1951. He finds that growth in household residential investment and growth in household consumer credit are very closely associated with contemporaneous growth in business profits, with the correlation between these variables being positive, while the growth in business investment and the growth in business profits are negatively correlated. Business investment clearly appears as an induced expenditure, which reacts with a lag to changes in profits and in rates of capacity utilization. Fiebiger goes so far as to conclude that the U.S. demand regime is one led by 'semi-autonomous household expenditures'. This is confirmed by two well-known students of business cycles—Edward Leamer (2009) and Howard Sherman (2010)—according to both of whom, despite using quite different approaches, the real estate industry is the most important advanced indicator of economic activity.

Most recently this question has been picked up by two young Italian economists, Girardi and Pariboni (2015). In four large European countries and in the United States, they look at the relationship between output and variables that one can consider as autonomous expenditures or proxy for these: exports, government expenditure, residential construction and consumer credit. With a vector error-correction model (VECM) they show that in the United States, if one excludes consumer credit, these autonomous expenditures can be said to 'cause' output in a unidirectional way. With consumer credit, the causality goes both ways. They also examine the relationship between autonomous expenditures and the share of investment in output, for the United States and four European countries (France, Germany, Italy, Spain). Conducting Granger-causality tests they conclude that causality is unidirectional, and that an increase in the growth rate of autonomous expenditures leads to a rise in the share of investment in output, and, thus, to a relative acceleration in the rate of capital accumulation, as the models presented above have suggested. Once again, there is, thus, some evidence that these non-capacity creating autonomous (or semi-autonomous) expenditures are inducing business investment, rather than the opposite.

## 6. CONCLUSION

We, thus, have reached a conditional proof that neo-Kaleckian results such as the paradox of thrift or the paradox of costs can be preserved even if the economy systematically comes back towards a constant normal rate of utilization, as long as we interpret neo-Kaleckian results as averages measured during the period of transition. This is achieved by taking into account an autonomous growth component, here autonomous consumption expenditures, by assuming short-run Keynesian stability and by incorporating to the investment function a Harrodian correcting mechanism which is not overly strong.

By embedding into a neo-Kaleckian model a mechanism akin to that of the Sraffian supermultiplier model suggested by Serrano (1995b), the change in income distribution or in the marginal propensity to save has no impact on the long-run rate of capacity utilization which is not endogenous anymore, because it eventually comes back to its normal or target rate. However, with a lower profit margin or a lower marginal propensity to save out of profits, the *average* rate of utilization and the *average* rate of growth achieved during the *traverse* from the initial equilibrium towards the new steady-state equilibrium will both be higher, as is being claimed from canonical neo-Kaleckian models.[10] As a consequence, the *level* of output and of capacity at all times will be higher than if there had been no increase in real wages or no decrease in the marginal propensity to save. Indeed, (nearly all) empirical works about wage-led and profit-led regimes that derive from the post-Kaleckian growth model are in fact based on calculations of *level* effects, where the impact of a change in the profit share on the *level* of GDP is being assessed, as in Onaran and Galanis (2012, 2013) for instance.[11]

Other post-Keynesians, also assume that non-capacity creating autonomous expenditures are the driving force, rather than investment. Serrano himself refers to Kaldor (1983, p. 9) to provide support for this reversal of causality. Fazzari *et al.* (2013) assume that there is some unidentified demand component that grows autonomously, in order to tame Harrodian instability; Godley and Lavoie (2007, ch. 11) and, as already pointed out Allain (2015), rely on autonomous government expenditures. Indeed, there is a large Kaldorian literature that relies on exogenous growth components other than business investment, most particularly the whole literature on Thirlwall's law with its

[10] This is in clear contrast with the so-called classical-Marxian view, which, as recently recalled by Duménil and Lévy (2014, p. 1288), asserts that a decrease in the real wage will lead to an increase in the normal profit rate and hence to an increase in the growth rate of the economy. One of the referees has reminded me that Skott (1989, pp. 81–4) also discusses level effects. The framework is different, however: the desired rate of utilization and the profit share are endogenous variables, while stronger labour unions lead to reduced rates of employment.

[11] Log level values are being used in the regressions, which allow to construe the regression coefficients as elasticities. Other authors, such as Storm and Naastepad (2012), regress the growth rate of real wages on the growth rate of GDP, thus, also obtaining coefficients that are elasticities.

exogenous exports (McCombie and Thirlwall, 1994), as well as Godley and Cripps (1983), with both government expenditure and export sales.[12]

With the obvious role played by consumer credit in the recent Global Financial Crisis, there have been a number of papers assuming the presence of autonomous consumption expenditures, such as that of Trezzini (2011a). With consumer credit and lines of credit based on the value of real estate, it is clear that consumption expenditures can grow independently of income to a large extent, at least for some time (Barba and Pivetti, 2009). This increase in autonomous consumption can also be tied to the attempt to keep up with the Joneses and to 'invest' in an appropriate lifestyle, as argued by a renewed and large literature on this topic (Brown, 2008).

As argued in the previous section, the mechanism first described by Serrano (1995b) and illustrated by equation (2) is far from being purely theoretical. There is empirical evidence that consumption can be considered as an autonomous component, or at least a component that is more exogenous than GDP or business investment. There is further empirical evidence that household residential investment plays a crucial role in driving economic activity, at least in the United States, with business investment reacting with a lag to the fluctuations in cash flows and in the rate of capacity utilization, so that investment in capacity is essentially an induced component of aggregate demand. A rise in household residential investment is also likely to be associated with a rise in the consumption of durable goods as households who purchase new dwellings are likely to purchase new furniture and all kinds of new household appliances.

There is no doubt that most post-Keynesians have not paid enough attention to the autonomous or semi-autonomous components of household consumption or household investment. This became obvious during the subprime financial crisis since, with a few exceptions such as Brown (2008), Dutt (2006) and Palley (1996), most post-Keynesian models of financial instability, for instance, were predicated on the destabilizing behaviour of banks and production firms, and not on that of households. To take residential investment seriously into account may also allow post-Keynesian researchers to solve another puzzle—the fact that the growth rate of employment roughly follows the growth rate of active population over the long run, that is, the fact that the rate of unemployment does not systematically rise or decrease.[13] Gowans

[12] Thus, adding to the confusion over terminology, Pérez-Caldentey and Vernengo (2013) refer to the Kaldorian tradition when discussing models based on induced investment and non-capacity creating exogenous growth components such as Serrano's Sraffian supermultiplier analysis.

[13] See Lavoie (2014, pp. 411–6) for an exposition of a non-exhaustive number of mechanisms purporting to solve this puzzle.

(2014) argues that in countries with advanced credit systems, where new households can get mortgages from the financial system, the growth in population generates a demand for real estate investment, which feeds back into aggregate demand. He constructs an overlapping-generation model which is stock-flow consistent and where investment is fully induced. He is, thus, able to derive a model where unemployment is demand-driven, but where the economy converges to a demand-led growth rate that turns out to be equal to the growth rate of (active) population, with the unemployment rate being constant, but positive and demand-dependent, while the actual rate of capacity utilization is equal to its normal value.

Ultimately, one may wonder whether changes of income distribution or in the propensity to save will only generate level effects rather than growth effects. If one finds the theoretical and empirical arguments of León-Ledesma and Thirlwall (2002) convincing, an increase in the average rate of growth generates an increase in the natural rate of growth, which might then also generate a feedback effect on the growth rate of autonomous consumption and real estate expenditures or on other autonomous expenditures, such as those of government.

## REFERENCES

Allain, O. (2015): 'Tackling the instability of growth: a Kaleckian-Harrodian model with an autonomous expenditure component', *Cambridge Journal of Economics*, 39 (5), pp. 1351–1371.

Amadeo, E. J. (1986): 'Notes on capacity utilisation, distribution and accumulation', *Contributions to Political Economy*, 5, pp. 83–94.

Barba, A., Pivetti, M. (2009): 'Rising household debt: its causes and macroeconomic implications – a long period analysis', *Cambridge Journal of Economics*, 33 (1), pp. 113–37.

Barbosa-Filho, N. (2000): 'A note on the theory of demand-led growth', *Contributions to Political Economy*, 19, pp. 19–32.

Bhaduri, A., Marglin, S. (1990): 'Unemployment and the real wage: the economic basis for contesting political ideologies', *Cambridge Journal of Economics*, 14 (4), pp. 375–93.

Bortis, H. (1997): *Institutions, Behaviour and Economic Theory: A Contribution to Classical-Keynesian Political Economy*, Cambridge University Press, Cambridge.

Brown, C. (2008): *Inequality, Consumer Credit and the Saving Puzzle*, Edward Elgar, Cheltenham.

Caserta, M. (1990): 'The steady-state model of capital utilisation: a comment', *Studi Economici*, 41 (2), pp. 139–53.

Cesaratto, S. (2015): 'Neo-Kaleckian and Sraffian controversies on the theory of accumulation', *Review of Political Economy*, 27 (2), pp. 154–82.

Chick, V., Caserta, M. (1997): 'Provisional equilibrium and macroeconomic theory', in Arestis, P., Palma, G., Sawyer, M. (eds): *Markets, Employment and Economic Policies: Essays in Honour of G.C. Harcourt, Volume Two*, Routledge, London.

Committeri, M. (1986): 'Some comments on recent contributions on capital accumulation, income distribution and capacity utilization', *Political Economy: Studies in the Surplus Approach*, 2 (2), pp. 161–86.

Dejuán, Ó. (2005): 'Paths of accumulation and growth: towards a Keynesian long-period theory of output', *Review of Political Economy*, 17 (2), pp. 231–52.

Dejuán, Ó. (2013): 'Normal paths of growth shaped by the supermultiplier', in Levrero, E. S., Palumbo, A., Stirati, A. (eds): *Sraffa and the Reconstruction of Economic Theory: Volume Two: Aggregate Demand, Policy Analysis and Growth*, Palgrave/Macmillan, Basingstoke.

Duménil, G., Lévy, D. (2014): 'A reply to Amitava Dutt: the role of aggregate demand in the long run', *Cambridge Journal of Economics*, 38 (5), pp. 1285–92.

Dutt, A. K. (1984): 'Stagnation, income distribution and monopoly power', *Cambridge Journal of Economics*, 8 (1), pp. 25–40.

Dutt, A. K. (1997): 'Profit-rate equalization in the Kalecki-Steindl model and the over-determination problem', *Manchester School*, 65 (4), pp. 443–51.

Dutt, A. K. (2006): 'Maturity, stagnation and consumer debt: a Steindlian approach', *Metroeconomica*, 57 (3), pp. 339–64.

Dutt, A. K. (2011): 'The role of aggregate demand in classical-Marxian models of economic growth', *Cambridge Journal of Economics*, 35 (2), pp. 357–82.

Fazzari, S. M., Ferri, P., Greenberg, E., Variato, A. M. (2013): 'Aggregate demand, instability, and growth', *Review of Keynesian Economics*, 1 (1), pp. 1–21.

Fiebiger, B. (2014): 'Semi-autonomous household expenditures as the causa causans of post-war U.S. business cycles: the stability and instability of Luxemburg-type external markets', working paper.

Freitas, F., Serrano, F. (2013): 'Growth, distribution and effective demand: a research report on the Sraffian supermultiplier and its alternative closure for heterodox growth models', working paper, Instituto de Economia, Federal University of Rio de Janeiro.

Freitas, F., Serrano, F. (2015): 'The Sraffian supermultiplier as an alternative closure to heterodox growth theory', working paper, Instituto de Economia, Universidade Federal do Rio de Janeiro (UFRJ).

Girardi, D., Pariboni, R. (2015): 'Autonomous demand and empirical growth: some empirical evidence', Working paper 714, Department of Economia Politica e Statistica, University of Sienna. Available at: http://www.deps.unisi.it/sites/st02/files/allegatiparagrafo/20-08-2015/714.pdf

Godley, W., Cripps, F. (1983): *Macroeconomics*, Fontana, London.

Godley, W., Lavoie, M. (2007): *Monetary Economics: An Integrated Approach to Credit, Money, Income, Production and Wealth*, Palgrave Macmillan, Basingstoke.

Gowans, D. (2014): 'Introducing population growth and demography in demand-led models of growth and accumulation', M.A. Major Paper, Department of Economics, University of Ottawa.

Halevi, J., Kriesler, P. (1991): 'Kalecki, classical economics and the surplus approach', *Review of Political Economy*, 3 (1), pp. 79–92.

Hein, E. (2014): *Distribution and Growth After Keynes*, Edward Elgar, Cheltenham.

Hein, E., Lavoie, M., Van Treeck, T. (2012): 'Harrodian instability and the normal rate of capacity utilization in Kaleckian models of distribution and growth – a survey', *Metroeconomica*, 63 (1), pp. 39–69.

Henry, J. (1987): 'Equilibrium as a process', *Économie appliqué*, 40 (3), pp. 463–82.

Kaldor, N. (1983): 'Keynesian economics after fifty years', in Worswick, D., Trevithick, J. (eds): *Keynes and the Modern World*, Cambridge University Press, Cambridge.

Lavoie, M. (1996): 'Traverse, hysteresis, and normal rates of capacity utilization in Kaleckian models of growth and distribution', *Review of Radical Political Economics*, 28 (4), pp. 113–47.

Lavoie, M. (2014): *Post-Keynesian Economics: New Foundations*, Edward Elgar, Cheltenham.

Leamer, E. E. (2009): 'Housing is the business cycle', NBER working paper. Available at: http://www.nber.org/papers/w13428

León-Ledesma, M. A., Thirwall, A. P. (2002): 'The endogeneity of the natural rate of growth', *Cambridge Journal of Economics*, 26 (4), pp. 441–59.

McCombie, J. S. L., Thirlwall, A. P. (1994): *Economic Growth and the Balance-of-Payments Constraint*, Macmillan, London.

Moudud, J. K. (2010): *Strategic Competition, Dynamics, and the Role of the State*, Edward Elgar, Cheltenham.

Onaran, Ö., Galanis, G. (2012): 'Is aggregate demand wage-led or profit-led: national and global effects', working paper # 40, Conditions of Work and Employment Series, International Labour Office. Available at: http://www.ilo.org/travail/whatwedo/publications/WCMS_192121/lang–en/index.htm

Onaran, Ö., Galanis, G. (2013): 'Is aggregate demand wage-led or profit-led: a global model', in Lavoie, M. Stockhammer, E. (eds): *Wage-led Growth: An Equitable Strategy for Economic Recovery*, Palgrave-Macmillan and the International Labour Office, Basingstoke.

Palley, T. (1996): *Post Keynesian Economics: Debt, Distribution and the Macro Economy*, Macmillan, London.

Palumbo, A., Trezzini, A. (2003): 'Growth without normal capacity utilization', *European Journal of the History of Economic Thought*, 10 (1), pp. 109–36.

Pariboni, R. (2015): 'Autonomous demand and the Marglin-Bhaduri model: a critical note', Working paper 715, Department of Economia Politica e Statistica, University of Sienna. Available at: http://www.deps.unisi.it/sites/st02/files/allegatiparagrafo/26-09-2015/715.pdf

Park, M. S. (1995): 'A note on the Kalecki-Steindl steady-state approach to growth and distribution', *Manchester School*, 63 (3), pp. 297–310.

Park, M. S. (2000): 'Autonomous demand and warranted rate of growth', *Contributions to Political Economy*, 19, pp. 1–18.

Pérez-Caldentey, E., Vernengo, M. (2013): 'Wage and profit-led growth: the limits to neo-Kaleckian models and a Kaldorian proposal', Working paper #775, Levy Economics Institute at Bard College, http://www.levyinstitute.org/pubs/wp_775.pdf

Rowthorn, B. (1981): 'Demand, real wages and economic growth', *Thames Papers in Political Economy*, Autumn, pp. 1–39.

Schoder, C. (2014): 'Effective demand, exogenous normal utilization and endogenous capacity in the long run: evidence from a cointegrated vector autoregression analysis for the USA', *Metroeconomica*, 65 (2), pp. 298–320.

Serrano, F. (1995a): 'Long period effective demand and the Sraffian supermultiplier', *Contributions to Political Economy*, 14, pp. 67–90.

Serrano, F. (1995b): The Sraffian Multiplier, PhD dissertation, Faculty of Economics and Politics, University of Cambridge.

Serrano, F., Freitas, F. (2015): 'Growth rate and level effects: the adjustment of capacity to demand and the Sraffian supermultiplier', working paper, Instituto de Economia, Federal University of Rio de Janeiro. Forthcoming in the *Review of Political Economy*, 2015.

Shaikh, A. (1991): 'Wandering around the warranted growth path: dynamic nonlinear solutions to the Harrodian knife-edge', in Nell, E. J., Semmler, W. (eds): *Nicholas Kaldor and Mainstream Economics: Confrontation or Convergence*?, Macmillan, London.

Sherman, H. J. (2010): *The Roller Coaster Economy: Financial Crisis, Great Recession and the Public Option*, M.E. Sharpe, Armonk.

Skott, P. (1989): *Conflict and Effective Demand in Economic Growth*, Cambridge University Press, Cambridge.

Skott, P. (2005): 'Fairness as a source of hysteresis in employment and relative wages', *Journal of Behavioral Economics'*, 57 (3), pp. 305–31.

Skott, P. (2012): 'Theoretical and empirical shortcomings of a Kaleckian investment function', *Metroeconomica*, 63 (1), pp. 109–38.

Steindl, J. (1952): *Maturity and Stagnation in American Capitalism*, Basil Blackwell, Oxford.

Storm, S., Naastepad, C. W. M. (2012): *Macroeconomics Beyond the NAIRU*, Harvard University Press, Cambridge, MA.

Taylor, L. (1983): *Structuralist Macroeconomics: Applicable Models for the Third World*, Basic Books, New York.

Trezzini, A. (1995): 'Capacity utilisation in the long run and the autonomous components of aggregate demand', *Contributions to Political Economy*, 14, pp. 33–66.

Trezzini, A. (1998): 'Capacity utilisation in the long run: some further considerations', *Contributions to Political Economy*, 17, pp. 53–67.

Trezzini, A. (2011a): 'The irreversibility of consumption as a source of endogenous-demand-driven economic growth', *Review of Political Economy*, 23 (4), pp. 537–56.

Trezzini, A. (2011b): 'Steady state and the analysis of long-run tendencies: the case of neo-Kaleckian models', in Ciccone, R., Gehrke, C., Mongiovi, G. (eds): *Sraffa and Modern Economics, Volume II*, Routledge, London.

Vianello, F. (1985): 'The pace of accumulation', *Political Economy: Studies in the Surplus Approach*, 1 (1), pp. 69–87.

Wen, Y. (2007): 'Granger causality and equilibrium business cycle theory', *Federal Reserve Bank of St. Louis Review*, May–June, pp. 195–205.

Marc Lavoie
Economics
University of Ottawa
Ottawa (Ontario)
Canada
E-mail: mlavoie@uottawa.ca

[10]

JOURNAL OF POST KEYNESIAN ECONOMICS
2017, VOL. 40, NO. 2, 223–238
https://doi.org/10.1080/01603477.2016.1262745

Routledge
Taylor & Francis Group

# Long-run convergence in a neo-Kaleckian open-economy model with autonomous export growth

Won Jun Nah and Marc Lavoie

**ABSTRACT**

This study combines a neo-Kaleckian growth and distribution model with a sort of Sraffian supermultiplier mechanism in which autonomous demand is driven by foreign exports. Short-, medium- and long-run equilibria are considered. In the long-run case, the expectations of sales growth governing investment change adaptively, and this, combined with the autonomous growth rate of exports, produces convergence of the actual rate of capacity utilization to its normal rate. It is demonstrated that some aspects of the main Kaleckian results can be preserved not only in the short or medium run but also in the long run, in the sense that both (1) a decrease in the propensity to save, and (2) a change in income distribution favoring labor, bring about higher *average* rates of production growth and capital accumulation. However, the impact of a change in the profit share is shown to be subjected to the condition that the responsiveness of the real exchange rate with respect to the profit share has to be bounded from above, confirming that the scope for wage-led demand or wage-led growth can be limited by open-economy considerations, even within the supermultiplier context.

**KEYWORDS**

Autonomous expenditures; capacity utilization; exports; growth; neo-Kaleckian; profit share

**JEL CLASSIFICATIONS**

E11; F41; O41

The purpose of the present study is to combine the features of the standard neo-Kaleckian model of growth and distribution (as could be found initially in Rowthorn [1981] and Dutt [1984], and later in Hein [2014] and Lavoie [2014, ch. 6]) with the mechanisms of the so-called Sraffian supermultiplier. These mechanisms are based on investment expenditures that are fully induced by sales, while there exists an autonomously growing component of aggregate demand that, in contrast to fixed investment, does not create capacity (as described initially in Serrano [1995a, 1995b] and Bortis [1997], and more recently formalized in Cesaratto [2015] and Freitas and Serrano [2015]). While this combination has already been done in Allain (2015) and Lavoie (2016), with the autonomous growth component being

Won Jun Nah is an associate professor in the School of Economics and Trade, Kyungpook National University, Daegu, Korea.

Marc Lavoie is emeritus professor at the University of Ottawa (Canada), and professor at the University of Paris 13 (CEPN), University of Sorbonne Paris Cité.

This study was presented at the meeting of the Korean Economic Association and at the workshop "Post-Keynesian Macroeconomics and Modelling," organized by Eckhard Hein at the Berlin School of Economics and Law in 2016, as well as at a seminar at Kingston University in 2017. The authors thank the participants as well as the referee of the journal for their questions and suggestions.

Color versions of one or more of the figures in the article can be found online at www.tandfonline.com/mpke.

government expenditure and capitalist consumption, respectively, here the noncapacity-creating component of aggregate demand will be foreign exports.

An open-economy version of the Sraffian supermultiplier has been presented by De Juan (2016); and Dutt (2015) has combined a neo-Kaleckian growth model with an autonomous export component. The peculiarity of the present model relative to those of De Juan and Dutt is that while exports do have an autonomous component, there is another component that is affected by the real exchange rate. Increasing the wage share thus changes the real exchange rate and allows for the possibility that an increase in the wage share may not have a favorable impact on economic activity. While this result is fairly well-known in the context of open-economy neo-Kaleckian models (Blecker 1989, 1999, 2011), it is a new result as far as the Sraffian supermultiplier model is concerned. Another interesting aspect of the model is the separation between the short, medium, and long runs, which makes the analysis of stability easier for each run.

A key feature of one variant of the present model is its convergence in the long run to the normal rate of capacity utilization. This is conditionally achieved by incorporating both the Harrodian principle of instability and an autonomous growth of the external demand that arises from world income growth. It is demonstrated that a critical aspect of the main Kaleckian results can be preserved not only in the short run but also over time, and finally in the long run. To focus on this issue while keeping our model as simple as possible, we introduce some inevitable simplifications. First, we assume away interest payments, those possibly arising from foreign debts or foreign assets.[1] Second, functional income distribution is assumed to be exogenous. Third, we assume away the feedback effects that changes in the real exchange rate could have on income distribution.

## The economic environment

Following Taylor (1983) and Dutt (1984), and more recently Hein and Vogel (2008), we assume an open economy that imports inputs or intermediate goods and then produces outputs for both domestic purposes and exports. The international markets are assumed to be competitive in the sense that countries can change neither import prices nor export prices: in other words, there is a 100 percent pass-through.[2] The price setting power of domestic firms is limited due to international competition. We assume that the threat of relocation of production facilities by entrepreneurs is credible enough to hinder any possible change in domestic functional income distribution that is due to the wage-setting power of labor unions, so that the income distribution between capital and labor is exogenously determined through the

[1]This should not be a problem as long as the interest rate on external debt does not rise.

[2]This is obviously a simplification, although Coutts and Norman (2013) argue from past empirical studies that while finished goods are subjected to a partial pass-through in advanced economies, intermediate products, which are considered by firms as a cost, are usually subjected to a full pass-through.

political process. We also assume that, for simplification purposes, there are no government activities.

In this open economy without a public sector, macroeconomic equilibrium can be characterized as the fundamental identity dictating that saving ($S$) should equal the sum of investment expenditures ($I$) and net exports, the latter being the trade balance $TB$:[3]

$$S = I + TB = I + (X - e_R M). \tag{1}$$

The variable $e_R$ denotes the real exchange rate, which is, by definition, $e_R = ep_f/p_d$, where $e$, $p_f$, and $p_d$ are the nominal exchange rate, the foreign price level, and the domestic price level, respectively. $X$ and $M$ are real exports and imports. Out of the exports $X$, we separate the autonomously growing part $X_0$ from the (stationary) part $X_1$, which is a function of the real exchange rate, so that $X = X_0 + X_1(e_R)$.

We employ the following linear specifications for investment expenditure and trade balance, both expressed in terms of the stock of capital. The investment function (2) below follows the standard neo-Kaleckian literature, where $g$ is the rate of accumulation of capital, $K$ the stock of capital, $u$ is a proxy of the rate of capacity utilization, $u_n$ the normal rate of capacity utilization, $\gamma$ the animal spirits of firms, and $\gamma_u > 0$ a parameter that captures the sensitivity of the rate of accumulation to changes in the rate of utilization. Note that if capacity utilization is at its normal or desired rate, then $g = \gamma$, and one would think that the rate of accumulation desired by firms corresponds to the expected growth rate of sales, so as to keep the rate of utilization at its target level, as was pointed out by Committeri (1986, p. 173) and Caserta (1990, p. 152), and more recently by Duménil and Lévy (2014, p. 1289).

$$g = I/K = \gamma + \gamma_u(u - u_n), \tag{2}$$

$$tb = \frac{TB}{K} = x + \phi_e e_R - \phi_u u. \tag{3}$$

The net export function (3) deserves some attention. Here the autonomous component of exports is represented by $x = X_0/K$. The other components of net exports are assumed to be increasing in the real exchange rate and decreasing in the domestic demand, which is $(X_1 - e_R M)/K = \phi_e e_R - \phi_u u$, where $\phi_e$ and $\phi_u$ are both positive.

Importantly, we assume that $X_0$ is exogenously increasing at the constant rate $\bar{g}_x > 0$, along with world income growth. In essence, we are considering the situation in which the model economy is too small to affect the rate of world income growth and thus we take the growth rate of autonomous exports, driven by world income growth, as a given. In this small economy, the exogenous and continuous growth in foreign demand becomes the driving

[3]Alternatively we could say that output net of intermediate imports has to equal consumption plus investment and exports.

force for sustained growth, as we shall see. In this vein, Kaldor (1970) has been explicit on the importance of the rate of export growth for the growth of national output. He claimed that "from the point of view of any particular region, the 'autonomous component of demand' is the demand emanating from outside the region; ... the rate of economic development of a region is fundamentally governed by the rate of its exports" (Kaldor 1970, p. 342).[4] It is in this regard that the global developments in effective demand may matter for the growth rate of an individual country in the long run.

The effects on net exports due to changes in the real exchange rate and domestic demand are reflected in the parameters $\phi_e$ and $\phi_u$, respectively. We assume that both are strictly positive. Positivity of $\phi_u$ is a standard assumption in that imports increase more often than not when domestic demand expands. The assumption that $\phi_e > 0$ is necessary for the Marshall–Lerner condition to hold so that real depreciation (appreciation) yields an increase (decrease) in net exports in this model economy.

Assuming away the possibility of saving out of wages, as is also standard in neo-Kaleckian models, we can normalize saving, which is on the far left-hand side of Equation (1), by dividing it by the stock of capital $K$:

$$S/K = s_p \pi u,$$

where $s_p$ denotes the propensity to save from capitalists' profits, $P$ is profits, $q$ is real income, $\pi = P/q$ is the share of profits out of national income, and $u = q/K$ is the proxy for the rate of capacity utilization. The equilibrium condition (1) can thus be rewritten as:

$$s_p \pi u = \gamma + \gamma_u (u - u_n) + x + \phi_e e_R - \phi_u u. \tag{4}$$

Isolating the investment function, we can rewrite this as $\sigma = g$:

$$\sigma = s_p \pi u + \phi_u u - x - \phi_e e_R = \gamma + \gamma_u (u - u_n) \tag{4A}$$

## Short-run consequences

The utilization rate $u^*$ and the growth rate $g^*$ in the short-run equilibrium are obtained from (4):

$$u^* = \frac{\gamma - \gamma_u u_n + x + \phi_e e_R}{s_p \pi - \gamma_u + \phi_u}, \tag{5}$$

and

$$g^* = \gamma + \gamma_u \left( \frac{\gamma + x + \phi_e e_R - (s_p \pi + \phi_u) u_n}{s_p \pi - \gamma_u + \phi_u} \right), \tag{6}$$

[4]This view was later developed in a slightly different direction through the balance-of-payment-constrained models of Thirwall (1979) and McCombie and Thirlwall (1994).

where superscript * denotes short-run equilibrium values of endogenous variables. In the context of the present model, the term "short run" can be understood as an instantaneous snapshot, before all level variables start growing away from their equilibrium values in a given short period, so that, in particular, the $x = X_0/K$ ratio is a given although its two components grow at different rates, in general, in the short run.

To define this short-run equilibrium as a stable one, we assume that the Keynesian stability condition holds, that is, saving should more strongly respond to the changes in the rate of utilization than the sum of investment and net exports:

$$s_p\pi > \gamma_u - \phi_u. \tag{7}$$

Also, since the rate of utilization of capacity should be nonnegative and smaller than unity, it is required that:

$$0 \leq \gamma - \gamma_u u_n + x + \phi_e e_R \leq s_p\pi - \gamma_u + \phi_u, \tag{8}$$

because otherwise the rate of capacity utilization could no longer be the adjusting variable.

The paradox of saving, understood as concerning both the short-run equilibrium rate of utilization and the rate of capital accumulation remains valid. This can be easily confirmed by checking that the partial derivatives $\partial u^*/\partial s_p$ and $\partial g^*/\partial s_p$ are both negative. On the other hand, the effects of a change in the functional distribution of income between capital and labor are ambiguous, thus depending on the values taken by the parameters of the model. However, we can derive the condition under which redistribution of income in favor of labor yields increases in demand and in the growth rate in a straightforward manner.

Making use of Equations (5) and (6), it follows that:

$$\frac{\partial u^*}{\partial \pi} = \frac{\phi_e \frac{\partial e_R}{\partial \pi} - s_p u^*}{s_p\pi - \gamma_u + \phi_u}$$

$$\frac{\partial g^*}{\partial \pi} = \gamma_u \frac{\partial u^*}{\partial \pi}.$$

Once again, from the above equation, it can easily be checked that the partial derivatives $\partial u^*/\partial \pi$ and $\partial g^*/\partial \pi$ are both negative if the short-run stability condition holds (the denominator is positive) while the numerator is negative. This will occur if and only if the following inequality holds:

$$\frac{\partial e_R}{\partial \pi} < \frac{s_p u^*}{\phi_e}.$$

Plugging the value of $u$* back into Equation (5), this implies the following inequality:

$$\frac{\partial e_R}{\partial \pi} < \frac{s_p(\gamma - \gamma_u u_n + x + \phi_e e_R)}{\phi_e(s_p\pi - \gamma_u + \phi_u)}, \tag{9}$$

With an exogenous growth in exports, a redistribution of income toward wages results in a higher utilization rate of capacity and a higher accumulation rate of capital in the short run if inequality (9) is fulfilled.

The argument above implies that for the model to generate wage-led rather than profit-led demand and growth regimes in the short run, the responsiveness of the real exchange rate with respect to a change in income distribution should be bounded from above. Open-economy considerations such as international competition seem to be able to limit the scope for wage-led demand and growth regimes. This result can be interpreted as being consistent with prevailing views in the Kaleckian literature, as found in Blecker (1989) and also Bhaduri and Marglin (1990).

Before moving on to the model dynamics, we briefly summarize the relationship between the real exchange rate and income distribution. As is well-known, the latter can fluctuate together with the change in the real exchange rate via three different channels in the present model environment. These are changes in (1) the nominal exchange rate $e$, (2) the nominal wage rate $w$, and (3) the markup $\theta$. Out of these three channels through which $\pi$ affects $e_R$, the real exchange rate becomes positively associated with the profit share when changes in income distribution are due to changes in either $e$ or $w$. To see this, from the relation identified by Hein and Vogel (2008):

$$\pi(e, w, \theta) = \frac{\theta(1 + j(e, w))}{1 + \theta(1 + j(e, w))}. \tag{10}$$

Let us define an implicit function:

$$e_R = \frac{ep_f y}{w(1 + \theta)(1 + j(e, w))} \equiv e_R(\pi(e, w, \theta);\ p_f,\ y), \tag{11}$$

where $y$ denotes labor productivity and $j = j(e, w)$ is the ratio of unit material costs to unit direct labor costs, which increases in $e$ and decreases in $w$, that is, $j_e > 0$ and $j_w < 0$. Recall that we are treating income distribution, and hence the profit share $\pi$, as a purely exogenous variable that is political in nature, and the value of which is realized together with $w$ and $\theta$, given $e$. Intuitively, if the price of imported material rises when $e$ goes up, then the share of wages should shrink, and thus $\pi$ should increase, while $e_R$ should rise. If $w$ goes up, other things being equal, then clearly $\pi$ should fall, while $e_R$ should also fall because domestic prices rise relative to foreign prices.

If, on the contrary, a change in $e_R$ is associated with a change in income distribution which comes about due to a change in $\theta$, then $e_R$ may respond negatively to $\pi$. Therefore, at least in theory, there seems to be an ambiguity in the relationship between the real exchange rate and income distribution. However, it is clearly documented by Hein (2014, p. 316) that "empirically, if there is any relationship between the profit share and international competitiveness, this relationship seems to be positive." Overall, it seems that we can confidently assume that real depreciation (appreciation) can be thought of as reflecting a corresponding rise (fall) in the profit share within the model environment of this study.

## Medium-run dynamics

However, the short-run equilibrium given by Equations (5) and (6) will get modified once $x$ starts to change over time. The autonomous component of export demand $X_0$ grows exogenously at the rate $\bar{g}_x$. As long as we stick to this exogenous growth component of effective demand within our model, it is helpful to distinguish conceptually between three different successive equilibria, which are the short-run, medium-run, and long-run equilibria, as in Allain (2015). In the short run, $x$ is constant and hence the effects of the autonomous export growth cannot be considered. In contrast, we define the medium run as being the period during which $X_0$ grows. Then the medium-run equilibrium can be defined as a point of rest where $x$ converges to a certain value. Finally, long-run issues will be discussed in the next section.

Considering the definition of $x$, we see that $x$ evolves through time as follows, where a hat on a variable denotes its instantaneous growth rate:

$$\hat{x} = \bar{g}_x - g^* = \bar{g}_x - \gamma - \gamma_u\left(\frac{\gamma + x + \phi_e e_R - (s_p\pi + \phi_u)u_n}{s_p\pi - \gamma_u + \phi_u}\right), \tag{12}$$

from which it is clear that if we assume short-run stability, that is, assuming that condition (7) is realized, we have:

$$\frac{\partial \hat{x}}{\partial x} = -\frac{\gamma_u}{s_p\pi - \gamma_u + \phi_u} < 0.$$

This implies that the behavior of $x$ is dynamically stable, and thus $x$ converges to its equilibrium value $x^{**}$ in the medium run, where superscript $^{**}$ represents the medium-run equilibrium value of a variable.

The medium-run rate of accumulation is obtained by using Equation (12) under the condition that $\hat{x} = 0$:

$$g^{**} = \bar{g}_x. \tag{13}$$

It follows from this that the medium-run rate of utilization becomes:

$$u^{**} = u_n + \frac{\bar{g}_x - \gamma}{\gamma_u}, \tag{14}$$

since it should be that $g^{**} = \gamma + \gamma_u(u^{**} - u_n)$. Also, in the medium-run equilibrium, the ratio of autonomous exports to capital stock, $x^{**}$, is obtained from (12):

$$x^{**} = (s_p\pi + \phi_u)u^{**} - \phi_e e_R - \bar{g}_x. \tag{15}$$

It seems natural for the next question to be whether our model economy can or cannot successfully reproduce the standard Keynesian and/or Kaleckian results in the long run. We have already investigated the short-run consequences of the model. It is shown that, in the short run, the paradox of saving is valid whereas the scope for wage-led growth becomes narrower than in a closed-economy environment. If it is the case, then what are the distinctive dynamic aspects of our model?

From Equations (13) and (14), we find that in the medium-run equilibrium, the rates of both accumulation and utilization are not affected by changes in the propensity to save or in income distribution. However, from Equation (15), it is straightforward to see that $\partial x^{**}/\partial s_P > 0$. The higher the propensity to save, the lower the *level* of capital stock for a given amount of autonomous exports. An increase in the propensity to save does not affect the medium-run growth rate of the capital stock, but decreases its level. This can be interpreted as implying that one of the key Kaleckian results is still valid in the medium run of our model.

We can also see that $\partial x^{**}/\partial \pi > 0$, under the condition that the following inequality holds. This inequality is exactly comparable to that given by (9) in the case of the short run.

$$\frac{\partial e_R}{\partial \pi} < \frac{s_p u^{**}}{\phi_e} = \frac{s_p}{\phi_e}\left(u_n + \frac{\bar{g}_x - \gamma}{\gamma_u}\right). \tag{16}$$

How can we interpret the economic meaning of this inequality? Decomposing the change in $x^{**}$ by totally differentiating (15), we have:

$$dx^{**} = s_p u^{**}\, d\pi - \phi_e \frac{\partial e_R}{\partial \pi}\, d\pi.$$

In the right-hand side of the above equation, an increase in the share of profits has a twofold effect on capital accumulation. The first term captures a direct negative effect from decreases in consumption demand (due to income redistribution toward capitalists), while the second term captures an indirect positive effect from increases in net exports (due to the higher real exchange rate). The former dominates the latter if:

$$s_p u^{**} - \phi_e \frac{\partial e_R}{\partial \pi} > 0,$$

which is exactly equivalent to condition (16) above.

Unless the real exchange rate is overly sensitive to changes in income distribution, then any change in income distribution favoring labor brings about a higher level of capital stock for a given amount of autonomous exports. In other words, the average growth rate of the capital stock, that is, the average accumulation rate, increases during the traverse following a decrease in the share of profits, until a new medium-run equilibrium is

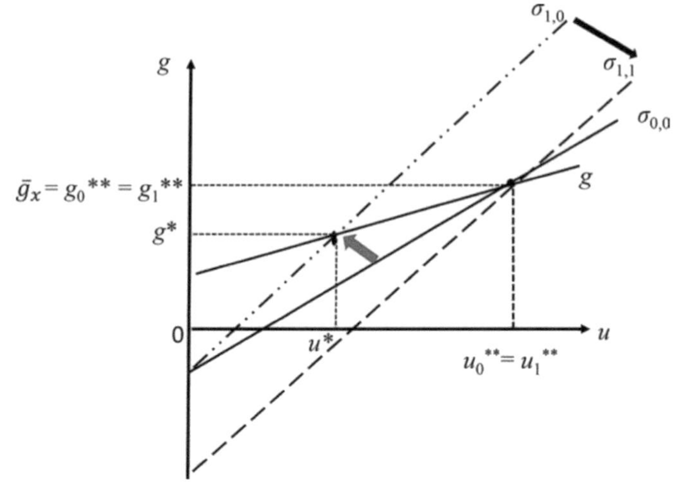


**Figure 1.** Short-run vs. medium-run impacts of an increase in the propensity to save

reached. It should be noted that this phenomenon should be more prominent when the propensity of capitalists to save is larger, or when the sensitivity of net exports to changes in the real exchange rate is lower.

The discussions so far clearly show that our simplified open-economy model with autonomous export growth can be successful in generating the well-known Kaleckian results concerning both the relationship between growth and the propensity to save, and the one between growth and income distribution. This point can be illustrated with the help of Figure 1.

Figure 1 exhibits the medium-run response of the hypothetical economy after a sudden rise in the propensity to save. The initial equilibrium is given at $\left(u_0^{**},\ g_0^{**}\right)$ in the figure. Now suppose $s_p$ increases from $s_{p0}$ to $s_{p1}$. The instantaneous short-run impact falls on the expanded saving curve, rotating it counterclockwise from $\sigma_{0,0}$ to $\sigma_{1,0}$. Thus, the economy moves from $\left(u_0^{**},\ g_0^{**}\right)$ to $(u^*, g^*)$. As we have seen in the previous section, both the rates of accumulation and utilization decrease in the short run.[5]

However, that cannot be the whole story. Since the autonomous component of exports increases continuously at the constant rate of $\bar{g}_x$ while the rate of accumulation of capital slows down, the ratio $x$ must increase. Over time, $x$ increases from $x_0$ to $x_1$. This in turn results in downward parallel shifts of the $\sigma$ curve (representing the left-hand side of Equation [4A]) in Figure 1 from $\sigma_{1,0}$ to $\sigma_{1,1}$.

[5]In Figure 1, we define $\sigma_{i,\,j} \equiv s_{pi}\pi u - tb(x_j)$. In the upper panel, the slopes of the $g$ curve and that of the $\sigma$ curve are $\gamma_u$ and $(s_p\pi + \phi_u)$, respectively. The values of the intercepts on the vertical axis are $(\gamma - \gamma_u u_n)$ and $-(x + \phi_e e_R)$, respectively.

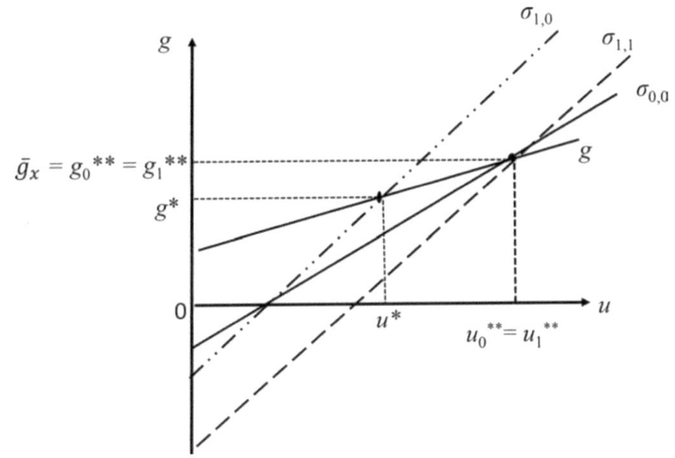


**Figure 2.** Short-run vs. medium-run impact of an increase in the profit share (wage-led demand regime).

Now let us turn to the effects of a redistribution of functional income between workers and capitalists. Figure 2 compares the short-run and medium-run responses of the rate of accumulation and the rate of utilization of capacity after an income distribution shock, which favors capital. Here, recall that we are implicitly assuming that the sensitivity of the real exchange rate with respect to changes in income distribution is small enough, the inequalities given by Equations (9) and (16) being assumed to be fulfilled.[6]

This time, let us suppose that the share of profits $\pi$ goes up from $\pi_0$ to $\pi_1$. In the short run, the expanded saving curve rotates and shifts down from $\sigma_{0,0}$ to $\sigma_{1,0}$, the shift reflecting the effects of an increase in the real exchange rate on the trade balance. Hence, in the short run, the economy moves to $(u^*, g^*)$.[7] Again over time, the ratio $x$ increases from $x_0$ to $x_1$. This yields further downward parallel shifts of the $\sigma$ curve from $\sigma_{1,0}$ to $\sigma_{1,1}$. All of these shifts continue until the economy reaches $(u_1^{**},\ g_1^{**})$, which is the new medium-run equilibrium, where the evolution of $x$ stops.

Figure 3 summarizes the responses of some important endogenous variables to a permanent increase in the propensity to save and in the share of profits over the short run and the medium run. Considering the whole traverse of variables over the medium run, and comparing their average rates of growth, we can claim that the main Kaleckian results are still

[6]It is sometimes argued that small open economies are more likely to be in a profit-led demand regime, and hence that since we assume the presence of a small open economy that has no feedback effect on world aggregate demand, we should describe the profit-led regime. But the results obtained by Onaran and Galanis (2012) seem to indicate that this is not necessarily the case, and that profit-led countries are sometimes countries that are specialized in exporting commodities, such as Canada, Australia, and South Africa.

[7]In Figure 2, we define $\sigma_{i,j} \equiv s_p\pi_i u - tb(\pi_i, x_j)$. All the values of slopes and intercepts are the same as in Figure 1.

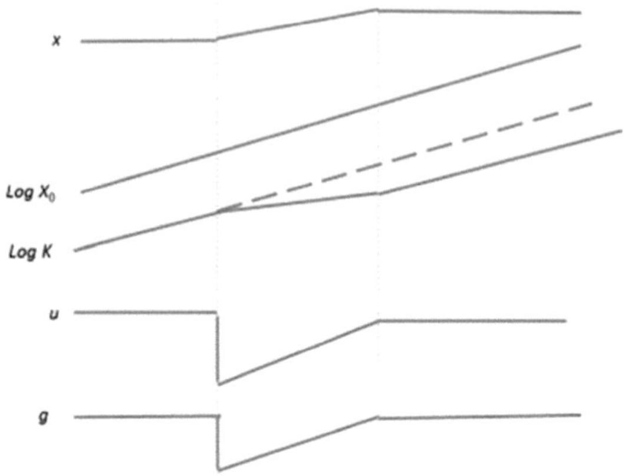


**Figure 3.** Short- vs. medium-run responses.

(conditionally) valid, even when we introduce autonomous growth in exports into an otherwise canonical open-economy neo-Kaleckian model.

## Long-run adjustments with Harrodian mechanism

From the standpoint of a number of Marxian authors, the medium-run equilibrium defined by Equation (14) can be subjected to criticism because the equilibrium rate of utilization generally will not coincide with its normal or desired rate.[8] Hence, assuming that such an equality is required to define a long-run equilibrium, we need a mechanism that will bring the equilibrium rate of capacity utilization, $u^{**}$, toward the normal rate of capacity utilization, $u_n$, over a longer horizon than the medium run we have defined so far.

As previously mentioned, in the present model the long-run adjustments of the rate of utilization toward its normal rate are driven by the action of the well-known Harrodian instability mechanism. It could seem unrealistic to assume that the growth rate of sales expected by firms, which is captured by the parameter $\gamma$ in the investment function, stays at the same value forever. Over time, it should slowly adjust to past changes in the growth rate of sales. In this regard, we can assume that $\gamma$, which so far, in the medium run, was considered as an exogenous constant, will begin to adjust. Within the context of a neo-Kaleckian growth model with an autonomous non-capacity-generating demand component growing at an exogenous rate, this

[8]The empirical argument is that the rate of utilization exhibits stationarity, although some authors argue instead that the normal rate shows historical trends (Duménil and Lévy 2014, p. 1289). Besides the fact that the rate of capacity utilization series seems to exhibit a break around 1980, a number of authors (e.g., Nikiforos 2016) argue that the series stationarity is an artifact, due to the way in which the rate is being measured by central banks or statistical agencies.

mechanism was first proposed by Allain (2015). Using the slightly modified version proposed by Lavoie (2014, 2016), the mechanism can be reformulated as the following Harrodian equation:

$$\hat{\gamma} = \Psi_0(u^{**} - u_n), \tag{17}$$

with $\Psi_0 > 0$ and where $u^{**}$ is the medium-run solution. This appeals to intuition in that, if the actual rate of utilization exceeds the desired or normal rate, then Equation (2) implies that the growth rate of the economy exceeds the expected growth rate of sales, so that firms ought to revise upward their expectations of future sales growth. Now using Equation (14), Equation (17) becomes:

$$\hat{\gamma} = \Psi_0\left(\frac{\bar{g}_x - \gamma}{\gamma_u}\right), \tag{18}$$

from which we can easily see that this long-run adjustment process in effect becomes stable. This stability is due to the interactive effects of the Harrodian mechanism with the growth of the autonomous demand components.[9]

$$\frac{\partial\hat{\gamma}}{\partial\gamma} = -\frac{\Psi_0}{\gamma_u} < 0.$$

The long-run equilibrium of the model is achieved when $\hat{\gamma} = 0$. Thus, it is described as follows:

$$g^{***} = \bar{g}_x, \tag{19}$$

$$u^{***} = u_n, \tag{20}$$

and plugging Equation (20) into Equation (15), we also have:

$$x^{***} = (s_p\pi + \phi_u)u_n - \phi_e e_R - \bar{g}_x. \tag{21}$$

Obviously, as also noted by Lavoie (2016), the growth rate of autonomous expenditures, here $\bar{g}_x$, cannot be too high otherwise the solutions of the autonomous exports to capital ratio, $x^{***}$, would be negative, which would seem to be meaningless.

It should be noted that we finally reached a long-run equilibrium where the rate of utilization of capacity converges to its normal, or desired rate, in the context of an open-economy neo-Kaleckian growth model. The task has been achieved by introducing both the autonomous growth of foreign aggregate demand and the Harrodian instability mechanism. We believe that it is plausible to assume that the sustained growth of a small open economy critically

[9] In fact, this is because the instability inherent to the Harrodian mechanism becomes more than offset by the exogenous growth of effective demand. The argument can be made more elaborate by replacing in Equation (17) $u^{**}$ by the value of $u^*$ as found in Equation (5). One then obtains a system of two differential equations with $\hat{x}$ and $\hat{\gamma}$. The mathematical and graphical stability analysis of this system, as well as the impact of an increase in the growth rate of autonomous exports, can be found in the Appendix of the working-paper version of the present study (Nah and Lavoie 2016).

hinges on the evolution of global effective demand. The autonomous growth in aggregate demand emanating from the external sector facilitates domestic growth in the long run—a point also made by the authors of Kaldorian growth models, as developed by McCombie and Thirlwall (1994). Moreover, together with the Harrodian mechanism, this growth component can contribute to bringing the economy into a fully adjusted position. This view is in stark opposition to the traditional belief that long-run economic growth depends solely on supply-side developments.

From Equations (19) and (20), it is evident that changes in neither the propensity to save nor the share of profits can affect the rates of accumulation or of capacity utilization in the long run. However, from Equation (21) we have $\partial x^{***}/\partial s_P > 0$, and $\partial x^{***}/\partial \pi > 0$ under the following inequality condition, which is simply a long-run version of Equations (9) or (16).

$$\frac{\partial e_R}{\partial \pi} < \frac{s_p u_n}{\phi_e}. \tag{22}$$

The long-run impact of a change in income distribution is subjected to the condition that the sensitivity of the real exchange rate to changes in the profit share has to be bounded from above, with this upper bound depending on both the propensity to save and the responsiveness of net exports to the real exchange rate.

Once we assume that the hypothetical model economy starts from a fully adjusted position with the actual rate of capacity utilization at $u_n$, that is, starting from an initial long-run equilibrium, then both a decrease in the propensity to save of capitalists and a redistribution of income favoring labor can be accompanied by a higher level of capital stock, a higher average rate of growth, and a higher average rate of utilization during the whole traverse until a new long-run equilibrium is reached. In this regard, most of the results obtained from our analyses dealing with the medium-run dynamics are maintained in the case of the longer run.

An additional experiment that requires some attention is the case where the exogenous growth rate of autonomous exports changes. Let us suppose that $\bar{g}_x$ increases from to $\bar{g}_x^0$ to $\bar{g}_x^1$. Now $X_0$ grows at a faster rate. What will happen in this case? Most notably, it is clear from Equation (19) that the rate of accumulation of capital will be higher in the long run. Also, from Equation (21) we have:

$$\frac{\partial x^{***}}{\partial \bar{g}_x} < 0,$$

which means that the faster growth of the autonomous demand component will be accompanied by an even faster rate of capital accumulation during at least part of the transition toward the long-run solution.

But, from Equation (15), and making use of Equation (14), we can see that due to the Keynesian stability condition given in Equation (7), we arrive at the following consequence for the autonomous exports to capital ratio when looking at the medium-run solution:

$$\frac{\partial x^{**}}{\partial \bar{g}_x} = \left(s_p\pi + \phi_u\right)\frac{\partial u^{**}}{\partial \bar{g}_x} - 1 = \frac{s_p\pi - (\gamma_u - \phi_u)}{\gamma_u} > 0.$$

An increase in $\bar{g}_x$ leads to a decrease of $x$ in the long run, but it increases $x$ in the medium run.[10] How can these seemingly contradictory observations be reconciled? The discussions so far reveal that in the long run, the faster growth rate of the autonomous demand component results in a permanent expansionary effect on the economy. However, for this long-run expansionary effect to occur, *at least for a while*, the growth rate of autonomous demand must surpass the rate of capital accumulation. This is what happens in the transition toward the medium run, along with the increase in the rate of capacity utilization, which induces the increase in the pace of capital accumulation. Otherwise, that is, if at all times aggregate demand increases more slowly or no faster than productive capacity, then there will not be any impetus for an induced acceleration of capital accumulation. Over the longer time horizon, during the transition toward the long run, through the Harrodian mechanism, as entrepreneurs raise the expected growth rate of sales and adjust their investment decisions in view of their revised long-run forecasts, for a while the rate of capital accumulation overcomes the growth rate of sales and autonomous demand. This brings down the rate of utilization back to its normal level while simultaneously also bringing down the $x$ ratio—the ratio of autonomous exports to capital—until finally the growth rate of capital and the growth rate of autonomous exports are brought back to equality in the long-run equilibrium.

## Concluding remarks

In this study, we have embedded the Sraffian supermultiplier argument of Serrano into an otherwise canonical open-economy neo-Kaleckian framework. The role of an autonomous component of export growth, which is determined by the growth in world demand, has been explored from a small open-economy perspective. The model has been shown to be conditionally successful in reproducing some aspects of the main Kaleckian results, not only in the short run but also over time. An increase in the propensity to save or in the share of profits can decrease the *average* rates of capital accumulation and economic growth. We also confirm that the scope for wage-led demand or wage-led growth can be limited by the sensitivity of the real exchange rate to changes in income distribution.

[10]Thus $\bar{g}_x$ can neither be too large nor too small. This is recognized in Lavoie (2017).

It should be noted that we have employed as simple a reduced-form model as is possible to clarify our findings. One thing that would need further consideration in our model is that the trade balance is not likely to be in equilibrium even in the long run. In fact, the ratio of the long-run trade balance to the stock of capital is constant and exogenously given by $tb^{***} = s_p\pi u_n - \bar{g}_x$, as can easily be deduced from Equation (21).[11] If our model economy was not growing but was instead in a stationary state, a permanent trade deficit would not be sustainable in the long run. However, in a constantly growing economy, this trade imbalance can be sustainable as long as it is increasing proportionally to economic expansion. This argument seems to be supported by real-life empirical observations.

We believe the discussions and analyses presented in this study can be enriched within a more realistic model environment by extending the study in at least three dimensions. First and foremost, we need to consider explicitly the interest payments possibly arising from foreign debts or from foreign assets. Second, the possible repercussions of changes in the real exchange rate on income distribution would need to be addressed. Third, the government sector would need to be added to our open-economy environment.

## References


Allain, O. "Tackling the Instability of Growth: A Kaleckian–Harrodian Model with an Autonomous Expenditure Component." *Cambridge Journal of Economics*, 2015, *39* (5), 1351–1371.

Bhaduri, A., and Marglin, S. "Unemployment and the Real Wage: The Economic Basis for Contesting Political Ideologies." *Cambridge Journal of Economics*, 1990, *14* (4), 375–393.

Blecker, R.A. "International Competition, Income Distribution and Economic Growth." *Cambridge Journal of Economics*, 1989, *13* (3), 395–412.

——. "Kaleckian Macro Models for Open Economies." In J. Deprez and J.T. Harvey (eds.), *Foundations of International Economics: Post Keynesian Perspectives*. London: Routledge, 1999, pp. 116–150.

——. "Open Economy Models of Distribution and Growth." In E. Hein and E. Stockhammer (eds.), *A Modern Guide to Keynesian Macroeconomics and Economic Policies*. Cheltenham: Edward Elgar, 2011, pp. 215–239.

Bortis, H. *Institutions, Behaviour and Economic Theory: A Contribution to Classical-Keynesian Political Economy*. Cambridge: Cambridge University Press, 1997.

Caserta, M. "The Steady-State Model of Capital Utilisation: A Comment." *Studi Economici*, 1990, *41* (2), 139–153.

Cesaratto, S. "Neo-Kaleckian and Sraffian Controversies on the Theory of Accumulation." *Review of Political Economy*, 2015, *27* (2), 154–182.

Committeri, M. "Some Comments on Recent Contributions on Capital Accumulation, Income Distribution and Capacity Utilization." *Political Economy: Studies in the Surplus Approach*, 1986, *2* (2), 161–186.


[11]Thus, we can claim from the model that a decrease in the propensity to save out of profits or in the profit margin will lead to an increase in the long-run trade deficit ratio, and obviously, that an increase in the autonomous growth rate of exports $\bar{g}_x$ will lead to a fall in this trade deficit ratio.

Coutts, K., and Norman, N. "Post-Keynesian Approaches to Industrial Pricing: A Survey and Critique." In G. C. Harcourt and P. Kriesler (eds.), *Oxford Handbook of Post-Keynesian Economics*, vol. *1*. Oxford: Oxford University Press, 2013, pp. 443–466.

De Juan, O. "Hidden Links in the Warranted Rate of Growth: The Supermultiplier Way Out." *European Journal of the History of Economic Thought*, 2016. doi:10.1080/09672567.2016.1186201.

Duménil, G. and Lévy, D. "A Reply to Amitava Dutt: The Role of Aggregate Demand in the Long Run." *Cambridge Journal of Economics*, 2014, *38* (5), 1285–1292.

Dutt, A. K. "Stagnation, Income Distribution and Monopoly Power." *Cambridge Journal of Economics*, 1984, *8* (1), 25–40.

———. "Growth and Distribution with Exogenous Autonomous Demand Growth and Normal Capacity Utilization." Mimeo, Notre Dame University, 2015.

Freitas, F., and Serrano, F. "Growth Rate and Level Effects: The Stability of the Adjustment of Capacity to Demand and the Sraffian Supermultiplier." *Review of Political Economy*, 2015, *27* (3), 258–281.

Hein, E. *Distribution and Growth After Keynes: A Post Keynesian Guide*. Cheltenham: Edward Elgar, 2014.

Hein, E., and Vogel, L. "Distribution and Growth Reconsidered: Empirical Results for Six OECD Countries." *Cambridge Journal of Economics*, 2008, *32* (3), 479–511.

Kaldor, N. "The Case for Regional Policies." *Scottish Journal of Political Economy*, 1970, *17* (3), 337–348.

Lavoie, M. *Post-Keynesian Economics: New Foundations*. Cheltenham: Edward Elgar, 2014.

———. "Convergence Towards the Normal Rate of Capacity Utilization in Neo-Kaleckian Models: The Role of Non-capacity Creating Autonomous Expenditures." *Metroeconomica*, 2016, *67* (1), 172–201.

———. "Prototypes, Reality, and the Growth Rate of Autonomous Consumption Expenditures: A Rejoinder." *Metroeconomica*, 2017, 68(1): 194–199.

McCombie, J. S. L., and Thirlwall, A. P. *Economic Growth and the Balance-of-Payments Constraint*. London: Macmillan, 1994.

Nah, W. J., and Lavoie, M. "Long Run Convergence in Neo-Kaleckian Open Economy Model with Autonomous Export Growth." Post-Keynesian Economics Study Group working paper 1604, 2016 (available at www.postkeynesian.net/downloads/working-papers/PKWP1604_Y57A0kM.pdf)

Nikiforos, M. "On the Utilisation Controversy: A Theoretical and Empirical Discussion of the Kaleckian Model of Growth and Distribution." *Cambridge Journal of Economics*, 2016, *40* (2), 437–457.

Onaran, Ö., and Galanis, G. "Is Aggregate Demand Wage-led or Profit-led? National and Global Effects." Working Paper no. 40, 2012. Conditions of Work and Employment Series.

Rowthorn, B. "Demand, Real Wages and Economic Growth." *Thames Papers in Political Economy*, 1981 (Autumn), 1–39.

Serrano, F. "Long Period Effective Demand and the Sraffian Supermultiplier." *Contributions to Political Economy*, 1995a, *14*, 67–90.

———. "The Sraffian Multiplier." Ph.D. diss., Faculty of Economics and Politics, University of Cambridge, 1995b.

Taylor, L. *Structuralist Macroeconomics: Applicable Models for the Third World*. New York: Basic Books, 1983.

Thirlwall, A.P. "The Balance of Payments Constraint as an Explanation of International Growth Rate Differences." *Banca Nazionale del Lavoro Quarterly Review*, 1979, *32* (128), 45–53.

Review of Keynesian Economics, Vol. 7 No. 3, Autumn 2019, pp. 275–291

# Convergence in a neo-Kaleckian model with endogenous technical progress and autonomous demand growth*

Won Jun Nah**
Associate Professor, School of Economics and Trade, Kyungpook National University, Daegu, Korea

Marc Lavoie***
Senior Research Chair, University of Sorbonne Paris Cité (University of Paris 13, CEPN), France and Emeritus Professor, Department of Economics, University of Ottawa, ON, Canada

*This paper introduces technical progress along the lines of the Kaldor–Verdoorn law within a neo-Kaleckian model of growth and distribution that incorporates the Sraffian supermultiplier mechanism. The key features of the model include the interactive effects of endogenous technical progress, the non-capacity-creating demand component that grows at an exogenous rate and, in its long-run version, a Harrodian adjustment mechanism. It turns out that, whereas the model converges towards the normal rate of capacity utilization, the main tenets of the Keynesian model are still valid in the long run as well as in the short run in the sense that all of the average rates of accumulation, capacity utilization, and technical progress are lower during the traverse after the propensity to save or the share of profits goes up. The conditions under which the productivity regime can be wage-led are examined, and the possible effects of an exogenous technical shift are also discussed.*

**Keywords:** *neo-Kaleckian, growth, capacity utilization, technical progress, autonomous expenditures*

**JEL codes:** *E11, F41, O41*

## 1 INTRODUCTION

Even with all the bustle of 'the 4th industrial revolution,' the recent decade has witnessed an apparent slowdown in productivity growth. In the United States, for instance, the annual rate of growth of labor productivity has been around 1.3 percent on average since 2007. Since 2010, it has become even lower, at 0.5 percent. It goes without saying that these figures are in stark contrast to the one corresponding to the Golden Age of capitalism, which amounted to 2.8 percent for a 26-year average. A couple of different explanations for the recent stagnation have been put forth, and one of them is based on the observation that the productivity slowdown is a by-product of the Great Recession

* We thank the referees for their useful advice. The paper was presented in February 2017 at a seminar at Kingston University, UK, and at a meeting of the Korean Association for Political Economy, Korea.

** Email: wjnah@knu.ac.kr.
*** Email: mlavoie@uottawa.ca.

in the aftermath of the global financial crisis. With demand depressed and the expected growth rate of sales falling, firms can be reluctant to expand productive capacity, and defer or even cancel the introduction of new technologies into production processes, resulting in a productivity slowdown, as in the so-called Kaldor–Verdoorn law (McCombie 2002).

The concept of the Kaldor–Verdoorn law has been provided recently with more empirical support. Reifschneider et al. (2015) argue that the sustained drop in productivity can be the result of a decline in investments, which implies that the recent productivity slowdown is an endogenous response to the contraction in economic activity. Anzoategui et al. (2019) embed the mechanism of the costly adoption of new technologies into a New Keynesian model and make the case that the fall in productivity following the Great Recession was an endogenous phenomenon reflecting the contraction in aggregate demand. In a similar vein, Mason (2017) emphasizes that the slow productivity growth in the recent decade can be understood as the result of weak demand.

The purpose of the present paper is to introduce technical progress along the lines of the Kaldor–Verdoorn law within a neo-Kaleckian model of growth and distribution that incorporates a non-capacity-creating demand component that grows at an exogenous rate. There has been a recent revival of interest among post-Keynesians for the role that this autonomous component of aggregate demand could play in the economy, arising from two strands. First, there are models that extend the arguments put forward by Serrano (1995a; 1995b) and by Bortis (1997) under the name of the Sraffian supermultiplier, as can be found in the recent works of Cesaratto (2015), Freitas and Serrano (2015), Pariboni (2016a), Dejuán (2017), and Serrano and Freitas (2017). Cesaratto et al. (2003) discuss the role of technical progress in this kind of model. Second, there are models that incorporate the autonomous growth component within a neo-Kaleckian model of growth and distribution, as can be found in the papers of Lavoie (2014; 2016), Allain (2015; 2019), Dutt (2015; 2019), Pariboni (2016b), Nah and Lavoie (2017; 2018; 2019), and Hein (2018). It is this second strand which is at the heart of the present paper.

The present work starts from Lavoie (2016), who shows how one can introduce an exogenously growing component of consumption into a neo-Kaleckian model of growth and distribution, with overall growth converging to the growth rate of exogenous demand. In this paper, we focus on the interactions between endogenous technical progress, the autonomous demand component, and a Harrodian instability mechanism. While the autonomous component of demand ultimately determines the long-run growth rate, endogenous technical progress amplifies the growth impact of capital accumulation in the traverse because faster capital accumulation raises the rate of technical progress. In addition, the paper endogenizes the parameters of the investment function so that the desired rate of accumulation responds to the actual rate of growth. It turns out that with this addition the model converges towards the normal rate of capacity utilization in the long run, but the main tenets of the Keynesian model are still valid in the short, medium, and long run, in the sense that the average rates of accumulation, capacity utilization, and technical progress are lower when we consider the whole duration of adjustments responding to an increase in the propensity to save or in the share of profits. Also we have examined the conditions under which the productivity regime can be wage-led, and long-run employment can be demand-determined.

We shall proceed as follows. In Section 2 we present the key elements of the model. Section 3 and 4 discuss the short-run and medium-run solutions respectively of the model. Section 5 discusses long-run solutions when the investment function incorporates a Harrodian mechanism. In all these sections we examine what happens if there is a change in some of the parameters, in particular the propensity to save, the share of profit, or the growth rate of the exogenous non-capacity-creating component of aggregate demand. In Section 6 we focus on the consequences of a change in the exogenous component of the growth rate of technical progress. Section 7 deals with the consequences of such a change for employment and Section 8 concludes.

## 2 THE ECONOMIC ENVIRONMENT

We extend a version of the neo-Kaleckian model of growth found in Lavoie (2016), by adding to it considerations linked to an endogenous technical progress function. Our model will ultimately encompass the interactive effects of technical progress, the autonomous growth of a component of expenditures, and a Harrodian investment function. For simplification, we consider a closed economy without a public sector.

The model economy is populated by capitalists who own capital and workers who do not. The functional income distribution between these two income groups is assumed to be determined by political and institutional factors, and hence assumed in the model to be exogenously given. The rate of profit, the rate of utilization of capacity and the rate of accumulation of capital, along with the rate of technical progress, will be endogenously determined.

We deal with only Harrod-neutral technical progress, which is capital-embodied and concomitant with a decrease in the labor-to-output ratio. To be specific, technical progress in our model is assumed to be described by the standard Kaldor–Verdoon equation, as can be found in Kaldor (1978), which can be interpreted as a variant of his technical progress function (Kaldor 1957).

$$\lambda = \lambda_0 + \lambda_g g, \tag{1}$$

where $\lambda_0 > 0$ and $\lambda_g > 0$. Here, $\lambda$ denotes the growth rate of output per labor, and $g$ the rate of accumulation. This specification postulates that the growth rate of labor productivity is positively associated with economic expansion due to dynamic increasing returns.

Let us assume that a part of capitalists' consumption is an autonomous component $Z$ and hence that the aggregate consumption of capitalists becomes

$$Z + (1 - s_p)P,$$

where $s_p$ is the marginal propensity to save of capitalists and $P$ stands for profits. With this kind of consumption by capitalists, and under the assumption that workers do not save and that there is no depreciation, the saving function can be specified as follows:

$$\sigma = s_p \pi u - z, \tag{2}$$

where $\sigma$ is capitalists' saving normalized by the capital stock $K$, $\pi$ the share of profits out of national income, $u$ the ratio of output to capital which is the proxy for the rate of utilization of capacity for a given $K$, and $z = Z/K$.

For the investment function, we employ the following specification:

$$g = \gamma + \gamma_u(u - u_n) + \gamma_\lambda \lambda, \tag{3}$$

where $g$ is the rate of accumulation, $\gamma$ the variable which captures the effects of animal spirits, $u_n$ the normal or the target rate of capacity utilization, and with $\gamma_u > 0$ and $\gamma_\lambda > 0$. This specification explicitly assumes that the rate of technical progress increases the rate of accumulation, other things being equal, as can be found in previous neo-Kaleckian models such as those of Rowthorn (1981, p. 23) and Lavoie (1992, p. 318). As long as productivity growth is fully embodied in the stock of capital, capitalists facing higher technical progress will increase the pace of investment in an attempt to gain from it. In other words, the pace of innovation is a shift parameter of the Kaleckian investment function. As recalled by Dutt (1990, p. 106), this is an argument that was made earlier by Kalecki (1971, ch. 15), and it was also supported by Steindl (1979, p. 7). There is also quite a lot of similarity with the views endorsed by neo-Schumpeterians, who contend that firms and their bankers ride on waves of innovation so that technical progress ought to have a positive effect on investment.

Plugging (1) into (3), we have:

$$g = \gamma + \gamma_u(u - u_n) + \gamma_\lambda(\lambda_0 + \lambda_g g).$$

Solving for $g$, we get:

$$g = \frac{\gamma - \gamma_u u_n + \gamma_\lambda \lambda_0}{1 - \gamma_\lambda \lambda_g} + \frac{\gamma_u}{1 - \gamma_\lambda \lambda_g} u. \tag{4}$$

## 3 SHORT-RUN EQUILIBRIUM

The basic characteristics of model dynamics can easily be seen with the help of the notion of short-run equilibrium, where saving adjusts to investment. In the model, the condition for short-run equilibrium, where both $z$ and $\gamma$ are constant, is given by

$$\dot{u} = 0, \tag{5}$$

with $\dot{u} = \phi_0(g - \sigma)$ and $\phi_0 > 0$. This implies:

$$u^* = \frac{\gamma - \gamma_u u_n + \gamma_\lambda \lambda_0 + z(1 - \gamma_\lambda \lambda_g)}{s_p \pi(1 - \gamma_\lambda \lambda_g) - \gamma_u} \tag{6}$$

$$g^* = \frac{\gamma - \gamma_u u_n + \gamma_\lambda \lambda_0}{1 - \gamma_\lambda \lambda_g} + \frac{\gamma_u}{1 - \gamma_\lambda \lambda_g} u^* \tag{7}$$

$$\lambda^* = \lambda_0 + \lambda_g g^*, \tag{8}$$

where * denotes the value of a variable in short-run equilibrium. Note that, as is standard in neo-Kaleckian models, we assume the following Keynesian stability condition to hold:

$$s_p \pi(1 - \gamma_\lambda \lambda_g) > \gamma_u. \tag{9}$$

Since $\gamma_u > 0$, a necessary but not sufficient condition for inequality (9) to hold is that $\gamma_\lambda \lambda_g < 1$.

It is straightforward to check that an increase in the marginal propensity to save, $s_p$, results in decreases in $u^*$ and $g^*$ in the short run. This confirms the paradox of thrift, which is a well-known result in the Keynesian/Kaleckian literature. Also a change in functional income distribution in favor of capital, to the detriment of labor, decreases

$u^*$ and $g^*$ in the short run. This means that the present model generates wage-led, instead of profit-led, demand and growth regimes in the short run. The negative effects of an increase in the profit share on demand and growth are exerted via consumption demand:

$$\frac{\partial u^*}{\partial \pi} = -s_p \cdot \frac{(1-\gamma_\lambda \lambda_g)u^*}{s_p \pi(1-\gamma_\lambda \lambda_g)-\gamma_u} < 0$$

$$\frac{\partial g^*}{\partial \pi} = \frac{\gamma_u}{1-\gamma_\lambda \lambda_g}\frac{\partial u^*}{\partial \pi} < 0.$$

In our model, the growth rate of labor productivity is positively affected by the rate of accumulation. Hence it follows that either an increase in $s_p$ or $\pi$ decreases $\lambda^*$ in the short run. The contractionary effect on aggregate demand caused by either an increase in the saving propensity or a redistribution of income away from wages lowers the rate of technical progress through the Kaldor–Verdoorn effect. We may thus conclude that the productivity regime also turns out to be wage-led.

## 4 MEDIUM-RUN EQUILIBRIUM

For analytical tractability, in this paper we define a short, medium and long run, according to which variables are adjusting and which are not. We assume that the short-run position of the model economy is achieved by the adjustments of the rate of utilization of capacity $u$, while holding both the autonomous consumption to capital stock ratio $z$ and the animal spirits $\gamma$ as constant. Now, in the case of the medium run, we allow for changes in $z$ while still taking $\gamma$ as given.

We assume that $Z$ increases at the exogenously given rate of $\bar{g}_z$ over time. This way the Sraffian supermultiplier mechanism can be embedded into the model. Then $z$ evolves according to the following law of motion:

$$\frac{\dot{z}}{z} = \bar{g}_z - g^*. \tag{10}$$

Using (7) and rearranging, we have:

$$\frac{\dot{z}}{z} = \bar{g}_z - \frac{\gamma - \gamma_u u_n + \gamma_\lambda \lambda_0}{1-\gamma_\lambda \lambda_g} - \frac{\gamma_u}{1-\gamma_\lambda \lambda_g}u^*.$$

As shown with the help of (11), we can observe that the evolution of $z$ follows a stable path owing to the short run stability condition (9). In other words, the same condition guarantees stability in both the short and medium run.

$$\frac{\partial}{\partial z}\left(\frac{\dot{z}}{z}\right) = -\frac{\gamma_u}{1-\gamma_\lambda \lambda_g}\frac{\partial u^*}{\partial z} = -\frac{\gamma_u}{s_p \pi(1-\gamma_\lambda \lambda_g)-\gamma_u} < 0 \tag{11}$$

It is natural to define the equilibrium condition in the medium run as:

$$\dot{z} = 0, \tag{12}$$

with $z > 0$. Plugging (6) and (10) into (12), we can solve for the medium-run equilibrium value of $z$:

$$z^{**} = \frac{\bar{g}_z[s_p\pi(1-\gamma_\lambda\lambda_g)-\gamma_u]-s_p\pi(\gamma-\gamma_u u_n+\gamma_\lambda\lambda_0)}{\gamma_u}, \tag{13}$$

where ** denotes the value of a variable in the medium-run equilibrium. It can be noted that for $z^{**}$ to be positive $\bar{g}_z$ must be large enough, as is argued in Lavoie (2017, p. 196):

$$\bar{g}_z > \frac{s_p\pi(\gamma-\gamma_u u_n+\gamma_\lambda\lambda_0)}{s_p\pi(1-\gamma_\lambda\lambda_g)-\gamma_u}.$$

Also we have:

$$g^{**} = \bar{g}_z \tag{14}$$

$$\lambda^{**} = \lambda_0 + \lambda_g\bar{g}_z \equiv \bar{\lambda} \tag{15}$$

$$u^{**} = u_n + \frac{\bar{g}_z(1-\gamma_\lambda\lambda_g)-\gamma-\gamma_\lambda\lambda_0}{\gamma_u}. \tag{16}$$

We can evaluate the medium-run effects of an increase in either $s_p$ or $\pi$. From (13) and (16), it follows that

$$\frac{\partial z^{**}}{\partial s_p} = \pi u^{**} > 0$$

$$\frac{\partial z^{**}}{\partial \pi} = s_p u^{**} > 0.$$

This medium-run adjustment to an increase in $s_p$ or $\pi$ can be graphically illustrated as shown in Figure 1.[1] Assume our economy is initially at a medium-run equilibrium. Once the share of profits increases, the rate of accumulation goes down in the short run. However, when we move beyond the short run, the curve representing equation (10) gets flattened and shifts up. At first $z$ increases because the rate of accumulation, that is, the growth rate of the capital stock, falls short of that of autonomous consumption. This is reflected in the small arrow in the upper panel of Figure 1. Now since $\dot{z} > 0$ at the current value of $z$, which is $z_0^{**}$, $z$ starts to increase along the new line, say to $z_1^{**}$. Then this in turn shifts down the saving curve from $\sigma_1(z_0^{**})$ to $\sigma_1(z_1^{**})$. At the new medium-run equilibrium, the rate of capacity utilization, the rate of accumulation, and the rate of technical progress simply come back to their initial positions.

The changes in the functional distribution of income do not affect the medium-run position of the economy *if* we compare only the initial and final positions. However, when we consider the whole traverse of the economy between the initial and the final position responding to a relevant change, it is apparent that non-neutral effects emerge

1. From now on we will omit the impact of changes in $s_p$ since they are symmetric to those in $\pi$.

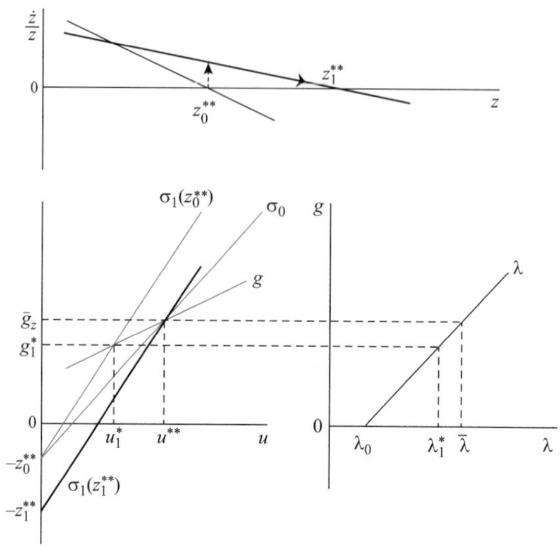

*Figure 1 Medium-run adjustments to an increase in $s_p$ or $\pi$*

on the *average* rate of accumulation, the average rate of capacity utilization, the average growth rate of labor productivity, and hence on both the level of capital stock and the level of labor productivity. This is surely consistent with some of the main tenets of the Keynesian perspective. In the case considered above, the redistribution of income favoring capital has a negative impact on average values without having an impact on the steady-state values achieved in the medium run.

Then what about the effects of an increase in $\bar{g}_z$? In the medium run, the line representing $\dot{z}/z = 0$ shifts up in a parallel fashion. The result is an increase in $z^{**}$. Note that $z$ increases whenever the average growth rate of the capital stock is lower than $\bar{g}_z$. However, when $\bar{g}_z$ itself increases, an increase in $z$ does not imply a lower growth rate of the capital stock. Indeed, from (13), we have:

$$\frac{\partial z^{**}}{\partial \bar{g}_z} = \frac{s_p\pi(1-\gamma_\lambda\lambda_g)-\gamma_u}{\gamma_u} > 0.$$

Comparing the initial and the new medium-run equilibrium, that is, after $z$ reaches $z_1^{**}$, and checking equations (14), (15), and (16), we can verify that the rate of utilization of capacity, the rate of accumulation and the rate of technical progress are all *positively* affected by an exogenous increase in $\bar{g}_z$. With $z$ adjusting from $z_0^{**}$ to $z_1^{**}$, all the *average* rates of utilization, accumulation, and technical progress are also *positively* affected.

This can be illustrated with the help of Figure 2. An increase in $\bar{g}_z$ from $\bar{g}_z^0$ to $\bar{g}_z^1$ brings about a bigger $z^{**}$, which in turn shifts down the saving curve. The new medium-run equilibrium has higher rates of accumulation, capacity utilization, and technical progress, which is $(\bar{g}_z^1, u_1^{**}, \bar{\lambda}_1)$ in the figure. This is true provided there is no adjustment to the $\gamma$ parameter, as we shall see next.

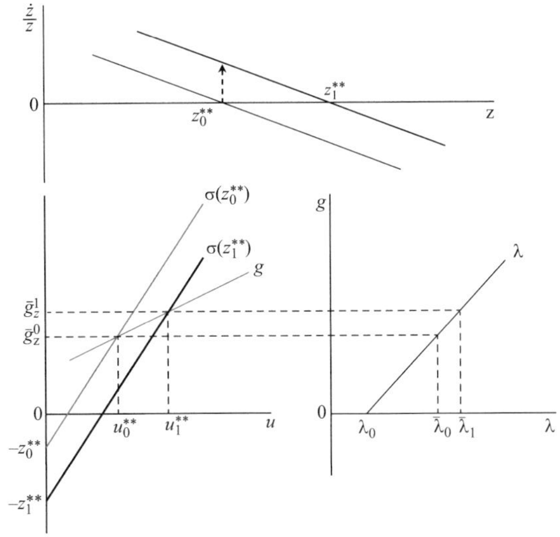


*Figure 2 Medium-run effects of an increase in* $\bar{g}_z$

## 5 LONG-RUN EQUILIBRIUM

It should be noted that in general the medium-run equilibrium rate of capacity utilization is not equal to its normal or target rate, $u^{**} \neq u_n$. This means that the introduction of the Sraffian supermultiplier on its own does not bring our model to a fully adjusted position.

Now let us consider the longer run. Although Kalecki (1971, p. 183) objected to theories based 'on such fallacious *a priori* assumptions as a constant degree of long-run utilisation of equipment,' it is often claimed that in the long run, all the endogenous variables – including the rate of capacity utilization – should converge to their fully adjusted values. As was first shown by Allain (2015), somewhat paradoxically, the combination of an exogenous growth demand component with a Harrodian instability mechanism can bring about a convergence towards a fully adjusted position within a neo-Kaleckian model. To be specific, the long run is defined as the time period during which a Harrodian investment variable $\gamma$ in the accumulation function (3) changes together with $z$ and other endogenous variables in the present model. Notably, Harrodian instability occurs when the parameter $\gamma$ becomes a variable which goes up whenever firms are confronted with a demand which is unexpectedly high, and hence if the rate of accumulation accelerates to any level that exceeds the sum of both the expected rate of sales growth in the absence of technical progress, which is $\gamma$, and the expected rate of growth of capital purely induced by technical progress, which is $\gamma_\lambda \lambda$. Conversely, if the actual rate of accumulation is less than the expected growth rate of capital when technical change is taken into account, $\gamma$ goes down.

$$\frac{\dot{\gamma}}{\gamma} = \psi(g^* - \gamma - \gamma_\lambda \lambda), \tag{17}$$

where $\psi > 0$ and $\gamma > 0$.

We interpret $\gamma$, which is a proxy for animal spirits – the sentiments and willingness among capitalists to invest – to be the expected rate of growth of capital when the effects of technical progress are ruled out. Here, because of the specification of our investment function as given by (3), it should be pointed out that $\gamma$ cannot be understood as the expected or trend growth rate of sales in the presence of technical change, as is the case in a number of neo-Kaleckian models which do not have explicitly considered technical change. In this regard, $\gamma$ must instead be only indirectly related to the growth rate of sales.

Straightforwardly from (3) we must have $\psi(g^* - \gamma - \gamma_\lambda \lambda) = \phi_1(u^* - u_n)$ with $\phi_1 = \psi\gamma_u > 0$. Putting this together with equations (17) and (6), we have:

$$\frac{\dot{\gamma}}{\gamma} = \phi_1\left[\frac{\gamma + \gamma_\lambda\lambda_0 + (1-\gamma_\lambda\lambda_g)z - s_p\pi u_n(1-\gamma_\lambda\lambda_g)}{s_p\pi(1-\gamma_\lambda\lambda_g) - \gamma_u}\right]. \tag{18}$$

Using this Harrodian equation, we can form a Jacobian which governs the dynamics of the present system in a slightly modified manner, as found in Lavoie (2014; 2016):

$$J = \begin{bmatrix} \frac{\partial(\dot{\gamma}/\gamma)}{\partial\gamma} & \frac{\partial(\dot{\gamma}/\gamma)}{\partial z} \\ \frac{\partial(\dot{z}/z)}{\partial\gamma} & \frac{\partial(\dot{z}/z)}{\partial z} \end{bmatrix} = \begin{bmatrix} \frac{\phi_1}{s_p\pi(1-\gamma_\lambda\lambda_g)-\gamma_u} & \frac{\phi_1(1-\gamma_\lambda\lambda_g)}{s_p\pi(1-\gamma_\lambda\lambda_g)-\gamma_u} \\ \frac{-s_p\pi}{s_p\pi(1-\gamma_\lambda\lambda_g)-\gamma_u} & \frac{-\gamma_u}{s_p\pi(1-\gamma_\lambda\lambda_g)-\gamma_u} \end{bmatrix}.$$

The determinant and the trace are reduced to:

$$DetJ = \frac{\phi_1}{s_p\pi(1-\gamma_\lambda\lambda_g)-\gamma_u} > 0$$

$$TrJ = \frac{\phi_1 - \gamma_u}{s_p\pi(1-\gamma_\lambda\lambda_g)-\gamma_u}.$$

For this dynamic system to exhibit stability around its long-run equilibrium, *DetJ* should be positive and *TrJ* negative. We can see that the conditions for long-run stability in the model are fairly weak. The conditions are that: (i) the short-run Keynesian stability condition given in (9) should be met; and (ii) $0 < \phi_1 < \gamma_u$.[2] Here, (ii) implies that Harrodian instability should be existent but not too severe, so that it can be tamed by the stabilizing forces of the co-evolution of $z$ in the model, that is, $\partial(\dot{\gamma}/\gamma)/\partial\gamma > 0$, and $\partial(\dot{\gamma}/\gamma)/\partial\gamma + \partial(\dot{z}/z)/\partial z < 0$.

Finally, our long-run equilibrium can be easily derived as follows:

$$g^{***} = \bar{g}_z \tag{19}$$

$$\lambda^{***} = \lambda_0 + \lambda_g\bar{g}_z = \bar{\lambda} \tag{20}$$

$$u^{***} = u_n \tag{21}$$

$$\gamma^{***} = \bar{g}_z(1-\gamma_\lambda\lambda_g) - \gamma_\lambda\lambda_0 \tag{22}$$

2. Because $\phi_1 = \psi\gamma_u$, the second condition means that $0 < \psi < 1$.

$$z^{***} = s_p \pi u_n - \bar{g}_z, \tag{23}$$

where *** denotes the value of a variable in the long-run equilibrium. It should be noted that we must assume the following inequality to have a meaningful long-run equilibrium. Otherwise, $z^{***}$ may take on non-positive values.

$$\bar{g}_z < s_p \pi u_n \tag{24}$$

We can examine the dynamics of the system using a phase diagram defined on the $(z, \gamma)$ space. From (18) and (10), we can derive two demarcation lines where $\dot{\gamma}/\gamma = 0$ and $\dot{z}/z = 0$, respectively, as follows:

$$\frac{\dot{\gamma}}{\gamma} = 0 : \gamma = -(1 - \gamma_\lambda \lambda_g) z + s_p \pi u_n (1 - \gamma_\lambda \lambda_g) - \gamma_\lambda \lambda_0 \tag{25}$$

$$\frac{\dot{z}}{z} = 0 : \gamma = -\left(\frac{\gamma_u}{s_p \pi}\right) z + \bar{g}_z \left(1 - \gamma_\lambda \lambda_g - \frac{\gamma_u}{s_p \pi}\right) + \gamma_u u_n - \gamma_\lambda \lambda_0. \tag{26}$$

It can be shown that the absolute value of the slope of the demarcation line for a constant $\gamma$, which is $(1 - \gamma_\lambda \lambda_g)$, exceeds the one for a constant $z$, which is given by $\gamma_u / s_p \pi$, as long as the short-run stability condition (9) is fulfilled. Thus, the demarcation line for a constant $\gamma$ is steeper than the one for a constant $z$. Also the vertical intercept of the demarcation line for a constant $\gamma$ must exceed the one for a constant $z$, since

$$s_p \pi u_n (1 - \gamma_\lambda \lambda_g) - \bar{g}_z \left(1 - \gamma_\lambda \lambda_g - \frac{\gamma_u}{s_p \pi}\right) - \gamma_u u_n$$

$$= \frac{z^{***}}{s_p \pi} [s_p \pi (1 - \gamma_\lambda \lambda_g) - \gamma_u] > 0,$$

again due to (9). Now we can illustrate the long-run co-evolution of $z$ and $\gamma$ using Figure 3, where the long-run equilibrium of our model is given by point $E$, which is unique and stable.

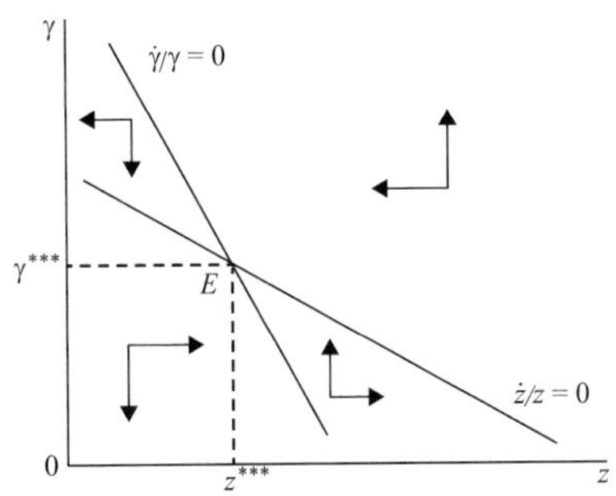


*Figure 3 Phase diagram: co-evolution of z* and $\gamma$

 

Most of the discussions about comparative analyses for the medium run carry over to the long run, as can be verified by checking equations (19) to (23). Clearly an increase in the share of profits, $\pi$, leads to an increase in the long-run value of the autonomous consumption-to-capital-stock ratio, $z^{***}$. However none of the long-run rates of accumulation, capacity utilization, and technical progress are affected by the increase in the share of profits, while all of the *average* rates of accumulation, capacity utilization, and technical progress are lower *during the traverse* towards the fully adjusted position. In this sense, we can say that some of the main features of the Keynesian model are still valid, not only in the short run but also in the long run.

We can also analyse the long-run effects of a permanent increase in $\bar{g}_z$. Suppose the growth rate of autonomous consumption increases from $\bar{g}_z^0$ to $\bar{g}_z^1$. In Figure 3, this would shift up the demarcation line for a constant $z$ in parallel fashion, while there is no change in the other demarcation line.[3] It is clear from (22) and (23) that in the new fully adjusted position $\gamma^{***}$ is larger while $z^{***}$ is smaller.

At first, an increase in the growth rate of autonomous consumption decreases saving by capitalists, which increases the rates of utilization, accumulation, and technical progress in the medium run. This adjustment process is represented by the gray downward arrow in Figure 4.

However, if we consider the longer time period, this should not be the whole story because now capacity is overutilized, at a rate which exceeds the target level. As a consequence, capitalists adjust their expectations, and this change in animal spirits in turn yields an upward shift of the accumulation curve. Moreover, this increase in the rate of accumulation pushes down the ratio of autonomous consumption to capital stock, again shifting the saving curve upward. The effects of this Harrodian adjustment are represented by the two black upward arrows in Figure 4.

Despite the fact that the rate of utilization is brought back to its normal value, the long-run rates of accumulation and of technical progress take on a permanent higher value. As to the rate of utilization, all that can be said is that its average value during the traverse is higher than the normal rate of utilization.

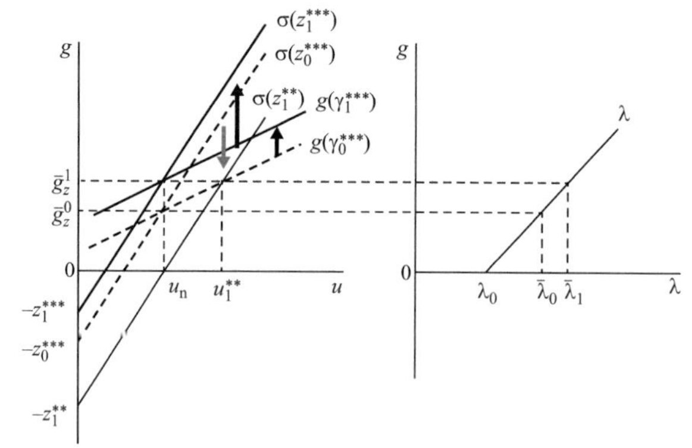


*Figure 4 The long-run effects of an increase in* $\bar{g}_z$

3. What then occurs in the phase diagram is identical to what is shown in fig. 5 of Lavoie (2016, p. 189).

## 6 THE EFFECTS OF PRODUCTIVITY SHIFTS

In their assessment of growth models based on autonomous demand components, Trezzini and Palumbo (2016, pp. 515–516) insist that it is important to take shifts in technical progress into account. Let us then examine the effects of an exogenous technological shift, that is, an increase in the growth rate of technical progress which presumably does not arise from the introduction of new machines. This is represented by an increase in $\lambda_0$ in our model. As is evident from (6), (7), and (8), there are positive effects on the rates of utilization of capacity, capital accumulation, and technical progress in the short run. Graphically, this change shifts the investment curve up, from $g_0$ to $g_1$, and the productivity curve to the right both in a parallel fashion, as in Figure 5, so that in the short run there is an increase in the rate of utilization, the rate of accumulation, and the rate of technical progress.

$$\frac{\partial u^*}{\partial \lambda_0} = \frac{\gamma_\lambda}{s_p\pi(1-\gamma_\lambda\lambda_g)-\gamma_u} > 0$$

$$\frac{\partial g^*}{\partial \lambda_0} = \frac{\gamma_u}{1-\gamma_\lambda\lambda_g}\frac{\partial u^*}{\partial \lambda_0} + \frac{\gamma_\lambda}{1-\gamma_\lambda\lambda_g} > 0$$

$$\frac{\partial \lambda^*}{\partial \lambda_0} = 1 + \lambda_g\frac{\partial g^*}{\partial \lambda_0} > 0$$

Moving on to the medium run, we should consider the effects on $z$, the autonomous consumption-to-capital-stock ratio. From (13), we see that

$$\frac{\partial z^{**}}{\partial \lambda_0} = -\frac{s_p\pi\gamma_\lambda}{\gamma_u} < 0.$$

Let us assume that the economy was initially at $(z_0^{**}, u_0^{**}, g_0^{**}, \lambda_0^{**})$ in Figure 5. After an increase in $\lambda_0$, the equilibrium changes to $(z_0^{**}, u_1^*, g_1^*, \lambda_1^*)$ at the intersection of $g_1$ and $\sigma_0$ in the short run. However, due to this increase in the rate of accumulation, $z$ decreases over time from $z_0^{**}$ to $z_1^{**}$. The adjustments in $z$ stop as soon as the rate

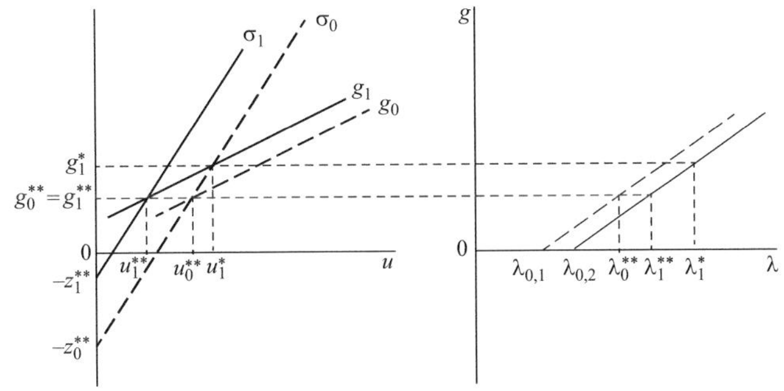


*Figure 5 The medium-run effects of an exogenous improvement in productivity growth*

 

of accumulation becomes $g_1^{**} = g_0^{**} = \bar{g}_z$ unless $\bar{g}_z$, which is exogenously given, itself changes. Now the changes in $z$, in turn, shift up the saving curve from $\sigma_0$ to $\sigma_1$. A new medium-run equilibrium is reached at $(z_1^{**}, u_1^{**}, g_1^{**}, \lambda_1^{**})$.

Apparently, there exist negative effects on the rate of capacity utilization, as can be confirmed algebraically from (16), and graphically from Figure 5.

$$\frac{\partial u^{**}}{\partial \lambda_0} = -\frac{\gamma_\lambda}{\gamma_u} < 0$$

The effects on the rates of both accumulation and technical progress need more consideration. Algebraically, from (14) and (15), we can see that an increase in $\lambda_0$ leads to no change in the medium-run rate of accumulation, $g^{**}$, and a one-to-one increase in the rate of technical progress, $\lambda^{**}$.

Thus, once more, comparing only the initial and terminal values of the rate of accumulation, we see that there is no change at all. However, when we consider the average values of the rate of accumulation during the whole duration after an exogenous increase in the growth rate of labor productivity in the medium run, we can conclude that there exist positive effects on the *average* rate of growth of the economy. Thus these results resemble those mentioned by Cesaratto et al. (2003, p. 49) in their discussion of the Sraffian supermultiplier mechanism, when they say that 'even when the effects of innovation on effective demand are positive, they are often level effects incapable of sustaining a higher growth rate of effective demand.'

The growth rate of labor productivity increases from $\lambda_0^{**}$ to $\lambda_1^{*}$ in the short run. This is due to both the exogenous increase in $\lambda_0$ from $\lambda_{0,1}$ to $\lambda_{0,2}$ and the increase in the rate of accumulation from $g_0^{**}$ to $g_1^{*}$. However, moving on to the medium run, while the actual rate of accumulation adjusts to the exogenously given growth rate of autonomous consumption, the short-run expansionary effects are contained and the rate of productivity growth decreases back to $\lambda_1^{**}$, which is still at a higher value than before the change in $\lambda_0$. This is the reason why the medium-run rate of productivity growth falls short of the short-run one.

Finally, let us consider the long-run effects. In the long run, the negative medium-run effect on the rate of capacity utilization is neutralized, and there is no effect left on the rates of either capacity utilization or accumulation, as is evident from (21) and (19). This is because the investment curve, which was shifted up in the medium run following the increase in productivity growth, comes back down to its original position while $\gamma$ adjusts to regain the normal rate of capacity utilization. All of this also occurs because the saving curve comes back down to its original position, reflecting the decrease in the rate of accumulation in the long run, as shown in Figure 6. This can also be seen by inspection of (23), which shows that $z^{***}$ is impervious to changes in the autonomous component $\lambda_0$ of technical progress, while $\lambda^{***}$ still has a one-to-one relation to $\lambda_0$ (equation (20)).

In Figure 7, it is demonstrated that an increase in $\lambda_0$ shifts down both demarcation lines by the same amount, as is clearly seen from (25) and (26). Hence there is no change in the long-run position of $z$, while $\gamma$ decreases. The latter result can be derived by examining equation (22).

Readers may be puzzled by the belief held by Cesaratto et al. (2003), as well as the result obtained here, to the effect that an exogenous increase in the rate of technical progress will only have a transitory positive effect on the rate of accumulation. *A contrario*, to quote a recent paper, 'technical innovations may have a role in determining the pace of accumulation, something that has been stressed by many historians and

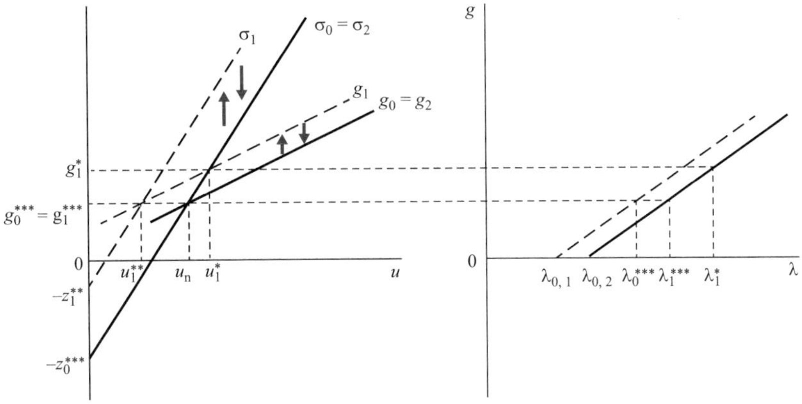


*Figure 6 The long-run effects of an exogenous improvement in productivity growth*

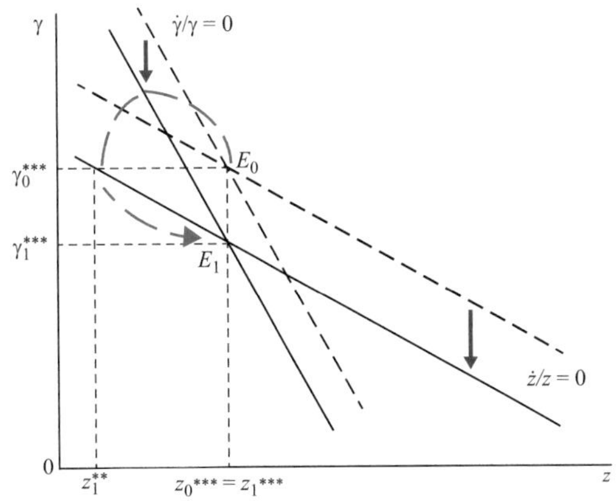


*Figure 7 Co-evolution of z and γ after an exogenous improvement in productivity growth*

economists in the analysis of historical processes of accumulation' (Trezzini and Palumbo 2016, p. 515). But as Dutt (2015, p. 35) points out, if we wish the rate of technological progress to help set the pace of long-run growth, 'technological change has to have some effect on aggregate demand in addition to its effect on investment.' This could occur, for instance, if faster technical change also generates an increase in the growth rate of the non-capacity-creating autonomous components of effective demand, for instance autonomous consumption, because of the accelerated pace in the introduction of novel and fashionable products. The very same possibility is raised by Dutt (ibid., p. 36) when he writes that one could 'interpret technological change as leading to product innovation and thereby determining the pace of autonomous capitalist consumption.'[4] This would imply making the 'autonomous' component of consumption a 'semi-autonomous component,' as Kalecki (1971, p. 174) would say, by writing it as a positive function of the rate of technical progress.

## 7 IMPLICATIONS FOR EMPLOYMENT

The present model provides additional implications for long-run employment, or rather the rate of growth of employment. Suppose our economy reaches its long-run equilibrium. Then the growth rate of output equals $\bar{g}_z$. Hence, in our model, the implied long-run growth rate of employment $g_e$ can be determined endogenously by subtracting the growth rate of labor productivity from the growth rate of output, as follows:

$$g_e = \bar{g}_z - (\lambda_0 + \lambda_g \bar{g}_z) = -\lambda_0 + (1 - \lambda_g)\bar{g}_z.$$

This relation implies that there exists a one-to-one relationship between the growth rate of employment and the growth rate of autonomous demand in the long run, with the latter determining the former, not the other way around. Moreover, we can say, provided the condition $\lambda_g < 1$ is fulfilled, that there will be a *positive* relationship between the growth rate of employment and the growth rate of autonomous demand in the long run. As one would expect, this condition is likely to be satisfied, because, as reported by McCombie (2002, p. 106), estimates of the Kaldor–Verdoorn effect, that is, of $\lambda_g$, are in the 0.3 to 0.6 range, with more recent findings tending towards the former number. However, it can also be seen from the equation above that an increase in the autonomous component of technical progress (the part of technical progress which is not incorporated through investment) will lead to a one-to-one fall in the long-run growth rate of employment. This is the case despite the introduction in our investment function (3) of the assumption that technical progress induces faster accumulation. As noted above, this conclusion can only be evaded within this kind of model if we assume that faster technical change also generates an increase in the growth rate of the non-capacity-creating autonomous components of effective demand.

## 8 CONCLUSION

The Kaldor–Verdoorn law asserts that faster growth will induce faster technical progress. The idea that the recent productivity slowdown is an endogenous phenomenon reflecting the contraction in demand in the aftermath of the Great Recession seems to be getting wider acceptance.[5] Along these lines, we have incorporated an endogenous technical progress function into a neo-Kaleckian model of growth with a non-capacity-creating autonomous growth component and the Harrodian instability mechanism.

It is demonstrated that the model converges towards the normal rate of capacity utilization in the long run under fairly weak conditions. However, even with this Classical feature, the main tenets of the Keynesian/Kaleckian model are shown to be valid, not

4. We do not believe, however, that it would be appropriate to write the investment equation as $g = \lambda + \gamma_u(u - u_n)$, for this would seem to reintroduce supply-side economics.
5. The idea that a slowdown in economic activity can cause a slowdown of the rate of technical progress, rather than the converse, can even be found in a recent article in *The New York Times* (see Irwin 2017).

only in the short run but also in the long run. A decrease in the propensity to save or in the profit share will lead to faster growth during the transition towards the new long-run steady state, and hence to a higher average rate of growth during the traverse to the new fully adjusted position. In other words, one observes positive level effects when the propensity to save and the profit share are decreased. In addition, we have shown, under the same conditions, that the productivity regime is wage-led, meaning again that while the long-run value of the growth rate of productivity will not be modified by a decrease in the profit share, the average growth rate of productivity during the traverse to the new fully adjusted position will be higher when the wage share is permanently raised.

We have also examined what happens to the economy of our model when there is an increase in the growth rate of the autonomous component of consumption. Not surprisingly, such a change leads to an increase in the rate of accumulation and in the growth rate of labor productivity in both the medium and long run. Finally, we have examined the consequences of an increase in the exogenous component of technical progress. As pointed out informally by previous authors, such an increase only leads to a temporary increase in the rate of accumulation despite the higher long-run rate of technical progress. To avoid such a result, which at first hand would seem to be counter-intuitive, one would need to modify the core of the model and make the autonomous component of consumption receptive to the growth rate of technical progress and to innovations, thus rendering this component *semi-autonomous*.

## REFERENCES


Allain, O. (2015), 'Tackling the instability of growth: a Kaleckian–Harrodian model with an autonomous expenditure component,' *Cambridge Journal of Economics*, 39(5), 1351–1371.

Allain, O. (2019), 'Demographic growth, Harrodian (in)stability and the supermultiplier,' *Cambridge Journal of Economics*, 43(1), 85–106.

Anzoategui, D., D. Comin, M. Gertler, and J. Martinez (2019), 'Endogenous technology adoption and R&D as sources of business cycle persistence,' forthcoming in *American Economic Journal: Macroeconomics*.

Bortis, H. (1997), *Institutions, Behaviour and Economic Theory: A Contribution to Classical–Keynesian Political Economy*, Cambridge, UK: Cambridge University Press.

Cesaratto, S. (2015), 'Neo-Kaleckian and Sraffian controversies on the theory of accumulation,' *Review of Political Economy*, 27(2), 154–182.

Cesaratto, S., F. Serrano, and A. Stirati (2003), 'Technical change, effective demand and employment,' *Review of Political Economy*, 15(1), 33–52.

Dejuán, O. (2017), 'Hidden links in the warranted rate of growth: the supermultiplier way out,' *European Journal of the History of Economic Thought*, 24(2), 369–394.

Dutt, A.K. (1990), *Growth, Distribution and Uneven Development*, Cambridge, UK: Cambridge University Press.

Dutt, A.K. (2015), 'Growth and distribution with exogenous autonomous demand growth and normal capacity utilization,' Mimeo, Notre Dame University.

Dutt, A.K. (2019), 'Some observations on models of growth and distribution with autonomous demand growth,' *Metroeconomica*, 70(2), 288–301.

Freitas, F. and F. Serrano (2015), 'Growth rate and level effects: the stability of the adjustment of capacity to demand and the Sraffian supermultiplier,' *Review of Political Economy*, 27(3), 258–281.

Hein, E. (2018), 'Autonomous government expenditure growth, deficits, debt and distribution in a neo-Kaleckian growth model,' *Journal of Post Keynesian Economics*, 41(2), 316–338.

Irwin, N. (2017), 'Maybe we've been thinking about the productivity slowdown all wrong,' *The New York Times*, 25 July, available at: https://www.nytimes.com/2017/07/25/upshot/maybe-weve-been-thinking-about-the-productivity-slump-all-wrong.html.

Kaldor, N. (1957), 'A model of economic growth,' *Economic Journal*, 67(268), 591–624.
Kaldor, N. (1978), 'Causes of the slow rate of economic growth in the United Kingdom,' in N. Kaldor, *Further Essays on Economic Theory*, London: Duckworth, pp. 100–138.
Kalecki, M. (1971), *Selected Essays in the Dynamics of the Capitalist Economy*, Cambridge, UK: Cambridge University Press.
Lavoie, M. (1992), *Foundations of Post-Keynesian Economic Analysis*, Aldershot, UK and Brookfield, VT: Edward Elgar Publishing.
Lavoie, M. (2014), *Post-Keynesian Economics: New Foundations*, Cheltenham, UK and Northampton, MA: Edward Elgar Publishing.
Lavoie, M. (2016), 'Convergence towards the normal rate of capacity utilization in neo-Kaleckian models: the role of non-capacity creating autonomous expenditures,' *Metroeconomica*, 67(1), 172–201.
Lavoie, M. (2017), 'Prototypes, reality and the growth rate of autonomous consumption expenditures: a rejoinder,' *Metroeconomica*, 68(1), 194–199.
Mason, J.W. (2017), 'What recovery? The case for continued expansionary policy at the Fed,' The Roosevelt Institute, available at: http://rooseveltinstitute.org/wp-content/uploads/2017/07/Monetary-Policy-Report.pdf.
McCombie, J. (2002), 'Increasing returns and the Verdoorn law from a Kaldorian perspective,' in J. McCombie, M. Pugno, and B. Soro (eds), *Productivity Growth and Economic Performance: Essays on Verdoorn's Law*, Basingstoke, UK: Palgrave Macmillan, pp. 64–114.
Nah, W.J. and M. Lavoie (2017), 'Long-run convergence in a neo-Kaleckian open-economy model with autonomous export growth,' *Journal of Post Keynesian Economics*, 40(2), 223–238.
Nah, W.J. and M. Lavoie (2018), 'Overhead labour costs in a neo-Kaleckian growth model with autonomous expenditures,' IPE Working Papers 111/2018, Berlin School of Economics and Law, Institute for International Political Economy (IPE).
Nah, W.J. and M. Lavoie (2019), 'The role of autonomous demand growth in a neo-Kaleckian conflicting-claims framework,' *Structural Change and Economic Dynamics*, Advanced Access, available at: https://doi.org/10.1016/j.strueco.2019.02.001.
Pariboni, R. (2016a), 'Household consumer debt, endogenous money and growth: a supermultiplier-based analysis,' *PSL Quarterly Review*, 69(278), 211–233.
Pariboni, R. (2016b), 'Autonomous demand and the Marglin–Bhaduri model: a critical note,' *Review of Keynesian Economics*, 4(4), 409–428.
Reifschneider, D., W. Wascher, and D. Wilcox (2015), 'Aggregate supply in the United States,' *IMF Economic Review*, 63, 71–109.
Rowthorn, R.E. (1981), 'Demand, real wages and economic growth,' *Thames Papers in Political Economy*, Autumn, 1–39.
Serrano, F. (1995a), 'Long period effective demand and the Sraffian supermultiplier,' *Contributions to Political Economy*, 14, 67–90.
Serrano, F. (1995b), *The Sraffian Multiplier*, PhD dissertation, Faculty of Economics and Politics, University of Cambridge.
Serrano, F. and F. Freitas (2017), 'The Sraffian supermultiplier as an alternative closure to heterodox growth theory,' *European Journal of Economics and Economic Policies: Intervention*, 14(1), 70–91.
Steindl, J. (1979), 'Stagnation theory and stagnation policy,' *Cambridge Journal of Economics*, 3(1), 1–14
Trezzini, A. and A. Palumbo (2016), 'The theory of output in the modern classical approach: main principles and controversial issues,' *Review of Keynesian Economics*, 4(4), 503–522.

Structural Change and Economic Dynamics 51 (2019) 427–444

Contents lists available at ScienceDirect

Structural Change and Economic Dynamics

journal homepage: www.elsevier.com/locate/sced

# The role of autonomous demand growth in a neo-Kaleckian conflicting-claims framework'

Won Jun Nah[a], Marc Lavoie[b,*]

[a] School of Economics and Trade, Kyungpook National University, 80, Daehakro, Bukgu, Daegu, 41566, Republic of Korea
[b] University of Sorbonne Paris Cité (University of Paris 13, CEPN), 99 ave. Jean-Baptiste Clément, 93430 Villetaneuse, France

ARTICLE INFO

*Article history:*
Received 18 September 2017
Received in revised form 28 March 2018
Accepted 1 February 2019
Available online 11 February 2019

*JEL classification:*
E11
F41
O41

*Keywords:*
Neo-Kaleckian
Growth
Capacity utilization
Autonomous expenditures
Conflicting-claims
Aggregate demand and supply reconciliation

ABSTRACT

This paper incorporates the role of an independently growing autonomous demand component into a neo-Kaleckian model of growth and distribution where the distribution of income is fully endogenized. A peculiar feature of these autonomous expenditures is that in contrast to investment they are non-capacity creating. The model presents the combined dynamic effects of a conflicting-claims theory of inflation, the Sraffian supermultiplier, the Harrodian instability mechanism and mechanisms based on a reserve army of labor effects. The key features of the model include the convergence towards a long-run steady state where the normal rate of utilization of capacity is being attained and where stable rates of employment and inflation are being achieved. Despite the achievement of a fully-adjusted position, the model vindicates some of the main Keynesian or Kaleckian tenets, in the sense that both the average rates of capital accumulation and capacity utilization decrease during the whole traverse after either an increase in the marginal propensity to save out of profits, an upward adjustment in the claims on profits, or an enhancement of the bargaining power of firms relative to workers.



## 1. Introduction

Recently, there has been a surge of interest among researchers over the role of autonomous expenditures in a neo-Kaleckian model of growth and distribution. This class of models, which has been first proposed by Allain (2015), and then by Lavoie (2014, 2016) and Dutt (2018), picks up the so-called "Sraffian super-multiplier" argument put forward by Serrano (1995a, 1995b), and introduces it into an otherwise canonical neo-Kaleckian model. Investment in capacity is regarded as an induced component of demand, which is itself attuned to the growth rate of the non-capacity creating autonomous component of demand. This approach enables neo-Kaleckian models to achieve the normal rate of utilization of capacity in the long run, while still preserving Keynesian results such as the paradox of thrift and the paradox of costs. There have already been a few extensions along this line of research in various directions, for example, Hein (2018); Dutt (2016); Lavoie (2017); Nah and Lavoie (2017, 2019); Fazzari et al. (2018). Whereas Allain (2015) and Hein (2018) focused on government spending as an independently growing demand component, Lavoie (2016) and Nah and Lavoie (2017) assumed a similar role of a non-proportional part of capitalists' consumption with respect to their profit income, and a part of export demand which is not explained by exchange rate fluctuations, respectively. Fazzari et al. (2018) examine the consequences of such an approach for the rate of unemployment. Also it should be noted that there have been recent empirical studies that provide support for the important role of autonomously or semi-autonomously growing expenditures, such as Girardi and Pariboni (2016) and Fiebiger (2018).

However, up until now, the distribution of income between capital and labor has always been assumed to be exogenously given in this class of models. The authors making this assumption were aware that income distribution is being affected by the extent of economic activity and the situation of the labour market, but the assumption was made as a first-step simplification. Income distribution is both affecting and, at the same time, affected by the course of economic growth. It follows that it would be best to consider all possible ramifications resulting from the endogenous and simultaneous interactions between the distribution of income and all the

* Corresponding author.
*E-mail addresses:* wjnah@knu.ac.kr (W.J. Nah), mlavoie@uottawa.ca (M. Lavoie).

https://doi.org/10.1016/j.strueco.2019.02.001
0954-349X/

other relevant variables within the economy when we examine the role of an autonomously-growing demand component.

We want to start to fill this gap. In this paper, we investigate the effects of an autonomously growing demand in an environment where the distribution of income is endogenous. For this purpose, we apply the framework of conflicting-claims inflation initially developed by Rowthorn (1977), and we embed price-setting and wage-setting relations by firms and labor unions into a version of Lavoie (2016). This essentially makes income distribution, i.e., the relative shares of wages and profits, endogenously determined. With this explicit consideration of the endogeneity of income distribution, we introduce feedback relations running from capacity utilization and accumulation to income distribution into a neo-Kaleckian growth model with autonomous expenditures and examine the issue of the long-run stability of the model, in a manner which is reminiscent of the approach previously taken by Stockhammer (2004).

The key results of the present study are not reproduced here and we will summarize them in Section 7 as concluding remarks. The Section 2 which follows lays out the basic assumptions of our model. For analytical clarity and tractability, the model is separated into its short-run, medium-run, and long-run versions. The properties of equilibrium and the related transitional dynamics are investigated analytically for each run in Sections 3 through 5. The main results will be confirmed in Section 6 with the help of numerical simulations.

## 2. The economic environment

We employ the following function for the saving equation, in consideration of the autonomous demand term which captures the consumption by capitalists which does not depend on their profit income.

$$\sigma = s_p \pi u - z \tag{1}$$

where $s_p$ denotes the propensity to save out of profits of capitalists, $\pi$ the share of profits, $u$ a proxy for the rate of utilization of capacity which is output $q$ divided by the stock of capital $K$, and $z$ the ratio of the autonomous consumption of capitalists $Z$ to the stock of capital. It is further assumed that workers spend all of their wages.

The accumulation function is specified in its simple neo-Kaleckian form.

$$g = \gamma + \gamma_u (u - u_n) \tag{2}$$

where $g$ is the rate of accumulation, i.e., the ratio of net investment to the stock of capital, and hence the rate of output growth in equilibrium. $\gamma$ represents the expected secular growth rate of sales and is assumed to take on a positive value. $\gamma_u$ is a positive parameter which relates the rate of accumulation to the rate of utilization of capacity. $u_n$ is the *normal*, i.e., targeted rate of utilization of capacity. The meaning of (2) is that when the rate of utilization is equal to its normal level, the capital stock of firms should grow at the same speed as expected sales.

We specify both wage inflation and price inflation in terms of the conflicting-claims argument initially found in Rowthorn (1977) and other Cambridge authors as Eqs. (3) and (4). For simplification, we do not consider technical progress in this paper.

$$\frac{\dot{w}}{w} \equiv \hat{w} = \Omega(\varpi_w - \varpi) \tag{3}$$

$$\frac{\dot{p}}{p} \equiv \hat{p} = \Psi(\varpi - \varpi_f) \tag{4}$$

where $w$, $p$, and $\varpi$ denote the nominal wage rate, price level, and real wage rate, respectively. $\varpi_w$ is the real wage target of labor unions while $\varpi_f$ is that of firms. The strengths of the bargaining position of workers and capitalists are represented by $\Omega$ and $\Psi$, respectively. Since $\Omega$ and $\Psi$ can be regarded as being relative to each other, we further assume that $\Omega = 1 - \Psi$ and $0 < \Psi < 1$. Also we can posit that $\varpi_f < \varpi_w$.

## 3. Short-run equilibrium

In this paper, the short run is defined as the time period during which both the level of autonomous consumption and the stock of capital are given. The growth rate of capital determines the level of investment at a moment of time. Hence, we have $z$ as a given constant in the short run. Also in the short run, we assume that, the expected secular growth rate of sales, and $n$, the growth rate of active population, are both exogenous constants. On the other hand, the rate of utilization of capacity, the rate of accumulation, the rate of inflation, the rate of profit and the share of profits are endogenously determined in the short run. As we shall see in the next two sections, the medium run is the period during which $z$ is allowed to adjust, while in the long run $\gamma$ and $n$ will be allowed to adjust as well.

The short-run equilibrium is conditioned by the two criteria given by Eqs. (5) and (8) below, the first of which equates saving to investment by adjusting $u$ such that

$$\dot{u} = \phi_u (g - \sigma) = 0, \ \phi_u > 0 \tag{5}$$

From (5), the equilibrium rates of capacity utilization and of capital accumulation are given by:

$$u^* = \frac{\gamma + z - \gamma_u u_n}{s_p \pi^* - \gamma_u} \tag{6}$$

$$g^* = \frac{s_p \pi^* \gamma + \gamma_u (z - s_p \pi^* u_n)}{s_p \pi^* - \gamma_u} \tag{7}$$

where * represents the short-run equilibrium. Here we assume that both the denominator and the numerator of (6) are positive so that Keynesian stability holds and the rate of utilization is positive in equilibrium.

The second criterion for the equilibrium is the constancy of the actual real wage rate, since we abstract from technical progress.

$$\dot{\varpi} = 0$$

In the equilibrium where the real wage rate is constant, it is obvious from (3) and (4) that both the rates of wage inflation and price inflation are equal and constant.

$$\hat{p}^* = \hat{w}^* = constant$$

The equilibrium real wage rate $\varpi^*$ can be solved for by equating (3) and (4).

$$\varpi^* = \Psi \varpi_f + (1 - \Psi) \varpi_w$$

Note here that $\pi^*$ and $\varpi^*$ are in close connection with each other since

$$\pi = \frac{pq - wE}{pq} = 1 - \frac{\varpi}{y}$$

and

$$\varpi = y(1 - \pi)$$

where $E$ and $y$ denote employment and average labour productivity, respectively. Hence we can rewrite the equilibrium criterion above as the constancy of the share of profit.

$$\dot{\pi} = 0 \tag{8}$$

Also, we can derive the equilibrium share of profits $\pi^*$.

$$\pi^* = \Psi \pi_f + (1 - \Psi) \pi_w \tag{9}$$

where

$$\pi_f \equiv 1 - \frac{\varpi_f}{y}$$

and

$$\pi_w \equiv 1 - \frac{\varpi_w}{y}$$

which implies that there is a one-to-one correspondence between the target real wage and the target profit share in the case where there is no change in productivity. Notice that targets for the real wage and the profit share move in opposite directions. As the former goes up, the latter goes down.

Assuming, as done by Lavoie (2014, ch. 8), that the target real wage of workers increases with faster growth rates of the employment rate, or equivalently assuming that the target profit share of workers is inversely related to the growth rate of the employment rate,[1] we have:

$$\pi_w = \nu_0 - \nu_1(\dot{e}/e)$$

where $e$ denotes the rate of employment which is the size of employment divided by the size of the labor force with $\nu_0 > 0$ and $\nu_1 > 0$. Then it follows that

$$\pi_w = \nu_0 - \nu_1(g - n) \tag{10}$$

where $n$ is the growth rate of the active population. We suppose that $\varpi_f$ and hence $\pi_f$ are exogenously set.

Plugging (10) into (9), we can express $\pi^*$ as a linear function either of $g^*$ or of $u^*$ as follows.

$$\pi^* = A - Bg^* \tag{11}$$

Or recalling the definition of Eq. (2),

$$\pi^* = C - Du^* \tag{12}$$

where

$$A \equiv \Psi\pi_f + (1 - \Psi)(\nu_0 + \nu_1 n)$$

$$B \equiv (1 - \Psi)\,\nu_1$$

$$C \equiv A - B(\gamma - \gamma_u u_n)$$

$$D \equiv B\gamma_u$$

A triplet $(\pi^*, u^*, g^*)$ of equilibrium profit share, equilibrium rate of capacity utilization, and equilibrium rate of accumulation can be simultaneously solved for from (6) and (12), or alternatively from (7) and (11). It is evident from (6) that $u^*$ is monotonically decreasing in $\pi^*$. Hence if we treat $u^*$ as a function of $\pi^*$, then it follows that

$$\frac{du^*}{d\pi^*} = -\frac{s_p u^*}{s_p\pi^* - \gamma_u} < 0$$

and

$$\frac{d(u^*)^2}{d^2\pi^*} = \frac{2s_p^2 u^*}{(s_p\pi^* - \gamma_u)^2} > 0$$

[1] This assumption looks similar to that of Cassetti (2003), but it is different. Cassetti (2003) assumed that the workers' bargaining power depends on the growth rate of the level of employment, whereas we assume that it depends on the growth rate of the employment rate. The difference in the assumptions will turn out to be consequential because we shall later assume that the growth rate of active population becomes an endogenous variable when we deal with the long run.

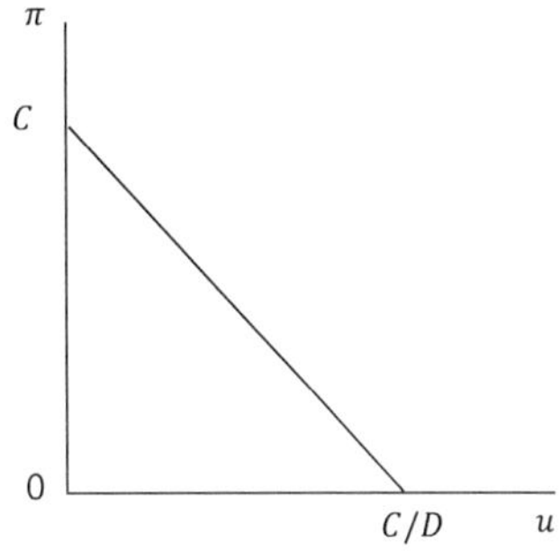


**Fig. 1.** Equilibrium constant-inflation share of profits.

This implies that the equilibrium rate of capacity utilization given by (6) can be depicted as a decreasing curve which is convex to the origin in the $(\pi, u)$ plane.

Eq. (12) is obviously a decreasing linear function in the $(\pi, u)$ plane, as shown in [Fig. 1]. This one-to-one function maps a constant-inflation share of profits to each of the rates of utilization of capacity. Both $\pi$ and $u$ should be positive and hence only the north-east quadrant is relevant. Hence, we need to assume that $C > 0$.

The short-run equilibrium $(\pi^*, u^*)$ can be represented as the points where the two curves representing Eqs. (6) and (12) intersect in [Fig. 2]. Three different cases emerge as in panels (a), (b) and (c).

From the equality of (3) and (4), we must have:

$$\Psi y\left(\pi_f - \pi^*\right) = (1 - \Psi)y\left(\pi^* - \pi_w\right)$$

Now if $\pi < \pi^*$, then it follows that

$$\hat{p} = \Psi y\left(\pi_f - \pi\right) > \Psi y\left(\pi_f - \pi^*\right)$$

and

$$\hat{w} = (1 - \Psi)y(\pi - \pi_w) < (1 - \Psi)y\left(\pi^* - \pi_w\right)$$

When the share of profits $\pi$ falls short of its equilibrium constant-inflation level $\pi^*$, price inflation exceeds wage inflation and hence the share of profits goes up, i.e.,

$$\pi < \pi^* \Rightarrow \dot{\pi} > 0 \tag{13}$$

and conversely

$$\pi > \pi^* \Rightarrow \dot{\pi} < 0 \tag{14}$$

Consider the case where there are two equilibria, as shown in panel (a) of [Fig. 2]. Suppose that we are on the demarcation line of $\dot{u} = 0$. Now moving along $\dot{u} = 0$, let us consider a perturbation around $(\pi_L, u_H)$. Clearly, we can see that even a tiny disturbance drives our economy away from the point $(\pi_L, u_H)$ due to (13) and (14). Any increase in $u$ results in $\pi > \pi^*$, lowering $\pi$. This in turn increases $u$ further away from $u_H$. Thus, $(\pi_L, u_H)$ is unstable. On the contrary, we can verify that the other combination, given by $(\pi_H, u_L)$, is a stable equilibrium by the same way of reasoning. Any increase in $u$ results in $\pi < \pi^*$, which in turn increases $\pi$ and decreases $u$.[2]

Panel (b) of [Fig. 2] exhibits the case with no equilibrium, while panel (c) is the case of tangency. In panel (c), there is a unique combination of $(\pi^*, u^*)$ satisfying (6) and (12) simultaneously.

[2] These results confirm those of Cassetti (2003) and Stockhammer (2004).

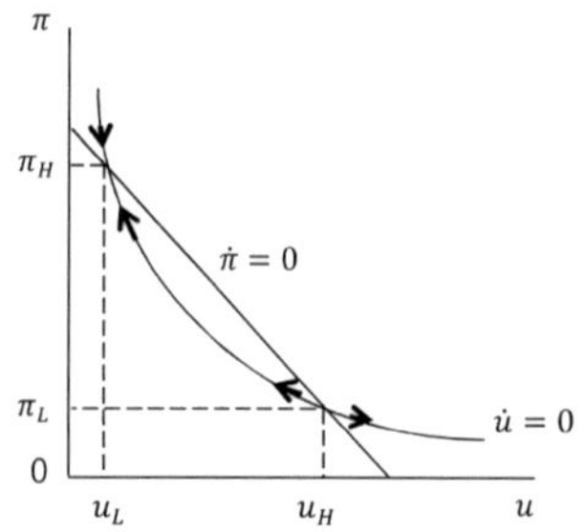


(a) Double-crossing: upper-left stable equilibrium and lower-right unstable equilibrium

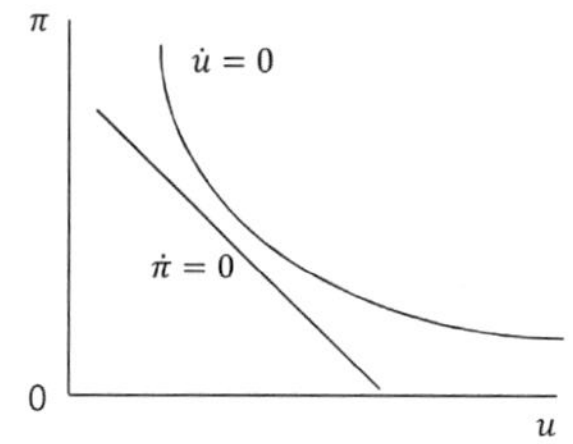


(b) No root

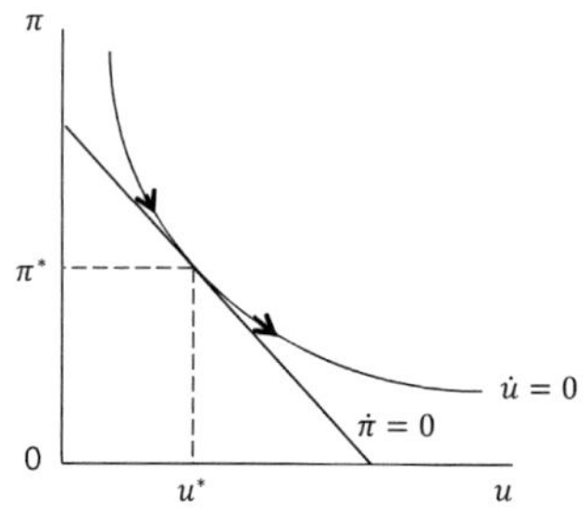


(c) Tangency: unique unstable equilibrium

**Fig. 2.** The short-run equilibrium of.($\pi^*$, $u^*$).
(a) Double-crossing: upper-left stable equilibrium and lower-right unstable equilibrium.
(b) No root.
(c) Tangency: unique unstable equilibrium.

However, based on the arguments in (13) and (14), we can conclude that this point of ($\pi^*$, $u^*$) is unstable. In this paper, we confine our attentions only to the case of stable equilibrium, which is in fact unique, and rule out the possibility of either panel (b) or (c). [Fig. 3] illustrates the determination of the short-run equilibrium of the present model.

The exact solution of ($\pi^*$, $u^*$, $g^*$) can be algebraically obtained from (6), (7), (11) and (12) as follows.

$$u^* = \frac{s_p C - \gamma_u - \sqrt{G}}{2 s_p D} \tag{15}$$

$$\pi^* = \frac{s_p C + \gamma_u + \sqrt{G}}{2 s_p} \tag{16}$$

$$g^* = \frac{F - \sqrt{H}}{2 s_p B} \tag{17}$$

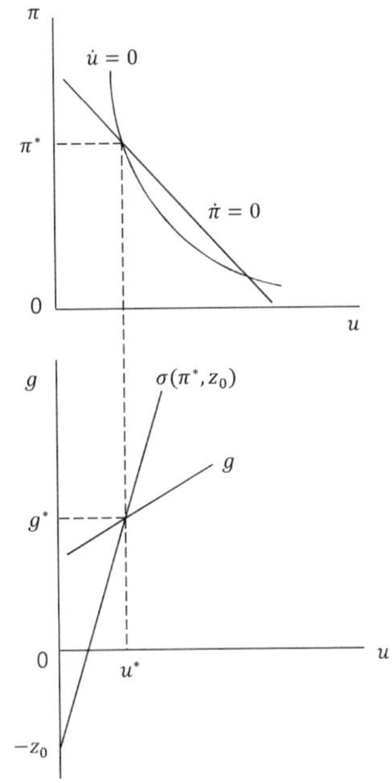


**Fig. 3.** Illustration of the short-run equilibrium of $(\pi^*, u^*, g^*)$.

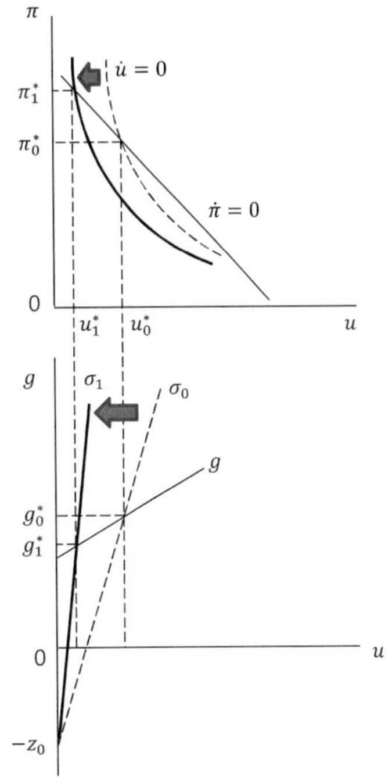


**Fig. 4.** The paradox of thrift in the short-run, where $\sigma_i = s_p^i \pi_i^* u - z_0\,(i = 0, 1)$.

where

$$F \equiv s_p\left[A + B(\gamma - \gamma_u u_n)\right] - \gamma_u$$

$$G \equiv (s_p C - \gamma_u)^2 - 4 s_p D(\gamma + z - \gamma_u u_n)$$

and

$$H \equiv F^2 - 4 s_p B\left[s_p A(\gamma - \gamma_u u_n) + \gamma_u z\right]$$

For this unique solution $(\pi^*, u^*, g^*)$ to be real and positive, we assume that the following strict inequalities hold.

$$s_p C > \gamma_u \tag{18}$$

$$G > 0 \tag{19}$$

$$H > 0 \tag{20}$$

Additionally, we can solve for the rate of equilibrium inflation using (4) and (11).

$$\hat{p} = \Psi y\left(\pi_f - \pi^*\right) = \Psi(1 - \Psi) y(\pi_f - \nu_0 + \nu_1(g^* - n))$$

It is easy to see that in the short run

$$\frac{\partial \hat{p}}{\partial g^*} = \Psi(1 - \Psi) y \nu_1 > 0$$

which vindicates the positive association between growth and inflation in the short run.

Now let us consider the characteristics of this equilibrium. Firstly, suppose there is an increase in the marginal propensity to save out of profit income. This indeed shifts the demarcation line of $\dot{u} = 0$ leftward in parallel fashion as in the upper panel of [Fig. 4]. Furthermore, this rotates the saving curve counterclockwise as in the lower panel. In the short run, a higher saving propensity is associated with a lower rate of utilization of capacity, a lower rate of accumulation and a higher share of profits. This can be interpreted as confirming the well-known Keynesian paradox of thrift.

We can see that a change in functional income distribution also affects the short-run equilibrium. An exogenous increase in either $\pi_f$ or $\nu_0$ shifts the demarcation line of $\dot{\pi} = 0$ upwards since, obviously from (12), we have

$$\frac{\partial \pi^*}{\partial \pi_f} = \Psi > 0$$

$$\frac{\partial \pi^*}{\partial \nu_0} = 1 - \Psi > 0$$

This upward adjustment in capitalists' claims for profit and the accompanying concessions by workers result in an increase in the equilibrium share of profits, which also brings about a pivot of the saving curve counterclockwise. The consequences are the lower rates of capacity utilization and accumulation. This is illustrated in [Fig. 5]. Conversely, we can expect that a downward adjustment in capitalists' claims for profits yields higher rates of utilization and accumulation in the short run.

A change in income distribution owing to a shift in the relative bargaining positions between capitalists and workers also affects the short-run equilibrium. Let us consider an increase in $\Psi$. The

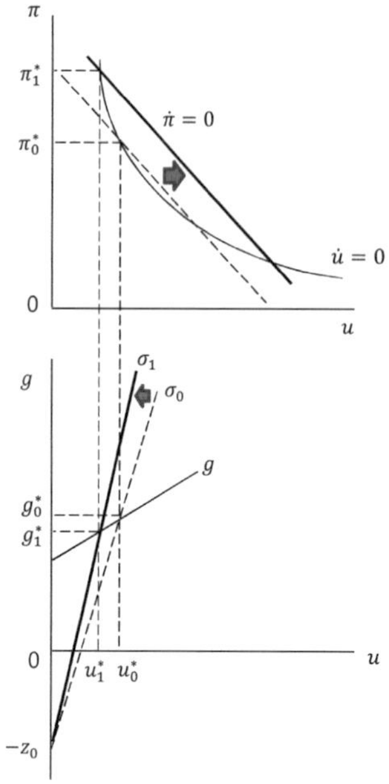


**Fig. 5.** The short-run effects of either an upward adjustment in capitalists' claims for profits or the stronger bargaining position of capitalists, where $\sigma_i = s_p\pi_i^* u - z_0\,(i = 0, 1)$.

effect of this enhancement of capitalists' bargaining power can be evaluated also from (12).

$$\frac{\partial \pi^*}{\partial \Psi} = \pi_f - \left(\nu_0 - \nu_1\left(\gamma + \gamma_u\left(u^* - u_n\right) - n\right)\right) = \pi_f - \pi_w > 0$$

Therefore, unless $\pi_f < \pi_w$, or equivalently, unless $\varpi_f > \varpi_w$, a stronger bargaining power of capitalists is associated with an upward parallel shift of the demarcation line of $\dot{\pi} = 0$ and also a counterclockwise pivot of the saving curve. These are illustrated with the help of [Fig. 5]. From this, we can infer that the present model with an endogenous profit share exhibits wage-led demand and growth regimes in the short run.

## 4. Medium-run equilibrium

Now, let us move on to a longer time horizon. To focus on the pure dynamic effects of autonomously growing expenditures, we define the *medium run* as a logical period which is a succession of short runs, yet this time with an independently growing consumption. We relax the constancy assumption of $z$ and, in order to allow for the Sraffian supermultiplier to work out, posit that $Z$ increases at an exogenous rate given by $\bar{g}_Z$. Note that we are still holding $\gamma$ and $n$ constant in our medium-run analysis.[3] It follows that $z$ grows in accordance with the following law of motion.

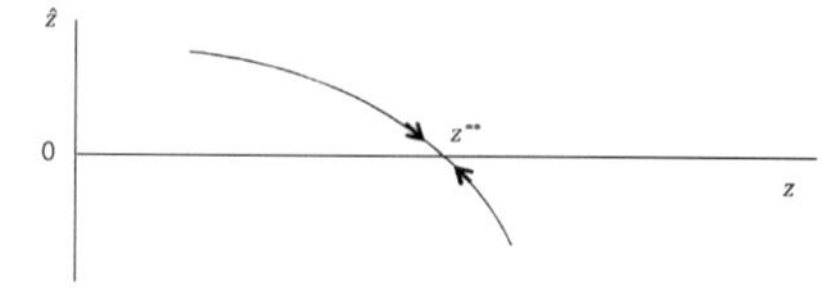


**Fig. 6.** The evolution of $z$.

$$\frac{\dot{z}}{z} \equiv \hat{z} = \bar{g}_Z - g^* \tag{21}$$

We can then define the medium-run equilibrium as being conditioned by

$$\hat{z} = 0$$

with $z > 0$. Thus, the medium-run equilibrium value of $z$, which we denote by $z^{**}$, can be solved for by combining Eqs. (17) and (21).

$$z^{**} = -\frac{s_p B}{\gamma_u}\bar{g}_Z^2 + \frac{F}{\gamma_u}\bar{g}_Z - \frac{s_p A \gamma}{\gamma_u} + s_p A u_n \tag{22}$$

where $^{**}$ represents the medium-run equilibrium. The stability of this equilibrium $z^{**}$ can be verified since

$$\frac{\partial \hat{z}}{\partial z} = -\frac{\partial g^*}{\partial z} = -\frac{\gamma_u}{\sqrt{H}} < 0 \tag{23}$$

where the denominator becomes real thanks to condition (20). From this inequality, we can also see in a highly straightforward manner that

$$\frac{\partial^2 \hat{z}}{\partial z^2} < 0$$

Therefore, the evolution of $z$ can be depicted graphically as in [Fig. 6].

The exact location and shape of this graph can be solved for. It is easy to confirm that they depend on the values of parameters $(\alpha_1, \alpha_2, \alpha_3, \alpha_4)$, as defined in the appendix.

Now the medium-run equilibrium, a new triplet $(\pi^{**}, u^{**}, g^{**})$ is such that

$$g^{**} = \bar{g}_Z \tag{24}$$

$$u^{**} = u_n + \frac{\bar{g}_Z - \gamma}{\gamma_u} \tag{25}$$

$$\pi^{**} = A - B\bar{g}_Z \tag{26}$$

We assume

$$\bar{g}_Z > \gamma - \gamma_u u_n \tag{27}$$

so that the rate of utilization cannot take non-positive values. [Fig. 7] demonstrates an example of adjustment process towards the medium-run position of the economy when the initial value of, $z_0$, was such that $z_0 < z^{**}$. In this case, when $z$ increases, the demarcation line of $\dot{u} = 0$ shifts to the right as is evident from (6) or (15), while the other demarcation line remains still. This lowers the equilibrium value of $\pi$, which in turn leads to a clockwise rotation of the saving curve in the medium run.

This is a novel result of the model. We have shown that an economy that exhibits a wage-led growth regime in the short run has a medium-run equilibrium which is stable. This can be

[3] The 'short-run' as we define it is conventional: the stock of capital, i.e., productive capacity, is assumed to be given and investment only generates an income effect. The 'medium-run' analysis here is designed to isolate the effects of the autonomously growing expenditures. The capacity effects of investment manifest themselves out in this stage since capital is accumulated along with the growing consumption which induces investment. The continuous increase in autonomous consumption also generates income effects, which should be sufficient to match the increasing productive capacity. In this way, the capacity and income effects interact with each other, both in the medium-run and long-run dynamics.

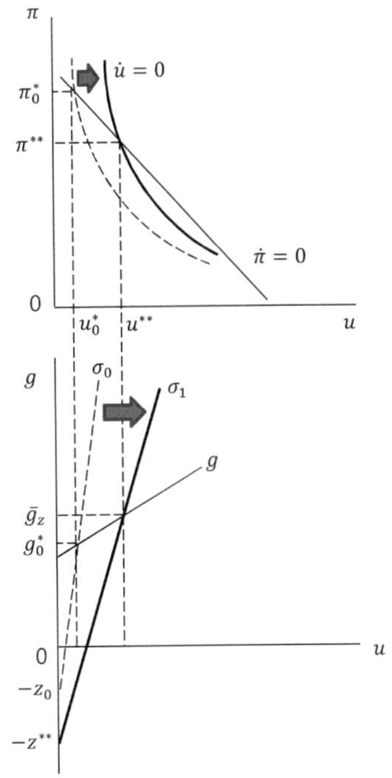


**Fig. 7.** An adjustment towards the medium-run equilibrium when $z_0 < z^{**}$, where $\sigma_0 = s_p\pi_0^*u - z_0$ and $\sigma_1 = s_p\pi^{**}u - z^{**}$.

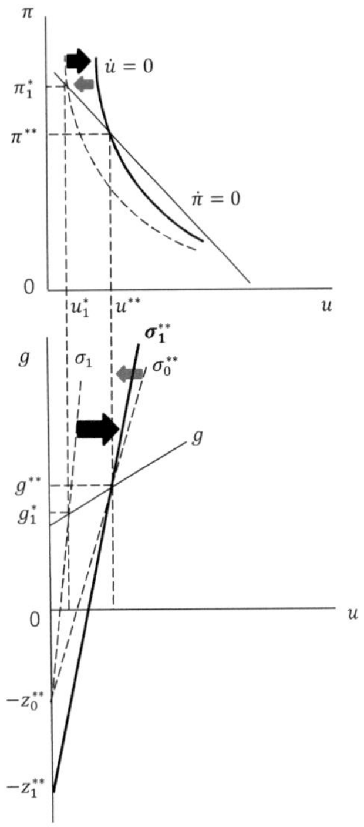


**Fig. 8.** The paradox of thrift in the medium-run or long-run, where $\sigma_i^{**} = s_p^i\pi^{**}u - z_i^{**}$ $(i = 0,\ 1)$.

contrasted with the result previously achieved by Stockhammer (2004) in a somewhat similar neo-Kaleckian model, but without an autonomous consumption component, where the profit share was a negative function of the rate of accumulation and hence a negative function of the growth rate of the employment rate, as is the case here. With such an assumption, Stockhammer (2004) has shown that the economy needs to be in a short-run profit-led regime for the longer run equilibrium to be stable; any economy in a stable short-run wage-led regime would turn out to have an unstable long-run equilibrium. It is not so here, because of the presence of a growing autonomous non-capacity creating demand component. The present model reinforces the claim made by Freitas and Serrano (2015) that the existence of an autonomous consumption component brings stability to the model economy, a claim also recently confirmed by Fazzari et al. (2018) in a model that incorporates expectations.

We can investigate some key features of this medium-run equilibrium with the help of comparative statics. Firstly, consider again an increase in the propensity to save out of profit income. As long as $\bar{g}_z$ is close enough to $\gamma$,[4] it follows from (22) that

$$\frac{\partial z^{**}}{\partial s_p} = \frac{z^{**} + \bar{g}_z}{s_p} > 0 \tag{28}$$

[4] We will see later that this relation holds in the neighborhood of the long-run equilibrium defined in this paper.

The higher is the value of $z^{**} = (Z/K)^{**}$, the lower is the rate of growth of $K$, once the rate of growth of $Z$ is held constant at $\bar{g}_z$. A description of the evolution of $z^{**}$ after an increase in $s_p$ can be found in [Fig. 6B] of the appendix.

Let us assume that our economy is initially at a medium-run equilibrium $(\pi^{**},\ u^{**},\ g^{**})$. An increase in $s_p$ shifts the demarcation line of $\dot{u} = 0$ to the left. This increases the share of profits and hence rotates the saving curve counterclockwise as indicated by grey arrows in [Fig. 8]. But, this is not the whole story. In the longer run now, as the increased saving propensity slows down capital accumulation, the ratio of the autonomous consumption to capital stock goes up from $z_0^{**}$ to $z_1^{**}$.

This increase in the value of $z^{**}$ brings about two changes, the first of which is the downward shift of the saving curve as is evident in (1). The second change is the rightward shift of the demarcation line of $\dot{u} = 0$ as is also clear from (6). Note that this shift of the line of $\dot{u} = 0$ is again associated with a decrease in the constant-inflation share of profits, and hence the saving curve evolves clockwise towards $\sigma_1^{**}$. All of the changes are illustrated in [Fig. 8] with dark arrows.

Comparing the new equilibrium with the initial one, we can conclude that, after an increase in $s_p$, in the medium run the economy recovers the exact same position of $(\pi^{**},\ u^{**},\ g^{**})$ from which it started. However, if we consider the whole duration of adjustments after the change, it is clear that the average rate of capacity utilization and the average rate of capital accumulation must be lower. In this sense, we can argue that the paradox of thrift is still valid in the medium run of the model.

We can also investigate the effects of changes in distribution parameters such as $\pi_f$ and $\nu_0$, which represent claims for profits, and $\Psi$, the bargaining power of capitalists. In accordance with the short-run analyses already noted, an increase in either $\pi_f$, $\nu_0$ or $\Psi$ instantly shifts the demarcation line of $\dot{\pi} = 0$ to the right and rotates the saving curve counterclockwise accordingly. This yields lower rates of utilization and of accumulation in the short run.

However moving on to the medium run, we should additionally take into account changes in $z$. The effect is that $z^{**}$ goes up due to the lower rate of accumulation, as can also be confirmed from the following inequalities, where $\pi_w(\bar{g}_z)$ is the value of $\pi_w$ evaluated at $g^* = \bar{g}_z$. To check the evolution of $z^{**}$ after each change, one can refer to [Fig. 6C] and [D] in the appendix.

$$\frac{\partial z^{**}}{\partial \pi_f} = s_p \Psi u^{**} > 0 \tag{29}$$

$$\frac{\partial z^{**}}{\partial \nu_0} = s_p(1 - \Psi)u^{**} > 0 \tag{30}$$

$$\frac{\partial z^{**}}{\partial \Psi} = s_p u^{**}(\pi_f - \pi_w(\bar{g}_z)) > 0 \tag{31}$$

With an increase in $z^{**}$, the saving curve shifts downward and the demarcation line of $\dot{u} = 0$ shifts to the right until the economy reaches the new medium-run equilibrium at $(\pi_1^{**}, u^{**}, g^{**})$. Note that the saving curve should rotate clockwise again, reflecting the changes in the profit share to $\pi_1^{**}$. Comparing this new equilibrium with the initial one at $(\pi_0^{**}, u^{**}, g^{**})$, we can notice that the equilibrium share of profits goes up whereas there is no change in the rates of utilization and accumulation after all. From (26), we can measure the degree to which the share of profits responds to each change.

$$\frac{\partial \pi^{**}}{\partial \pi_f} = \Psi > 0$$

$$\frac{\partial \pi^{**}}{\partial \nu_0} = 1 - \Psi > 0$$

$$\frac{\partial \pi^{**}}{\partial \Psi} = \pi_f - \pi_w(\bar{g}_z) > 0$$

The overall effects are illustrated in [Fig. 9].

At first glance, this may seem to mean that distribution parameters are neutral in their effects on the economy. This would be true if we were only to compare the initial and final end positions, without considering the transitional dynamics. However, taking account of the transition process from the initial to the final positions, and thus the resulting level effects generated during the whole traverse of the adjustments towards the new medium-run equilibrium, we can conclude that the present model exhibits wage-led demand and growth regimes.

Let us now consider the medium-run effects of an exogenous increase in $\bar{g}_z$, the rate of growth of autonomous consumption. In (22), $z^{**}$ is represented as a quadratic equation of $\bar{g}_z$. Two different values for $\bar{g}_z$ which make $z^{**}$ zero are given by

$$\frac{F \pm \sqrt{F^2 - 4s_p^2 AB(\gamma - \gamma_u u_n)}}{2s_p B} \equiv \Delta_1, \Delta_2$$

with $\Delta_1 < \Delta_2$. It should be noted that both $\Delta_1$ and $\Delta_2$ are strictly bigger than zero due to (20). Since the coefficient for the first term

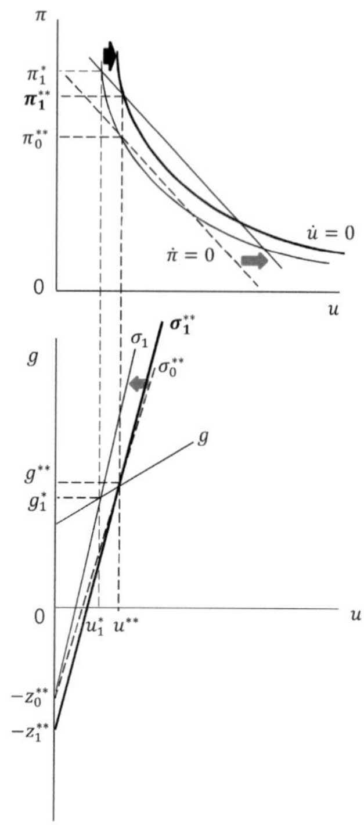


**Fig. 9.** The medium-run or long-run effects of either an upward adjustment in capitalists' claims for profits or the stronger bargaining position of capitalists, where $\sigma_i^{**} = s_p \pi_i^{**} u - z_i^{**}$ $(i = 0, 1)$.

on the right-hand side of (22) is negative, for $z^{**}$ to be positive, $\bar{g}_z$ should be such that

$$\Delta_1 < \bar{g}_z < \Delta_2$$

However, we have already seen from (17) that in the medium run

$$\Delta_1 < \bar{g}_z < \frac{F}{2s_p B}$$

Note that the fraction on the far right amounts to the exact middle point between $\Delta_1$ and $\Delta_2$. This implies that $z^{**}$ must be in the range within which it increases in $\bar{g}_z$.

$$\frac{\partial z^{**}}{\partial \bar{g}_z} > 0 \tag{32}$$

The evolution of $z^{**}$ after an increase in $\bar{g}_z$ is depicted in [Fig. 6E] in the appendix, where the graph of $\hat{z}$ shifts up in a parallel fashion.

Then what will happen to the rates of utilization and accumulation and the share of profits in the medium run? It follows from (24–26) that

$$\frac{\partial g^{**}}{\partial \bar{g}_z} = 1 > 0$$

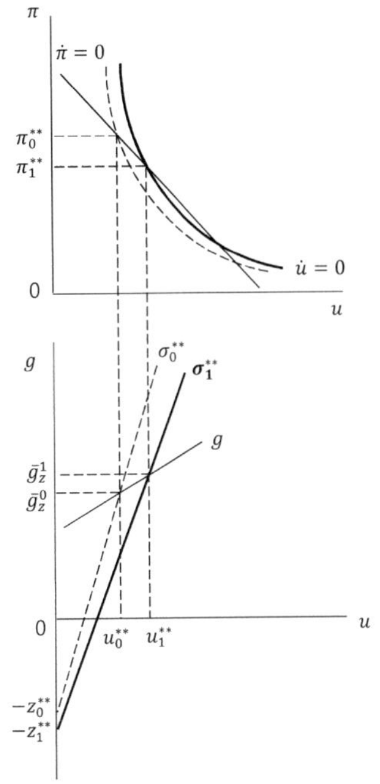


**Fig. 10.** The medium-run effects of an increase in $\bar{g}_z$, where $\sigma_i^{**} = s_p\pi_i^{**}u - z_i^{**}$ ($i = 0, 1$).

$$\frac{\partial u^{**}}{\partial \bar{g}_z} = \frac{1}{\gamma_u} > 0$$

$$\frac{\partial \pi^{**}}{\partial \bar{g}_z} = -(1 - \Psi)\nu_1 < 0$$

Clearly, a higher rate of growth of autonomous expenditures is associated with higher rates of utilization and accumulation together with a lower share of profits.

These medium-run adjustments can be explained graphically. Let's look at [Fig. 10]. An increase in $z^{**}$ due to an increase in $\bar{g}_z$ from $\bar{g}_z^0$ to $\bar{g}_z^1$ has two distinct direct effects. Firstly, in the upper panel of the figure, it shifts the demarcation line of $\dot{u} = 0$ to the right over time. Note that this yields both a decrease in $\pi^{**}$ and an increase in $u^{**}$. Meanwhile in the lower panel, the increase in $z^{**}$ shifts the saving curve downward in a parallel fashion, and then there is a rotation of the saving curve clockwise reflecting the decrease in $\pi^{**}$. The medium-run position of our economy was initially at $(\pi_0^{**}, u_0^{**}, g_0^{**})$, but over time it moves to $(\pi_1^{**}, u_1^{**}, g_1^{**})$.

## 5. Long-run equilibrium

So far, our model economy stabilizes the share of profits, the rate of accumulation and the rate of capacity utilization in its medium run where autonomous demand leads growth. However, it is not certain that the medium-run equilibrium defined in this paper brings the rate of (un)employment to a steady level. Unless the medium-run growth rate $\bar{g}_z$ happens by fluke to equal the given growth rate of active population $n$, the rate of (un)employment will increase or decrease indefinitely, as has been pointed out by Cassetti (2002) and Dutt (2006), just to name a few of the authors who have made this point.

As summarized in Lavoie (2014, pp. 411–416), several possible mechanisms have been proposed that reconcile the actual growth rate and the *natural* growth rate of the economy so that the rate of (un)employment reaches some constant value in the long run. To this end, we propose the following equation to help achieve the long-run equilibrium of the model:

$$\frac{\dot{n}}{n} \equiv \hat{n} = \phi_n \hat{e} = \phi_n(g^* - n) \qquad (33)$$

with $\phi_n > 0$ and $n > 0$. This would pull the growth rate of active population towards the long-run equilibrium growth rate. It should be noted that the long-run *natural* growth rate is simply nothing but the growth rate of active population, since we assume that there is no technical progress in this paper.

This long-run adjustment mechanism can be justified on the following grounds. Firstly, economic growth can be demand-led. Within our neo-Kaleckian framework, the supply-side factors adjust to the evolution of effective demand. In the literature, it has been argued that the endogeneity of the so-called *natural* rate is quite plausible. Secondly, the key determinants of the size of active population can indeed be regarded as being endogenous. It is very well known that the size of active population fluctuates not only with birth and death but also with migration movements into and out of the reservoir of the labor force. This can be an effect emanating from the reserve army of labor. In addition, economic fluctuations do have an impact on the rate of participation, an effect which is referred to as the *extensive margin of labor supply* and which has been emphasized in the mainstream macro labor literature. In their parlance, the decision of individual workers on whether to participate in the labor market or not is based on their *reservation wage*. In a sense, this is lending support to the idea of the endogeneity of the size of active population. To summarize, we can argue that, perhaps not all, but at least some important factors affecting the growth rate of active population can be endogenously determined by the evolution of the economy within society instead of being just exogenously given.

The only remaining condition that we need to add with a view to having a fully-adjusted position in the long run is for the targeted or normal rate of capacity utilization to be achieved. To this end, we introduce a Harrodian investment adjustment mechanism and allow $\gamma$ to change in accordance with the following equation suggested by Lavoie (2014, 2016):

$$\hat{\gamma} = \phi_\gamma(g^* - \gamma) \qquad (34)$$

with $\phi_\gamma > 0$. This equation reflects the argument that the growth rate of sales expected by firms, which is proxied by $\gamma$, should adjust to the realized growth rate of sales over time (which is the same as the rate of accumulation once transitions are achieved).

With the introduction of the additional adjustments of $n$ and $\gamma$ besides that of $z$, the long-run dynamics of the model is now governed by the system of Eqs. (21),(33), and (34). The conditions under which this system exhibits stability in the long-run can be examined based on a Jacobian matrix, $J$, defined as below:

$$J = \begin{bmatrix} \frac{\partial \hat{z}}{\partial z} & \frac{\partial \hat{z}}{\partial n} & \frac{\partial \hat{z}}{\partial \gamma} \\ \frac{\partial \hat{n}}{\partial z} & \frac{\partial \hat{n}}{\partial n} & \frac{\partial \hat{n}}{\partial \gamma} \\ \frac{\partial \hat{\gamma}}{\partial z} & \frac{\partial \hat{\gamma}}{\partial n} & \frac{\partial \hat{\gamma}}{\partial \gamma} \end{bmatrix} = \begin{bmatrix} (-) & & (-) \\ 0 & (-) & 0 \\ (+) & & (+) \end{bmatrix}$$

where

$$\frac{\partial \hat{n}}{\partial n} = -\phi_n < 0$$

$$\frac{\partial \hat{n}}{\partial z} = \frac{\partial \hat{n}}{\partial \gamma} = 0$$

$$\frac{\partial \hat{\gamma}}{\partial \gamma} = \frac{\partial \hat{\gamma}}{\partial z} = \frac{\phi_\gamma}{\sqrt{G}} > 0$$

$$\frac{\partial \hat{z}}{\partial \gamma} = -\frac{1}{2}\left(1 + \frac{s_p C + \gamma_u}{\sqrt{H}}\right) < 0$$

and $\partial \hat{z}/\partial z$ is given by (23). Note that the growth of active population is a stable process as is the evolution of $z$, whereas that of $\gamma$ alone is not. However, the present system as a whole can be stable when both the trace and the determinant of $J$ are negative, even with the Harrodian instability embedded in the dynamics of $\gamma$.

It is very clear that the trace of $J$ can be negative under the condition that

$$\left|\frac{\partial \hat{\gamma}}{\partial \gamma}\right| < \left|\frac{\partial \hat{z}}{\partial z}\right| + \left|\frac{\partial \hat{n}}{\partial n}\right|$$

i.e., as long as the instability due to $\gamma$ can be tamed by the stability due to the growth of both autonomous expenditures and the active labor force.

It is also evident that we can define some parametric conditions under which the determinant of $J$ becomes negative.[5]

$$\mathrm{Det}(J) = -\phi_n\left(\frac{\partial \hat{z}}{\partial z}\frac{\partial \hat{\gamma}}{\partial \gamma} - \frac{\partial \hat{z}}{\partial \gamma}\frac{\partial \hat{\gamma}}{\partial z}\right)$$

Notice that the required condition is such that

$$\left|\frac{\partial \hat{z}}{\partial \gamma}\frac{\partial \hat{\gamma}}{\partial z}\right| > \left|\frac{\partial \hat{z}}{\partial z}\frac{\partial \hat{\gamma}}{\partial \gamma}\right|$$

Hence, we can conclude that the present model is conditionally stable around its long-run equilibrium position defined as ($z^{***}$, $n^{***}$, $\gamma^{***}$), where *** denotes long-run value of a relevant variable. The equilibrium can be solved for as follows:

$$g^{***} = \gamma^{***} = n^{***} = \bar{g}_z \tag{35}$$

$$u^{***} = u_n \tag{36}$$

$$\pi^{***} = \Psi\pi_f + (1 - \Psi)\nu_0 \tag{37}$$

$$z^{***} = s_p \pi^{***} u_n - \bar{g}_z \tag{38}$$

The long-run equilibrium rate of inflation turns out to depend on the relative bargaining power of capitalists and workers and also on their aspiration gap with respect to the target share of profits. In the long run, the rate of inflation does not depend on the rate of (employment) growth.

$$\hat{p}^{***} = \Psi(1 - \Psi)y(\pi_f - \nu_0) \tag{39}$$

Starting from the initial long-run equilibrium where $g_0^{***} = \bar{g}_z^0$, we shall consider the effects of an increase in $\bar{g}_z$ from $\bar{g}_z^0$ to $\bar{g}_z^1$ as an interesting comparative statics. From (35–38), it can be shown that

$$\Delta g^{***} = \Delta \gamma^{***} = \Delta n^{***} = \Delta \bar{g}_z = \bar{g}_z^1 - \bar{g}_z^0 > 0$$

$$\Delta u^{***} = \Delta \pi^{***} = 0$$

[5] For a $(n \times n)$ Jacobian $J$, the stability condition requires that $(-1)^n Det(J) > 0$.

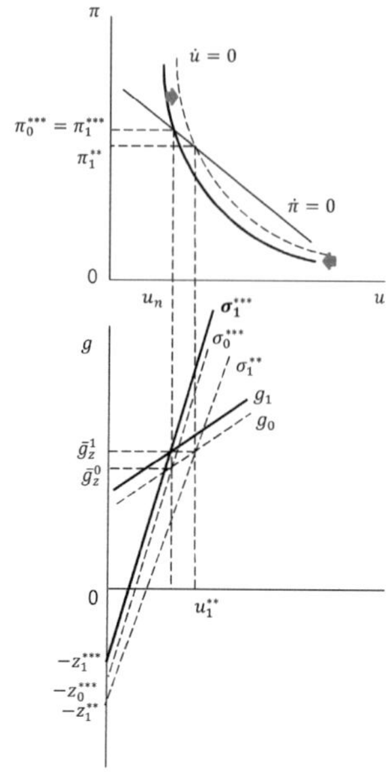


**Fig. 11.** The long-run effects of an increase in $\bar{g}_z$, where $\sigma_i^{***} = s_p \pi_i^{***} u - z_i^{***}$ ($i = 0, 1$).

$$\Delta z^{***} = -\Delta g^{***} < 0$$

The long-run equilibrium rate of accumulation increases with the growth rate of autonomous demand. However, the rate of utilization does not change (unless there is a change in the normal rate). Also it is clear that neither the long-run profit share nor the long-run rate of inflation change after an increase in the long-run growth rate. This can be explained in the following way. Recall first that in the medium run the share of profits has fallen after an increase in $\bar{g}_z$. However, as the growth rate of active population increases over a longer time horizon, the target wage share of workers is exposed to downward pressures, reflecting the weaker bargaining power of their unions. This ends in the unchanged share of profits.

[Fig. 11] illustrates these long-run adjustments. In the upper panel, the line of $\dot{u} = 0$ which once shifted rightward due to the higher value of $z^{**}$ in the medium run shifts back to its original position since the changes in $\gamma^{***}$ and $z^{***}$ cancel out each other, i.e., $\Delta\gamma^{***} + \Delta z^{***} = 0$. Note that an increase in $\bar{g}_z$ increases the value of $z$ in the medium run at first, but over the longer time horizon the value of $z$ should decrease due to the expansionary effects from the increased rate of accumulation of capital. Also it can be noted that the effects from an increase in $n$ which pushes the line of $\dot{\pi} = 0$ to the right and up are exactly offset by the effects from a decrease in $\gamma$, and hence in this case there will be no shift at all of the line given by $\dot{\pi} = 0$. Moving to the lower panel, we can see that the saving curve recovers its original slope. This is because $\Delta\pi^{***} = 0$. The vertical intercept once lowered in the medium run gets higher than even its initial position as we go to the long run. Again, this is due to the response of $z$.

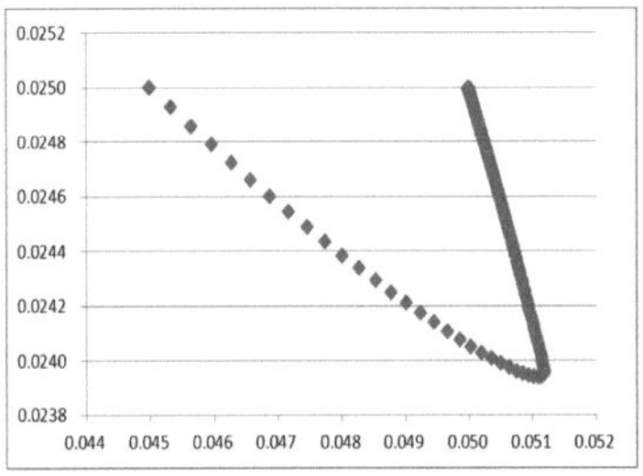


(a) $\gamma$ (vertical) versus $z$ (horizontal)

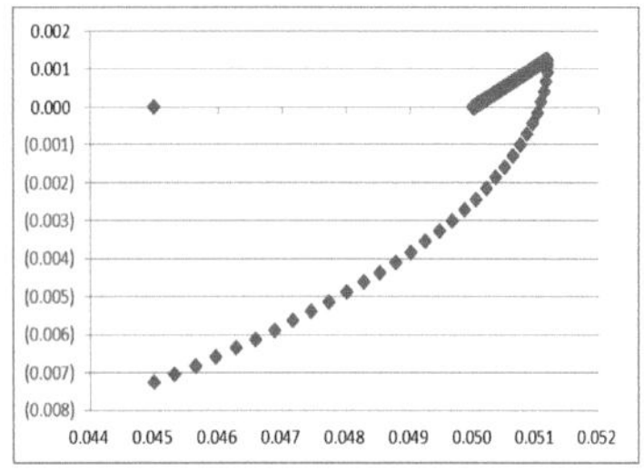


(b) $\dot{e}/e$ (vertical) versus $z$ (horizontal)

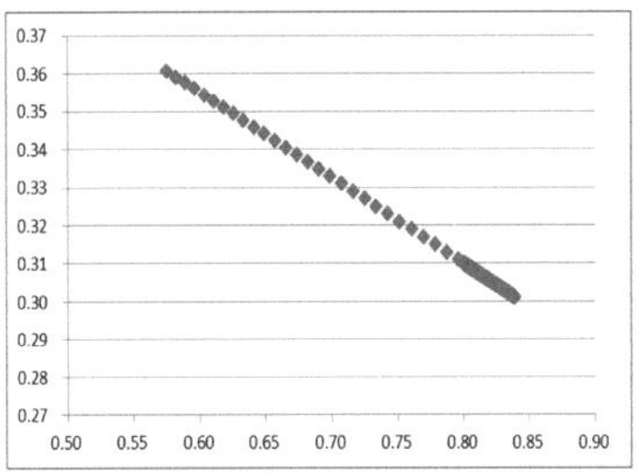


(c) $\pi$ (vertical) versus $q/qf$ (horizontal)

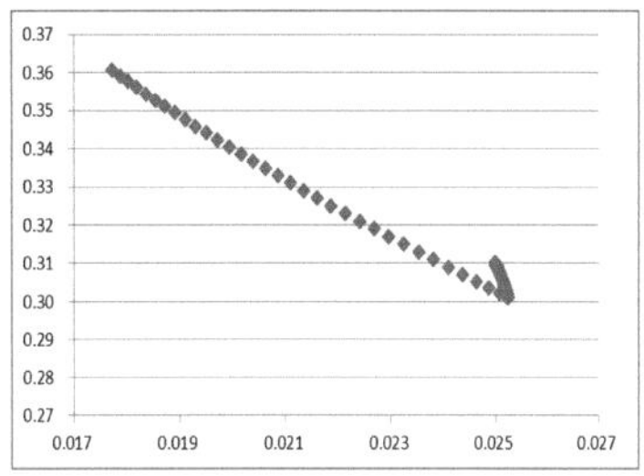


(d) $\pi$ (vertical) versus $g$ (horizontal)

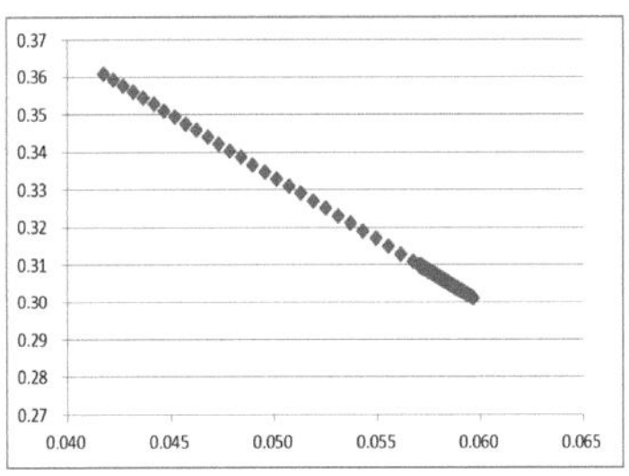


(e) $\pi$ (vertical) versus $\hat{p}$ (horizontal)

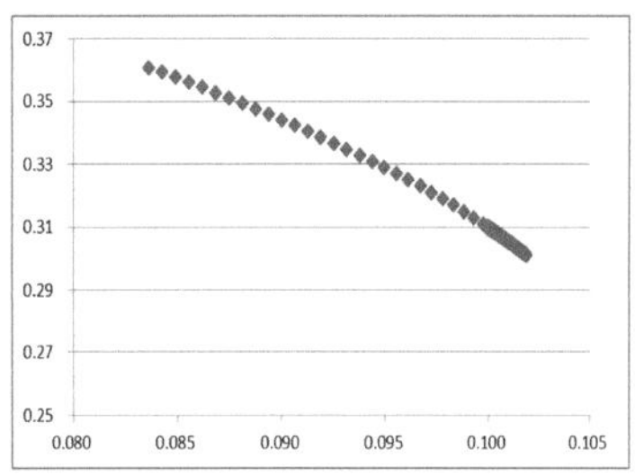


(f) $\pi$ (vertical) versus $r$ (horizontal)

**Fig. 12.** Long-run transitional dynamics after an increase in.$s_p$.
(a) $\gamma$ (vertical) versus z (horizontal).
(b) e /e (vertical) versus z (horizontal).
(c) $\pi$ (vertical) versus q/qf (horizontal).
(d) $\pi$ (vertical) versus g (horizontal).
(e) $\pi$ (vertical) versus $\hat{p}$ (horizontal).
(f) $\pi$ (vertical) versus r (horizontal).

**Table 1**
An artificial economy: long-run assumptions.

| Profit share | Profit rate | Output to full-capacity output | Growth rate |
|---|---|---|---|
| 0.310 | 0.100 | 0.800 | 0.025 |

## 6. A numerical example

The analytical results obtained so far can be demonstrated by numerical simulations. We assume an artificial economy which has long-run characteristics as summarized in Table 1. The assumptions for the long-run share of profits and the long-run rate of growth are consistent with the values found in Franke (2017).

From the assumptions for the profit share and the profit rate in the long run, we compute $u_n$, the normal rate of utilization of capacity, which corresponds to the long-run average ratio of output to capital[6] as being 0.323. We assume the propensity to save out of profits, $s_p$, to be 0.700, which is close to the value chosen by Sasaki

[6] In the model, the variable $u$ proxies the rate of utilization, but in fact is the ratio of output to capital, $q/K$, as defined in (1) and, strictly speaking, differs from the ratio of output to full-capacity output, $q/qf$.

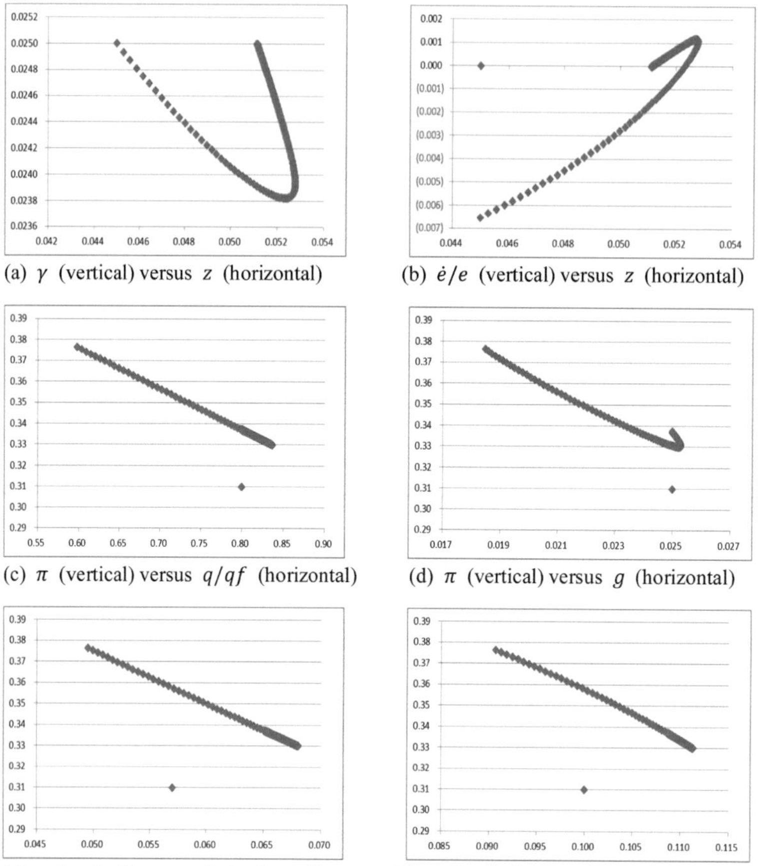

(a) $\gamma$ (vertical) versus $z$ (horizontal) (b) $\dot{e}/e$ (vertical) versus $z$ (horizontal)

(c) $\pi$ (vertical) versus $q/qf$ (horizontal) (d) $\pi$ (vertical) versus $g$ (horizontal)

(e) $\pi$ (vertical) versus $\hat{p}$ (horizontal) (f) $\pi$ (vertical) versus $r$ (horizontal)

**Fig. 13.** Long-run transitional dynamics after an increase in $\Psi$
(a) γ (vertical) versus z (horizontal).
(b) e /e (vertical) versus z (horizontal).
(c) π (vertical) versus q/qf (horizontal).
(d) π (vertical) versus g (horizontal).
(e) π (vertical) versus p̂ (horizontal).
(f) π (vertical) versus r (horizontal).

(2011). Consistent with this assumption for $s_p$, the long-run value of $z$ is computed to be 0.045 in accordance with (38).[7] The values for the other parameters in the model are assumed to be as follows: $\gamma_u = 0.080$, $\Psi = 0.3000$, $\pi_f = 0.5000$, $\nu_1 = 10$, and $\phi_n = 0.4$. Then we can compute $\nu_0$ in turn as being equal to 0.2285 so that the long-run share of profits can become 31%. The assumption for $\gamma_u$ is also based on Sasaki (2011). The values chosen for these parameters of the model are rather provisional and can be regarded justifiably as being somewhat arbitrary. However, concerning the *qualitative* aspects of the achieved numerical results, they appear to be robust, at least when parameter values are modified within a reasonable range.[8]

[7] Recall that workers do not save in this paper. A propensity to save out of profits of 70% with a profit share of 31% implies that the share of saving (or investment) out of national income is 21.7%. It is well-known that the historical long-run investment-to-output ratio in the U.S. varies from 18.7% (Maddison, 1992) to 24% (Summers and Heston, 1984).

[8] Since the important endogenous variables such as the share of profits are solved for from a set of quadratic equations as shown in (15) through (17), we can have complex roots for them. In the theoretical model, this possibility is ruled out thanks

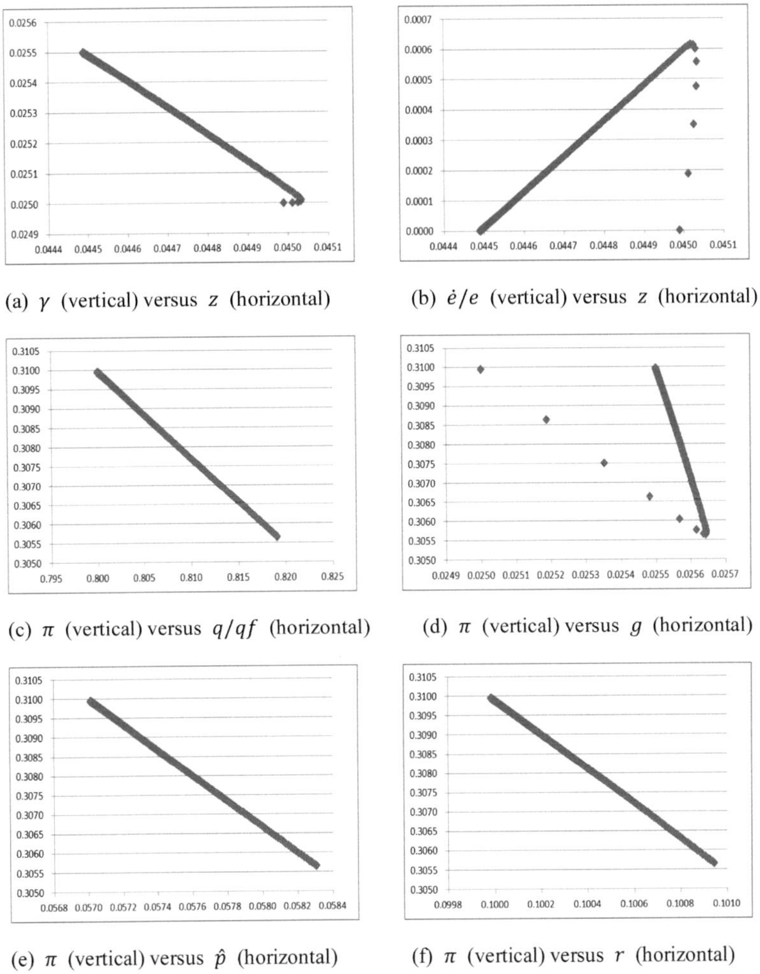


**Fig. 14.** Long-run transitional dynamics after an increase in $\bar{g}_z$
(a) γ (vertical) versus z (horizontal).
(b) e /e (vertical) versus z (horizontal).
(c) π (vertical) versus q/qf (horizontal).
(d) π (vertical) versus g (horizontal).
(e) π (vertical) versus p̂ (horizontal).
(f) π (vertical) versus r (horizontal)

Based on these calibrations, we can perform comparative static analyses either for the short, medium, or long run. Here, we present some of the results. The second, third and fourth columns of Table 2 compare an initial long-run equilibrium with the new short-run (SR) and the new long-run (LR) equilibrium following an increase in the propensity to save of capitalists $s_p$ from 0.700 to 0.750. The second, fifth, and sixth columns do the same exercise, but this time following an increase in the relative bargaining position of capitalists $\Psi$ from 0.300 to 0.400. Note that $qf$ denotes the full-capacity

to assumptions (19) and (20). However, while doing simulations, we cannot just assume away the possibility of complex roots. This problem indeed turned out to be severe and constrained our choice of parameter values. This is why we suggest that our numerical results should be understood as an illustrative example.

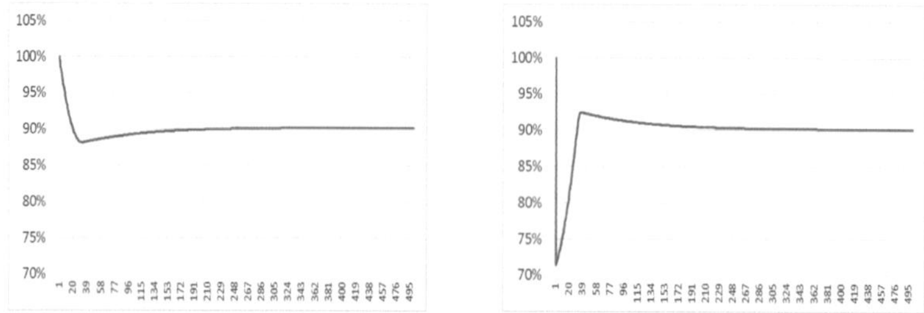


(a) Long-run effects of an increase in $s_p$ on the level of capital (left) and output (right)

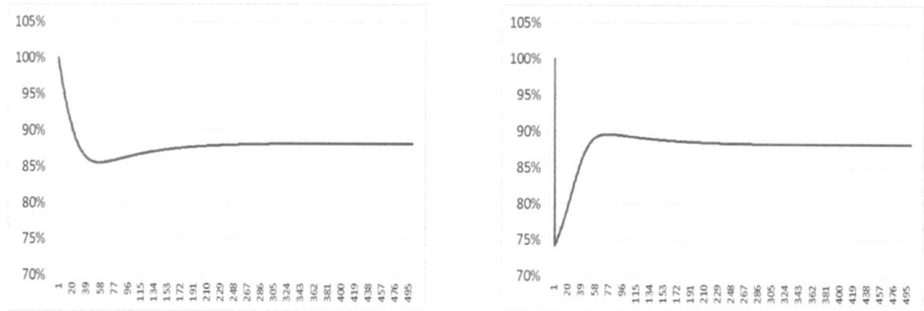


(b) Long-run effects of an increase in $\Psi$ on the level of capital (left) and output (right)

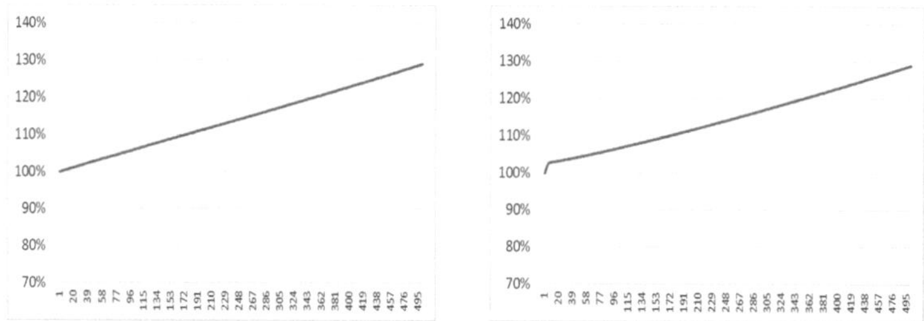


(c) Long-run effects of an increase in $\bar{g}_z$ on the level of capital (left) and output (right)

**Fig. 15.** Comparison of the long-run level of capital and output.
(a) Long-run effects of an increase in $s_p$ on the level of capital (left) and output (right).
(b) Long-run effects of an increase in $\Psi$ on the level of capital (left) and output (right).
(c) Long-run effects of an increase in $\bar{g}_z$ on the level of capital (left) and output (right).

level of output. Finally, the second and seventh columns compare the initial long-run position with the new long-run one after an increase in the growth rate of autonomous consumption $\bar{g}_z$ from 0.0250 to 0.0255.

However, these results compare only the initial and final positions of the model economy. We believe that the whole transitional dynamics along the traverse from the initial steady state to the new one after a change in parameter values should be computed to fully examine the properties of the model. [Fig. 12–14] summarize our computational results.

Panel (a) of [Fig. 15] compares the levels of capital and output when there is a permanent increase in $s_p$ with those when there is no change in the propensity to save. The latter is shown as 100% in the figure. Likewise, panel (b) and panel (c) contrast the cases of a permanent increase in $\Psi$ and $\bar{g}_z$, respectively, from the cases of no change.

Last but not least, another notable feature of the present model is that the rate of employment converges to a stable value in the long run. Conventional neo-Kaleckian models of growth and distribution, which are not subject to any explicit labor supply constraints, usually do not discuss the value taken by the rate of employment. In general, if the growth rate of the labor force is assumed to be exogenously given, it is likely to deviate permanently from the growth rate of labor demand since the latter is endogenously determined,

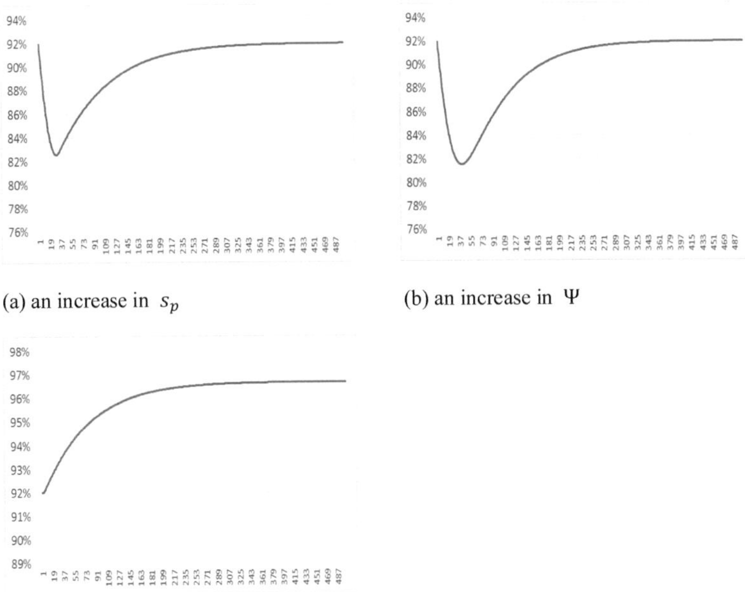


(a) an increase in $s_p$

(b) an increase in $\Psi$

(c) an increase in $\bar{g}_z$

**Fig. 16.** Long-run effects on the rate of employment. (a) an increase in $s_p$. (b) an increase in $\Psi$. (c) an increase in $\bar{g}_z$.

**Table 2**
Comparative statics.

| | Initial | $ds_p > 0$ | | $d\Psi > 0$ | | $d\bar{g}_z > 0$ |
|---|---|---|---|---|---|---|
| | | SR | LR | SR | LR | LR |
| $s_p$ | 0.7000 | 0.7500 | 0.7500 | 0.7000 | 0.7000 | 0.7000 |
| $\Psi$ | 0.3000 | 0.3000 | 0.3000 | 0.4000 | 0.4000 | 0.3000 |
| $\bar{g}_z$ | 0.0250 | 0.0250 | 0.0250 | 0.0250 | 0.0250 | 0.0255 |
| $z = Z/K$ | 0.0450 | 0.0450 | 0.0500 | 0.0450 | 0.0511 | 0.0445 |
| $\gamma, n$ | 0.0250 | 0.0250 | 0.0250 | 0.0250 | 0.0250 | 0.0255 |
| $\pi = P/q$ | 0.3100 | 0.3608 | 0.3100 | 0.3763 | 0.3371 | 0.3100 |
| $q/qf$ | 0.8000 | 0.5750 | 0.8000 | 0.5974 | 0.8000 | 0.8000 |
| $g$ | 0.0250 | 0.0177 | 0.0250 | 0.0185 | 0.0250 | 0.0255 |
| $e$ | 0.9200 | 0.9133 | 0.9200 | 0.9140 | 0.9200 | 0.9660 |
| $\hat{p}$ | 0.0570 | 0.0418 | 0.0570 | 0.0495 | 0.0652 | 0.0570 |
| $r = P/K$ | 0.1000 | 0.0836 | 0.1000 | 0.0906 | 0.1087 | 0.1000 |

meaning that the rate of employment would move up or down forever. But this is not the case of the present model, thanks to Eq. (33). [Fig. 16] illustrates the long-run effects on the rate of employment as a consequence of an increase in $s_p$, $\Psi$, and $\bar{g}_z$, respectively. The evident wage-led nature of employment stands out in the present model.

## 7. Concluding remarks

We investigated the role of a non-capacity creating autonomous expenditure in the process of growth of an artificial economy which is demand-constrained in its nature. In this paper, we have assumed that a part of aggregate consumption by capitalists is not proportional to their profit income and is an independently growing demand component, as in Lavoie (2016). The novelty of our model, which makes it distinct from the previous literature dealing with the super-multiplier effects of autonomous expenditures, lies in that we have applied the framework provided by the conflicting-claims theory of inflation in order to make the distribution of income between capital and labor fully endogenous. We conclude by summarizing the three main results of our study as follows.

Firstly, our model combines the dynamic effects of the conflicting-claims model of inflation and income distribution that depends on changes in the employment rate, the Sraffian super-multiplier, the Harrodian investment adjustment mechanism and an endogenous labor force. All of these turn out to contribute to a kind of classical convergence towards the fully-adjusted state in the long run where the normal rate of capacity utilization is achieved, while generating rich dynamics along the transitional path. One thing to note is that the rate of employment reaches a stable value in the long run. This is one of the most peculiar feature of our model (and of that of Fazzari et al., 2018). This convergence is facilitated by the endogenous adjustments in the growth rate of active population.

Secondly, our model demonstrates that some of the main Keynesian tenets such as the paradox of thrift and wage-led demand (the paradox of costs) still hold not only in the short run but also in the long run. These paradoxes hold in the restricted sense that both the average rate of accumulation and that of capacity utilization decrease when we consider the whole traverse after an increase in the marginal propensity to save out of profits, an upward adjustment in the claims on profits, or an enhancement of the bargaining power of firms relative to that of workers.

Thirdly, our model contains an important message concerning the long-run stability of the wage-led demand/growth regime. Under a specific assumption about the determinants of the endogenous share of profits which was similar to our own, Stockhammer (2004) had shown that there is no stable long-run equilibrium in any economy operating within a wage-led regime. By contrast, our model demonstrates that this defect can be successfully addressed by considering the effects of an autonomously-growing and non-capacity creating component of effective demand. In this respect, autonomous expenditures, or semi-autonomous expenditures as Fiebiger (2018) calls them, seem to play an important role, as they provide the needed medium-run or long-run stabilizing forces in a wage-led economy, and this has been shown with the help of a numerical simulation of the model.

This being said, in response to the comments of a referee, mathematical modelling inevitably abstracts from some of the economic reality that we observe. The main achieved result, that the economy could reach a fully-adjusted long-run position, is clearly counterfactual as such a full equilibrium is never reached in reality. This can be explained in part by the simple fact that while here we assumed the growth rate $\bar{g}_z$ to be a constant, in reality the growth rate of autonomous or semi-autonomous expenditures is likely to change substantially from period to period. One only needs to think of household expenditures in real estate. In addition, there could be a multiplicity of demand components that grow autonomously, at different rates. Also, we assumed that firms were reacting to the expected growth rate of sales and to rates of capacity utilization, but they could also be reacting to several other determinants, such as the profit rate. Their expectations about future sales may differ from the way they were formalized here, and the $\gamma$ variable could be permanently shifted without achieving any rest point.

Our position on all this is similar to that of Fazzari et al. (2018: 8–9) who write that: "...[W]e do not assert that the steady-state growth path is necessarily some kind of *fully adjusted* or *long run* equilibrium to which the system converges. Again, a necessary condition for such convergence is the dynamic stability of the model, which is not guaranteed for all parameter values. Furthermore, long-run convergence would require a long-run constant rate of growth of autonomous demand, which is empirically unlikely. Indeed, there may be different sources of autonomous demand with different growth rates. ... [E]ven if the system does not converge to the steady-state path, the steady state can function as a 'center of gravity' for actual dynamics". In this sense, we believe that the model presented in this paper provides a perspective with which we can understand some, but not all, aspects of the longer-term evolution of a modern economy, especially with regards to the relationship between growth and income distribution. And we believe that it provides important and useful insights about the stabilizing role of non-capacity creating autonomous or semi-autonomous expenditures.

## Appendix A. Changes in the graph of $\hat{z}$ against $z$

The equation governing the evolution of $z$ is given by

$$\hat{z} = \bar{g}_z - \alpha_1 + \alpha_2\sqrt{\alpha_3 - \alpha_4 z}$$

where

$$\alpha_1 = \frac{F}{2s_pB}$$

$$\alpha_2 = \frac{1}{2s_pB}$$

$$\alpha_3 = F^2 - 4s_p^2AB(\gamma - \gamma_u u_n)$$

$$\alpha_4 = 4s_pB\gamma_u$$

This function can be graphed in the $(\hat{z}, z)$ plane as in [Fig. A17(A)].

Now we consider the effects of an increase in $s_p$. It can be easily seen that

$$\frac{\partial \alpha_1}{\partial s_p} > 0$$

$$\frac{\partial \alpha_2}{\partial s_p} < 0$$

$$\frac{\partial \alpha_4}{\partial s_p} > 0$$

Together with (28) $\partial z^{**}/\partial s_p > 0$, these inequalities imply that

$$\frac{\partial}{\partial s_p}\left(\frac{\alpha_3}{\alpha_4}\right) > 0$$

[Fig. A17 (B)] shows how the graph of $\hat{z}$ evolves for two different values of $s_p$.

Secondly, we consider the effects of an increase either in $\pi_f$ or $\upsilon_0$. Easily, we can see that

$$\frac{\partial \alpha_1}{\partial \pi_f} > 0$$

$$\frac{\partial \alpha_2}{\partial \pi_f} = \frac{\partial \alpha_4}{\partial \pi_f} = 0$$

$$\frac{\partial \alpha_1}{\partial \upsilon_0} > 0$$

$$\frac{\partial \alpha_2}{\partial \upsilon_0} = \frac{\partial \alpha_4}{\partial \upsilon_0} = 0$$

Again since $\partial z^{**}/\partial \pi_f > 0$ and $\partial z^{**}/\partial \upsilon_0 > 0$, the partial derivatives above imply that

$$\frac{\partial}{\partial \pi_f}\left(\frac{\alpha_3}{\alpha_4}\right) > 0$$

and

$$\frac{\partial}{\partial \upsilon_0}\left(\frac{\alpha_3}{\alpha_4}\right) > 0$$

[Fig. A17(C)] shows how the graph of $\hat{z}$ gets modified when there is a change in either $\pi_f$ or $\upsilon_0$.

Finally, it is evident that both $\alpha_2$ and $\alpha_4$ increase in $\Psi$.

$$\frac{\partial \alpha_2}{\partial \Psi} > 0$$

$$\frac{\partial \alpha_4}{\partial \Psi} > 0$$

[Fig. A17(D)] sketches some of the changes in the graph of $\hat{z}$ after an increase in $\Psi$.

W.J. Nah and M. Lavoie / Structural Change and Economic Dynamics 51 (2019) 427–444 443

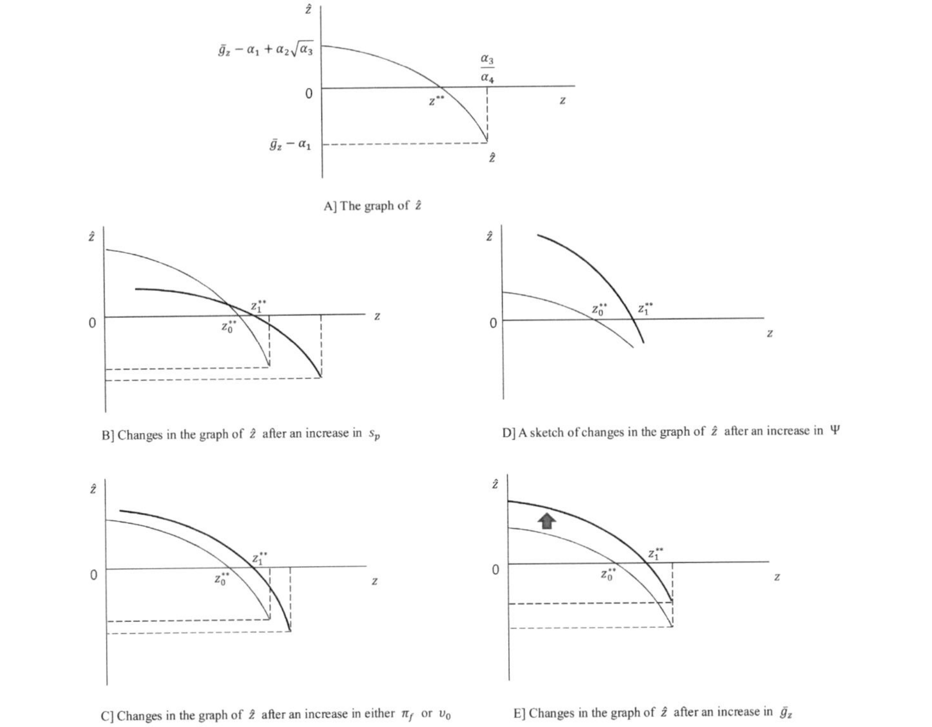


**Fig. A17.** (A) The graph of $\hat{z}$, (B) Changes in the graph of $\hat{z}$ after an increase in $s_p$, (c) Changes in the graph of $\hat{z}$ after an increase in either $\pi_f$ or $\upsilon_0$, (D) A sketch of changes in the graph of $\hat{z}$ after an increase in $\Psi$, (E) Changes in the graph of $\hat{z}$ after an increase in $\bar{g}_z$.

## Appendix B. List of symbols in the approximate order of appearance

$\sigma$ saving to capital stock ratio
$s_p$ propensity to save out of profits
$\pi$ share of profits out of national income
$q$ output: real national income
$K$ stock of capital
$u$ output to capital stock ratio: proxy for the rate of capacity utilization
$Z$ autonomous consumption of capitalists
$z$ ratio of autonomous consumption of capitalists to the capital stock
$u_n$ normal rate of capacity utilization
$g$ rate of accumulation
$\gamma$ expected secular growth rate of sales
$\gamma_u$ responsiveness of investment to the rate of capacity utilization
$p$ price level
$w$ nominal wage rate
$\varpi$ real wage rate
$\varpi_w$ real wage rate target of labor unions
$\varpi_f$ real wage rate target of firms
$\Omega$ bargaining power of labor unions
$\Psi$ bargaining power of firms
$\phi_u$ adjustment parameter relating changes in $u$ to the gap between $g$ and $\sigma$
$E$ employment level
$e$ rate of employment: the employment to labor force ratio
$n$ growth rate of active population
$y$ average labor productivity
$\pi_f$ profit share target of firms
$\pi_w$ profit share target of labor unions
$\upsilon_0$ autonomous factor determining $\pi_w$
$\upsilon_1$ parameter relating $\pi_w$ to the growth rate of the employment rate
$\bar{g}_z$ growth rate of autonomous consumption of capitalists
$qf$ full-capacity output
$r$ rate of profit on the capital stock
$\phi_n$ adjustment parameter relating changes in $n$ to the gap between $g$ and $n$
$\phi_\gamma$ adjustment parameter relating changes in $\gamma$ to the gap between $g$ and $\gamma$

## References

Allain, O., 2015. Tackling the instability of growth: a Kaleckian-Harrodian model with an autonomous expenditure component. Cambridge J. Econ. 39 (5), 1351–1371.

**Cassetti, M., 2002.** Conflict, inflation, distribution and terms of trade in the Kaleckian model. In: Setterfield, M. (Ed.), The Economics of Demand-Led Growth, Challenging the Supply-Side Vision of the Long Run. Edward Elgar, Cheltenham, pp. 189–211.

**Cassetti, M., 2003.** Bargaining power, effective demand and technical progress: a Kaleckian model of growth. Cambridge J. Econ. 27 (May (3)), 449–464.

**Dutt, A.K., 2006.** Aggregate demand, aggregate supply and economic growth. Int. Rev. Appl. Econ. 20 (3), 319–336.

**Dutt, A.K., 2018. Some observations on models of growth and distribution with exogenous autonomous demand growth. Metroeconomica,** http://dx.doi.org/10.1111/meca.12234.

**Fazzari, S., Ferri, P., Variato, A.M., 2018.** 'Demand-led Growth and Accommodating Supply', FFM Working Paper No 15. Hans-Böckler-Stiftung.

**Fiebiger, B., 2018.** Semi-autonomous household expenditures as the causa Causans of postwar US business cycles: the stability and instability of Luxemburg-type external markets. Cambridge J. Econ. 42 (1), 155–175.

**Franke, R., 2017.** A simple approach to overcome the problems arising from the Keynesian stability condition. Eur. J. Econ. Econ. Policies Interv. 14 (1), 48–69.

**Freitas, F., Serrano, F., 2015.** Growth rate and level effects: the stability of the adjustment of capacity to demand and the Sraffian supermultiplier. Rev. Political Econ. 27 (3), 258–281.

**Girardi, D., Pariboni, R., 2016.** Long-run effective demand in the US economy: an empirical test of the Sraffian Supermultiplier model. Rev. Political Econ. 28 (4), 523–544.

**Hein, E., 2018.** Autonomous government expenditure, growth, deficits, debt and distribution. J. Post Keynes Econ. 41 (2), 316–338.

**Lavoie, M., 2014.** Post-Keynesian Economics: New Foundations. Edward Elgar, Cheltenham.

**Lavoie, M., 2016.** Convergence towards the normal rate of capacity utilization in neo-Kaleckian models: the role of non-capacity creating autonomous expenditures. Metroeconomica 67 (1), 172–201.

**Lavoie, M., 2017.** Prototypes, reality and the growth rate of autonomous consumption expenditures: a rejoinder. Metroeconomica 68 (1), 194–199.

**Maddison, A., 1992.** A long-run perspective on saving. Scand. J. Econ. 94 (2), 181–196.

**Nah, W.J., Lavoie, M., 2017.** Long-run convergence in a neo-Kaleckian open-economy model with autonomous export growth. J. Post Keynes. Econ. 40 (2), 223–238.

**Nah, W.J., Lavoie, M., 2019.** Convergence in a neo-Kaleckian model with endogenous technical progress and autonomous demand growth. Rev. Keynes. Econ. 7 (3).

**Rowthorn, R.E., 1977.** Conflict, inflation and money. Cambridge J. Econ. 1 (September (3)), 215–239.

**Sasaki, H., 2011.** Conflict, growth, distribution, and employment: a long-run Kaleckian model. Int. Rev. Appl. Econ. 25 (5), 539–557.

**Serrano, F., 1995a.** Long period effective demand and the Sraffian supermultiplier. Contrib. Polit. Econ. 14, 67–90.

**Serrano, F., 1995b.** The Sraffian Multiplier, PhD dissertation, Faculty of Economics and Politics. University of Cambridge.

**Stockhammer, E., 2004.** Is there an equilibrium rate of employment in the long-run? Rev. Political Econ. 16 (1), 59–74.

**Summers, R., Heston, A., 1984.** Improved international comparisons of real product and its composition: 1950-1980. Rev. Income Wealth 30 (2), 207–262.

REVIEW OF POLITICAL ECONOMY
2020, VOL. 32, NO. 4, 511–537
https://doi.org/10.1080/09538259.2020.1810875



# Overhead Labour Costs in a Neo-Kaleckian Growth Model with Autonomous Non-Capacity Creating Expenditures

Marc Lavoie [a,b] and Won Jun Nah [c]

[a]University of Ottawa, Ottawa, Canada; [b]University of Sorbonne Paris Nord (CEPN, France), Villetaneuse, France; [c]Kyungpook National University, Daegu, Korea

**ABSTRACT**

A notable feature of income distribution is the widening wage differential among workers: there is a redistribution in favour of managers at the detriment of ordinary workers. The paper incorporates this distinction between overhead managerial labour and direct labour into a neo-Kaleckian growth model with target-return pricing, where an autonomously growing demand component ultimately determines the long-run path of an economy. Our aim is to explore the role of overhead labour costs in the coevolution of income distribution and economic growth. We find that the profit share becomes an increasing function of the rate of capacity utilization, implying that empirical research based on the post-Kaleckian specification of investment is likely to be biased in finding a profit-led regime. Our model also features convergence to a fully adjusted position. We examine the parametric conditions under which the model achieves a wage-led growth regime in the long run, in the restricted sense that both the average rates of accumulation and utilization decrease during the transitional dynamics arising from an upward adjustment of the normal profit rate. Moreover, it is shown that a more equitable wage distribution between managers and ordinary workers will strengthen the wage-led nature of the economy.

**ARTICLE HISTORY**
Submitted 20 February 2020
Accepted 22 June 2020

**KEYWORDS**
Neo-Kaleckian; growth; overhead labour; autonomous expenditures; target-return pricing

**JEL CODES**
E11; E37; O41

## 1. Introduction

The popular success of the book of Thomas Piketty (2014) has rekindled interest in the study of income inequality (and possibly wealth inequality) among all strands of economic thought. One of the key features of post-Keynesian economics is its concern with the effects of changes in functional income distribution on economic activity as well as the impact of the evolution of economic activity on income distribution. Over the last twenty years, an enormous literature has been developed by post-Keynesian authors on the relationship between the profit share, or the wage share, and economic activity or economic growth, both from a theoretical angle and through empirical studies (Lavoie and Stockhammer 2013). What the work of Piketty and his colleagues throughout the world has however also underlined is the importance of income inequality arising from an

**CONTACT** Marc Lavoie mlavoie@uottawa.ca

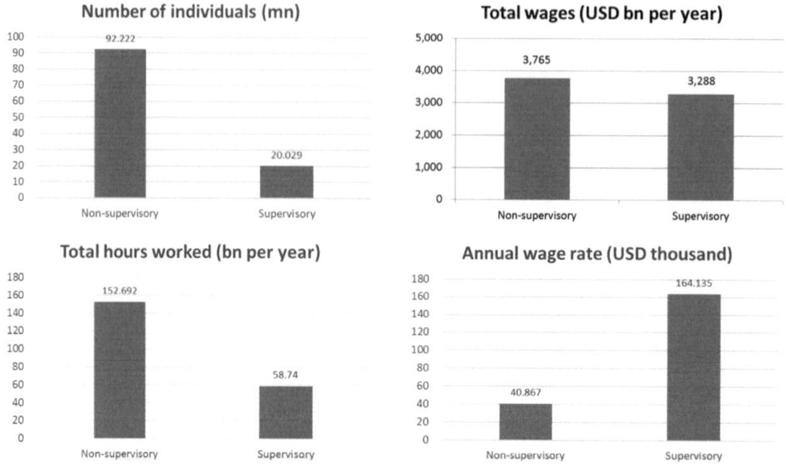


**Figure 1.** Labour indices of non-supervisory and supervisory workers. Source: Mohun (2014), Computations based on data provided by Simon Mohun.

unequal income distribution within wage-earners — a feature that had been left relatively unexplored by post-Keynesian authors.

Thus one of most notable feature of income distribution over the last 40 years is the widening wage differential among workers: there is a redistribution in favour of top management at the detriment of ordinary workers. How can this be taken into account within a macroeconomic model of growth and income distribution which, by tradition, only distinguished between wages and profits, or at best between wages, net profits and rentier income? In this paper we propose to subdivide wage-earners into two categories, overhead labour and direct labour. Overhead labour, or white-collar workers, will be associated with persons holding managerial positions or what the Bureau of Labor Statistics (BLS) in the United States calls supervisory workers. By contrast, direct labour, or blue-collar workers, will be associated with persons designated as non-supervisory workers.

Simon Mohun is one of the few scholars who has taken interest in this distinction at the empirical level. Figure 1 below shows numbers for the year 2010 and is taken from data that he collected from the BLS and that he to one of the current authors, and which is at the origin of the study found in Mohun (2014). Figure 1 shows that the distinction between non supervisory and supervisory workers is not innocuous and has a substantial sociological and economic meaning. While supervisory workers represent less than 20 per cent of all workers (more exactly, 18 per cent), their average annual salary is over four times that of non-supervisory workers, so that they gather nearly half of all the wages and salaries that were paid out in 2010.[1] As one would expect from the work of Piketty, there has been a huge evolution through the years. Back in 1964, while supervisory

[1]A large part of this discrepancy in annual salary income can be attributed to the big difference in the number of hours worked per year. On the basis of a 50-week year, non-supervisory workers work 33.1 hours per week, while supervisory workers appear to compile no less than 58.6 hours per week. The discrepancy in worked hours is similar throughout the 1964–2010 period.

workers also represented slightly less than 18 per cent of the workforce, their annual wage income was only 2.3 times that of non-supervisory workers, so that their share of total wages and salaries was less than one third. This is a further justification for devising macroeconomic models that can take some account of this evolution in the widening annual wage differential between workers.

Our intent in this paper is to introduce the distinction between non-supervisory (direct labour) and supervisory workers (overhead labour) into a neo-Kaleckian model of growth and distribution. While there are dozens of such models, only very few of them incorporate this distinction. The first authors to do so, but in static models, were Asimakopulos (1970) and Harris (1974). In growth models, the distinction was introduced by Rowthorn (1981), Kurz (1990), Nichols and Norton (1991), Lavoie (1992, 1995, 1996, 2009, 2014), Dutt (1992, 2012) and Nikiforos (2017). In all these works, overhead labour is indeed a fixed cost and 'assumed to move in proportion to production capacity' (Steindl 1979, 3).[2] A second set of authors — Tavani and Vasaudevan (2014), Ederer and Rehm (2020) as well as Palley (2005, 2015, 2017) — also consider two classes of wage earners (workers and managers), but the relative wage revenue of the two classes remains constant whatever the level of economic activity, thus implicitly assuming that employment in both classes move in proportion to output. We believe this is a shortcoming, as it cannot capture the short-run fluctuation of the profit share. We shall follow instead the lead of the first set of authors, where the salaries of managers are truly considered as a fixed cost.

Relative to these previous works, the peculiarity of our paper is that this distinction between overhead and direct labour is set within a neo-Kaleckian growth model with autonomously growing expenditures that do not by themselves create production capacity. There is now a general recognition that this may be an appropriate way to model basic stylized facts of modern economies with access to credit, as argued in particular by Fiebiger (2018), who claims that what he calls semi-autonomous expenditures — household investment made possible by mortgages and debt-financed personal consumption expenditures — are the main drivers of the US economy (cf. Leamer 2015). Published papers developing this new approach, which is related to the so-called Sraffian supermultiplier of Freitas and Serrano (2015) and Serrano and Freitas (2017), can first be found in Allain (2015) and Lavoie (2016). A number of other papers have extended this line of research in various directions and with different autonomous expenditures, as in Allain (2019), Dutt (2019), Hein (2018), Fazzari, Ferri, and Variato (2020), Lavoie (2017a), Pariboni (2016), and Nah and Lavoie (2017, 2019a, 2019b). All these papers provide a new closure consistent with fundamental Keynesian features, where saving adjusts to investment through an endogenous average propensity to save despite constant marginal propensities to save, while requiring neither an endogenous rate of capacity utilization nor an endogenous pricing mark-up.

The next section presents the key equations of our model, notably how the amount of direct and overhead labour are determined, and it calculates the algebraic values of the various shares of income that go to profits, the salaries of managers and the wages of direct labour when firms set prices on the basis of a target-return pricing formula. We

[2]As far as we know, Rolim (2019) is the only empirical work on wage-led and profit-led demand regimes that splits the wage share into the shares going to supervisory and non-supervisory personnel. More about this will be said in the conclusion.

shall see that the profit share and the share of wage income going to managers depend on the realized rate of capacity utilization. As Steindl (1979, p. 3) puts it, 'we need to distinguish between those shifts to or from profits which are due to effective demand, and those that result from changed price-cost relations independent of demand'. This means that in a neo-Kaleckian model with overhead costs the profit share can no longer be considered as an exogenous parameter, being instead an endogenous variable. This means that a slightly different definition of wage-led demand is needed, one that in our model will depend on the target rate of return of firms. In the third section we analyse the determinants of the short-run equilibrium, having previously discussed the shape of the saving and investment functions. In particular we discuss the conditions under which an increase in the target rate of return or in the wage rate of managers relative to that of direct workers has a negative impact on the rate of capacity utilization. We also study the impact of such changes on the profit share, taking note that an increase in the target rate of return does not necessarily lead to an increase in the profit share. In the fourth section, we shall study the long-run equilibrium of the model. At this stage we introduce a path-dependent adjustment, such that the growth rate of sales expected by firms react to realized values. We examine what happens in the long run when a less equitable wage distribution between supervisory and non-supervisory workers is being imposed to our model economy. We also examine the conditions under which the model achieves a wage-led demand regime, in the restricted sense that both the average rates of accumulation and of utilization decrease during the transitional dynamics arising from an upward adjustment of the target rate of return in the pricing equation. The last section will recap the main features of the model and its main results, relating some of these to two very recent empirical studies.

## 2. The Model Economy

The model economy is a closed economy with no government, where households and monopolistically competitive firms interact. We borrow the basic assumptions from Lavoie (2009) for our artificial economy. Firms are owned and managed by a subset of households, who are the shareholders of firms while at the same time providing managerial, or supervisory, i.e., overhead labour services for the firms. On the other hand, the rest of households, do not save and provide ordinary, i.e., direct labour services for the firms. The (nominal) wage rate is given by $w$ for direct labour and $\sigma w$ for overhead labour, where $\sigma$ is the wage premium of overhead labour over that of direct labour, with $\sigma > 1$.[3]

The number of direct workers, $L_d$, varies proportionally to the level of production, $q$, while that of overhead workers, $L_f$, for *fixed* labour, hinges on productive capacity, $q_{fc}$ i.e., *full*-capacity output. For some constants $y_d$ and $y_f$, we have $q = y_d L_d$ and $L_f = q_{fc}/y_f$ . This implies that direct labour costs are variable and overhead labour costs are fixed with respect to $q$, once the stock of capital, $K$, is given. With $f \equiv y_d/y_f$, we can measure the size of $L_f$ relative to $L_d$ when the economy is operating at full capacity (when $q = q_{fc}$). The productivity of direct labour is given by $y_d$. As to the overall labour

[3]Other formulations of the wage remuneration of overhead labour are possible. Lavoie (2009, p. 390) suggests that the real wage of overhead workers be a given, thus avoiding that autonomous increases in the mark-up of firms reduce their real remuneration.

productivity $y$, taking both direct and overhead labour into account, it is a pro-cyclical variable as it depends positively on the rate of capacity utilization, $u = q/q_{fc}$, as shown below:[4]

$$y = \frac{q}{L_d + L_f} = \frac{y_d}{1 + f/u} \tag{1}$$

National income is divided into profits and wages, and the latter is again divided into wages to overhead labour and wages to direct labour. Let $\pi$ denote the *net* share of profits out of national income, while $m$, where $m$ stands for '*m*anagers', denotes the share of national income that goes to overhead labour. Hence, $(\pi + m)$ amounts to what we can call the gross share of profits, as it is determined by the percentage gross costing margin of firms over direct unit costs (Lee et al. 1986). From now on we will refer to $\pi$ as simply the share of profits.

Let us assume that workers involved with direct labour, save nothing and consume all their wages.[5] In our model economy, total saving is then made up of three components: saving from the retained earnings of firms; saving out of the salaries of the managers and out of received dividends; and a negative component, which is dissaving due to autonomous consumption.[6] Let us further assume that firms retain a proportion $s_f$ of their net profits, and that households who receive overhead salaries and dividends save a constant proportion $s_h$ of both components of these revenues.[7] These dividends are thus a proportion $(1 - s_f)$ of net profits. We assume that $0 < s_f < 1$ and $0 < s_h < 1$.

With $Z$ the real autonomous consumption expenditure, total saving can then be expressed as:

$$s_f \pi q + s_h[mq + (1 - s_f)\pi q] - Z \tag{2}$$

Dividing equation 2 by $K$, the capital stock, we have a saving function expressed in growth terms, $g_s$, such that:

$$g_s = s_f \frac{\pi u}{v} + s_h\left[\frac{mu}{v} + (1 - s_f)\frac{\pi u}{v}\right] - z \tag{3}$$

[4]As Kaldor (1964, p. xvi) puts it, 'short-period labour costs per unit of output are not constant, but falling (mainly on account of the influence of "overhead labour")'.

[5]Of course, some of the non-supervisory workers may dissave, but we shall assume that as a group they neither save nor dissave. Similarly, a fraction of supervisory workers may be dissaving by getting access to credit. Explicit dissaving by direct workers would require an analysis of household debt and wealth dynamics, which would greatly complicate the model, as others who have dealt with poor and rich households have found out in previous articles, and it would lead us away from our main task.

[6]These two components of saving and dissaving by managers are among the peculiarities of our model compared to Lavoie (1995, 2014) for instance.

[7]This comes down, as mentioned earlier, to assume that shareholders are at the same time managers. Making a distinction between managers (who earn salaries, save and hence receive profits on their accumulated financial wealth) and pure capitalists (who only receive capital income) would imply the consideration of three classes and the addition of the dynamics of the shares of capital accumulated by managers on one hand and pure capitalists on the other, and thus make our model even more complex. Ederer and Rehm (2020) have something of the sort, with either workers who save and capitalists who don't work in their basic model, or with both workers and managers who work and save in their extended model, thus considering in both models the determinants of their respective shares of financial capital with differential rates of return. Dutt (1990), assuming the presence of pure capitalists and workers who save, as did Pasinetti (1962), was the first author to examine the endogenous determination of the shares of wealth in a neo-Kaleckian model. Palley (2017) has a structure similar to Ederer and Rehm's extended model, but his shares of wealth are exogenous.

where $v = K/q_{fc}$ is the capital-to-capacity output ratio which is assumed to be constant, and where $z = Z/K$ is the relative magnitude of non-capacity creating autonomous expenditures compared to the volume of capital.

There is quite a bit of empirical evidence that firms use target-return pricing (Lee 1998). Under this pricing procedure, the price is set in such a way that a normal rate of profit $r_n$ will be achieved when the economy is running at the normal rate of utilization of capacity, i.e., when $u = u_n$.[8] Lavoie (2014, p. 333) shows that under these conditions the price is given by:

$$p = \left[1 + \frac{r_n v}{u_n - r_n v}\right]\left[\left(1 + \frac{\sigma f}{u_n}\right)\left(\frac{w}{y_d}\right)\right] = \left[1 + \frac{r_n v + \sigma f}{u_n - r_n v}\right]\frac{w}{y_d} = \left[\frac{u_n + \sigma f}{u_n - r_n v}\right]\frac{w}{y_d} \quad (4)$$

The first expression reflects the necessary percentage net costing margin on the normal unit cost which is the sum of the unit direct labour cost and of the unit normal overhead labour cost. The next two expressions reflect the percentage gross costing margin on the unit direct labour cost $(w/y_d)$. Obviously, any increase in the target rate of return $r_n$ or in the relative overhead cost $\sigma f$ requires a higher mark-up. For equation 4 to be positive, it must be that:

$$u_n > r_n v \quad (5)$$

Notice that the inverse of the last term inside the squared bracket, given by $(u_n + \sigma f)/(u_n - r_n v) > 1$, happens to be the income share of direct labour, $d$, where $d$ is for '*d*irect labour', since the numerator of equation 6 is the revenue (in real terms) of direct labour while the denominator is total output:

$$d = \frac{(w/p)L_d}{q} = \frac{(w/p)}{y_d} = \frac{u_n - r_n v}{u_n + \sigma f} \quad (6)$$

From equation 6, we can see that an increase in the target rate of return — the normal rate of profit $r_n$ — will lead to a fall in the share of income going to direct labour. Similarly, when there is an increase in the proportion of supervisory workers (measured by $f$ at full capacity) or in the wage premium going to managers (measured by $\sigma$), the share of income going to direct labour gets reduced. This is because the percentage mark-up on unit direct costs, as can be ascertained from equation 4, is raised.

In a similar way, the income share that goes to overhead salaries, $m$, becomes:

$$m = \frac{(\sigma w/p)L_f}{q} = \frac{\sigma f}{u}\left[\frac{u_n - r_n v}{u_n + \sigma f}\right] \quad (7)$$

It follows that the share of profits is equal to:

$$\pi = 1 - d - m = 1 - \left[1 + \frac{\sigma f}{u}\right]\left[\frac{u_n - r_n v}{u_n + \sigma f}\right] \quad (8)$$

We may thus gather from the above that the overall share of income that goes into the hands of the managers/shareholders is equal to $M = m + (1 - s_f)\pi$. But we will not

[8]Target-return pricing is a specific version of normal-cost pricing, where the estimated unit cost is calculated at the standard rate of capacity utilization, which corresponds to normal output, also called nowadays *budgeted output* (Lee 2013).

deal with this measure anymore, except to say that it can be shown that this share becomes smaller with a higher rate of capacity utilization, all else equal.

From equations 7 and 8, it is clear that the share of profits, $\pi$, is an increasing function of the rate of utilization of capacity, $u$, while the share of overhead salaries, $m$, decreases in $u$. With overhead labour present, an increase in the rate of utilization due to an increase in effective demand brings about changes in the composition of labour, increasing the relative proportion of direct labour and decreasing that of overhead labour. Thus, as Steindl (1952, p. 46) made clear,

> the net profit margin can, in fact, change for two quite different reasons: either because of a change in utilisation of capacity, with an otherwise unchanged structure of costs and prices; or the net profit margin can change at a *given level of utilisation of capacity*. The latter type of change will take place, for example, if the gross profit margins change.[9]

This will happen in particular if the target rate of return $r_n$ changes or if there is a change in the relative overhead labour cost, represented by the combined parameters $\sigma f$.

That the profit share has a contemporaneous positive response to an increase in the actual rate of capacity utilization implies that the share of profits itself can be a poor indicator either of the expected profitability or of the relative bargaining position of capital in the class conflict. The point was made early on by Rowthorn (1981, p. 21) when he noted that there was no necessary positive relationship between the mark-up and the profit share, and it was reasserted by Lavoie (1995, 2014, p. 422, 2017b). And as Palley (2017, p. 50) puts it: 'If the profit share is a positive function of capacity utilization, shifts of the IS schedule can make it look empirically as if the economy is profit-led when it is in fact wage-led'. It was in this vein that Weisskopf (1979) suggested the concept of the 'corrected share of profits', which here we denote by $\pi_c$, and which we define as follows:

$$\pi_c = 1 - d - m\frac{u}{u_n} \tag{9}$$

Evidently, $\pi_c$ corrects the actual share of overhead salaries by making it proportional to the actual utilization rate relative to its normal rate.[10] Hence, the uncorrected share of profits seen from the cost (or supply) side, which we shall call $\pi^s$, and the corrected one $\pi_c$ can be contrasted by comparing equations 10 and 11 below, obtained after some manipulations of equations 8 and 9, respectively:

$$\pi^s = \frac{(\sigma f + r_n v)u - (u_n - r_n v)\sigma f}{u(u_n + \sigma f)} \tag{10}$$

$$\pi_c = \frac{r_n v}{u_n} \tag{11}$$

Notably, out of $(d,\ m,\ \pi^s,\ \pi_c)$, only $d$ and $\pi_c$ are independent of the rate of utilization while the others are not. In this respect, we argue that, when we consider the post-Kaleckian investment function of the Bhaduri-Marglin (1990) type, the true indicator of the expected profitability or of the relative power of capital in the class struggle should be

[9]Original emphasis.

[10]Weisskopf (1979) defined the corrected profit share by multiplying the income share of overhead labour by the ratio of output relative to full-capacity output, but consistency with the target-return formula requires that it be multiplied by the ratio of output relative to normal output.

$\pi_c$ (or inversely $d$), or rather $r_n$ itself, instead of the traditional measure $\pi$. This is because, in the presence of overhead labour, the traditional share of profits $\pi$ will not succeed in isolating the pure effects of profitability on accumulation, as has been repeatedly argued by Weisskopf (1979), Sherman and Evans (1984), and most recently by Lavoie (2017b), to name a few.

It is interesting to note that the corrected share of profits $\pi_c$ is impervious to any change in the wage differential between supervisory and non-supervisory workers. By contrast, the share of profits $\pi$ will move up or down as a consequence of an increase in the wage premium going to managers, measured by $\sigma$,[11] depending on whether the actual rate of capacity utilization is higher or lower than the normal rate of utilization, as the following equation shows:

$$\frac{\partial \pi^s}{\partial \sigma} = \frac{f(u - u_n)(u_n - r_n v)}{u(u_n + \sigma f)^2} \tag{12}$$

Note that this partial derivative is valid for a given rate of utilization. This means that the profit-share curve seen from the supply side (equation 10), drawn in $(u, \pi)$ space, shifts down if $u < u_n$ and shifts up if $u > u_n$ as $\sigma$ increases. This is illustrated in Figure 2.

We may now deal with the last elements of the model. The saving function can be reformulated with an explicit consideration of our target-return pricing formula as can be found in Appendix 1. In this paper, we assume that the investment function takes the standard form of those neo-Kaleckian models that are concerned with a possible convergence towards the normal rate of capacity utilization:[12]

$$g_i = \gamma + \gamma_u(u - u_n) \tag{13}$$

$g_i$ is the rate of accumulation of capital, i.e., investment divided by $K$. The first term on the right-hand side, $\gamma$, represents the secular expected growth rate of sales. The coefficient $\gamma_u$ captures the sensitivity of induced investment to changes in effective demand, i.e., to changes in the rate of capacity utilization.

## 3. Equilibrium in the Short Run

For analytical tractability, we introduce a distinction between the short and the long run into our model economy. We define the short run as the time period during which the capital stock, $K$, does not change, thus implying that there is no expansion of production capacity as of yet. It is also assumed that over the short run there is no change in the expectation of the firms about future sales growth, $\gamma$, and in the autonomous consumption of managers, $Z$. All these variables will be allowed to adjust in the long run.

[11]This is also true of a change in the proportion of supervisory workers, measured by $f$ at full capacity. However, we focus on $\sigma$ because, as recalled in the introduction, the variable $f$ seems to have hardly changed through time.

[12]Some readers may wonder why we don't use the investment function advocated by Bhaduri and Marglin (1990), with the share of profits as an additional component to the function used here. Besides the reason given in the main text, with overhead costs the share of profits becomes an endogenous variable that does not measure profitability at normal capacity utilization. Furthermore, Pariboni (2016, p. 426) has shown that in a model with autonomous non-capacity creating expenditures and the Bhaduri-Marglin investment function, the profit-led regime 'is no longer a feasible option: an increase in the profit share leads to a reduction in the equilibrium degree of capacity utilization, regardless of the relative magnitude of the parameters involved'. There is thus no advantage in making use of this more complicated investment function.

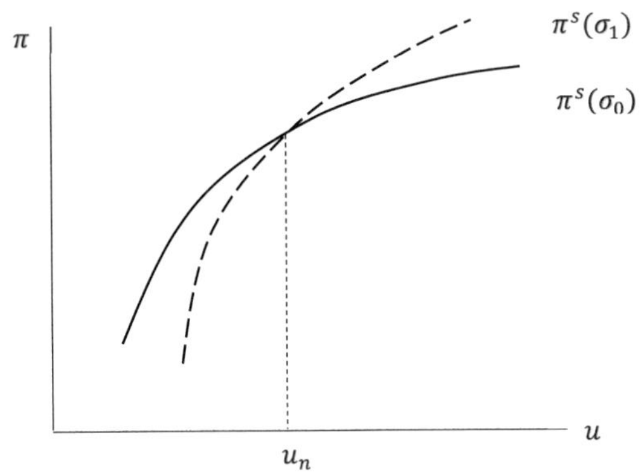


**Figure 2.** Profit curves seen from the supply side for a larger overhead wage premium, $\sigma_0 < \sigma_1$.

The short-run equilibrium is achieved by adjustments in the rate of utilization of capacity so as to equate $g_s$ to $g_i$ (so that saving equals investment, or alternatively, so that aggregate supply equates aggregate demand). The equilibrium rate of utilization of capacity will be denoted by $u^*$, as determined in Appendix 1. For the short-run equilibrium to be stable, the following Keynesian stability condition must be met, derived from the fact that the slope of the saving curve (equation A2) must be steeper than that of the investment curve (equation 13), which also implies that the denominator of $u^*$ as determined in Appendix 1 must be positive:

$$[s_f(1-s_h)+s_h](\sigma f + r_n v) - \gamma_u v(u_n + \sigma f) \equiv A > 0 \tag{14}$$

We can also obtain the short-run equilibrium values of the share of profits, $\pi^*$, the rate of profit, $r^*$, and the rate of accumulation, $g^*$, as found in Appendix 1.

A simple comparative statics exercise shows that both the short-run equilibrium values of the rate of capacity utilization and of the rate of accumulation are lower when there is a higher normal rate of profit $r_n$. This reveals, as expected from the chosen investment function, the wage-led nature of demand and accumulation of the present model in the short run:

$$\frac{\partial u^*}{\partial r_n} = \frac{-\sigma f v\{s_f(1-s_h) + u^*[s_f(1-s_h)+s_h]\}}{A} < 0 \tag{15}$$

$$\frac{\partial g^*}{\partial r_n} = \gamma_u \frac{\partial u^*}{\partial r_n} < 0 \tag{16}$$

Furthermore, we can evaluate the short-run effects of widening the gap $\sigma$ between the wage rate obtained by overhead labour and the wage rate of direct labour. We have:

$$\frac{\partial u^*}{\partial \sigma} = \frac{f(u_n - r_n v)\{u_n s_f(1-s_h) - u^*[s_f(1-s_h)+s_h]\}}{A(u_n+\sigma f)} \tag{17}$$

Three cases need to be considered:

(a) $\partial u^*/\partial\sigma > 0$ and $\partial g^*/\partial\sigma > 0$, if

$$u^* < \left[\frac{s_f(1-s_h)}{s_f(1-s_h)+s_h}\right] u_n \tag{18}$$

(b) $\partial u^*/\partial\sigma < 0$ and $\partial g^*/\partial\sigma < 0$, if

$$u^* > \left[\frac{s_f(1-s_h)}{s_f(1-s_h)+s_h}\right] u_n \tag{19}$$

And finally, (c) $\partial u^*/\partial\sigma = 0$ and $\partial g^*/\partial\sigma = 0$, if

$$u^* = \left[\frac{s_f(1-s_h)}{s_f(1-s_h)+s_h}\right] u_n \tag{20}$$

A permanent increase in $\sigma$ has a twofold effect. Obviously, it directly increases overhead expenses incurred by firms. This reallocates income from the firms to their managers. With income going to firms, only the ratio $(1-s_f)(1-s_h)$ gets to be spent on consumption by managers; with income going directly to managers, the ratio $(1-s_h)$ gets spent. The former is strictly less than the latter. Moreover, when the value of $s_f$ is higher, the difference between the former and the latter gets bigger. Thus, an increase in $\sigma$ may lead to an increase in consumption and in the rate of utilization as in the (a) case, and this positive redistribution effect is amplified with a bigger $s_f$. We can see that, the higher is $s_f$, the more likely is the (a) case, since the term inside the squared bracket on the far right of (18) increases in $s_f$. The (a) case is more likely once the term inside the bracket is big enough, and vice versa:

$$\frac{\partial}{\partial s_f}\left[\frac{s_f(1-s_h)}{s_f(1-s_h)+s_h}\right] > 0 \tag{21}$$

However, this is not the whole story. As is evident from equation 6, an increase in $\sigma$ lowers the income share that goes to direct labour, whose propensity to consume is assumed to be unitary. This is because of the target-return pricing strategy: as equation 4 shows, an increase in overhead costs will lead to an increase in the percentage mark-up over unit direct labour costs and hence to a fall in the real wage of direct labour. A widening gap in wage rates shifts income away from the poor to the rich. Due to the difference in their respective propensities to save, this change yields a shrinking effect on the economy as in the (b) case. This is to be expected because if managers receive higher wages but save most of it, the potential positive effect of this change will be that much smaller. Also, it is apparent that, as $s_h$ gets smaller, the difference in the propensities to consume of direct labour and overhead labour diminishes, and hence the negative effect caused by the redistribution towards the overhead labour is dampened. This makes the (b) case less likely. It is consistent with the fact that the term in the squared bracket on the far right of (19) decreases in $s_h$:

$$\frac{\partial}{\partial s_h}\left[\frac{s_f(1-s_h)}{s_f(1-s_h)+s_h}\right] < 0 \tag{22}$$

These two effects are in conflict with each other. The former positive effect is due to the redistribution towards the managers away from the retained earnings of the firms, and the latter negative effect is due to the redistribution towards managers away from direct labour. Unless the former dominates the latter, the less equitable structure of wages resulting from an increase in $\sigma$ turns out to reduce effective demand in the short run, as in the (b) case. From the discussions above, we can conclude that the (b) case is more likely to occur than the (a) case when the marginal propensity to save of managers, which is $s_h$, is high and when the retention ratio of firms, which is $s_f$, is low. We can also conclude from the fact that the term inside the bracket of the right hand side of either equation 18 or 19 is smaller than unity that in the neighbourhood of the normal rate of capacity utilization $u_n$, the effect on economic activity of an increase in wage dispersion will be negative.[13]

Coming now to the effects on the profit share as a consequence of an increase in the wage premium obtained by overhead labour, i.e., of an increase in wage dispersion, we plug (equation 7) into the saving function (equation 3), thus obtaining a saving function with only the profit share and the rate of utilization as endogenous variables, and then equate this saving function to the investment function (equation 13) to get the profit share as a function of the rate of utilization:

$$\pi^d = \frac{1}{s_f + s_h(1 - s_f)}\left[\nu\gamma_u - s_h\sigma f\left(\frac{u_n - r_n\nu}{u_n + \sigma f}\right)\right] + \frac{\nu(\gamma - \gamma_u u_n + z)}{u[s_f + s_h(1 - s_f)]} \tag{23}$$

Equation 23 is the profit share seen from the demand side and can be contrasted with equation 10, which is seen from the opposite cost side. Evaluating the partial derivative with respect to $\sigma$, while holding the rate of utilization constant in equation 23, we have:

$$\frac{\partial\pi^d}{\partial\sigma} = -\frac{fs_h u_n(u_n - r_n\nu)}{[s_f + s_h(1 - s_f)](u_n + \sigma f)^2} < 0 \tag{24}$$

This implies that the profit-share curve seen from the demand side (equation 23), drawn in $(u,\ \pi)$ space, shifts down in a parallel fashion when the wage premium of managers, $\sigma$, increases. This is illustrated in either Figure 3(A or B), depending on whether the term $(\gamma - \gamma_u u_n + z)$ in equation 23 is positive or negative.[14]

Table 1 summarizes the effects of an increase in $\sigma$ (the wage premium of overhead labour) on the rate of utilization and on the share of profits when the combined effects on the demand and supply sides are taken into consideration. With regards to the impact of an increase in the wage differential on the short-run equilibrium share of profit, an analytical discussion is provided in Appendix 2. As to the impact of this increase on the rate of capacity utilization, the possible cases were explained above with the help of equation 17. The detailed graphical illustrations corresponding to the various cases of Table 1 can be found in Figure 4(A and B).

[13]As an illustration if the retention ratio of firms is 0.6 while the propensity to save of managers is 0.1, and with a normal rate of utilization equal to 0.8, an increase in $\sigma$ will have a negative impact on the rate of utilization as long as $u^* > 0.675$. So this should be the more frequent case.

[14]Obviously, in the case where managers do not save ($s_h = 0$), there will be no shift of the demand-side profit-share curve, as occurred in Lavoie (1995). Note that we consider only the case where the profit-share curve (equation 10) is steeper than (equation 23) as in Figure 4(B) because the rate of utilization must decrease when there is an increase in the target rate of return, as shown by the sign of the derivative given by equation 15, and this can only happen if the slope of equation 10 is steeper than that of equation 23.

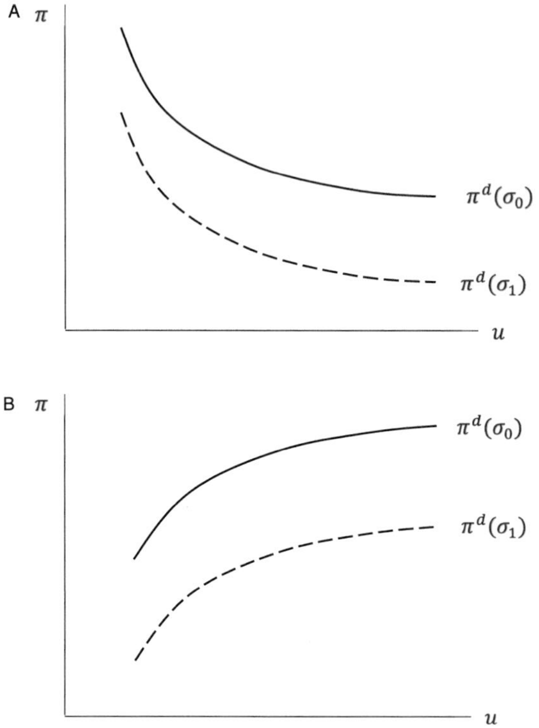


**Figure 3.** (A) Profit curves seen from the demand side for a larger overhead wage premium, with $\gamma - \gamma_u u_n + z > 0$ and $\sigma_0 < \sigma_1$. (B) Profit curves seen from the demand side for a larger overhead wage premium, with $\gamma - \gamma_u u_n + z < 0$ and $\sigma_0 < \sigma_1$.

We may also briefly examine what happens to the rate of capacity utilization and to the share of profit in the short-run equilibrium when there is an increase in the target rate of return. We already know from equation 15 that the rate of capacity utilization will be lower. What happens to the share of profits can be ascertained by checking Figure 5

**Table 1.** The short run effects of an increase in $\sigma$, the wage premium of overhead labour.

| | Utilization rate | $du$ | $d\pi$ | Figure |
|---|---|---|---|---|
| $\gamma - \gamma_u u_n + z > 0$ | $u > u_n$ | (−) | ? | 4(A1) |
| | $\left[\frac{s_f(1-s_h)}{s_f(1-s_h)+s_h}\right]u_n < u \leq u_n$ | (−) | (−) | 4(A2) |
| | $u < \left[\frac{s_f(1-s_h)}{s_f(1-s_h)+s_h}\right]u_n$ | (+) | (−) | 4(A3) |
| $\gamma - \gamma_u u_n + z < 0$ | $u > u_n$ | (−) | (−) | 4(B1) |
| | $\left[\frac{s_f(1-s_h)}{s_f(1-s_h)+s_h}\right]u_n < u \leq u_n$ | (−) | (−) | 4(B2) |
| | $u < \left[\frac{s_f(1-s_h)}{s_f(1-s_h)+s_h}\right]u_n$ | (+) | ? | 4(B3) |

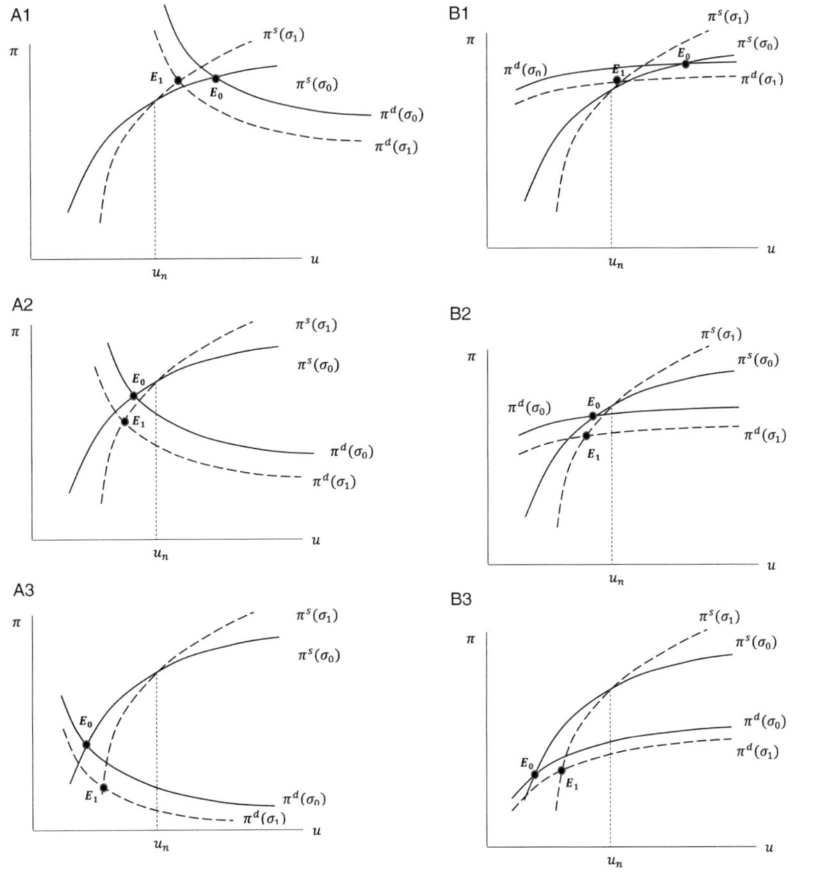


**Figure 4.** (A1) The effects of an increase in the overhead wage premium $\sigma$ for the case of $\gamma - \gamma_u u_n + z > 0$ and $u > u_n$. Note: Due to an increase in $\sigma$, the $\pi^s$ curve tilts counterclockwise and the $\pi^d$ curve shifts down. The economy moves to point $E_1$ once it starts from point $E_0$. The same explanation applies to Figure 4(A2, A3, B1, B2 and B3). (A2) The effects of an increase in the overhead wage premium $\sigma$ for the case of $\gamma - \gamma_u u_n + z > 0$ and $\left[\frac{s_f(1-s_h)}{s_f(1-s_h)+s_h}\right]u_n < u < u_n$. (A3) The effects of an increase in the overhead wage premium $\sigma$ for the case of $\gamma - \gamma_u u_n + z > 0$ and $u < \left[\frac{s_f(1-s_h)}{s_f(1-s_h)+s_h}\right]u_n$. (B1) The effects of an increase in the overhead wage premium $\sigma$ for the case of $\gamma - \gamma_u u_n + z < 0$ and $u > u_n$. (B2) The effects of an increase in the overhead wage premium $\sigma$ for the case of $\gamma - \gamma_u u_n + z < 0$ and $\left[\frac{s_f(1-s_h)}{s_f(1-s_h)+s_h}\right]u_n < u < u_n$. (B3) The effects of an increase in the overhead wage premium $\sigma$ for the case of $\gamma - \gamma_u u_n + z < 0$ and $u < \left[\frac{s_f(1-s_h)}{s_f(1-s_h)+s_h}\right]u_n$.

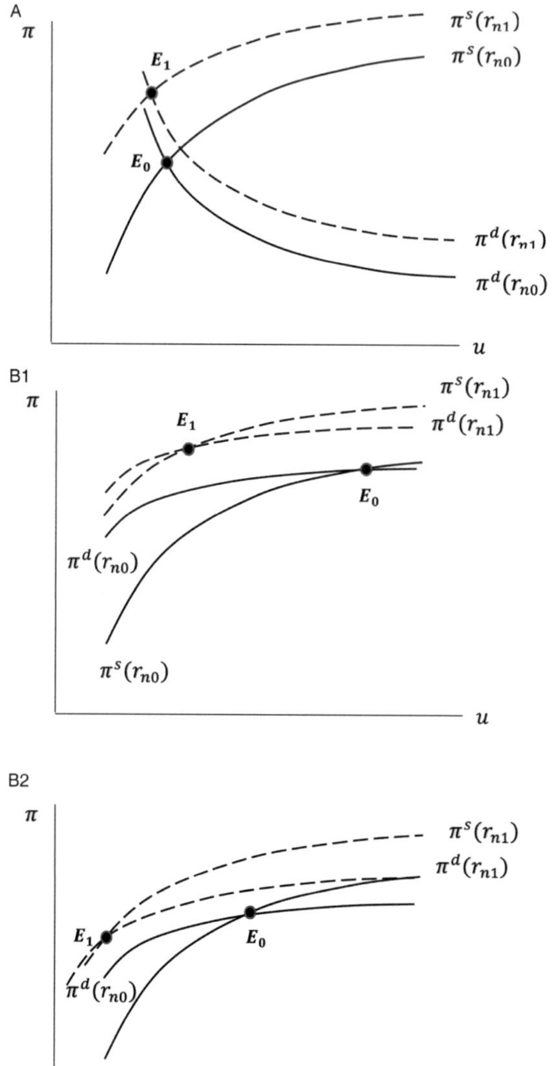


**Figure 5.** (A) The effects of an increase in the target rate of return $r_n$ for the case of $\gamma - \gamma_u u_n + z > 0$. Note: Due to an increase in $r_n$, both the $\pi^s$ curve and the $\pi^d$ curve shift up. The economy moves to point $E_1$ once it starts from point $E_0$. The same explanation applies to Figure 5(B1 and B2). (B1) The effects of an increase in the target rate of return $r_n$ for the case of $\gamma - \gamma_u u_n + z < 0$: $\Delta\pi^* > 0$. (B2) The effects of an increase in the target rate of return $r_n$ for the case of $\gamma - \gamma_u u_n + z < 0$: $\Delta\pi^* < 0$.

(A and B). From equation 10, it is obvious that a rise in the normal rate of profit $r_n$ shifts up the curve representing the profit share $\pi^s$ seen from the cost side:

$$\frac{\partial \pi^s}{\partial r_n} = \frac{(\sigma f + u)v}{u(u_n + \sigma f)} > 0 \tag{25}$$

From equation 23, we can ascertain that a rise in the normal rate of profit also shifts up the curve representing the profit share $\pi^d$ seen from the demand side:

$$\frac{\partial \pi^d}{\partial r_n} = \frac{s_h \sigma f v}{[s_f + s_h(1 - s_f)](u_n + \sigma f)} > 0 \tag{26}$$

However, it can be worthwhile to emphasize that, for any value of $u$, the $\pi^s$ curve seen from the cost side shifts upward vertically more than does the $\pi^d$ curve seen from the demand side, when responding to an increase in $r_n$. This can be verified by comparing the relative magnitude of the two partial derivatives as follows:

$$\frac{\partial \pi^s}{\partial r_n} - \frac{\partial \pi^d}{\partial r_n} = \frac{v}{u_n + \sigma f}\left[\left(1 + \frac{\sigma f}{u}\right) - \frac{s_h}{s_h + s_f(1 - s_h)}\sigma f\right] > 0 \tag{27}$$

The very last fraction in the squared brackets is smaller than unity and it is multiplied by $\sigma f$ which we can also safely assume to be smaller than unity, on the basis of the data provided in Figure 1[15] in the introduction of this paper.[16] Furthermore, it is also evident that the degree with which the $\pi^s$ curve moves up when responding to an increase in $r_n$ decreases in $u$ while the $\pi^d$ curve shifts upward in a parallel fashion, since

$$\frac{\partial}{\partial u}\frac{\partial \pi^s}{\partial r_n} < 0 \tag{28}$$

$$\frac{\partial}{\partial u}\frac{\partial \pi^d}{\partial r_n} = 0 \tag{29}$$

Figure 5(A) corresponds to the case where the term $(\gamma - \gamma_u u_n + z)$ in equation 23 is positive. A rise in the target rate of return is necessarily associated with a higher equilibrium profit share $\pi^*$. Hence in that case the evolution of the profit share will adequately represent the evolution of the stronger bargaining position of firms and this will allow researchers to appropriately assess that the economy is in a wage-led demand regime since the rate of utilization is necessarily lower.

By contrast, in the case where the term $(\gamma - \gamma_u u_n + z)$ in equation 23 is negative, a rise in the target rate of return could associate a lower rate of capacity utilization with a lower equilibrium profit share $\pi^*$, as illustrated with Figure 5(B2). This is apparent due to the

[15]Considering the data presented in Figure 1, we can assume that the employment share of overhead labour at full capacity is 0.2. This implies we can pinpoint the value of $f$ being close to 0.2. Also, considering that the overhead salary rate is close to the quadruple of the wage rate obtained by direct workers, we can pinpoint the value of $\sigma$ being close to 4. Hence, we may safely assume that $\sigma f < 1$, in accordance with the empirical facts.

[16]If the $\pi^s$ curve shifts upward less than the $\pi^d$ curve does, i.e., $\partial \pi^s/\partial r_n < \partial \pi^d/\partial r_n$, then the rate of utilization *increases* after an increase in $r_n$. If the degree to which the two curves shift is the same, i.e., $\partial \pi^s/\partial r_n = \partial \pi^d/\partial r_n$, then the rate of utilization stands still, since the increase in the utilization rate due to the upward shift of the $\pi^d$ curve exactly offsets the decrease in it due to the same amount of vertical shift of the $\pi^s$ curve. However, these two cases are ruled out because equation 15 must hold.

fact that the $\pi^s$ curve shifts up more than the $\pi^d$ curve does after an increase in $r_n$. This is more likely to happen when the propensity to save of managers is close to zero.[17] Empirical researchers would then mistakenly assess that the economy is in a profit-led demand regime.

This can be analysed algebraically. The effect of an increase in the target rate of return $r_n$ upon the equilibrium profit share $\pi^*$ in Appendix 1, is not uniquely determined. It can be shown that it depends on the magnitude of the effect of $r_n$ on $u^*$, and hence on the value of $u^*$, since from:

$$\frac{\partial\pi^*}{\partial r_n} = \frac{(\sigma f/u^*)(u_n - r_n\nu)\dfrac{\partial u^*}{\partial r_n} + \nu(u^* + \sigma f)}{u^*(u_n + \sigma f)} \tag{30}$$

it follows that

$$\frac{\partial\pi^*}{\partial r_n} > 0 \quad \Leftrightarrow \quad \frac{u^*\nu(u^* + \sigma f)}{\sigma f(u_n - r_n\nu)} > \left|\frac{\partial u^*}{\partial r_n}\right| \tag{31}$$

and

$$\frac{\partial\pi^*}{\partial r_n} \leq 0 \quad \Leftrightarrow \quad \frac{u^*\nu(u^* + \sigma f)}{\sigma f(u_n - r_n\nu)} < \left|\frac{\partial u^*}{\partial r_n}\right| \tag{32}$$

## 4. Equilibrium in the Long Run

We now move on to a longer time horizon, and let autonomous consumption, $Z$, increase at the exogenously given rate of $\bar{g}_z$. In this paper, we define the 'long run' as the time period during which our artificial economy ultimately reaches a fully adjusted position, in the sense that the growth rate of sales expected by firms, $\gamma$, is allowed to adjust, while the flow of autonomous consumption relative to the stock of capital, given by $z$, is allowed to move through time. These two variables change through time according to the laws of motion given by equations 33 and 34, where '^' represents the rate of change,

$$\hat{z} = \bar{g}_z - g^* \tag{33}$$

$$\hat{\gamma} = \phi_\gamma(g^* - \gamma) \tag{34}$$

Equation 33 arises straightforwardly from the definition of $z = Z/K$. The assumed given rate of growth of autonomous consumption expenditures is represented by $\bar{g}_z$. Equation 34, where we assume that $\phi_\gamma > 0$, implies that the sales expectations of firms in growth terms react positively to the realized rate of growth. For instance, when the actual growth rate of the economy turns out to be surprisingly high, the expected growth rate of sales will be modified upwards accordingly. This reaction function is often referred to as the Harrodian instability mechanism.

[17] When $s_h = 0$, the $\pi^d$ curve given by equation 23 does not shift at all when there is a change in $r_n$ and hence an increase in $r_n$ necessarily leads to a fall in the profit share.

From equations 33 and 34, the long-run equilibrium solutions are given by:

$$g^{**} = \bar{g}_z \tag{35}$$

$$\gamma^{**} = \bar{g}_z \tag{36}$$

$$u^{**} = u_n \tag{37}$$

The long-run values of other variables can be determined. Straightforwardly from equation 10, the long-run share of profits, $\pi^{**}$, is equal to:

$$\pi^{**} = \frac{r_n v}{u_n} \tag{38}$$

As to the long-run income shares of direct wages, $d^{**}$, and overhead salaries, $m^{**}$, they are:

$$d^{**} = \frac{u_n - r_n v}{u_n + \sigma f} \tag{39}$$

$$m^{**} = \frac{\sigma f}{u_n}\left[\frac{u_n - r_n v}{u_n + \sigma f}\right] \tag{40}$$

Then from equation 3, we have:

$$z^{**} = [s_f(1 - s_h) + s_h]\, r_n + s_h \frac{\sigma f}{v}\left[\frac{u_n - r_n v}{u_n + \sigma f}\right] - \bar{g}_z \tag{41}$$

It is shown in Appendix 3 that, essentially, in this model of autonomously growing non-capacity creating expenditures with overhead labour costs, just as in the standard model without such costs, the presence of the short-run Keynesian stability condition, which is $A > 0$, given by equation 14, also guarantees dynamic stability towards a long-run fully adjusted position, provided there exists a Harrodian adjustment mechanism tied to the investment function and provided this Harrodian instability mechanism is sufficiently weak so that it gets tamed by the growth of autonomous expenditures.

Finally, we evaluate some of the important partial derivatives of $z^{**}$:

$$\frac{\partial z^{**}}{\partial r_n} = s_f(1 - s_h) + \frac{s_h u_n}{u_n + \sigma f} > 0 \tag{42}$$

$$\frac{\partial z^{**}}{\partial \sigma} = \frac{s_h f u_n d^{**}}{v(u_n + \sigma f)} > 0 \tag{43}$$

Recall that the numerator of $z$ grows at a constant rate. Hence, equation 42 implies that when there is an upward adjustment to the target rate of return set by firms, on average the stock of capital grows more slowly than do autonomous expenditures (which grow at the rate $\bar{g}_z$) during the whole traverse between the old and the new long-run equilibrium. Considering the transition dynamics after the change, we can say that the average rate of accumulation has gone down. This is indicative of the wage-led nature of growth in the long run, in the restricted sense that the rate of capital accumulation *on average* gets reduced during the traverse, until it reaches a new long-run position after an increase in the normal rate of profit. This means that the *level* of output will be lower than otherwise it would have been if firms had not decided to raise the target rate of return. What we have is a level effect.

Likewise, for the same reasons, equation 43 implies that a widening gap in the wage obtained by overhead workers relative to that attained by direct workers slows down the accumulation of capital during the traverse to the new long-run solution. During the transition period from the initial to the final state, the average rate of accumulation goes down after an increase in the wage differential between supervisory and non-supervisory workers. This can be interpreted as supporting the prospect for the 'income (or wage) equality-led growth'.[18]

Last but not least, the wage-led nature of growth in the present model economy, which is evident from equation 42, can be shown to be more prominent when wage distribution is more equitable, and hence when the relative wage gap is smaller. This can be demonstrated by the inequality below:

$$\frac{\partial}{\partial \sigma}\left[\frac{\partial z^{**}}{\partial r_n}\right] = -\frac{s_h u_n}{(u_n + \sigma f)^2} < 0 \tag{44}$$

In words, an economy where wage distribution is highly unequal, all else equal, will turn out to be less strongly wage-led in the long run. The positive association that our paper reveals between the wage-led feature of growth and a more equal wage distribution is in line with the recent claims of Carvalho and Rezai (2016) and Palley (2017).

## 5. Conclusion

We have devised a neo-Kaleckian model of growth and distribution where capital accumulation depends on the expected growth rate of sales and on the discrepancy between the actual and the normal rate of capacity utilization, but where the economy is driven by the growth rate of autonomous non-capacity creating expenditures, more specifically by the growth rate of autonomous consumption expenditures, those that Fiebiger (2018) and Fiebiger and Lavoie (2019) call semi-autonomous household expenditures.

The novelty in this neo-Kaleckian model with autonomous expenditures arises from combining three features. First, we distinguish between managerial labour — overhead labour or supervisory workers — on the one hand, and direct labour — or non-supervisory workers — on the other hand. Non-supervisory workers do not save, whereas managers have a given marginal propensity to save out of their salaries and out of the capital income they receive from firms. Managers are the social class that has autonomous consumption expenditures. The saving function is thus more complex than usual in this kind of model.

The employment of direct labour moves proportionately with the level of actual output whereas the employment of managers is tied to the level of full-capacity output. In accordance with the stylized facts noted in the introduction, there is a substantial differential between the wage rate received by overhead labour compared to that obtained by direct labour. It follows that the profit share becomes an endogenous variable, which is a positive function of the level of capacity utilization in the short run, as is often observed in the early

[18]This point has been recognized from the recent experiences in South Korea, where the policies for 'income-led growth' have been implemented, but where it has been observed that the fragmentation of the labour market is a major structural obstacle to the success of the policies. For more on this, see Nah (2018) and Joo et al. (2020).

phase of the business cycle. In addition, because of the presence of overhead labour, the overall labour productivity is a pro-cyclical variable. A possible implication of this feature for future empirical research on wage-led and profit-led demand regimes is that econometricians should be using the corrected profit share $\pi_c$ of equation 9 instead of the actual profit share when doing their estimations.

The second key feature of our model is that we suppose that firms set prices on the basis of a target-return pricing formula. As a consequence, an increase in the wage rate of overhead labour relative to that of direct labour will lead to an increase in the percentage mark-up set by firms, thus modifying in general the income distribution between profits and wages, as well as the distribution between wages going to managers and wages going to direct workers.

The third key feature of the present model with autonomous non-capacity creating expenditures is that in the long run we introduce a slow Harrodian instability mechanism, whereby firms increase the expected growth rate of sales when the actual growth rate is above the one expected by firms.

Several interesting results directly arise from the target-return pricing formula combined to the distinction between overhead and direct labour. First an increase in the target rate of return or in the relative real wage of overhead labour, at a given rate of capacity utilization, leads to a fall in the income share of direct labour. Second, at a given rate of capacity utilization, this increase in the relative real wage of overhead labour will lead to an increase (decrease) in the profit share if this given actual rate of capacity utilization is bigger (smaller) than the normal rate.

Third, in an economy with overhead labour, all else equal, that is, with no change whatsoever in the percentage mark-up over unit direct labour costs, an increase in the rate of utilization leads to a fall in the income share of overhead labour and an increase in the share of profits. Thus, unless the measures of the profit share are corrected for this effect, statistical enquiries will be biased towards finding that the aggregate demand regime is profit-led. We have computed an amended version of the corrected profit share suggested by Weisskopf (1979), where the income share of overhead labour is corrected by the actual rate of utilization relative to the normal rate, and have shown that this measure is both impervious to a change in the actual rate of capacity utilization and in the wage differential between supervisory and non-supervisory workers, as it ought to be when firms use a target-return pricing formula.

Combining now the above supply-side with the demand-side effects, we have shown that in the short run an increase in the bargaining power of firms as reflected by their target rate of return always leads to a fall in the equilibrium rate of capacity utilization and in the rate of accumulation. The model is thus wage-led in the short run, in the sense that an autonomous increase in the costing margin of firms calculated at the normal rate of capacity utilization, i.e., an autonomous increase in the mark-up, leads to a fall in the rate of utilization. In general, this will be accompanied by a rise in the profit share, as one would expect from a wage-led model; but the higher target rate of return may also be associated with a fall in both the rate of utilization and the profit share, thus yielding a false profit-led result.

We have also identified the conditions under which an increase in the wage differential favouring overhead labour (necessarily accompanied by an increase in the mark-up and a fall in the income share of direct labour) will lead in the short run to a fall in the rate of capacity utilization and in the rate of accumulation. This will necessarily occur when the actual rate of utilization is higher than the normal rate of utilization, but it may also happen if the actual rate of utilization is smaller than the normal rate of utilization, provided the actual rate is greater than a certain fraction of the normal rate. This fraction depends on the retention ratio of firms and on the marginal propensity to save of managers. The higher is their marginal propensity to save, the smaller will that fraction be, and hence the more likely it is that more inequality in the distribution of wages will generate lower rates of utilization and of accumulation. This result is intuitive because the redistribution of income from direct labour, who do not save, towards overhead labour, who do save, will reduce aggregate demand, so this negative effect will be particularly strong if the marginal propensity to save of overhead labour is high.

As to the effect of a redistribution of income towards overhead labour on the short-run equilibrium profit share, we have shown that its effect is particularly uncertain. The only thing that can be said with certainty is that if the actual rate of utilization is in-between the same fraction of the normal rate of utilization evoked above and the normal rate of utilization, then more wage inequality will generate a fall in the short-run equilibrium value of the profit share. Otherwise the effect of this redistribution on the profit share can go one way or another. However, it can be asserted that the consequence of an increase in the relative wage of overhead labour is more likely to have a negative than a positive impact on the profit share. Changes in the way wages are split between managers and direct labour thus has effects on the rate of utilization and the profit share, and this ought not to be omitted when doing empirical work on demand regimes.

Finally, we consider the results obtained for the long-run equilibrium of the model. The adjustment mechanism involving the expected growth rate of sales (the Harrodian instability mechanism), combined with the dynamic behaviour of the relative weight of the autonomous consumption expenditures, drives the economy towards a fully adjusted state, at a normal rate of capacity utilization, provided the Keynesian short-run stability condition holds and provided Harrodian instability is not overly strong.

We have shown that an increase in the target rate of return set by firms leads to a fall in the average growth rate during the traverse to the new long-run equilibrium — a result which is consistent with what we had observed in the short run. The economy is thus clearly wage-led, a result which is not really surprising given the formulation of the investment function, given by equation 13, which does not include a term ascertaining expected profitability (at the normal rate of capacity utilization), in contrast to the post-Kaleckian model of Bhaduri and Marglin (1990).

What is more surprising and particularly interesting in the study of the long-run effects of our model is that, despite the ambiguous short run effect on the rate of capacity utilization and the rate of accumulation of an increase in the wage differential favouring supervisory workers, there is no ambiguity with respect to the long-run effect. We have demonstrated that increased inequality in wage distribution necessarily leads to a fall in the average rate of growth of the economy during the traverse from the old to the new long-run equilibrium, thus implying a lower level of economic activity and lower potential output in the long run compared to a situation with no change in wage dispersion.

The main implication of these results, if the model is sufficiently faithful to reality, is that governments should pursue policies that tend to reduce wage dispersion between managerial jobs and non-supervisory jobs, as Palley (2017) also advocates. This calls for a return to egalitarian wage policies or solidarity wage policies. In other words, besides the possibility of a wage-led growth regime, our long-run results provide support for a growth strategy based on wage equality and the imposition of constraints on the perks and salaries obtained by executive managers, such as the imposition of a maximum ratio between executive income and the average or median wage of the other employees of a firm. Efforts to shrink the dispersion of wages by raising the remuneration of those workers at the bottom of the scale also ought to be pursued.

Some final remarks ought to be made regarding the main assumption of our model, which is that by construction the model has a wage-led demand regime. Neo-Kaleckian models of growth and distribution, as well as their empirical versions based on structural equations, have been criticized, among other features, for omitting the possible distributive impact of changes in the rate of utilization on the wage share. Empirical studies conducted with the so-called aggregative VAR approach, which entertain the simultaneous impact of rates of capacity utilization on the wage share and of wage shares on the rate of utilization, used to find systematic evidence of profit-led demand regimes and of profit-squeeze effects (meaning that positive shocks to the rate of utilization lead to a fall in the profit share) — neo-Goodwinian results as alluded to above. But these aggregative results have recently been questioned by new research, which provides support for the Kaleckian model with overhead labour costs that has been presented here, or at least its short-run results.

Michael Cauvel (2019) has pointed out that these aggregative studies use a restrictive specification, such that 'the utilization rate does not have a contemporaneous effect on the wage share'. When that restriction is removed, 'an increase in the wage share is generally found to have a positive effect on the utilization rate … The response of the wage rate to a utilization rate shock is generally small and insignificant' (2019, p. 30). Recall that it is a key feature of the Kaleckian model with overhead labour costs that the rate of utilization has a contemporaneous effect on the wage and profit shares. Furthermore, when dealing with an adjusted wage share and adding the cyclical component of labour productivity, Cauvel (2019, pp. 37–38) finds that 'demand appears to be wage-led and the effects of demand on distribution are found to be mixed or insignificant. Therefore, the results of this disaggregated analysis suggest that the relationship between these variables would be better characterized by wage-led demand and cyclical effects of demand on productivity, rather than a Goodwin cycle pattern'.[19]

Lilian Rolim (2019) has provided further evidence that the Goodwinian profit-led demand regimes and profit-squeeze distributive effects may be spurious. Using the wage and profit shares based on the same data provided by Mohun (2014) as done here, Rolim has verified that using the standard aggregative approach yields the usual Goodwinian results. The results are misleading because they fail to take into account the impact and role of overhead costs. When the wage share is split into the income shares of non-supervisory and supervisory workers, this alternative specification yields results which are quite consistent with the model that has been presented here:

> A positive shock of the workers' share will lead to a decrease in the supervisors' share and to an increase in capacity utilization. A positive shock on the supervisors' share will lead to a

[19]In the working paper version of this article (Nah and Lavoie 2018), we have provided figures illustrating numerical simulations which show that changes in the target rate of return or in the wage premium of overhead labour can produce transitional dynamics that generate a clockwise loop in the $(u, \pi)$ space, and thus loops similar to those defending the neo-Goodwinian profit-led/profit-squeeze story, thus generating a pseudo-Goodwin loop.

> decrease in both the workers' share and in capacity utilization. Finally, a positive shock in capacity utilization will lead to an increase in both the workers and the supervisors' share, but in the first period, there is a small decrease in the latter ... There is evidence that both the workers' and supervisors' shares Granger-cause capacity utilization and that capacity utilization Granger-causes the supervisors' share. (Rolim 2019, pp. 765–766)

Thus, both Caudel and Rolim provide empirical evidence that supports the neo-Kaleckian wage-led model of growth and distribution with overhead labour costs the details of which have been presented here.

Taking into account the strength of the accumulated response functions found by Rolim, there does seem to exist a profit-squeeze mechanism, but the squeeze is done through the supervisors' remuneration, and not through the wages obtained by the non-supervisory workers. The increase in capacity utilization leads to a (non-significant) small increase in the income share of non-supervisory workers and a Granger-caused substantial increase over time in the income share of managers, and thus to a fall in the share of profits. It is the increase in the wage-income share of managers, presumably obtained through various bonuses and salary increases when the economy is doing well, that leads to an eventual fall in the rate of capacity utilization. Thus the political implications that we have already mentioned in our conclusion can be reasserted: to raise aggregate demand, governments should pursue wage-led policies and policies that tend to reduce wage dispersion between managerial jobs and non-supervisory jobs. This conclusion is of course reinforced when considering that a more equal wage distribution could be said to be desirable, on its own, based on ethical grounds.

## Acknowledgments

We thank the two anonymous referees of the journal for their detailed comments which certainly helped to clarify some of the statements of our paper. This research has benefitted in the past from a grant for the study of income distribution issues provided by the Institute for New Economic Thinking (INET). The paper was presented at the 22nd Conference of the Forum for Macroeconomics and Macroeconomic Policies (FMM) in October 2018.

## Disclosure Statement

No potential conflict of interest was reported by the author(s).

## ORCID

*Marc Lavoie* http://orcid.org/0000-0002-9942-1803

## References

Allain, O. 2015. 'Tackling the Instability of Growth: A Kaleckian-Harrodian Model with an Autonomous Expenditure Component.' *Cambridge Journal of Economics* 39 (5): 1351–1371.

Allain, O. 2019. 'Demographic Growth, Harrodian (In)Stability and the Supermultiplier.' *Cambridge Journal of Economics* 43 (1): 85–106.

Asimakopulos, A. 1970. 'A Robinsonian Growth Model in One-Sector Notation – an Amendment.' *Australian Economic Papers*, December: 171–176.

Bhaduri, A., and S. Marglin. 1990. 'Unemployment and the Real Wage: the Economic Basis for Contesting Political Ideologies.' *Cambridge Journal of Economics* 14 (4): 375–393.

Carvalho, L., and A. Rezai. 2016. 'Personal Income Inequality and Aggregate Demand.' *Cambridge Journal of Economics* 40 (2): 491–505.

Cauvel, M. 2019. 'The neo-Goodwinian Model, Reconsidered.' FMM Working paper, No 47, https://www.econstor.eu/bitstream/10419/213403/1/1670248771.pdf.

Dutt, A. K. 1990. 'Growth, Distribution and Capital Ownership: Kalecki and Pasinetti Revisited.' In *Economic Theory and Policy*, edited by B. Datta, S. Gangopadhyay, D. Mookherjee, and D. Roy. Bombay: Oxford University Press.

Dutt, A. K. 1992. 'Stagnation, Growth and Unproductive Activity.' In *The Economic Surplus in Advanced Economies*, edited by J. B. Davis. Aldershot: Edward Elgar.

Dutt, A. K. 2012. 'Growth, Distribution and Crises.' In *From Crisis to Growth? The Challenge of Debt and Imbalances*, edited by H. Herr, T. Niechoj, C. Thomasberger, A. Truger, and T. van Treeck. Marburg: Metropolis.

Dutt, A. K. 2019. 'Some Observations on Models of Growth and Distribution with Autonomous Demand Growth.' *Metroeconomica* 70 (2): 288–301.

Ederer, S., and M. Rehm. 2020. 'Making Sense of Piketty's "Fundamental Laws" in a Post-Keynesian Framework: The Transitional Dynamics of Wealth.' *Review of Keynesian Economics* 8 (2): 195–219.

Fazzari, S., P. Ferri, and A. M. Variato. 2020. 'Demand-led Growth with Accommodating Supply.' *Cambridge Journal of Economics* 44 (3): 583–605.

Fiebiger, B. 2018. 'Semi-Autonomous Household Expenditures as the Causa Causans of Postwar US Business Cycles: The Stability and Instability of Luxemburg-Type External Markets.' *Cambridge Journal of Economics* 42 (1): 155–175.

Fiebiger, B., and M. Lavoie. 2019. 'Trend and Business Cycles with External Markets: Non-Capacity Generating Semi-Autonomous Expenditures and Effective Demand.' *Metroeconomica* 70 (1): 247–262.

Freitas, F., and F. Serrano. 2015. 'Growth Rate and Level Effects: The Stability of the Adjustment of Capacity to Demand and the Sraffian Supermultiplier.' *Review of Political Economy* 27 (3): 258–281.

Harris, D. J. 1974. 'The Price Policy of Firms, the Level of Employment and Distribution of Income in the Short Run.' *Australian Economic Papers* 13 (22): 144–151.

Hein, E. 2018. 'Autonomous Government Expenditure Growth, Deficits, Debt and Distribution in a Neo-Kaleckian Growth Model.' *Journal of Post Keynesian Economics* 41 (2): 316–338.

Joo, S. Y., K. K. Lee, W. J. Nah, and S. M. Jeon. 2020. *The Income-led Growth in Korea: Status, Prospects and Lessons*. Korea Institute for International Economic Policy. (Forthcoming).

Kaldor, N. 1964. 'Introduction.' In *Essays on Economic Policy, Volume 1*, edited by N. Kaldor. London: Duckworth.

Kurz, H. D. 1990. 'Technical Change, Growth and Distribution: A Steady State Approach to Unsteady Growth.' In *Capital, Distribution and Effective Demand: Studies in the Classical Approach to Economic Theory*, edited by H. D. Kurz. Cambridge: Polity Press.

Lavoie, M. 1992. *Foundations of Post-Keynesian Economic Analysis*. Aldershot: Edward Elgar.

Lavoie, M. 1995. 'The Kaleckian Model of Growth and Distribution and its Neo-Ricardian and Neo-Marxian Critiques.' *Cambridge Journal of Economics* 19 (6): 789–818.

Lavoie, M. 1996. 'Unproductive Outlays and Capital Accumulation with Target-Return Pricing.' *Review of Social Economy* 54 (3): 303–321.

Lavoie, M. 2009. 'Cadrisme Within a Kaleckian Model of Growth and Distribution.' *Review of Political Economy* 21 (3): 371–393.

Lavoie, M. 2014. *Post-Keynesian Economics: New Foundations*. Cheltenham: Edward Elgar.

Lavoie, M. 2016. 'Convergence Towards the Normal Rate of Capacity Utilization in Neo-Kaleckian Models: The Role of Non-Capacity Creating Autonomous Expenditures.' *Metroeconomica* 67 (1): 172–201.

Lavoie, M. 2017a. 'Prototypes, Reality and the Growth Rate of Autonomous Consumption Expenditures: A Rejoinder.' *Metroeconomica* 68 (1): 194–199.

Lavoie, M. 2017b. 'The Origins and Evolution of the Debate on Wage-led and Profit-led Regimes.' *European Journal of Economics and Economic Policies: Intervention* 14 (2): 200–221.

Lavoie, M., and E. Stockhammer. 2013. *Wage-led Growth: An Equitable Strategy for Economic Recovery*. Basingstoke: Palgrave Macmillan.

Leamer, E. E. 2015. 'Housing Really is the Business Cycle: What Survives the Lessons of 2008–09?' *Journal of Money, Credit and Banking* 47 (1) supplement: 43–50.

Lee, F. S. 1998. *Post Keynesian Price Theory*. Cambridge: Cambridge University Press.

Lee, F. S. 2013. 'Post-Keynesian Price Theory.' In *The Oxford Handbook of Post-Keynesian Economics: Volume I: Theory and Origins*, edited by G. C. Harcourt and P. Kriesler. Oxford: Oxford University Press.

Lee, F. S., J. Irving-Lessman, P. Earl, and J. E. Davies. 1986. 'P.W.S. Andrews's Theory of Competitive Oligopoly: A New Interpretation.' *British Review of Economic Issues* 8 (19): 13–39.

Mohun, S. 2014. 'Unproductive Labor in the U.S. Economy: 1964–2010.' *Review of Radical Political Economics* 46 (3): 355–379.

Nah, W. J. 2018. 'The First Year of Income-led Growth Policies in Korea: a Post-Keynesian View.' *Journal of Korean Economic Development* 24 (3): 35–64.

Nah, W. J., and M. Lavoie. 2017. 'Long-Run Convergence in a neo-Kaleckian Open-Economy Model with Autonomous Export Growth.' *Journal of Post Keynesian Economics* 40 (2): 223–238.

Nah, W. J., and M. Lavoie. 2018. 'Overhead Labour Costs in a Neo-Kaleckian Growth Model with Autonomous Expenditures.' Working Paper, No. 111/2018, Hochschule für Wirtschaft und Recht Berlin, Institute for International Political Economy (IPE), Berlin. https://www.econstor.eu/bitstream/10419/188924/1/1041257600.pdf.

Nah, W. J., and M. Lavoie. 2019a. 'Convergence in a Neo-Kaleckian Model with Endogenous Technical Progress and Autonomous Demand Growth.' *Review of Keynesian Economics* 7 (3): 275–291.

Nah, W. J., and M. Lavoie. 2019b. 'The Role of Autonomous Demand Growth in a Neo-Kaleckian Conflicting-Claims Framework.' *Structural Change and Economic Dynamics* 51 (December): 427–444.

Nichols, L. M., and N. Norton. 1991. 'Overhead Workers and Political Economy Macro Models.' *Review of Radical Political Economy* 23 (1-2): 47–54.

Nikiforos, M. 2017. 'Uncertainty and Contradiction: An Essay on the Business Cycle.' *Review of Radical Political Economics* 49 (2): 247–264.

Palley, T. 2005. 'Class Conflict and the Cambridge Theory of Distribution.' In *Joan Robinson's Economics: A Centenial Celebration*, edited by B. Gibson. Cheltenham: Edward Elgar.

Palley, T. I. 2015. 'The Middle Class in Macroeconomics and Growth Theory: A Three-Class neo-Kaleckian-Goodwin Model.' *Cambridge Journal of Economics* 39 (1): 221–243.

Palley, T. I. 2017. 'Wage- vs Profit-led Growth: the Role of the Distribution of Wages in Determining Regime Character.' *Cambridge Journal of Economics* 41 (1): 49–61.

Pariboni, R. 2016. 'Autonomous Demand and the Marglin-Bhaduri Model: A Critical Note.' *Review of Keynesian Economics* 4 (4): 409–428.

Pasinetti, L. L. 1962. 'Rate of Profit and Income Distribution in Relation to the Rate of Economic Growth.' *Review of Economic Studies* 29 (4): 267–279.

Piketty, T. 2014. *Capital in the Twenty-First Century*. Cambridge, MA: Harvard University Press.

Rolim, L. N. 2019. 'Overhead Labour and Feedback Effects Between Capacity Utilization and Income Distributions: Estimations for the USA Economy.' *International Review of Applied Economics* 33 (6): 756–773.

Rowthorn, B. 1981. 'Demand, Real Wages and Economic Growth.' *Thames Papers in Political Economy*, Autumn: 1–39.

Serrano, F., and F. Freitas. 2017. 'The Sraffian Supermultiplier as an Alternative Closure for Heterodox Growth Theory.' *European Journal of Economics and Economic Policy: Intervention* 14 (1): 71–90.

Sherman, H. J., and G. R. Evans. 1984. *Macro-Economics: Keynesian, Monetarist and Marxist Views*. New York: Harper & Row.

Steindl, J. 1952. *Maturity and Stagnation in American Capitalism*. Oxford: Blackwell.

Steindl, J. 1979. 'Stagnation Theory and Stagnation Policy.' *Cambridge Journal of Economics* 3 (1): 1–14.

Tavani, D., and R. Vasaudevan. 2014. 'Capitalists, Workers, and Managers: Wage Inequality and Effective Demand.' *Structural Change and Economic Dynamics* 30 (December): 120–131.

Weisskopf, T. E. 1979. 'Marxian Crisis Theory and the Rate of Profit in the Postwar U.S. Economy.' *Cambridge Journal of Economics* 3 (4): 341–378.

## Appendices

### Appendix 1. Characterization of the short-run equilibrium

Taking an explicit account of our target-return pricing formula, we can rewrite our saving function as equation A1, by making use of equations 7 and 8 into equation 3 and rearranging.

$$g_s = \frac{[s_f(1-s_h)+s_h](\sigma f + r_n v)u - s_f(1-s_h)\sigma f(u_n - r_n v)}{v(u_n+\sigma f)} - z \tag{A1}$$

The equilibrium rate of utilization, $u^*$, is then solved for from equations A1 and 13, for given values of $z$ and $\gamma$.

$$u^* = \frac{\gamma - \gamma_u u_n + z + \dfrac{s_f(1-s_h)\sigma f(u_n - r_n v)}{v(u_n+\sigma f)}}{\dfrac{[s_f(1-s_h)+s_h](\sigma f + r_n v)}{v(u_n+\sigma f)} - \gamma_u} \tag{A2}$$

Applying $u^*$, we can solve for the short-run equilibrium values of the share of profits, $\pi^*$, the rate of profit, $r^*$, and the rate of accumulation, $g^*$ as follows.

$$\pi^* = \frac{(\sigma f + r_n v)u^* - (u_n - r_n v)\sigma f}{u^*(u_n+\sigma f)} \tag{A3}$$

$$r^* = \frac{(\sigma f + r_n v)u^* - (u_n - r_n v)\sigma f}{v(u_n+\sigma f)} \tag{A4}$$

$$g^* = \gamma + \gamma_u(u^* - u_n) \tag{A5}$$

Note that for $\pi^*$ and $r^*$ to take on positive values, for otherwise unit direct and overhead costs will not be covered by the value of sales, $u^*$ must be such that:

$$u^* > \left[\frac{u_n - r_n v}{\sigma f + r_n v}\right]\sigma f\ . \tag{A6}$$

### Appendix 2. The effect of an increase in the wage premium going to overhead labour on the short-run equilibrium profit share

Starting from equation 8, we can write

$$\frac{\partial \pi^*}{\partial \sigma} = \frac{u_n - r_n v}{u^{*2}(u_n+\sigma f)^2}\left[\sigma f\frac{\partial u^*}{\partial \sigma} + u^*(u^* - u_n)\right]. \tag{A7}$$

This indicates that, if there is an increase in $\sigma$, the short-run equilibrium share of profits may either increase or get reduced, depending on the sign of the sum of the terms found inside the squared brackets on the far right. It can easily be shown that $\partial\pi^*/\partial\sigma < 0$ if

$$\left[\frac{s_f(1-s_h)}{s_f(1-s_h)+s_h}\right]u_n \leq u^* \leq u_n\,. \tag{A8}$$

This makes sense because we have already seen that, for a given rate of utilization which is lower than its normal level, an increase in the wage differential will generate a decrease in the profit share, while we have just found that if the left-hand side inequality in the relation shown above is verified, then the actual rate of utilization will fall, which means a further fall in the profit share. Otherwise, the sign of $\partial\pi^*/\partial\sigma$ is indeterminate. The first term in the bracket is positive, while the second term is negative, if

$$u^* < \left[\frac{s_f(1-s_h)}{s_f(1-s_h)+s_h}\right]u_n \tag{A9}$$

Contrarily, the first term is negative, while the second is positive, if this time

$$u^* > u_n\,. \tag{A10}$$

This relates to the determination (or indetermination) of the signs of $d\pi$ in Table 1.

## *Appendix 3. Long-run stability*

Equation 41 in the text implies another inequality constraint for autonomous expenditures $Z$ to be positive in the long run. Its growth rate $\bar{g}_z$ cannot be too high:

$$\bar{g}_z < [s_f(1-s_h)+s_h]\,r_n + s_h\frac{\sigma f}{v}\left[\frac{u_n - r_n v}{u_n+\sigma f}\right] \tag{A11}$$

We can also see that the long-run share of saving from firms out of total saving is given by the following relation:

$$\Omega^{**} = \frac{s_f \pi u_n/v}{(\pi + s_h m)u_n/v - z} \tag{A12}$$

This is because both the firms and managers/shareholder should save equal proportions of their own capital stocks in the steady state, so that $\Omega$ converges to a certain constant, $\Omega^{**}$.

$$\frac{s_f\pi q}{\Omega K} = \frac{s_h[mq + (1-s_f)\pi q] - Z}{(1-\Omega)K} \tag{A13}$$

To evaluate the long-run stability of the model, let us form a Jacobian $J$ to be:

$$J = \begin{bmatrix} \dfrac{\partial\hat{z}}{\partial z} & \dfrac{\partial\hat{z}}{\partial\gamma} \\ \dfrac{\partial\hat{\gamma}}{\partial z} & \dfrac{\partial\hat{\gamma}}{\partial\gamma} \end{bmatrix} \tag{A14}$$

Now, we can evaluate each element of $J$ using equations 33 and 34.

$$J = \begin{bmatrix} -\dfrac{\gamma_u}{B} & -1-\dfrac{\gamma_u}{B} \\ \dfrac{\phi_\gamma\gamma_u}{B} & \dfrac{\phi_\gamma\gamma_u}{B} \end{bmatrix}, \tag{A15}$$

where

$$B \equiv \frac{v(u_n+\sigma f)}{A} \tag{A16}$$

with $A$ being the denominator of the short-run rate of utilization as computed in Appendix 1, which must be positive as implied by the short-run stability condition (equation 14) of the main text. From this it follows that

$$Det(J) = \phi_\gamma \gamma_u v(u_n + \sigma f)\, A > 0 \tag{A17}$$

$$Tr(J) = \frac{(\phi_\gamma - 1)\ \gamma_u}{B}\ . \tag{A18}$$

The determinant of $J$ is necessarily positive as long as the usual short-run Keynesian stability condition is fulfilled. It is easy to see that the trace of $J$ can be negative, so that our system turns out to be dynamically stable in its long run, under the condition that

$$\phi_\gamma < 1. \tag{A19}$$

This proves that the long-run stability of the current system of two differential equations is guaranteed by the usual short-run Keynesian stability condition (which implies in particular that the growth rate of capital accumulation of firms does not react too strongly to the discrepancy between the realized and the standard rate of capacity utilization), as long as Harrodian instability is not too severe, i.e., as long as the secular growth rate of sales does not react too strongly to the discrepancy between the actual and the expected growth rate of the economy.

[14]

Received: December 2016 | Revised: September 2017

DOI: 10.1111/meca.12192

ORIGINAL ARTICLE

WILEY METROECONOMICA INTERNATIONAL REVIEW OF ECONOMICS

# Trend and business cycles with *external markets*: Non-capacity generating semi-autonomous expenditures and effective demand

**Brett Fiebiger** | **Marc Lavoie**[1,2]

[1]University of Paris 13 (CEPN)

[2]University of Ottawa

**Correspondence**
Marc Lavoie, Centre d'Économie de Paris Nord, University of Paris 13, 93430 Villetaneuse, France.
Email: mlavoie@uottawa.ca

**Abstract**

The Global Financial Crisis has underlined the importance of developments in the household sector to explaining macro patterns. Some recent papers have discussed the role of non-capacity generating semi-autonomous expenditures in growth theory. This literature ties together several aspects of heterodox thought: growth and distribution; the Sraffian supermultiplier; Duesenberry's relative income hypothesis; the endogenous money approach and Kalecki–Luxemburg external markets. The basic message is that non-wage sources of effective demand, based on mortgage and consumer credit, can play a key role in inducing capacity investment and driving long-run output growth. This article gives a broad overview of the role of financed-induced semi-autonomous expenditures in growth, cycles and crises, and thus criticizes some of the previous approaches that claim to mimic actual cycles while abstracting from these crucial determinants of economic activity.

## 1 | INTRODUCTION

For many post-Keynesians, the principle of effective demand applies just as well in the long run as it does in the short run. Demand growth is reasoned to be the primary determinant of output growth as labour force growth and productivity growth are both responsive to demand growth. Most Marxian-oriented authors concur with post-Keynesians about the short run but doubt that the principle of effective demand reigns supreme in the long run. In an effort to engage with other strands of post-Keynesian economics, Lavoie (2016) has presented a neo-Kaleckian model where accumulation is entirely induced by non-capacity generating semi-autonomous consumption expenditures, along the lines of the Sraffian supermultiplier.[1] These semi-autonomous expenditures can be associated with

[1]See Serrano (1995), Bortis (1997), Cesaratto, Serrano, and Stirati (2003), Cesaratto (2015), Freitas and Serrano (2015), Serrano and Freitas (2017).

  

residential investment, which is heavily financed by mortgages, and with consumer expenditures financed by credit. An extension of the model provides an adjustment mechanism that brings the rate of utilisation back to its normal level, which may provide comfort to those who believe that Harrodian instability mechanisms are at work in real economies. The Great Recession was, however, a crisis with underlying causes that do not fit neatly with Harrodian instability or even Minskyan fragility. Neither Roy Harrod nor Hyman Minsky gave much consideration to household-centred financial dynamics in growth and cycles.

The crisis has revived interest in Veblen-Duesenberry positions on consumer spending as a relatively independent growth motor. If we add that dwelling investment is quasi-consumption, and does not generate capacity, we have some pieces of the macroeconomy to which post-Keynesians perhaps did not give sufficient attention in the past. What components of effective demand are more stable than others may be country and time period specific. Exports have provided a stable source of demand growth over long periods in open developing economies (e.g., the East Asian tigers). In the United States, there is evidence that public expenditures and consumption expenditures are more stable in cyclical dimensions than business investment. Dwelling investment is complex. The early decades of the post-WWII era saw large and sustained cycle-over-cycle rises in the rate of U.S. homeownership. A supermultiplier mechanism is capable of giving insight into the effects of secular trends in dwelling investment on the secular growth rate. There is however also an unstable cyclical dimension to dwelling investment that appears to be an overlooked factor in generating Keynesian unemployment and crises. The recent Global Financial Crisis, which was triggered by rising default rates in U.S. mortgage markets, is a good example of what we mean. As was pointed out a long time ago by Sherman and Evans (1984, p. 158), 'distress in the housing industry has important linkage effects in the economy'. All of this underlines the pragmatic point that the merit of any set of modelling and behavioural assumptions are contingent on the analytical task under investigation.

The analysis proceeds with Section 2 highlighting some of the recurrent issues debated in growth theory. Section 3 discusses differing explanations of business cycles. In Section 4, attention is given to the role of dwelling investment in growth and cycles in U.S. data. Concluding remarks are presented in Section 5.

## 2 | RECURRENT THEMES DEBATED IN GROWTH THEORY

Roy Harrod's (1939) essay on economic dynamics has been subjected to numerous interpretations. Robinson (1949) interpreted Harrod as a growth theorist of a rather uncertain Keynesian pedigree. Among her complaints was Harrod's neglect of income distribution. Robinson also objected to Harrod's replacement of Keynesian unemployment with Marxian unemployment, which he did through his concept of a natural growth rate that is impervious to the level of effective demand and to any policymaking influence. Harrod's immutable natural growth rate provided the inspiration for the neo-classical/Keynesian synthesis. The assumptions of constant technical progress and a constant labour participation rate were also taken up by Goodwin (1967).

Heterodox economists thus have mixed views about Harrod. On the one hand, a case can be made that Harrod sought to extend Keynes' ideas on effective demand to long period analysis. On the other hand, critics point out that Harrod reached the conclusion that thrift drives growth, which is inconsistent with the Keynesian principle of effective demand.[2] We will focus on two broad issues debated by

[2]This claim is stated succinctly by Shaikh (2009, p. 476): 'in HT [Harrodian-type] theory it is the savings rate (thrift) that principally drives growth'.

heterodox economists. A first debate is whether output growth in the long run is driven by the supply side or the demand side. A second debate concerns the stability of growth processes.

## 2.1 | Supply-side or demand-side economics

For post-Keynesians the task of extending the principle of effective demand into the long run requires a recognition of the channels through which demand-derived effects positively impact the supply-side growth in productive capacity. Kaldor's (1957) technical progress function was a seminal contribution. The positive relationship between demand growth and productivity growth is known as the Kaldor-Verdoorn Law. For Kaldor increasing returns to scale can be static or dynamic by affecting technical progress.[3] Labour participation rates are known to be responsive to demand growth. Unemployment hysteresis is another channel. The endogeneity of the natural growth rate forms part of the post-Keynesian reply to the supply-side focus of other traditions (León-Ledesma & Thirlwall, 2002). Kaldor's (1983, 1996) 'cumulative causation' places expansions in effective demand as the main engine of long-run output growth.

What explains a rising trend in the Harrodian economy is unclear. Kalecki (1962) saw Schumpeterian innovation as necessary to explain a rising trend, while remaining sceptical that technical progress would always occur on a sufficient scale to preclude 'the phenomenon of long-run excess capacity, which to a varying degree makes its appearance in a "normal" capitalist economy' (Kalecki, 1962, p. 153). Kalecki (1968b, 1971) would later point to what he called 'external markets' as important to enabling expanded reproduction.

Authors from a Marx-Harrod perspective favour supply-side explanations of growth and cycles. Along these lines Peter Skott (1989) is a long-standing proponent of the Harrodian economy and its underlying hypothesis of Marxian unemployment. In Skott (2010, 2017b) and Skott and Zipperer (2012), the Marxian reserve army takes the explicit form of the employment rate being a negative determinant of the firm sector's investment function (via a so-called 'output expansion function'). High (low) values of the rate of employment beyond some threshold are theorized to cause a deterioration (improvement) of the business climate. As Skott and Zipperer (2012, p. 286) put it: 'we assume that high employment rates (associated with strong workers and a poor business climate) put a damper on accumulation'.[4] It would seem more reasonable to assume that labour shortages, possibly associated with accelerating wage inflation, would 'generate policy responses in the form of increasing interest rates and/or contractionary fiscal policy' (Ryoo & Skott, 2008, p. 361).But this is not the mechanism that Skott endorses in his theoretical work, as he prefers to argue that entrepreneurs will stop producing or investing when the labour market tightens.

## 2.2 | Stability of growth processes

Harrod (1939) is seen as concerned with two instability puzzles: (a) the inconsistency between the warranted and natural growth rates; and, (b) the instability of the warranted growth rate itself. Two distinct modelling approaches to mitigating the second instability puzzle can be identified. One approach nullifies the 'knife edge' instability of the multiplier-accelerator mechanisms. Examples include endogenous

[3] Cesaratto et al. (2003, p. 50) summarise some of the logic: 'Economic growth induces a greater division of labour, facilitates the penetration of new products, and fosters innovative activities by accelerating the recovery of their costs before innovations are imitated ... What historical experience seems to be showing is that fast aggregate demand growth allows more inventions to turn into innovations and that makes output per worker grow faster'.

[4] There are strong similarities with the profit-led and profit-squeeze explanation of business cycles, often associated with Goodwin cycles, as discussed by members of the Social Structure of Accumulation school (see Lavoie, 2017b).

distribution (Kaldor, 1955–1956), endogenous utilisation (Dutt, 1984; Rowthorn, 1981) and endogenous technical change (Dutt, 2006). The second approach can be traced to Hicks (1950) who sought to tame Harrodian instability by imposing ceiling and floors.

In Hicks' trade cycle model, the ceiling is provided by some bottleneck constraint. The floor is provided by the *supermultiplier*. A floor is set at the 'level of income generated by the multiplier when induced investment is zero and only autonomous investments are made' (Trezzini, 1995, p. 43). The supermultiplier concept underpins Kaldorian open-economy models where exogenous exports are the floor and the balance-of-payments constraint is the ceiling (McCombie & Thirlwall, 1994). For Godley and Cripps (1983), it is exports and government expenditures that drive output growth in the long run. Hicks (1950) explained an upward trend by rising autonomous business investment. Duesenberry (1950, p. 472), in his review article, suggested such an explanation was not very plausible: 'It can easily be replaced by introducing an irreversible consumption function which keeps the income in a depression from falling back to the level of the previous depression'.

Several Sraffian economists have extended the Hicks/Kaldor concept of the supermultiplier to long-run accumulation paths.[5] This literature is partly inspired by James Duesenberry insofar as it dispenses with autonomous business investment. Instead, the long-run growth rate of output and accumulation is determined by the growth rate of the semi-autonomous expenditures that do not create any productive capacity. In Cesaratto (2015), Freitas and Serrano (2015) and Lavoie (2016), it is some portion of personal consumption expenditures that is designated as the non-capacity generating semi-autonomous expenditures. That these expenditures represent financial dis-saving, and are significantly financed through debt, ties in with the endogenous money approach and the credit-creating powers of banks. Cesaratto (2015) and Fiebiger (in press) highlight that household sector debt-financed expenditures, while internal to the dynamics of a private capitalist economy, are analogous to an *external market*, as defined by Rosa Luxemburg and Michał Kalecki.

> Nor should the significance of "external markets" in the development of capitalism be disregarded. In particular, in present-day capitalism the "external markets" in the form of government expenditure, especially on armaments, play an important role in the functioning of capitalist economies. This expenditure to the extent that it is financed by loans, or even by taxation of capitalists, contributes to the solution of the problem of effective demand because its effect is not offset by the decline in investment and consumption. (The latter would be the case if this expenditure were financed by indirect or direct taxation of workers.) Thus today the "external markets"; in this particular form are even of greater significance for expanded reproduction than at the time when Rosa Luxemburg propounded her theory (Kalecki, 1968b, p. 79).

Kalecki's (1968b, 1971) appreciation of how Luxemburg's *external markets* can provide a means to temporarily thwart the realisation problem and promote expanded reproduction appears to have been overlooked. Heterodox growth models often posit the simplifying assumptions that capacity investment is financed exclusively by retained profits, worker consumption by wages and capitalist consumption by dividends (and interest income). If households are able to borrow from a financial sector which creates money, and thus do not merely borrow intermediated funds from other households amassed by

[5]See the authors mentioned in footnote 1. Allain (2015) presents a neo-Kaleckian model with the supermultiplier and with public expenditures as the semi-autonomous expenditures. In another contribution Fazzari, Ferri, Greenberg, and Variato (2013) use the supermultiplier to provide a floor under downswings without specifying which expenditures are the semi-autonomous expenditures.

not spending out of income (and by subtracting from firms' revenues), then such debt-financed expenditures will provide an external source of profits.[6]

Sraffian supermultiplier authors focus on non-capacity generating expenditures that have a low volatility (as it is this property which allows the rate of capacity utilisation to adjust to its normal level in the theoretical model). In principle, these *autonomous* expenditures could be consumer spending financed by debt (or by drawing on accumulated financial resources), residential investment, government expenditures and exports. Fiebiger (in press) calculates a measure of *semi-autonomous* household expenditures comprised of household gross fixed investment and the change in consumer credit (with the latter a proxy for debt-financed consumption). In U.S. data, these expenditures are unstable in cyclical dimensions. Thus, expenditures which do not create productive capacity and which correspond to an 'external market' need not have cyclical stability.

A noteworthy contribution of the Sraffian supermultiplier is that it provides another basis for extending the principle of effective demand into a medium- to long-run setting. Such extensions had previously relied on endogenous income distribution, endogenous utilisation rates or endogenous technical change. In models with the Sraffian supermultiplier an increase in the growth rate of semi-autonomous expenditures has level effects during the transition as well as permanent growth effects. Critics of this approach have wondered whether any component of effective demand would ever be *fully* autonomous in the real world; hence, the prefix of *semi* as found in Kalecki (1968a) seems preferable. Obviously, no one believes that the growth rate of the semi-autonomous expenditures would be a constant value in the real world, even on average.

We make these points as some critics of the literature on autonomous and semi-autonomous expenditures advance objections that to us seem misplaced. The context for understanding Skott's (2017a) criticisms is that he believes heterodox economists should be modelling limit cycles which merge destabilising Harrodian investment dynamics with a stabilising Marxian reserve army function. We have a different reading of U.S. data as it concerns the propagating mechanisms in downturns. Part of Skott's (2017a) difficulties appears to be that he mistakes simple models built for expositional and heuristic purposes as suitable for empirical testing (Lavoie, 2017a).[7] There is, for example, no explicit financial relations (and financial constraints) in models with the Sraffian supermultiplier. Most of the canonical growth models have no explicit financial relations. Few would defend the empirical realism of those assumptions although Skott and Zipperer (2012) and Skott (2017b) appear to do so.

Skott and Zipperer (2012) report that their preferred model finds strong support in U.S. data. Their model has no financial stocks (and no channel for interest rates), no public sector (and no channel for proportional taxes), no foreign sector, no inventory dynamics, no dwelling investment, no debt-financed consumption, no overhead labour and an investment function that reduces decisions on output and accumulation down to a negative relation with the rate of employment. It would be remarkable if such a model did have strong empirical support, given its abstraction from the world of complexity in which we live. Skott (2017a, p. 193) wonders if it is realistic to suppose that the 'trajectory of a

[6]With workers providing a non-wage source of effective demand and profits comes many complexities from debt servicing. Evidently, while workers must service debts (over multiple periods), there must be a positive propensity by rentiers to spend out of the interest income (Setterfield and Kim, 2016). The most depressing part of worker borrowing is principal repayments. Those payments curb worker expenditures. Principal repayments to banks are 'destroyed'. For non-bank lending, as principal repayments represent a return of financial capital to creditor agents, such payments are likely to be reinvested in a financial asset (instead of spent on output).

[7]Nor are models with a supermultiplier mechanism presented as opposing the stabilising empirical role played by some counter-cyclical macro policy. Godley and Lavoie (2007) show in a stock-flow consistent model that a functional finance approach to fiscal policy is capable of achieving an equivalent level of macro stabilisation that orthodox economists attribute to monetary policy.

**TABLE 1** Annual growth rate of U.S. output components (in percent), 1955–2015

| | Mean | Standard deviation | Max | Min |
|---|---|---|---|---|
| Gross domestic product | 3.1 | 2.2 | 7.3 | −2.8 |
| Personal consumption expenditures | 3.3 | 1.9 | 7.4 | −1.6 |
| Gross private domestic investment | 4.3 | 9.0 | 27.3 | −21.6 |
| Fixed investment* | 3.4 | 6.4 | 15.1 | −18.2 |
| Non-residential* | 3.7 | 6.2 | 15.9 | −16.5 |
| Residential* | 3.1 | 13.2 | 39.9 | −26.5 |
| Exports | 6.0 | 6.1 | 18.9 | −13.5 |
| Imports | 6.0 | 6.5 | 24.4 | −13.7 |
| Government consumption and investment | 1.9 | 2.5 | 8.7 | −3.2 |

*Adjusted for inflation using a deflator calculated from Tables 1.1.5 and 1.1.6. Source: U.S. Bureau of Economic Analysis, *NIPA*, Tables 1.1.5 and 1.1.6.

significant proportion of aggregate demand would be independent of past, current and expected future income'. One may reply by asking Skott whether it is realistic to suppose that all of the relevant macro dynamics originate within the firm sector and, hence, that there is no role whatsoever for *external markets* to influence growth and cycles. Assigning an exogenous growth rate to a portion of demand is a simplifying assumption. It is a means to investigate an economy where some demand components are less explained than others.

Does anyone believe that the growth rate of public expenditures is induced, and determined, by multiplier-accelerator mechanisms?[8] Possibly Skott's (2017a) concerns may be with the private and foreign sectors. Are there any takers for the view that personal consumption expenditures are more autonomous than business investment? Such a proposition has remained a stylized fact since Duesenberry (1949) drew attention to it. Table 1 illustrates the stability of personal consumption expenditures, but it also shows that residential investment is much more volatile than non-residential investment. As to exports, the possibility of exports driving demand is particularly plausible for open developing economies (Pacheco-López & Thirlwall, 2014).

Consumption is by far the largest component of U.S. output. That it tends to be more stable than output and private investment should be reflected in theory. The renewal of interest in the work of Veblen and Duesenberry has come to be known shorthand as 'keeping up with the Joneses' (Brown, 2008). Duesenberry (1949) advanced an irreversible consumption function. The idea is that once households become accustomed to the higher consumption levels obtained in upswings, it is their reluctance to curb spending, which provides a floor under national income (Trezzini, 2011). Consumption emulation motivated by social status may be a factor in the upward trend in the consumption share of U.S. output since the early 1980s. The rise in the consumption share posed an empirical puzzle as it occurred alongside an increase in wealth and personal income inequality. We now know that rising debt enabled household spending to expand beyond income growth for an extended time period (Barba & Pivetti, 2009, Kim, Setterfield, & Mei, 2014). Stagnating-tendencies from the secular worsening in distribution were masked. As put by Cynamon and Fazzari (2015, pp. 170–171): 'household borrowing postponed the full brunt of inequality-induced demand drag for decades prior to the Great Recession'.

[8]Franke (2017) points to proportional tax rates as another way to tame Harrodian instability.

Obviously, the growth rate of semi-autonomous consumption is not exempt from secular reversions in a balance-sheet recession.

## 3 | WAGE-LED VERSUS PROFIT-LED DEMAND

The paper by Bhaduri and Marglin (1990) gave rise to an empirical debate on whether demand regimes are wage-led or profit-led.[9] The existence of a pro-cyclical profit share, as in the U.S. economy, is often taken as providing support for a Marx-Goodwin interpretation. One concern is that the omission of overhead labour costs (supervisory workers) biases opinion towards a profit-led conclusion. It also debatable whether the phenomenon of growth and cycles can be adequately explained in a framework that focuses only on real wage dynamics. The alternative viewpoint is that financial-real interactions—including a role for Kalecki-Luxemburg 'external markets'—matter on the empirical front.

### 3.1 | The Goodwin cycle view

Goodwin's (1967) 'profit-squeeze' theory of the business cycle has proven popular amongst heterodox economists with a Marxian inclination. Along these lines is the structuralist-Goodwin model of Barbosa-Filho and Taylor (2006) and the preferred model of Skott and Zipperer (2012). Their limit-cycle models posit the classical saving assumptions in the form:

$$P=s_{\pi}P=I=S,\ s_{\pi}=1 \tag{1}$$

where $P$ is profits, $s_{\pi}$ is the propensity to save out of profits, $I$ is capacity investment and $S$ is aggregate saving. In national accounts, the net lending of any group of $i$ sectors is equal to the change in a sectors' net financial assets ($\Delta NFA_i$).[10] An often overlooked implication of the classical saving assumptions is that the $\Delta NFA_i$ of each sector is equal to zero. That is a dubious assumption.

Skott and Zipperer's (2012) preferred model generates a pro-cyclical profit share within the prism of the classical saving assumptions where $\Delta NFA_i=0$ is posited for all sectors. The model has two sectors: firms and workers. A rise in the profit share occurs through a causal process running from some unexplained 'shock' that causes 'excess demand', leading to an 'instantaneous' price inflation (above wage inflation), thus generating an increase in output and a higher profit share 'ex post'. Besides Skott's weird assumption of flex-prices with prices clearing markets in the very short run (also criticized by von Arnim and Barrales, 2015), it is not obvious how workers could create 'excess demand' given that their expenditures are limited to, and always exactly equal to, the wage bill. A more realistic proposition would be to suppose that workers have access to credit. That the $\Delta NFA_i$ of all sectors must sum to zero (i.e., $\sum_i \Delta NFA_i \equiv 0$) does not justify a behavioural hypothesis of $\Delta NFA_i=0$ for each sector. In practice: $\Delta NFA_i \lesseqgtr 0$. One can wonder if abstracting from the financial sphere has any behavioural and empirical plausibility.

From a Keynesian perspective explaining growth and cycles through a negative relationship between the rate of employment and the rate of accumulation is a narrow prism. It is akin to a theory of spontaneous collapse/ignition. Unlike Hicks (1950), who assigned a role to autonomous business investment as providing a floor under downswings, there are no semi-autonomous expenditures in the models of Skott (2010) and Skott and Zipperer (2012). It follows therefore that capacity investment is induced spontaneously by itself and assumed to *lead* cycles. The crucial puzzle from the standpoint of

[9]See Blecker (2016) for a recent overview.

[10]In national accounts, a sector's $\Delta NFA_i$ is equal to its net acquisition of financial assets minus its net issuance of liabilities (before revaluation gains/losses); and, equivalently to its expenditures minus revenues.

an outsider to this approach is the following: why would firms expand productive capacity at troughs when they are bulging in idle capacity? There is a second puzzle within this storyline. Unless firms are able to raise costing margins in a downturn, when taking fixed overhead costs into consideration, low rates of capacity utilisation and low rates of employment should be associated with low profit shares and low profits. Skott's storyline must thus be abstracting from an important feature of real economies —the presence of overhead costs. Going back to Thomas Weisskopf's (1979) classic study, it is shown that profitability is 35% lower in the through of the cycle than it was at the beginning of the second phase of the expansion, when presumably low profitability starts discouraging corporate investment. Why low profitability should encourage firms to speed up investment, as must be the case in Skott's world, is beyond us.

## 3.2 | Alternatives to Goodwin prey-predator mechanisms

The existence of a pro-cyclical profit share is insufficient evidence to claim the relevance of Goodwinian predator-prey mechanisms, where increases in the wage share (and real wage rates), are theorized to crowd-out capacity investment. An alternative explanation is provided by Stockhammer and Michell (2017), who present a formal model where pseudo-Goodwin cycles are generated by financial fragility in the firm sector. Fiebiger (in press) focuses on household-centred financial dynamics in U.S. data. He reports evidence of consistent short-run clockwise cycles in U.S. business cycles over 1954(II)–2009 (II) for the output share of corporate profits and the output shares of household fixed investment and semi-autonomous household expenditures vis-à-vis the rate of employment and the rate of utilisation. It turns out that the output share of corporate fixed investment does not closely follow the profit share, especially around troughs, as is assumed by the classical saving assumptions. Divergent cyclical movements between corporate fixed investment and profits present an empirical conundrum to models based on the classical saving assumptions.

Fiebiger (in press) also shows that the measure of semi-autonomous household expenditures is inversely related to the U.S. household net lending balance, that is, with the financial component of the sector's saving. The household sector's net lending balance is negatively associated with economic activity. Similarly, Barbosa-Filho, Rada, Taylor, and Zamparelli (2008, p. 630) had observed on the U. S. household sector's net *borrowing* balance—the inverse of the net *lending* balance—that the U.S. demand regime is 'household net borrowing led'. Most housing literature points to 'wealth effects' as spurring consumption. Fiebiger (in press) suggests instead that homeownership may create a need for consumer credit, to furnish housing, and to maintain consumption levels at socially-desired norms given the additional drain on income from mortgage servicing (and the costs of the down payment).

Finally, Fiebiger (in press) reports that the growth in household gross fixed investment, and in the proxy for overall semi-autonomous household expenditures, has a strong contemporaneous relation with the growth of corporate profits and economic activity, while the growth of corporate gross fixed investment is a lagged and apparently induced variable. In our opinion, such findings provide support for the role played by Kalecki-Luxemburg's *external markets*. A story about the generation of domestic demand and macro profits is rather different when some portion of expenditures originates from *outside* the firm sector (and this is true regardless of whether those expenditures are 'stable' or 'unstable' in cyclical dimension).

We conclude this section with some remarks on how the supermultiplier alters the neo-Kaleckian model. In the canonical neo-Kaleckian model, faster output growth is associated with a lower investment share. That facet is considered inconsistent with empirical data according to Cesaratto (2015, p. 172): 'A positive relation between the rate of growth and the investment share $I/X$ is a widely recognised stylised fact of economic growth'. A few caveats are actually needed on Cesaratto's stylized fact.

First, if we disaggregate private investment, it turns out that cycles in household fixed investment typically precede those of corporate fixed investment at least in U.S. data, as we will establish below. Second, out of troughs, fast increases in capacity utilisation tend to occur while the output share of corporate fixed investment is falling or stable as per the canonical neo-Kaleckian model. What the supermultiplier adds to the neo-Kaleckian framework is a plausible mechanism for explaining phases of the business cycle when the output share of capacity investment is rising amidst robust rates of output growth.

Consider now the profit relation in models with a supermultiplier mechanism, either the model presented by Freitas and Serrano (2015) or its neo-Kaleckian version as presented by Lavoie (2016). In both versions, the profit share is assumed to be a constant, and there is no internal mechanism to make it change even if the growth rate of autonomous expenditures increases. The inclusion of a supermultiplier mechanism taken on its own is therefore unable to explain a pro-cyclical profit share which many consider to be an important stylized fact in U.S. data. What is often forgotten and what must be underlined is that neo-Kaleckian models with overhead labour costs can account for a pro-cyclical profit share (Lavoie, 1992, 1995, 1996, 2009, 2014, pp. 423–427; Nichols & Norton, 1991; Rowthorn, 1981).[11] Cyclical shifts in $\Delta NFA_i$ are also important to understanding sectoral contributions to effective demand and hence movements in the profit share.

## 4 | CYCLICALLY UNSTABLE DWELLING INVESTMENT AS A GROWTH MOTOR?

Housing markets are clearly important to U.S. cyclical fluctuations. As Leamer (2009) puts it in the title of his paper on U.S. business cycles: 'Housing *Is* the Business Cycle' [emphasis is in original]. Sherman (2010), a Marxian economist with Keynesian longings, likewise reports that dwelling investment tends to be the leading indicator of U.S. real economy activity. This section will begin with some observations on secular trends in U.S. housing markets during the post-WWII era.

The early decades of the post-WWII era is renowned for its stability and general prosperity. Important drivers of the *Golden Age* were high rates of population growth and a large surge in the U.S. homeownership rate, from an average of 43.6% during the 1940s, to 61.9% during the 1960s. It is perhaps no coincidence that the *crisis of overaccumulation* of the 1970s followed the end in the upward trend in the homeownership rate. The *Golden Age* homeownership boom also saw an expansion in household debt relative to income, as shown in Figure 1. At the end of WWII, the U.S. financial sector emerged with a portfolio heavily weighted with low-yielding government securities. Expanding credit access to households was an avenue to higher profitability. A Minskyan dynamic was also at play: expanding credit access to households helped to generate a booming economy and that in turn fed back into a positive credit performance.

From the mid-1960s, until the early 1990s, the U.S. homeownership rate was broadly stable. Again, it was a change in financial practices that pushed the U.S. homeownership rate to new peaks during the U.S. housing market bubble, which began in the mid-1990s, and started to unravel from mid-2006. This time it was an expansion in credit access to subprime borrowers. Finance and financial practices are essential to a story about residential investment and homeownership rates. Dwelling investment can function as an *external market* because such expenditures will usually require external sources of finance, and the banking system extends credit by creating new money, thus creating ex

[11] Skott and Zipperer (2012, p. 294) choose to critique a straw person: 'The Kaleckian model says nothing about the movements in π however'. As Hein (2017) notes, Skott's 'claim that Kaleckians have not thought about feedbacks of demand and growth on income distribution is therefore unwarranted'.

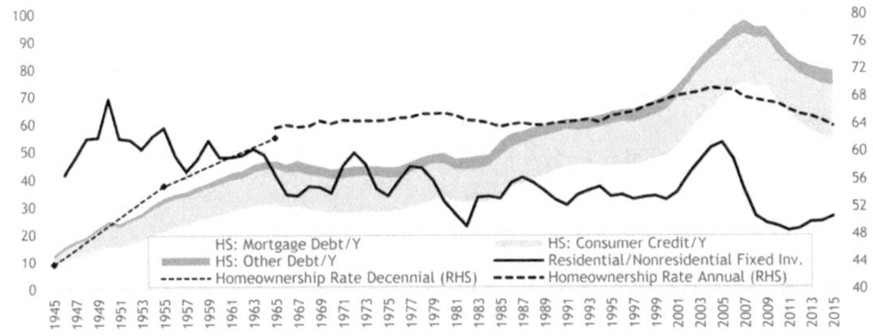


**FIGURE 1** Selected variables for U.S. housing and household sector debt (in percent), 1945–2015
*Sources*. U.S. Federal Reserve, *Financial Accounts of the United States*, Tables F.2 and B.102. U.S. Bureau of Census

nihilo purchasing power that requires no abstinence on the part of other agents.[12] That finance can be extended with some independence from current income is why dwelling investment and debt-financed personal consumption expenditures can lead upswings in the business cycle (even while income growth is weak and the rate of unemployment is relatively high).

A supermultiplier-type mechanism is capable of giving insight into how secular trends in dwelling investment and the homeownership rate affects the secular growth rate. Accordingly, during the transition to a higher secular rate of homeownership, the growth rate of dwelling investment can rise above that of active population. There are level effects during the transition as well as permanent growth effects from the secular rise in the rate of homeownership. It is possible to argue that dwelling investment, while volatile in cyclical dimensions, can be stable in secular dimensions. Clusters of housing activity are a persistent feature of U.S. cycles. Can a component of demand have severe amplitude in cyclical dimensions and yet still be viewed as a driver of the secular growth rate? Such a role is assigned to capacity investment in the Goodwinian limit-cycle models. Still, to the extent that there are housing cycles, this raises questions of endogeneity.

The main point we make on this issue is that the capacity of households to borrow can be relatively independent from income for long periods: the U.S. household debt to output ratio rose from 12.9% in 1945 to a peak of 97.8% in 2007. If during a recession the rise in the rate of unemployment is fairly contained, there may be minimal credit rationing.[13] If there is a large and sustained rise in the rate of unemployment there may be nonlinear feedbacks. Beyond a certain threshold, the rate of unemployment will feed into higher default rates, potentially eroding the buffers of the financial sector and generating a more system-wide credit squeeze.

Panel A in Figure 2 shows the evolution of the rate of employment ($e$) and the real growth rate of corporate gross fixed investment (C-GFI^).[14] Panel B does likewise for the real growth rate of household gross fixed investment (H-GFI^). The positive relation between $e$ and C-GFI^ tends to be fairly contemporaneous. That peaks (lows) in $e$ are followed by falls (rises) in C-GFI^ could possibly support a Harrod-Goodwin explanation of U.S. unemployment and business cycles. Skott and Zipperer (2012) report that high (low) values of $e$ have strong negative (positive) effects on rates of output growth and

[12]For the typical worker, the cost of buying a home will exceed their annual wage and dwarf whatever funds they may be able to save in any given year (including the portion that is inaccessible in pension funds).

[13]In the cycles since 1954(II), the average deterioration in the US employment rate is 3.0 percentage points. The decrease in the creditworthiness of households directly affected by falls in $e$ can be more than offset by the positive effects of counter-cyclical monetary policy on the creditworthiness of households in aggregate.

[14]Note that the symbol ^ denotes the growth rate of variables in real terms. Variables are adjusted for inflation using a deflator calculated from the U.S. Bureau of Economic Analysis' National Income and Production Account Tables 1.1.5 and 1.1.6.

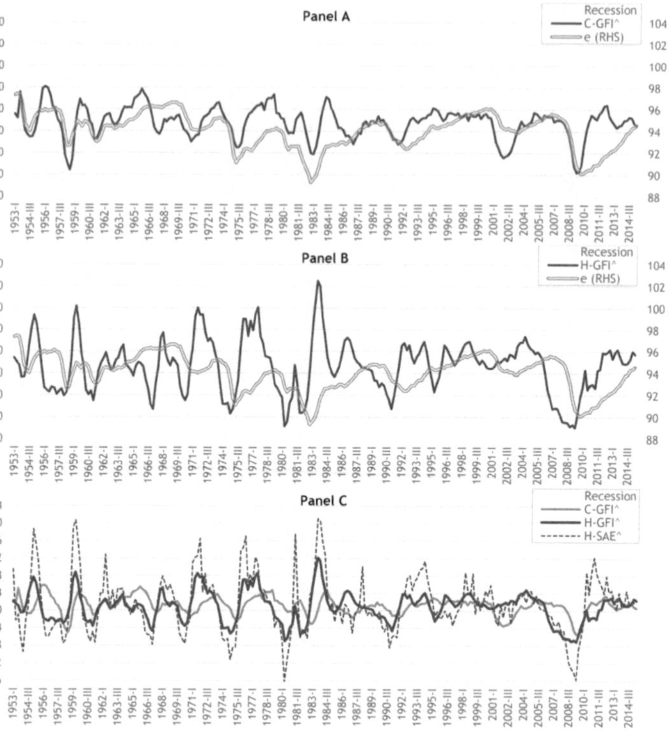


**FIGURE 2** Quarterly annualized real growth rates of selected variables vis-à-vis e (in percent), 1953(I)–2015(II)
*Sources.* St. Louis Federal Reserve, *FRED*. U.S. BEA, *NIPA*, Tables 1.1.5 and 1.1.6

accumulation in U.S. data. What they ignore is the pro-cyclicality of household investment and the attending effects on the level of demand and profitability. Household fixed investment cycles are of greater amplitude than corporate fixed investment cycles. Clusters in household investment occur at the start of cycles, preceding those of the corporate sector, except in the most recent upswing. Typically, in the early phases of cyclical expansion, H-GFI^ expands rapidly even while *e* is low. Low values of *e* do not trigger a spontaneous ignition of corporate fixed investment; instead, it is an increase in aggregate demand from outside the corporate sector which first pushes up rates of capacity utilisation, with induced effects on capacity investment.

Additionally, in every downswing without exception, H-GFI^ collapses while *e* is either stable or rising. Indeed, it is the waning of H-GFI^ that characteristically provides the impetus to contraction in U.S. business cycles (and undermines profitability), not a spontaneous collapse due to high values of *e*. The strong pro-cyclicality of household fixed investment is due partly to counter-cyclical monetary policy. Zezza (2008) presents a stock-flow consistent growth model with residential investment and two types of households: rich and other. Housing demand for the former depends on the return from properties comprised of rents and expected capital gains (and is part of a Tobinesque portfolio allocation of their financial wealth). For the latter, it depends positively on population growth and expected real income growth and negatively on lagged mortgage servicing. Those assumptions appear reasonable. Speculative demand was partly fulfilled in the recent crisis by mortgage-backed securities, nonetheless, a role for speculative buyers in the housing market who are crowded-in by housing price appreciation during booms and wait for a bottom during busts is surely a factor that adds to the magnitude of persistent housing boom and bust cycles.[15]

Panel C in Figure 2 enables comparison between C-GFI^, H-GFI^ and H-SAE^ (recall that H-SAE adds the change in consumer credit to H-GFI). Two points are worth making. First, it does not seem plausible to explain U.S. cycles, including a pro-cyclical profit share, without a role for *external markets* as we have defined them. Those with Marxian proclivities will have to do more than point to a pro-cyclical profit share to justify assumptions of the Marx-Goodwin type.

Second, given the amplitude in household fixed investment cycles (augmented by booms in debt-financed consumption), it is clear that such growth processes are unstable in local dynamics. Can clusters of household fixed investment provide a stabilising role in global dynamics? The answer is yes if household fixed investment cycles are a persistent feature of the economy and their timing is not fully synchronized with corporate fixed investment cycles.[16] The bigger point here is that household-centred financial dynamics can provide a persistent source of cyclical fluctuations and output growth. The dispersal of household fixed investment cycles are not random: the peaks tend to occur during the early phases of the business cycle.[17] All of this may seem very counter-intuitive to those who think that firm-centric multiplier-accelerator mechanisms (and a simple period-over-period accelerationist behavioural hypothesis) capture the essential aspects of dynamic instability and growth processes. Firms finance the majority of fixed investment out of retained profits, by a recycling of yesterday's income. To understand dynamic growth processes we must focus on agents who borrow and spend new money into existence: 'in a dynamic growth process someone must first borrow in excess of any pre-existing amount of financial resources' (Seccareccia, 2011−2012, p. 72).

How can crises and stagnation be explained? Supermultiplier models are not designed to give insight into the nonlinear disruptions of a balance-sheet recession. The simplifying assumption that changes in the growth rate of non-capacity generating semi-autonomous expenditures do not affect distribution can be queried. If workers are undertaking the semi-autonomous expenditures, having recourse to debt, a higher growth rate of those expenditures is likely to be allied with a rise in the financial sector and thereby a shift in distribution.[18] Rising worker debt may have counteracted the stagnating tendencies from the adverse trend in inequality, but it may also have contributed to that trend.

[15]The extent to which dwelling investment can feedback on itself, and beget more dwelling investment by creating booming conditions, may depend on the potential for increases in the homeownership rate such as in the *Golden Age*. If the homeownership rate is already comparatively high, and less elastic, it may be that a cluster of dwelling investment above the growth rate of the active population would run out of steam on its own accord (if the demand for housing units is ultimately linked to the growth rate of the active population). There is, of course, no homogeneous home unit. A story about housing demand is not one solely of home units but add-ons as well (e.g., more expensive fixtures and landscaping, a second or third storey, pools, etc.). Additional complexities arise from existing housing sales which have similar macro-effects to margin lending.

[16]When fixed investment cycles by the household and corporate sectors overlap, as they do for some phases of the business cycle, such growth processes will amplify global divergence. To the extent that peaks and troughs in H-GFI^ cycles (and H-SAE^ cycles) do occur at different times than C-GFI^ cycles, with the former tending to precede the latter, there is also the possibility that two unstable growth processes will at times promote global convergence by having nonsynchronous cycles.

[17]It is worth pointing out that H-GFI^, H-SAE^ and C-GFI^ collapsed mid-cycle in the 1960s. A recession did not ensue due to a large expansion in public expenditures related to the Vietnam War.

[18]One reason is because the distribution of functional income in financial firms is more skewed to profits than in nonfinancial firms (and perhaps also for that between managers and workers). Further, as debt requires interest servicing, there will also be an increase in the income share going to the rentier class. That increase will be in addition to higher dividends that nonfinancial firms may distribute (assuming that an increase in worker debt-financed expenditures bodes for higher profits in the productive sector).

Cynamon and Fazzari's (2015, p. 180) analysis that the stagnating tendencies of rising inequality were postponed for decades in the U.S. economy implies that increasing equality would most likely be pro-growth: 'Demand generation would be stronger if lower income groups received a higher share of total income'. Several post-Keynesians have endorsed this view and provided some empirical evidence (Lavoie & Stockhammer, 2013). Skott (2017b, p. 356) is sceptical: 'It is dangerous to base policy recommendations for lower inequality on their growth-enhancing benefits'. Addressing inequality can be considered an end in itself. It also matters, however, that there is empirical evidence indicating that if policymakers wish to address inequality it 'may serve both equity and growth at the same time' (Ostry, 2015, p. 156).

Why is there crisis and stagnation in the Goodwinian limit-cycle models? The answer is the rate of employment is too high, real wage rates are too high and the profit share is too low. Those who endorse this answer also ask us to imagine that *all* expenditures on current output originate within the firm sector (so consumption is only possible via payments of wages, dividends and interest payments) and to disregard who the financial sector lends to. On our part, we would query any explanation of growth and cycles that excludes channels for financial-real interactions and *external markets*.

## 5 | CONCLUSION

Harrod (1939) provided the impetus to growth theory. Over the decades many post-Keynesians have sought to present an alternative view about the medium run or the long run—a view different from Harrod's underlying hypothesis of Marxian unemployment, with his unexplained trend and no financial-real interaction. The literature on non-capacity generating semi-autonomous expenditures has explored another means to extend the principle of effective demand beyond the short run. At the pedagogical level, models with a Sraffian supermultiplier provide an accessible and coherent story on how expenditures originating in the household, government or foreign sectors can stabilize as well as drive growth processes. Dwelling investment and the complications of a balance-sheet recession are undoubtedly complex. We echo Franke's (2017) sentiment that the perceived problem of taming Harrodian instability can be considered as mastered and it is time to consider other methodological issues.

Over the years, Peter Skott has written a long series of papers criticising the Kaleckian approach to growth and distribution. He seems to believe that everyone should tell a story about Marxian unemployment, and that all models except his are implausible or unconvincing. A limited number of replies have been written, defending the Kaleckian model and expressing reservations with Skott's approach, for example, his instantaneous price adjustments assumed to equate aggregate demand to aggregate supply. Reasons were also given as to why a convergence towards a normal rate of utilisation was either not required or not possible, or alternatively that the normal rate of utilisation could itself be endogenous. Skott and Zipperer (2012) claim that U.S. data supports their preferred model and invalidates the Kaleckian approach. It is disquieting to see that these authors think that simple models with no financial variables could substantiate such claims. Skott (2010) and Skott and Zipperer (2012) also fail to mention the contributions in the Kalecki-Steindl tradition that have considered a more complex macroeconomy with features such as overhead labour and financial variables (including the role of the rentiers).

This paper has built on Kalecki's (1968b, 1971) observations on the contemporary role of *external markets* in enabling expanded reproduction. There is evidence that personal consumption expenditures and government expenditures are more stable than private investment. Many developing economies have made the transition to a more industrialized economy through the path of export-led growth. Those who have studied the characteristics of U.S. business cycles during the post-WWII era tell us that household-centred financial dynamics have always mattered to turning points. In particular, household fixed investment and its associated debt-financed consumption appear to play a key role. The case for Kalecki-Luxemburg *external markets* is compelling. The case for reducing the complexity of firms' decisions on accumulation down to a negative relation with the rate of employment is weak.

## ACKNOWLEDGMENTS

We would like to thank the two referees for their suggestions, which led to some substantial changes. A version of the paper was presented at the Fourth Nordic post-Keynesian conference held in Aalborg in April 2017.

## REFERENCES

Allain, O. (2015). Tackling the instability of growth: A Kaleckian-Harrodian model with an autonomous expenditure component. *Cambridge Journal of Economics*, *39*(5), 1351–1371.

Barba, A., & Pivetti, M. (2009). Rising household debt: Its causes and macroeconomic implications—A long period analysis. *Cambridge Journal of Economics*, *33*(1), 113–137.

Barbosa-Filho, N., Rada, C., Taylor, L., & Zamparelli, L. (2008). Cycles and trends in US net borrowing flows. *Journal of Post Keynesian Economics*, *30*(4), 623–647.

Barbosa-Filho, N., & Taylor, L. (2006). Distributive and demand cycles in the US economy—A structuralist Goodwin model. *Metroeconomica*, *57*(3), 389–411.

Bhaduri, A., & Marglin, S. A. (1990). Unemployment and the real wage: The economic basis for contesting political ideologies. *Cambridge Journal of Economics*, *14*(4), 375–393.

Blecker, R. A. (2016). Wage-led versus profit-led demand regimes: The long and the short of it. *Review of Keynesian Economics*, *4*(4), 373–390.

Bortis, H. (1997). *Institutions, behaviour and economic theory: A contribution to classical-keynesian political economy*. Cambridge: Cambridge University Press.

Brown, C. (2008). *Inequality, consumer credit and the saving puzzle*. Cheltenham: Edward Elgar.

Cesaratto, S. (2015). Neo-Kaleckian and Sraffian controversies on the theory of accumulation. *Review of Political Economy*, *27*(2), 154–182.

Cesaratto, S., Serrano, F., & Stirati, A. (2003). Technical change, effective demand and employment. *Review of Political Economy*, *15*(1), 33–52.

Cynamon, B. Z., & Fazzari, S. M. (2015). Rising inequality and stagnation in the US economy. *European Journal of Economics and Economic Policies: Intervention*, *12*(2), 170–182.

Duesenberry, J. J. (1949). *Income, saving and the theory of consumer behavior*. Cambridge: Harvard University Press.

Duesenberry, J. J. (1950). Hicks on the trade cycle. *Quarterly Journal of Economics*, *64*(3), 464–476.

Dutt, A. K. (1984). Stagnation, income distribution and monopoly power. *Cambridge Journal of Economics*, *8*(1), 25–40.

Dutt, A. K. (2006). Aggregate demand, aggregate supply and economic growth. *International Review of Applied Economics*, *20*(3), 319–336.

Fazzari, S. M., Ferri, P. E., Greenberg, E. G., & Variato, A. M. (2013). Aggregate demand, instability, and growth. *Review of Keynesian Economics*, *1*(1), 1–21.

Fiebiger, B. (in press). Semi-autonomous household expenditures as the *causa causans* of post-war U.S. business cycles: The stability and instability of Luxemburg-type external markets. *Cambridge Journal of Economics*, https://doi.org/10.1093/cje/bex019

Franke, R. (2017). A simple approach to overcome the problems arising from the Keynesian stability condition. *European Journal of Economics and Economic Policies: Intervention*, *14*(1), 48–69.

Freitas, F., & Serrano, F. (2015). Growth rate and level effects, the stability of the adjustment of capacity to demand and the Sraffian supermultiplier. *Review of Political Economy*, *27*(3), 258–281.

Godley, W., & Cripps, F. (1983). *Macroeconomics*. London: Fontana.

Godley, W., & Lavoie, M. (2007). Fiscal policy in a stock-flow consistent (SFC) model. *Journal of Post Keynesian Economics*, *30*(1), 79–100.

Goodwin, R. M. (1967). A growth cycle. In C.H. Feinstein (Ed.), *Socialism, capitalism and economic growth*. Cambridge: Cambridge University Press.

Harrod, R. F. (1939). An essay in dynamic theory. *The Economic Journal*, *49*(193), 14–33.

Hein, E. (2017). Post-Keynesian macroeconomics since the mid 1990s: Main developments. *European Journal of Economics and Economic Policies: Intervention*, *14*(2), 131–172.

Hicks, J. R. (1950). *A contribution to the theory of the trade cycles*. Oxford: Clarendon Press.

Kaldor, N. (1955–1956). Alternative theories of distribution. *Review of Economic Studies*, *23*(2), 83–100.

Kaldor, N. (1957). A model of economic growth. *Economic Journal*, *67*(268), 591–624.

Kaldor, N. (1983). Keynesian economics after fifty years. In D. Worswick & J. Trevithick (Eds.), *Keynes and the modern world* (pp. 1–28). Cambridge: Cambridge University Press.

Kaldor, N. (1996). *Causes of growth and stagnation in the world economy*. Cambridge: Cambridge University Press.

Kalecki, M. (1962). Observations on the theory of growth. *Economic Journal*, *72*(285), 134–153.

Kalecki, M. (1968a). Trend and business cycles reconsidered. *Economic Journal*, *78*(310), 263–276.

Kalecki, M. (1968b). The Marxian equations of reproduction and modern economics. *Social Science Information*, *7*(6), 73–79.

Kalecki, M. (1971). *The problem of effective demand with Tugan-Baranovsky and Rosa Luxemburg*. In M. Kalecki, Selected essays on the dynamics of the capitalist economy (pp. 146–155). Cambridge: Cambridge University Press.

Kim, Y. K., Setterfield, M., & Mei, Y. (2014). A theory of aggregate consumption. *European Journal of Economics and Economic Policies: Intervention*, *11*(1), 31–49.

Lavoie, M. (1992). *Foundations of post-Keynesian economic analysis*. Aldershot: Edward Elgar.

Lavoie, M. (1995). The Kaleckian model of growth and distribution and its neo-Ricardian and neo-Marxian critiques. *Cambridge Journal of Economics*, *19*(6), 789–818.

Lavoie, M. (1996). Unproductive outlays and capital accumulation with target-return pricing. *Review of Social Economy*, *54*(3), 303–321.

Lavoie, M. (2009). Cadrisme within a Kaleckian model of growth and distribution. *Review of Political Economy*, *21* (3), 371–393.

Lavoie, M. (2016). Convergence towards the normal rate of capacity utilization in neo-Kaleckian models: The role of non-capacity creating autonomous expenditures. *Metroeconomica*, *67*(1), 172–201.

Lavoie, M. (2017a). Prototypes, reality and the growth rate of autonomous consumption expenditures: a rejoinder. *Metroeconomica*, *68*(1), 194–199.

Lavoie, M. (2017b). The origins and evolution of the debate on wage-led and profit-led regimes. *European Journal of Economics and Economic Policies*, *14*(2), 200–221.

Lavoie, M., & Stockhammer, E. (Eds.) (2013). *Wage-led growth: An equitable strategy for economic recovery*. Basingstoke: Palgrave Macmillan.

Leamer, E. E. (2009). *Housing is the business cycle*. NBER Working paper. Retrieved from http://www.nber.org/papers/w13428

León-Ledesma, M. A., & Thirlwall, A. P. (2002). The endogeneity of the natural rate of growth. *Cambridge Journal of Economics*, *26*(4), 441–459.

McCombie, J. S. L., & Thirlwall, A. P. (1994). *Economic growth and the balance-of-payments constraint*. London: Macmillan.

Nichols, L. M., & Norton, N. (1991). Overhead workers and political economy macro models. *Review of Radical Political Economics*, *23*(1–2), 47–54.

Ostry, J. D. (2015). Inequality and the duration of growth. *European Journal of Economics and Economic Policies: Intervention*, *12*(2), 147–157.

Pacheco-López, P., & Thirlwall, A. P. (2014). A new interpretation of Kaldor's first growth law for open developing economies. *Review of Keynesian Economics*, *2*(3), 384–395.

Robinson, J. (1949). Mr. Harrod's dynamics. *Economic Journal*, *59*(233), 68–85.

Rowthorn, B. (1981). *Demand, real wages and economic growth* (pp. 1–39). Autumn: Thames Papers in Political Economy.

Ryoo, S., & Skott, P. (2008). Financialization in Kaleckian economies with and without labor constraints. *European Journal of Economics and Economic Policies: Intervention*, *5*(2), 357–386.

Seccareccia, M. (2011–2012). The role of public investment as principal macroeconomic tool to promote long-term growth: Keynes's Legacy. *International Journal of Political Economy*, *40*(4), 62–82.

Serrano, F. (1995). *The Sraffian multiplier* (PhD dissertation), Faculty of Economics and Politics, Cambridge: University of Cambridge.

Serrano, F., & Freitas, F. (2017). The Sraffian supermultiplier as an alternative closure to heterodox growth theory. *European Journal of Economics and Economic Policies: Intervention*, *14*(1), 68–91.

Setterfield, M., & Kim, Y. K. (2016). Debt servicing, aggregate consumption, and growth. *Structural Change and Economic Dynamics*, *36*(1), 22–33.

Shaikh, A. (2009). Economic policy in a growth context: A classical synthesis of Keynes and Harrod. *Metroeconomica*, *60*(3), 455–494.

Sherman, H. J. (2010). *The roller coaster economy: Financial crisis, great recession and the public option*. Armonk: M.E. Sharpe.

Sherman, H. J., & Evans, G. R. (1984). *Macroeconomics: Keynesian, Monetarist and Marxist views*. New York: Harper & Row.

Skott, P. (1989). *Conflict and effective demand in economic growth*. Cambridge: Cambridge University Press.

Skott, P. (2010). Growth, instability and cycles. In M. Setterfield (Ed.), *Handbook of alternative theories of economic growth* (pp. 108–131). Cheltenham: Edward Elgar.

Skott, P. (2017a). Autonomous demand and the Harrodian criticisms of the Kaleckian model. *Metroeconomica*, *68*(1), 185–193.

Skott, P. (2017b). Weaknesses of 'wage-led growth. *Review of Keynesian Economics*, *5*(3), 336–359.

Skott, P., & Zipperer, B. (2012). An empirical evaluation of three post-Keynesian models. *European Journal of Economics and Economic Policies: Intervention*, *9*(2), 277–308.

Stockhammer, E., & Michell, J. (2017). Pseudo-Goodwin cycles in a Minsky model. *Cambridge Journal of Economics*, *41*(1), 105–125.

Trezzini, A. (1995). Capacity utilisation in the long run and the autonomus components of aggregate demand. *Contributions to Political Economy*, *14*, 33–66.

Trezzini, A. (2011). The irreversibility of consumption as a source of endogenous demand-driven economic growth. *Review of Political Economy*, *23*(4), 537–556.

Von Arnim, R., & Barrales, J. (2015). Growth cycles: A response to Peter Skott. *Review of Keynesian Economics*, *3* (3), 387–391.

Weisskopf, T. E. (1979). Marxian crisis theory and the rate of profit in the postwar U.S. *Economy', Cambridge Journal of Economics*, *3*(4), 341–378.

Zezza, G. (2008). U.S. growth, the housing market, and the distribution of income. *Journal of Post Keynesian Economics*, *30*(3), 375–401.

**How to cite this article:** Fiebiger B, Lavoie M. Trend and business cycles with *external markets*: Non-capacity generating semi-autonomous expenditures and effective demand. *Metroeconomica*. 2019;70:247–262. https://doi.org/10.1111/meca.12192

# PART III

# TWO-SECTOR GROWTH MODELS

ELSEVIER Structural Change and Economic Dynamics 8 (1997) 157–175

STRUCTURAL CHANGE AND ECONOMIC DYNAMICS

# The Hicksian traverse as a process of reproportioning: some structural dynamics

J. Henry, M. Lavoie *

*Department of Economics, University of Ottawa, 550 Cumberland Street, Ottawa, Ontario, Canada K1N 6N5*

**Abstract**

The paper picks up the well-known theme of the neoclassical traverse, with full employment of labour and full utilization of capacity maintained throughout the transition, as first developed by Hicks. The focus here is on: the dynamics of the required reproportioning of the capital stock and of the labour force for full employment to be maintained; the dynamics of the subsequent changes in relative prices and distribution variables for effective demand conditions to be fulfilled; and on the graphical representation of such a process of reproportioning. In addition, the unsuccessful traverse in the lesser-discussed cases of unsustainable growth and dynamic instability is also ascertained and graphically illustrated. © 1997 Elsevier Science B.V.

*Keywords:* Traverse; Structural dynamics; Decumulation; Historical path

## 1. Introduction

While many of Hicks's contributions have been extensively developed and even incorporated into textbooks, the notion of traverse analysis, which he presented in 1965, has only been picked up by a handful of authors. This did not distract Hicks from attaching importance to the notion of the traverse until the very end (Hicks, 1990). The reason for this is that Hicks was anxious to place economic analysis *in time*, or what Joan Robinson called historical time. For while economists may spend most of their time studying models at their equilibrium steady states, economies are usually moving along some transitory path, on a traverse.[1]

* Corresponding author.

[1] That traverse is the rule rather that the exception is well argued by Hicks (1983, pp. 61–62): "When one turns to questions of policy, looking toward the future instead of the past, the use of equilibrium methods is still more suspect (...). It may be hoped that, after the change in policy, the economy will somehow, at some time in the future, settle into what may be regarded [in a 'loose' sense] as a new equilibrium; but there must necessarily be a stage before that equilibrium is reached. There must always be a problem of traverse. For the study of a traverse, one has to have recourse to sequential methods of one kind or another." Joan Robinson (1979, p. 52) makes the same point. Whenever a change occurs, "the position is no longer one of equilibrium...[and] to find a new equilibrium (if there is one) we have to fill in a whole story about the behaviour of the economy when it is out of equilibrium...".


*PII* S0954-349X(96)00075-6

The phenomenon known as traverse – or transient passage, as Samuelson (1975, p. 41) calls it – can be viewed as a transition taking place either between two steady states or out of steady states altogether. The present paper will be mainly concerned with traverse as the *attempted passage* between two steady states. As was done by Hicks, a *neoclassical* traverse will be considered, i.e. a traverse where full capacity of utilization and full employment of labour is maintained throughout. As in most previous presentations, the complementarity of factors of production (i.e. fixed coefficients of production) will be assumed, but already installed machines, and their accompanying labour force, will be allowed to move from one sector to the other.

The economic literature on the traverse is not very extensive and, with few exceptions, mainly takes the form of a purely mathematical exercise.[2] The purpose of the paper, when compared with previous contributions, is to provide an explicit account of the actual path taken by the various variables during the traverse. In doing so, we shall show that the Hicksian traverse may be seen as a process of reproportioning. This will be done for the dynamically stable cases but also for the dynamically unstable ones, which had previously been relegated to obscurity.

The paper is organized as follows. In Section 2, the quantity and price equations of the standard two-sector model are recalled, with one slight modification; in Section 3, the conventional Hicksian traverse is shown within the new framework; in Section 4, the dynamics of reproportioning are assessed; in Section 5 we present a graphical illustration of the traverse in the dynamically stable case; in Section 6, a peculiar subset of the dynamically stable case is discussed; and in Section 7, the dynamics of reproportioning and the failed traverse are illustrated in the dynamically unstable case. Section 8 concludes.

## 2. Standard quantity and price equations

In the analysis to follow it is assumed that there exists one own-produced means of production taking the form of a *super-machine* that does not depreciate, whose current production is denoted by $I$ in physical terms, and whose already accumulated stock is $K$, where obviously $I = \Delta K$. The unit price of the super-machine is $p_i$. There will be one 'primary' means of production, *labour* ($L$), whose nominal wage is $w^*$. The rate of growth of labour is exogenous, where $nL = \Delta L$. There is one commodity produced for *final consumption* ($C$), and its unit price is $p_c$. The *super-machine* is a basic commodity: it can both produce a final commodity for consumption and reproduce itself.

[2] See Shinkai (1960); Hicks (1965); Spaventa (1973); Samuelson (1975); Bhaduri (1975); Lowe (1976); Craven (1977); O'Connell (1978); Nagatani and Neher (1978); Belloc (1980); Bhaduri and Robinson (1980); Magnan de Bornier (1980); Halevi (1985); Hagemann (1992); Halevi (1992).

The technology is denoted by the symbol $T(\cdot)$:

$$\begin{aligned} T(\cdot) &= T(a_c, a_i, \ell_c, \ell_i) \\ &= T(a_c/\ell_c, a_i/\ell_i) \\ &= T(k_c, k_i), \end{aligned} \tag{1}$$

where $a_j$ = super-machine per unit of output $j$, and $\ell_j$ = labour per unit of output $j$. We shall assume that the technique given by the above coefficients constitutes the only available technique. The quantity equations are now given below (in absolute terms and relative terms):

$$a_c C + a_i I = K, \quad a_c c + a_i i = k, \tag{2}$$

$$\ell_c C + \ell_i I = L, \quad \ell_c c + \ell_i i = 1, \tag{3}$$

$$I = gK, \qquad i = gk, \tag{4}$$

where the lower-case letters refer to the physical elements per unit of labour, and $g$ is the rate of capital accumulation.

Likewise, with the classical savings assumption (no savings out of wages while profits are entirely saved), the price equations are given by below (in absolute and relative terms):

$$p_c = \ell_c w^* + a_c p_i r, \quad p = \ell_c w + a_c r, \tag{5}$$

$$p_i = \ell_i w^* + a_i p_i r, \quad 1 = \ell_i w + a_i r, \tag{6}$$

$$p_i I = r p_i K, \qquad i = rk, \tag{7}$$

$$p_c C = w^* L, \qquad pc = w, \tag{8}$$

where obviously the super-machine is used as *numéraire*; $p$ is the relative price of the consumption good and $w$ is the real wage rate, in terms of the super-machines.[3]

In a properly accounted production system, value added is equal to the value of the net product, so that:

$$i + pc = w + rk, \tag{9}$$

which makes either Eq. (7) or Eq. (8) redundant.

The ratio $k = K/L$ of own-produced to primary means of production will play a crucial role in the analysis to follow: on the one hand, the current value of $k$ reflects

[3] Using the price of machines as numéraire will simplify computations. In particular, the wage–profit frontier remains linear, whatever the technique in use. Furthermore, in contrast to many articles based on two-sector models, changes in techniques – and hence in kinds of capital goods – are not considered here. In such exercises, the consumption good needs to be chosen as the numéraire if comparisons are to be meaningful. In general, there is no reason to choose the consumption good as numéraire in a model where there is no utility function. See Henry (1991, pp. 36–39).

the past history of the system; on the other hand, the value of $k$ can be used to monitor the process of reproportioning during the traverse.[4] Both $K$ and $L$ are assumed to be homogeneous and non-specific, i.e. they can be used in either line of production. The process of reproportioning within the structure will precisely consist in shifting $K$ and $L$ from one line of production to another within the production system. Differentiating $k$ totally and remembering that $I=\Delta K$ and $nL=\Delta L$, we have

$$dk = i - kn = (g-n)k, \tag{10}$$

where $g$ is defined in Eq. (4). Eq. (10) neatly describes the process of structural adaptation. Given that the value of $n$ is exogenous and can therefore fluctuate for unexplained reasons, the *fluctuations* of $n$ will force the system to reproportion itself, and that is precisely the problem of the traverse we wish to study. So long as the fluctuations of $n$ do not exceed a certain range to be defined later, Eq. (10) will govern the macro behaviour of the production system in the context of structural stability.

The reproportioning caused by fluctuations in $n$ can be both quantitatively and qualitatively determined, if we remember that the overall ratio of the own-produced to non-produced means of production ($k$) is by definition equal to a weighted average of the similar ratios ($k_c$, $k_i$) in both lines of production, with the sum of the weights $\lambda_c+\lambda_i=1$, where $\lambda_c=L_c/(L_i+L_c)$.

$$k=\frac{K_c+K_i}{L_c+L_i}=\frac{K_c}{L_c+L_i}\cdot\frac{L_c}{L_c}+\frac{K_i}{L_c+L_i}\cdot\frac{L_i}{L_i}=\frac{K_c}{L_c}\cdot\frac{L_c}{(L_c+L_i)}+\frac{K_i}{L_i}\cdot\frac{L_i}{(L_c+L_i)},$$

$$k=\lambda_i k_i+\lambda_c k_c=(1-\lambda_c)k_i+\lambda_c k_c=k_i+(k_c-k_i)\lambda_c.$$

Differentiating the above equation and remembering that $k_c$ and $k_i$ are fixed, we have

$$dk=(k_c-k_i)\,d\lambda_c, \tag{11}$$

which defines the needed reproportioning quantitatively and qualitatively. Eqs. (10) and (11) will play a crucial role in the analysis of the next section.

## 3. Stability analysis versus reproportioning

Traditional theory looks at traverse as a phenomenon affecting the economy 'as a whole', strongly relies on mathematical analysis, and barely, if ever, makes use of graphical exposition. It typically proceeds crisply in four steps:[5]

*Step 1.* From Eqs. (2) and (4), a maximum value of $g$ is determined that ensures positivity of outputs ($c$ and $i$).

*Step 2.* After substitution into Eq. (10) for the value of $g$ obtained from Eqs. (2)–(4), a differential equation in $k$ is obtained.

[4] Note that state variable $k$ also plays an important role in traditional theory where it is the main argument in 'well-behaved' production functions, whose assumed properties (e.g. instantaneous technical substitutability) thereafter dominate all the results.

[5] Bhaduri (1975) provides a very clear exposition of the traditional approach.

*Step 3*. Inspection of the differential equation in $k$ reveals that the equilibrium value of $k$ can only be positive if the production of $C$ is more mechanized than the production of $I$, i.e. if $k_c > k_i$. This is the dynamic stability condition.

*Step 4*. Starting from a position where $g = n > 0$ and letting $n$ fluctuate, it is shown that a successful traverse exists if and only if the dynamic stability condition is met. What happens to the system when a traverse does not exist is usually left unexplained, even though the system then undergoes a qualitative change affecting its very functions.

Note that the traditional analysis of traverse could be fully and more simply conducted in terms of Eqs. (10) and (11) above. Hicks's (1965, pp. 187–190) four cases are neatly summarized in Table 1.[6]

For example, consider case 1 in Table 1. Starting from an equilibrium situation ($g = n$), let $n$ fall for one reason or another, so that $g > n > 0$ for a while, thus making $dk > 0$. Since the super-machines are now being own-produced faster than labour is being 'imported' to man them, the system can only remain at full employment of labour and capacity if it reproportions itself, giving more weight to the production of $C$ that is more machine-intensive ($k_c > k_i$). Thus, $\lambda_c$ increases, $\lambda_i$ decreases pari passu and this obviously reduces the current output of super-machines and also the rate of accumulation ($g$), until $g = n$ is restored again.

Now consider case 4 in the table, where this time $k_i > k_c$, so that preservation of full capacity utilization and full employment of labour requires an expansion of the production of $I$, which is the most machine-intensive. As can be seen from column F of the table, this will increase the discrepancy between endogenous $g$ and exogenous $n$. Attempts to keep the system at full capacity utilization and full employment would soon lead to complete specialization of the system in the production of super-machines. Consideration of cases 2 and 3 is left to the reader.

## 4. The dynamics of reproportioning

In the following sections we wish to tell the story of a traverse. Our objective is to describe mathematically the process of reproportioning in a way such that the dynamic sequence of events that constitutes a traverse can be seized at a glance.

Table 1
Hicks's four cases

| | External disturbance | $(g-n)k$ (A) | $dk$ (B) | $(k_c-k_i)d\lambda_c$ (C) | $d\lambda_i$ (D) | $di$ (E) | $dg$ (F) |
|---|---|---|---|---|---|---|---|
| Case 1 | $n$ falls | + | + | (+) (+) | − | − | − |
| Case 2 | $n$ increases | − | − | (+) (−) | + | + | + |
| Case 3 | $n$ increases | − | − | (−) (+) | − | − | − |
| Case 4 | $n$ falls | + | + | (−) (−) | + | + | + |

6 The signs of the various columns are given: column A, by definition; column B, by Eq. (10); column C, by Eq. (11); column E, by considering that $i = I/L = (I/L_i)(L_i/L) = (1/l_i)(\lambda_i)$ and hence that $di = (1/l_i)d\lambda_i$; column F, by considering that $g = i/k$.

Let us adopt the following conventions to simplify notations:

$$P^- = (k - k_i)/(k_c - k_i) \geq 0 \tag{12}$$

$$P^+ = (k_c - k)/(k_c - k_i) \geq 0. \tag{13}$$

Now let us go back to Eqs. (2)–(7) and solve to obtain:

$$c = (1/\ell_c)P^-, \tag{14}$$

$$i = (1/\ell_i)P^+, \tag{15}$$

$$g = (1/\ell_i k)P^+, \tag{16}$$

$$w = (k_c/\ell_i k)P^- = k_c(P^-/P^+)g = (a_c/\ell_i)(c/k), \tag{17}$$

$$p = (a_c/\ell_i k) = w/c, \tag{18}$$

$$r = g, \tag{19}$$

which describes the state of the production system at one point in time.[7] Let us assume that the system is in a quasi-stationary state with $r = g = n$. Mere inspection of the solution above now allows us to observe the system in the action of reproportioning itself following an exogenously imposed fluctuation in $n$.

The 'backbone' of the production system is given by Eq. (16), which can be rewritten as:

$$g = g(k;T) = (1/\ell_i k)P^+ \geq 0. \tag{16a}$$

We have seen that the overall $k$ ratio must be somewhere between $k_c$ and $k_i$. We can verify that

$P^+ \to 1$ and $g \to 1/a_i$, as $k \to k_i$,

$P^+ \to 0$ and $g \to 0$, as $k \to k_c$,

which gives the range of variability for the rate of accumulation, while the limits $k_c$ and $k_i$ give the range of possible reproportioning. Moreover, taking the derivative of Eq. (16a) with respect to $k$ and remembering that $P^+$ also depends on $k$, we have

$$(\mathrm{d}g/\mathrm{d}k) = -(a_c/zk^2), \tag{20}$$

where the above derivative is negative if $z = \ell_c \ell_i (k_c - k_i) > 0$, i.e. if $(k_c - k_i) > 0$. Thus, to a negative relationship between the rate of accumulation $g$ and the overall capital to labour ratio $k$ corresponds Hicks's dynamically stable cases 1 and 2 discussed above. The dynamically unstable cases will be discussed in Section 7.

From now on in this section and the following one we shall deal exclusively with

[7] Note the recursive nature of the solution. Given technology and the story of past accumulation, $c$, $i$ and then $g$ are determined first, which enables us to know $w$ and then $p$, $r$ being known as soon as $g$ is known. This is a classical (Sraffian) structure in which quantities determine prices or causality runs from quantities to prices. See Henry (1993, p. 6) and Halevi (1992, p. 279).

the stable cases. In these stable cases, the 'backbone' of the production system, which defines the possibilities for reproportioning within a given structure, is the downward-sloping curve drawn in Fig. 1(a).

Let us now see how the production of the consumption good behaves during the process of reproportioning. Remembering Eq. (12), we obtain from differentiating Eq. (14) and dividing by $c$ the following:

$$(\mathrm{d}c/c) = \{k/(k-k_i)\}(\mathrm{d}k/k).$$

Since $c=C/L$, $k=K/L$ and $nL=\Delta L$, the above expression can be modified to read

$$\hat{C} = C(k;T,n) = (kg - k_i n)/(k-k_i), \tag{21}$$

which gives the rate of change $\hat{C}=(\mathrm{d}C/C)$ of the output of consumption goods as reproportioning is taking place. Recalling the range of variability of $g$, in Hicks's cases 1 and 2, we have

$$\hat{C} \to +\infty, \text{ as } k \to k_i,$$

$$\hat{C} \to -\{nk_i/(k_c - k_i)\} < 0, \text{ as } k \to k_c,$$

and the slope of Eq. (21) is

$$(\partial\hat{C}/\partial k) = k_i\{n-(1/a_i)\}/(k-k_i)^2. \tag{22}$$

That curve is drawn in Fig. 1(a). Note that the sign of its slope does not depend on technology, but depends instead on the condition that the exogenous value of $n$ be smaller than $1/a_i$, which is the maximum value that a sustained rate of accumulation $g$ can take.

We may similarly derive from Eq. (15) an expression for the rate of change in the output of super-machines:

$$\hat{I} = I(k;T,n) = (k_c n - kg)/(k_c - k), \tag{23}$$

whose slope is

$$(\partial\hat{I}/\partial k) = (\ell_i k_c n)/(k_c - k)^2 > 0. \tag{24}$$

Its extreme points in Hicks's cases 1 and 2 are

$$\hat{I} \to +\infty, \text{ as } k \to k_c,$$

and $\hat{I}$ approaches a value that can be positive or negative as $k \to k_i$. That curve is also drawn in Fig. 1(a).

Using Eqs. (17) and (18), we perform the same operations as above, which results in

$$\hat{w} = w(k;T,n) = k_i(g-n)/(k-k_i), \tag{25}$$

$$\hat{p} = p(k;T,n) = n - g, \tag{26}$$

$$\hat{w} - \hat{p} = \hat{c} = k(g-n)/(k-k_i). \tag{27}$$

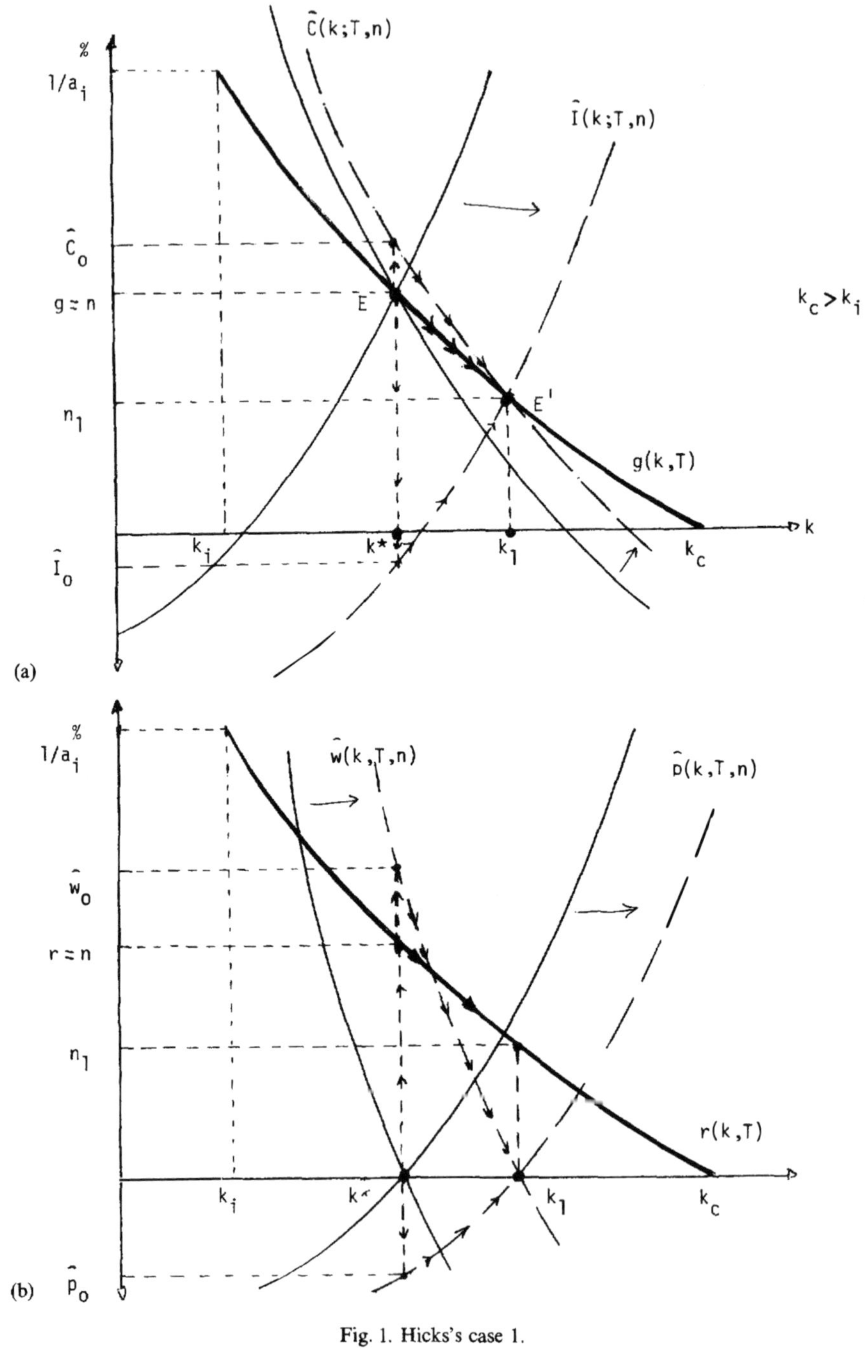


Fig. 1. Hicks's case 1.

Remembering that $r=g$ by Eq. (19), we may draw the price changes in Fig. 1(b). The 'backbone' of the production system is identical (in this case because of the classical saving assumption) in the physical and value spaces. The evolution of the purchasing power of workers, i.e. consumption per worker, is given precisely by Eq. (27), and is approximated by that of Eq. (25).

When the production system is in a steady state ($g=n$), we have from Eqs. (16), (19), (21), (23), (25) and (26) above that $dk=0$ and

$$1/a_i \geq g=(1/\ell_i k^*)P^+ = n=\hat{I}=\hat{C}=r\geq \hat{w}=\hat{p}=0. \tag{28}$$

All quantities grow at the same percentage rate, while all (absolute and relative) prices remain constant. In such a state defined by the coordinates of points $E$ and $E'$ in Fig. 1(a), the system grows proportionately at a constant rate without structural change. The steady state is illustrated by the horizontal lines in Fig. 2(a).

## 5. A graphical analysis of the dynamically stable Hicksian traverse

The steady state described by Eq. (28) will remain undisturbed so long as the interaction between the production system and its wider environment is not changed, i.e. so long as $n$ remains constant. If the rate of growth $n$ of the labour force suddenly changes while technology ($T$) remains constant, then the 'backbone' curves $g(k;T)=r(k;T)$ will not be affected, but all the other curves, except $\hat{p}$, will shift in a direction that depends on the dynamic stability condition (i.e. on the character of technology). Note that wages in terms of the investment good and real consumption always shift in the same direction.

$$\partial\hat{C}/\partial n\,|\bar{k}= -\{k_i/(k-k_i)\}, \tag{29}$$

$$\partial\hat{I}/\partial n\,|\bar{k}= \{k_c/(k_c-k)\}, \tag{30}$$

$$\partial\hat{w}/\partial n\,|\bar{k}= -\{k_i/(k-k_i)\}, \tag{31}$$

$$\partial\hat{p}/\partial n\,|\bar{k}=1, \tag{32}$$

$$\partial(\hat{w}-\hat{p})/\partial n=\partial\hat{c}/\partial n\,|\bar{k}= -\{nk/(k-k_i)\}. \tag{33}$$

Let us consider Hicks's case 1 where $k_c>k_i$ and there occurs a sudden fall in the value of $n$, with the result that $g>n$ instantaneously. By the same token, the $\hat{C}(k;T,n)$ and $\hat{w}(k;T,n)$ curves instantaneously shift upwards to accommodate the lower value of $n$, while the $\hat{I}(k;T,n)$ and $\hat{p}(k;T,n)$ curves shift downwards for the same reason, as shown by the dotted lines in Fig. 1. The production system must now adjust to a lower rate of growth of its labour force. About the adjustment to take place, we know two things.

First, $g$ must adjust to $n$, i.e. the endogenous rate of accumulation must adjust to the exogenous rate of increase of labour. In other words, if the new equilibrium ratio of own-produced to non-produced means ($k_1$) is to be achieved in time, $g=i/k$ must fall and this can only be achieved if the production of new super-machines

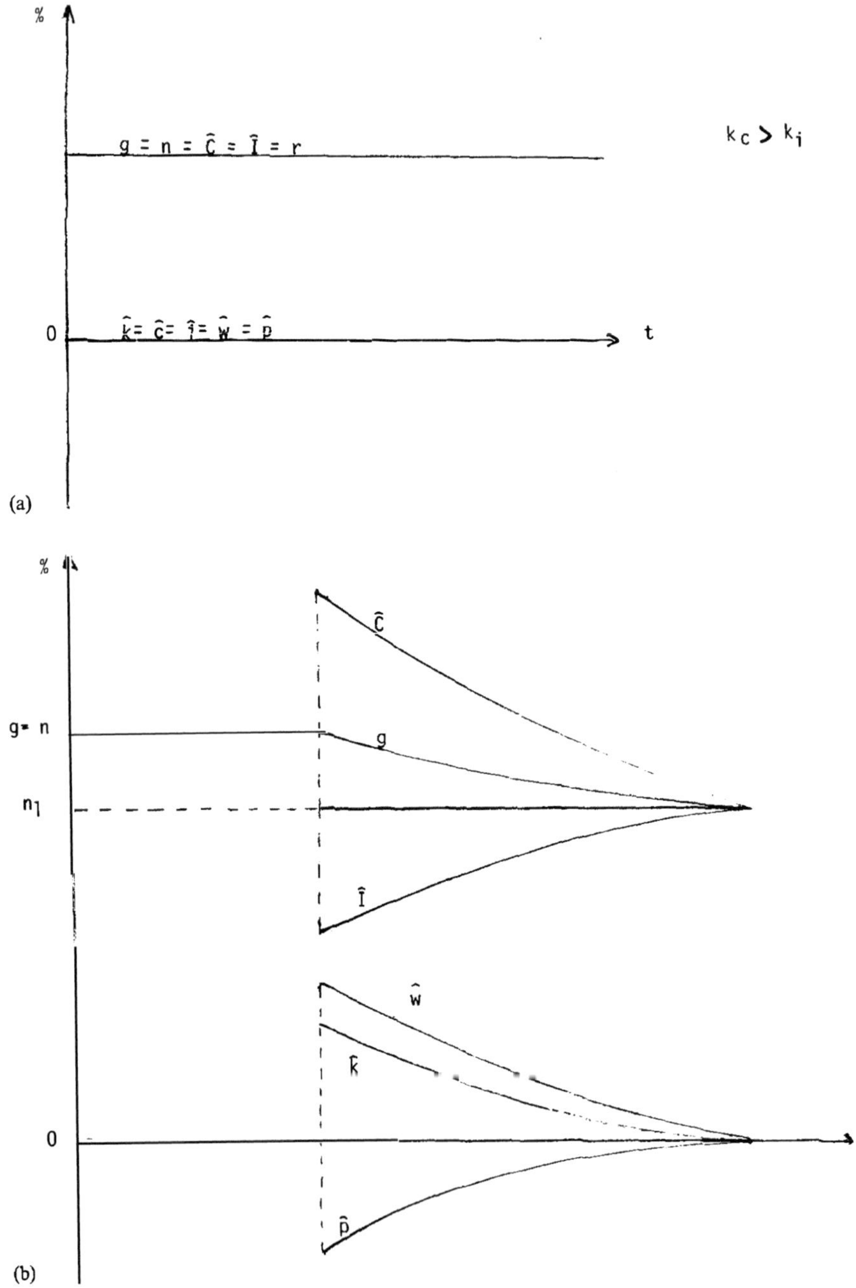


Fig. 2. Hicks's case 1.

is reduced while that of consumption goods is increased. Thus, within an invariant structure $T(\cdot)$, adjustment is made through reproportioning in favour of the production of $C$.

Secondly, the adjustment to the new situation cannot conceivably be instantaneous. Even if we assume that the reallocation of workers and super-machines from the production of $I$ to that of $C$ can be instantaneous, the actual production of more super-machines (albeit at the reduced rate) must take time as the transition is made from $k^*$ to $k_1$.

The 'quantity traverse' is shown in Fig. 1(a). Immediately following the fall of $n$ (which has been somewhat exaggerated to gain graphical clarity), we can read vertically above and below the old ratio $k^*$ that the rate of growth in the production of consumption goods ($\hat{C}_0$) has been stepped up, while the rate of growth in the production of super-machines ($\hat{I}_0$) has fallen (in this case, it becomes negative). As time goes by and adjustment takes its course, these dramatic initial changes are gradually toned down until adjustment is complete and Eq. (28) holds again at $k_1$.

Similarly, the 'price traverse' can be visualized in Fig. 1(b). Initially, there is a sudden fall in the relative price of consumption goods ($\hat{p}_0$) and a sudden increase in the real wage rate ($\hat{w}_0$); in a market-clearing sense, the changes in $w$ and $p$ provide support to the expansion of the production of consumption goods and also to the contraction of the production of super-machines. Since wages are all consumed while profits are all saved, an increase in real wages allows workers to purchase the relatively larger amount of consumption goods required to keep the system at full employment of labour and capacity.

For full employment and full capacity utilization to be maintained at all times during the traverse, the above changes in prices and rates of growth of quantities must take place. The price traverse helps to fulfil the requirements of effective demand, while the quantity traverse helps to achieve the supply-side constraints of full employment. During the traverse, the production system loses its homogeneous character summarized by Eq. (28), as rates of change of the physical and value elements become differentiated. However, homogeneity is gradually reintroduced as the system approaches its new steady state at point $(n_1, k_1)$.

Fig. 2(b) is also quite revealing concerning what occurs during the traverse. Starting from an initial position of steady-state growth, at rate $g = n \geq 0$, the production system is shocked by a sudden fall in $n$ and, judging by the pulsating lines on the graph, the system really comes to life during the traverse. Is it not paradoxical that traditional economic theory has devoted so much time to studying steady states that resemble clinical deaths while badly neglecting the analysis of traverse?[8]

## 6. Unsustainable growth in the dynamically stable case

The detailed analysis of Hicks's case 2 ought to be left to the reader. It holds no additional difficulty, except, however, when $n > 1/a_i$. In standard analyses of the

[8] A notable exception to this are the efforts by Pasinetti (1981, 1993) to develop non-homothetic models of growth.

traverse, this subcase is excluded altogether, since it is shown mathematically, from Eqs. (2) and (4), that equilibrium would require output in one of the two sectors to be negative. We are not told, however, what would occur to the economic system if, starting from a sustainable steady-state rate of accumulation $n=g$, the rate of growth of the labour force were suddenly jacked up to a level $n_1 > 1/a_i$. To describe such a transition and its dissipative consequences is the purpose of the present section.

As was pointed out in Section 4, the rates of change in the production of both consumption goods and investment goods depend on the exogenous rate of growth of the labour force. However, whereas the slope of the $\hat{I}$ curve is always positive with respect to $k$, the slope of the $\hat{C}$ curve depends on the sign of $\{n-(1/a_i)\}$. When the growth rate of labour is sustainable, i.e. below $(1/a_i)$, the $\hat{C}$ curve is downward sloping. Yet when the exogenous $n$ is too high, the $\hat{C}$ is upward sloping, as can be seen from Eq. (22). Between $k_i$ and $k_c$, as can be computed from Eq. (21), the $\hat{C}$ curve rises from $-\infty$ to a negative value. Thus, when an unsustainable rate of growth of the labour force is newly imposed on an economy, even when this economy is normally dynamically stable, (i.e. Hicks's case 2), the production of consumption goods must necessarily decrease forever.

What actually occurs in this case of excessive population growth is illustrated in Fig. 3, which shows the quantity traverse only. It is assumed that the system is initially in a steady state given by $g=n<1/a_i$. There is then a sudden increase in the rate of growth of the labour force, such that $n_1 > 1/a_i$. The $\hat{I}$ curve will shift upwards, as shown by Eq. (24). As to the $\hat{C}$ curve, it will take an entirely new form, as can be seen in Fig. 3. To maintain the full employment of the now abundant labour, production will need to be shifted towards the labour-intensive sector, that of the investment-producing goods. There will be a brisk increase in the rate of growth of the investment-producing sector ($\hat{I}_0$), accompanied by a brisk decrease in the rate of growth of the consumption-producing sector ($\hat{C}_0$). Actually, the rate of growth in the production of consumption goods becomes negative. There is an immediate reduction in the produced amount of consumption goods, despite the strong increase in the labour force. As the overall rate of accumulation $g$ speeds up towards its new target $n_1$, the rate of growth in the production of investment goods gradually slows down. However, the rate of decrease in the production of consumption goods will worsen. Soon almost the entire production will be devoted to investment goods and little or no consumption goods will be produced. The excessive rate of the labour force, tied to the requirement of continuous full employment, has led to a system devoid of consumption goods.

## 7. A graphical analysis of the dynamically unstable Hicksian traverse

We shall now study the dynamically unstable situation, given by Hicks's cases 3 and 4. It is interesting to observe that, in these cases, not only is traditional theory rather silent about the ultimate fate of the system following a disturbance, as it was in the subcase of the previous section, but, more importantly, it is completely silent on how, in fact, the production system could conceivably have entered 'into' such

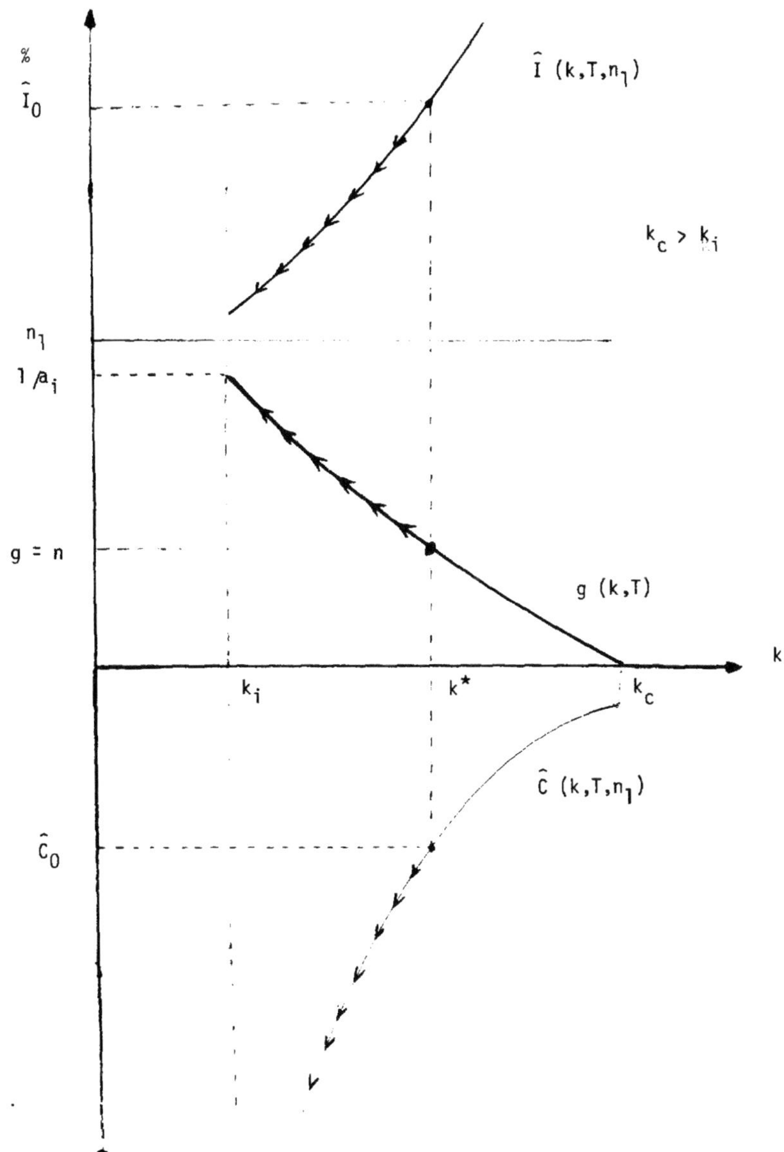


Fig. 3. Unsustainable growth in Hicks's case 2.

an equilibrium in the first place! While unable to answer this second question, we shall attempt to tackle the first issue.

In the dynamically unstable situation, given by Hicks's cases 3 and 4, the reader will note that the backbone $g(k;T)=r(k;T)$ of the production system presents a serious deformity: it has a positive slope, as shown by Eq. (20). In traditional theory, such a deformity is called by some an 'irregularity'. In other words, a structure characterized by $k_i \geq k_c$ is *dissipative*, implying that the slightest fluctuation of $n$ will be amplified and will soon force the system to reorganize its mode of insertion and of interaction with its wider environment.[9]

This can be seen by looking at Fig. 4, based on Hicks's case 4. As pointed out above, the $g(k;T)$ and $r(k;T)$ curves are upward sloping rather than downward sloping. However, the other two curves depicting the evolution of the rate of growth of consumption output and investment output, $\hat{C}$ and $\hat{I}$, are, respectively, downward sloping and upward sloping, as they were in the stable case, and as follows from the derivatives of Eqs. (22) and (24). The shapes of these two curves are, however, different from the shapes observed in the stable case. This can be seen by checking on the extrema of $\hat{C}$ and $\hat{I}$ when $k$ approaches its limits $k_i$, and $k_c$. We have

$$\hat{C} \to -\infty, \text{ as } k \to k_i,$$

$$\hat{C} \to -\{nk_i/(k_c - k_i)\} > 0, \text{ as } k \to k_c,$$

$$\hat{I} \to -\infty, \text{ as } k \to k_c,$$

$$\hat{I} \to -(nk_c - k_i/a_i)/(k_c - k_i) > 0, \text{ as } k \to k_c.$$

Similarly, the $\hat{w}$ curve has a slope with the same sign, but has a different shape, in the unstable cases when compared with the stable cases. However, the slope of the $\hat{p}$ curve depends on the shape of the backbone of the production system, and hence depends on whether the economy is in the stable or the unstable situation. The shapes of the $g(k,T)$, $\hat{C}$, $\hat{I}$, $\hat{w}$ and $\hat{p}$ curves are shown in Fig. 4, which describes Hicks's case 4. Let us assume, as before with case 1, a permanent fall in the rate of growth $n$ of the labour force. As shown by Eqs. (29) and (30), the two curves $\hat{C}$ and $\hat{I}$ will now shift in a direction opposite to that of the stable case. The fall in the rate of growth of labour will now induce an increase in the rate of production of the super-machines, since the investment-producing sector is more machine-intensive, while the rate of growth of the consumption-goods sector will be lower. Symmetrically, accompanying the slowdown in the production of consumption goods, there will be a fall in the wage rate and in the purchasing power of workers, as shown in Fig. 4(b). Whereas the capital–labour ratio that would be required by a new balanced configuration falls from $k^*$ to $k_1$, the actual overall capital labour ratio takes off. As the economy reproportions itself towards the more machine-intensive sector, the overall rate of accumulation increases, thus drifting away from the rate of growth of the labour force, while the rates of growth of the consumption and the investment sectors continue to wander apart.

At the end of this process, such a production system ends up specializing in the production of super-machines. The production of consumption goods per labour

[9] As pointed out by Halevi (1985), a structure characterized by $k_c = k_i$ is just as dissipative, since it offers no scope for reproportioning.

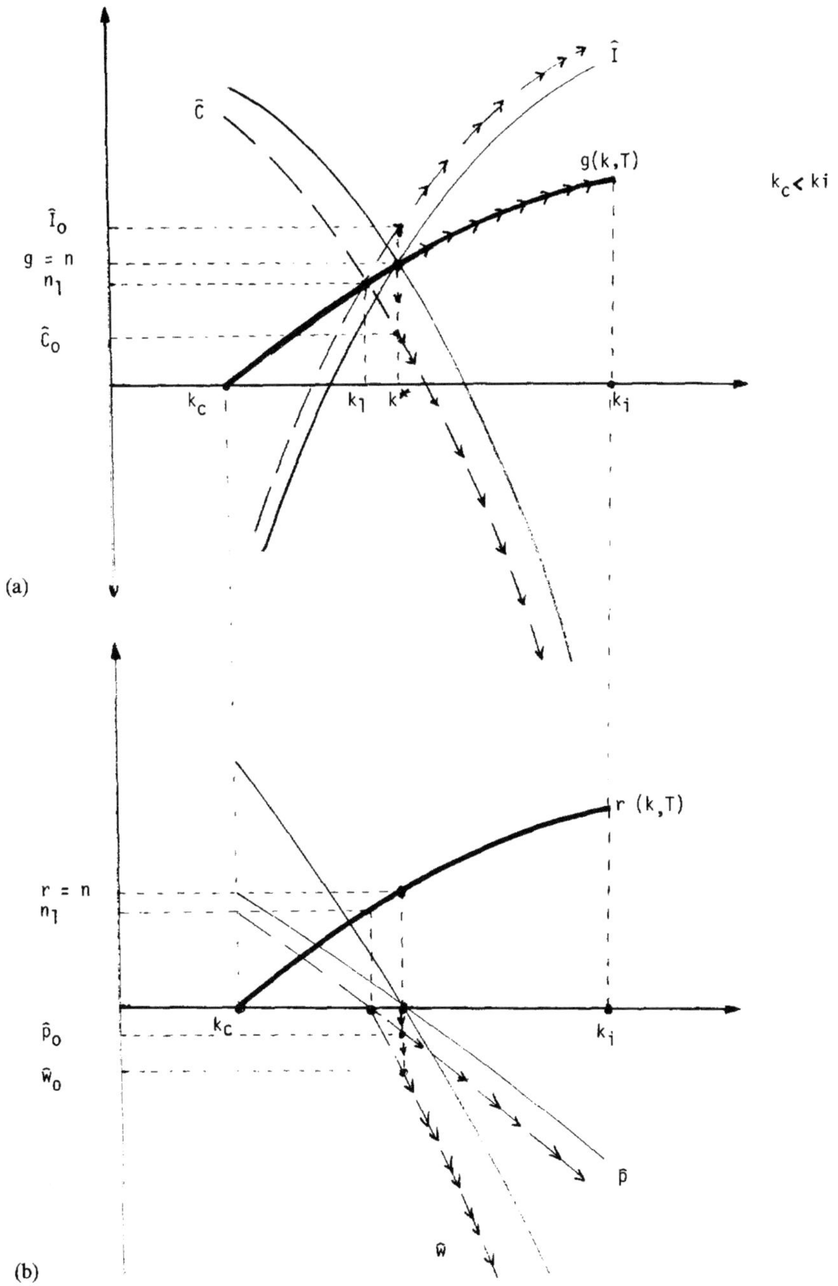


Fig. 4. Hicks's case 4.

will decline, and it may even decline in absolute terms, reaching a zero level. To be truly sustainable, such an economy would need to export its investment goods and to import consumption goods. Otherwise, the only way out for this economy is to change its production structure or its objectives of full employment of labour and capacity.

We may also consider Hicks's case 3, when the rate of growth of the labour force increases. This is illustrated in Fig. 5. Only the (failed) quantity traverse is shown. Since labour is now becoming abundant, the decisions of planners aiming to retain the full utilization of capital and full employment of labour will induce decision-makers to redirect production towards the more labour-intensive sector, the one producing consumption goods.[10] This will lead to a continuous decline in the overall rate of accumulation, as illustrated in Fig. 5, accompanied by an increase in the rate

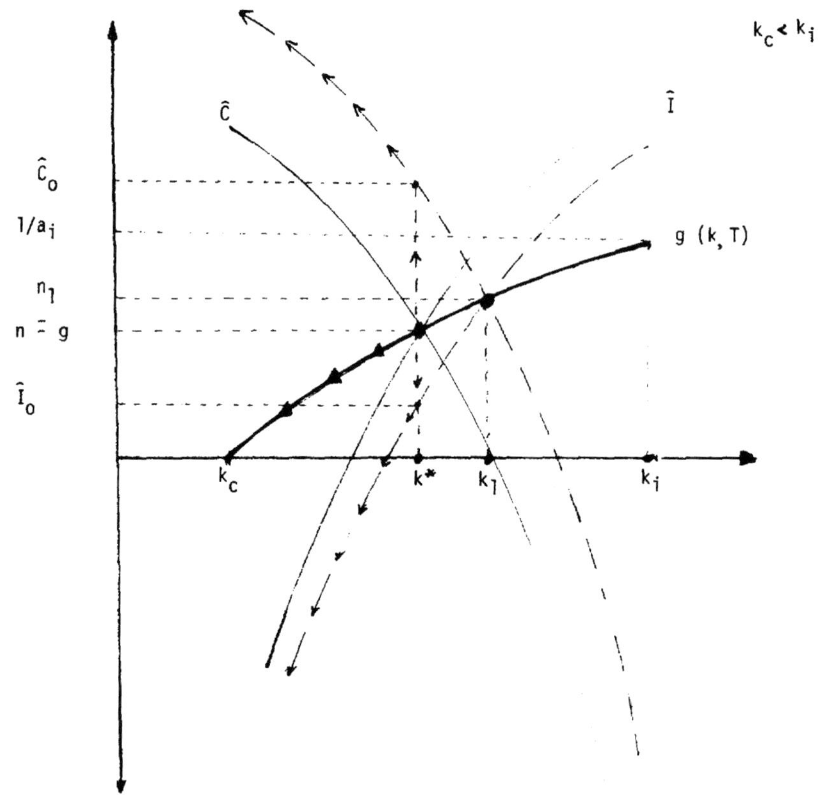


Fig. 5. Hicks's case 3.

[10] According to Halevi (1985, p. 232), a similar fate would await a capitalist economy, for the relative scarcity of machines "would compel producers to invest in the [most] labour-intensive sector, namely the consumption-goods one".

of production of consumption goods and a decline in the rate of production of machines. Eventually, the rate of growth in the production of investment goods $\hat{I}$ will become negative: despite the exponential increase in population, the absolute amount of machines being produced will decline. Increasingly more resources will be diverted to the production of consumption goods. At some point, the spree in consumption per labour (as a result of the positive discrepancy between $\hat{C}$ and $n$) will come to an end.[11] When almost all existing machines are devoted to the production of consumption goods, i.e. when $k$ approaches $k_c$, it becomes impossible for this economy to increase its capacity to produce consumption goods. Consumption per labour will have to fall, or else the system will have to import machines and export its consumption goods, or restructure its economy. If neither of the latter two paths are possible, the fall in the standard of living will become irreversible as the economy decumulates.

## 8. Conclusion

Whereas the Hicksian traverse, i.e. the issue of whether or not a new balanced growth rate can be achieved without giving up full employment of labour and full utilization of capital, has been extensively studied from the stability angle, little had been done about the actual path being followed by such an economy. The present paper has shown what happens to various quantity variables, not only in the stable cases where the traverse is generally achieved, but also in the case of unsustainable growth and in the unstable cases, when a successful traverse cannot occur. The consequences of such unsuccessful traverses have been clearly spelled out: either the system produces less and less consumption goods or the economy is bound to decumulate. In all cases the purpose of the system disappears. The ultimate fate is that the economy is eventually unable to produce any consumption good.

In addition, in contrast to Hicks's own analysis, the price traverse has also been explicitly spelled out: in particular, it has been shown that the price traverse is an offspring of the required quantity traverse. While the latter safeguards full employment of both labour and capacity, the former provides the required changes in aggregate demand to match the changes in the quantities supplied.

The analysis of the dynamically unstable cases highlights the warnings of those who worked out the comparative dynamics of growth models. As Spaventa (1970, p. 147) points out, for instance, the results arising from the comparison of steady-state growth equilibria "should not be automatically applied to dynamic movements from one equilibrium position to the other due to, say, a change in the natural rate

[11] Paradoxically, as labour becomes more abundant, real wages are rising. Coming back to the comments made in the previous footnote, we may wonder whether a capitalist economy would continue to follow the described path. Capitalists might soon decide to stop investing in the labour-intensive sector (the one producing consumption goods), although the relative price of consumption goods is going up compared with that of investment goods – when they realize that the cost of labour (real wages) is continuously rising. However, if they were to invest in the more mechanized sector (the one producing the super-machines), the full employment condition would not be realized.

of growth". It is clear that these results become irrelevant for all economies where the dominant technique is such that $k_c < k_i$: the steady-state equilibria can only be attained by chance.

Another way out has, however, been offered by Hicks (1965, p. 194; 1990, p. 102): installed capacity may be over-utilized or under-utilized during the traverse, but then labour may also not be fully employed.[12] As noted before, it is difficult to imagine how economies with technologies such that $k_c < k_i$ could even take off. However, in a world where full capacity utilization and full employment is not a necessary constraint, or at least, not a condition that is always fulfilled, the economies adopting such technologies, and then attempting to retain full employment of their labour force and of their installed capacity, could suffer the fate that has been outlined in the previous section.

## Acknowledgements

This article is a revised and extended version of a working paper, originally written by Jacques Henry in November 1985, and presented at a conference on growth theory held at the University of Ottawa in March 1987. Jacques Henry died from a heart disease in June 1989. I wish to thank my colleague Mario Seccareccia for his comments, as well as the anonymous referees of the journal. The usual caveat applies.

## References

Belloc, B., 1980. Croissance Économique et Adaptation du Capital Productif. Economica, Paris.

Bhaduri, A., 1975. On the analogy between the quantity- and the price-traverse. Oxford Economic Papers 27 (3), 455–461.

Bhaduri, A., Robinson, J., 1980. Accumulation and exploitation: An analysis in the tradition of Marx, Sraffa and Kalecki. Cambridge Journal of Economics 4 (2), 103–115.

Craven, J., 1977. A comment on Bhaduri's traverse analogy. Oxford Economic Papers 29 (1), 156–157.

Hagemann, H., 1992. Traverse analysis in a post-classical model, in: Halevi, J., Laibman, D., Nell, E.J. (Eds.), Beyond the Steady State: A Revival of Growth Theory. St Martin's Press, New York, 235–263.

Halevi, J., 1985. Switching and employment. Eastern Economic Journal 11 (3), 229–234.

Halevi, J., 1992. Accumulation and structural disequilibrium, in: Halevi, J., Laibman, D., Nell, E.J. (Eds.), Beyond the Steady State: A Revival of Growth Theory. St Martin's Press, New York, 264–288.

Henry, J., 1991. La Théorie du Commerce Extérieur dans le Temps Historique: Une Analyse Post-Keynésienne, Presses Universitaires de France, Paris.

Henry, J., 1993. Post-Keynesian methods and the post-classical approach. International Papers in Political Economy 1 (2), 1–26.

Hicks, J., 1965. Capital and Growth. Oxford University Press, London.

Hicks, J., 1983. IS-LM: An explanation, in: Fitoussi, J.P. (Ed.), Modern Macroeconomic Theory. Blackwell, Oxford. 49–63.

Hicks, J., 1990. Ricardo and Sraffa, in: Bharadwaj, K., Schefold, B. (Eds.), Essays on Piero Sraffa: Critical Perspectives on the Revival of Classical Theory. Unwin Hyman, London, 99–102.

[12] See Lavoie and Ramirez-Gastón (1997) for the analysis of a demand-led traverse in an otherwise similar two-sector model.

Lavoie, M., Ramírez-Gastón, P., 1997. Traverse in a Two-sector Model of Growth with Target Return Pricing. The Manchester School 65 (2), 145–169.
Lowe, A., 1976. The Path of Economic Growth. Cambridge University Press, Cambridge.
Magnan de Bornier, J., 1980. Capital et Déséquilibres de la Croissance: Essai sur L'économie de la Traverse. Économica, Paris.
Nagatani, K., Neher, P.A., 1978. On adjustment dynamics: An exercise in traverse, in: G. Schwodiauer (Ed.), Equilibrium and Disequilibrium in Economic Theory. Reidel, Boston, MA, 369–396.
O'Connel, J., 1978. Savings and prices in a full-employment traverse. Oxford Economic Papers 30 (3), 458–463.
Pasinetti, L.L., 1981. Structural Change and Economic Growth. Cambridge University Press, Cambridge.
Pasinetti, L.L., 1993. Structural Economic Dynamics. Cambridge University Press, Cambridge.
Robinson, J., 1979. History versus equilibrium, in: Collected Economic Papers 5. Basil Blackwell, Oxford, 48–58.
Samuelson, P.A., 1975. Steady-state and transient relations: A reply on reswitching. Quarterly Journal of Economics 89 (1), 40–47.
Shinkai, Y., 1960. On equilibrium growth of capital and labour. International Economic Review 1, 107–111.
Spaventa, L., 1970. Rate of profit, rate of growth, and capital intensity in a simple production model. Oxford Economic Papers 22 (2), 129–147.
Spaventa, L., 1973. Notes on problems of transition between techniques, in: Mirlees, Stern (Eds.), Models of Economic Growth. Macmillan, London, 168–202.

*Cambridge Journal of Economics* 1997, **21**, 453–467

# Pasinetti's vertically hyper-integrated sectors and natural prices

Marc Lavoie*

Hyper-vertically integrated sectors and their natural prices, as presented by Pasinetti (1988), are re-examined in a slightly different framework and with the help of a very simple three-industry model. It is shown that while Pasinetti's analysis takes into account basic commodities and interdependences, it short-circuits them. It is then asked whether such an approach is required to analyse growing sub-systems.

## 1. Introduction

The concept of vertical integration, although extensively but implicitly used in macroeconomic analysis, has always been difficult to seize intuitively. In an article of this journal, Pasinetti (1988) has proposed a generalisation of his previous work on vertical integration (Pasinetti, 1973). The paper was published, following exhortations from pupils who wanted to work on vertically hyper-integrated sectors, i.e., on models of vertical integration encompassing accumulation. One of the main feature of the model is to develop the so-called *natural* price sub-systems—a notion that had first been presented in Pasinetti (1981), but within a model where capital goods are only produced by labour. The fact that these various issues are not easily understood can be attested by the publication of a new book by Pasinetti (1993), where the author proceeds to further simplifications by taking out capital goods altogether.

The main purpose of the present paper is pedagogical. It is meant to explore some of the most surprising contentions of Pasinetti (1988), within the simplest model that can handle Pasinetti's framework. This will allow those of us who are not at ease with linear algebra or with input–output models to understand better Pasinetti's natural price sub-systems. In particular, it will illustrate clearly what has left many readers pondering, i.e., his result that the same capital good may have different prices in different sub-systems.[1] The simplest of such models is one with a single capital good and two consumption goods, the demand for which is growing at different rates. The model will allow us to understand better some criticisms that have been addressed against the later versions of Pasinetti's

Manuscript received 7 April 1995; final version received 12 February 1996.

*University of Ottawa, Canada. The paper follows numerous discussions I had with Tom Rymes. I also benefited from comments by Gary Madden, Angelo Reati, Bertram Schefold, Ian Steedman, Luigi Pasinetti, and an anonymous referee. Without implication, I would like to thank them for their help. The paper was in part written while I was Visiting Professor at Curtin University, in Perth, Western Australia.

[1] Pasinetti (1981, 1988) also deals with units of productive capacity. One easily understands that a unit of productive capacity in one vertically integrated sector has a price which is different from that of a unit of productive capacity in another sector. But this is *not* the point at stake. What is at issue is the law of one price.

vertical integration, i.e., that these versions do not incorporate basic commodities. It might also help us appreciate the practical reasons why Pasinetti proceeds in the way he does.

## 2. A standard view of vertical integration

Let us start with the usual neo-Ricardian price system, at its most general level:

$$\boldsymbol{pB} = \boldsymbol{a_n}w + \boldsymbol{pA} + \boldsymbol{pA}\pi$$

where $\boldsymbol{p}$ is the row vector of prices, $\boldsymbol{B}$ is the output matrix, $\boldsymbol{A}$ is the input matrix including fixed and circulating capital, $\boldsymbol{a_n}$ is the row vector of labour input, $w$ is the wage rate scalar, and $\pi$ is *the* uniform rate of profit. Assuming away, for simplification, circulating capital and depreciation on fixed capital, assuming away joint production, and defining physical units appropriately ($\boldsymbol{B}$ is the identity matrix $\mathbf{I}$), we are left with:

$$\boldsymbol{p} = \boldsymbol{a_n}w + \boldsymbol{pA}\pi$$

We may now add a slight complication by assuming a non-uniform rate of profit for each industry and for each sort of fixed capital good. These rates of profit are now given by the matrix $\Pi$, whereas the returns to capital per unit of output are now given by the direct product (or Schur product) $\boldsymbol{A}\star\Pi$, where a typical element of $\boldsymbol{A}\star\Pi$ is $[a_{ij}\pi_{ij}]$.[1] We have:

$$\boldsymbol{p} = \boldsymbol{a_n}w + \boldsymbol{p}(\boldsymbol{A}\star\Pi)$$

This (almost) standard price equation can now be solved to obtain:

$$\boldsymbol{p} = w\boldsymbol{a_n}(\mathbf{I} - \boldsymbol{A}\star\Pi)^{-1}$$

What we are concerned with are the properties of the natural economy, as defined by Pasinetti. In the very special case defined by the natural economy, the matrix set of rates of profit on fixed capital is equal to the matrix set of rates of growth of fixed capital, here called $\boldsymbol{G}$. The above equation can thus be rewritten as:

$$\boldsymbol{p} = w\boldsymbol{a_n}(\mathbf{I} - \boldsymbol{A}\star\boldsymbol{G})^{-1} \qquad (1)$$

where, as with $\boldsymbol{A}\star\Pi$, $\boldsymbol{A}\star\boldsymbol{G}$ is a direct product of the two matrices, here $\boldsymbol{A}$ and $\boldsymbol{G}$, with $\boldsymbol{A}\star\boldsymbol{G} \equiv [a_{ij}g_{ij}]$.

In the special case of the natural economy, i.e., when the rates of growth and the rates of profit for each capital stock are equated, $\boldsymbol{G} = \Pi$, it turns out that prices are proportional to the vertically hyper-integrated labour coefficient $\boldsymbol{l}$. This coefficient is the ***unweighted*** sum of the direct and hyper-indirect requirements in labour to produce one unit of consumption good.[2] Setting $w = 1$, the vector of prices *is equal* to the vector of vertically hyper-integrated labour coefficient: $\boldsymbol{p} = \boldsymbol{l}$.[3]

Let us then assume, as Pasinetti (1988) does, an economy with constant technical coefficients (say, because of constant returns to scale and no technical progress). Suppose

[1] The rates of profit differ both across production processes and across kinds of produced inputs. See Cas and Rymes (1991, pp. 20–23).

[2] Indirect labour requirements are excluded, since there are no intermediary inputs and since there is no depreciation on fixed capital.

[3] Similarly, besides the vector of hyper-vertically integrated labour coefficient $l$, one could identify a matrix $\boldsymbol{H} = \boldsymbol{A}(\boldsymbol{I} - \boldsymbol{A}\star\boldsymbol{G})^{-1}$, each column-vector of which is a composite commodity representing one unit of vertically hyper-integrated productive capacity for the final good $i$. Here, as in Pasinetti (1973), such a unit would depend on what is going on in the rest of the economy.

that this economy has three industries, each producing a single good. Two consumption goods ($c_1$ and $c_2$) and one capital good ($k_3$) are being produced. The same capital good is used as the means of production in all three industries. Note that this capital good is a basic good. Because there is no change in the technical coefficients, *any increase in output is equivalent to an increase in the inputs*. Let us call $g_1$ the rate of growth of the first consumption good, and hence the rate of growth of the capital stock related to the first industry. Similarly, $g_2$ is the rate of growth of the second consumption good and of its capital stock, while $g_3$ is the rate of growth of the investment good and of the capital stock of the investment-good industry. Thus growth rates (and natural profit rates) now differ only across industries (production processes). We may now leave out the Schur product $\boldsymbol{A}\star\boldsymbol{G}$, and make use of standard matrix multiplication to define $\boldsymbol{A}\hat{\boldsymbol{G}}$, where the rates of growth are now given by the following diagonal matrix:

$$\hat{\boldsymbol{G}} = \begin{bmatrix} g_1 & 0 & 0 \\ 0 & g_2 & 0 \\ 0 & 0 & g_3 \end{bmatrix}$$

Similarly, the labour coefficient vector and the price vector are given by:

$$\boldsymbol{a_n} = (a_{n1}, a_{n2}, a_{n3})$$

$$\boldsymbol{p} = (p_{c1}, p_{c2}, p_{k3})$$

while the technological matrix $\boldsymbol{A}$ of capital/output ratios is the following:

$$\boldsymbol{A} = \begin{bmatrix} 0 & 0 & 0 \\ 0 & 0 & 0 \\ a_{31} & a_{32} & a_{33} \end{bmatrix}$$

and where the $(\mathbf{I} - \boldsymbol{A}\hat{\boldsymbol{G}})$ term is equal to:

$$(\boldsymbol{I}\text{–}\boldsymbol{A}\hat{\boldsymbol{G}}) = \begin{bmatrix} 1 & 0 & 0 \\ 0 & 1 & 0 \\ -g_1 a_{31} & -g_2 a_{32} & 1-g_3 a_{33} \end{bmatrix}$$

Solving the price equation (1) above in the standard manner, with $w = 1$ as already assumed, one gets the following:

$$p_{c1} = a_{n1} + \frac{a_{n3} g_1 a_{31}}{1 - g_3 a_{33}} \quad (2)$$

$$p_{c2} = a_{n2} + \frac{a_{n3} g_2 a_{32}}{1 - g_3 a_{33}} \quad (3)$$

$$p_{k3} = \frac{a_{n3}}{1 - g_3 a_{33}} \quad (4)$$

What should be noted is that the price of each consumption good depends on the rate of growth of the investment-good industry, $g_3$. There is only one price for the capital good, $p_{k3}$. That price is valid for both hyper-vertically integrated sectors; just like the other prices, it depends on the overall rate of growth of the investment-good industry. Under this view of vertical integration, prices in one vertically integrated sector do not depend solely on the rate of growth of that sector. They also depend on the accumulation which is going on in the other sectors. Another way to put it is to say that natural prices in this vertically integrated sector do not depend only on the rate of profit in its consumption-good industry: it also depends on the rate of profit required in the other sectors.

### 3. Pasinetti's view of vertical integration

The above is not Pasinetti's view. The view of vertical integration that he presents in his 1988 paper is analogous to the model that he presented in his 1981 book. In the latter, the reader may recall that most of the chapters are based on the assumption that capital goods are produced by labour alone. This, however, is not crucial. What is important is that, even in the more complex model involving capital goods for the production of capital goods, it is assumed that each sort of capital good is only used in one vertically integrated sector. This may be linked to Pasinetti's decision to measure capital in units of vertically integrated productive capacity (Pasinetti, 1981, p. 36). To each consumption good corresponds a specific unit of productive capacity. Therefore, each consumption good is matched with a specific composite capital good. As Pasinetti (1981, p. 43) puts it, 'each of the capital goods sectors makes capital goods for itself and for the corresponding consumption goods sector'. In the formalisation adopted by Pasinetti, each consumption good is fitted with a single particular capital good, and that capital good has no relationship with the other consumption goods. Quite obviously, as has been pointed out by several readers, within such a system there are no basic goods, since any given capital good is only relevant for a single sector. In the special case of the natural economy, prices in each sector are proportional to the sum of the direct, indirect and hyper-indirect labour requirements. The latter, by construction so to speak, only depend on the growth rate of the relevant sector.

One of the main aims of Pasinetti's 1988 paper is to recover the same independent price structures, but within a more general model where a given capital good may be required to produce several different consumption goods, the output of which is growing at different rates.[1] Our simplified model, with its two consumption goods, corresponds to such a model, since its single capital good is required to produce itself and both consumption goods. What Pasinetti does, conceptually, is to split the machines of this single capital good into two separate and independent groups, as if they were two firms, each autonomously feeding a different consumption-good industry. The machines of the first group are only used to produce the first consumption good or to expand the stock of machines required for the production or the expansion of this first consumption-good industry. Similarly, the machines of the second group are only used to produce the second consumption good, or to expand the required stock of machines related to that second consumption good. By doing so, Pasinetti gets rid of the interdependence inherent to the presence of a basic good, i.e., the capital good that enters all three industries. Although there is a single capital good, it is as if that good had been separated into two different independent goods, each relevant to a distinct consumption-good industry.

For each hyper-vertically integrated sector, Pasinetti is then able to define a hyper-vertically integrated labour coefficient, which depends only on the growth requirement of the consumption good corresponding to that sector. In the case of the natural economy, one has:

[1] Such a general framework had been presented in Pasinetti (1973), again in answer to questions. The framework was more general in the sense that it allowed for basic commodities, but it considered the issue of accumulation only briefly.

$$p^{(i)} = l^{(i)} = a_n(\mathbf{I} - g_i A)^{-1}$$

where $g_i$ is a scalar representing the rate of growth of the ith consumption good and of its capital stock. Only one component of that $l^{(i)}$ labour coefficient vector is actually relevant for each consumption good, its ith component, which is a scalar and which we may call $l^{(i)}_i$. That component will determine the price of the consumption good concerned. However, the capital good of our little model appears in two different vertically integrated sectors, and as Pasinetti (1988, p. 129) points out, there will be in such a case two different natural prices for the same means of production, each natural price being specific to a particular hyper-sub-system. In our simplified model, the relevant prices for the first sector are:

$$p_{c1}^{(1)} = a_{n1} + \frac{a_{n3}g_1a_{31}}{1 - g_1a_{33}} \tag{5}$$

$$p_{k3}^{(1)} = \frac{a_{n3}}{1 - g_1a_{33}} \tag{6}$$

In the second sector, the relevant prices are:

$$p_{c2}^{(2)} = a_{n2} + \frac{a_{n3}g_2a_{32}}{1 - g_2a_{33}} \tag{7}$$

$$p_{k3}^{(2)} = \frac{a_{n3}}{1 - g_2a_{33}} \tag{8}$$

We are now in a position to compare Pasinetti's view of vertical integration with the previous view, which was simply based on Leontief's inverse, and which, for lack of a better term, I called the standard view. In the latter (equations (2) to (4)), although prices take into account the direct and hyper-indirect labour requirements, prices reflect what is going on in the rest of the economy. This is illustrated by the appearance of the $g_3$ variable in the prices $p_{c1}$ and $p_{c2}$ of the two consumption goods. In Pasinetti's framework (equations (5) to (8)), every sub-system is truly isolated from the rest of the economy. Prices, or vertically integrated labour requirements, only depend on the rate of growth of the sub-system in question. For instance, the price of the first consumption good, $p_{c1}{}^{(1)}$ only depends on the rate of growth $g_1$. Similarly, still in the natural economy, the price of a unit of hyper-vertically integrated productive capacity is defined without ambiguity, since it only depends on the rate of growth of its corresponding consumption good (Pasinetti, 1988, p. 134).

The 'price' to pay for this hypothetical independence is that the same capital good must have two different prices in the two sub-systems, here given by the two values taken by $p_{k3}$ in equations (6) and (8). In Pasinetti's view of vertical integration, the cost of providing new capital goods to sustain growth in the first sub-system is presumed to be independent of what is going on elsewhere in the economy. This is not the case in the standard view. The choice between the standard view and Pasinetti's view of vertical integration would thus seem to depend on the relative benefits of avoiding messy interdependences and of taking them explicitly into account.

## 4. Interdependence in the standard view

One may wonder what the relationship is between the various rates of growth, i.e., between $g_1$, $g_2$ and $g_3$. Even within our simple three-industry model, the answer may be relatively complex. Let us call $\Delta K = I$ the overall investment in capital goods and call $K$ the current overall stock of machines. The stocks of machines in each industry are respectively $K_1$, $K_2$ and $K_3$. It follows that:

$$I = g_1K_1 + g_2K_2 + g_3K_3$$

and that:

$$g = I/K = g_1(K_1/K) + g_2(K_2/K) + g_3(K_3/K)$$

The proportion of the overall capital stock that can be found in each industry is thus equal to $K_i/K = \lambda_i$, and we can rewrite the above equation as:

$$g = I/K = g_1\lambda_1 + g_2\lambda_2 + g_3\lambda_3 \tag{9}$$

There exists a supply constraint on this overall rate of accumulation. This constraint is the amount of investment goods that can be produced under existing conditions. This amount depends on the current stock of machines in the investment industry, $K_3$, and the capital to output ratio of the investment producing industry, $a_{33}$. We have:

$$I = K_3/a_{33} \tag{10}$$

and hence:

$$g = I/K = (K_3/K)/a_{33} = \lambda_3/a_{33} \tag{11}$$

The overall rate of accumulation is thus by definition a positive function of the proportion of machines in the investment industry and an inverse function of the capital to output ratio of this industry. At a moment of time, once these two elements are historically given, there can only be a single overall rate of capital accumulation.[1] There are thus seven variables ($g_1$, $g_2$, $g_3$, $g$, $\lambda_1$, $\lambda_2$, $\lambda_3$) and five equations: the three historically given shares of machines $\lambda_i$, and equations (9) and (11). Two of the three sectoral growth rates may thus be chosen as exogenous variables. The choice of the exogenous variables is *not* indifferent, as we shall soon see.

While the $\lambda_i$ variables are fixed at a moment of time, they are endogenous over time, unless one assumes that the rates $g_1$, $g_2$ and $g_3$ are all equal. From the definition of $\lambda_i$, the evolution of the relative proportions of capital in each $i$ sector is given by the following equation:

$$\frac{d\lambda_i/dt}{\lambda_i} = \hat{\lambda}_i = g_i - g \tag{12}$$

Similarly, while the overall rate of accumulation $g$ is fixed by the supply constraint at a given moment of time, this overall rate is endogenous through time. Any change in $\lambda_3$—the share of capital held by the investment-good industry—must induce a proportional change in $g$, as can be seen from equation (11), having supposed from the very beginning that there is no change in technical coefficients (the parameter $a_{33}$ is constant and there is no excess capacity in the investment-good industry). From equations (11) and (12), it can easily be shown that:

$$dg/dt = g(g_3 - g) \tag{13}$$

Two cases must now be distinguished. Let us first assume that the rate of growth of the

[1] If the rate of capacity utilisation can be different from unity, then the overall rate of accumulation can be anything, up to its maximum value given by equation (11). This case will be covered in the next section.

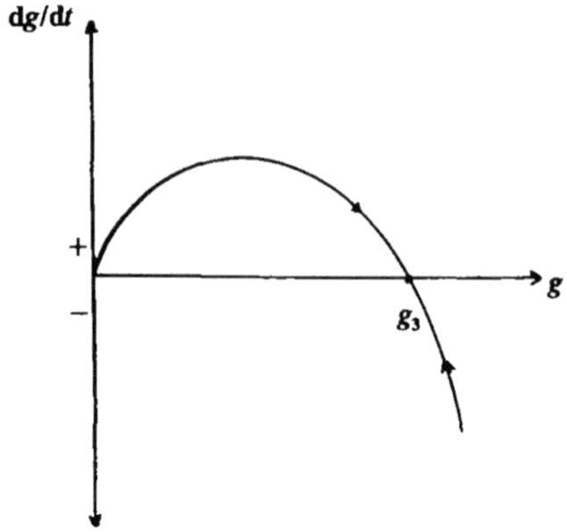


**Fig. 1.** *The growth rate of the investment sector is a constant: stability.*

investment sector, $g_3$, is one of the two exogenous variables among $g_1$, $g_2$, $g_3$. From equation (13), the phase diagram shown in Figure 1 can be derived. Equation (13) reveals that there are two equilibria, $g = 0$ and $g = g_3$. Only the latter is a stable equilibrium, as can be seen from the phase diagram. Thus, for instance, if the overall rate of accumulation $g$ is below the given growth rate of the investment-good industry $g_3$, $g$ will converge towards the fixed $g_3$.

Let us now consider more closely the end result of this convergence process. Let us assume that $g = g_3$. Substituting $g_3$ for $g$ in equation (9), we get the following solution where, as one might expect, the rate of growth of the investment good industry (or the overall rate of growth) must equal the weighted average of the two rates of growth of the two consumption good industries. We have:

$$g^\star = g_3{}^\star = \frac{g_1\lambda_1 + g_2\lambda_2}{1 - \lambda_3} \tag{14}$$

where $\lambda_i/(1 - \lambda_3)$ is the share of the machines being held by the $i$th consumption good industry among all the machines being held by the consumption good industries.

While in a two-sector model the above condition would be sufficient, there is an additional condition that the growth variables must fulfil in a three-sector model.[1]

[1] Things are neater when there is only one consumption-good industry with the investment-good industry. The reader may wish to skip the remainder of the present section, and read only its last paragraph and the present footnote, which deals with the much simpler two-sector case. When the rate of growth of the investment industry ($g_3$) is the given variable, then it can be shown with the help of equation (12) that the time-derivative of the endogenous rate of growth of the single consumption good is given by:

$$dg_1/dt = g_1(g_3 - g_1)$$

This implies without any ambiguity that the rate of accumulation of the consumption-good industry converges towards that of the investment-good industry (the phase diagram is similar to that of Fig. 1). However, when the rate of growth of the single consumption-good industry ($g_1$) is the fixed variable, then it can be shown that the time-derivative of the endogenous rate of growth of the investment-good industry is given by:

$$dg_3/dt = g_1(g_3 - g_1)(\lambda_1/\lambda_3)$$

The above clearly shows that any discrepancy between the two growth rates will be amplified. If, for instance, $g_3$ is greater than $g_1$, $g_3$ will be growing (the phase diagram is similar to that of Figure 2, with $g_1$ being substituted for $g^{\star\star}$). The model becomes unstable.

Because of equations (11) and (12), and the assumed constancy of the technical coefficients, the equality $g = g_3$ implies that the proportion of capital $\lambda_3$ held by the investment sector does not change, as shown by equation (12). This also implies, as can be seen through equation (11), that both of these growth rates remain constant, as can be seen explicitly in equation (13), despite changes in the $\lambda_1$ and $\lambda_2$ variables. As a result the following condition must hold:

$$dg^*/dt = g_1 \frac{d\lambda_1}{dt} + g_2 \frac{d\lambda_2}{dt} = 0$$

Making use of equation (12), the above condition can be solved for $g$ and requires that:

$$g^{**} = \frac{\lambda_1 g_1^2 + \lambda_2 g_2^2}{\lambda_1 g_1 + \lambda_2 g_2} \tag{15}$$

The overall rate of accumulation $g$ must thus equal the values given by both equations (14) and (15). It is easily shown that both equations are fulfilled only if $g_1 = g_2$, or if one of the two consumption industries vanishes. Starting out from an arbitrary position, with unequal $g$ and $g_3$, two situations arise. Either one of the consumption industries is assumed to grow at the rate of accumulation of the investment industry (say $g_1 = g_3$), in which case the endogenous growth rate of the other consumption industry ($g_2$) will converge towards the growth rate of the first, but then we are eventually back to balanced growth—which is precisely what vertically integrated sectors were designed to avoid. Or else—the more general case—neither equation (14) nor equation (15) will ever be realised, except at the limit, when the importance of the consumption industry with the exogenous slow-growing rate has approached zero ($\lambda_1/(1-\lambda_3) \approx 0$). During the transition the faster-growing consumption industry will see the importance of its weight increase, while the weight of the slower-growing consumption industry will decrease. Without any additional changes, the weighted average of the growth rate of the consumption industries would thus increase through time, until it catches up with the growth rate of the investment industry (when $\lambda_1 = 0$).

Let us now deal with the second case, where one assumes that both of the consumption-good industries grow at some exogenous rate, while the rate of growth of the investment industry is the endogenous variable. Making use of equations (9) and (11), for given $g_1$ and $g_2$, we find what the rate of growth of the investment-good industry must be to fulfil the supply constraint. The rate of growth $g_3$ is thus a residual:

$$g_3 = \frac{1}{a_{33}} - \frac{g_1\lambda_1 + g_2\lambda_2}{\lambda_3} \tag{16}$$

Note, from the above equation, that if $g_3 > g$, we have the following inequality:

$$\lambda_1(g_3 - g_1) + \lambda_2(g_3 - g_2) > 0 \tag{17}$$

Taking the time derivative of equation (16) allows us to follow the evolution of the rate of accumulation of the investment industry. Recall that $a_{k3}$, $g_1$ and $g_2$ are constants, while all three $\lambda_i$s are endogenous variables. We have:

$$\frac{dg_3}{dt} = \frac{-[g_1(d\lambda_1/dt) + g_2(d\lambda_2/dt)]\lambda_3 + [g_1\lambda_1 + g_2\lambda_2](d\lambda_3/dt)}{\lambda_3^2}$$

Making use of equation (12), the above equation comes down to:

$$dg_3/dt = g_1(g_3 - g_1)(\lambda_1/\lambda_3) + g_2(g_3 - g_2)(\lambda_2/\lambda_3) \tag{18}$$

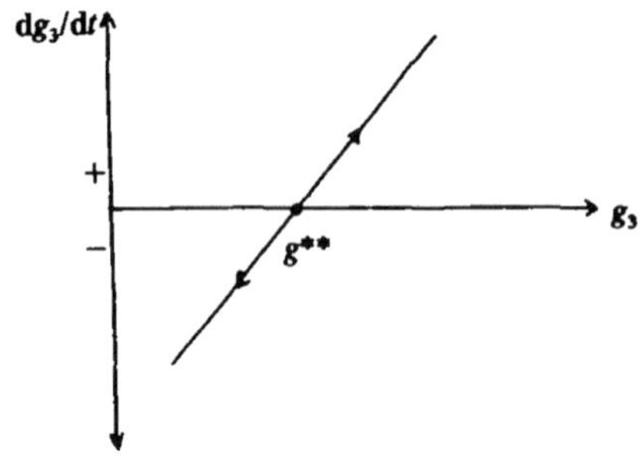


**Fig. 2.** *The growth rate of the investment sector is a variable: instability.*

It can be shown from equation (18) that $dg_3/dt > 0$ if $g_3 > g^{**}$ (the $g^{**}$ of equation (15)). Figure 2 illustrates the phase diagram of this unstable second case. Instability is obvious when the rate of growth of the investment industry is larger than both exogenously given rates of growth of the consumption industries ($g_3 > g_1, g_3 > g_2$, and hence $g_3 > g$). Then the rate of growth of the investment industry and that of the overall rate of accumulation—the latter trailing $g_3$ because of equation (13)—are forever increasing, until $g$ hits its upper limit at $g = 1/a_{k3}$, when almost all machines are located in the investment industry. Reciprocally, if, at a moment in time, the residual rate of growth of the investment industry is below both rates of growth of the consumption industries ($g_3 < g_1, g_3 < g_2$, and hence $g_3 < g$), then the rate of growth of the investment industry tends towards zero. Eventually, the share of machines in that industry will tend towards zero ($\lambda_3 = 0$), at which point the exogenous rates of accumulation $g_1$ and $g_2$ will become unsustainable, as a result of a lack of machines being produced.[1]

It follows from the above that two sets of hypotheses may be considered. In the first set, one assumes that the rates of accumulation of the consumption industries are constants, as one would be tempted to do in a model based on vertical integration. But then one encounters a problem similar to Harrod's instability problem. The accumulation of such a system is unsustainable. The share of the investment-good industry and its rate of growth are either ever-increasing or ever-decreasing. This implies that the economic system ends up producing either no consumption goods or no investment goods in relative terms. No such instability problem is encountered with the second set of hypotheses, when the rate of accumulation of one of the consumption-good industries is assumed to be endogenous, while the rate of growth of the investment-good industry is a given. But this assumption is not a very tempting one in a model devoted to vertically integrated sectors. There are only two ways out: either to assume Pasinetti's view of interdependence, or to forsake the assumption of fixed coefficients. We deal with the latter first.

## 5. The standard view with flexible technical coefficients

Let us again assume that the rates of accumulation of both consumption-good industries are given exogenously, while the rate of growth of the investment-good industry is endogenous. We shall now assume that there is excess capacity in the investment-good

[1] Things are more complicated when $g_3$ is somewhere between $g_1$ and $g_2$, as a comparison of equations (17) and (18) shows.

industry, i.e., the rate of capacity utilisation of the investment industry is $u_3$, and can be anywhere between zero and unity.[1] The technical coefficient $a_{33}$ must now be reinterpreted as a constant capital to capacity ratio, instead of the usual capital to output ratio. The true capital to output ratio is now given by $a_{33}/u_3$. The presence of excess capacity in the investment industry now yields some flexibility to the overall rate of capital accumulation. Whereas before this rate was unique, once the share of machines in the investment-good industry was given at a moment in time, as in equation (11), there is now a multiplicity of possible overall rates of accumulation, as can be seen from the new constraint:

$$g = I/K = u_3\lambda_3/a_{33} \tag{19}$$

Let us again focus our attention on the special case where the rate of accumulation of the investment industry is equal to the overall rate of accumulation. This implies, as we saw with equation (14), that these rates are a weighted average of the rates of accumulation going on in the consumption-good industry. Hence we need:

$$g^\star = g_3{}^\star = \frac{g_1\lambda_1 + g_2\lambda_2}{1 - \lambda_3} \tag{14}$$

Whereas before—with constant technical coefficients—such an equality could be achieved but not sustained, this condition can remain realised as long as there are reserves of excess capacity which allow the investment-good industry to increase the rate of growth of its output, thus allowing the overall rate of accumulation to increase through time. The rate of capacity utilisation of the investment industry is the variable that will allow unbalanced growth to proceed, for the historically given shares of machines. Combining equations (14) and (19), this required rate of capacity utilisation is:

$$u_3{}^\star = \frac{(g_1\lambda_1 + g_2\lambda_2)a_{33}}{(1 - \lambda_3)\lambda_3}$$

Provided the required rate of capacity utilisation is smaller than unity, the values of $g^\star$ and $g_3$ can be equated and realised and the share of machines held by the investment-good industry ($\lambda_3$) remains a constant. In the general case, where both rates of accumulation have not yet been equated, the following time derivative follows from equation (19):

$$dg/dt = g[(g_3 - g)u_3 + \hat{u}_3] \tag{20}$$

where $\hat{u}_3$ is the rate of change of the rate of capacity utilisation in the investment-good sector.

This equation can be contrasted with equation (13), when excess capacity was assumed away. Here, as before, any discrepancy between $g$ and $g_3$ will tend to be reduced. However, in contrast to the cases discussed in the previous section, the overall rate of accumulation need *not* be a constant when it is equal to the rate of accumulation of the investment industry, i.e., when $g = g_3$. Indeed, we see from equation (20) that when these two rates of growth are equal, the overall rate of accumulation must be non-negative and its own rate of increase must be:

$$\hat{g}^\star = \hat{u}_3{}^\star \tag{21}$$

The rate of change of this special rate of accumulation can itself be computed by taking

[1] This is, of course, an assumption akin to Kaleckian economics. See Dutt (1990).

the time-derivative of equation (14), recalling that $\lambda_3$ is a constant, as was done in the previous section. One gets:

$$\hat{g}^{\star} = \frac{\lambda_1\lambda_2(g_1 + g_2)^2}{(g_1\lambda_1 + g_2\lambda_2)(\lambda_1 + \lambda_2)} > 0 \tag{22}$$

As the faster-growing consumption industry increases its share of the machines, the overall rate of accumulation and the rate of accumulation of the investment-good industry must increase. This is accommodated by the increase in the rate of capacity utilisation of the investment-good industry.

Finally, this section should be concluded by making some remarks about the natural prices in the standard view of vertical integration. Whereas before—when there was no excess capacity—natural prices had to change through time, the same natural prices may remain constant through time when the rate of capacity utilisation in the investment-good sector is endogenous. Take, for instance, the natural price of the first consumption good, which was previously given by equation (2) and which is now given by:

$$p_{c1} = a_{n1} + \frac{a_{n3}g_1a_{31}}{1 - g_3(a_{33}/u_3)} \tag{23}$$

When the rate of accumulation of the investment-good industry is a correctly weighted average of the rates of growth of the two consumption-good industries, $g_3$ is equal to its $g_3^{\star}$ value, and equation (21) holds. This implies that the expression $g_3(a_{33}/u_3)$ in equation (23) remains constant, and hence that all natural prices remain constant through time. Adding the possibility of excess capacity thus provides the standard view of vertical integration with coherence and simplicity.

## 6. Interdependence in Pasinetti's view

Pasinetti's framework also allows the provision of coherence and simplicity in the analysis of vertical integration. It retains sustainable growth without fixing in advance the rate of accumulation in the investment industry, while assuming given rates of growth for the consumption-good industries and holding on to fixed technical coefficients. By splitting the investment industry into two independent groups, Pasinetti introduces two constraints which replace equation (10). This gives to his system of equations an additional degree of liberty, which plays the role of the endogenous rate of capacity utilisation in the previous section, but without having to assume the existence of excess capacity. The stock of capital in the investment industry is now split in two:

$$K_3 = K_{31} + K_{32}$$

where $K_{31}$ and $K_{32}$ are the stocks of capital used in the two groups of the investment industry, to allow growth and reproduction of the machines used in each of the two vertically integrated sectors.

Let us concentrate our attention on the first vertically integrated sector, knowing that symmetric conditions apply to the second sector. From the definition of vertically integrated sectors, we know that *within* each vertically integrated sector, all rates of accumulation are equal. This implies that the overall rate of accumulation of the first sub-system is $g_1$. It also implies that $\lambda_{31}$ is a constant, where $\lambda_{31}$ is the share of the machines held by the investment sub-industry among all the machines being held in the first vertically integrated sector, and is defined as:

$$\lambda_{31} = K_{31}/(K_1 + K_{31}) \tag{24}$$

In the first vertically integrated sector, a supply condition, similar to that of equations (10) and (11), needs to apply:[1]

$$g_1 = \lambda_{31}/a_{33} \tag{25}$$

Equation (25) tells us that the growth of demand for the first consumption good determines what value the $\lambda_{31}$ parameter must take for supply-side issues to be kept in the background. Or, reciprocally, for an historically given $\lambda_{31}$, the equation tells us what the rate of growth of demand in that sub-system could be. Similar relations are required for the second vertically integrated sector, where, with symmetric notations, $g_2 = \lambda_{32}/a_{33}$. The overall rate of accumulation of the economy, $g$ in the Pasinetti model, is now given by:

$$g = g_1[(K_1 + K_{31})/K] + g_2[(K_2 + K_{32})/K]$$

The terms between square brackets represent the proportion of machines that are to be found in each vertically integrated sector. With the previous definitions, and equations (24) and (25), the above equation can now be rewritten as:

$$g = \frac{g_1\lambda_1}{1 - \lambda_{31}} + \frac{g_2\lambda_2}{1 - \lambda_{32}} \tag{26}$$

The macroeconomic rate of growth $g$ is thus a weighted average and will change through time.[2] However, the proportion of machines being held by the investment-good industry is also an endogenous variable, the value of which can be found through the definitions of the $\lambda_i$s and the definition given by equation (24). This proportion $\lambda_3$ is again a weighted average which is bounded:

$$\lambda_3 = \frac{K_{31} + K_{32}}{K} = \frac{\lambda_{31}\lambda_1}{1 - \lambda_{31}} + \frac{\lambda_{32}\lambda_2}{1 - \lambda_{32}} \tag{27}$$

The proportion of capital being held in the investment-good industry is a variable because $\lambda_1$ and $\lambda_2$ will vary through time as long as $g_1$ and $g_2$ are unequal. Provided the series of sectoral supply constraints given by equation (25) are fulfilled, then the supply constraint on the overall value of the rate of accumulation will also be fulfilled. With the appropriate substitutions, it can be verified that the values of $g$ and $\lambda_3$ given by equations (26) and (27) always validate the overall supply constraint given by equation (11). In addition, whereas before the rate of accumulation of the investment industry was either a constant or a residual, the rate of growth $g_3$ is now a weighted average, as is the case for $g$ in equation (26). The rate of accumulation of the investment industry is endogenous and, from equations (9) and (26), given by:

$$g_3 = \frac{\lambda_{31}\lambda_1 g_1}{(1 - \lambda_{31})\lambda_3} + \frac{\lambda_{32}\lambda_2 g_2}{(1 - \lambda_{32})\lambda_3} \tag{28}$$

In contrast to what happened in equation (16), in the standard case of section 4, the rate of growth of the overall investment industry is now bounded, somewhere between the

[1] As Pasinetti (1981, p. 47) points out, 'a *series* of sectoral conditions' have to be fulfilled. 'Each sector *i* must be endowed with that stock of productive capacity which is necessary to produce the amount of commodity *i* which is demanded.'

[2] This is what Englmann (1987) calls the heterogeneity of capital over time.

values taken by $g_1$ and $g_2$, as one would expect.[1] Provided equation (25) is fulfilled, Pasinetti's vertical integration framework allows the analysis of unbalanced growth, with given rates of growth in the consumption industries, while avoiding the instability that plagues other approaches with fixed coefficient assumptions. Pasinetti's device, so to speak, is to suppose that within each sub-system the historically given supply constraints are compatible with sectoral demand growth, as in equation (25). By doing so, Pasinetti solves the so-called problem of reproportioning, without having to forsake fixed technical coefficients. In addition, while considering exogenously given rates of sectoral growth, Pasinetti is able to put aside the complex variations of the overall rate of accumulation and of the rate of accumulation of the overall investment industry, as given by equations (26) and (28).[2] This may help to understand why Pasinetti is so keen to develop his interpretation of vertical integration, in contrast to what I have called the standard view.

The consequences of the above for prices in a natural economy are straightforward. Under Pasinetti's view of vertical integration, if $g_1$ and $g_2$ are the exogenous elements, Pasinetti's natural prices remain constant through time, despite continuous changes in the weighted averages which happen to be the rates of accumulation in the investment industry and in overall capital. This is the case where Pasinetti's view of vertical integration, which allows the avoidance of cumbersome weighting procedures, would seem to bring the most substantial dividends, for one would be hard-pressed to give an account of Pasinetti's natural prices when the overall rate of accumulation is assumed to be the exogenous variable. Under the more traditional view of vertical integration, that given by equations (2) to (4), the relative natural prices of consumption goods will have to vary through time in any case, since they depend on the various rates of growth, one of which at least must change. However, as we saw with equation (23) of the previous section, natural prices in the standard view can also be constant, despite changes in the overall rate of accumulation, when endogenous rates of capacity utilisation are taken into account. One wonders then which are the truly relative natural prices: Pasinetti's hyper-vertically integrated prices or those of the standard view of vertical integration.[3]

## 7. Conclusion

We have seen that there are two views of vertical integration: one where interdependence is still present, and one where interdependence is short-circuited. Pasinetti (1988, p. 125) claims that the intent of his 1988 paper is to generalise the analysis of vertical integration that could be found in Pasinetti (1973), where basic commodities are present but where growth is absent. What should now be clear is that Pasinetti (1988) is really trying to generalise the analysis of vertical integration developed in Pasinetti (1981) and which

[1] Note, by comparing equation (26) with equation (28), that the overall rate of accumulation $g$ and the rate of accumulation of the investment-good industry $g_3$ are different, unless the rates of growth of the two vertically integrated sectors are identical.

[2] Pasinetti (1988) sometimes leaves some ambiguity as to the necessary variability of at least one of $g_1$, $g_2$ and $g$, for within the interval of a page he assumes both the constancy of the overall rate of growth and that of the demand for consumption goods: 'Suppose, to begin with, constant technical coefficients and population growth' (p. 126); 'Each [consumption good] is expanding through time at its particular rate of growth ($g + r_i$), which we assume to be steady for the time being' (p. 127).

[3] Pasinetti (1988, p. 132) points out that the natural economy of equations (5) to (8) has the normative property of leading to the choice of technique which entails the minimisation of labour inputs. But the price system presented in equations (2) to (4)—or in its revised form with excess capacity— urely also has this property. Which prices are truly the most efficient ones: those partitioning capital goods into autonomous production processes or those taking into account what is going on in the overall economy?

arises from his earlier work in the 1960s, where accumulation is at the centre stage but where there are no basic commodities. The paper of 1988, as argued by its author, is thus 'one step further in the direction of the complete generalisation of the concepts of sub-system and vertically integrated sector', but because basic commodities are neutralised, it generalises the presentation of the 1981 book instead of that of the 1973 article. Rather, it is the so-called standard view, presented here in Section 1, with its interdependences, which is closest to the spirit of the 1973 article. We have seen, however, that there are good reasons for sticking to Pasinetti's view of vertical integration, because of the added flexibility that such a view procures. In particular, it allows the circumvention of complex weighting procedures, it averts unsustainable results, and it bypasses the requirements of excess capacity.

At the end of his paper, Pasinetti (1988, p. 134) hints of further developments of his model in the case of technical progress. In his book (1981), technical progress seems to be introduced exogenously in the various sub-systems. It is clear, however, that technical progress occurs at the level of the industry. In our simplified model, technical progress in the capital-good industry would affect equally both conceptually constructed groups producing the single capital good. The rate of technical progress in one sub-system thus cannot be assumed to be independent of the rate of technical progress occurring in other sub-systems.[1] Indeed, as the weight of the various components of a given unit of productive capacity will be changing, the rate of technical progress occurring in an investment-good-producing industry will have varying repercussions in two different hyper-integrated sectors.

The point is obvious when one thinks of basic goods in Sraffian analysis. Splitting the economy into sub-systems 'does not mean that there are no interconnections between these sub-systems, given that the system contains basic goods' (Englmann, 1985, p. 88). Some of the problems arising from the absence of these connections appear when technical progress must be measured and correctly assessed (Cas and Rymes, 1991, pp. 90–93). To adopt a view of vertical integration which seeks to avoid weighting complexities may thus be—for some purposes—excessively artificial, despite its obvious mathematical advantages for the analysis of unbalanced growth.

## Bibliography

Cas, A. and Rymes, T. K. 1991. *On Concepts and Measures of Multifactor Productivity in Canada: 1961–1980*, Cambridge, Cambridge University Press

Dutt, A. K. 1990. *Growth, Distribution and Uneven Development*, Cambridge, Cambridge University Press

Englmann, F. 1985. Pasinetti on the choice of technique: a note, *Cambridge Journal of Economics*, vol. 9, no. 1, 85–8

Englmann, F. 1987. Structural change, heterogeneity of capital over time and the non-uniqueness of 'the' uniform rate of profit, *Manchester School of Economics and Social Studies*, vol. 55, no. 2, 184–96

Hagemann, H. 1990. Capital goods, pp. 123–7 in Eatwell, J., Milgate, M. and Newman, P. (eds), *The New Palgrave: Capital Theory*, London, Macmillan

[15] This was pointed out right away: 'Technical change takes place at the industry level so that rates of productivity growth in the different integrated sectors cannot be thought of as being independent of each other' (Schefold, 1982, p. 549), and it has recently been underlined again. 'The *industry-specific nature of technical change* also implies that, contrary to Pasinetti's assumption, rates of productivity growth in the different vertically integrated sectors cannot be thought as being independent of each other' (Hagemann, 1990, p. 126). Most likely, Pasinetti assumes that the rates of productivity growth in each vertically integrated sector are, by definition, the result of the rates of productivity growth in each industry.

Pasinetti, L. L. 1973. The notion of vertical integration in economic analysis, *Metroeconomica*, vol. 25, no. 1, 1–29

Pasinetti, L. L. 1981. *Structural Change and Economic Growth*, Cambridge, Cambridge University Press

Pasinetti, L. L. 1988. Growing sub-systems, vertically hyper-integrated sectors and the labour theory of value, *Cambridge Journal of Economics*, vol. 12, no. 1, 125–34

Pasinetti, L. L. 1993. *Structural Economic Dynamics: A Theory of the Economic Consequences of Human Learning*, Cambridge, Cambridge University Press

Schefold, B. 1982. Review of Pasinetti's *Structural Change and Economic Growth*, *Kyklos*, vol. 35, no. 3, 548–50

*The Manchester School Vol LXV No. 2 March 1997*
*0025–2034 145–169*

# TRAVERSE IN A TWO-SECTOR KALECKIAN MODEL OF GROWTH WITH TARGET-RETURN PRICING*

by
MARC LAVOIE
and
PABLO RAMÍREZ-GASTÓN†
*University of Ottawa*

The first purpose of this article is to extend the Kaleckian model of growth and distribution to a two-sector framework, taking into account the fact that the investment good is a basic good. The second objective is to present an analysis of the traverse. It is shown that such a traverse exists when for instance profit margins are changed or when inducements to invest change. The Kaleckian traverse does not require the restrictions on technology that the standard Hicksian traverse needs.

## I Introduction

Kaleckian growth models, with oligopolistic industries, cost-plus prices, excess capacities and endogenous rates of capacity utilization, now seem to have superseded the standard Cambridgian growth models *à la* Robinson and Kaldor, where variations in demand are met in the long run by changes in prices at a normal rate of capacity utilization. The main purpose of this paper is to extend the so-called Kaleckian model of growth and distribution to a two-sector framework, with an investment good and a consumption good. The main objective in doing so is to present an analysis of the traverse from one steady growth path to another. The traverse of the Kaleckian model, where full employment is assumed away and where the real wage rate does not change during the traverse, will thus be contrasted with that of the neoclassical Hicksian traverse in the standard two-sector Cambridgian model, where

* Manuscript received 26.10.93; final version received 21.9.95.
† This paper was initially presented in May 1993 at the Rencontres de l'ISMEA, at the University of Marne-la-Vallée (France), and then at seminars at Aarhus University (Denmark), at the University of Paris X-Nanterre and at the New School for Social Research in New York. We wish to acknowledge the helpful comments of the participants as well as those of the anonymous referees, and those of Michel Rosier (University of Paris VII), Tom Rymes (Carleton University) and Mario Seccareccia (University of Ottawa).


Published by Blackwell Publishers Ltd, 108 Cowley Road, Oxford OX4 1JF, UK, and 350 Main Street, Malden, MA 02148, USA.

full employment is assumed to be maintained both before and during the transition.[1]

There have been few previous attempts at modelling such two-sector Kaleckian growth models. Some authors have discussed the issue informally, for instance Bhaduri (1985), or without behavioural equations, for instance Halevi and Kriesler (1991). The most advanced formulations, however, are those of Taylor (1989) and Dutt. Dutt arrives at two main results. First, it is shown that higher real wages lead to higher rates of profit and of accumulation, even in a two-sector model (Dutt, 1987). Second, it is shown that, even though growth rates of the two sectors will converge, their profit rates will not converge unless investment functions are arbitrarily designed to make them do so (Dutt, 1988).

Taylor's and Dutt's models have one drawback however, a drawback which has been underlined lately by Steedman (1992) in his critique of Kaleckian models in general. Steedman points out that mark-ups in various sectors cannot be independent of each other.[2] For instance, the profit margins on the costs of basic goods should enter the determination of the mark-ups for all goods. In Taylor's and Dutt's models, where there is a basic good—the investment good—it is assumed that the mark-up on unit wage costs of the consumption sector is independent of the price of the investment good. This may be a legitimate assumption to make, to simplify the analysis, in short-run analysis, or if one assumes that profit margins only depend on variable costs. However, if "these mark-ups are designed to cover, over time, both overhead costs and profits" as Asimakopulos (1975, p. 319) and many Kaleckians would argue, then it is clear that mark-ups in the consumption sector cannot be considered independent of the mark-up in the investment sector.

In the next section we thus present what we consider to be an appropriate Kaleckian pricing model within a two-sector framework. This will be followed by the presentation of the investment functions and the short-run solutions of the model. We shall then discuss the main result of the paper, that of the traverse from one steady-state rate of growth to another, when the profit margins of the investment sector or of the consumption sector are being modified. The induced changes in the sectoral rates of profit will also be discussed. The paper will conclude with a short discussion of possible extensions of the present Kaleckian traverse. Needless to say, the conclusions which we arrive at need not extend beyond two-sector models.

In the end, the reader might notice that there is a certain extent of

[1]Bhaduri (1975) has proposed calling such a specific sort of transition a "neoclassical traverse".

[2]It must be recognized that all Kaleckians are not equally at fault in this regard. Eichner (1987), for instance, takes interdependence into account in his pricing model.

complementarity with the work carried on by Boggio (1980, 1986). Just as we do, Boggio (1990, p. 57) considers that the full cost approach, or rather a specific version of it based on target-return pricing, is the proper and most realistic explanation of price formation. But whereas Boggio's work is mainly concerned with the possible convergence of full cost prices towards Sraffian prices of production, rates of accumulation and of capacity utilization are the focus of our model.

## II The Model

### *Assumptions of the Model*

The assumptions of the model are the following.

(a) There are two sectors in the economy: one produces an investment good and the other produces a consumption good.
(b) The investment good is a basic good: it enters in the production of the other good as well as in its own production.
(c) There is only fixed capital; circulating capital is set aside.
(d) There is no depreciation of capital goods.
(e) Capital goods are specific, i.e. they are bolted down: once installed, they cannot be moved from one sector to another.
(f) The other factor required for the production process is labour, the supply of which is assumed never to be scarce: either there is a reserve army of unemployed workers, or labour can be imported.
(g) There is no fixed (overhead) labour.
(h) There are constant returns to scale, and there is no technical progress.
(i) There is only one technique of production for the system.
(j) There is excess capacity: firms can increase production by increasing the rate of utilization of capacity, i.e. by starting up idle segments of plants.
(k) The supply of output can be immediately adapted to demand, as is usually assumed in Keynesian models.[3]
(l) When the degree of capacity utilization varies, the employment of labour varies proportionately.[4]

[3]In the terms of Duménil and Lévy (1987, p. 140), the model is one of "equilibrium dynamics", where "the market for commodities always remains in equilibrium, since in each period supply is immediately set equal to the level of demand".

[4]This may be linked to the "bolted down" assumption. When dealing with equipment and labour, Kaldor (1960, p. 104) points out the following: "It is a significant fact of modern technique that *given the type of equipment in existence* there is a relation of strong complementarity between them; that is to say, the extent to which the proportions of these factors can be varied in production is highly limited."

(m) There are no savings out of wages, but a proportion $s_p$ of the profits is being saved.
(n) The economy is a closed one, without government.
(o) Uncertainty is introduced by assuming the presence of rules of thumb, for instance target-return pricing, and investment decisions dependent on animal spirits and current rates of capacity utilization.
(p) Firms act in an oligopolistic framework, using normal cost pricing procedures.
(q) Profit margins over unit labour costs in each sector depend on a target rate of return over fixed capital.
(r) The nominal wage rate is the same for the two sectors.
(s) Capital goods are always valued at their replacement cost, rather than at their historical cost.
(t) There is one firm in each sector, in which case the firm in the investment sector values its capital stock according to the price charged for investment goods sold to the firm of the consumption sector; or there are many identical firms in each sector, in which case it is assumed that they behave just like one vertically integrated firm in each sector.

Some of the assumptions have been made to simplify computations. For example, many Kaleckian models include overhead labour (Asimakopulos, 1975; Rowthorn, 1981; Lavoie, 1992), but here its presence has been assumed away. Similarly, most proponents of normal cost pricing procedures would argue that capital must be valued at its historical cost (Lee, 1985), but here replacement cost is being assumed. Many of the above assumptions can be found in the central part of Robinson's *The Accumulation of Capital* (1956, ch. 8). For instance, with respect to the last assumption made, Robinson writes that "capital goods produced by an entrepreneur for his own use are valued at a price exceeding their wages cost by a notional profit margin" (1956, p. 75).

There are four assumptions which make the present model of the traverse different from the standard neoclassical Hicksian traverse. Here prices are fixed, capital is bolted down once installed, full employment is not assumed, and the rate of capacity utilization is an endogenous variable. In the typical Hicksian traverse, prices are flexible, capital can be moved from one sector to the other, while full employment and full (or normal) use of capacity are required throughout.[5]

[5]See O'Connell (1978) and Henry and Lavoie (1997) among many others. Sometimes the hypothesis of flexible prices and real wages, with given propensities to save, is replaced by one of flexible propensities to save, with fixed prices and wage rates. See O'Connell (1978) and Hicks (1965, p. 195).

*Target-return Pricing*

It will be assumed that firms in both sectors follow normal cost pricing procedures, according to a target-return pricing formula. This is a variant of cost-plus prices, more precisely a variant of full cost prices, since fixed costs are taken into consideration.[6] More specifically, to set the profit margin, fixed costs at a *standard* rate of capacity utilization are taken into account. As Bhaduri and Robinson (1980, p. 107) put it, "gross margins in each line are fixed up in such a way as to cover costs and yield a 'subjective-normal' rate of net profit at a standard level of utilisation of capacity". This corresponds to what Robinson (1956, pp. 185–186) had defined earlier as a "*subjective-normal price*, which is such that the gross margin entering into it is calculated as to yield a profit that the entrepreneurs concerned have come to regard as attainable . . . calculated upon the basis of an average or standard rate of output". Note that her pricing procedure coincides with Lanzillotti's definition of target-return pricing: "The margins added to standard costs are designed to produce the target rate of profit on investment, assuming standard volume to be the long-run average rate of plant utilization" (1958, p. 923).

In both sectors $j$, $j \equiv \mathrm{i, c}$ (i for investment goods and c for consumption goods), and for given unit labour costs $wa_{\ell j}$, with $w$ the nominal wage rate and $a_{\ell j}$ the labour–output ratio in sector $j$, prices thus depend on a profit margin $\theta_j$:

$$p_j = (1 + \theta_j)wa_{\ell j} \tag{1}$$

This profit margin, in each sector, must be such that sales ($q_j^{\mathrm{s}}$) corresponding to the standard degree of capacity utilization must provide enough profits to fulfil the *target rate of return* ($r_j^{\mathrm{s}}$). The corresponding normal flow of profits for each sector $j$, in any given period, may thus be written, from equation (1), either as

$$\Pi_j^{\mathrm{s}} = \theta_j wa_{\ell j} q_j^{\mathrm{s}} \tag{2}$$

or as

$$\Pi_j^{\mathrm{s}} = r_j^{\mathrm{s}} p_{\mathrm{i}} K_j \tag{3}$$

where $p_{\mathrm{i}}$ is the price of investment goods and $K_j$ is the stock of capital of each sector. Defining, for each sector $j$, the capital to full-capacity output ratio

$$a_{kj} = K_j / q_j^{\mathrm{f}} \tag{4}$$

and the standard rate of utilization of capacity

[6]According to Lee (1985, p. 206) full cost pricing is a "theoretically consistent and more realistic theory of prices", since there is "a tendency for present day firms to adopt full cost or target return pricing procedures over the mark up pricing procedure".

$$u_j^s = q_j^s / q_j^f \tag{5}$$

equation (3) can be rewritten as

$$\Pi_j^s = r_j^s p_i a_{kj} q_j^s / u_j^s \tag{6}$$

Combining equations (2) and (6), we find

$$\theta_j = \frac{r_j^s a_{kj} p_i}{u_j^s a_{\ell j} w} \tag{7}$$

Taking into account equation (1) as it applies to the investment sector, the profit margin of the investment sector is equal to

$$\theta_i = \frac{r_i^s a_{ki}}{u_i^s - r_i^s a_{ki}} \tag{8}$$

Under the assumptions of the model, the profit margin in the investment sector thus depends solely on its own standard rate of capacity utilization and target rate of return, as well as on its own capital to full-capacity ratio. By contrast, making use again of the price equations given by (1), it is obvious that the profit margin in the consumption sector depends on the profit margin in the investment sector. We have

$$\theta_c = \frac{r_c^s a_{kc}}{u_c^s} \frac{a_{\ell i}}{a_{\ell c}} (1 + \theta_i) \tag{9}$$

Taking equation (8) into account, the profit margin in the consumption sector becomes

$$\theta_c = \frac{u_i^s}{u_c^s} \frac{a_{\ell i}}{a_{\ell c}} \frac{r_c^s a_{kc}}{u_i^s - r_i^s a_{ki}} \tag{10}$$

Equation (10) indicates explicitly the direct relationship between the profit margin of the consumption sector and the target rate of return of the investment sector.[7] In a cost-plus model that takes fixed capital costs into account, the profit margin in the consumption sector depends on the parameters determining the profit margin in the investment sector. Any change in the determinants of the profit margin of the basic good will have an impact on all profit margins and hence on all prices. In particular, it should be noted that an increase in any profit margin, be it that of the consumption sector or the investment sector, will have a negative impact on the real wage rate of workers, provided it is assumed that firms of the consumption sector will not reduce their target rate of return when faced with higher prices for their capital goods.

[7]For expressions (8) and (10) to be economically meaningful, the following condition must hold: $u_i^s > r_i^s a_{ki}$. This inequality simply means that the value of output in the investment sector at normal use of capacity has to be greater than its normal amount of profits. Obviously, this must be the case, otherwise labour costs would have to be negative.

*Effective Demand*

The demand equations of the model are similar to those of Dutt (1988). It is assumed that any discrepancy that could arise between supply and demand is quickly corrected by a change in produced output, i.e. by a change in the level of capacity utilization. First note that, on the income side, the value of output can be divided into realized wages and realized profits. This is shown in equations (11) and (12), for the consumption and investment sectors respectively, where $r_j$ is the realized rate of profit, in contrast to the target rate of return $r_j^s$, of each sector.

$$p_c q_c = w a_{\ell c} q_c + r_c p_i K_c \tag{11}$$

$$p_i q_i = w a_{\ell i} q_i + r_i p_i K_i \tag{12}$$

Demand in the consumption sector is equal to total wages plus consumption out of realized profits. In real terms, when supply and demand are equated in the short run in the consumption sector, we have

$$q_c = (w/p_c)(a_{\ell c} q_c + a_{\ell i} q_i) + (1 - s_p)(p_i/p_c)(r_i K_i + r_c K_c) \tag{13}$$

Supply and demand in the investment sector are equated when the output of the investment sector equals the demand for capital goods arising from the consumption sector plus the demand for capital goods arising from the investment sector. Calling $g_j$ the rate of accumulation of each sector, we have the following condition:

$$q_i = g_c K_c + g_i K_i \tag{14}$$

We now discuss the investment function of each sector. In most Kaleckian models, desired accumulation depends on the expected rates of profit and of capacity utilization (Rowthorn, 1981; Dutt, 1988). It is generally assumed that these expected rates are the currently realized rates.[8] There are also some models where the rate of accumulation is said to depend on the rate of utilization and some measure of the normal rate of profit (Vianello, 1989; Bhaduri and Marglin, 1990; Kurz, 1990). In these models, despite the rate of utilization being endogenous, it is possible for the real wage rate and the rate of accumulation to move in opposite directions. Here, mainly because of the complexities added by the consideration of two sectors and the addition of target-return pricing, it will be assumed that the desired accumulation of each sector only depends on an autonomous element and its own rate of capacity utilization.[9] We thus have, for each sector $j$,

[8]See Amadeo (1987) for a model where the dynamics between the expected and the previously realized rates is made explicit. His results, and our assumption (k), explain why investment may be considered as an endogenous variable, even in the short period.

[9]Such an investment function, or a variation thereof, can be found in one-sector notation in the papers of Amadeo (1986) and Dutt (1990).

$$g_j = \alpha_j + \tau_j u_j \tag{15}$$

where $u_j$ is the realized rate of utilization of sector $j$, given by

$$u_j = q_j/q_j^{\mathrm{f}} \tag{16}$$

Taking equation (4) into consideration, the above equation can also be rewritten as

$$u_j = (q_j/K_j)(K_j/q_j^{\mathrm{f}}) = (q_j/K_j)a_{kj} \tag{17}$$

Desired accumulation in each sector $j$, equation (15), may thus be rewritten as

$$g_j = \alpha_j + \tau_j a_{kj}(q_j/K_j) \tag{18}$$

Ignoring for now the target-return pricing formula, i.e. taking into account only equations (1), (11), (12) and (18), the demand conditions given by equations (13), (14) and (17) yield the solutions for the rate of utilization of each sector:[10]

$$u_{\mathrm{c}}^* = a_{k\mathrm{c}}(\alpha_{\mathrm{c}} + \alpha_{\mathrm{i}}/\kappa)\Omega_{\mathrm{c}} \tag{19}$$

$$u_{\mathrm{i}}^* = a_{k\mathrm{i}}(\alpha_{\mathrm{c}}\kappa + \alpha_{\mathrm{i}})\Omega_{\mathrm{i}} \tag{20}$$

with the simplifying notation

$$\Omega = (1 - \tau_{\mathrm{i}}a_{k\mathrm{i}})s_p\theta_{\mathrm{c}} - \tau_{\mathrm{c}}a_{k\mathrm{c}}(a_{\ell\mathrm{i}}/a_{\ell\mathrm{c}})[1 + (1 - s_p)\theta_{\mathrm{i}}] \tag{21}$$

$$\Omega_{\mathrm{c}} = (a_{\ell\mathrm{i}}/a_{\ell\mathrm{c}})[1 + (1 - s_p)\theta_{\mathrm{i}}]/\Omega \tag{22}$$

$$\Omega_{\mathrm{i}} = (s_p\theta_{\mathrm{c}})/\Omega \tag{23}$$

$$\kappa = K_{\mathrm{c}}/K_{\mathrm{i}} \tag{24}$$

*Stability Analysis*

Dutt shows that the above solutions are stable, provided the denominator $\Omega$ of the solutions is positive.[11] This also ensures that the solutions themselves are positive. Obviously, $1 - \tau_{\mathrm{i}}a_{k\mathrm{i}}$ must be assumed to be strictly positive, i.e. the $\tau_{\mathrm{i}}$ reaction parameter must be sufficiently small ($\tau_{\mathrm{i}} < 1/a_{k\mathrm{i}}$). This condition being fulfilled, let us see what else short-run stability implies in the case of target-return pricing. Substituting $\theta_{\mathrm{c}}$ by its value in equation (9), we get $\Omega$ in terms of $\theta_{\mathrm{i}}$ only. After some manipulations, it can be shown that the denominator $\Omega$ is positive, and hence the solutions are stable, provided the following condition is fulfilled:

[10]See also Dutt (1988, pp. 149–150).

[11]Actually, Dutt (1988, p. 148) uses an adjustment rule which states that the supply of output responds to excess demand, assuming the adjustment coefficient to be unity. This comes down to assumption (k) of our model.

$$s_p > \frac{\tau_c a_{kc}}{(1 - \tau_i a_{ki})R_c + \tau_c a_{kc} R_i} \tag{25}$$

with

$$R_j = r_j^s a_{kj} / u_j^s \tag{26}$$

This is similar to the standard stability condition in one-sector Keynesian or Kaleckian growth models, where the parameters have to be such that the savings function is more sensitive to changes than the investment function. Here the propensity to save out of profits has to be larger than some combination of the parameters related to desired accumulation. The smaller the $\tau_j$s, the parameters representing the sensitivity of the investment functions to variations in the rates of capacity utilization, the higher the probability that the model is stable. Note that, provided the $\tau_i$ parameter is sufficiently small as defined above, the model is always stable when the $\tau_c$ coefficient is equal to zero, i.e. when the rate of accumulation of the consumption sector is exogenous. It can further be shown, substituting $R_c$ by its value in equation (26), that the stability condition does not depend on the capital to full-capacity output ratio of the consumption sector.

### *Other Solutions*

We may also easily derive the equations for the solutions of the rates of accumulation, using equations (15), (19) and (20). These solutions, as well as those pertaining to the rates of utilization, are valid both during the traverse and when the economy is in a steady state.

$$g_c^* = \alpha_c + \tau_c a_{kc}(\alpha_c + \alpha_i/\kappa)\Omega_c \tag{27}$$

$$g_i^* = \alpha_i + \tau_i a_{ki}(\alpha_c \kappa + \alpha_i)\Omega_i \tag{28}$$

These two equations are crucial. They tell us that, the other parameters being given, the rate of accumulation of the consumption sector is an inverse function of the variable $\kappa$, the ratio of the capital stocks being held in each sector, while the rate of accumulation of the investment sector is a direct function of that variable $\kappa$. This should be expected for, everything else being equal, the greater $\kappa$ is, the smaller the proportion of capital in the investment sector, and hence the higher the rate of capacity utilization of that sector. In the short run, the variable $\kappa$ is a constant, since the stocks of capital are given. But in the long run, because once they are installed the capital goods are immobile, $\kappa$ will vary according to the difference in the rate of accumulation of each sector.

Similarly, the solutions for the realized rates of profit may be found. First recall that the realized rates of profit are given by equations (11) and (12). The realized rate of profit in sector $j$ is thus

$$r_j^* = \frac{p_j q_j^* - w a_{\ell j} q_j^*}{p_i K_j} \tag{29}$$

where capital goods, as noted in the initial hypotheses, are valued at their replacement cost.[12] With the help of equation (1), and with a few manipulations, equation (29) can be rewritten

$$r_j^* = [\theta_j/(1+\theta_i)](a_{\ell j}/a_{\ell i})(q_i^*/q_j^f)(q_j^f/K_j) \tag{30}$$

The definitions given by (4) and (5) yield

$$r_j^* = [\theta_j/(1+\theta_i)](a_{\ell j}/a_{\ell i})(u_j^*/a_{kj}) \tag{31}$$

With the definition of $\theta_c$ (equation (9)) for the consumption sector and with the definition of $\theta_i$ (equation (8)) for the investment sector, the above equation yields a very simple formula for the realized rates of profit:

$$r_j^* = r_j^s(u_j^*/u_j^s) \tag{32}$$

As Bhaduri and Robinson (1980, p. 107) put it, "the ex-post rate of profits for each [sector] will be normal when the standard rate of output is realised. If actual output were higher than standard, profits would be more than normal, and vice versa." Such a result is not surprising. It clearly illustrates the importance of the realized rate of capacity utilization once the standard degree of utilization and the target rate of return have been set.

## III Comparative Statics

### *Dynamic Stability*

The set of equations (27) and (28) pertaining to the rates of accumulation are illustrated in Fig. 1, with the upward-sloping curve $g_i$ and the downward-sloping hyperbola $g_c$. There is a ratio $\kappa^*$ of the sectoral capital stocks for which the two sectoral rates of accumulation are equal, at $g^*$. This is the steady state, where both sectors are growing at the same rate. It can be shown that there is a tendency for such a steady state to occur, regardless of the relative capital intensity of the two sectors. This is the so-called dynamic stability issue. It can be studied by looking at the evolution through time of the $\kappa$ ratio. Taking the logarithmic derivative with respect

[12]As recalled by Kurz (1994, p. 409), there is a certain ambiguity in defining *realized* rates of profit. According to Robinson (1962, pp. 29–30), "the realised rate of profit is vague because there are various conventions that can be used to assess it". The present definition corresponds to what Robinson (1962, p. 29) calls the *current* rate of profit, "that is, the ratio of current gross profits, minus depreciation, to the value of the stock of capital at current replacement costs".

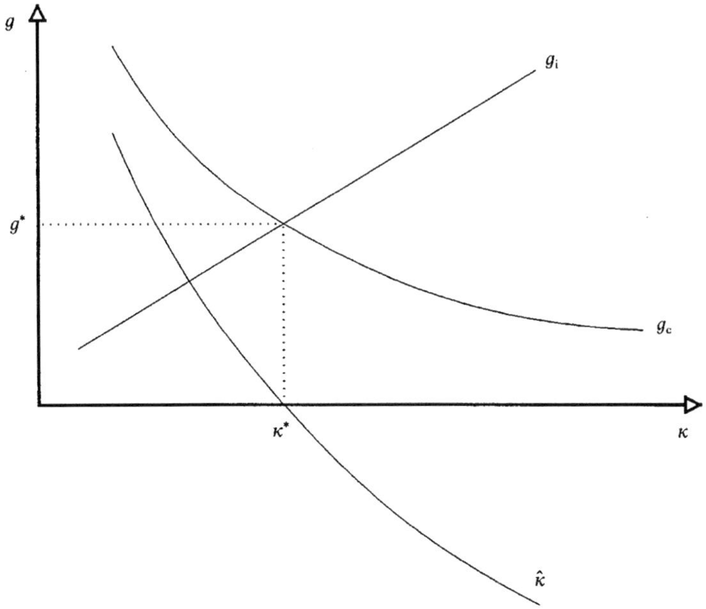


FIG. 1

to time of equation (24), where the circumflex denotes a rate of growth, we have

$$\hat{\kappa} = \hat{K}_c - \hat{K}_i = g_c^* - g_i^* \tag{33}$$

Obviously, whether the $\kappa$ ratio increases or not depends on whether the rate of accumulation of the consumption sector exceeds that of the investment sector. Making use of equations (27) and (28), we have

$$\frac{d\hat{\kappa}}{d\kappa} = -\frac{\tau_c a_{kc}\alpha_i\Omega_c}{\kappa^2} - \tau_i a_{ki}\alpha_c\Omega_i < 0 \tag{34}$$

The model is dynamically stable since an increase in $\kappa$ leads to a slowdown in its growth rate $\hat{\kappa}$. Hence, in contrast to what is asserted by Halevi and Kriesler (1991, p. 90), Kaleckian models in which there is a tendency towards a steady state can be constructed. The present Kaleckian two-sector model is always dynamically stable when its short-period solutions are stable. There is no need to assume, as in the Cambridgian or Hicksian two-sector model, that the consumption sector is more mechanized than the investment sector, i.e.

$a_{kc}/a_{\ell c} > a_{ki}/a_{\ell i}$.[13] In a sense this difference between the two models is not surprising since the Hicksian steady state assumes full employment of capital and labour, and attempts to preserve it during the traverse. There is no such assumption in the Kaleckian traverse: the full-employment constraints are replaced by behavioural restrictions on the investment functions, and indeed their values are relevant for stability analysis. More will be said on this matter when we deal with the issue of reproportioning.

Equation (33) is represented in Fig. 1 by the downward-sloping $\kappa$-curve, which is just the vertical distance between the $g_c$ and the $g_i$ curves. $\kappa$ is zero when the two sectoral growth rates are equal, i.e. when the steady state has been achieved.

### *A Change in the Profit Margin of the Investment Sector*

We now wish to know what happens to accumulation rates when there is a change in the profit margins. One may wonder whether it is correct to assume that prices are the causal factor and that prices can be constant during the traverse. Bhaduri and Robinson (1980, p. 106) argue that in the real world the share of profits, i.e. profit margins, is the causal factor. Furthermore, Hicks (1965, p. 195) asserts that when entrepreneurs set prices according to the full-cost principle, "they stick to those prices even when they are out of equilibrium". Under the present model, this can be interpreted as meaning that prices do not vary although accumulation accelerates or decelerates and although the degree of capacity utilization may be over or under its normal rate.

Before we begin the analysis of the traverse, it should be pointed out that the results with regard to the sectoral rates of capacity utilization and capital accumulation are qualitatively similar, whether there is an initial change in $\theta_c$ or in $\theta_i$. Let us consider then an increase in the profit margin of the investment sector, with its feedback effect on the profit margin of the consumption sector. This implies, for instance, an increase in the target rate of return $r_i^s$ of the investment sector, with no change in the target rate of return $r_c^s$ of the consumption sector. We must thus take the partial derivatives of equations (27) and (28) with respect to $\theta_i$, taking into account that with target-return pricing $\theta_c$ depends on $\theta_i$, i.e. taking into account equation (9). With $A = a_{\ell i}/a_{\ell c}$, we get

[13]See Hicks (1965, p. 187) or Bhaduri (1975) and Henry and Lavoie (1997) when the rate of growth of the labour force is changing, or see Spaventa (1973) when techniques are improved. The same condition is required in the usual classical models of convergence towards prices of production, as underlined by Boggio (1992), although more recent formulations incorporating supplemental adjustment processes (often of the Keynesian/Kaleckian type, as assumed here) do not require any restriction on input proportions (Caminati, 1990; Duménil and Lévy, 1993).

$$\frac{\mathrm{d}g_{\mathrm{c}}}{\mathrm{d}\theta_{\mathrm{i}}}=-\overset{\rho}{\frac{a_{kc}\tau_{\mathrm{c}}A}{\Omega^{2}}}\,\Omega[1+(1-s_{p})\theta_{\mathrm{i}}]\frac{\alpha_{\mathrm{i}}}{\kappa^{2}}\frac{\mathrm{d}\kappa}{\mathrm{d}\theta_{\mathrm{i}}}+\overset{\theta}{\;}\alpha_{\mathrm{c}}+\overset{\iota}{\frac{\alpha_{\mathrm{i}}}{\kappa}}\,\overset{\sigma}{[R_{\mathrm{c}}A(1-a_{ki}\tau_{\mathrm{i}})s_{p}^{2}]} \tag{35}$$

$$\frac{\mathrm{d}g_{\mathrm{i}}}{\mathrm{d}\theta_{\mathrm{i}}}=\overset{\kappa}{\frac{s_{p}R_{\mathrm{c}}Aa_{ki}\tau_{\mathrm{i}}}{\Omega^{2}}}\,\Omega\alpha_{\mathrm{c}}s_{p}(1+\theta_{\mathrm{i}})\frac{\mathrm{d}\kappa}{\mathrm{d}\theta_{\mathrm{i}}}-\overset{\lambda}{(\alpha_{\mathrm{c}}\kappa+\alpha_{\mathrm{i}})As_{p}a_{kc}\tau_{\mathrm{c}}} \tag{36}$$

Let us first consider the short-run effects of this increase in the profit margin of the investment sector. In the short run, there is no change in the sectoral stocks of capital: the variable $\kappa$ is constant and hence $\mathrm{d}\kappa/\mathrm{d}\theta_{\mathrm{i}}=0$. The partial derivatives show without ambiguity that an increase in the profit margin will thus induce a fall in the rates of accumulation of both sectors. This is shown graphically in Fig. 2. In the initial situation, it is assumed that the rate of accumulation is $g^{*}$ and that the sectoral stocks of capital ratio is $\kappa^{*}$. That ratio being given in the short run, the sectoral rates of accumulation fall to $g_{\mathrm{c}0}$ and $g_{\mathrm{i}0}$, which in general will not be equal. In the long run, these two sectoral rates of accumulation will converge to $g^{**}$, along the paths indicated by the arrows.

This is the path of the traverse from the initial steady state to the new steady state. Both sectoral rates of accumulation suddenly fall off in the short run as a result of the higher profit margins. During the traverse,

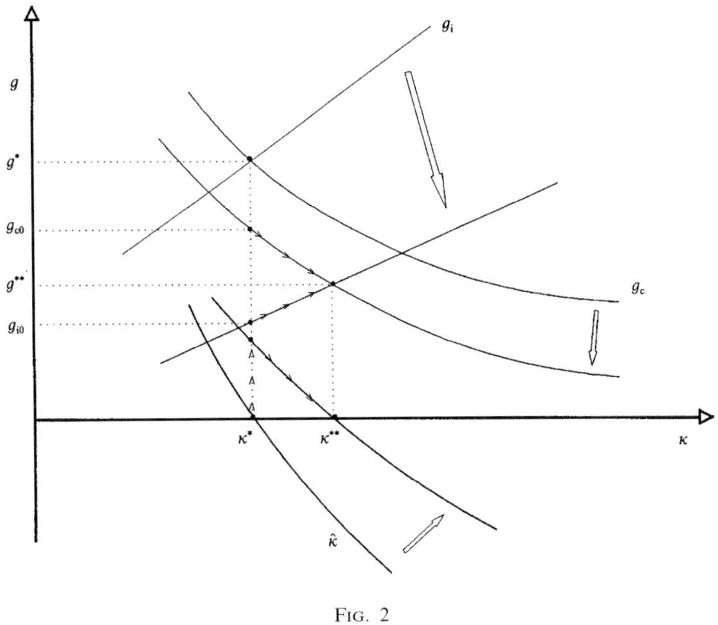


FIG. 2

the accumulation rate of one of the sectors continues to fall off, while the accumulation rate of the other sector regains some speed. In the case described by Fig. 2, since there is a growing proportion of the labour force working in the investment sector, consumption demand coming from workers outside the consumption sector grows, generating an increasing rate of capacity utilization and an increasing rate of accumulation in the consumption sector. In the new steady-state equilibrium, however, the growth rate of both sectors is necessarily smaller than the initial growth rate, as can be seen graphically. Similarly, the new steady-state rates of utilization of both sectors must have fallen compared with the initial steady-state rates.[14] Further tedious computations show that an autonomous increase in the profit margin of the consumption sector, for instance an increase in the target rate of return in the consumption sector, with no change in the target rate of return in the investment sector, leads to the same results.

The results obtained in this section are thus in partial contrast with those procured by Dutt (1987, p. 64). Dutt concludes that while increases in the mark-up of the consumption sector unambiguously lead to a slowdown of the steady-state rate of accumulation, an increase in the mark-up of the investment sector may lead to an increase in the steady-state rate of accumulation. This result is possible only because the properties of basic goods—here investment goods—have been overlooked. In our model, an increase in any of the profit margins leads to a decrease in the real wage rate and in the demand for consumption goods. The validity of Baran and Sweezy's monopoly power view does not depend on the sectoral origin of profit margin increases, in contrast to what Dutt (1987, p. 71) is led to conclude.

The causal mechanism at work in the present model is straightforward. If the $\tau_c$ parameter were to be equal to zero, i.e. if the change in income distribution and its accompanying slowdown in consumption demand have no impact on the accumulation decisions of the firms located in the consumption sector, no change in growth rates would occur. The $g_c$ curve would be flat and neither the $g_c$ nor the $g_i$ curves would shift down, as can be verified from equations (35) and (36). By contrast, when the $\tau_c$ parameter is positive, the fall in the rate of capacity utilization in the consumption sector will induce a fall in its desired rate of accumulation and hence a drop in the demand for investment goods. The fall in the rate of capacity utilization in the investment sector will in turn induce a slowdown in the rate of accumulation of the investment sector.

Such a causal story has been told by Joan Robinson, in a well-known passage of her major work, *The Accumulation of Capital*. Although she

[14]This is due to the form of the investment functions, equation (15). For a given $\alpha_j$, a fall in $g_j$ requires a fall in $u_j$.

closes off her analysis with an unwarranted statement about back-to-normal rates of utilization, she provides an excellent economic account of the Kaleckian traverse being formalized here. Compared with our analysis, it seems that Robinson starts out with an increase in the profit margins of the consumption sector, while assuming the rate of investment to be exogenous in the short period.

> Now let us suppose that Alaph entrepreneurs begin to form themselves into rings and raise prices. We will suppose that the process takes place gradually, so that the economy is not subject to a violent shock. As prices rise, with constant money wages, the volume of sales of consumption goods gradually falls (or rather fails to rise at its former rate). Workers become unemployed, and the utilisation of capital equipment in the consumption sector falls below capacity . . . . Initially employment in the investment sector is unaffected, and the quasi-rent in the consumption sector is therefore initially unchanged; quasi-rent per man employed has risen in the proportion in which employment per unit of capital has fallen. But with redundant equipment in the consumption sector the demand for replacements falls off, there is unemployment in the investment sector and a fall in the rate of profit. (Robinson, 1956, pp. 77–78).

*Reproportioning in the Kaleckian Traverse*

The question that arises from the above algebraic and graphical analysis is whether the $d\kappa/d\theta_i$ term is positive or negative. Does an increase in the profit margin of the investment sector lead to an increase in the $\kappa$ ratio? In the case depicted in Fig. 2, the increased profit margin induces a larger fall in the accumulation rate of the investment sector, which implies a shift upward of the $\kappa$-curve. This means that the new steady-state ratio, $\kappa^{**}$, is higher than the initial one, $\kappa^{*}$. It must thus be concluded that the $\kappa$ ratio rises in the long run whenever $g_c$ exceeds $g_i$ in the short run, for a given $\kappa$. What we are looking at is whether

$$\left.\frac{d\kappa}{d\theta_i}\right|_{\kappa=\mu} > 0 \tag{37}$$

Making use of equations (33), (35) and (36), we find that the derivative of equation (37) yields a positive expression provided the following condition is fulfilled:

$$\kappa > \frac{1 - \tau_i a_{ki}}{\tau_i a_{ki}} \tag{38}$$

Noting that we can rewrite $\kappa$, with $K$ the overall stock of capital ($K = K_c + K_i$), as

$$\kappa = \frac{1 - K_i/K}{K_i/K} \tag{39}$$

the above condition can be simplified to the following:

$$\lambda_i = K_i/K < \tau_i a_{ki} \tag{40}$$

This condition is quite remarkable. It says that the evolution of the relative importance of the sectoral stocks of capital only depends on parameters related to the investment sector, more specifically the sensitivity of accumulation to changes in the rate of utilization and the capital to full-capacity output ratio. In a sense, this result should not surprise us. That the basic good plays a peculiar role, even in a Kaleckian growth model, should be expected. Again it should be noted that there is symmetry between the consequences of an increase in the profit margin of either sector. Indeed, it can be shown that the condition warranting an increase in the $\kappa$ ratio following an increase in the profit margin of the consumption sector is identical to that of equation (38). It is the parameters of the *investment* sector which determine whether or not an increase in the profit margin of the *consumption* sector will be followed by an increase in the proportion of capital located in the consumption sector.

In the standard Cambridgian or Hicksian two-sector model, when the model is dynamically stable, a fall in the steady-state rate of accumulation must be accompanied by a fall in the proportion of the capital stock located in the investment sector, otherwise the traverse becomes impossible. This is not so here, since a fall in the steady-state rate of accumulation, induced by a rise in profit margins, may induce a rise in the proportion of the capital stock located in the investment sector when conditions (38) or (40) are not fulfilled, as shown in Fig. 3. It should be noted from equation (40) that the probability of such a paradoxical event increases the lower the $\tau_i$ and $a_{ki}$ parameters are. Hence, recalling the results of equation (25), the more stable the model the more the paradox is likely to occur.[15] In the extreme case where $\tau_i = 0$, i.e. when the $g_i$ curve is horizontal, condition (40) is never fulfilled and an intuitive result arises: an increase in profit margins induces a fall in $\kappa$ or in the proportion of the capital stock located in the consumption sector, while the steady-state growth rate is constant at $\alpha_i$. This is what should be expected when the rate of accumulation remains constant: the fall in real wages and hence in consumption should reduce the relative importance of the consumption sector.

It may help to understand the peculiarity of the Kaleckian traverse

[15]Note that a comparable paradox arises in the Hicksian traverse. The closer the model is to being unstable while still being stable, the faster adjustments are achieved (Bhaduri, 1975, p. 458).

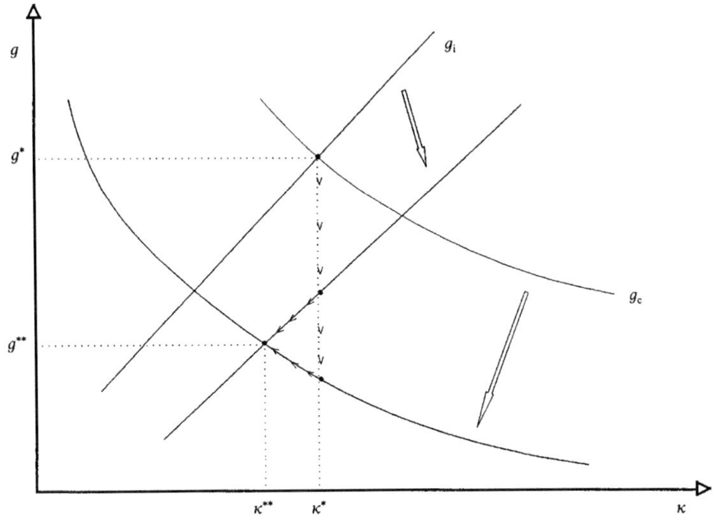


FIG. 3

by looking at it from another angle. Consider the following definition of the overall rate of accumulation, valid both in the steady state and during a traverse:

$$g = \frac{\Delta K}{K} = \frac{q_i}{K} = \frac{q_i}{q_i^f}\frac{q_i^f}{K_i}\frac{K_i}{K} \tag{41}$$

where $K$ as before is the overall stock of capital. Using the definitions provided in equations (4) and (16), and noting the reciprocal of equation (39),

$$\lambda_i = K_i/K = 1/(1+\kappa) \tag{42}$$

we have the following relation, various accounts of which can be found in Halevi (1985, p. 231), Vianello (1985, p. 75) and White (1989, p. 132):

$$g = \frac{u_i}{a_{ki}(1+\kappa)} \tag{43}$$

This relation does not depend on price equations and hence it is equally valid both in a Kaleckian and in the Cambridgian two-sector models, whatever the propensity to save. The equation shows neatly that if $u_i$, the rate of capacity utilization in the investment sector, is a given, fixed for instance at its normal or standard level, any increase in the rate of accumulation must be accompanied by a decrease in the proportion of capital held by the consumption sector. This equation thus allows us to rediscover a result which is of importance for the possible occurrence of the Hicksian traverse, a result that has been analysed by Robinson (1956, p. 77) and also underlined by Marxist authors dealing with the *proportionality* problem (Bhaduri, 1986, p. 211).[16]

*Acceleration of Accumulation and Excess Capacity Requirements*

The analysis above has shown that the Kaleckian traverse has more flexibility than the Hicksian traverse. This, of course, is not surprising given the possibilities offered by idle capacity. Indeed, Hicks (1965, p. 193) himself pointed out that the difficulties of the standard two-sector traverse could be alleviated by giving away the condition that "goods should not be used to more than a normal degree of utilization".[17] Still, a Kaleckian economy is also facing a constraint: the rate of capacity utilization cannot exceed unity in any one of the sectors, both in the long run *and in the short run*. To look at the requirements of the steady state is insufficient to assess whether or not the new steady state is possible; the rate of capacity utilization must also remain below unity *at all times during the traverse*.

This particular constraint of the Kaleckian traverse may be illustrated with the help of Fig. 4. As before it is assumed that the original steady state is given by the growth rate $g^*$ and a $\kappa^*$ ratio, as shown in Fig. 4(a). In general the sectoral steady-state rates of utilization will be different. Here we suppose that the rate of utilization in the investment sector is particularly high, higher than that of the consumption sector. Let us now assume a decrease in one or both profit margins, i.e. an increase in real wages. As can be seen in Fig. 4(b), this will lead in the short run to a sudden increase in both sectoral rates of utilization, from $u_i^*$ to $u_{i0}$ in the case of the investment sector. Under the conditions defined by equation (40), the rate of utilization of the investment sector will then decline continuously during the traverse until it reaches its new steady-state level at $u_i^{**}$. Figure 4 illustrates the fact that the short-term lack of excess capacity may prevent the traverse to a higher pace of accumulation. Not only must $u_i^{**}$ be below unity, $u_{i0}$ must also remain below unity. As is recognized by Dutt (1988, p. 149), the solutions given by equations (19) and (20) must thus be constrained below unity, both in the short run and

[16]The issue of reproportioning from one steady state to another can also be handled with the help of equation (43) by equating, as one can do in a steady state, the differentials of both equations (15) and (43).

[17]Hicks (1990, p. 102) recently did press the issue again: "We need not only permit underutilization along a traverse; overutilization also can be permitted. That makes quite a bit of difference. For, if scarce goods can be overused, surplus goods can be used more fully. Both overutilization and underutilization make traverse easier. I am hopeful that extension, more or less in the direction I have been describing, would have had some appeal to Sraffa." Neo-Ricardians have concurred with this suggestion, thus agreeing with Kaleckians on this issue. See Vianello (1990, p. 107).

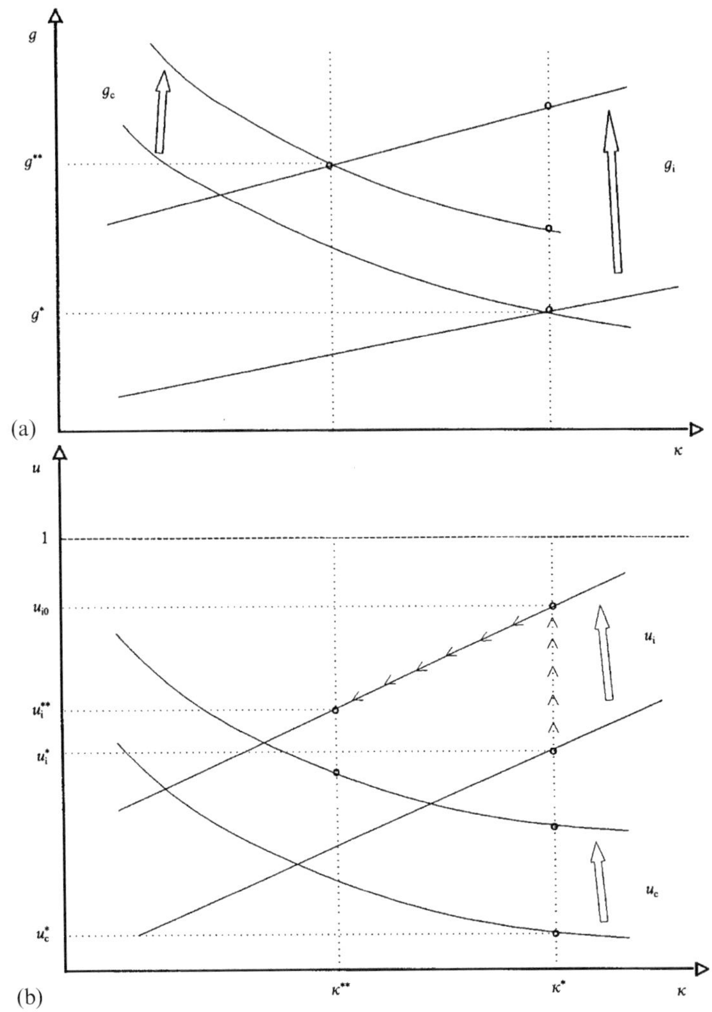


FIG. 4

in the long run. This analysis shows the importance of traverse analysis: comparing the equilibrium solutions and their stability may not be enough to assess whether or not a transition is possible.

It should further be noted that the same capacity constraints operate whenever effective demand increases. For instance, suppose there is an increase in the inducement to invest, i.e. an increase in either of the $\alpha_j$s, following a change in animal spirits or in long-run growth expectations.

This will induce a higher steady-state rate of capital accumulation without any change in the real wage rate. The traverse from one steady state to another will look precisely like that described by Fig. 4, except that the conditions defining the direction of reproportioning are different.[18] As in the previous case, because of the presence of idle capacity, it is possible for the rate of accumulation to increase without a fall in the real wage.

### *Rates of Profit*

At this stage, not much has been said about sectoral profit rates. At the aggregate level, it is clear that, provided there is no change in the propensity to save, any fall in the rate of accumulation will, in the long run, lead to a fall in the macroeconomic rate of profit, through the Cambridge formula $r = g/s_p$. The long-period positive connection observed in the one-sector Kaleckian model between the realized rate of profit and the real wage rate is thus preserved in the two-sector version. This macroeconomic rate of profit is not, however, the uniform rate of profit. Rather it is a weighted average of the two sectoral rates of profit:

$$r = \frac{r_i K_i + r_c K_c}{K_i + K_c} = \frac{r_i + r_c \kappa}{1 + \kappa} \tag{44}$$

Since the weight $\kappa$ may change in either direction, a fall in the rate of accumulation need not be accompanied by a fall in both sectoral rates of profit. Indeed, what happens to the realized sectoral rates of profit when there is a change in the margins of profit is not obvious. We know nevertheless that any increase in the target rate of return of one sector will lead to a fall in the realized rate of profit in the other sector, both in the short run and in the long run. This can be seen by looking at equation (32), and remembering that realized rates of capacity utilization are lower when margins of profit are higher. There is thus some antagonism between capitalists operating in different sectors.[19] Formally, with the bar over the $j$ denoting "not $j$", this can be written as

$$\frac{dr_j}{dr^s_{\bar{j}}} = \frac{r^s_j}{u^s_j}\frac{du_j}{dr^s_{\bar{j}}} \tag{45}$$

The issue still to be determined is whether an increase in the profit margin of a given sector might lead to an increase in the realized rate of

[18]This can be shown by taking the derivatives of equations (27) and (28) with respect to the $\alpha_j$. It can also be shown that if $\kappa$ is such that $dg_i/d\alpha_c > dg_c/d\alpha_c$, then $dg_i/d\alpha_i > dg_c/d\alpha_i$—an intuitive result.

[19]This result has some similitude with a claim made by Sweezy within the informal context of a Kaleckian model and the result arrived at by Steedman (1977, p. 181) within a Sraffian model.

profit of that sector, despite the fall in the rate of capacity utilization. There are no definite results with respect to long-run values, when the traverse is complete. This is due again to the uncertainty with regard to the sign and the amplitude of the $\mathrm{d}\kappa/\mathrm{d}\theta_j$ factor. In the short run, i.e. taking $\kappa$ as a constant, an increase in the target rate of return of the consumption sector always leads to a decrease in its realized rate of profit. Taking the derivative $\mathrm{d}r_\mathrm{c}/\mathrm{d}\theta_\mathrm{c}$, at $\kappa = \psi\mu$, from equations (19) and (32), we get

$$-s_p R_\mathrm{c}(\alpha_\mathrm{c} + \alpha_\mathrm{i}/\kappa)(1 - \tau_\mathrm{i} a_{k\mathrm{i}})\Omega_\mathrm{c} < 0$$

On the other hand, an increase in the profit margin of the investment sector may lead to an increase in the realized rate of profit of that sector. Taking the derivative $\mathrm{d}r_\mathrm{i}/\mathrm{d}\theta_\mathrm{i}$, at $\kappa = \psi\mu$, from equations (20) and (32), we get

$$[s_p R_\mathrm{c}(1 - a_{k\mathrm{i}}\tau_\mathrm{i}) - a_{k\mathrm{c}}\tau_\mathrm{c}]s_p R_\mathrm{c} A^2(\alpha_\mathrm{c}\kappa + \alpha_\mathrm{i})/\Omega^2$$

The derivative is positive if the expression between brackets is positive, i.e. if

$$s_p > \frac{\tau_\mathrm{c} a_{k\mathrm{c}}}{(1 - \tau_\mathrm{i} a_{k\mathrm{i}})R_\mathrm{c}} \tag{46}$$

Comparing this inequality with equation (25) yielding the stability condition, it follows that the derivative may be positive or negative. Firms in the investment sector may thus have some incentive to increase their profit margin, at least in the short run, a move which would be detrimental to the capitalists of the consumption sector. This is more likely to occur, as one would expect, if the lower rates of capacity utilization induced by lower consumption only have a small impact on the demand for investment goods (the case of low $\tau_j$). In the long run, since $r_\mathrm{i}$ is a positive function of $\kappa$, an increase in $r_\mathrm{i}^\mathrm{s}$ will lead to further increases in the realized profit rate of the investment sector provided condition (38) is not fulfilled, i.e. provided $\tau_\mathrm{i}$ is sufficiently small. One may thus conclude that, under the circumstances that lead to paradoxical reproportioning, there is some likelihood that, as a consequence of an increase in the mark-up of the investment sector, the realized rate of this sector will be higher while that of the other sector will be lower in the new steady-state equilibrium.

## IV CONCLUSIONS

We have shown that it is possible to design a coherent two-sector Kaleckian model of accumulation, with excess capacity, where the profit margin of the non-basic good—consumption—depends on the profit margin of the basic good—investment. Such a model has been built on the basis of target-return pricing procedures, and under the assumption that investment decisions mostly depend on the realized rate of capacity utilization. It has been shown that an increase in *any* of the target rates of return leads to a downfall in the rates of accumulation in both sectors in the short run. This result is preserved in the long run, in contrast to what may happen in the simple mark-up model.

It was also established, when profit margins are raised, that the sectoral rates of accumulation converge towards each other until a steady state is achieved, at a lower rate of accumulation than the one prevailing with the lower margins of profit. A similar process occurs when there is a drop in the animal spirits of the entrepreneurs operating in any of the two sectors. In contrast, it was shown that lower rates of accumulation did not necessarily entail lower sectoral rates of profit. A relation of antagonism may exist between the capitalists of the two sectors of the economy. In particular, it was shown that while a higher mark-up in the investment sector necessarily induced a lower realized rate of profit in the consumption sector, it could produce an increase in the realized rate of profit in the investment sector when the decisions of firms relative to accumulation are not very sensitive to changes in rates of capacity utilization.

A peculiar feature of the Kaleckian traverse is that its occurrence does not depend on any conditions related to technological characteristics. Provided the model is stable in the short period, it will exhibit stability in the dynamic sense, at least within the two-sector framework. There is another feature which is in contrast with the Hicksian traverse within the framework of the two-sector Cambridgian model: in a successful traverse, the evolution in the proportion of capital held by each of the sectors cannot be predicted by the direction of the change in the rate of accumulation. Higher rates of accumulation may be associated with a lower proportion of capital in the investment sector. This is due to the fact that in the Kaleckian model the rates of capacity utilization are endogenous, instead of being fixed to a normal level as in the standard Cambridgian model.

An issue that remains to be explored is whether Kaleckian models in general are an appropriate representation of capitalism in the long period, since these models do not fulfil some form of profit rate equalization. As it stands, the present Kaleckian model of the traverse does not lead towards profit rate equalization (neither targeted nor realized), while normal levels of capacity utilization could only be achieved by fluke. Various forms of profit rate convergence could be considered, involving for instance endogenous target rates of return or endogenous standard rates of capacity utilization. In the meantime, we believe, as do Halevi and Kriesler, that an analysis based on various variants of profit rate equalization or on steady growth models set at normal use of capacity is doubtful unless "some coherent dynamic adjustment process is specified which can describe the traverse from one equilibrium position to another, without the traverse itself influencing the final equilibrium position, that is, without the equilibrium being path determined" (1991, p. 86). Indeed, some recent efforts on the part of the members of various non-orthodox traditions have proceeded, more or less explicitly, to identify and inspect these processes.[20]

## References

Amadeo, E. J. (1986). "The Role of Capacity Utilization in Long-Period Analysis", *Political Economy: Studies in the Surplus Approach*, Vol. 2, No. 2, pp. 147–185.

Amadeo, E. J. (1987). "Expectations in a Steady-state Model of Capacity Utilization", *Political Economy: Studies in the Surplus Approach*, Vol. 3, No. 1, pp. 75–89.

Asimakopulos, A. (1975). "A Kaleckian Theory of Income Distribution", *Canadian Journal of Economics*, Vol. 8, No. 3, pp. 313–333.

Bhaduri, A. (1975). "On the Analogy between the Quantity and the Price Traverse", *Oxford Economic Papers*, Vol. 27, No. 3, pp. 455–461.

Bhaduri, A. (1985). "L'accumulation du capital: temps logique et temps historique", *Economie Appliquée*, Vol. 38, No. 2, pp. 453–470.

Bhaduri, A. (1986). *Macroeconomics: The Dynamics of Commodity Production*, Armonk, NY, M. E. Sharpe.

Bhaduri, A. and Marglin, S. (1990). "Unemployment and the Real Wage: the Economic Basis for Contesting Political Ideologies", *Cambridge Journal of Economics*, Vol. 14, No. 4, pp. 375–393.

Bhaduri, A. and Robinson, J. (1980). "Accumulation and Exploitation: an Analysis in the Tradition of Marx, Sraffa and Kalecki", *Cambridge Journal of Economics*, Vol. 4, No. 2, pp. 103–115.

Boggio, L. (1980). "Full Cost and Sraffa Prices: Equilibrium and Stability in a System with Fixed Capital", *Economic Notes*, Vol. 9, No. 1, pp.3–32.

Boggio, L. (1986). "Stability of Production Prices in a Model of General Interdependence", in W. Semmler (ed.), *Competition, Instability, and Nonlinear Cycles*, Berlin, Springer-Verlag.

Boggio, L. (1990). "The Dynamic Stability of Production Prices: a Synthetic Discussion of Models and Results", *Political Economy: Studies in the Surplus Approach*, Vol. 6, No. 1–2, pp. 47–58.

Boggio, L. (1992). "Production Prices and Dynamic Stability: Results and Open Questions", *The Manchester School*, Vol. 60, No. 3, pp. 264–294.

Caminati, M. (1990). "Gravitation: an Introduction", *Political Economy: Studies in the Surplus Approach*, Vol. 6, No. 1–2, pp. 11–44.

Deprez, J. and Dalendina, P. D. (1994). "The Monetary Determinants of (In)stability: Some Contrasts of Duménil/Lévy and the Post-Keynesians", *Review of Radical Political Economics*, Vol. 26, No. 3, pp. 66–75.

Duménil, G. and Lévy, D. (1987). "The Dynamics of Competition: a Restoration of the Classical Analysis", *Cambridge Journal of Economics*, Vol. 11, No. 2, pp. 133–164.

[20]See Duménil and Lévy (1994), Deprez and Dalendina (1994), Dutt (1996) and Lavoie (1995, 1996) among others.

Duménil, G. and Lévy, D. (1993). *The Economics of the Profit Rate: Competition, Crises and Historical Tendencies in Capitalism*, Aldershot, Edward Elgar.

Duménil, G. and Lévy, D. (1984). "Being Keynesian in the Short Term and Classical in the Long Term: the Traverse to Classical Long-term Equilibrium", CEPREMAP, Preliminary draft, April.

Dutt, A. K. (1987). "Competition, Monopoly Power and the Uniform Rate of Profit", *Review of Radical Political Economics*, Vol. 19, No. 4, pp. 55–72.

Dutt, A. K. (1988). "Convergence and Equilibrium in Two-sector Models of Growth, Distribution and Prices", *Journal of Economics—Zeitschrift für Nationalökonomie*, Vol. 48, No. 2, pp. 135–158.

Dutt, A. K. (1990). "Growth, Distribution and Capital Ownership: Kalecki and Pasinetti Revisited", in B. Datta, S. Gargopadhyay, D. Mookherjee and D. Roy (eds), *Economic Theory and Policy*, Bombay, Oxford University Press.

Dutt, A. K. (1996). "Equilibrium, Path Dependence and Hysteresis in Post-Keynesian Models", prepared for a volume of essays in honour of Geoffrey Harcourt, edited by P. Arestis and M. Sawyer.

Eichner, A. S. (1987). *The Macrodynamics of Advanced Market Economies*, Armonk, NY, M. E. Sharpe.

Halevi, J. (1985). "Switching and Employment", *Eastern Economic Journal*, Vol. 11, July–September, pp. 229–234.

Halevi, J. and Kriesler, P. (1991). "Kalecki, Classical Economics and the Surplus Approach", *Review of Political Economy*, Vol. 3, No. 1, pp. 79–92.

Henry, J. and Lavoie, M. (1997). "The Hicksian Traverse as a Process of Reproportioning: Some Structural Dynamics", *Structural Change and Economic Dynamics*, Vol. 8, No. 2, forthcoming.

Hicks, J. R. (1965). *Capital and Growth*, Oxford, Oxford University Press.

Hicks, J. R. (1990). "Ricardo and Sraffa", in K. Bharadwaj and B. Schefold (eds), *Essays on Piero Sraffa: Critical Perspectives on the Revival of Classical Theory*, London, Unwin Hyman.

Kaldor, N. (1960). "Stability and Full Employment", in *Essays in Economic Stability and Growth,* London, Duckworth; first published 1938.

Kurz, H. D. (1990). "Technical Change, Growth and Distribution: a Steady State Approach to Unsteady Growth", in *Capital, Distribution and Effective Demand: Studies in the Classical Approach to Economic Theory*, Cambridge, Polity Press.

Kurz, H. D. (1994). "Growth and Distribution", *Review of Political Economy*, Vol. 6, No. 4, pp. 393–420.

Lanzillotti, R. F. (1958). "Pricing Objectives in Large Companies", *American Economic Review*, Vol. 48, No. 5, pp. 921–940.

Lavoie, M. (1992). *Foundations of Post-Keynesian Economic Analysis*, Aldershot, Edward Elgar.

Lavoie, M. (1995). "The Kaleckian Model of Growth and Distribution and its Neo-Ricardian and Neo-Marxian Critiques", *Cambridge Journal of Economics*, Vol. 19, No. 6, pp. 789–818.

Lavoie, M. (1996). "Traverse, Hysteresis, and Normal Rates of Capacity Utilization in Kaleckian Models of Growth and Distribution", *Review of Radical Political Economics*, Vol. 28, No. 4, pp. 113–147.

Lee, F. S. (1985). "Full Cost Prices, Classical Price Theory, and Long Period Method Analysis: a Critical Evaluation", *Metroeconomica*, Vol. 37, No. 2, pp. 199–219.

O'Connell, J. (1978). "Savings and Prices in a Full-employment Traverse", *Oxford Economic Papers*, Vol. 29, No. 3, pp. 458–463.

Robinson, J. (1956). *The Accumulation of Capital*, London, Macmillan.

Robinson, J. (1962). *Essays in the Theory of Economic Growth*, London, Macmillan.

Rowthorn, B. (1981). "Demand, Real Wages and Economic Growth", *Thames Papers in Political Economy*, Autumn, pp. 1–39. Reprinted in *Studi Economici* (1982), No. 18, pp. 3–54, and also in M. C. Sawyer (ed.), *Post-Keynesian Economics*, Aldershot, Edward Elgar.

Spaventa, L. (1973). "Notes on Problems of Transition between Techniques", in J. A. Mirlees and N. H. S. Stern (eds), *Models of Economic Growth*, London, Macmillan.

Steedman, I. (1977). *Marx after Sraffa*, London, New Left Books.

Steedman, I. (1992). "Questions for Kaleckians", *Review of Political Economy*, Vol. 4, No. 2, pp. 125–151.

Taylor, L. (1989). "Demand Composition, Income Distribution and Growth", in G. R. Feiwel (ed.), *Joan Robinson and Modern Economic Theory*, New York, New York University Press.

Vianello, F. (1985). "The Pace of Accumulation", *Political Economy: Studies in the Surplus Approach*, Vol. 1, No. 1, pp. 69–87.

Vianello, F. (1989). "Effective Demand and the Rate of Profits: Some Thoughts on Marx, Kalecki and Sraffa", in M. Sebastiani (ed.), *Kalecki's Relevance Today*, New York, St Martin's Press.

Vianello, F. (1990). "Comment on John R. Hicks", in K. Bharadwaj and B. Schefold (eds), *Essays on Piero Sraffa: Critical Perspectives on the Revival of Classical Theory*, London, Unwin Hyman.

White, G. (1989). "Normal Prices and the Theory of Output: Some Significant Implications of Recent Debates", *Political Economy: Studies in the Surplus Approach*, Vol. 5, No. 2, pp. 129–149.

# [18]



*The Korean Economic Review*
Volume 33, Number 1, Summer 2017, 179-206.

# Demand-led Growth and Long-run Convergence in a Neo-Kaleckian Two-sector Model

Jung Hoon Kim* · Marc Lavoie**

*This paper analyzes a two-sector model, with consumption and investment sectors, which incorporates both Kaleckian and Classical views. Starting from a model where investment depends on actual profit rates and rates of capacity utilization, we characterize three regimes with different investment functions and specific adjustment mechanisms to bring about a uniform rate of profit and convergence between the actual and the normal rates of capacity utilization. We find that the paradox of thrift holds in the long run for all regimes. With regards to income distribution, results concerning wage-led growth and the paradox of costs are more ambiguous. The reproportioning of the capital stock between the two sectors is also discussed. We conclude that our analysis provides some justification for using simple one-sector Kaleckian models, since the results achieved with the two-sector model are roughly in conformity with those of the one-sector model, depending on the closure being used.*

JEL Classification: B51, E11, E12
Keywords: Two-sector Model, Kaleckian Growth Model, Profit Rate Equalization, Paradox of Thrift, Paradox of Costs

## I. Introduction

The Kaleckian growth and distribution model is now at the heart of the empirical work that has been pursued by post-Keynesian economists to assess whether increases in the profit share in national income have favorable or negative effects on economic activity and productivity (Storm and Naastepad, 2012; Onaran and Galanis, 2012). The Kaleckian model of growth and distribution was formally

*Received: Jan. 24, 2016. Revised: Oct. 31, 2016. Accepted: May 15, 2017.*

* First Author, Research Fellow, Gyeonggi Research Institute, 1150 Gyeongsu-daero, Jangan-gu, Suwan, Gyeonggi-do 16207, Korea. E-mail: jh6911@gri.re.kr

** Corresponding Author, Emeritus Professor, Department of Economics, University of Ottawa, 120 University Street, Social Sciences Building, Ottawa, Ontario K1N 6N5, Canada; and Senior Research Chair of Université Sorbonne Paris Cité, Centre d'Économie de l'Université Paris-Nord (CEPN), University of Paris 13, 99 avenue Jean-Baptiste Clément, 93430 Villetaneuse, France. E-mail: mlavoie@uottawa.ca. We thank two anonymous referees for their helpful comments.

suggested and developed in the 1980s, in particular, by Rowthorn (1981), Dutt (1984), Taylor (1985) and Amadeo (1986). The canonical Kaleckian growth model has four crucial features, which are the following: "First, there is the investment function, which may depend on several variables, one of which must be the rate of capacity utilization. Second, prices relative to direct costs are assumed to be given, dependent on conventional forces instead of market forces. Prices are of the cost-plus type. Third, saving out of wages is often assumed to be nil, although it is sufficient to assume that the propensity to save out of wages is smaller than that out of profits, as in the neo-Keynesian growth model. Fourth, the rate of utilization of capacity is assumed to be generally below unity, and labour is assumed not to be a constraint." (Lavoie, 2014, p. 360).

Besides its use for empirical work, the Kaleckian model of growth and distribution has provided a useful common framework which has allowed heterodox authors of various persuasions to interact with each other on matters of growth and distribution. But there exist unresolved gaps between neo-Kaleckian views on one hand and classical views on the other hand, meaning here neo-Marxian and Sraffian authors. In multi-sector models, disagreements are mainly related to the possible existence of long-run positions and of adjustment mechanisms towards those. The issue, in particular, is whether or not profit rates are equalized among industrial sectors and whether or not there exists convergence between the actual and the normal rates of capacity utilization.

Hein, Lavoie and van Treeck (2011, 2012) have examined the various mechanisms that have been proposed to handle the second issue, that of the possible discrepancy between actual and normal rates of capacity utilization. Arguments have also been offered as to why the equality between these two rates may not necessarily be expected, even in the long run. Although we do not wish to rehearse this debate, it should be pointed out that the debate has occurred within the context of simple one-sector models. Here we wish to examine what can be said within the framework of a multi-sector model. In their extension to a two-sector Kaleckian model, Dutt (1988, 1990) and Lavoie and Ramírez-Gastón (1997) show that the incongruity between the actual and the normal rates still prevails in the long run. Moreover, they insist that a uniform rate of profit could be achieved only under some specific conditions, adding that it is dubious that these conditions would be satisfied, particularly in a modern oligopolistic economy, as described by monopoly power theorists such as Kalecki (1939, 1971), Sweezy (1942), Steindl (1952), Spence (1977) and Cowling (1982).

Most neo-Marxists and some Sraffians would object to these claims, as do Auerbach and Skott (1988), claiming that rational firms would not want to keep undesired excess capacity, and hence would act in such a way that the normal or optimal rate of capacity utilization would be achieved in the long run (or that the actual rate would gravitate around the normal rate).[1] Furthermore, they argue that profit rates among industries tend to be equalized in the long run, since competition between capitalists would lead to the mobility of (financial) capital from an industrial sector with a low profit rate to one with a high rate (Duménil and Lévy, 1995, 1999; Glick and Campbell, 1995; Semmler, 1984).

The purpose of this paper is to explore whether in a two-sector model there exist qualitative, significant, differences in long-run relationships and traverses towards long-run positions when adjustment mechanisms are incorporated in a simple model.[2] To conduct this task, we characterize regimes with different investment functions and specific adjustment mechanisms, reflecting neo-Kaleckian and classical views. We then examine whether the paradox of thrift, the wage-led regime, and the paradox of costs hold in the long run. While some authors in the past have examined some of the issues and some of the mechanisms that we deal with here, we believe that this is the first paper that does so in a systematic fashion.

The paper is organized as follows. In the next section we develop a dynamic Kaleckian two-sector model with target-return pricing. In the third section, we specify two additional regimes by introducing adjustment mechanisms that intend to reconcile Kaleckian and classical concerns. The last section summarizes and concludes.

## II. A Basic Two-sector Kaleckian Model

In this section, we set a simple two-sector model in an analytical framework, which will then be used to develop more specific investment functions and adjustment mechanisms. Stability conditions and long-run relationships are then analyzed. To do so, in particular, we suppose that a uniform rate of profit depends on whether there exist any barriers to the free mobility of (financial) capital when there are profit rate differentials between industrial sectors,[3] while convergence between the actual and the normal rates depends on whether costing margins and prices change in response to a gap between the actual and the normal rates of

[1] However, there are a number of Sraffians such as Garegnani (1992), Kurz (1994), Park (1995), Palumbo and Trezzini (2003) and Trezzini (2011) who agree that there could be persistent divergence between the normal and the actual rates of utilization, on average, even in the long run.

[2] The multi-sectoral model is a useful framework in which we can analyze structural economic dynamics that change the production structure and affect economic variables such as the growth rate (Araujo and Lima, 2007). For example, in a multi-sectoral neo-Kaleckian model, Araujo and Teixeira (2011) and Nishi (2014) show that sectoral heterogeneity and reallocation could result in different growth regimes.

[3] Harris (1978, p. 46) points out that 'a uniform rate of profit is then a consequence of the assumption of competition in this sense [the free mobility of capital] and of the tendencies associated with competition'.

capacity utilization.[4]

## 2.1. Basic Pricing Equations

To keep the model simple, we assume the following: the economy consists of a consumption sector (denoted $i=1$) and an investment sector (denoted $i=2$), and there is one firm (or identical firms) in each sector; there are two factors to produce goods, fixed capital and labour; there is no overhead or fixed labour; the investment good is a basic good; capital stocks are non-transferable between both industrial sectors, and have constant efficiency and no depreciation; firms operate plants under constant returns to scale; all wages are consumed and the propensity to save of capitalists is $s_p$; the wage rate is the same in both sectors. Also, let us suppose that firms in both industrial sectors set the prices of their products by following the target-return pricing procedures described by Lanzillotti (1958) and adopted by Lavoie and Ramírez-Gastón (1997). Target-return pricing is a variant of cost-plus pricing, where the price is set by adding a costing margin to some measure of unit cost. Other variants of cost-plus pricing include normal-cost pricing, full-cost pricing and markup pricing. In the case of target-return pricing, the margin depends on a target rate of return, to be achieved when the firm is running at its standard rate of capacity utilization. According to Kaplan et al. (1958), this pricing procedures is the most prevalent one, with Lee (1998) arguing in his review of the pricing literature that it is particularly the case of large firms.

In addition to its realistic feature, an advantage of target-return pricing is that it explicitly takes into account the intersectoral dependence of costing margins among sectors. This pricing procedure will also allow the introduction of explicit adjustment mechanisms that bring about fully-adjusted positions, where productive capacity is utilized at its normal level, with a uniform profit rate.

A simple mark-up pricing rule can be written as

$$p_i = (1+\theta_i)w\alpha_i \tag{1}$$

where $p$ is the price level, $\theta$ is the costing margin, $\alpha$ is the labour-output ratio that is assumed to be fixed, and $w$ is the nominal wage rate.

The actual real outputs $S$ are defined as follows:

$$S_1 \equiv C \tag{2.1}$$

[4] Neo-Marxists may disagree with these dichotomic assumptions because competition among capitalists would lead to a change in markups and hence it might be a force to bring about convergence between actual and normal rates of capacity utilization. We believe that Regime 3, to be described below, can be considered as illustrating this case.

$$S_2 \equiv I_1 + I_2 \equiv g_1 K_1 + g_2 K_2 \tag{2.2}$$

where $C$ is consumption in real terms; $I_i$ is investment in real terms, that is, sales of machines to the consumption sector and to the machine-producing sector; the $K_i$ are the capital stocks of the two sectors and $g_i$ is the rate of accumulation of each sector. From the assumption of target-return pricing, the standard sales $S^s$ correspond to the standard (or normal) rate of capacity utilization $u^s$ of each sector; this rate is such that it must provide enough profits to fulfill the target rate of return $r^s$. The full-capacity output $S_{fc}$ and the standard sales are defined respectively as

$$S_{fc,i} \equiv K_i / \sigma_i \tag{3}$$

$$S_i^s \equiv u_i^s S_{fc,i} \tag{4}$$

where $\sigma$ is the capital to full-capacity output ratio that is assumed to be fixed.

Equating the two equations that define total profits targeted in sector $i$, $F_{T,i}^s = \theta_i w \alpha_i S_i^s$ and $F_{T,i}^s = r_i^s p_2 K_i$, the costing margin of each sector is derived as

$$\theta_1 = \sigma_1 \alpha_2 r_1^s u_2^s / [\alpha_1 u_1^s (u_2^s - \sigma_2 r_2^s)] \tag{5.1}$$

$$\theta_2 = \sigma_2 r_2^s / [u_2^s - \sigma_2 r_2^s] \tag{5.2}$$

The condition ensuring positive costing margins (and hence positive prices) is $u_2^s > \sigma_2 r_2^s$ for each sector. This condition is necessarily fulfilled by equations (3) and (4) when the standard output of the investment sector is greater than target real profits in that sector ($S_2^s > r_2^s K_2$). Note that the costing margin (and hence the price) in the consumption sector depends on pricing in the investment sector, whereas the costing margin in the investment sector is independent of pricing in the consumption sector as it should be for a basic good. An increase in the price of investment goods leads to a higher costing margin in the consumption sector because firms in the latter sector would try to offset losses due to the increased purchasing price of investment goods by raising their costing margin, for a given target rate of return. Substituting equations (5.1) and (5.2) into (1), the price equation of each sector can be rewritten as:

$$p_1 = \alpha_1 w + A p_2 \tag{1.1'}$$

$$p_2 = B w \tag{1.2'}$$

where $A = \sigma_1 r_1^s / u_1^s$ and $B = \alpha_2 u_2^s / (u_2^s - \sigma_2 r_2^s)$.

The actual rate of capacity utilization $u$ is defined as

$$u_i \equiv S_i / S_{fc,i} \equiv \sigma_i S_i / K_i \tag{6}$$

and, from equation (1), the actual total profits $F_T$ are given by

$$F_{T,i} = \theta_i w \alpha_i S_i = m_i p_i S_i \tag{7}$$

where $m = \theta / (1+\theta)$ is the gross profit margin, the so-called 'degree of monopoly' in Kalecki's terminology.

Using equations (1.1)', (1.2)', and (6), we obtain the actual profit rate, which is defined by $r = F_T / (p_2 K)$,

$$r_i = r_i^s (u_i / u_i^s) \tag{8}$$

With target-return pricing, therefore, the actual profit rate changes proportionally with the actual rate of capacity utilization, for a given target rate of return and a given standard rate of capacity utilization (so do the ratio of the actual to the target rate of profit with the ratio of the actual to the standard rate of utilization). This relationship also implies that the existence of undesired excess capacity ($u < u^s$) results in the actual profit rate being less than the desired rate ($r < r^s$). Also, in the two-sector economy, when $(u_1 / u_2) = (r_2^s / r_1^s)(u_1^s / u_2^s)$, the actual profit rates are equalized in both sectors, while when $r_i = r_i^s$, the actual rate of capacity utilization is equal to the standard rate.[5][6]

## 2.2. Regime 1: Short-run Solutions with no Adjustment Mechanism[7]

Regime 1 embodies the argument of monopoly power theorists, in line with Dutt

[5] If firms try to operate at full capacity utilization ($u^f = 1$) at least in the long run, that is, $u^s = 1$, then the adjustment mechanism to bring about $r_i^s \rightarrow r_i$ would also result in a uniform rate of profit ($r_1 = r_2$) at the same time, without an additional adjustment mechanism.

[6] With equations (5.1) and (5.2), the gross profit margin (or the net share of profits) of each sector is $m_i = \sigma_i (r_i^s / u_i^s)$, and thus the actual profit rate of equation (8) can be rewritten as $r_i = m_i u_i / \sigma_i$. This implies that even though the actual profit rates are equalized in both sectors and the actual rates converge toward their standard rates, the net shares of profits in both sectors are not same, because of the structural differences between those sectors.

[7] This subsection is mainly based on Lavoie and Ramírez-Gastón (1997). In the present paper, however, we assume that an investment function depends on both the profit rate and the utilization rate, as in Rowthorn (1981), while in the former model it was a sole function of the rate of capacity utilization. Also, we explicitly derive long-run solutions and mathematically examine whether the paradox of thrift and the paradox of cost hold in the long run, introducing a specific assumption which leads to a different result with respect to how the reproportioning of the capital stocks occurs in our model relative to the former model.

(1988) and Lavoie and Ramírez-Gastón (1997). The regime does not incorporate any adjustment mechanism to bring about the equalization between the actual and the standard rates. Hence, in the long run, profit rates do not converge, actual profit rates are not equal to the target rate, and the actual rate of capacity utilization diverges from the standard rate. In other words, costing margins and prices are chosen on the basis of the target rate of return and the standard rate of capacity utilization determined by the 'rules of thumb' of entrepreneurs, regardless of the state of effective demand.

We suppose that the investment function depends on the animal spirits of entrepreneurs $\gamma_{i0}$,[8] the actual profit rate and the actual rate of capacity utilization, such that

$$g_i = \gamma_{i0} + \gamma_{i1} r_i + \gamma_{i2} u_i \tag{9}$$

This type of investment function has been used in many Kaleckian models since Rowthorn (1981) and Dutt (1984) adopted it. Here, the rate of capacity utilization reflects the level of effective demand and the rate of profit is an indicator of the actual profitability of firms and hence an indicator of the capacity of firms to obtain funds from banks and financial markets (Lavoie, 1995). Fazzari and Mott (1986-87), Chamberlain and Gordon (1989) and Arestis et al. (2012) all provide empirical evidence showing that capacity utilization (or sales) and profitability (or retained earnings) have a significant positive impact on the investment of firms.

Substituting equation (8) into (9), the investment function can be reduced to a function of the rate of capacity utilization only.

$$g_i = \gamma_{i0} + \gamma_{i3} u_i \tag{9'}$$

where $\gamma_{i3} = \gamma_{i1} r_i^s / u_i^s + \gamma_{i2}$. Therefore, an increase [decrease] in the rate of capacity utilization raises [reduces] both the rate of accumulation and the profit rate, that is, these rates move together in the same direction, for a given target rate of return and standard rate of capacity utilization.

In the short run we assume that the distribution of the capital stock between the two sectors is a given and hence that the variable $k = K_1 / K_2$ is a constant. Assuming that supply adjusts to demand within the period, that is, assuming that output adjusts to the quantities that are being demanded and hence that the rate of capacity utilization is an endogenous variable, we obtain the short-run equilibrium

[8] The autonomous parameter is also sometimes interpreted as the secular growth rate of sales which is expected by entrepreneurs, but only when investment is a function of the discrepancy between the actual and the normal rates of capacity utilization (Committeri, 1986; Caserta, 1990).

rates of capacity utilization and equilibrium rates of accumulation:[9]

$$u_1^* = \sigma_1 u_1^s (u_2^s - s_p \sigma_2 r_2^s)(\gamma_{10} + \gamma_{20} / k) / \Phi_1 \tag{10.1}$$

$$u_2^* = s_p \sigma_1 \sigma_2 r_1^s u_2^s (\gamma_{10} k + \gamma_{20}) / \Phi_1 \tag{10.2}$$

$$g_1^* = \gamma_{10} + \gamma_{13} \sigma_1 u_1^s (u_2^s - s_p \sigma_2 r_2^s)(\gamma_{10} + \gamma_{20} / k) / \Phi_1 \tag{11.1}$$

$$g_2^* = \gamma_{20} + \gamma_{23} s_p \sigma_1 \sigma_2 r_1^s u_2^s (\gamma_{10} k + \gamma_{20}) / \Phi_1 \tag{11.2}$$

where $\Phi_1 = s_p \sigma_1 r_1^s u_2^s (1 - \gamma_{23} \sigma_2) - \gamma_{13} \sigma_1 u_1^s (u_2^s - s_p \sigma_2 r_2^s)$ and the local stability condition of short-run equilibrium is $\Phi_1 > 0$.

To sum up, here is what happens in the short run. Prices are set by firms, on the basis of their unit wage cost, their target rate of return and the various technical coefficients, such as the capital to capacity ratio and the standard rate of capacity utilization. Prices are thus assumed to be given. The stock of machines in each sector is also assumed to be given (as well as the financial value of the capital in each sector, since the price of machines is a given), so that the new machines being produced in a given period are added to the existing stocks only before the next period starts. Produced output and hence sales in each sector is determined by desired purchases, assuming that there is always enough spare capacity to respond to any increase in demand. Parameters such as the profit shares, which arose from the pricing procedures, and the propensity to save out of profits help determine the actual rates of capacity utilization and the actual rates of profit in each sector, which retroact on the demand for investment goods, and hence on the demand for consumption goods, and hence on the realized rates of profit and of utilization.[10]

## 2.3. Long-run Dynamic Adjustment Mechanism

In the long run, $k$ is not constant and changes over time. Let us consider the dynamics of $k$ over time, where $\dot{k} = dk / dt$. Substituting equations (11.1) and (11.2) into equation (12) below and differentiating it with respect to $k$, we have $d\hat{k} / dk < 0$ and hence the long-run equilibrium rate of accumulation $g_1^{**} = g_2^{**} = g^{**}$ is stable.[11] Figure 1 shows the convergence of the two rates of

[9] For the proof, see the Appendix.

[10] While the profit share in our model is determined by exogenous factors, shown in equation (5.1) and (5.2), such as the monopolistic power of firms and the respective bargaining power of workers and capitalists, in a neo-classical model it is endogenously determined as a result of the profit maximization of firms, that is, by the marginal product of capital. Also, a change in the propensity to save in our model affects the rate of profit through a change in the rate of utilization (thus through the demand side), but in the neo-classical model, it changes the rate of profit through a change in the marginal product of capital under full capacity utilization (through the supply side).

[11] Therefore, in contrast to Park's (1998, p. 285; 1998-1999, p. 304) argument, in a two-sector

accumulation.

$$\hat{k} = \dot{k} / k = g_1^* - g_2^* \tag{12}$$

**[Figure 1]** Dynamics of rates of accumulation

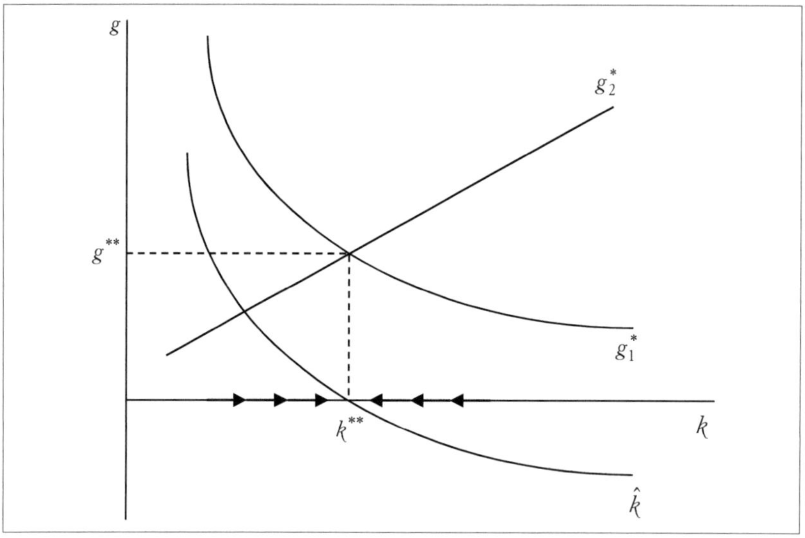


To examine whether there exist a paradox of thrift and a paradox of cost, we need to find the long-run equilibrium ratio of sectoral capital stocks $k^{**}$. For the sake of simplicity, we assume that the entrepreneurs' animal spirits on investment are the same in both sectors, that is, $\gamma_{10} = \gamma_{20}$.[12] Then, by equalizing the two equations (11.1) and (11.2), we obtain the long-run equilibrium ratio of sectoral capital stocks as follows:

$$k^{**} = \gamma_{13} u_1^s (u_2^s - s_p \sigma_2 r_2^s) / (\gamma_{23} s_p \sigma_2 r_1^s u_2^s) \tag{13}$$

Here, $k^{**}$ is always greater than zero because $u_2^s > s_p \sigma_2 r_2^s$. This follows from the assumptions that $u_2^s > \sigma_2 r_2^s$ and $s_p < 1$.

Substituting equation (13) into (10.1) and (10.2), the long-run equilibrium rate of capacity utilization is given by:

---

Kaleckian model, a uniform rate of accumulation is achieved and is stable in the long run without an additional equation or condition for a uniform rate of profit.

[12] For the analysis of a general case, through the use of graphs, see Lavoie and Ramírez-Gastón (1997).

$$u_i^{**} = (\Omega / \Phi_1) / \gamma_{i3} \tag{14}$$

where $\Omega = \sigma_1[\gamma_{10}\gamma_{13}u_1^s(u_2^s - s_p\sigma_2 r_2^s) + \gamma_{20}\gamma_{23}s_p\sigma_2 r_1^s u_2^s]$ Hence, we find a long-run relationship between the rates of capacity utilization of the two sectors

$$u_1^{**} = (\gamma_{13} / \gamma_{23})u_2^{**} \tag{15}$$

which implies that the rate of capacity utilization of one sector is associated positively to that of the other sector. Hence, with a given target rate of return and standard rate of capacity utilization, a positive shock on the rate of capacity utilization in the consumption sector will bring about an increase in the rate of accumulation and the profit rate of that sector through equations (8) and (9)', as well as an increase in the rate of accumulation and the profit rate of the investment sector through equation (15), and *vice versa*.

Putting equations (8), (9)' and (15) together, the long-run profit rate and the long- run rate of accumulation are given respectively as follows:[13]

$$r_i^{**} = [r_i^s / (\gamma_{i1}r_i^s + \gamma_{i2}u_i^s)](\Omega / \Phi_1) \tag{16}$$

$$g^{**} = g_i^{**} = \gamma_{i0} + \Omega / \Phi_1 \tag{17}$$

Differentiating equations (14), (16) and (17) with respect to the propensity to save and the target rate of return,[14] we eventually obtain Table 1, along with the first derivatives of equation (13). Therefore, the paradox of thrift holds in the long run, that is, a higher propensity to save leads to a lower rate of accumulation. The model is still wage-led, that is, an increase in real wages has a favourable impact on the rate of accumulation and the rate of capacity utilization (or an increase in the target rate of return has a negative impact on economic variables). However, a change in the target rate of return in a sector has an uncertain impact on the profit

[13] Note that in the present model a change in labour productivity does not have any effect on the rate of capacity utilization, the profit rate and the rate of accumulation, both in the short run and in the long run. This result arises because a change in real wage rates is offset by a change in the share of wages. For instance, a rise in labour productivity of the consumption sector (a decrease in $\alpha_1$) decreases the price of consumption goods in equation (1.1)', with the constant price of investment goods. This causes the real wage rate to increase, for a given nominal wage rate. But, a rise in labour productivity reduces the share of wages because the costing margin of the consumption sector increases in equation (5.1). The two opposite forces are offset by each other as shown in equations (A2.1) and (A3.1) in the Appendix, so that a change in labour productivity has no real effect.

[14] In our model, income distribution refers to the distribution between workers and capitalists. An increase in the target rate of return ($r_i^s$) leads to an increase in the costing margins of equations (5.1) and (5.2), as well as to an increase in the profit shares (or the gross profit margins) as shown in equation (7).

rate of that sector (as indicated by the ? sign).

[**Table 1**] Long-run effects in an economy with no adjustment mechanism

| | $s_p$ | $r_1^s$ | $r_2^s$ |
|---|---|---|---|
| $u_i^{**}$ | – | – | – |
| $r_1^{**}$ | – | ? | – |
| $r_2^{**}$ | – | – | ? |
| $g^{**}$ | – | – | – |
| $k^{**}$ | – | – | – |

As can be seen from the last row of Table 1, the ratio of sectoral capital stocks is associated negatively with an increase in costing margins, i.e., a higher costing margin induces a rise in the proportion of the capital stock located in the investment sector. This implies that the case of $dk^{**}/dr_2^s > 0$ is ruled out, when assuming that the entrepreneurs' animal spirits about investment are the same in both sectors ($\gamma_{10} = \gamma_{20}$), whereas this was possible under specific conditions in Lavoie and Ramírez-Gastón (1997, pp. 159-160). In other words, unexpectedly (when having in mind the stable case of the Hicksian traverse (Hicks, 1965)), a higher rate of accumulation is associated with a lower proportion of the capital stock being located in the investment good industry.

# III. Alternative Regimes with Adjustment Mechanisms

## 3.1. Regime 2: A Uniform Rate of Profit

Next, we specify Regime 2 as a case where there is an intersectoral mobility of (financial) capital so that profit rates in both industrial sectors are equalized. In this regime, we modify the investment function by assuming that investment decisions in the consumption sector follow equation (9), whereas investment decisions in the investment sector depend on the rate of accumulation of the consumption sector, modulated however by the difference between actual profit rates (Lavoie and Ramírez-Gastón, 1993).[15] This assumption is reasonably realistic since the

[15] This idea originates from Dutt (1988, p. 154, fn. 31), but he suggests equation (18.1) for the investment sector and equation (18.2) for the consumption sector. If we were to adopt Dutt's choice in Regime 2, the main results that we obtain, such as the paradox of thrift and the paradox of costs, would still hold: in particular, when $r_1^s = r_2^s$ and $u_1^s = u_2^s$, the two sets (ours and Dutt's) of investment functions yield exactly the same results. This implies that whether growth regimes are wage-led or profit-led does not depend on whether the consumption sector or the investment sector is assumed to

investment sector essentially responds to the demand for investment goods arising from the consumption sector, which in turn depends on its own rate of accumulation.[16] In this case, we can replace the investment function (9) by:

$$g_1 = \gamma_0 + \gamma_1 r_1 + \gamma_2 u_1 \tag{18.1}$$

$$g_2 = g_1 + \beta(r_2 - r_1) \tag{18.2}$$

where $\beta > 0$ is a reaction coefficient which measures the speed of adjustment to profit rate differentials.[17] With target-return pricing, as shown in equation (8), the equalization between the two actual profit rates takes place through a change in the actual rates of capacity utilization (that is, through quantity adjustment processes, but not price adjustment processes), for given standard rates. In this regime, since there is no impact on costing margins and prices, i.e., since the monopoly power to control prices is kept constant in each sector, firms have undesired excess capacity even in the long run.

We find the short-run equilibrium rate of profit as follows:[18]

$$r_1^* = \sigma_1 \gamma_0 r_1^s u_1^s u_2^s (u_2^s - s_p \sigma_2 r_2^s)(1 + 1/k)/\Phi_2 \tag{19.1}$$

$$r_2^* = s_p \sigma_1 \sigma_2 \gamma_0 r_1^s r_2^s u_1^s u_2^s (1 + k)/\Phi_2 \tag{19.2}$$

where $\Phi_2 = s_p \sigma_1 r_1^s u_1^s u_2^s (u_2^s - \beta \sigma_2 r_2^s) - \sigma_1 u_1^s u_2^s (u_2^s - s_p \sigma_2 r_2^s)[(\gamma_1 r_1^s + \gamma_2 u_1^s)(1 + 1/k) - \beta r_1^s / k]$ and the short-run stability condition is $\Phi_2 > 0$.

In the long run, the two sectoral rates of profit are equalized, when the following

base its investment decisions on equation (18.2) of our model. Rather, it is more likely to be related to the specification of the investment function itself. For instance, Bhaduri and Marglin (1990) show that different potential regimes could exist in a one-sector model when the profit rate in the investment function is replaced by the profit share. On the other hand, Dutt (1995; 1997) assumes that (identical) firms in both sectors choose their total rate of accumulation dependent on the average (or generalized) rate of capacity utilization and the average rate of profit, in order to induce a uniform rate of profit. Meanwhile, Duménil and Lévy (1999) suppose that a centralized capitalist agency controls the total amount of capital and distributes it to each industry according to the difference in profit rates. In both cases, equalization between profit rates is ensured by adopting equation (18.2).

[16] The assumption is also reminiscent of Pasinetti's (1981) hyper-vertically integrated sectors.

[17] Park (1997B, 1998, 1998-1999), even though investment functions equations (18.1) and (18.2) ensure a uniform rate of profit, claims that two questions remain to be answered: why is it that the investment function in the consumption sector fails to reflect differences in profit rates among industries; and why do capitalists of the investment sector ignore their own growth rates when making their investment decisions? Although his critique may be valid, it is not realistic to assume that firms take investment decisions regardless of the overall level of economic activity. Entrepreneurs should incorporate economy-wide factors in their investment decisions because they provide information about 'future profitability' and about whether the performance of individual firms results from 'chance events' (Dutt, 1990, p. 223, fn. 51).

[18] For the proof, see the Appendix.

condition is fulfilled:

$$k^{**} = (u_2^s / s_p \sigma_2 r_2^s) - 1 \tag{20}$$

Note that the long-run ratio of sectoral capital stocks depends only on the propensity to save and the parameters of the investment sector. This remarkable result indicates that the evolution of the sectoral capital stocks is associated closely to the pricing decision of the investment sector.[19] Intuitively, it comes from the specific investment function of the investment sector that is exactly the same as that of the consumption sector in the long run. With this specification, the impact of the investment behaviour of each sector on the ratio of sectoral capital stocks will offset each other in the long run, so that this ratio will be related only to the parameters of the investment sector which produces basic goods.

Let us consider the stability condition. By using equation (18.2), the rate of change in the ratio of sectoral capital stocks can be represented as a function of profit rates as follows:

$$\hat{k} = g_1^* - g_2^* = \beta(r_1^* - r_2^*) \tag{21}$$

Using equations (19.1) and (19.2), we have $d\hat{k} / dk < 0$, provided the following condition is satisfied

$$(\gamma_2 u_1^s / r_1^s) + \gamma_1 < \beta < s_p \tag{22}$$

That is, a condition for long-run stability is that the speed of adjustment of profit rate differentials must be smaller than the propensity to save.[20] Figure 2 shows the convergence of the two profit rates. Assuming that the economy is in the steady state, if $k > k^{**} [k < k^{**}]$ in a given period, then $r_2 > r_1 [r_2 < r_1]$ by equations (19.1) and (19.2), and hence $g_2 > g_1 [g_2 < g_1]$ by equation (18.2). Since it leads to $\hat{k} < 0$ $[\hat{k} > 0]$ until $k = k^{**}$, the economy will converge towards the steady state over time. Therefore, profit rates (and hence the rates of accumulation) in both sectors converge towards a locally stable equilibrium rate.

---

[19] This is compatible with the result obtained in Lavoie and Ramírez-Gastón (1997, pp. 159-161). However, while they prove it in Regime 1 as specified in this paper, we find it in Regime 2, not in Regime 1.

[20] This condition is consistent with the standard condition for stability in one-sector Kaleckian growth models, 'where the parameters have to be such that the savings function is more sensitive to changes than the investment function' (Lavoie and Ramírez-Gastón, 1997, p. 153).

**[Figure 2]** Dynamics of profit rates

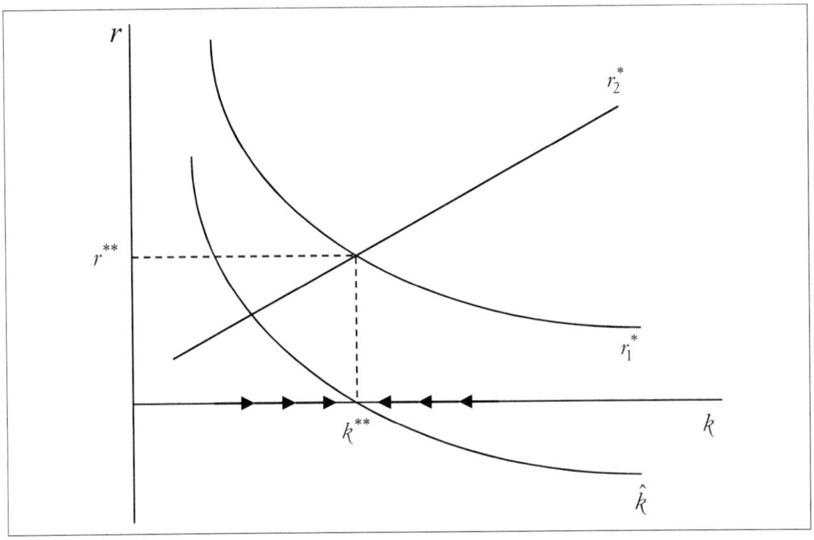


Substituting equations (20) into (19.1) and (19.2), we obtain a uniform rate of profit as follows:

$$r^{**} = r_1^{**} = r_2^{**} = \gamma_0 r_1^s / [(s_p - \gamma_1) r_1^s - \gamma_2 u_1^s] \tag{23}$$

where $s_p > (\gamma_2 u_1^s / r_1^s) + \gamma_1$ is satisfied by the stability condition. This result shows, somewhat surprisingly, that in this simple model the long-run equilibrium (uniform) rate of profit does not depend on the variables of the investment sector. Furthermore, the long-run equilibrium rate of profit is exactly identical to the one obtained in a one-sector Kaleckian model.[21] As mentioned above, this is because in Regime 2 the long-run investment function of the investment sector gets reduced to that of the consumption sector, so that the latter plays a crucial role in the determination of long-run positions.

In turn, substituting equation (23) into (8) and (18.1), the long-run rate of capacity utilization and the long-run rate of accumulation are obtained

$$u_1^{**} = \gamma_0 u_1^s / [(s_p - \gamma_1) r_1^s - \gamma_2 u_1^s] \tag{24.1}$$

$$u_2^{**} = \gamma_0 r_1^s u_2^s / \{r_2^s [(s_p - \gamma_1) r_1^s - \gamma_2 u_1^s]\} \tag{24.2}$$

[21] For instance, see a one-sector model with target-return pricing in Lavoie (2003).

$$g^{**} = g_1^{**} = g_2^{**} = s_p\gamma_0 r_1^s / [(s_p - \gamma_1)r_1^s - \gamma_2 u_1^s] \tag{25}$$

The first derivatives of equations (23) - (25) with respect to the propensity to save and the target rate of return are given in Table 2, along with the first derivatives of equation (20). An increase in the propensity to save lowers both the rate of accumulation and the profit rate, and hence the paradox of thrift still holds, even when we modify the investment function in order to bring about a uniform profit rate in a simple two-sector model. Also, an increase in the target rate of return of the consumption sector lowers the rate of accumulation, the rate of utilization and the rate of profit. The economy is thus wage-led and tied to the paradox of costs when considering increases in the costing margin of the consumption sector. By contrast, the target rate of return of the investment sector has no impact on the rate of accumulation and the profit rate, despite its negative impact on the rate of utilization of that sector.

**[Table 2]** Long-run effects in an economy with a uniform rate of profit

| | $s_p$ | $r_1^s$ | $r_2^s$ |
|---|---|---|---|
| $u_1^{**}$ | – | – | 0 |
| $u_2^{**}$ | – | – | – |
| $r^{**}$ | – | – | 0 |
| $g^{**}$ | – | – | 0 |
| $k^{**}$ | – | 0 | – |

In the last row of Table 2, we see that an increase in the costing margins of the consumption sector does not modify the ratio of sectoral capital stocks in the long run, while this ratio has an inverse relationship with the costing margins of the investment sector. The latter result is compatible with what was obtained in Regime 1.

It should further be noted that actual profit rates get equalized in this regime despite the fact that target rates of return remain exogenously set. The profit rate equalization obtained in this regime is thus unlikely to be the one described by Sraffian authors, who most likely assume the realization of equalized target rates of return in the pricing equations, and thus an additional mechanism is required to fully reconcile the Kaleckian and Sraffian views.

### 3.2. Regime 3: A Fully-Adjusted Economy

Regime 3 presents a classical model, that is, a fully-adjusted economy 'in which a uniform rate of profit prevails, and the productive capacity installed in each industry is exactly sufficient to produce the quantities that the market absorbs when commodities are sold at their natural prices' (Vianello, 1985, p. 71). Following Lavoie (1995; 1996; 2003), we assume that the economy arrives at fully-adjusted positions in the long run through an adjustment of target rates of return towards actual profit rates, i.e., through the endogenous target rates. Reading from equation (8), we know that when the actual rate of capacity utilization is above the standard rate, the actual profit rate is higher than the target rate. In that case, firms will slowly raise the target rate of return until the actual rate of capacity utilization arrives at the standard rate with a decrease in effective demand, and *vice versa*. Eventually, an economy achieves fully-adjusted positions as the actual rate of capacity utilization converges towards the standard rate.

We specify the adjustment mechanism as follows:

$$\dot{r}_i^s = \pi_i (r_i - r_i^s) \tag{26}$$

where $\pi > 0$ is a reaction coefficient. Thus, the target rate of return of an industrial sector is influenced by the profit rate realized in that sector. This kind of adjustment process, associated to a normal-cost pricing formula, has close similarities to the full-cost pricing model presented by Boggio (1986).

In this regime, changes in effective demand lead only to changes in the *size* of productive capacity, not to changes in the *rate* of capacity utilization in the long run (Vianello, 1985, pp. 72-73).[22] With the fully-adjusted target rate of return, the fluctuation of actual profit rates leads to changes in costing margins and in prices of goods: for instance, if the actual rate of capacity utilization is above the standard rate, then the price of a product will increase due to rising costing margins.[23] In this case, relative prices depend on the given values of the parameters. Using equations (1), (5.1) and (5.2), the long-run equilibrium relative price can be written as

$$(p_1 / p_2)^{**} = \alpha_1 / \alpha_2 + [(\sigma_1 \alpha_2 u_2^s - \sigma_2 \alpha_1 u_1^s) / (\alpha_2 u_1^s u_2^s)] r^{**}$$

Hence, if $(\sigma_1 / \alpha_1) / (\sigma_2 / \alpha_2) > u_1^s / u_2^s$, then $\partial (p_1 / p_2)^{**} / \partial r^{**} > 0$, and *vice versa*. In this regime, therefore, relative prices depend on the income distribution

[22] This is also pointed out by Garegnani (1983, p. 75); 'a satisfactory long-period theory of output does not require much more than (a) an analysis of how investment determines saving through changes in the level of *productive capacity* (and not only through changes in the *level of utilization* of productive capacity)...'

[23] It is compatible with a price equation suggested by Duménil and Lévy (1995; 1999). They suggest that in a neo-Kaleckian model it can be presented as $p_i = p_{i(-1)} + \phi(u_{i(-1)} - u_{i(-1)}^s)$ (in the present model, through equation (26)). Therefore, higher price levels correspond to actual rates of capacity utilization being higher than standard rates.

between workers and capitalists, but the direction of the change in relative prices depends on the chosen technology of the economy and the standard rates of capacity utilization set by firms.

Here, it is not easy to show mathematically the stability of this regime because the substitution of equation (23) into (26) leads to a non-linear form. Instead of finding a stability condition, we show that there exists a locally stable long-run position by using a phase diagram. Since $\dot{r}^s = 0$ in the steady state,

$$r^{**} = r_i^{**} = r_i^s \tag{27}$$

To draw the $\dot{r}_1^s = 0$ curve, replacing $r_1$ in the left hand side of equation (23) with $r_1^s$ and solving for $r_1^s$, we have

$$r_1^s = (\gamma_0 + \gamma_2 u_1^s)/(s_p - \gamma_1) \tag{28}$$

Since the $\dot{r}_1^s = 0$ curve is independent of $r_2^s$, it is drawn as a vertical line on a plane with axes given by $r_1^s$ and $r_2^s$. If the target rate of return in the consumption sector is larger than the actual profit rate of that sector, i.e., on the right hand side of the $\dot{r}_1^s = 0$ curve in Figure 3, the target rate of return will decrease over time ($\dot{r}_1^s < 0$) by equation (26), and *vice versa*.

Let us consider the $\dot{r}_2^s = 0$ curve. Replacing $r_2$ in the left hand side of equation (23) with $r_2^s$, we obtain

$$r_2^s = \gamma_0 r_1^s / [(s_p - \gamma_1) r_1^s - \gamma_2 u_1^s] \tag{29}$$

Since $dr_2^s / dr_1^s < 0$ and $d^2 r_2^s / (dr_1^s)^2 > 0$, the $\dot{r}_2^s = 0$ curve is convex to zero. If the target rate of return in the investment sector is greater than the actual profit rate of that sector, it will increase over time ($\dot{r}_1^s < 0$) by equation (26), and *vice versa*.

As shown in Figure 3, the target rates of return converge towards point E where the two curves intersect, and hence a uniform target rate of return is locally stable at that point.[24] In other words, the long-run target rate of return converges towards a uniform rate of profit over time, and it results in the fully adjusted economy in the

[24] Strictly speaking, we must simultaneously show that the ratio of sectoral capital stocks also converge towards the (locally) stable long-run position when there exists a deviation from the initial steady-state level. Intuitively, in the short period, a shock that pushes the economy away from its initial steady state will immediately change the actual profit rate and the ratio of sectoral capital stocks without a change in the target rate of return. As the adjustment mechanism works over time, this ratio would converge towards the new steady state as shown in Regime 2, with the adjustment of the target rate of return. Kim (2007) shows that there are locally stable long-run positions through simulation of Regime 3 within a stock-flow consistent framework.

long run.

**[Figure 3]** Dynamics of target rates of return

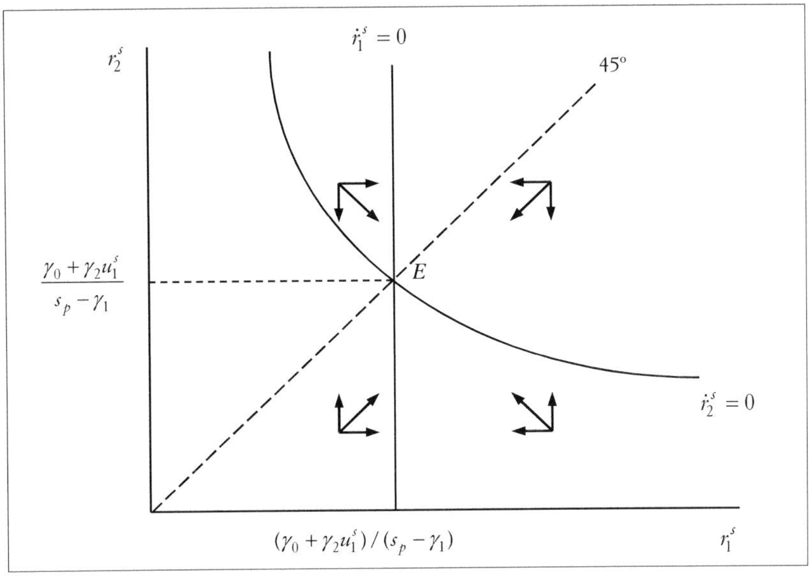


Therefore, the long-run ratio of sectoral capital stocks and the long-run uniform rate of profit are respectively

$$k^{**} = u_2^s(s_p - \gamma_1)/[s_p\sigma_2(\gamma_0 + \gamma_2 u_1^s)] - 1 \tag{30}$$

$$r^{**} = r_1^{**} = r_2^{**} = r_1^{s**} = r_2^{s**} = (\gamma_0 + \gamma_2 u_1^s)/(s_p - \gamma_1) \tag{31}$$

Thus, whereas the long-run ratio of sectoral capital stocks is not independent of the standard rate of capacity utilization of the consumption sector, the long-run (uniform) rate of profit is still independent of the variables of the investment sector and its value is the same as that in a one-sector model (due to the reason presented in Regime 2).

The long-run actual rate of capacity utilization converges towards the standard rate,

$$u_i^{**} = u_i^s \tag{32}$$

and substituting equation (31) into (25), the long-run rate of accumulation is obtained

$$g^{**} = g_1^* = g_2^{**} = (\gamma_0 + \gamma_2 u_1^s) / [1 - (\gamma_1 / s_p)] \tag{33}$$

In a fully adjusted economy, the long-run actual rate of accumulation therefore depends only on the propensity to save and the parameters of the consumption sector, as was already the case in Regime 2, with its value being also the same as that found in a one-sector model.

Differentiating equations (31) and (33) with respect to the propensity to save, we have:

$$dr^{**} / ds_p < 0 \,; \quad dg^{**} / ds_p < 0$$

An increase in the propensity to save will shift both the $\dot{r}_1^s = 0$ curve and the $\dot{r}_2^s = 0$ curve to the left by equations (28) and (29), and as shown in Figure 4, profit rates in both sectors will go down over time. Intuitively, we can see that this occurs because in the initial period an increase in the propensity to save induces lower actual rates of capacity utilization in the consumption sector first, and then lower rates in the investment sector with a time lag, which bring about lower actual profit rates. Since the target rates of return are higher than actual profit rates in the short run, the target rates will decrease towards the actual rates by the adjustment mechanism, and eventually the long-run profit rate in the new steady state will be lower than in the initial steady state. Therefore, an increase in the propensity to save leads to a lower long-run profit rate even in a fully-adjusted economy. A lower long-run profit rate lowers the long-run rate of accumulation and hence the 'paradox of thrift' still holds in this regime, although there is no long-run impact on capacity utilization rates. The 'paradox of thrift' is sustained even in this 'classical' regime because of the presence of hysteresis effects: there is hysteresis in growth due to the flexible target rate of return.

The first derivative of equation (30) yields

$$dk^{**} / ds_p > 0$$

and hence, unlike Regime 1 and Regime 2, the higher propensity to save leads to a rise in the ratio of sectoral capital stocks. This is what one would normally expect: a lower rate of accumulation is associated with a higher proportion of the capital stock being allocated to the consumption sector.[25]

We can further note, checking equations (31) and (33), that changes in income distribution have no more long-run effects on the accumulation rate and the profit

[25] Indeed it cannot be otherwise if the rate of utilization is exogenously given in the long run, as it is here, because, as Lavoie and Ramírez-Gastón (1997, p. 161) recall, by definition $g = u_i / \sigma_i (1 - k)$.

rate. The accumulation rate only depends on the coefficients of the investment function of the consumption sector, on its standard rate of utilization, and on the propensity to save. However, a temporary increase in real wages will have positive effects on economic activity in the short run. Hence, while the assumed adjustment mechanisms will bring the economy to a steady state with no undesired excess capacity, where changes in income distribution have no effect on accumulation and utilization rates, their average values over the transition period will be higher than their steady-state values. This is a major point, made repeatedly by Sraffians (Garegnani, 1992; Serrano, 1995; Park, 1997A; Cesaratto, 2015; Freitas and Serrano, 2015), and recently reasserted and proven within the context of a standard Kaleckian model with the help of a different converging mechanism (Allain, 2015; Lavoie, 2016).[26]

**[Figure 4]** Dynamics of the higher propensity to save

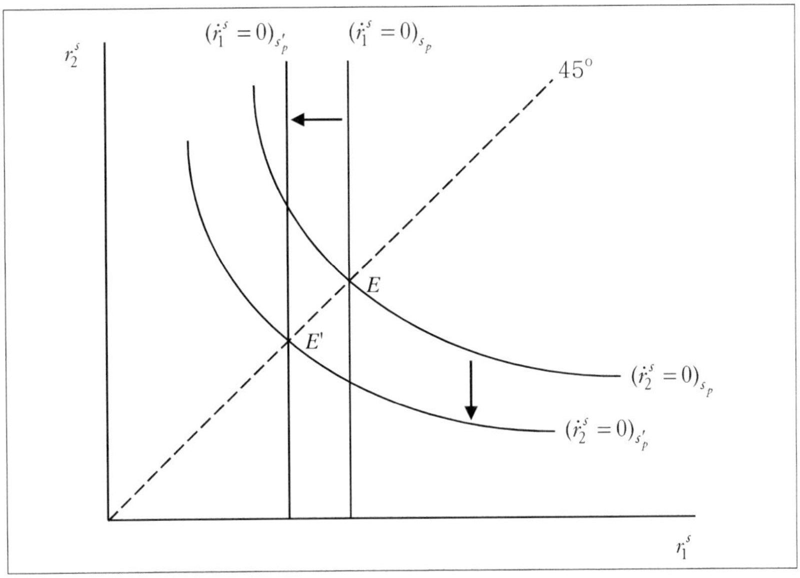


# IV. Conclusion

In this paper, we have analyzed three regimes specified by different investment functions and specific adjustment mechanisms, incorporating the arguments of both

[26] This mechanism relies on a non-capacity creating autonomous component of aggregate demand combined with the addition of a weak Harrodian component in the investment function.

neo-Kaleckians and neo-Marxists/Sraffians into a two-sector model.

We find that the 'paradox of thrift' holds for all regimes in the long run, as summarized in Table 3, whether there exists or not an adjustment mechanism. It is compatible with the result obtained in canonical neo-Kaleckian models, so that economic growth is 'demand-led' or 'consumption-led' in the short run as well as in the long run.

**[Table 3]** Long-run effects of the higher propensity to save

| | Regime 1 | Regime 2 | Regime 3 |
|---|---|---|---|
| $g^{**}$ | – | – | – |
| $u_i^{**}$ | – | – | 0 |
| $r_i^{**}$ | – | – | – |

As to the impact of changes in income distribution, things are more ambiguous. In the regime deprived of a classical adjustment mechanism, the economy remains wage-led, but the paradox of costs may or may not apply, meaning that a sector that increases its target rate of return may indeed achieve a higher realized profit rate in the long run. With a mechanism designed to equalize realized profit rates, the economy remains wage-led only when costing margins of the consumption sector are modified; when changes in real wages arise as a consequence of a change in the costing margin of the investment sector, this has no long-run consequences on the realized profit rate and the rate of accumulation. When adding a mechanism adjusting target rates of return to realized profit rates, changes in the parameters determining income distribution have no effect on long-run profit rates and growth rates.

Our analysis also shows that in regimes with a uniform rate of profit, where firms in the investment sector adjust to investment decisions in the consumption sector, the long-run profit rate and the long-run rate of accumulation depend only on parameters of the consumption sector and the propensity to consume, which are exactly the same as those obtained in a one-sector neo-Kaleckian model. In addition, for non-fully adjusted regimes, the ratio of sectoral capital stocks is associated negatively with an increase in the target rate of return, that is, the proportion of the capital stock located in the investment sector is related inversely to the long-run rate of accumulation. However, the reproportioning that occurs in the dynamically-stable two-sector Cambridgian or Hicksian model with full capacity is restored in the fully-adjusted regime described here.

Therefore, although there still exist debates about long-run positions and the existence of adjustment mechanisms, our analysis suggests that aggregate demand plays a crucial role in the determination of the growth path, both in the short and in the long run, and hence that economic growth could be consumption-led and wage-led. Our analysis also offers some justification for using simple one-sector neo-Kaleckian growth models, since most of the key results of these models are sustained in more sophisticated two-sector models with various closures; this however needed to be demonstrated, and this is what we have done here.

Finally, we have explored long-run relationships in a simple two-sector model, but growth regimes in multi-sector models could be sensitive to the model specification and the chosen values of parameters because of complicated dynamics due to sectoral heterogeneity. This means that we need to examine multi-sector models including various economic sectors such as financial and overseas sectors,[27] and to investigate characteristics of growth regimes through empirical analysis, using multi-sectoral data. These topics are left for future research.

[27] For example, Kim and Lavoie (2016) explore the dynamics towards long-run positions as well as the impact of changes in various parameters within a multi-sector Kaleckian growth model that incorporates endogenous labour-saving technical progress and price inflation arising from the conflicting claims of workers and firms over income distribution.

## Appendix. Short-run equilibria in Regime 1 and 2

### (1) Regime 1

From pricing equation (1), the national accounts yield

$$p_i S_i = w\alpha_i S_i + r_i p_2 K_i \tag{A1}$$

Assuming that supply adjusts to demand within the period, we can rewrite the actual real output equations (2.1) and (2.2) as follows:[28]

$$S_1 = (w / p_1)(\alpha_1 S_1 + \alpha_2 S_2) + (1 - s_p)(p_2 / p_1)(r_1 K_1 + r_2 K_2) \tag{A2.1}$$

$$S_2 = g_1 K_1 + g_2 K_2 \tag{A2.2}$$

Using equations (1.1)', (1.2)' and (A1), equation (A2.1) can be rewritten as

$$(s_p \sigma_1 r_1^s u_2^s) S_1 - u_1^s (u_2^s - s_p \sigma_2 r_2^s) S_2 = 0 \tag{A3.1}$$

and substituting equations (6) and (9)' into (A2.2),

$$-\gamma_{13}\sigma_1 S_1 + (1 - \gamma_{23}\sigma_2) S_2 = (\gamma_{10} K_1 + \gamma_{20} K_2) \tag{A3.2}$$

Hence, by putting equations (A3.1) and (A3.2) together,

$$\begin{bmatrix} s_p \sigma_1 r_1^s u_2^s & -u_1^s (u_2^s - s_p \sigma_2 r_2^s) \\ -\gamma_{13}\sigma_1 & (1 - \gamma_{23}\sigma_2) \end{bmatrix} \begin{bmatrix} S_1 \\ S_2 \end{bmatrix} = \begin{bmatrix} 0 \\ (\gamma_{10} K_1 + \gamma_{20} K_2) \end{bmatrix} \tag{A4}$$

and by solving equation (A4) on $S_1$ and $S_2$, we obtain

$$S_1 = u_1^s (u_2^s - s_p \sigma_2 r_2^s)(\gamma_{10} K_1 + \gamma_{20} K_2) / \Phi_1 \tag{A5.1}$$

$$S_2 = s_p \sigma_1 r_1^s u_2^s (\gamma_{10} K_1 + \gamma_{20} K_2) / \Phi_1 \tag{A5.2}$$

where $\Phi_1$ is the determinant of the first matrix on the left hand side of equation (A4), given by:

[28] Equation (A2.1) is equivalent to saying that investment must be equal to saving, implying that: $p_2 S_2 = s_p (r_1 p_2 K_1 + r_2 p_2 K_2)$.

$$\Phi_1 = s_p\sigma_1 r_1^s u_2^s(1-\gamma_{23}\sigma_2) - \gamma_{13}\sigma_1 u_1^s(u_2^s - s_p\sigma_2 r_2^s)$$

and the short-run stability condition is $\Phi_1 > 0$, while the numerator of equation (A5.1) is positive at all times since we already assumed $u_2^s > \sigma_2 r_2^s$ for outputs to be positive.

Substituting equations (A5.1) and (A5.2) into (6), we obtain equations (10.1) and (10.2), and then equations (11.1) and (11.2).

## (2) Regime 2

Substituting equations (6), (8), (18.1) and (18.2) into (A2.2), we obtain

$$-\sigma_1 u_2^s[(\gamma_1 r_1^s + \gamma_2 u_1^s)(1+1/k) - \beta r_1^s/k]S_1 + u_1^s(u_2^s - \beta\sigma_2 r_2^s)S_2 = \gamma_0 u_1^s u_2^s(K_1+K_2) \quad \text{(A6)}$$

and with equation (A3.1),

$$\begin{bmatrix} s_p\sigma_1 r_1^s u_2^s & -u_1^s(u_2^s - s_p\sigma_2 r_2^s) \\ -\sigma_1 u_2^s[(\gamma_1 r_1^s + \gamma_2 u_1^s)(1+1/k) - \beta r_1^s/k] & u_1^s(u_2^s - \beta\sigma_2 r_2^s) \end{bmatrix}\begin{bmatrix} S_1 \\ S_2 \end{bmatrix} = \begin{bmatrix} 0 \\ \gamma_0 u_1^s u_2^s(K_1+K_2) \end{bmatrix} \quad \text{(A7)}$$

Hence, by solving equation (A7), we have

$$S_1 = \gamma_0(u_1^s)^2 u_2^s(u_2^s - s_p\sigma_2 r_2^s)(K_1+K_2)/\Phi_2 \quad \text{(A8.1)}$$

$$S_2 = s_p\sigma_1\gamma_0 r_1^s u_1^s(u_2^s)^2(K_1+K_2)/\Phi_2 \quad \text{(A8.2)}$$

where $\Phi_2$ is the determinant of the first matrix on the left hand side of equation (A7), given by:

$$\Phi_2 = s_p\sigma_1 r_1^s u_1^s u_2^s(u_2^s - \beta\sigma_2 r_2^s) - \sigma_1 u_1^s u_2^s(u_2^s - s_p\sigma_2 r_2^s)[(\gamma_1 r_1^s + \gamma_2 u_1^s)(1+1/k) - \beta r_1^s/k]$$

and the short-run stability condition is $\Phi_2 > 0$.

Using equations (6), (8), (A8.1) and (A8.2), we obtain equations (19.1) and (19.2).

# References

Allain, O. (2015), "Tackling the Instability of Growth: A Kaleckian-Harrodian Model with an Autonomous Expenditure Component," *Cambridge Journal of Economics*, Vol. 39, No. 5, 1351-1371.

Amadeo, E. (1986), "Notes on Capacity Utilization, Distribution and Accumulation," *Contributions to Political Economy*, Vol. 5, No.1, 83-94.

Araujo, R. A. and G. T. Lima (2007), "A Structural Economic Dynamics Approach to Balance-of-payments Constrained Growth," *Cambridge Journal of Economics*, Vol. 31, No. 5, 755-774.

Araujo, R. A. and J. R. Teixeira (2015), "A Multi-sector Version of the Post-Keynesian Growth Model," *Estudos Econômicos* (São Paulo), Vol. 45, No. 1, 127-152.

Arestis, P., A. R. Gonzáles and O. Dejuán (2012), "Modeling Accumulation: A Theoretical and Empirical Application of the Accelerator Principle under Uncertainty," *Intervention: European Journal of Economics and Economic Policy*, Vol. 9, 255-276.

Auerbach, P., and P. Skott (1988), "Concentration, Competition and Distribution," *Inter national Review of Applied Economics*, Vol. 2, No. 1, 42-61.

Bhaduri, A. and Marglin, S. (1990), "Unemployment and the Real Wage: The Economi c Basis for Contesting Political Ideologies", *Cambridge Journal of Economics*, Vol. 1 4, No. 4, 375–393.

Boggio, L. (1986), "Stability of Production Prices in a Model of General Interdependence," in W. Semmler, ed., *Competition, Instability and Nonlinear Cycles*, New York: Springer-Verlag, 83-102.

Caserta, M. (1990), "The Steady-state Model of Capital Utilization: A Comment," *Studi Economici*, Vol. 41, No. 2, 139-153.

Cesaratto, S. (2015), "Neo-Kaleckian and Sraffian Controversies on the Theory of Accumulation," *Review of Political Economy*, Vol. 27, No. 2, 154-182.

Chamberlain, T. W. and M. J. Gordon (1989), "Liquidity, Profitability, and Long-run Survival: Theory and Evidence on Business Investment," *Journal of Post Keynesian Economics*, Vol. 11, No. 4, 589-610.

Committeri, M. (1986), "Some Comments on Recent Contributions on Capital Accumulation, Income Distribution and Capacity Utilization," *Political Economy: Studies in the Surplus Approach*, Vol. 2, No. 2, 161-186.

Cowling, K. (1982), *Monopoly Capitalism*, London: John Wiley & Sons.

Duménil, G. and D. Lévy (1995), "Post-Keynesian Long-term Equilibrium with Equalized Profit Rates? A Rejoinder to Amitava Dutt's Synthesis," *Review of Radical Political Economics*, Vol. 27, No. 2, 135-141.

__________________ (1999), "Being Keynesian in the Short Term and Classical in the Long Term: The Traverse to Classical Long-term Equilibrium," *The Manchester School of Economic and Social Studies*, Vol. 67, No. 6, 684-716.

Dutt, A. K. (1984), "Stagnation, Income Distribution and Monopoly Power," *Cambridge Journal of Economics*, Vol. 8, No.1, 25-40.

________ (1988), "Convergence and Equilibrium in Two Sector Models of Growth,

Distribution and Prices," *Journal of Economics*, Vol. 48, No. 2, 135-158.

_________ (1990), *Growth, Distribution, and Uneven Development*, Cambridge: Cambridge University Press.

Fazzari, S. M. and T. L. Mott (1986-87), "The Investment Theory of Kalecki and Keynes: An Empirical Study of Firm Data, 1970-1982," *Journal of Post Keynesian Economics*, Vol. 9, No. 2, 171-187.

Freitas, F. and F. Serrano (2015), "Growth and Level Effects, the Stability of the Adjustment of Capacity to Demand and the Sraffian Multiplier," *Review of Political Economy*, Vol. 27, No. 3, 258-281.

Garegnani, P. (1983), "Two Routes to Effective Demand: Comment on Kregel," in J. Kregel, ed., *Distribution, Effective Demand and International Economic Relations*, London: Macmillan, 69-80.

__________ (1992), "Some Notes for an Analysis of Accumulation," in J. Halevi, D. Laibman and E. J. Nell, eds., *Beyond the Steady State: A Revival of Growth Theory*, New York: St. Martin's Press, 47-71.

Glick, M., and D. A. Campbell (1995), "Classical Competition and the Compatibility of Market Power and Uniform Rates of Profit," *Review of Radical Political Economics*, Vol. 27, No. 2, 124-153.

Harris, D. J. (1978), *Capital Accumulation and Income Distribution*, Stanford: Stanford University Press.

Hein, E., M. Lavoie and T. van Treeck (2011), "Some Instability Puzzles in Kaleckian Models of Growth and Distribution: A Critical Survey," *Cambridge Journal of Economics*, Vol. 35, No. 3, 587-612.

________________________________ (2012), "Harrodian Instability and the Normal Rate of Capacity Utilization in Kaleckian Models of Distribution and Growth: A Survey," *Metroeconomica*, Vol. 63, No. 1, 39-69.

Hicks, J. (1965), *Capital and Growth*, Oxford: Oxford University Press.

Kalecki, M. (1939), *Essays in the Theory of Economic Fluctuations*, London: Allen & Unwin.

________ (1971), *Selected Essays on the Dynamics of the Capitalist Economy: 1933-1970*, Cambridge: Cambridge University Press.

Kaplan, A. D. H., J. B. Dirlam and R. F. Lanzillotti (1958), *Pricing in Big Business: A Case Approach*, Brookings Institution.

Kim, J. H. (2007), *Three Essays on Effective Demand, Economic Growth and Inflation*, Ph.D. Dissertation, University of Ottawa.

Kim, J. H. and M. Lavoie (2016), "A Two-sector Model with Target-return Pricing in a Stock-flow Consistent Framework," *Economic Systems Research*, vol. 28, no. 3, 403-427.

Kurz, H. D. (1994), "Growth and Distribution," *Review of Political Economy*, Vol. 6, No. 4, 393-420.

Lanzillotti, R. F. (1958), "Pricing Objectives in Large Companies," *American Economic Review*, Vol. 45, No. 5, 921-940.

Lavoie, M. (1995), "The Kaleckian Model of Growth and Distribution and Its Neo-Ricardian and Neo-Marxian Critiques," *Cambridge Journal of Economics*, Vol. 19, No. 6, 789-818.

________ (1996), "Traverse, Hysteresis, and Normal Rates of Capacity Utilization in Kaleckian Models of Growth and Distribution," *Review of Radical Political Economics*, Vol. 28, No. 4, 113-147.

________ (2003), "Kaleckian Effective Demand and Sraffian Normal Prices: Towards a Reconciliation," *Review of Political Economy*, Vol. 15, No. 1, 53-74.

________ (2014), *Post-Keynesian Economics: New Foundations*, Edward Elgar.

________ (2016), "Convergence towards the Normal Rate of Capacity Utilization in Neo-Kaleckian Models: The Role of Non-capacity Creating Autonomous Expenditures," *Metroeconomica*, Vol. 67, No. 1, 172-201.

Lavoie, M., and P. Ramírez-Gastón (1993), "Traverse in a Two-sector Kaleckian Model of Growth with Target-return Pricing," Working Paper, University of Ottawa. .

____________________________ (1997), "Traverse in a Two-sector Kaleckian Model of Growth with Target-return Pricing," *The Manchester School of Economic and Social Studies*, Vol. 65, Issue 2, 145-169.

Nishi, H. (2014), "Income Distribution and Economic Growth in a Multi-sectoral Kaleckian Model," Research Project Center Discussion Paper, E-14-011, Kyoto University.

Onaran, Ö. and G. Galanis (2012). "Is Aggregate Demand Wage-led or Profit-led: National and Global Effects," Working Paper # 40, Conditions of Work and Employment Series, International Labour Office. http://www.ilo.org/wcmsp5/groups/public/---ed_protect/---protrav/---travail/documents/publication/wcms_192121.pdf

Palumbo, A. and A. Trezzini (2003), "Growth without Normal Capacity Utilization," *European Journal of the History of Economic Thought*, Vol. 10, No. 1, 109-135.

Park, M.-S. (1995), "A Note on the "Kalecki-Steindl" Steady-state Approach to Growth and Income Distribution," *The Manchester School of Economic and Social Studies*, Vol. 63, No. 3, 297-310.

_________ (1997A), "Normal Values and Average Values," *Metroeconomica*, Vol. 48, No. 2, 188-199.

_________ (1997B), "Accumulation, Capacity Utilisation and Distribution," *Contributions to Political Economy*, vol. 16, 87-101.

_________ (1998-1999), "Individually Identical or Collectively Autonomous? Questioning the Representation of Investment Behavior in the Kaleckian Multisector Model of Growth," *Journal of Post Keynesian Economics*, Vol. 21, No. 2, 299-313.

_________ (1998), "The Cambridge Theory of Income Distribution: A Partial Critique," *Review of Political Economy*, Vol. 10, No. 3, 277-298.

Pasinetti, L. L. (1981), *Structural Change and Economic Growth*, Cambridge: Cambridge University Press.

Rowthorn, B. (1981), "Demand, Real Wages and Economic Growth," *Thames Papers in Political Economy*, Autumn, 1-39; reprinted in M. C. Sawyer, ed., *Post-Keynesian Economics*, Aldershot: Edward Elgar, 1988.

Semmler, W. (1984), *Competition, Monopoly, and Differential Profit Rates,* New York: Columbia University Press.

Serrano, F. (1996), *The Sraffian Multiplier*, PhD dissertation, Faculty of Economics and

Politics, University of Cambridge.

Spence, A. M. (1977), "Entry, Capacity, Investment and Oligopolistic Pricing," *The Bell Journal of Economics*, Vol. 8, No. 2, 534-544.

Steindl, J. (1952), *Maturity and Stagnation in American Capitalism*, Oxford: Blackwell, reprinted in 1976 by the Monthly Review Press.

Storm, S. and C. W. M. Naastepad (2012), *Macroeconomics Beyond the NAIRU*, Cambridge (Mass.): Harvard University Press.

Sweezy, P. (1942), *The Theory of Capitalist Development: Principles of Marxian Political Economy*, New York: Monthly Review Press, reprinted in 1970.

Taylor, L. (1985), "A Stagnationist Model of Economic Growth," *Cambridge Journal of Economics*, Vol. 9, No. 4, 383-403.

Trezzini, A. (2011), "Steady State and the Analysis of Long-run Tendencies: The Case of Neo-Kaleckian Models," in R. Ciccone, C. Gherke and G. Mongiovi, eds., *Sraffa and Modern Economics, Volume II,* London: Routledge, 129-151.

Vianello, F. (1985), "The Pace of Accumulation," *Political Economy: Studies in the Surplus Approach*, Vol. 1, No. 1, 67-87.